D1234312

ECONOMICS
OF
LABOR

ECONOMICS
OF
LABOR

RICHARD A. LESTER

Chairman, Department of Economics
Princeton University

SECOND EDITION

THE MACMILLAN COMPANY, NEW YORK
COLLIER-MACMILLAN LIMITED, LONDON

To D.

THE MACMILLAN COMPANY, NEW YORK
COLLIER-MACMILLAN CANADA, LTD., TORONTO, ONTARIO

Printed in the United States of America

PREFACE

As THE TITLE indicates, this book deals primarily with the economic aspects of labor problems. It is a complete revision of a textbook for college courses in labor published in 1941.

Emphasis throughout is on economic analysis, applied to the main issues in the labor field. For that purpose an economics of collective activity in the labor area is developed, based on up-to-date concepts of management, trade unionism, and the employment process. This collective economics is compared with the individualistic approach of classical economics, showing the contrasting implications for public policy.

On the basis of this new analytical framework, an attempt has been made to present a well integrated view of the entire field. Three themes run through the book and help to unify it. They are: (1) the importance of an evolutionary orientation for an understanding and analysis of labor developments; (2) the need for an economics of collective action, not only for analyzing negotiated wages and union policies but also for theorizing about the behavior of management in the labor area; and (3) the use of an evolutionary perspective and a collective type of analysis as a basis for understanding and judging issues of public policy in the labor field.

The first theme is introduced in Chapter 2 and is expanded and illustrated in Chapters 3, 4, 5, and 13, dealing with historical evolution and trends. The second theme, also briefly discussed in Chapter 2, is fully developed in Chapters 6, 7, and 8, and is applied in subsequent chapters. The third theme, which involves the economic basis for public policies, is outlined in Chapter 13 and is illustrated and elaborated in Chapters 14 through 18. Some of its implications are also indicated in Chapters 11 and 12.

The development of an economics of management, unions, and collective bargaining permits an integrated treatment of both traditionally "labor economics" subjects (wages, work hours, labor supply) and "labor relations" subjects (union-management negotiations, work rules, and employee benefits). That approach is also useful for dealing with questions of manpower policy (employment exchanges, vocational training, and unemployment).

In addition to the analysis and themes already mentioned, special

v

features of the book include: an extensive examination of the evolution of management's labor policies, an analysis of the rapid growth of employee benefits, a systematic study of employment experience under minimum-wage legislation, a discussion of the economics of fair employment practices legislation, and an analytical survey of the manpower program under the Manpower Development and Training Act and the annual Manpower Report of the President.

Focus of attention on the economics of labor has, however, necessitated the omission of discussion of such interesting subjects as the political activities of organized labor, white-collar unionism, corruption in American unions, and the handling of individual workers' grievances in the shop. Good articles on those subjects are available in books of readings, labor and management periodicals, and the scholarly journals.

Although this book is highly integrated, considerable flexibility is possible in its use. Chapters 6, 7, 8, and 9 are basic to the volume, and Chapter 13 is an introduction to those that follow it. However, other chapters can be assigned in a variety of sequences. A number could be omitted and yet one could cover the central material of the introductory course in labor economics or labor problems.

To aid the reader to review a chapter as a whole in a concise fashion, each chapter closes with a brief summary in outline form. Discussion questions at the end of each chapter provide a basis for testing one's grasp of the subject matter. The selected readings furnish suggestions for further exploration of particular topics.

The writing of a book involves the accumulation of many obligations. My colleague, William G. Bowen, has read and helpfully criticized Chapters 2, 6, 7, 8, 9, 10, 11, 16, and 17. Hazel Benjamin, the librarian of the Industrial Relations Section at Princeton in which I am a Faculty Associate, cheerfully aided in the search for material and also read proof. Others on the Section staff have helped in a variety of ways. Doris McBride, Anne Seitz, Mary A. Sweeney, and Alberta Thomas typed parts of the manuscript. My wife read proof and helped make the index. Above all, the hundreds of students in my classes and precepts since 1936 have helped to sharpen my thinking on labor issues.

Perhaps a personal note is appropriate for ending this preface. After teaching an introductory labor course in Economics Departments in three institutions over a period of 25 years, one cannot complete a text like this without feeling that much of a life's work is embodied in it. The reader must decide how well the professor has "learned from experience."

R.A.L.

Princeton, N.J.
January 1964

CONTENTS

ix

industry differentials. Local differentials. Geographical
differentials. WAGE LEVEL CHANGES: *Collective*
bargaining and prices. Unemployment and wage
change. Labor's share in the national income.

PART THREE   *PUBLIC POLICY*

Part *ONE*
BACKGROUND
and DEVELOPMENTS

I.
Introduction

PEOPLE, IT IS said, are a nation's richest resource. Certainly the operation of the American economy depends, in large measure, upon the employment of people—on the purchase, sale, and performance of labor services.

It is the work of persons on payrolls that builds our cities and factories, that makes the things we buy, and that supplies us with services of all sorts, from transportation and garbage collection to television programs and the opera. And employment provides not only the wherewithal to purchase the products of industry but also the satisfaction that stems from accomplishment and contribution to the welfare of society.

THE IMPORTANCE OF EMPLOYMENT

This book centers on the problems of paid employment in our economy. It analyzes the various aspects of work for pay and the economic issues arising out of employee-employer and union-management relationships.

In America, employment has pregnant implications not only for economic magnitudes such as production, income, and prices but also for our whole way of life. During much of our lives we are a people at work, and as workers we are largely a nation of employees.

Primarily, we work for money; the major element in the cash nexus is payrolls. Of all persons gainfully occupied (or commercially engaged), five out of every six get their living, not as independent or self-employed operators like farmers or storekeepers, but by hiring out their services in return for pay envelopes and employee benefits of various sorts. Consequently, wages and salaries represent over 70 per cent of all money income and about the same percentage of the total costs of production of American industry.

A "Laboristic Economy"?

So pervasive and potent is the employment relationship that the late Professor Sumner H. Slichter of Harvard contended that America has already become, or at least is rapidly becoming, a "laboristic economy."[1] By that term he meant a situation where employees are the most influential group in the community and their viewpoints tend to dominate the society's values and are the major factor determining government policy.

Undoubtedly, Slichter's conclusion concerning labor supremacy represents an exaggeration, perhaps purposely so, in order to attract attention to a long-term trend. In our economy, management still largely directs production and employment, and the ideology of business continues to exert more influence on American culture and politics than that of organized labor.

Nevertheless, the perspective of history clearly reveals that labor has been ascending; employee concerns and problems have received increasing consideration. As explained in Chapter 4, during the past four decades a shift has occurred from a cold "com-

---

[1] Sumner H. Slichter, *The American Economy, Its Problems and Prospects* (New York: Knopf, 1948), pp. 7–13.

modity" to a warm "welfare" concept of employment in American industry.

Concern for Employees' Welfare

The care and attention given labor's needs are evident from the proliferation of company programs for employees. They include employee safety, health, counseling, communication, training, life insurance, sickness benefits, pensions, lay-off benefits, and grievance settlement.

Worker considerations also explain the increase in the number of persons serving full time as staff members in personnel or industrial relations activity.[2] Annual surveys covering a group of companies rather representative of American industry show that manufacturing firms have an average of one personnel staff member for every 150 employees; the ratio is about one for every 100 employees in banking-finance-insurance and in public utilities and one for every 220 employees in trade and transportation. In recent years the salaries of people who administer employee programs apparently have amounted to three to four cents per hour worked by each employee.[3]

Increased solicitude and pressure for labor's viewpoint is also evidenced by the great expansion in worker representation. Labor unions in this country have about eighteen million members, who pay over half a billion dollars a year in union dues and assessments, or an annual average of about thirty dollars per member.

Most of this money is used to meet the cost of representing employees in negotiations with employers, in employee grievance presentation, and in propaganda and political activities on behalf of the membership of organized labor. It is estimated that in this country some two million full- and part-time labor officials, agents, and shop stewards are engaged in various sorts of union activities. If the United States becomes a laboristic economy (more accurately, a laboristic society), it will be mainly through the efforts

---

[2] Including clerical and other assistants to the staff and professional personnel.

[3] See R. J. Nelson, G. W. England, and D. Yoder, "Personnel Ratios and Costs, 1962," *Personnel*, XL (January–February 1963), pp. 17–26 and earlier issues reporting on this annual survey.

of this administrative staff (the management?) of the American labor movement.

SCOPE AND AIMS OF OUR INQUIRY

Employment is not merely a matter of wages and working hours. As already suggested, it has ramifications throughout the economy and society.

Although this book focuses on the employment relationship, it includes within its purview many of the challenging issues of our time. We will examine the implications that organized labor, collective bargaining, management's labor policies, and government policies in this area have for economic development and social change. We will be interested not only in the present but also the past and the future. One of our aims will be to understand where we are headed. For that purpose we will investigate long-run trends as well as short-run variations and current conditions.

The Big Questions

What such an analysis may mean in more concrete terms is indicated by the following outline, chiefly in the form of broad questions.

1. THE IMPACT OF UNIONS. Is organized labor strengthening or strangling our economy? Are unions promoting or retarding employment, productivity, and the efficient allocation of economic resources?

Are union leaders promoting the public welfare by stressing high standards of living on the job, or are they doing so at the expense of potentially higher standards of consumption and stimulation of wage-price inflation? Are labor organizations impeding economic growth by discouraging capital investment, limiting technological change, and restricting management freedom and individual initiative, or are they enhancing the national product by prodding management to improve its procedures and techniques, by raising the self-respect and morale of employees, and by promoting worker participation and cooperation in industrial progress?

Is the American labor movement stimulating class conflict and carrying the country down the road to co-determination, the corporate state, or some other radical reform of the economy, or is it serving to improve the operation of American capitalism and raise the prestige of private enterprise both at home and abroad?

Are our unions advancing democratic values, or are they substituting for one authority (management) another (the union) which is more costly and more subject to corruption?

These are the kinds of questions about American trade unionism to which this book will address itself.

2. THE IMPLICATIONS OF MANAGEMENTS' LABOR POLICIES. With respect to the industrial relations practices and policies of American management a similar set of questions arises.

In attempting to attach workers to the firm by employee programs, are managements so reducing labor mobility as to restrict the adaptability and productivity of our economy, or is the resulting improvement in employee security and contentment a net social gain?

Do wage scales established unilaterally by management have a more or less favorable effect on employee productivity than those fixed by collective bargaining?

To what extent is management justified in charging unions with responsibility for price inflation, and to what extent do its own policies (such as pricing methods, wage formulas in long-term contracts, and high administrative expenses) account for upward bias in the price level?

Does American management in its employment policies and political positions fail to take sufficient account of the social investment in human resources, or has the shift toward a welfare concept of employment and toward fairly mature relations with unions adequately remedied any weaknesses in managements' programs on that score? Is the opposition of most of American management to labor standards legislation (such as minimum wages, hours of work, better unemployment benefits, and nondiscrimination in employment) shortsighted, or is a program of reliance on market determination and collective bargaining—on private settlement rather than legislation—now a valid position from the point of view of the general welfare?

Are managements' labor policies helping to guide American capitalism along proper lines, or is American management establishing precedents and pursuing programs in industrial relations that will hamper the future development of our economy?

3. THE CONSEQUENCES OF GOVERNMENT POLICIES.   As the power of organized labor has expanded and national administrations have sought through public programs to maintain economic stability and a high level of employment, the labor policies of government, especially the Federal Government, have become of increasing importance.

What role should government play with respect to union-management relations, the establishment of labor standards, and the provision of economic security? Should the government attempt to promote or curb collective bargaining? Should it follow a policy of seeking a balance of power between the parties by government regulation?

Is national economic planning to promote full employment and price stability compatible with free collective bargaining on a sectional basis?

What legal limits should be placed on the use of union power and strikes, especially work stoppages that threaten to create national emergencies? Are unions monopolies that should be subject to the antitrust laws?

Has the government a responsibility to promote democracy and financial integrity in unions and to prevent a host of "unfair practices" in union-management relations?

Will detailed government regulation of unions tend to make them mere creatures of the state and destroy an important element in the pluralism of American society? And will the heavy hand of government serve to rob collective bargaining of its flexibility and self-governing values?

With respect to the conservation of human resources and security, what should be the function of government in the development and effective utilization of the nation's manpower and womanpower? How far should it go in promoting vocational training, public employment exchanges, and public programs to prevent discrimination in employment?

What are the economic consequences of government intervention in the market through the setting of legal minimum wages, maximum daily and weekly work hours, and fair employment practices?

What should be the respective roles of the Federal Government, the States, and private industry in providing economic security for workers, and how do programs of the three units differ in their economic effects on mobility, incentive, and consumption patterns?

Finally, what about the power of organized labor and business management to influence or control government labor policies? What are the prospects for domination of the government by the labor movement, so that governmental manpower programs may become instruments for achieving the special interests of labor groups?

With that question we are back again to the subject of a laboristic (in contrast to a capitalistic) economy.

The Total View

These comprehensive questions indicate the aims and scope of our study. They should help us see the forest from the trees as we proceed, chapter by chapter, to examine individual topics. And they supply a general background into which to place a particular analysis or set of facts.

This preview in question form also suggests the complex nature of the subject and the many obstacles to neat answers. The purpose in devoting the next chapter to a discussion of analytical methods and to sources of facts and errors, is to guard against common pitfalls and one-sided conclusions in a subject with so many dimensions and ramifications.

In the final chapter, after we have examined and analyzed the many facets of labor economics, we will return to these broad questions asked at the outset. There it will be our task to attempt, so to speak, to mount the summit and, with wide-angle vision, seek to construct from the separate branches of our inquiry a balanced and integrated structure of general conclusions.

THE SELLERS AND BUYERS OF LABOR

Some of the confusion in the field of industrial relations arises from a failure to define terms. For instance, use of the expression "laboristic economy" raises a question whether salaried employees, including corporation executives, are a part of "labor." With employment playing such a crucial role in our economy and giving rise to such serious policy issues, it is appropriate at the beginning of our inquiry to delineate the sellers and buyers of labor. As we shall see, this is not easy to do.

Some Definitions

Labor, in the broad sense of the term, may refer to any hand or brain work. It can be performed for money income or for love and personal satisfaction (as the chores of a housewife). To the extent that work is done for pay or consists of the making of items for sale, the person is considered to be "gainfully occupied." However, the self-employed (such as farmers, professional men practicing under a personal shingle, and other individuals operating their own businesses) have no "labor problems." Labor issues arise only when persons sell their services and work, as directed, on the premises of the buyer (employer).

Any attempt to define the term "labor" in a meaningful manner runs into difficulty where persons are both salaried employees and actual employers at the same time. That is true of the hired managements of firms, ranging all the way from the foremen to corporation presidents. They have the power to hire and fire workers, and they plan and direct the work. As a consequence, they tend to have attitudes and viewpoints characteristic of "the management" in contrast to those of "the men."

In any consideration of labor matters, the distinction between the supervisors and those who are supervised is crucial. Significant differences in economic outlook, in group interests, and in social relationships develop between the labor-buying, order-giving managers and the labor-selling, order-taking workers.

The gap between managers and managed may be especially

marked in the case of "blue-collar" factory employees in plants of some size. Their status is usually that of "wage earners," who are paid on an hourly basis and generally subject to fairly close supervision. The distinction between management and men may be more blurred in the case of technicians and white-collar employees, who work in an office, are on a salary, and seem less conscious of being "bossed."

Such gradations and blending make it difficult to apply a term like "the working class" to employed groups in this country. Certainly skilled craftsmen, technicians, and white-collar employees think of themselves as part of a great middle class. Even unskilled and semiskilled factory workers on hourly pay do not visualize themselves as belonging to a distinct working class, set apart economically and socially. In America, differences in industrial rank and prestige have not sharply crystallized attitudes along class lines.

With this brief background, we are now ready to define some terms frequently used in this textbook. The reader should be warned that these definitions are for purposes of clarity. They may not conform exactly with common usage, which is apt to be loose and sometimes ambiguous.

Let us start with some simple ones. "Employee" is a general term meaning any person who works for an employer and in return receives compensation—wages, salary, or other items of value. The person, corporation, or other business unit buying the services is the "employer." In a corporation, the employer is the "management," and all who have the power to hire, lay off, recall, and discharge are part of such a collective employer.

1. LABOR. More indefinite and confusing is the term "labor." Sometimes it is employed as shorthand for organized labor. That is its meaning in such expressions as "the labor movement," "the views of labor," or "the labor press." The term is practically synonymous with "employee" when used with reference to "the labor supply" or "labor standards." The difference between these two definitions of "labor" is evident from the fact that in this country organized labor includes only about eighteen million union members (a small fraction of whom are foremen in management),

whereas some 65 million persons received the bulk of their income in the form of wages or salaries during 1962.

The term "labor" has been used in still a third, more all-inclusive sense. In speaking of "the labor force," "labor mobility," and "labor as a factor of production," the meaning of labor is the same as "gainfully occupied" or "seeking gainful employment." This definition would include (on the average) 75 million persons during 1962.

Amidst such definitional confusion, consistent usage is almost impossible. Nevertheless we will try. Henceforth, where the term "labor" is used without some qualification or modifier, it will mean all nonmanagerial employees who earn their living primarily by selling their services directly to employers. Or it will refer to the services that they sell. The context will indicate whether reference is to the services or to the persons selling them. Thus defined, the term "labor" excludes all who have the power to hire, fire, and supervise.

"Labor problems," then, are the economic and social issues that grow out of work for pay. They include not only industrial unrest, labor unions, and slowdowns or strikes but also threats of wage loss from unemployment or other forms of economic insecurity. A broader term than labor problems is "industrial relations," which includes all aspects of labor in the economy—practices and policies as well as problems.

2. THE LABOR FORCE. Another term requiring definition is "labor force." The "civilian labor force" of the nation is the total working population. It consists of all nonmilitary personnel fourteen years of age or more, who are either gainfully occupied or are unemployed but seeking a job. The "total labor force" is the civilian force plus persons in the Armed Services. Included in the labor force are the self-employed and employers as well as employees. The expression "in the labor market" is sometimes used to mean in the labor force. However, as later explained, such usage may serve to create mistaken impressions.

The average size of the civilian labor force in 1962 was 71.8 million. Of that number, it is estimated that 8.9 million were in the category of employers and self-employed, that 61.4 million were employees (including hired managers) and the unemployed, and 1.5 million were unpaid family workers.[4] When economists speak of labor as a factor of production, they include the work services performed by all persons in the civilian labor force. The economics of labor analyzes their employment and the interrelations among workers, unions, management, and other economic variables.

3. LABOR SUPPLY. The total supply of labor services for sale is a more restricted concept than the labor force. Excluded from the labor supply are the self-employed and nonemployee employers, such as individually owned and managed enterprises and business partnerships. Hired managers, as both sellers and buyers of labor services, wear two hats, so to speak. As sellers they are part of the labor supply. The labor-supply concept also includes the factor of the work day and work week—the hours of work offered for sale.

For some purposes, the labor-supply concept is more useful than the less limited concept of the labor force. Unfortunately, the official statistics are all in terms of the labor force. Estimates of the nation's total labor supply can, however, be derived from labor-force data. Approximately six-sevenths of the labor force are employees, and expansion and contraction in the labor force is largely in the employee categories.

In the next section we will examine the components of the country's labor supply as well as variations in the total and the different categories. Because the components are not interchangeable parts, labor supply in general may not be too meaningful, particularly from a short-run viewpoint. In this connection, the short run assumes no change in the total population or in basic training, whereas, the long run takes into account population growth and education or training that requires over a year to complete. In a later chapter we will analyze more fully the factors affecting short-run and long-run changes in the labor supply.

---

[4] *Manpower Report of the President and A Report on Manpower Requirements, Resources, Utilization, and Training by the U.S. Department of Labor* (Washington: U.S. Government Printing Office, March 1963), pp. 139, 141. The figures are annual averages.

Sellers of Labor

With employment playing such a significant role in our whole economy, it is important to know something about the sellers of labor—their characteristics and the kinds of jobs they occupy.

Our understanding of the behavior of labor-supply components has been greatly enriched by the decennial census and the *Monthly Report on the Labor Force.* The latter, collected by the Bureau of the Census each month since the beginning of 1942, is based on interviews with a carefully selected sample of about 35,000 households in 330 areas of the country.

1. LABOR-FORCE PARTICIPATION RATE.   Perhaps the most significant over-all figure is the labor-force participation rate; that is, the proportion of the population over fourteen years of age who are actually in the labor force. (Bear in mind that this means either gainfully occupied or seeking a job and is not, therefore, identical with the labor supply.)

During the half century before World War II, our labor-force participation rate showed considerable stability from one decennial census to the next. From 1890 to 1940, close to 55 per cent of the working-age population was in the nation's work force.[5] For European nations with lower living standards and different work mores, the participation rates were somewhat higher. As a result of such apparent stability of the labor force relative to population in the United States, it was assumed that the labor supply was inflexible, if not invariant.

Actually the stability in the over-all participation rate in the pre-World War II censuses was achieved by significant offsetting changes in different components of the labor force. Under the impact of child-labor and compulsory school-attendance laws, the full-time employment of children practically disappeared between 1900 and 1940. Whereas in 1900 as many as 26 per cent of the boys and 10 per cent of the girls between ten and fifteen years of age were gainfully employed, in 1940 less than 2 per cent of the four-

---

[5] When the crude figures are adjusted according to a standardized distribution by age and sex and also are adjusted for the fact that the Census figures before 1940 were in terms of the population ten years of age or older instead of fourteen years or older.

teen and fifteen year olds were in the labor force, and the number under fourteen was so negligible that the Bureau of the Census ceased to enumerate them.

Labor-force participation rates have also declined at the other end of the life span. Largely due to systematic arrangements for retirement income (especially social security) and a decline in self-paced types of employment (especially on the farm), the work-force participation of the population sixty-five years of age and over declined from 39 per cent in 1890 to 25 per cent in 1940 and 19 per cent in 1962.

The drop in labor-force participation among the youth and senior citizens has been more than offset by increased participation by females, especially married women, in work outside the home. The percentage of adult women gainfully employed rose from 17 to 28 per cent between 1890 and 1940. Female participation rates since 1940 are indicated for selected years in Table 1.

TABLE 1

Total Labor-Force Participation Rates for Persons over Fourteen Years of Age, by Sex for Selected Years

Year	Both Sexes	Male	Female
1940	55.9	83.9	28.2
1944	63.1	89.7	36.8
1946	57.2	83.7	31.3
1951	58.8	84.8	33.8
1954	58.4	83.9	33.7
1956	59.3	83.7	35.9
1958	58.7	82.1	36.0
1960	58.3	81.2	36.7
1961	58.0	80.3	36.9
1962	57.4	79.3	36.7

Source: *Manpower Report of the President, op. cit.,* Table A–2, p. 140.

Obviously, total labor-force participation rates, which include the military, were greatly affected by World War II. After the war, as shown in Table 1, they dropped sharply for both sexes. However, since 1947 the long-term upward trend in the female participation rate has again become prominent. The male rate, on the other hand, has been declining since 1956 due largely to a marked decline in the participation rate of males fourteen to nine-teen years of age and males sixty-five and over.

The factors accounting for the century-old upward trend in female participation rates are complex, but technological change is certainly an important element. Housework has been eased by labor-saving devices and automatic equipment (e.g., washers, stoves, and other instruments in the "kitchen revolution"). Work once done in the home has moved to the factory (e.g., ready-made clothes and baked, frozen, and canned goods) and to the service shop (e.g., the beauty parlor and clothes cleaning and pressing establishments). In addition, jobs in industry have become lighter and cleaner—better adapted to female qualifications and tastes. For such reasons, one out of every three gainful workers is now a woman; almost three-fifths of them are married, nearly one-third are employed only part time. Half of all women in the forty-five-to-fifty-four-year age bracket are in paid employment, and the more education women have, the more they are gainfully working. Over half the women with a college degree were gainfully occu-pied in 1959, compared with less than one-third of the women who had left school after completing the eighth grade.

The growth in female participation is indicated by the fact that women constituted only one-sixth of the nation's labor force in 1890, one-fifth in 1920, one-fourth in 1940, 29 per cent in 1950, and 33 per cent by 1962.

Year-to-year changes in participation rates for both sexes in peacetime seem to have been chiefly economic in origin. The labor supply—the hours of labor services available—tends to expand and contract with business conditions. In periods of prosperity (like the boom of 1955–56), workers with relatively weak labor-force propensities are drawn into gainful employment. Mostly they are women—often on part-time work under rearranged work schedules and lower hiring standards. In recessions, some of these "marginal" labor resources withdraw and temporarily cease to seek paid employment. (Note the lower average increase in the total labor force in the recession years of 1953–54 and 1957 and 1962 in Figure 1.)[6]

---

[6] The labor-force statistics, of course, include the unemployed. The figures are subject to interview and sampling shortcomings and should be interpreted in light of the Census definitions. For example, should the following be counted as in or out of the labor force: persons who are absent from work because of sick-

Wide fluctuations in the rate of labor-force growth from year to year characterize the postwar period. One can observe in Figure 1 that the labor force expanded over two million in the two years following 1949, 1954, and 1959. On the other hand, from 1953 to 1954 and from 1956 to 1958, the expansion was less than half a million a year. From 1959 to 1961, both employment and unemployment increased about a million each. The explanation is to be found mainly in the fact that the expansion of many industries drew people into the labor force, while the simultaneous contraction of some other industries created unemployment.

FIGURE 1   ANNUAL AVERAGE INCREASES IN THE
TOTAL LABOR FORCE, 1947-62

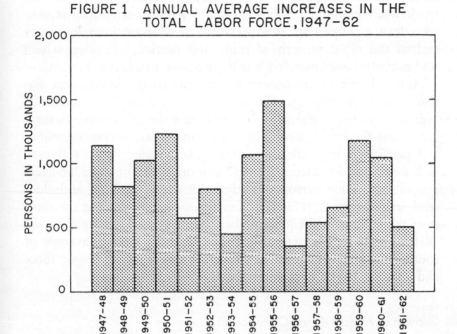

The American labor force has come to be characterized by a high degree of partial and intermittent attachment. Of the 78 million different persons who worked at some time in 1959, 30 per cent (or 23.6 million) worked at part-time jobs or at full-time jobs for only 1 to 26 weeks. Some ten million more worked at some

ness, strikes, paid or unpaid vacations, or bad weather; persons who are on temporary lay-off; persons who are not looking for work but would accept a job if a suitable one were offered to them? The Census excludes only the last two (on lay-off and passively selective) from the labor force.

time during the year than were employed at the seasonal peak in July. In the summer months, students seeking vacation jobs and housewives accepting work in agricultural lines swell the nation's work force to three or four million above the January-February figures.

The decade from 1950 to 1960 witnessed a 40 per cent increase in part-time employment compared with a rise of only 8 per cent in full-time employment. Such relative expansion in part-time employment can be traced largely to the great influx of workers seeking less than full-time employment (students who combine school attendance and part-time employment, housewives who work while children are in school, and workers sixty-five or over who draw a pension but seek part-time or occasional employment) and to the rapid growth of trade and service industries, which traditionally have provided much part-time employment.[7]

Intermittent or temporary attachment to the labor force has also been expanding, and the same groups are largely responsible. Married women frequently enter and leave the labor force to meet home and family responsibilities, students work during vacations, and pensioners may take temporary jobs. A study of the Bureau of Labor Statistics states: "In 1957 and other recent years, an average of 3¼ million persons—mostly housewives, students, and older semi-retired men—entered the labor force each month (on the average) while an almost equal number withdrew."[8] Data for the year 1959 indicate that between one month and the next an average of about 10 per cent of married women workers left the labor force and another 10 per cent entered it.[9]

Growth in Middle-Class Occupations

Another significant trend during the past fifty years has been the marked expansion in white-collar and middle-class occupations.

---

[7] See R. L. Stein and J. L. Meredith, "Growth and Characteristics of the Part-Time Work Force," *Monthly Labor Review,* LXXX (November 1960), pp. 1166–75.

[8] *The Extent and Nature of Frictional Unemployment,* Study Paper No. 6, Joint Economic Committee, Eighty-sixth Congress, 1st Session, November 19, 1959, p. 33.

[9] Sophia Cooper, "Work Experience of the Population in 1959," *Monthly Labor Review,* LXXX (December 1960), pp. 1279–80.

That, of course, has come about largely through shifts in industry and, therefore, in demand. However, on the supply side, it has necessitated sufficient adaptation to provide the qualified personnel for the expanding professional, technical, administrative, and clerical positions.

TABLE 2

Education and Median Wage or Salary Income of Year-Around, Full-Time Male Workers by Occupational Groups, 1961 and 1962

Occupational Group	School Years Completed (median) March, 1962	Income (median) 1961
Mental Work		
White-collar workers		
Professional, technical, and kindred workers	16.4	$7,339
Managers, officials, and proprietors (nonfarm)	12.5	7,343
Clerical and kindred workers	12.5	5,387
Sales workers	12.7	6,163
Hand Work		
Manual workers		
Skilled craftsmen, foremen, and kindred workers	11.2	6,067
Semiskilled operatives and kindred workers	10.2	5,108
Unskilled laborers, except farm and mine	8.9	4,330
Service workers, except private household	10.1	4,203
Private household workers	8.7	—
Farm workers		
Farmers and farm managers	8.8	558*
Farm Laborers and Farm Foremen	8.3	1,793*

* Farmer's income would, of course, be largely nonwage in form, and the figure for farm laborers and foremen is unduly low because it includes farm laborers who are "unpaid family workers."

Source: Income figures from 1960 Census of Population, *United States Summary: Detailed Characteristics*, 1963, Table 208, pp. 1-553-554 and Part 5, Chapter B, *Income of Families and Persons in the United States: 1961, Current Population Reports*, Bureau of the Census, Series P–60, No. 39, February 28, 1963, Table 42, p. 44.

Generally speaking, such "mental work" types of jobs require a higher level of education and training and usually carry relatively high compensation. This is indicated in Table 2 by the Census figures for male members of the civilian labor force who worked the full year on a full-time basis. (Median means the midpoint, or the figure that divides a series of numbers in half.) In 1961 the average *total* money income of *families* by education of the family head was as follows: college graduate, $9,264; high-school graduate, $6,032; grade-school graduate, $4,772; those with less than eight years of elementary school, $3,279.[10]

For all age groups and both sexes, a close association exists between levels of education and occupation. The professional, technical, and related workers are mostly college graduates. The other three "mental work" groups are composed mostly of high-school graduates. Elementary-school graduates are largely concentrated in the less skilled handwork occupations requiring little preparation and yielding low incomes. That distribution held true in 1960 for those who only recently had completed their formal schooling as well as for older workers.

While educational levels have been advancing, a shift toward middle-class types of jobs has taken place. During the past half century, three major transformations have occurred in the distribution of the labor force by occupational groups: (1) the proportion of professional and clerical workers has expanded rapidly; (2) farmers and farm laborers have declined to a much smaller fraction of the gainfully occupied; and (3) skilled and semiskilled workers have gained at the expense of unskilled laborers. These main shifts, which apply for both sexes, are brought out by Table 3, comparing 1900, 1950, and 1960.

The shift toward jobs requiring more education is further illustrated by figures for growth in occupational employment by educational levels and by rates of unemployment by educational levels. Between 1953 and 1962, employment in occupations with a median educational level of less than nine years declined by 8.2 per cent, whereas it expanded by 20 per cent in occupations with a median educational level of twelve to sixteen years, and by 48 per cent for occupations with an educational median of sixteen years or more.[11] The figures for unemployment in the civilian labor force in 1959 showed a direct inverse correlation with educational attainment. The unemployment rate was 9.9 per cent for those with less than eight years of schooling and 7.0 per cent for those with eight years,

---

[10] *Ibid.*, Table 8, p. 20.

[11] Calculated from figures on p. 13 and in Table A-7 in *Manpower Report of the President, op. cit.*

TABLE 3

Occupational Distribution of Employed Persons, 1900, 1950, and 1960 in Percentages

Occupational Group	1900	1950	1960
White-collar workers	17.6%	36.6%	43.2%
Professional, technical, and kindred workers	4.3	8.6	11.8
Managers, officials, and proprietors (nonfarm)	5.8	8.7	8.8
Clerical and kindred workers	3.0	12.3	15.1
Sales workers	4.5	7.0	7.5
Manual workers	35.8	41.1	38.7
Skilled craftsmen, foremen, and kindred workers	10.5	14.1	14.2
Semiskilled operatives and kindred workers	12.8	20.4	19.4
Unskilled laborers, except farm and mine	12.5	6.6	5.1
Service workers	9.0	10.5	11.7
Service workers, except private household	5.4	7.9	8.9
Private household workers	3.6	2.6	2.8
Farm workers	37.5	11.8	6.5
Farmers and farm managers	19.9	7.4	4.1
Farm laborers and foremen	17.7	4.4	2.4
Total	100.0%	100.0%	100.0%

Source: *Occupational Trends in the United States—1900 to 1950*, U.S. Bureau of the Census, U.S. Department of Commerce, 1958, Working Paper No. 5; and *U.S. Census of Population: 1960, Detailed Characteristics, United States Summary*, Final Report PC (1)–1D (Washington: U.S. Government Printing Office, 1963), p. XXXV.

compared with an unemployment rate of only 1.8 per cent for college graduates and 0.7 per cent for those with five years or more of college.[12]

Behind the occupational trends lies a comparative expansion in service types of industry. Between 1900 and 1962, the percentage of all gainful workers represented by trade, government, professional service (including amusement), and finance, insurance, and real estate, more than doubled in each category. At the same time, manufacturing only rose from 22 to 25 per cent of the labor force. In fact, in 1962 about three-fifths of all workers were engaged in the various types of service industry; whereas in 1870 only one-quarter of the work force was so occupied and three-quarters were

[12] See Harold Katz, *Educational Attainment of Workers*, Special Labor Force Report No. 1 (U.S. Department of Labor, Washington: U.S. Government Printing Office, 1960), p. A-6.

producing physical goods (in manufacturing, farming, mining, forestry, and fishing).

The relative decline in employment in goods-producing industries and expansion in service-supplying industries is indicated in Table 4. Actually, the goods-producing industries had 1.5 million fewer workers in 1962 than in 1947. Automation was a big factor in that drop.

TABLE 4

Percentage Distribution of Employment, by Industry Division,
1947, 1957, and 1962

Industry Division	1947	1957	1962
Goods-producing industries	51.3%	45.9%	41.8%
Manufacturing	29.8	29.0	27.7
Mining	1.8	1.4	1.1
Construction	3.8	4.9	4.5
Agriculture	15.8	10.5	8.6
Service-producing industries	48.7	54.1	58.2
Transportation and other utilities	8.0	7.2	6.5
Trade	17.2	18.4	19.1
Finance, insurance and real estate	3.4	4.2	4.6
Services and miscellaneous	9.7	11.4	12.8
Government	10.5	12.9	15.2

Source: *Manpower Report of the President, op. cit.,* p. 17.

Also, within the goods-producing industries, a marked growth has occurred in office and other white-collar employments relative to manual work. As a result, manual workers in manufacturing, mining, and building construction combined represented a smaller percentage of the nation's work force in 1962 than in 1900. Even more significant is the fact that, since the mid-1950's, white-collar workers have surpassed the blue-collar manual workers.

The relative expansion in middle-class occupations has had significant labor implications. That is especially true when combined with the increased labor-force participation by married women. One consequence has been a greater concentration of family incomes in the middle-income categories and, therefore, a stimulus not only to suburban living but also to moderation in political and social views.[13] Many skilled manual workers (with the wife work-

---

[13] See Sumner H. Slichter, "The Growth of Moderation," *Atlantic Monthly,* CXCVIII (Octobr 1956), pp. 61–64.

ing) have achieved a family income and standard of living exceeding that of the lower quarter of certain professional and management groups. Those manual workers have "lived like Republicans" and certainly do not feel exploited.

Expansion of white-collar and female employment has also had adverse implications for unions. Generally speaking, those groups are more difficult to organize and keep organized than are male, manual workers. Actually, it is estimated that about six-sevenths of all union members in the United States in 1960 were manual workers.

Buyers of Labor

The problem of defining the employer, especially in the case of a corporation or governmental unit, has already been indicated. Technically, perhaps, the stockholders and the consumers are the ultimate employers (buyers of labor) in the case of corporations. Nevertheless, the employees think of the management—the foremen, supervisors, and other executives—as their employers. The statistics, however, are in terms of employing units and do not give the total number of persons with authority to hire and fire employees.

Frequently, we think of the employer as some local businessman who employs a few workmen. That is the typical situation still in certain lines of business like retailing, farming, and building construction. The bulk of employment, however, is supplied by corporations and governments. And it is the large corporate enterprises that tend to set industrial relations patterns in this country.

1. NUMBER AND SIZE OF EMPLOYERS. If the term "employer" is confined to enterprises employing at least the equivalent of one man for a whole year, there are, it is estimated, some 2.5 million employers in this country. Roughly two million of them are nonfarm enterprises, and half a million are employing farmers.[14] On

---

[14] Estimates in W. S. Woytinsky and Associates, *Employment and Wages in the United States* (New York: Twentieth Century Fund, 1953), p. 342. This source estimates that during any year at least six million units (three million farmers and three million nonfarm establishments) supply some employment, and that employers hiring three man-years or more of labor amount to 1.25 million.

TABLE 5

Distribution of Employees by Size of Firm, 1956

Size Class (number of employees)	Number (in 000's)	Employees Per Cent
1–3	3,084	6.5
4–7	2,906	6.6
8–19	4,544	10.6
20–49	4,291	10.1
50–99	3,136	7.6
100–499	6,346	15.0
500–999	2,303	5.5
1,000–9,999	7,205	20.3
10,000–or more	7,192	17.8
Total	41,006	100.0

Source: *Statistical Abstract of the United States, 1962* (U.S. Department of Commerce, Washington: U.S. Government Printing Office, 83rd ed., 1962), p. 490. The data represent employers reporting under the Social Security Act.

the basis of this definition, the sellers of labor outnumber the buyers by about twenty-two to one.

The size of the employing units has increased during the past two decades as American industry has marched forward on bigger and bigger corporate feet. The largest dozen corporations have a combined employment of about three million. The fifty largest corporations alone account for about one-tenth of all private employment in the country.

Employer reports under the Federal Old Age and Survivors' Insurance program provide a good picture of the distribution of employees by size of employing firm. This program covers employers of one or more, includes some 41 million workers, and embraces practically all commercial and industrial establishments privately operated except for the railroads. Table 5 gives the figures for 1956. It shows that almost two-fifths of the employees are connected with concerns employing at least one thousand workers, and that firms with one hundred or more employees account for three-fifths of all the covered employment. Inclusion of government and the railroads would increase the percentages represented by the larger employing units.

In industrial relations, plant size and firm size may be signifi-

cant variables. Studies indicate that large plants are more susceptible to unionization and have a higher strike propensity than small
plants.[15] That is understandable. In small shops and companies, the
top management and the men are likely to be in intimate contact.
Generally, the plant atmosphere is more informal and personal, and
industrial relations decisions can be quickly made on the spot.
Large firm size means many layers to the management hierarchy,
more decisions from a distant headquarters, more problems of communication between top management and plant employees, and,
often, a more impersonal atmosphere in the shop.

2. SHIFTS IN DEMAND. As already explained, the composition
of the demand for labor has altered with technological advance,
with changes in the structure of industry, and with increases in living standards. The demand for professional, technical, and other
trained white-collar workers has increased as industry has placed
more emphasis on education, research, administration, and distribution, and as service lines have expanded relative to goods production.

The demand for labor is a derived demand. Hours of work are
bought for the goods and services they help produce. Therefore,
the purchases of labor reflect consumer demand and the demand
of industry for plant and equipment. Employment rises and falls
with seasonal variations, business-cycle fluctuations, and secular
changes in industry. The different approaches for analyzing various employment changes are considered in the next chapter.

To some extent, labor demand and supply are interrelated and
influence each other. As already explained, increased demand in
prosperous times tends to bring forth additional ("marginal") supply. Moreover, employers may adjust the skill composition of their
demand to fit the characteristics of the available supply. Employers'
hiring standards may be lowered when qualified labor is short and
raised when unemployment increases. For the most part, however,
supply adjusts to demand by such means as training and new recruits entering the labor force. The adaptation of demand to
supply is often only a temporary expedient.

---

[15] For some supporting evidence, see Sherrill Cleland, *The Influence of Size on
Industrial Relations* (Industrial Relations Section, Princeton University, 1955).

SUMMARY

This introductory chapter has presented some facts, issues, and conclusions that may be briefly summarized as follows:

1. Employment is a central fact of our existence. Many economic and social problems stem from it.

2. Concern for employees' welfare has increased to such an extent that one authority predicts we will soon have a "laboristic economy."

3. A look at the "big questions" that we will tackle provides a framework for subsequent examination of particular subjects.

4. The term "labor" is so loosely used that clear distinctions need to be drawn. The "labor force" and "labor supply" are technical terms requiring careful delineation.

5. A measure of stability in the country's labor-force participation rate has been achieved by compensating factors. A rise in the female participation rate has more than offset the practical elimination of child labor and the increased rate of retirement of older workers. The changing job composition and the "kitchen revolution" have encouraged married women to enter paid employment.

6. The past half century has witnessed a marked expansion in service industries and in middle-class occupations that require a good education, carry relatively high rates of pay, and are not so susceptible to unionization.

7. The suppliers of labor outnumber the buyers by about twenty-two to one. Employing units have expanded in size, which has tended to accentuate labor problems and to stimulate labor organization.

DISCUSSION QUESTIONS

1. Discuss the notion that the United States is rapidly becoming a "laboristic economy."
2. What are some of the problems one encounters in attempting to define the following terms: labor, labor supply, the employer, the working class?

3. Explain the changes that have occurred in different components of the labor force during the past half century. From that experience, what do you conclude concerning labor-force participation rates during the next two decades? Explain.
4. How do economic conditions and fluctuations affect the size of the labor force and the supply of labor? Support your conclusions by citing experience during particular years.
5. Discuss the claim that labor-force changes during recent decades have helped promote moderation in political and social views.
6. How are labor demand and supply interconnected?

SELECTED READINGS

Galbraith, J. K., *The Affluent Society* (Boston: Houghton, Mifflin, 1958).

Long, Clarence D., *The Labor Force under Changing Income and Employment* (Princeton: Princeton University Press, 1958).

Manpower Report of the President and A Report on Manpower Requirements, Resources, Utilization, and Training by the United States Department of Labor, transmitted to Congress, March 1963 (Washington: U.S. Government Printing Office, 1963).

Phelps Brown, E. H., *The Economics of Labor* (New Haven: Yale University Press, 1962).

Scherer, Joseph, "Labor Force: Concepts, Measurements, and Use of Data," *Journal of Business*, XXXI (January 1958), pp. 38–62.

Slichter, Sumner H., *The American Economy, Its Problems and Prospects* (New York: Knopf, 1948).

———, "The Growth of Moderation," *Atlantic Monthly*, CXCVIII (October 1956), pp. 61–64.

U.S. Department of Labor, *The American Workers' Fact Book* (Washington: U.S. Government Printing Office, 1956).

Woytinsky, W. S. and Associates, *Employment and Wages in the United States* (New York: Twentieth Century Fund, 1953).

2.
Keys to Labor Knowledge

IN FACTORIES AND workplaces all over the country, employee-employer problems and union-management discussions are an everyday occurrence. Practitioners and students of industrial relations seek to understand how labor problems arise, why certain developments take place, what actions will lead to which predictable results. They desire, for example, to judge the effectiveness of particular wage structures and to determine the economic consequences of different wage changes. For such purposes, they need a tested set of concepts and generalizations that will help make sense out of a seemingly confused mass of incidents and data.

Empirical knowledge consists of facts. Ideas about how facts relate to one another is theoretical knowledge. Mental images of interrelationships and simplified systems of thought serve as sort of operational road maps to orient us in the complex world of facts. Of course, abstract theory never explains all the nuances of reality; it is not intended to fit exactly the detailed facts. A theory is sufficiently effective if it embodies principles or truths that illuminate obscurity and lead to approximately correct conclusions. For understanding the inner links between events, nothing is so practical as theoretical guides that reveal the significance and unity in apparent diversity.

SYSTEMATIC INQUIRY IN THE LABOR FIELD

The means of arriving at such a body of abstract knowledge is, of course, scientific research. Science is both a method and an attitude. The method is that of systematic search, honest reporting, and objective analysis, in contrast to wishful thinking and reliance on traditional biases. True, the application of the scientific method to social affairs may involve more field observation and less controlled experimentation, more variables and less stable elements, more qualification and less quantification, than in natural science research. But, some of the natural sciences, such as astronomy and geology, are largely observational, and the data of genetics do not lend themselves to precise quantification. As Dr. Vannevar Bush (one of the elder statesmen among contemporary American scientists) has pointed out, "there has been great science which involved very little in the way of measurement and mathematical formulation. Science does not always lean on the deflection of a needle, or a dip of a balance"[1]—or the concoction of an algebraic equation.

A part of the scientific method is conceptualizing and theorizing —defining terms, forging tools of analysis, formulating hypotheses and simplified models of reality, and testing theoretical constructs. A theory is a statement about significant relationships within the subject matter under study. The discovery of an interdependence between two variables may permit a prediction of the way a change in one of the variables (say, the supply or demand) may alter the other (say, the price). Systematic theory is the development of a whole structure or set of relationships that is logically consistent and linked together through observations or experiments. Without a growing body of theory, a science stagnates.

The attitude of scientific research is one of open-mindedness, persistent self-examination, and tolerance of alternative conceptions. It also involves a willingness to revise or discard theoretical

---

[1] "A Matter of Degree," Carnegie Corporation of New York, *Quarterly Report*, II (July 1954), p. 7.

formulations in the light of new findings. A science progresses not only by the creation of new theories but also by the elimination of old errors. It needs to be self-corrective. Especially in a new and rapidly developing field like labor, conclusions are likely to be provisional, subject to some change with the discovery of new interrelationships or with alterations in institutional and environmental conditions.

Types of Economic Analysis

Like other social scientists, the economist formulates theories in an effort to explain the inner operation of our complex economy and society. Broadly speaking, the theoretical structures or approaches of economists can be grouped into three general types: partial analysis (both orthodox and collective), national-income analysis, and development analysis. A brief examination of the characteristics and limitations of each type will help to orient the analytical sections in subsequent chapters.

1. ORTHODOX PARTIAL ANALYSIS. This traditional approach focuses on particular markets, enterprises, and individuals. It is also known as microeconomics, competitive price theory, or partial equilibrium analysis. The analysis is partial in that it reasons about the consequences of change in one variable in a section of the economy on the assumption that other sections of the economy remain unchanged. Such "thought experimentation" is apt to overlook various repercussions, despite efforts to check its conclusions against actual experience. In any event, its conclusions cannot legitimately be assumed to apply to the economy as a whole.[2]

The orthodox version of partial analysis rests on a model in which each enterprise operates on the principle of maximizing its profits, and each person is an economic man maximizing his net satisfactions. Both enterprises and individuals are supposed to adjust in the market by incremental calculation and adaptation (marginal analysis), so as to bring demand and supply into balance or equilibrium. The process is mechanistic; the results are deceptively precise.

---

[2] The fallacy involved in using the results of partial analysis for national-income problems is discussed in this chapter under "Some Pitfalls."

Orthodox partial equilibrium analysis makes few (if any) allowances for the special institutional features of the purchase and sale of labor. It is presumed to apply to all types of purchases and all types of markets. Such presumed universality is an advantage for some purposes but is a serious shortcoming for much research and analysis in the labor field.

Orthodox theorists using partial analysis generally have an individualistic economic philosophy and favor market solutions of labor problems. In their theoretical framework, nonmarket values are largely disregarded, and the collective decision-making process within large firms and unions is more or less ignored. Neglected also are many of the dimensions of management, competition, and employment. The narrow focus of this body of theory predisposes its adherents to condemn labor unions and minimum-wage legislation as uneconomic interferences with the competitive price mechanism. The validity of the policy conclusions drawn from partial analysis employing the traditional or orthodox approach will be considered at many points in this volume.

Here it may simply be noted that, despite its limitations, the traditional type of partial analysis has many uses for labor economics. Subject to significant ranges of tolerance, it is valuable for some types of long-range prediction. For instance, it helps to explain marked differences in wage scales between occupations, regions, or countries. Also it points to the economic consequences (in terms of surpluses and shortages and employment and investment changes) that will follow if the wage scales of a particular firm, occupation, industry, or area are fixed at an excessively high or an unduly low figure.

2. COLLECTIVE PARTIAL ANALYSIS.   Increasingly, our economy is composed of collective units. For that reason, partial analysis, especially for the short run but also for long-run purposes,[3] needs to be based on broader conceptions of business management, competition, and the process of wage determination than those postulated in the orthodox type of analysis. Such a collective approach

---

[3] The short run is the immediate future, during which adjustments involve changes in production and employment at existing plant capacity. The long run is a period sufficiently long for complete adjustment to an economic change to take place, including changes in the capital investment in the firm or industry.

for partial analysis stresses the corporation as a combination of capitalists who bargain collectively through the corporate unit. Corporate management is visualized as a group operation, faced with sets of probabilities and with options permitting adjustments in a variety of ways and not merely on a price-quantity plane. Competition is conceived as rivalry among collectives, not only in markets but also in terms of institutional prestige, political influence, and public esteem.

In an economy of collectives, unions and collective bargaining play a significant role, and employment is a many dimensional and evolving concept, difficult to encompass in the narrow channel of demand and supply curves. As the analytical sections of Part II will amply demonstrate, partial analysis in a collective framework is more complex and unprecise than the orthodox variety. It has areas of indeterminacy (zones of no-reaction or unpredictable response), and its concept of management (the entrepreneur) includes multioptional adaptation. Although it is less abstract and, therefore, less simple and universal in its pretensions, collective analysis is, as we will see, more appropriate and useful for analyzing the behavior of large units.[4]

3. NATIONAL-INCOME ANALYSIS.   In contrast to partial analysis, this approach focuses on the whole economy as a unit. It operates with a few national aggregates—total consumption, total savings, and total investment. These key variables determine the total flow of income, production, and employment in the national economy. Simply stated, full employment can occur only if the output at that level is disposed of through planned consumption and planned investment—by the purchases of individuals and households, by the purchases of businesses (investing in capital equipment and inventories), by the purchases of governmental units, and by the purchases of foreigners (net foreign investment). If those purchases combined are insufficient to absorb the full-employment output at

---

[4] In addition, there is general equilibrium analysis which deals with the interrelations among many individual markets throughout the economy. Because it is so general and ambitious in its coverage, it is not very useful for analysis of most labor problems, but it can be helpful in tracing rather general repercussions through different sections of the economy.

existing prices, unemployment occurs and business slumps. The immediate cause of the idleness of men and machines can be called either "oversaving" or "underinvestment and underconsumption"; they are essentially the same thing expressed differently. When total demand exceeds the full-employment output at current prices, an inflationary gap exists, and prices rise.

This sort of general theory of income and employment is also known as macroeconomics, aggregate analysis, or Keynesian theory, after the late J. M. Keynes, whose *General Theory of Employment, Interest and Money* (1936) laid the foundation for it. Subsequently, simple econometric models of the economy have been developed, assuming certain patterns of interrelationships among the aggregates.

National-income analysis arose out of the Great Depression of the thirties. It is particularly useful for indicating the roads that will lead to increased income and employment. Its predictive power, however, is still not impressive, because the aggregates are less well behaved than Keynes and his followers imagined. For instance, surveys of consumer spending plans show that people's propensity to buy consumer goods varies significantly with their expectations, and that savings patterns are more complex and unstable than had been supposed. Thus, the relationships stressed by Keynesian analysis may not have such key significance, and the aggregates themselves seem to conceal some important relationships. In short, this approach may suffer from overaggregation.

With its focus on aggregates and the economy as a whole, income analysis has tended to neglect underlying behavior patterns and structural features. As an example, employment practices and the detailed processes of wage and price determination (even the activities of unions themselves) are largely ignored. Indeed, income analysis has tended to accept unquestioningly certain assumptions of partial analysis, namely, that the behavior of firms and individuals is governed by the principles of maximum net profit and maximum net satisfaction—whatever those two terms may mean. Hence, business management continues to be visualized as the bloodless calculator of marginal analysis, and the light thus shed on the economics of collective units or organized activity is somewhat dim.

4. DEVELOPMENT ANALYSIS. This type of approach is also referred to as "economic dynamics" and "growth economics."[5] It recognizes that a single decision or event is only one element in an extended and evolving process. Consequently, instead of searching for the one cause or mechanically analyzing short-term adjustments, it focuses on the structural features that influence the process of economic adaptation and the interactions and institutional adjustments that occur as change proceeds over time. In short, it is concerned with economic evolution.

The aim of development analysis is to construct theories of long-term economic change, either for the economy as a whole or significant sections of it. Since in this type of approach one is dealing with many variables interacting over a long time span, the analysis is bound to be less rigorous than partial or national-income analysis. Also it must, of necessity, draw more heavily on other social sciences like history, sociology, and political science.

Economic development is, to a considerable extent, cumulative and nonrepetitive. In that respect, economics differs from the natural sciences, which deal with matter or cells rather than people. Only man is conscious of changes over time—of past history and future prospects—and modifies his behavior accordingly. Thus, it frequently is not possible in economics, and certainly not for the economy as a whole, to revert exactly to a previous set of conditions. Yet most mechanistic types of theory like traditional partial and national-income analysis, assume reversibility.[6] In contrast, development analysis emphasizes evolutionary change, much of which is a one-way street. Consequently, its conclusions may tend to be historically and geographically conditioned. For such reasons, long-term change remains a relatively underdeveloped area in economics.

A basic characteristic of our economy, however, is innovation

---

[5] For a discussion of aspects of this approach, see W. J. Baumol, *Economic Dynamics, An Introduction* (New York: Macmillan, 2nd ed., 1959); and M. Abramovitz, "Economics of Growth" in B. F. Haley (ed.), *A Survey of Contemporary Economics* (Homewood, Ill.: Irwin, 1952), pp. 132–78.

[6] This limitation of mechanistic types of theory is pointed out in K. E. Boulding, "Economic Theory: The Reconstruction Reconstructed," in Boulding, *et al.*, *Segments of the Economy* (Cleveland: Allen, 1957), pp. 17 and 24. The contrast between physical and social sciences in this respect is also made in E. H. Carr, *The New Society* (London: Macmillan, 1951), p. 5. This is not to deny that some mechanistic types of theory are irreversible.

and growth. Certainly, evolutionary change is a significant feature of the labor aspects of economic affairs. Therefore, considerable use is made of development analysis in this book. It is applied to such short-run problems as the process of wage-setting and collective bargaining and the process of management adjustment to cost changes. Stress is on the process itself rather than on a cross-sectional analysis at one moment of time.

Mainly, however, the time focus of development analysis is the long run—evolutionary change in economic institutions and magnitudes over a period of a decade or more. Such analysis is concerned with growth patterns, trends, and continued interaction among groups of variables. Examples of such groups of variables are: wage levels, living standards, and workers' aspirations; or production techniques, labor-force composition, and labor organization; or union-management relations, the political activities of organized labor, and the role of government in industrial relations. Note that the variables become so broad that they are difficult to define, measure, or even observe. Also, the network of their interrelations and interactions can be highly complex. Therefore, simple models will not suffice. The numerous hazards have not, however, stopped some economic philosophers (like Karl Marx or Joseph Schumpeter) from taking whole economies as their oyster and constructing a comprehensive theory of economic evolution for capitalism, the working class, and the structure of the economy. Such grandiose economic speculations have been called by some "magnificent dynamics,"[7] and by others, "magnificent illusions." It will be part of our interest, of course, to examine the development of theories of wages and labor—to see how they grew out of a particular (economic and intellectual) environment and how they, in turn, influenced economic developments.

Contribution of Other Social Sciences

Understanding is often enhanced by expanding the dimensions of an analysis. To the study of labor economics, other social science disciplines can contribute their particular approaches and theoretical knowledge. Their concepts and orientation may direct attention

---

[7] See Baumol, *op. cit.*

to variables that might otherwise be disregarded or oversimplified. A fairly comprehensive focus is important where, as is the case in the labor field, development plays an impressive role. As an illustration, enlargement of the concept of competition to include different types of institutional rivalry may serve to indicate the significance of certain social and political factors in economic evolution.

1. HISTORY. Obviously, history can contribute to a well-rounded view of economic change and sequence. For its knowledge and understanding, history draws on all of the social sciences. In other words, it is interdisciplinary. Thus, it helps to correct myopia from single-disciplinary vision (such as an exclusively economic interpretation of labor relations), and shows how changing social patterns (noneconomic variables) may influence economic results. Also, a knowledge of historical factors helps to explain the relations between economic doctrines and contemporary economic structures and institutions. And histories of unions, union-management relations, and union leaders, and even broad labor histories, may supply useful data for rough testing of hypotheses concerning labor and economic developments.

2. POLITICAL SCIENCE. In economic life, politics is a pervasive influence. Indeed, the subject of economics used to be called "political economy" before political science became established as a separate academic discipline. Political science studies the government of men, including the competitive struggle for votes, leadership, and power. In both policy determination and its administration, the interrelations and overlap of politics with economics are extensive. To a considerable extent, the policies of economic institutions (e.g., corporations and unions) are formed through the processes of their internal government, whether they are democratic, oligarchic, or authoritarian in nature. Business management uses political concepts when it talks of its "authority" and "prerogatives." Labor unions have even been referred to as political instrumentalities engaged primarily in economic activity. Also, of course, they engage in political activity, and one does not need to subscribe to the doctrine that economic interests completely determine political action in order to appreciate the impact of organized labor on national, state, and local politics and on foreign affairs.

Another reason for interdependence between the two disciplines is that, in the solution of economic issues, political decisions (elections, legislation, and administrative and judicial determination) are an alternative to market settlement. The significance of political decision-making and operations is indicated by the fact that government directly provides almost one-eighth of all gainful employment in our economy.[8]

3. PSYCHOLOGY AND SOCIOLOGY. The disciplines of history and politics may contribute to labor analysis at various levels—the single institution (firm or union), an industry or area, the nation (interstate), or the world (international). Because of their focus and tools of analysis, psychology and sociology are especially useful at the in-plant, intraunion, and local-community levels. The analytical tools of these two disciplines include attitude surveys, public opinion polling, employee interviewing and counseling, and clinical techniques. Psychology and sociology are particularly concerned with individuals and interactions within small groups, in contrast to the bold use of aggregation in economics.

To the analysis of employment and labor relations, psychology and sociology bring their own special insights and modifications of purely economic interpretations. Psychology helps in understanding personal motivation and the psychological needs of workers. The findings of group and social psychology are applicable to such matters as collective bargaining, strikes, and corporate decision-making.[9] With respect to employment, sociology stresses status, class, and other distinctions. Those factors help to explain how differences in social position arise among sellers of labor services (e.g., between factory and professional employees) and how such differences affect work goals, work satisfaction, and wages.

Sociologists are interested in the work place as a "social system." Under "group dynamics" they analyze the structure and functioning of small groups within industrial plants and the influence of such factors upon labor unrest and productivity. On a broader scale, sociology deals with the theory of organization, theories of institutional development including bureaucratization,

---

[8] Based on about nine million Federal civilian and State and local government employees in 1962.

[9] See, for example, G. Katona, *Psychological Analysis of Economic Behavior* (McGraw-Hill, New York, 1951).

and organized labor as a social movement. In view of our interest in adequate concepts and in development analysis, we will have occasion to make use of the findings of these two disciplines, as well as those of political science and history.

EMPIRICAL STUDIES

The collection, selection, and presentation of facts about labor may take various forms. In industrial relations, most empirical work can be classified as history, topical surveys, case studies, statistical material, or experimental results. Labor history marshals facts in a time sequence; topical surveys represent a cross-section slice through many units at one particular time. Case studies focus microscopically on one unit, usually treating the detailed facts both historically and cross-sectionally. Statistics offer facts in quantitative terms, which are summarized numerically. Laboratory experiments under properly controlled conditions are relatively rare in industrial relations. Ordinarily, the investigator must make his observations while industry is performing its regular functions and must use data that are a by-product of normal activity. A report of the results of any more-or-less controlled experiment could take the form of historical sequence or statistics.

Brief comment on each of these five types of empirical study may help explain some of their virtues and limitations. Needless to say, no economic generalization has ever jumped out of a collection of facts. The human mind is required to read causal relations into the accumulating mass of empirical data.

Historical Studies

Much of the recorded data in industrial relations are in historical form. They consist of such material as narratives of union and bargaining experience, reports of company developments in industrial relations, stories of organizational campaigns and strikes, and biographies of labor leaders.

Study of labor history brings home the complexity of reality and the diversity of viewpoints in our society. It also reveals change and growth as a more or less continuous sequence, an unfolding process in which preceding conditions influence succeeding events. Actual developments are, of course, subject to changes of pace as material advance and mental adjustment interact. Part of the appeal of history arises from speculation about such fluctuations—the rise, reduced momentum, and decline in programs, institutions, and leadership.

Historical research provides a significant part of the raw material for deductive conclusions. The authors of such studies themselves usually attempt some explanation of the events they chronicle. Indeed, the facts of history are rather barren and meaningless without some generalizing concepts to guide the selection and perception of them. However, the theoretical preconceptions underlying the writing of a narrative introduce an element of bias. Consequently, with theoretical advance as well as the discovery of additional material, the rewriting of parts of labor history may prove rewarding. In much historical material, the web of causation is far too complex to unravel with complete assurance. One must, of course, guard against the simple error of assuming that, because one event follows another in time, the first causes the second (sometimes called the *post hoc, ergo propter hoc* fallacy). Historical data are perhaps best adapted to revealing trends. They are also useful for the framing and testing of broad generalizations concerning the development of employment, wages, unions, and industrial management.

Topical Surveys

Much of the factual research in labor consists of the collection of data on particular topics. Such single-subject surveys are usually unified and manageable. Many of the studies of the United States Department of Labor, published in the *Monthly Labor Review* or as special *Bulletins*, fall into this category.

The possible subjects for such topical surveys are almost limitless. They range from the seniority clauses in agreements to the provisions of sickness benefit plans, from work stoppages to profit-sharing. The method of data collection may be by questionnaire, by interview, or from records (such as collective agreements, arbitration decisions, company reports, union documents, or social-insurance and employment-office records). They cover actual practices as well as official pronouncements or monetary sums.

Because topical surveys generally involve a current slice across

many industrial units in terms of the chosen subject focus, they
are likely to suffer from one or more limitations. If the study rests
on a sample of firms, the representativeness of the sample may be
questioned. In addition, the heterogeneity of the sample may raise
a question whether important differences are being concealed by
aggregation, unless the material is broken down into more homogeneous categories (e.g., by size of firm, industry or type of operation, etc.). Even though the data have been gathered and classified
by most impeccable techniques, their validity may be dated. Discrete investigations of the facts may be limited to the time of the
survey and hence lack the virtue of comparability over time. Consequently, they may be of little use in determining trends or long-
period changes. For such reasons, cross-section surveys of a single
topic generally yield findings that are qualified or are only approximately accurate. And such surveys are better suited to the
testing of hypotheses when they are specifically designed with that
aim in view.

Case Studies

Because labor relations occur continuously in hundreds of thousands of firms, the possibilities for the collection and interpretation
of case data are immense. A case—covering a single plant, firm, or
local union—can be investigated both historically and cross-sectionally, and the focus can be confined to one aspect of industrial
relations.

Intense examination of one unit at the local level has a number
of advantages. Not only is one able to gain familiarity with all the
pertinent facts and the important persons involved, but also in
doing so he tends to develop a feeling for the concrete situation,
an appreciation of the richness of reality, and an awareness of the
many facets of a problem that comes from field study. One result
of such microscopic scrutiny often is an added recognition of the
role of psychological and sociological factors—the personalities of
the leaders and the special characteristics in the groups.[10] Case

---

[10] As an example of the importance of the personal attitudes and other personality factors possessed by key persons in the bargaining relationship, see Chapter
5 by Douglas McGregor in *Fundamentals of Labor Peace: A Final Report*, sum-
marizing and analyzing the National Planning Association's series on *Causes of
Industrial Peace under Collective Bargaining*, Case Studies No. 14, December 1953,
pp. 72–83.

studies also permit a comparison of the facts, either before and after a change has been instituted, or currently between two or more situations that are quite similar except for one or two particulars. As a teaching device, cases may be most instructive. By presenting the complexity of experience, they can be used to indicate the alternative ways of selecting, presenting, and weighing the facts to arrive at different interpretations.

The limitations of case studies are likewise evident. The selection of particular cases for investigation raises a question of how representative, or typical, they are. Furthermore, the presentation of facts and their interpretation may simply represent one investigator's results, not readily subject to verification. Especially are such studies discrete and difficult to confirm if different concepts and theoretical frameworks guided the persons making them. Indeed, case studies may serve as a sort of intellectual refuge for the researcher appalled by obstacles to the development of an adequate theoretical structure or even by the difficulties of discovering and testing causal connections. And, through concentration on cases, the student may fail, so to speak, to see the forest from the near-by trees. He may overlook the fact that impersonal forces (especially economic factors) are at work underneath the surface, controlling or influencing the more dramatic actions of individuals. Moreover, although each case may be different, some understanding of the common elements in cases is necessary in order both to communicate knowledge through generalization and to provide a basis for prediction.

Statistics

In the labor field, we are blessed by an abundance of statistical material. For over seventy years, the United States Bureau of Labor Statistics[11] has been collecting and processing data. The Bureau provides statistical information on a great variety of subjects—employment, hours of work per week, wage scales, hourly and weekly earnings, cost of living for workers' families, labor turnover in industry, work stoppages, productivity and unit labor costs, and so forth. The statistics are usually gathered periodically

---

[11] Established in 1884, the agency was originally named the United States Bureau of Labor.

(monthly, yearly, or less frequently), and are broken down by industry, by region, and (for some series) by state or city.

Such a systematic compilation of facts provides useful summaries of a mass of observations. Collected by a single source that is expert and remarkably objective, they are useful for comparisons over considerable periods of time despite difficulties of comparability arising from changes in the content of jobs, in the methods and kinds of compensation, and in other industrial practices. By analyzing wage statistics, for example, one can tell what has happened to the level of wages in different industries and cities or to the wage differentials between industries, occupations, and regions; he can correlate wage changes with variations in productivity or calculate the change in wages during different phases of the business cycle. Statistics can prove valuable for testing theories, provided the theories are framed in such a way as to lend themselves to statistical verification.

Statistics are, however, tricky. Different statistics, and even the same statistical series, can be used as proof of opposite conclusions. Consequently, the limitations of statistics are worthy of respect. One should be on guard against such defects as a bias in the method of collection or in the sample, or a misleading summary figure which conceals significant variations, or the use of a year characterized by abnormal conditions as a base or standard of comparison for subsequent years. To illustrate, a part of the 1954 wage arbitration case of the Brotherhood of Locomotive Engineers, on which the union reputedly spent one-quarter of a million dollars, was vitiated by a failure to appreciate that the Bureau of Labor Statistics indexes of wages for skilled and unskilled building workers were affected by expansion of the sample to include new low-wage areas during the decade after 1945. False impressions can also be created by stress on certain statistics and omission of others, by the use of absolute numbers where relatives (percentages) are more appropriate, or by the supposition that correlations between numerical series prove cause and effect.

Attitude surveys and opinion-polling in industry provide statistics that afford some notion of workers' beliefs and even the intensity with which they hold their views. Despite the difficulties of formulating questions that will not bias answers and of reducing to numbers as intricate an entity as people's feelings, the polling technique is a real improvement over introspection as a means of determining the opinions and aspirations of wage-earners and managers. The results, however, must be interpreted with caution by persons who understand the pitfalls and appreciate the range of possible interpretations.

Often, commercial pollsters have taken opinion surveys on issues too complex to be handled by their techniques and have drawn general conclusions from completely inadequate data. One of the leading polling firms, for example, attempted to determine whether American workers favored or opposed the thirty-page Taft-Hartley Act by asking a small sample of workers ten specific questions right after the Act was passed in 1947. Unfortunately, even on those ten subjects, the questions did not correspond in detail to the provisions of the Act, and many important restrictions in the Act were not (and could not be) covered by the questions. Because each of the ten questions separately received a majority of favorable answers, the head of the polling firm jumped to the unwarranted conclusion that a majority of all the workers in the country actually favored the Taft-Hartley Act *in toto*. Handled in such a crude and indefensible manner, statistics may lead to a perversion of the truth.

Experiments

As already indicated, experiments under conditions controlled by the investigator are difficult to achieve in industrial relations. An approximation to controlled experimentation may be possible in relatively simple matters that are part of normal business operations, such as comparing the results from the use of different tests in selecting employees or the use of different items of equipment. For most labor problems, however, the laboratory type of testing is impractical. Companies and unions are reluctant to be used as guinea pigs so that the numerous variables can be kept constant while one is altered as the investigator wishes. Moreover, people are not standard products. The results are likely to be influenced by the operators' awareness that they are participating in an experiment. Strict comparability is difficult to assure with so many human variables in the picture.

Such difficulties were largely responsible for the rather negative results of the "scientific" experiments at the Hawthorne plant of the Western Electric Company near Chicago. Conducted over a five-year period between 1927 and 1932, the total cost of the experiments was reported to be approximately a million dollars.[12] A measure of productivity was the assembling of "relay" units. A "test group" of six girls was selected to perform the operation in a separate room, and a "control group" of six other girls (identical in all apparent respects) was maintained as an integral part of a large group also assembling relays. The conditions were changed only for the test group.

First, rest pauses were introduced and varied in frequency and amount over a seven-month period, and a midmorning lunch was tried. Then other variations were introduced successively, and combinations of changes were experimented with: a reduction of half an hour in the work day, the five-day instead of the six-day work week, and payment by results (piecework) instead of by the hour (time rates). Experiments were also conducted with changes in the candlepower of the lighting. Careful measurements of output and workers' physical condition were made for both groups before and after each variation was applied to the test group. After every innovation, the output of the test group increased and that of the control group did not. Finally, all the variations were withdrawn; the test group was returned to the original conditions; nevertheless, their output increased further to some 25 per cent above their productivity before the whole experiment began.

The investigators were puzzled. Time after time unsuspected complexities seemed to be vitiating their experiments. Finally, they concluded that the most potent factors affecting their results were variables that they could not measure: social and psychological influences in the working environment, especially informal group relationships and attitudes. The output of the test group rose in part because they enjoyed special attention. The recognition, consultation, and status accorded the test group gave them a feeling of importance and affected their work attitudes. In short, human factors spoiled the experiment as originally designed but led to another set of generalizations about worker behavior, stress-

---

[12] The results were most completely reported in F. J. Roethlisberger and W. J. Dickson, *Management and the Worker* (Cambridge: Harvard University Press, 1939).

ing the importance of individual recognition and participation, the morale of the small group, and the "human relations" abilities of the supervision.[13]

SOME PITFALLS

Certain sources of error in reasoning about labor matters have already been pointed out. Conclusions may be invalid because important factors were omitted from the analysis, the statistics used contain a bias, or more adequate data point to a different result. A brief explanation of other common pitfalls may help in avoiding elementary mistakes and unsound reasoning.

Reasoning from the Particular to the General

In labor economics, one must be chary of common-sense conclusions and solutions that are derived from personal experience. That is especially true for national-income type problems like wage-price inflation or general unemployment. One cannot derive the answers to such issues simply from case studies. The reason is that conclusions based on particular cases may be invalid for the entire economy; and conversely, what is true for the nation may be incorrect for individual application.

This common source of economic error has been called the "fallacy of composition." The fallacy consists of assuming that what is true of a part is, on that account alone, also true for the whole. As early as 1726, Francis Rawle (alleged to be the first writer on political economy in America) pointed out: "It is false Reasoning to make general Conclusions from particular Cases."[14] The layman, however, finds it difficult to believe that the lessons of business or personal experience may be absolutely incorrect when applied to the whole economy.

It has been said that economics is only common sense dressed

---

[13] For a report on some experiments in bargaining behavior, see Myron L. Joseph, "An Experimental Approach to the Study of Collective Bargaining," in Gerald G. Somers (ed.), *Proceedings of the Thirteenth Annual Meeting of the Industrial Relations Research Association* (Madison, Wisconsin, 1961), pp. 139–55.

[14] *A Just Rebuke to a Dialogue Betwixt Simon and Timothy, Shewing What's therein to be found*, Philadelphia, 1726, p. 15.

up in technical language. But, as M. S. Eccles (former chairman of the Board of Governors of the Federal Reserve System) has explained, "the economics of the system as a whole differs profoundly from the economics of the individual; what is economically wise behavior on the part of a single individual may on occasion be suicidal if engaged in by all individuals collectively."[15] When business begins to decline, common sense would seem to indicate that the appropriate policy for individual businessmen to pursue is one of curtailed expenditures in order to avoid inflated inventories and an illiquid position. However, costs to one man are income to others, so that reduced expenditures mean shrinking incomes. Consequently, policies that seem so sound to individuals—to reduce expenditures, increase one's cash position, and save although the savings temporarily lie idle—are ruinous when followed by almost everyone. Paradoxically, attempts by individuals to save more in a business recession may so reduce incomes as to lead to less saving altogether. Thus, "sound" finance can bring about widespread bankruptcy, and personal economy, by causing economic resources to be idle, may result in social waste.

In reasoning on labor problems, one must bear in mind that wage costs are a large part of the nation's income. Normally, a fairly close correlation exists between payroll expenditures and sales of consumer products. Therefore, partial demand-and-supply analysis, which appropriately applies only to single markets (and assumes that demand in general remains the same), is well-nigh useless for broad national issues such as the proper wage level or the best program to increase total employment. That explains why it is illegitimate to utilize the microeconomic principle of marginal analysis and individual demand curves for macroeconomic problems.

Furthermore, a company or union policy that works well in one situation may lose its effectiveness if it is generalized. This is true where the effectiveness of the policy depends on a differential advantage. Some companies, for example, are convinced from experience that it pays them, in terms of employee morale and the

---

[15] "Controlling Booms and Depressions," in A. D. Gayer (ed.), *The Lessons of Monetary Experience* (New York: Farrar and Rinehart, 1937), p. 6.

selection of job applicants, to have a wage scale 5 or 10 per cent above the average for the community or their industry. However, all firms cannot at the same time pay wages above the average, nor can all have their pick of the available workers. Similarly, one worker may solve his unemployment problem by getting a job through agreeing to acquire more training at night school or by offering to work for lower pay; but all unemployed workers cannot solve their problem by the same method.

The economic advantages of one group in society are sometimes won at the expense of other groups. Suppliers benefit when their product or service becomes relatively scarce; but their gain harms others, and general scarcity is economically detrimental to all. Where demand is inelastic (relatively inflexible to price changes), particular firms or union members may, by restricting supply and raising prices, increase their net income. They improve their living standards at the cost of lower living standards for the rest of society. Consequently, such slogans as "What helps business helps you" and "What helps labor helps everybody" lack general validity. Because individual or group advantage may conflict with the social good, it is a questionable practice to generalize on the basis of the selfish interest of some person or bloc.

The contention that industrial harmony will prevail providing people are sufficiently righteous overlooks such conflicts of interest between economic groups. It also ignores differences between individual and social loss, often illustrated by innovations. The introduction of a new machine, for example, may cause a financial loss to some firms owning equipment thereby made obsolete, and a loss of earning power may be suffered by highly paid skilled workers needed for the old process but not on the new equipment. It would be fallacious, however, to reason from such individual losses to the conclusion that society as a whole also suffers a net loss. On the contrary, new techniques usually increase total output and raise the living standards of the community at large.

Perhaps these examples have sufficiently illustrated the need at times to subordinate the particular to the general viewpoint. In any event, they indicate the importance of understanding the economic level—the part or the whole—to which a particular type of analysis and reasoning can appropriately be applied.

The Selective Fallacy

Another common source of error in the labor field is to pick particular examples which fit a conclusion and to ignore experience in conflict with one's preconceptions or theories. Because industrial relations are human relations, particular cases can readily be found to support any position or opinion. All sorts of people constitute labor and management, so that it is easy to cite some instance to prove any conclusion, and exceptions can be found to almost every generalization in the subject of labor.

It is necessary, therefore, to try to arrive at a balanced view of the whole situation and to avoid overstressing exceptional cases or the peculiar circumstances in one's own locality. By living in various sections of the country—in coal-mining towns, in nonunion rural areas, in swanky suburbs, or in cities where unions alone or in league with employers are forcing the public to pay high costs for local services and construction—one soon learns to what a large extent a person's opinions on labor questions are conditioned by his immediate surroundings. One purpose of a course in the subject should be to expand one's vision and knowledge so that he will not be bigoted and parochial. The fact that so much of the published material on labor matters is a mixture of truth, prejudice, and rationalization makes it all the more necessary to be discerning and balanced in drawing conclusions.

Misuse of Analytical Tools

Improper employment of the tools of economic analysis is a common failing. A number of illustrations of such misuse have already been presented in the discussions of statistics and of partial and national-income analysis. The fallacy of composition is actually an example of the use of a form of analysis inappropriate for the level of the problem, namely, application of partial analysis to the economy as a whole.

Other examples of this kind of pitfall may serve to guard against falling into it. A not infrequent error is to use highly abstract, long-run types of theory to describe and explain actual developments during a short-run period—a year or two. As an example, the so-called marginal productivity theory[16] (part of the traditional partial analysis) has sometimes been employed in explanations of wage determination under collective bargaining. Actually, collective partial analysis or a short-run bargaining theory is better suited for that purpose. Marginal productivity theory is much too abstract and formal, lacking a realistic conception of either the operation of business management or union functioning and behavior. That theory is more appropriate for explaining gross differences in wages between areas or from one period to another and for the prediction of such gross differences. Also it can properly be used as one possible standard for judging the fitness of wage structures from a long-run viewpoint.

A related pitfall is the misapplication of analytical concepts. Of late, it has become fashionable to refer to "the labor market." Sometimes it is simply a shorthand way of saying "either employed or seeking employment." But to the analyst the concept of "the market" has a much more exact meaning and formulation. He thinks in terms of the area in which competition and the forces of demand and supply converge to enforce a single price and an equilibrium that clears the market. Market theory has been developed with respect to commodities; its logic may not fit too well the process of employment. That may be particularly true where, as in many large firms, employment has evolved into a complex bundle of rights, long-term obligations, work-life attachments, and even lifetime protections for the employee and his family. At a later point we will examine this evolution of employment from a commodity concept (still appropriate for harvest and some other types of short-term hiring) to a welfare concept with many new dimensions—dimensions that cannot be left out or squeezed into the market concept. Use of the term "labor market" tends to ignore that evolution and, hence, is likely to nurture false conclusions.

Clearly, analytical tools, like mechanical tools, have their particular uses. Likewise, such powerful aids can be misapplied. One is reminded of the March Hare in *Alice's Adventures in Wonderland,* who tried to fix his watch with butter and was troubled that

---

[16] This theory is discussed in Chapter 9.

it did not work despite the fact, as he said, that he used "the best butter." For some purposes and situations, the best butter is not good enough.

The Fallacy of Single Causation

Social thinkers have repeatedly sought a single organizing principle, some one master key that would unlock all doors.

Unfortunately, our society and economy are pluralistic and exceedingly complex. No one factor so dominates all others that they are completely dependent on it and lack any causative power of their own. Therefore, to single out and attribute sole causal potency to one factor is to oversimplify social relationships and to neglect interactions within the processes of social change. This sort of mistake underlies Karl Marx' materialistic interpretation of history. In the Marxian model, economic factors are assumed to be the "true" cause of everything. Political, cultural, and religious developments hinge on production and exchange; they are devoid of any influence of their own. The result often is a one-sided view that supplies simple answers and creates an illusion of understanding.

In partial analysis, one can fall into the same sort of a trap with respect to complex institutions. It is naive, for example, to assume that union action is determined solely by wage objectives or that corporations relentlessly pursue the long-run aim of maximum net profit. Use of a collective approach for partial analysis is designed to avoid this pitfall of the all-embracing cause or sole determinant.

Value Judgments

As a nation we hold to certain ideas and ideals and to conventional precepts and a common folklore, which we live by and, on occasion, are ready to die for. To us they are self-evident truths or unquestioned principles. It makes little difference that the values we espouse may be somewhat inconsistent, like democracy and efficiency, equality and individualism, economic freedom and industrial authority, competition and economic security, or limited government and promotion of the common welfare. Such inconsistency permits an appeal to whichever value best suits the occasion or the argument. For example, idleness resulting from a business recession (or idleness caused by a strike) can be condemned as creating needless waste and insecurity or can be condoned as part of the costs of a free economy.

Naturally, persons who grow up in a civilization absorb its dominant cultural values, and their views on labor issues are colored accordingly. The student obviously cannot completely avoid value judgments, nor should he fruitlessly seek some strictly neutral position with respect to the great issues of the day. Our traditional values are an integral part of the American way of life.[17] One should, however, make his value assumptions explicit, be aware of their limitations and inconsistencies, and recognize the fact that our social values are continually changing and being redefined.

The weight one gives to different social values depends, of course, on his economic and social philosophy and also his personal interests. Industrialists are likely to stress freedom from governmental interference in economic affairs, efficiency measured in market terms, and individual self-reliance. Labor leaders, on the other hand, are prone to emphasize full employment, collective protections from management authority, and the welfare state. Nevertheless, business management generally proposes detailed government regulation of unions, and labor leaders frequently recommend more strict government regulation of business. Such interest-inspired inconsistency is understandable.

No one value or goal can be considered the "supreme good." All are relative. And society is continually working out, through practical compromises, the "best" balance among competing goals and conflicting values. In a democracy, any such balance is temporary, for emphases on the different values change with conditions, and concepts of welfare and social justice alter over time. Consequently, the correctness of any particular social balance or economic philosophy is not provable by scientific methods. Of course, interest blocs and pressure groups such as business associations and organized labor are constantly striving to influence public opinion and

---

[17] The values of American society are elaborated and examined in Max Lerner, *America as a Civilization, Life and Thought in the United States Today* (New York: Simon and Schuster, 1957).

government policy so that they conform more closely to the current value pattern of the interest group.[18]

In this connection, one must also beware of the "tyranny of words." Slogans can confuse; verbal disguises may mislead. In the struggle for men's minds (basically, for conversion to a particular value pattern) words and ideas are weapons. The labor field especially has been plagued with emotionally charged phrases like "right to work," "labor bosses," "closed shop," "yellow dog contract," "labor exploitation," and "scabbing on workers." In examining ideas, we must strive to eliminate the emotional connotations and analyze dispassionately.

Of course, it is extremely difficult to shun all personal bias in the labor field. A student's attitude toward a particular issue or toward labor problems in general is likely to be influenced by his own experience, the experience of relatives and friends, or his hopes and ambitions—by the position in society he expects to occupy after graduating from the campus.

SUMMARY

In looking back over the contents of this chapter one cannot help but be impressed by the interrelatedness of things, by the complexities of our economy and society. Nevertheless, keys that unlock knowledge can be forged, and, as we will see in subsequent chapters, many forward steps toward tested knowledge have been made.

1. Much of our understanding in the labor field rests on useful theories developed by means of the methods of scientific research.

2. In economics, orthodox partial analysis is a useful tool for long-run problems and gross predictions. It suffers, however, from a narrow focus and obsolete concepts. Collective partial analysis, by enlarging some of the concepts, seeks to overcome certain defects in the traditional approach.

3. Income analysis, operating in terms of national aggregates,

---

[18] For a good discussion of the problem of balance between different social values, see J. M. Clark, *Guideposts in Time of Change* (New York: Harper, 1949), Chapter 3, and *Alternative to Serfdom* (New York: Knopf, 1948), Chapter 1.

is useful for problems of "the level"—the level of employment, the wage level and the business cycle, or wage and price level changes.

4. A still different approach is represented by development analysis. It focuses on dynamic change, especially the complex problem of long-term evolution, which is largely irreversible.

5. Especially to collective and development analysis, the tools and insights of other social sciences can make a contribution. Psychology and sociology are most useful for supplemental application at the local level; history and political science are of more general analytical assistance.

6. The collection and processing of facts in the labor field take a variety of forms—historical studies, cross-sectional surveys on a particular topic, case studies, and statistical surveys. Controlled experimentation is rarely feasible.

7. Perhaps the most frequent error in labor economics is switching between levels of analysis—to apply partial or particular reasoning to general or "level" problems and *vice versa*. This pitfall involves the familiar fallacy of composition. Other misapplications of analytical tools include use of long-run theory for descriptive purposes and use of a technical "labor market" concept for analyzing the complex relationship into which much of the employment in this country has evolved.

8. Another possible pitfall is the selection of one factor as the sole source of causation or the only aim of complex organizations.

9. The social values of a nation influence judgments concerning union and management policies. Value judgments must be faced, for they cannot be avoided. However, one should guard against personal bias and verbal confusions.

DISCUSSION QUESTIONS

1. What are some of the problems of applying scientific methods to the field of labor? Why are experiments difficult to arrange in industrial relations and what substitutes for controlled experimentation can be used?
2. Explain the uses and limitations of each of the following: orthodox partial analysis, collective partial analysis, national-income analysis, and development analysis.

3. Explain some of the ways that other social sciences can aid in the analysis of labor matters and at what level—local, industry, or national—different social sciences can most effectively be used.
4. Give some examples of "empirical studies." How can statistics and polling techniques be misused and, thus, prove misleading?
5. What is "the fallacy of composition"? Give an example of the misapplication of partial analysis. Of the misuse of national-income analysis.
6. Comment on the following statement: "Lower wages, and thus lower production costs, enable local employers to expand their employment and help to overcome unemployment locally. The same thing is, of course, true nationally. General wage reduction is the answer to nationwide unemployment."
7. Explain two other pitfalls besides the fallacy of composition.
8. What can be said about value judgments in the field of labor?

SELECTED READINGS

Baumol, W. J., *Economic Dynamics, An Introduction* (New York: Macmillan, 2nd ed., 1959).
Boulding, K. E., *The Skills of the Economist* (Cleveland: Allen, 1958).
———, "Economic Theory: The Reconstruction Reconstructed," in *Segments of the Economy* by K. E. Boulding, *et al.* (Cleveland: Allen, 1957).
Clark, J. M., *Economic Institutions and Human Welfare* (New York: Knopf, 1957).
Dubin, Robert, *The World of Work: Industrial Society and Human Relations* (New York: Prentice-Hall, 1958).
Katona, George, *The Psychological Analysis of Economic Behavior* (New York: McGraw-Hill, 1951).
Lerner, Max, *America as a Civilization, Life and Thought in the United States Today* (New York: Simon and Schuster, 1957).
Wilensky, Harold L., *Syllabus of Industrial Relations: A Guide to Reading and Research* (Chicago: University of Chicago Press, 1954).

3.
Development of
Organized Labor
before the New Deal

THIS AND THE next chapter examine the development of organized labor in America. It is a long and involved story, extending back some 180 years to 1778. In that year, the journeymen printers of New York City temporarily combined to demand and obtain an increase in wages.

In fact, during the decade following the inauguration of George Washington as the first President in 1789, unions of shoemakers, printers, and carpenters were organized in New York, Philadelphia, and Boston; negotiations were conducted with employers; and strikes occurred. In this country, local unions were functioning in a fairly modern fashion for some time before the first American business corporation was chartered.

Contrary to common presumptions, it was the skilled workers having strong bargaining power who pioneered the trade union movement in this and other countries. The "aristocrats" of labor, not the poorly paid proletariat, challenged the authority and control of employers during the early days of labor organization. This fact about the formative years of unionism is of considerable

significance for an understanding of the American labor movement
prior to the New Deal of the thirties, and even for a proper com-
prehension of the labor movement in America today.

In a survey of the history of organized labor in America, a
number of key questions call for some sort of an answer. They are:

1. What conditions stimulated the rise and growth of labor
unions? Why, at various times, were some areas and industries
organized and others not?

2. What factors explain the changes in orientation and structure that have occurred within organized labor? What types of
labor organization and philosophy of unionism were best fitted
to thrive and survive during different historical periods?

3. How does one account for the periods of rapid advance,
plateau, and decline in the strength of organized labor during the
180 years of its history?

4. Why have violence and corruption been more prevalent in
the history of American labor than in that of most other industrial
nations?

5. What explains the shift from a fairly militant to a more
mature unionism?

6. Has the American labor movement, on balance, been a radical, progressive, or conservative force?

THE SHAPING FORCES

The answers to these questions are not easy. Organized labor
in America is too complex and diverse to be explained by any simple model or formula or by any unitary interpretation.

It is clear that unions did not arise solely from competition and
expansion of product markets, from specialization and the dilution
of work skills, from factory techniques and conditions, or from
growth in the size of employing units. Yet each of those factors
was, at times, influential in union development. Rather, American
unionism, like the labor movements of most countries, grew out
of the combination of factors generated by the process of industrialization. And the pattern of its development has been condi-

tioned by the special economic, political, and social characteristics of this country.

To a considerable extent, a country's labor movement is the product of its environment. It adapts to the circumstances and problems it encounters. That explains why the labor movements of different countries do not duplicate one another, why each has its distinctive characteristics. ("Labor movement" is a broader term than "labor union"; it presupposes some solidarity between workers in different trades and industries—the association of a number of individual unions for common action.)

Some Basic Influences

Three fundamental factors have helped mold the American labor movement. As these factors have experienced secular change, the nature of their influence has altered over time. A brief discussion of each factor will suggest the sort of influence it has exerted on union development.

1. IMMIGRATION AND THE CHANGING CHARACTER OF THE WORK FORCE. In American labor history, immigration has been a major consideration. Its importance is indicated by the fact that some 38 million immigrants, mostly male workers,[1] entered this country between 1820 and 1930.

Table 6 shows the importance of this added labor supply in terms of the ratio of immigration (during a decade) to the nation's labor force (at the end of that decade). During the ten-year period 1881–90, the immigrant inflow averaged over half a million a year, and in the peak decade 1904–14 it averaged a million a year. In relation to the labor force, however, 1851–60 was the peak decade, as Table 6 indicates.

The immigrants, a ready prey for exploitation, frequently represented a threat to existing wage and labor standards. Some were even important as strikebreakers. Arriving bewildered and

---

[1] Some four-fifths of all immigrants were workers, fifteen years of age or older, and males constituted, on the average, perhaps three-fourths of the total. See C. Taeuber and I. B. Taeuber, *The Changing Population of the United States* (New York: Wiley, 1958), pp. 67–68.

TABLE 6

Immigration by Decades and Expressed as a Percentage of Total Labor Force, 1821–1930

Decade	Number of Immigrants (in 000's)	Ratio to Labor Force at End of Decade
1821–30	143	4%
1831–40	599	11
1841–50	1,713	22
1851–60	2,598	25
1861–70	2,315	18
1871–80	2,812	16
1881–90	5,247	23
1891–1900	3,688	13
1901–10	8,795	24
1911–20	5,736	14
1921–30	4,107	8

Source: *Statistical Abstract of the United States,* 1957, pp. 92 and 195; and J. Frederick Dewhurst and Associates, *America's Needs and Resources: A New Survey* (New York: Twentieth Century Fund, 1955), Table 306, p. 725.

practically penniless, the male immigrant was forced to obtain work at any pay and any working conditions in order to sustain life. As a costless source of cheap labor, immigration promoted a short-run commodity concept of employment, and helped keep a wide differential between the wages of skilled and unskilled workers.

Other economic consequences stemmed from immigration. By supplying an inflow of unskilled labor at the bottom of the occupational pyramid, it aided labor mobility and rapid occupational advancement for the earlier settlers. Also, by stimulating movement of workers and creating a labor force with diverse cultural, language, and racial characteristics, immigration produced obstacles for labor organization. Yet immigrants, handicapped for promotion into management positions, supplied much of the leadership for certain American unions, such as the Mineworkers, the Clothing Workers, and the Cigar Makers.

With the decline of immigration to a trickle in the twenties and the continued rise in educational levels, the nation's labor force has tended to become more homogeneous—in culture, language, and training. After the large inflow of workers considered "inferior" stopped, many employers came to have more concern for the long-run welfare of all their employees.

2. STEADY IMPROVEMENT IN REAL WAGES.   Another pervasive influence has been the rather continuous rise in the buying power of the wages workers have received. This, of course, has meant a steady increase in their living standards. By 1958, the purchasing power of an hour of labor in this country was well over four times what it had been a century earlier.

The course of hourly real wages from the 1820's to the 1850's is depicted in Figure 2.[2] Real wages are money wages divided by an index of the cost of living so as to eliminate the effect of changes in the buying power of the dollar. In the chart, a five-year average for the first half and for the second half of each decade has been used in order to show the changes on a semidecade basis. The chart, plotted on ratio scale so that line slopes everywhere represent equivalent percentage changes, shows that real wages have experienced a marked upswing since the outbreak of World War I. Before that there were three periods (1830–39, 1850–65, and 1873–83) when the average worker's living standard failed to rise. As we will see, worker unrest was especially prevalent during the first and third of those three plateau periods.

A progressive rise in real wages encourages economic optimism and serves as a solvent for some labor problems. In an economy with improving real wages, collective bargaining seems to pay off in the form of a better life on and off the job.

3. ECONOMIC EXPANSION AND TECHNOLOGICAL CHANGE.   Largely responsible for rising real wages has been the increase in average output per hour worked. During the past century, output per

---

[2] The data in Figure 2 are five-year averages centered at the second and seventh years of each decade; 1860 is the base year. Sources of data: For the period 1820–40 use was made of the statistics in Alvin Hansen, "Factors Affecting the Trend of Real Wages," *American Economic Review*, XV (March 1925), p. 32 converted to an 1860 base year. For 1840–1945 use was made of W. S. Woytinsky and Associates, *Employment and Wages in the United States, op. cit.*, Appendix Tables 15 and 18, pp. 582–83 and 586. In Table 15 Tucker's Series was used; the Composite Wage in Table 18 was converted to an 1860 base; the United States Bureau of Labor Statistics figures of average hourly earnings in manufacturing deflated and adjusted to the 1947 index figure were used for 1948 to 1963; and, of course, five-year averages were calculated for the whole series.

FIG. 2   HOURLY REAL WAGES IN THE UNITED STATES, 1820-1963

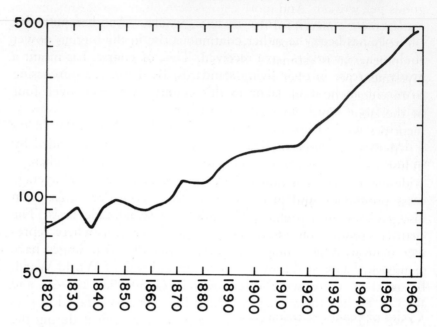

man hour has increased about sixfold, and has been rising at an average rate of 1.7 per cent a year compounded.[3] Although this output increase is often called "labor productivity," it has been due largely to technological improvement, greater capital investment per worker, and large-scale production.

Technological advance has meant the application of machinery and mechanical power in place of manpower and horse power. Indeed, modern technology in the form of automatic devices (automation) is tending to eliminate "muscle work" from industry. As explained in Chapter 1, this is a basic factor in the shift from manual work to middle-class, white-collar types of employment, which are less susceptible to unionization.

---

[3] For the period 1850–1900 see J. F. Dewhurst and Associates, *America's Needs and Resources* (New York: Twentieth Century Fund, 1948), Table 3, p. 23. For other estimates and later years, see W. S. Woytinsky and Associates, *op. cit.,* Table 32, p. 84; John W. Kendrick, *Productivity Trends in the United States* (Princeton: Princeton University Press, 1961), Chapter 3; and *Staff Report on Employment, Growth, and Price Levels,* Joint Economic Committee, U.S. Congress, December 24, 1959, pp. 34–36.

More advanced methods of production have, of course, required a steady increase in the quantity and quality of capital goods per worker. And more capital investment has meant greater management concern for the welfare and effectiveness of the workers responsible for operating the more elaborate and expensive equipment. It is estimated that in the past eighty years capital investment per worker increased threefold and in 1963 amounted to an average of about $9,000 (at current prices) for each member of the labor force.[4] In manufacturing, the average capital investment per worker was over $16,000 in 1958.[5]

Methods of large-scale production hinged on the expansion of industry—from local to national markets and from local to nationwide companies. A national market, continental in size, facilitated mass production and promoted the large, multiplant concern. It also gave unions a problem of organizing the whole area of competitive production. Otherwise they faced the undermining effects of nonunion competition and interstate differences in labor standards.

Cycles of Economic Disturbance and Political Transition

American history has witnessed seven periods of rapid growth in union membership. Four of them partially coincided with a war—1836–72 (Civil War), 1896–1904 (Spanish-American War), 1917–20 (World War I), and 1940–45 (World War II). These war periods were generally characterized by a rising price level, booming business, and relative shortage of labor.

Rapid union expansion has also occurred during periods marked by almost the opposite conditions. Three major waves of union growth took place following a decline in the price level, wage cuts, and business depression with widespread unemployment. They were eras of political and industrial unrest—1827–36 (the

---

[4] For estimates of capital (except land and its improvement) for the period 1879–1944, valued at 1929 prices, see S. S. Kuznets, *Long-Term Changes in the National Income of the United States of America Since 1870* in S. S. Kuznets (ed.), *Income and Wealth of the United States; Trends and Structure*, Income and Wealth, Series II (England: Bowes and Bowes, Cambridge, 1952), Table 11, p. 78. A 1963 figure of $9,000 is a rough estimate by the author.

[5] See H. J. Weinberger, "Capital Invested Per Production Worker," *The Conference Board Business Record*, XV (March 1958), pp. 98–99.

age of Jacksonian Democracy), 1881–86 (the rise of Populism), and 1933–39 (the New Deal).

In those years, the clash of class interests sharpened, and shifts occurred in the political power of economic groups. John T. Dunlop attempts to demonstrate that each of these three periods coincided with the bottom of a Kondratieff long wave (representing economic growth and averaging fifty years in duration).[6] In any event, they were times of transition toward a new balance between individual values and collective action.

Retarding Factors

Many explanations have been offered for the delayed development of trade unionism in America after a strong upsurge in the 1820's and 1830's. Then this country pioneered, achieving a number of world firsts in the labor field—the first effective city-central organization of local unions, the first trade-union journal, and allegedly the first labor party all arose in Philadelphia in 1827 and 1829. Yet the next half century was spent in groping for a stable form of organization and in oscillating from political to economic activity and back to preoccupation with politics.

This fumbling and fluctuation occurred in large measure because America in the nineteenth century did not present fertile ground for continued union organization. The labor movement was held back by a number of uncongenial factors—economic, social, and political. Three of them have already been mentioned. They were: immigration (providing a working population with wide racial, linguistic, and cultural differences), the size and diversity of the country (creating handicaps for unionization), and labor mobility (keeping local work groups in a state of flux).

Actually, a fairly continuous group of employees is needed for unionism to achieve some permanency. An "open society," with movement of labor geographically and up and down the occupational ladder, is so fluid that little class stratification occurs. People do not consider themselves continuously part of a separate "working class."

---

[6] See John T. Dunlop, "The Development of Labor Organization: A Theoretical Framework" in R. A. Lester and Joseph Shister (eds.), *Insights Into Labor Issues* (New York: Macmillan, 1948), pp. 187–92.

Free land and frontier conditions gave the country a social philosophy and a distinctly individualistic flavor. Individualism colored the Federal and State constitutions and held sway here longer than in other countries. Many of our factory workers were recruited from rural areas, where a rugged sort of individualism was rife and the birth rate high. Workers from rural backgrounds were reluctant to join in the collective activities of labor unions.

Our form of government has been another retarding factor. American political democracy diffused power and served as a solvent for class friction. Political parties were not drawn on class lines, and no class has held political rule by virtue of heredity. In the first decades of the 1800's, universal male suffrage was established, unencumbered by property qualifications. Consequently, wage-earning groups were not solidified by political injustice and oppression. Yet, a Federal structure meant that labor unions were subject to differing State laws and court rulings, and often were considered unwelcome in localities by reason of intercommunity and interstate competition for industry.

Indeed, hostility to unions on the part of employers and other elements in the community has been an important factor limiting union growth. In this country, vigorous (even ruthless) employer resistance to labor organization continued for almost a century and a half prior to World War II. Such opposition was much more prolonged and bitter here than in other industrial countries. As explained in Chapter 5, it helped to give our labor relations history its own special strands of physical violence and private warfare.

Finally, wage-paid labor was only a minority of the total labor force (or voting public) during much of the nineteenth century. Farmers, small businessmen, and other middle-class groups tended to dominate. In the early 1800's, four-fifths of the nation's work force were self-employed or employers. In the decades before 1870, industrial wage-earners and their families accounted for less than a quarter of the nation's total population, while persons engaged in farming and their families represented about half of the citizenry. Only in 1880 did wage-earners in all types of economic activity expand enough to become a bare majority of all gainful workers.[7]

---

[7] See Spurgeon Bell, *Productivity, Wages, and National Income* (New York: National Bureau of Economic Research, 1940), p. 10.

The wage-earners were too much a part of the fluid, diffuse, and pluralistic society to respond to a purely working-class appeal. It is not surprising that in the nineteenth century political combinations of groups with diverse economic interests—labor, farmers, and small business—proved highly impermanent, shifting with the next phase of the business cycle.

SEARCH FOR A STABLE FORM OF ORGANIZATION

The labor history of the nineteenth century is characterized by recurrent shifts of means and objectives. Labor programs fluctuated between economic and political action, between collective bargaining and major social reform, largely with changes in business conditions.

During prosperous periods, unions would thrive, with emphasis on negotiation with employers and protection of investment in craft skill. As prosperity yielded to depression, the membership of unions would melt away and interest would shift to political action, radical or utopian schemes, and more inclusive programs that might attract support from less skilled labor and also farmers and other nonemployee groups. Early establishment of manhood suffrage served to encourage frequent diversion of workers' interests from unionism to political programs.

Trade unionism revived and expanded during the following periods of prosperity: 1810–15, 1824–37, 1850–57, 1863–73, and 1879–85. On the other hand, labor unions were either wiped out or practically eliminated during the depression years of 1816–20, 1837–43, 1857–62, and 1873–79. It was only in the late 1880's, with the triumph of craft unionism, following the founding of the American Federation of Labor, that labor organizations achieved sufficient strength and tenacity to weather severe depression without losing most of their membership.

Colonial Regulations

Before the American Revolution, industry was in the handicraft stage, with master craftsmen and their apprentices. The master owned his own shop and tools, combining in one person the functions of capitalist, merchant, and worker.

Largely in the interest of producer craftsmen and of consumers, the colonial legislatures passed laws regulating industry. In addition to fixing the quality and price of a variety of manufactured products, colonial statutes specified the fees to be charged by tanners of leather, blacksmiths, millers of grain, sawmill owners, carters, and others. It was against a municipal ordinance fixing the price for removing a cartload of dirt from the streets that the New York teamsters (entrepreneurs, not wage-earners) struck in 1677.[8]

Because prices for services seemed "excessive" in the colonies, some of these early laws fixed maximum fees as a means of keeping down wage rates. From 1630 to 1635, the Massachusetts legislature attempted to fix maximum wage rates for "Carpenters, Joyners, Bricklayers, Sawers, Thatchers, Wheelwrights, Tylers, Mowers, Master and inferior taylors, and labourers," stipulating a fine to be paid by all offending employers.[9] In 1638 the towns of Massachusetts were given the authority by the legislature to fix "the prices & rates for all workmen, laborers, & servants wages." Records show that in 1651 a worker was haled into court for "taking excessive wages."[10] Such statutory action was taken because "excessive rates" charged by workmen had become "a general complaint."

"High American wages" date from the founding of Jamestown and Plymouth. In all the colonies at various dates, from 1625 to 1776, there were complaints that "Labour is dear" and, according to statements made in 1651 and 1698, wages in the northern colonies were from two to three times as high as in England.[11]

Although apprenticeship was almost as familiar in the colonies as in England and was regulated by numerous colonial statutes, the scarcity of labor caused the term of apprenticeship to be reduced below the seven-year requirement in the mother country. For example, the City of New York adopted an ordinance in 1680 providing that "coopers, carpenters and smiths, &c., serve five years

---

[8] J. R. Commons, *et al.*, *History of Labour in the United States* (New York: Macmillan, 1918), Vol. I, p. 25.

[9] *Ibid.*, pp. 51–52; and United States Bureau of Labor Statistics, *History of Wages in the United States from Colonial Times to 1928*, Bulletin No. 499, 1929, p. 9.

[10] United States Bureau of Labor Statistics, *loc. cit.*; and Commons, *et al.*, *op. cit.*, p. 50.

[11] V. S. Clark, *History of Manufactures in the United States* (New York: McGraw-Hill, 1929), Vol. I, pp. 64–66.

before being allowed to set up business" for themselves.[12] Just before the Revolutionary War it was customary for American mechanics to serve a regular apprenticeship.

Rise of the Merchant Capitalist

By the time of the Revolution, cities had grown and markets had so expanded that master craftsmen were employing numbers of journeymen (already through their apprenticeship) to work in central workrooms or in the worker's own home, making the complete product. As a consequence, the number of wage-earning employees was increasing, and the workers gradually lost contact with the customers and the suppliers of raw material. They became labor specialists. And, with competition displacing custom, price became more important than the personal reputation of the producer, especially in "shop" work for a general market.

As markets widened toward the end of the eighteenth century, a class of wholesale merchants arose who bought the products of the different workshops and sold them to retailers in that locality and elsewhere. These wholesale merchants soon achieved the role of merchant capitalists, by virtue of the fact that they concentrated on merchandising and on furnishing raw materials and orders to home workers doing piecework. Master employers became dependent upon such merchant capitalists for the sale of their output. By playing one employer against another, either in the same city or in different cities, the merchant wholesalers put considerable pressure upon employers to reduce their costs of production.

Such impersonal competition between producers and between communities caused employers to attempt to cut the wages of skilled workers and to subdivide the work in their shops in order both to speed up production and to use cheaper, unskilled workers (including women and children) on some phases of the work. The apprenticeship system began to disintegrate as one former trade became half a dozen separate tasks. In that way, many "green hands" who had not served an apprenticeship could be employed. In 1811 the New York printers complained that skilled craftsmen were being "turned out of their places by miserable botches because they will work for what they can get."[13]

---

[12] Commons, *et al., op. cit.,* p. 46.
[13] Commons, *et al., op. cit.,* p. 114.

In some types of manufacture such as cloth and garment making, merchant capitalists supplied farmers' wives and daughters with both the raw materials and the equipment. In shoemaking, not only did a craftsman tend to specialize on one operation (e.g., heeling or stitching soles), but not infrequently he worked at home with the aid of his family on the orders and material furnished by a merchant capitalist. Thus, by the first decades of the nineteenth century there was a distinct wage-earning class, which frequently did not own the handtools with which it worked.

Early Unions: Generating Forces and Modern Features

American trade unions antedate the factory system and machine methods of production. It was the competition and conflict generated by merchant capitalists that caused craftsmen to form unions and call strikes. Skilled tradesmen like printers, shoemakers, tailors, and carpenters combined to combat employer resort to wage-cutting and use of nonapprentice labor. The first strike of wage-earners in a single trade seems to have been that of the journeymen printers in Philadelphia in 1786 against a reduction of wages below six dollars a week.[14] In 1799, the journeymen shoemakers' union in Philadelphia struck for nine weeks against a wage cut and hired one of their members to picket outside the employers' shops.

Similar competitive pressures and conditions gave rise to the formation of the first unions in other industrial countries (England, Sweden, Norway, Denmark, Australia, etc.). In these nations also the better-paid skilled workers, not the low-wage factory and home workers, led the way in labor organization.

The problem of the skilled craftsman early in the century (around 1810) was to protect their wages and work jurisdictions. Available data seem to indicate that the average level of real wages failed to increase from 1800 to 1820, and may even have declined slightly during that period.[15] However, the lot of the unskilled improved somewhat, while craftsmen's living standards tended to fall.

---

[14] *Ibid.*, pp. 25 and 123.

[15] United States Bureau of Labor Statistics, *op. cit.*, p. 58; J. B. McMaster, *A History of the People of the United States* (New York: Appleton, 1895), pp. 510–13; and H. A. Millis and R. E. Montgomery, *Labor's Progress and Some Basic Labor Problems* (New York: McGraw-Hill, 1938), p. 80.

To combat the competitive pressure of merchant capitalists, the skilled craftsmen attempted to fix a wage below which none of them would work. They also demanded strict observance of apprenticeship rules, which would eliminate the competition of unskilled workers (including women and children) in the making of products that craftsmen normally had manufactured.

However, after the Revolution there were no statutes of apprenticeship to be enforced by law. Apprenticeship then was only a custom. Its enforcement depended on the economic strength of the craftsmen and their organizations. The skilled workers could only refuse to work in the same shop with a person who had not served an apprenticeship and complain that their skill was "a thing of property," which must be protected if they were to support their families in the manner to which they were accustomed.[16]

These early unions were remarkably modern in their characteristics and tactics. Exclusively craft organizations, they adopted a scale of wages ("book of prices") below which they would not work and attempted to force employers to hire only members of the organization, who had served an apprenticeship. Probably more effort was exerted then by unions to establish the principle of the closed shop (exclusive employment of union members) than in any subsequent period. In some cases, collective bargaining negotiations were conducted with employers; a few simple agreements covering wages were signed; picketing during strikes was practiced; and sympathetic strikes and the payment of strike benefits occurred.

Most of these craft-protective organizations had benefit features (such as accident, sickness, and death benefits) to protect members and to aid widows and orphans. Indeed, benefit features were a prominent aspect of many of the early labor organizations in this country. However, written agreements negotiated with employers were relatively rare until the 1880's. Such agreements seemed unnecessary when union demands consisted of a single journeyman's rate, the ten-hour day, and the closed shop, all of which the union could try to impose on employers by unilateral action.

---

[16] Commons, *et al., op. cit.*, p. 449.

The Organizational Surge (1824–37)

By the mid-1820's, the less skilled workers in the factories had begun to organize, and the first strike conducted solely by female workers had occurred. In 1827, a strike by the Philadelphia building trades for the ten-hour work day led to the formation of a city federation of the local unions in separate trades—the first in the world, antedating similar city-central associations in England by three years. In that same city in 1829, the publication of the first trade-union journal in the world commenced.

Out of the movement for a ten-hour day emerged the Working Men's Party, which is alleged to have been the first known labor party anywhere in the world. It began in Philadelphia in 1828 and flourished in New England, New York, and Ohio in the years from 1829 to 1832. Appealing to persons outside the wage-earning class, its demands included: a free and universal system of tax-supported schools (at that time one-third of the children between the ages of five and fifteen were not in school; children in that age group then constituted one-third of all factory workers), the ten-hour day, abolition of monopolies, more just taxation, and opposition to protective tariffs.

From the early 1820's to the late 1830's, as Figure 2 indicates, the level of real wages apparently did not increase. Labor, especially skilled craftsmen, continued to struggle against the competitive pressures generated by merchant capitalism. Divisions within society seemed to be deepening as industrial unrest increased. This was the period of the rise of Jacksonian democracy, following the removal of property qualifications for voting in the States.

Disillusioned by the lack of political success, workers turned again to trade-union action between 1833 and the economic panic of 1837. Over 160 strikes were recorded in contemporary newspapers during those five years. The strike wave developed with a business boom and especially with a sharp rise in consumer prices from 1834 to 1837.

At the time of this reversion from political to economic action, New York City had twenty-nine trades with labor organization, Philadelphia had twenty-one, and Baltimore seventeen. By 1836, the number of local trade unions had increased to fifty-eight in Philadelphia, fifty-two in New York, twenty-three in Baltimore, sixteen in Boston and in Newark, fourteen in Cincinnati, and thirteen in Pittsburgh. In that peak year practically every urban community had some labor organization.

Intertrade association was indicated by the existence of city centrals in at least thirteen cities at that time. These local union federations served to provide the affiliated unions with mutual aid in strikes and sought to promote union-made goods and to gain favorable publicity for such labor causes as the ten-hour day.

During the 1833–37 period, union membership reached a remarkable peak. In those years, five trades (the shoemakers, printers, carpenters, comb makers, and hand-loom weavers) held national conventions and organized on a national basis, and the first national federation, composed of local unions, city centrals and national unions, was established and existed for three years. National organization, however, was economically premature.

Some two-thirds of New York City's workers were said to have been union members in 1836, and the nation's total trade-union membership for that year has been estimated at 300,000. That figure is half the total then employed in manufacturing.[17] It was almost forty years before as many as 300,000 were again enrolled in unions, and exactly a century (1936) before such a high ratio of union membership to total persons employed in manufacturing occurred again.

Table 7 gives estimates of union membership for selected years from 1836 to 1960 in terms of absolute numbers and percentage of the labor force. In interpreting the percentages of the labor force one has to bear in mind the much larger role of agriculture in the early years. Manufacturing constituted but one-eighth of all gainful employment in 1836 compared with a figure of one-fourth by 1900. Yet, union membership in terms of percentage of the labor force was higher in 1836 than in any subsequent year until World War I.

The Era of "Utopianism" (1838–49)

The labor organization and the Working Men's Party that had mushroomed in the mid-1830's soon disintegrated in the panic of

---

[17] *Ibid.*, p. 424. Not half of the manufacturing employees were organized because some union members (e.g., the building trades) were engaged in non-manufacturing pursuits.

TABLE 7

Estimated Membership of Labor Unions in Selected Years,
1836–1960

Year	No. of Members	Per Cent of Labor Force
1836	300,000	6.5%
1869	170,000	1.4
1872	300,000	2.1
1878	50,000	.3
1883	200,000	1.1
1885	300,000	1.5
1886	1,000,000	5.0
1890	400,000	1.7
1897	440,000	1.6
1900	791,000	1.6
1910	2,116,000	5.9
1920	5,034,000	12.1
1930	3,632,000	7.5
1940	8,944,000	16.8
1950	14,751,000	23.4
1960	18,607,000	26.2

Source: Membership estimates taken from W. S. Woytinsky and Associates, *op. cit.*, Tables 67 and 68, pp. 233–34, where the variety of sources from which they were drawn is indicated. For slightly different estimates by decade from 1870 to 1900 see Lloyd Ulman, *The Rise of the National Trade Union* (Cambridge: Harvard University Press, 1955), Table 3, p. 19. The figures for 1950 and 1960 are from Irving Bernstein, "The Growth of American Unions," *Labor History*, II (Spring 1961), p. 135.

1837 and the long depression of 1839–43. Indeed, the price level declined from 1820 to 1843, except for the years 1834–37. Wages were also under heavy pressure from increased immigration.[18] Table 6 shows that, relative to the current labor force, the 1840's and 1850's were years of great immigration, coming especially from Ireland, England, and Germany.

As low-wage immigrant labor helped intensify job competition, even serving as strikebreakers, the unions found themselves losing strikes and recently won gains. Lack of success in the economic sphere stimulated a swing toward all sorts of schemes for reforming the economy and eliminating the wage system of hired employees.

The proposed panaceas ranged from producers cooperatives and socialistic communities to profit-sharing and a free farm for

---

[18] See Norman Ware, *The Industrial Worker: 1840–1860* (Boston: Houghton Mifflin, 1924), Chapters 2, 3, 4, and 9.

every industrial worker from the public lands. The hope was that workers might become independent producers or part of management. So widespread at this time were utopian schemes designed to solve labor's problems that Emerson wrote Carlyle in 1840: "We are all a little wild here with numberless projects of social reform. Not a reading man but has a draft of a new Community in his waistcoat pocket."[19]

Most of these programs for restructuring the economy, however, proved visionary; the model communities (like New Harmony, Indiana) soon shed most of their novel features. With the return of general prosperity in the 1850's, the pendulum swung back to trade unionism and collective bargaining.

The Emergence of National Unions (1850–78)

The return to economic action in the 1850's was more narrowly based in the skilled crafts than was true in the 1830's. Railroad networks were knitting the country into national markets and, thus, broadening the area of competitive production. Mechanization was threatening elimination of the need for some craft skills.

Craftsmen, therefore, sought to organize nationally along trade lines in order to enforce craft protective devices (apprenticeship, the closed shop, work jurisdictions, and a standard journeyman's wage rate). This objective was partly achieved through agreements with employers' associations, which were becoming more prevalent in several trades. Beginning with the printers in 1850, local unions in more than a dozen trades formed national craft unions during the following decade.

The emphasis in the 1850's was more on national organization than on city centrals. A national union composed of locals in a single craft aims at economic action and negotiation with employers. In contrast, union federations (city, state, or federal) are structured more for political activity. For that reason it has been suggested that the triumph of the national union over the local federation reflected the victory of collective bargaining over political reform.[20]

---

[19] C. E. Norton (ed.), *The Correspondence of Thomas Carlyle and Ralph Waldo Emerson, 1834–1872*, vol. 1 (Boston: Osgood, 1883), p. 308.

[20] Ulman, Lloyd, *The Rise of the National Union* (Cambridge: Harvard University Press, 1955).

However, union leaders in the 1850's and 1860's were still not committed to negotiated agreements as labor's chief objective over the long run. Most of them continued to view collective bargaining with employers as a short-run expedient. They believed that labor's ultimate salvation lay in a radical change in the economic system that would eliminate the possibility of a permanent wage-earning class.

The fortunes of national unions, of course, varied with the business cycle. A depression like that in 1857 brought wage cuts and the collapse of weak national unions and many of the locals. However, the national unions began to show greater resistance to economic adversity than had been true earlier of the unattached local unions. Three unions now in existence—those of the printers, molders, and machinists—date their founding in the 1850's.

The rise of national unions should be kept in proper perspective. Organized labor remained narrowly confined to trades outside the factories. The mills were manned mainly by women, children, and recent immigrants. In the 1850's and 1860's, less than 2 per cent of the nation's labor force were union members.

The Civil War did, however, give labor organization a strong impetus. Rising living costs and labor shortages stimulated economic action. By 1864, union membership had risen to a total exceeding 200,000, which was larger than at any time during the 1840's or 1850's.

Subtle changes occurred as organized labor moved toward a national orientation along craft lines. Before the Civil War, strikes generally were local, short-lived, and peacefully conducted.[21] During the war, numerous strikes occurred. However, the Lincoln Administration, sympathetic toward labor, opposed suppression of the freedom to strike. After the war, strikes tended to encompass a larger area and, on occasion, were quite violent.

With a considerable section of skilled labor organized on a national scale and a revival of city centrals during the war, many labor leaders thought the time was ripe for some sort of national federation. In 1866, a National Labor Union was established after the French pattern, with city centrals (called "trade assemblies") and national unions both represented, together with farmers' societies and other political groups. So motley was the membership

---

[21] An exception was a strike of shoemakers in 1860 which spread to various New England communities and involved some 20,000 workers.

that one writer described it as a "typical American politico-reform organization, led by labor leaders without organizations, politicians without parties, women without husbands, and cranks, visionaries and agitators without jobs."[22]

In addition to the eight-hour day, the leaders of the National Labor Union sought to promote producers' cooperatives, homesteading on public lands, an increase in greenback money, and other means of avoiding a permanent wage-earning class. The cooperative ventures, like previous ones, generally failed, and the trade unionists lost interest in the political program. By 1870, the national unions had seceded from the National Labor Union, after which it rapidly declined and disappeared.

The survival power of national unions was severely tested in the hard times from 1873 until 1879. During the four years 1871–75, the cigar-makers union lost 54 out of 78 strikes; 64 of the strikes were against employer attempts to reduce wages.[23] Despite the prolonged business depression, at least eleven national unions are known to have weathered it, and eight new nationals were formed during the slump. Thus, the national unions evidenced greater staying qualities than had the earlier local unions and city centrals. Nevertheless, the membership of the surviving national unions declined sharply; the cigar-makers union lost almost five-sixths of its members, the barrel makers about four-fifths, the machinists around two-thirds, and the printers over a half. Consequently, as Table 7 indicates, total membership in 1878 was but one-sixth of the 1872 figure.

As during previous depression periods, labor leaders again turned to political action. In these years of economic adversity, workingmen's parties were active in industrial regions. In some cases, they joined forces with farmers who were agitating for the issuance of greenback currency to increase prices, which fell 50 per cent from 1865 to 1879. The Socialists also appeared as active participants in the labor movement at this time.

Although they were successful in electing some labor and farmer candidates, the strength of labor-farmer political groups

---

[22] N. J. Ware, *The Labor Movement in the United States: 1860–95* (New York: Appleton, 1929), p. 11.

[23] Clarence E. Bonnett, *History of Employers' Associations in the United States* (New York: Vantage Press, 1956), p. 100.

began to wane with the return of prosperity in 1879. Higher prices for three years caused farmers to lose interest, and, with increasing employment, the workers turned again to organization and bargaining for wage increases.

During the depression from 1873 to 1879, employers sought to eliminate unions by a systematic policy of lockouts,[24] black lists, labor espionage, use of strikebreakers, and legal prosecution. As a consequence, sections of labor organized more or less secretly, and stimulus was given to the physical violence that characterized labor strikes during this period. A secret miner's organization (the "Molly Maguires") engaged in terroristic tactics during the 1874–75 strike in anthracite coal. The railroad strikes in July 1877 resulted in widespread rioting and bloodshed,[25] the burning of many millions of dollars of railroad property, and the use of Federal troops to quell disorders in several cities. Jobless demonstrations, mob violence, and the destruction of property caused popular concern and fears for the future.

The Structural Issue: Craft vs. All-Inclusive Unionism (1879–87)

Under the banner of the Noble and Holy Order of the Knights of Labor, an attempt was made to develop one all-embracing, nationwide labor organization, which would include the workers in all industries and occupations. The national trade unions had organized on craft lines, so that they appealed to skilled craftsmen. The Knights not only admitted to membership any person who worked for wages but also former wage-earners, except for liquor dealers, lawyers, bankers, stockbrokers, and professional gamblers. Into "one fold" were to be gathered "all branches of honorable toil." It represented the first significant attempt in this country to establish one big, general union.

From a small secret organization, the Knights under a new constitution became a national organization with secrecy completely eliminated in 1878 and 1879. Its objectives were similar to those of the National Labor Union—the eight-hour day, producers' cooperatives, homesteading on public lands, monetary expansion,

---

[24] The refusal of an employer to furnish any further employment until his workers agree to the terms of employment that he insists upon.

[25] A dozen persons were killed in Baltimore and 25 in Pittsburgh.

prohibition of child labor, compulsory arbitration, income and inheritance taxes, adult education, and a number of other progressive proposals. Although its heterogeneous program seemed largely reformist and political, the leaders sought to control collective bargaining and industrial action, supporting strikes and boycotts even though opposed in principle to strike action. One difficulty with the Knights was the ambiguous and uncertain position of its leadership. The central office actually could not control matters, although the constitution provided for a high degree of centralization of authority. On the assumption of common interests among the common people, many of the local units of the Knights were "mixed," including persons of diverse occupation, race, and sex. Until 1887, however, most of the local "assemblies" seem to have been single trade or single industry units, and the Order admitted, as "trade assemblies," a number of national craft unions without loss of identity or any change in their structure.

The period of rising prices and prosperity from 1879 to 1883 witnessed the usual increase in the number of national trade unions and their membership. By 1884 they had at least 300,000 members. The great expansion of the Knights began with depression and wage-cutting in 1884. It was accelerated by the remarkably successful strikes in 1885 against railroads controlled by Jay Gould and the epidemic of almost two hundred boycotts in the same year, nearly all of which were supported by the Knights. From 52,000 members in 1883, the Knights mushroomed to a membership of 700,000 in 1886. Unskilled and semiskilled workers, small-town merchants and mechanics, and farmers accounted for much of the expansion, thereby diluting the membership with elements possessing little interest in the problems agitating urban wage-earners.

The polyglot membership of the Knights resulted in disunity of purpose, internal conflict, and vacillation. Differences of interest arose between the farmers, shopkeepers, and small employers, who were for the most part politically minded, and the trade unionists in the large cities, who stressed economic action. The unions in the skilled trades were interested in trade autonomy and craft-protective devices, such as enforcement of apprenticeship rules and prevention of invasion of the craftsmen's work by "green hands." Their objective was to organize all competing employers in the same line of business or trade in order to control conditions of labor throughout the whole area of competitive production. The skilled craftsmen were a stable and cohesive group whose indispensability gave them considerable bargaining strength. The Knights, however, tended to disregard craft lines, and the leaders directed the organization's resources toward assisting the less skilled workers who flocked into and out of it. By 1885 the craft unionists in the Knights were dissatisfied with the lack of regard for their interests, and the craft unions began to abandon the Noble and Holy Order. In the end, even the industrial unions, like the miners and brewery workers whose jurisdictions included a whole industry, were opposed to a general labor organization such as the Knights.

The conflict between the craft unionists and the Knights proved irreconcilable. In 1881, the trade unionists had helped to form a Federation of Organized Trades and Labor Unions of the United States and Canada, which had a constitution taken almost verbatim from that of the British Trades Union Congress. Primarily a political organization, with less than 50,000 members in the affiliated unions in 1884, it afforded little protection to the craft unions against the growing Knights of Labor, which admitted seceding factions of national unions and even boycotted the label of such unions. In October 1886, the Knights refused to accept a proposed "treaty" under which it would have agreed to abandon all jurisdictions where craft unions were established. This refusal, accompanied by further acceptance of rival unions into the Knights, caused the craft unionists, for self-protection, to establish the American Federation of Labor, with which the Federation of Organized Trades and Labor Unions was merged. The new federation, unlike its predecessor, had economic as well as legislative functions. The national or international (North American) unions were made the basic units of the federation, which in 1886 represented a membership of about 150,000. Following refusal of the Knights to agree to refrain from interfering with the national unions and from signing up locals in their trades, open warfare broke out that even resulted in one side "scabbing" on the other in strikes. A second attempt in 1888 to negotiate some compromise between the Knights and the Federation also failed, revealing anew the fundamental differences in purpose and philosophy between the two organizations.

After mid-1886, membership in the Knights of Labor started to decline almost as rapidly as it had expanded. A series of unsuccessful strikes, including one on another part of Gould's Southwest system, revealed weaknesses in the organizational structure. The leadership proved timid and vacillating, and parts of the membership became irresponsible and uncontrollable. In addition, the Knights, although in no way responsible, reaped some of the odium of the Haymarket Square bombing in May 1886. The basic difficulty, however, was incompatibility of interests within the organization's membership base, resulting in disregard of the economic needs of the workers. As the membership fell to 222,000 in mid-1888 and to 100,000 in 1890, the leaders of the Knights turned toward political activity, and it became predominantly an agrarian and small-town organization, having lost its hold on the wage-earners in the large cities.

The experience of the Knights of Labor again proved the difficulties of founding in nineteenth-century America a strong and stable organization on a working-class basis for either economic or political action. The American wage-earner has lacked the political and class solidarity of European workers. Skilled workers could develop cohesive and disciplined organizations for economic action, centering around their common interests in preserving and enhancing the value of their craft skill. They could not, however, be induced to subordinate that craft interest to a program for elevating the mass of unskilled workers, whose ranks were being constantly replenished by immigration. The unskilled and semi-skilled workers lacked the bargaining strength, the unity of interests and ideology, or the political power, upon which to base a strong and stable organization. Repeated attempts to achieve labor goals by political action were hampered by the diverse politics of urban wage-earners and the political importance of rural areas and small towns.

The decline of the Knights of Labor and the rise of the American Federation of Labor in the late 1880's was to mark the beginning of half a century during which conservative craft unionism predominated. After almost one hundred years of oscillation between trade unionism and political action, between craft-con-

sciousness and all-inclusive organization, between collective bargaining and schemes for eliminating the wage system, business
unionism had triumphed.

THE ERA OF AFL UNIONISM

Prior to the founding of the American Federation of Labor,
the national unions had been strengthened by changes in policy.
In the late 1870's, the leaders of the Union of Cigar Makers
(namely Samuel Gompers and Adolph Strasser) had reorganized
the union along British lines. To ensure stability and permanency
of the organization, they adopted high dues, a system of sickness
and death benefits, and centralized control. The national officers
had complete authority over locals and strict discipline over use
of the strike weapon, with fairly adequate financial support for
officially sanctioned strikes.

Other trade unions followed the lead of the cigar makers in
adopting the new union philosophy of businesslike methods and
centralization of authority. Recognizing a real conflict of interest
between employers and employed, reliance was placed on trade
organization, job control, and the negotiation of written agreements.

Taking to heart the lessons of a century of experience, the
new unionism shunned direct participation in political organizations and in programs of radical reform. Instead, emphasis was
placed on the economic strength and sectional interests of each
craft. The craftsmen, who occupied strategic positions in the productive process or in the market, sought to promote their own
cohesiveness and coercive power rather than dissipate their economic advantages in attempts to elevate the status of the less
skilled.

The creed of the new unionism became the philosophy of the
American Federation of Labor. In considerable measure that came
about through the influence and efforts of Samuel Gompers, who
was the Federation's president for all save one of the first 38 years
of its existence. The national trade unions were the key units in the
reoriented labor movement. In order to curtail the influence of the
city centrals, little voting power in the AFL was granted to them.
Leaders of the new unionism distrusted the city organizations,

because in numerous instances they were under the domination of Socialists and other reformers.

In sharp contrast to the Knights of Labor, the Federation's principles involved strict autonomy for the national unions. That meant no meddling in their internal affairs—in admission policies, apprenticeship, disciplining of members, or government of the union. With the major stress on economic action, an important function of the AFL was to lend support to the national unions in their strikes, boycotts, and organizing activities.

Politically, the Federation's policy was to avoid any party alignment and in elections to "reward labor's friends and defeat its enemies." As a pragmatist, Gompers distrusted abstract reasoning and fine-spun political programs. Of the Socialists he once said: "Economically, you are unsound; socially, you are wrong; and industrially, you are an impossibility."[26] It is not surprising, therefore, that Gompers was reported to have defined the aims of the Federation as "More, more, more—now!"

The Formative Years (1886–1904)

The craft unions that established the AFL had found a labor philosophy and a structural form that facilitated continued organization. Stress on craft-protective regulations, benefits for members, and negotiation and application of written agreements gave the unions functions to perform and services to provide on a day-to-day basis.

The result was a slow but steady growth of the total membership of unions affiliated with the AFL. From 140,000 at its founding, the total affiliated membership rose to 225,000 in 1890, 250,000 in 1892, and 278,000 in 1898. It is significant that, for the first time, no important decline in total membership occurred during the depression years from 1892 to 1898. The unions, aided by their new policies, were generally able to weather the economic storm.

This was true despite a strike peak that included some 750,000 workers and two violent and unsuccessful strikes (Homestead in 1892 and Pullman in 1894). Homestead involved one of the strongest AFL affiliates (The Amalgamated Association of Iron and

---

[26] *AFL Convention Proceedings*, 1903, p. 198.

Steel Workers with over 24,000 members). Pullman did not directly concern an AFL organization, since the railroad unions were not affiliated with the AFL. The Federation did, however, have an interest in the Pullman strike because the defeat of the American Railway Union (a year-old industrial union of 150,000 members threatening to displace the craft unions with a single union in the railroad industry) served to eliminate a rival type of unionism.

Probably the greatest achievement of the 1890's was the widespread use of the trade agreement, and particularly the development of national negotiations between a national union and an employers' association in such industries as glassware, stoves, printing, and bituminous coal. Written agreements, renewed year after year, involved a conception of unions as continuous-service organizations, gradually achieving labor's aims by means of gains wrested from management at the bargaining table.

Until the Homestead strike, the relations between the Carnegie Steel Company and the union had been friendly. Working conditions had been governed by a three-year agreement covering skilled workers who were members of the Amalgamated. It was, therefore, somewhat surprising to find that the strike, which followed failure to renegotiate the agreement, led to a twelve-hour pitched battle between some three hundred Pinkerton detectives and the striking workers, in which ten persons were killed. Thereafter some two thousand strikebreakers were brought in to run the mill. The Amalgamated Association of Iron and Steel Workers never regained its strength and steadily lost ground, faced by the opposition of the Carnegie Company and its successor, the U.S. Steel Corporation.

Most of the big strikes in the nineteenth century arose out of wage cuts instituted by employers during economic slumps. That was true of the Homestead and Pullman strikes as well as the railroad strikes in 1877. Pullman cars were made in a company town, and wages were cut 25 to 40 per cent without a corresponding reduction in rents for company housing. The American Railway Union spread the strike by attempting to boycott Pullman cars on all railroads. In the resulting conflict, rioting broke out, railway cars and other property were destroyed, and 25 persons were killed. The strike failed when the Federal Government arranged not only for special deputies and Federal troops to keep the trains running, but also obtained a blanket injunction from a Federal judge outlawing the strike. The union's leader, Eugene V. Debs, and three of his associates were jailed for disobeying the court injunction. With the railroads refusing to employ its members, the union disintegrated within a year.

These violent strikes were followed by a period of rising prices, prosperity, and comparative industrial peace from 1898 to 1904. Partly as a result of the shock from the Homestead and Pullman strikes, labor leaders and many industrialists sought (by such means as the tripartite National Civic Federation) to promote the peaceful settlement of labor problems. Acceptance of collective bargaining became more widespread. A growing number of trade agreements was the fruit of the AFL's rather conservative program of "business unionism" and the sympathetic efforts of public figures to promote stable labor relations. In the anthracite coal strike of 1902, President Roosevelt pressured the employers into accepting arbitration by a Presidential commission. Thereafter, the United Mine Workers (an industrial union) expanded into one of the best organized and largest affiliates of the AFL.

The combined membership of AFL affiliates grew from 278,000 in 1898 to 1,682,000 in 1904—a sixfold increase. This membership expansion represented mostly growth of unions already established. Between 1898 and 1904, the AFL expanded from representing 55 per cent to accounting for 80 per cent of all union membership. From 1904 to the founding of the CIO in 1935, the dominance of the AFL is evidenced by the fact that its affiliates accounted for 75 to 85 per cent of all organized labor during each of those 31 years. The largest unaffiliated group were the railroad brotherhoods in the engine and train service, who maintained friendly relations with the Federation.

The Solidification of Craft Unionism (1905–14)

By 1904, a stable form of labor organization had been achieved. "Business unionism," based on collective bargaining, had triumphed. Economic in aim and conservative in ideology, it so dominated the labor movement that radical reform groups thereafter were peripheral—outside the main core of organized labor.

Nevertheless, the rate of growth in union membership was

most gradual during the decade from 1904 to 1914. In fact, as Figure 3 indicates, total union membership was almost stationary between 1904 and 1910.[26a] That stability occurred despite such favorable circumstances as a rising price level and the upswing of a fifty-year-long wave. During those years, immigration greatly increased (see Table 6). But, undoubtedly, the chief retarding influence was stiffening employer opposition to labor organization. Sharp advances in union conquests usually stimulated a reaction in the form of employer campaigns, such as the "open shop" drive during the decade prior to World War I.

Even as craft unionism solidified and its leadership became entrenched, new developments were afoot in other sections of organized labor. Following two major strikes in the women's clothing industry in New York City, an industrial union of all manual workers in the factory was founded in 1911. This union, the International Ladies' Garment Workers, affiliated with the AFL. In the men's clothing industry, a group within the lethargic United Garment Workers Union (a craft organization) rebelled and founded a new industrial union, independent of the AFL, the Amalgamated Clothing Workers. Both unions were vigorous and grew rather rapidly.

Despite employer opposition to labor organization, the Socialists were unable to make headway within the AFL, and the attempt by radical and dissident elements to establish a rival general union (the Industrial Workers of the World) in 1905 failed to threaten the dominant position of the AFL. In this new single union (commonly known as the IWW), the militant metal miners, lumberjacks, and migratory workers of the West joined hands with Eastern socialistic groups and proponents of broad-based unionism.

[26a] In Figure 3 the line showing membership in percentage of the total labor force begins in 1900 above the line for total union membership in millions and moves below the total membership line after 1931, declining below 28 per cent by 1960. The line for total membership begins with 447,000 in 1897 and rises to above eighteen million for the years 1956–60.

The sources of data for Figure 3 are: W. S. Woytinsky and Associates, *op. cit.*, Appendix Table 53, p. 642; Irving Bernstein, "The Growth of American Unions," *American Economic Review*, XLIV (June 1954), Table 1, pp. 303–304 and "The Growth of American Unions, 1954–1960," *Labor History*, II (Spring 1961), Table 1, p. 135; *Monthly Labor Review*, LXXXIII (January 1960), pp. 2–4; and *Monthly Labor Review*, LXXXIV (December 1961), p. 1302.

Advocating both the elimination of capitalism and the goal of working class solidarity, the IWW bitterly attacked the policies of the AFL while engaging in violent strikes, industrial sabotage, and other dramatic tactics. Like the Knights of Labor, the membership of the IWW was highly unstable; probably it never exceeded 60,000 or 70,000 paid members at its peak before World War I. This union was practically eliminated during the war, in which its leaders strongly opposed America's participation.[27]

By the turn of the century, corruption had crept into the American labor movement on an important scale. Employer collusion and extortion from employers for "strike insurance" were especially prevalent in the building trades, where local union agents or officials were able to acquire considerable power and to develop personal empires. Prime examples of such extortion were Sam Parks in New York City (1896–1903) and "Umbrella Mike" Boyle of Chicago (prior to World War I). Even an idealist such as Peter J. McGuire, president of the Carpenters Union and founder of Labor Day, succumbed in 1901 to the practice of taking union funds for personal use and doctoring the books to conceal it.[28]

Advance in World War I (1914–20)

By 1916 the boom caused by World War I had begun to raise total union membership well above the plateau of the prewar decade. The war strengthened the hand of organized labor in a number of ways. Military orders and the draft created labor shortages at a time when immigration practically ceased. The push of rising living costs was added to the pull of job opportunities. Thus, the position of workers improved, and their fears of such employer weapons as discriminatory discharge and the black list were dulled. Indeed, the employers' antiunion drive was suspended, and various concessions to labor were made.

The government also became more favorable to organized labor. Anxious to avoid unrest and work stoppages, the Federal Government established special labor adjustment boards for such

---

[27] For a history of the IWW up to 1917, see P. F. Brissenden, *The IWW; a Study of American Syndicalism* (New York: Columbia University Press, 1919).

[28] See Robert A. Christie, *Empire in Wood: A History of the Carpenters Union* (Ithaca: Cornell School of Industrial and Labor Relations, 1956), pp. 98–99.

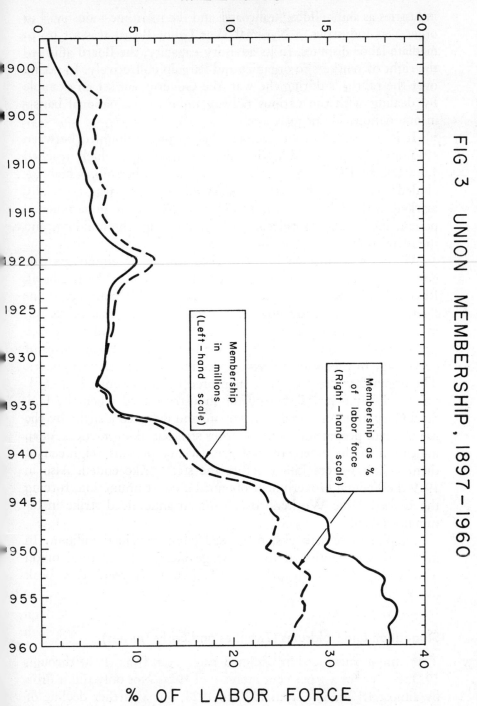

FIG 3 UNION MEMBERSHIP, 1897-1960

MILLIONS

% OF LABOR FORCE

Membership
in millions
(Left—hand
scale)

Membership as %
of labor force
(Right—hand
scale)

industries as shipbuilding, railroads, and the maritime industry. For other war industries, a National War Labor Board was set up to mediate labor disputes. In its advisory capacity, the Board affirmed the right of workers to organize and bargain collectively. In taking over the railroads during the war, the Government set an example by dealing with the various railway unions on a national basis—in one nationwide negotiation.

It is not surprising, therefore, that as prices doubled between 1915 and 1920, so did trade-union membership, which reached 5,000,000 in 1920. The increase in union membership, which included many unskilled and semiskilled workers, was especially marked in those industries most directly affected by governmental policy, including the railroads, ocean shipping, shipbuilding, and the metal trades.

With the Armistice in 1918, the attitude of employers, the government, and the public commenced to change. The Bolshevik Revolution in Russia caused a Red scare in this country. It influenced public attitudes toward the rash of strikes that broke out in 1919, particularly the general strike in Seattle and the police strike in Boston. In fact, 1919 is the all-time peak year in terms of percentage of the industrial workforce involved in work stoppages. The organizing drive in steel, sponsored by the twenty-four AFL unions claiming jurisdiction in the industry, failed when the U.S. Steel Corporation refused to negotiate and defeated a strike by the use of scare propaganda and vigorous strikebreaking tactics. As an indication of the extent of violence, twenty persons (eighteen of them strikers) were killed before the steel strike ended. Also in 1919 the Federal Government obtained a court injunction, forcing the United Mine Workers to call off an announced strike in bituminous coal.

Despite these setbacks, organized labor remained militant. In many areas it continued to win wage increases, and total union membership rose with prices until they both reached a peak in 1920.

Stagnation and Doldrums (Twenties and Early Thirties)

Total union membership declined each year from 1920 through 1933, except for a 1 per cent increase in 1927. Not only did it drop by almost 1.5 million from 1920 to 1923, but a further decline of

180,000 occurred between 1923 and 1929, a period of high prosperity. For the first time, the labor movement suffered a numerical contraction during a business boom. When the 1929 slump began, total union membership was lower than at any time during the preceding twelve years. From 1924 to 1929, over half of all national unions affiliated with the AFL experienced some decline in membership.

A drop in the numerical strength of organized labor in the 1921–22 slump was to be expected. Indeed, the industries accounting for three-fourths of the wartime expansion were also responsible for three-quarters of the membership loss between 1920 and 1923. In 1921 the United States Shipping Board helped bring about a strike defeat and the decline of the Seamen's Union by refusing to let the Board's vessels be used by any operator renewing the agreement with the union. The railroad shop crafts suffered a membership reduction of over 40 per cent as a result of their unsuccessful strike in mid-1922, in which hundreds of college students served as strikebreakers. The strike was doomed when the Attorney General of the United States obtained a sweeping court injunction that prohibited any statements to the public, any aid to the strikers, or any attempts to persuade anyone to stop work.

A variety of explanations have been offered for the failure of union membership to increase after 1922. They include: failure of living costs to rise so as to stimulate membership; an open-shop campaign by employers under the slogan of "the American Plan"; the rise of management programs for employee welfare; physical changes within industry; and weaknesses in union structure and union leadership.

A swing toward a welfare concept of employment began in the twenties, especially in some of the large firms in mass-production lines. Dubbed "welfare capitalism," it included a variety of employee benefit and welfare programs as well as "employee representation plans." Stimulating this movement were such influences as the wartime labor shortages, the decline in immigration, the rise in levels of education, a desire to reduce labor turnover, and, in some cases, the intent to avoid unionization.

In industry, expansion in the twenties was chiefly outside the "job territory" of the unions, which were largely craft based. In manufacturing, the unorganized mass-production lines expanded most. New machinery and other technological changes were reducing the importance of craft types of skill. As a result, semi-skilled operatives increased in numbers compared with skilled workers. In addition, production in a number of industries, such as coal and clothing, tended to move away from the centers controlled by the unions.

The relative reduction in the industrial base of craft unionism found the leadership of the AFL clinging to its traditional outlook and seeking to woo employers by conciliatory and cooperative overtures. But the olive-branch program failed to win over the employers and lacked the inspirational qualities necessary to gain enthusiastic support among the workers. The dominant unionism seemed too complacent and too rigid—mentally and structurally— to cope with the changes occurring in industry and in government. Special circumstances help to explain disruption and demoralization in individual unions. For example, the clothing unions were weakened by Communist disruption in the twenties, and the leadership of the United Mine Workers, the largest union in 1923, could offer nothing better than an economically unsound program of "no backward step," as more and more soft-coal mines went nonunion.

With the stock-market crash in 1929 and the ensuing unemployment, organized labor appeared to be too demoralized and bewildered to take advantage of the situation. Despite widespread wage reductions between 1929 and 1933, there were relatively few strikes or other aggressive actions on the part of organized labor. And the dominant type of unionism was ineffective politically as well as economically. Not only did it oppose unemployment insurance and wage or hours legislation for men, but in the 1932 campaign the AFL declined to support either Roosevelt or Hoover for the Presidency. Its neutrality indicated that organized labor, like the rest of the country, was unable to adjust its thinking to the sweep of the depression.

SUMMARY

The story of organized labor's development is continued in the next chapter. The transformation that occurred in the labor movement with the New Deal and the Great Depression does, however, stimulate one to look backward and make a few general observations concerning the first century of union history.

1. Unions initially developed among skilled workers in response to the competitive pressures generated with the rise of merchant capitalists. Thereafter, wage reductions frequently led to labor protest and strikes.

2. The form and policies of labor organization in America remained unsettled until near the end of the nineteenth century. The long search for a stable underpinning ended with the triumph of craft unionism of the Gompers' type, with stress on businesslike methods, authority in the national union, job control, and negotiated agreements.

3. Union insecurity became a traditional concern of labor leaders in America. Stress on survival was understandable in an "open society," characterized by heavy immigration, great labor mobility, rapid technological change, rising living standards, and marked cyclical swings in business conditions.

4. Narrowly based unionism, although demonstrating survival values, tended to be conservative and, except during periods of disturbance like wars or deep depressions, was inclined to stagnate (witness the plateaus of total membership in the decades 1904–14 and 1921–31). And in the face of great change (such as the depression of the thirties), the Gompers' type of unionism lacked sufficient adaptability to avoid a cultural lag and structural obsolescence.

5. Even with the New Deal, as explained in the next chapter, union development experienced, not a marked mutation, but a partial alteration and expansion in leadership, tactics, and jurisdiction. The adjustment in basic union philosophy was neither profound nor completely permanent.

DISCUSSION QUESTIONS

1. Discuss the conditions under which the first local unions were formed in this country.
2. How did immigration affect wages and the possibilities of labor organization?
3. How was labor organization affected by technological change during the half century ending in 1930?
4. Why did fluctuations in business conditions have so much influence on labor organization throughout the nineteenth century?

5. Why has the issue of "union security" (the closed shop and other arrangements for tying employment and union membership together) played such a significant role in American industrial relations?

6. It has been said that organized labor could have grown more steadily and much larger between 1830 and 1890 if its leadership had been less reform-minded and more businesslike. Do you agree? Justify your position.

7. What was the union philosophy and program of Samuel Gompers and the AFL during his presidency?

8. Why was craft unionism generally more successful than industrial unionism prior to the 1930's?

9. What factors were most influential in changes in total union membership during the century from 1830 to 1930? Explain the extent to which the influence of different factors altered with developments in the economy.

SELECTED READINGS

Commons, John R., *et al.*, *History of Labour in the United States* (New York: Macmillan, 1918, 4 vols.).

Dulles, Foster R., *Labor in America, A History* (New York: Crowell, 1949).

Dunlop, John T., "The Development of Labor Organization: A Theoretical Framework," in R. A. Lester and Joseph Shister (eds.), *Insights Into Labor Issues* (New York: Macmillan, 1948), pp. 163–93.

Lerner, Max, *America as a Civilization: Life and Thought in the United States Today* (New York: Simon and Schuster, 1957).

Perlman, Selig, *The History of Trade Unionism in the United States* (New York: Macmillan, 1937).

Ulman, Lloyd, *The Rise of the National Union* (Cambridge: Harvard University Press, 1955).

United States Department of Labor, *Brief History of the American Labor Movement*, Bureau of Labor Statistics, Bulletin No. 1000, 1957 revision (Washington: United States Government Printing Office, 1957).

Ware, N. J., *The Labor Movement in the United States, 1860–1895* (New York: Appleton, 1929).

4.

The Great Transformation and Union Growth

DURING THE 1930's, labor in general in America experienced a remarkable transformation. Although that transformation had many facets, three were particularly noteworthy because of their long-run implications: (1) the shift from a commodity to a welfare concept of employment; (2) widespread intervention of government in the employment relationship, with emphasis on humanitarian considerations and expansion of purchasing power; and (3) the spread of industrial unionism, with accompanying innovations in organizing methods, leadership, and political policies. For labor, the New Deal meant a new dispensation.

Of course, the roots of many New Deal changes extended back into the twenties and earlier. The New Deal did not represent a clean break with the past, but it did run contrary to much traditional thinking. That was especially true of its economic philosophy of raising wages and increasing government spending in order to expand employment, its promotion of the rights and welfare of workers, and its encouragement to labor organization. As Foster Rhea Dulles explains, "For the first time in our history a national administration was to make the welfare of industrial workers a direct concern of the government and act on the principle that only organized labor could deal on equal terms with organized capital in bringing about a proper balance between those two rival forces in a capitalistic society."[1]

The Federal Government intervened in favor of industrial labor, farmers, and low-income groups in general. It was argued that individuals who were not organized in some collective form were at a disadvantage in selling their services (in the case of workers) or their products (in the case of farmers). A theory of countervailing power was later developed to explain how organized strength can beget its own offsets. The theory assumed that collective organization and action by one functional group (say, capital and management in the large corporation) stimulated countervailing collective organization and pressure by groups (say, employees or customers) dealing with it.[2] Where countervailing power failed to develop naturally, the government would be under political pressure to promote its development. Thus, government intervention to maintain a balance of economic forces was viewed as a more or less continuing matter. In the labor field, the emphasis was on equality of bargaining power between management and labor.

ALTERATION IN THE CONCEPT OF EMPLOYMENT

Until the New Deal, a commodity concept of employment generally prevailed. Except for some progressive firms that adopted employee welfare programs in the twenties, factory "hands" were regarded by management much like other agents of production—materials, land, and machinery. Indeed, land and machinery had capital value, and management, therefore, had to be concerned about their depreciation. Not so of the men (except under slavery), since their depreciation was not a calculated cost of production to the company.

---

[1] *Labor in America: A History* (New York: Crowell, 1955), p. 264.

[2] See J. K. Galbraith, *American Capitalism, the Concept of Countervailing Power* (Boston: Houghton Mifflin, 1952), esp. pp. 121–3, 133, and 141–57. Certainly it is not a general rule that countervailing power develops naturally in markets, or will be provided with government aid to do so where there are large and powerful corporations in those markets.

Under the commodity view, labor was exposed to unrestrained competition on the supply side and callous treatment by dominant employers. The consequences can be illustrated by two examples. In 1904, Cyrus Ching, later vice-president of U.S. Rubber Company, was nearly electrocuted when working as a repair troubleshooter for the Boston Elevated Railroad Company. The minute that word of the accident reached company headquarters, Ching was removed from the payroll and no one from the company even got in touch with him or offered any help during the subsequent four months that he spent in the hospital.[3] In the twenties, it was the practice at the Ford Motor Company and other automobile manufacturers to close down for a model change-over, pay off all production employees, and, upon reopening the plant, the hourly workers were hired in at the wage of a beginner regardless of the length of their past employment with the company.[4] In lay-offs and rehiring, preference often was given workers under thirty-five years of age, with length of previous service with the company completely disregarded. Experienced hands over thirty-five were frequently the first ones dismissed when the workforce was released.

Beginning in the twenties, however, a number of factors caused company managements to pay more attention to workers' welfare and to shift from a short to a long employment basis. Among them were: changes in the character of the labor force, with sharp curtailment of immigration and advances in the educational level of factory workers; the stress on employee responsibility, with the rising value of capital equipment; recognition of company investment in employees, including the cost of training and the wastes of labor turnover; and the climate of public opinion, influenced by democratic and self-respecting treatment of workers and their

---

[3] Cyrus S. Ching, *Review and Reflection, A Half-Century of Labor Relations* (New York: Forbes, 1953), pp. 9–10. See also pp. 5–6 on commodity treatment of labor by large companies.

[4] See Harry Bennett, *We Never Called Him Henry* (New York: Fawcett, 1951), pp. 108–109; also A. Nevins and F. E. Hill, *Ford: Expansion and Challenge, 1915–1933* (New York: Scribner's, 1957), p. 534. It should be stressed that Ford had pioneered in labor matters by instituting the five dollar pay for an eight-hour day in 1914, despite condemnation from employers for upsetting low standards, and by hiring handicapped and Negro workers. See Nevins and Hill, Chapter 10, pp. 508–40. For an interesting discussion of the treatment of the mass of job applicants after announcement of the five dollar minimum pay, see A. Nevins, *Ford: The Times, the Man, the Company* (New York: Scribner's, 1954), Chapter 21, pp. 542–67.

families in the community, the church, politics, and some social activities. The shock to American management arising from the rapid spread of labor organization in the thirties also stimulated companies to extend their employment horizon and to adopt a "welfare concept" in place of a "commodity concept" of labor. The results of psychological studies were still another factor influencing management to alter its perspective and practices.

The New Deal Revolution in Industrial Employment

Since World War I, noteworthy new dimensions have been added to the workshop relationship. Around manual employment has grown a network of employee rights and employer obligations that involve not only the dignity and welfare of the individual worker but also the security and well-being of the members of his family. And as a part of this revolutionary development, many of the rights and privileges of salaried (office) employees have been spread to hourly paid (plant) workers.

Among the privileges extended from the office to the factory have been a series of "fringe," or welfare, benefits. They include company-financed pensions, company-paid vacations, paid holidays, sickness pay, and company-supported hospital benefits and medical care. Through private and public pension programs, the employer has assumed part of the burden of worker depreciation —caused by wearing out and obsolescence. By covering not only the employee but also his dependents under programs like hospitalization and medical care, the employment relationship has been stretched to a family welfare obligation.

A metamorphosis also has occurred with respect to compensation. Not only have pay differentials between blue-collar and white-collar employees been reduced, but manual workers are compensated in various ways for lack of work: reporting pay, dismissal compensation, and (public and private) unemployment benefits. In a few instances (e.g., the International Business Machines Corporation), all factory workers were put on a salary basis or its equivalent.

The eclipse of the commodity concept of employment in various sections of the economy did not occur all at once or just in the thirties. It was a gradual, step-by-step process in which unions and collective bargaining supplied part of the generating pressures.

Through negotiated agreements, plant pay scales and work rules were jointly determined, and the objective criterion of seniority (length of service with that company) established the order of priority in lay-offs, in recall to work, and even in opportunity to qualify for promotion. Also, labor agreements, fixing wage scales and other terms of employment for one to five years, tended to isolate wage rates from the immediate pressures of short-term market forces. Furthermore, the agreements contained a judicial machinery (bipartisan grievance procedures ending in arbitration) to settle alleged violations of the agreement and other job complaints. All this, of course, sharply limited autocracy in the industrial plant.

The result of enlargement of the employment concept far beyond the cash nexus was to expand the workforce horizon of company managements. Instead of a hard-boiled, day-to-day basis, newly hired workers were looked upon as potential work-life employees. Employment became a career with the company. With a longer-run outlook on the firm's workforce, stress was placed on employee selection and training, foreman training in human relations, employee contentment on the job (employee counseling even covered family worries), and educational and recreational activities. Instead of providing employees with merely a means of wage income, companies began to take on some of the aspects of a community center, a psychiatric clinic, a school, and an insurance company—all in the cause of promoting good employee relations.

The need for development analysis, as explained in Chapter 2, is evident from the alteration in employment and factory life that gained momentum under the impact of the New Deal. While practice has traveled great distances, orthodox partial analysis still postulates the *status quo ante*. Thus, it applies a type of market analysis to employment matters that, in significant parts of the American economy, may be unwarranted and misleading.[5] The theoretical implications of this marked alteration in the composition of employment are investigated in Part II.

---

[5] The shift from a commodity to a welfare concept of employment has, generally speaking, progressed much further in the United States, especially in large manufacturing concerns, than is true in most foreign countries. That is one reason why British and Swedish economists often have difficulty in fully comprehending the employment analyses and assumptions of some American economists.

Landmarks in Labor Legislation

Some of the enlarged employment obligations were adopted voluntarily by company managements as good business. It was assumed that they paid for themselves in terms of employee morale and productivity. Other new dimensions, like seniority and old-age and unemployment insurance, were forced on firms by labor unions and government action. And labor organization and collective bargaining were protected and fostered by legislation.

Widespread economic collapse eliminated taboos against government intervention and created an intellectual climate receptive to labor organization and labor legislation. The change in economic attitudes resulted in a series of path-breaking statutes, providing for marked Federal intervention into the employment relationship. Partly, their purpose was to expand mass purchasing power by raising pay scales and putting people back to work. Another motive was the humanitarian aim to improve the lot of the "underprivileged"—"the ill-fed, ill-clad, and ill-housed."

An indication of the shift in public sentiment in a prounion direction was the passage of the Norris-LaGuardia Act in 1932, just before Franklin D. Roosevelt's Presidency. It made "yellow-dog" contracts unenforceable and severely circumscribed the issuance of labor injunctions by the Federal courts. Union organization thereby gained significantly in freedom from legal restraint. However, the promotion of industrial relations reform for recovery purposes began with the New Deal.

The National Industrial Recovery Act of 1933 (invalidated in 1935) provided that workers were to enjoy "the right to organize and bargain collectively through representatives of their own choosing," and industry codes were to be drafted containing wage and hour standards. Subsequently, those two basic ideas (self-organization plus collective bargaining and wage-hour standards) were more fully established by the National Labor Relations (or Wagner) Act of 1935 and the Fair Labor Standards (or Wage and Hour) Act of 1938.[6]

Under Section 7(a) of the Recovery Act, employees were to be free "from the interference, restraint, or coercion of employers"

---

[6] The Walsh-Healey Public Contracts Act (1936) provided for wage and hour standards by private concerns producing items for the Federal Government.

in exercising their right of self-organization and collective bargaining. Discrimination against unionists in hiring and firing had generally been an effective employer weapon against organization of the plant or firm. Lacking enforcement teeth, Section 7(a) could not prevent some antiunion actions. For example, although company-dominated unions were ostensibly banned by Section 7(a), the number of workers covered by employee representation plans (promoted and supported by employers) rose from 1,250,000 in 1933 to 2,500,000 in 1935 just before the National Industrial Recovery Act was declared unconstitutional.[7] Nevertheless, the Recovery Act enhanced the prestige of labor unionism and enabled union organizers to assert: "President Roosevelt wants you to join."

The Wagner Act strongly supported the new faith in collective bargaining as a means of improving economic balance. The right of employee self-organization was protected against management interference by providing that antiunion activities on the part of management (including the establishment and support of company-controlled unions) were legally banned as "unfair labor practices." Also, provision for employee elections, with management obligated to bargain in good faith with a union selected by majority vote, enabled unions to obtain recognition and status without striking to win an economic endurance contest. Under subsequent interpretation of the law, employers were forced to share with that union authority over various aspects of the employment relationship including pensions and other benefits. The act became fully effective when its constitutionality was upheld in the Spring of 1937.

In addition to labor organization and collective bargaining, the Federal Government promoted worker aspirations and intervened in the employment relationship by enacting the Social Security Act of 1935 and the Fair Labor Standards Act of 1938. The Social Security Act established a whole new program of social insurance. The Fair Labor Standards Act, for the first time, legislated a minimum-wage standard for men as well as women on a nationwide basis. Both of these laws ran counter to the rather narrow creed of the AFL founding fathers. However, repeated public opinion polls showed that the labor legislation adopted between 1933 and 1938 enjoyed widespread popular support.

[7] A. L. Bernheim, *et al., Labor and the Government* (New York: Twentieth Century Fund, 1935), p. 79.

UNION REJUVENATION AND MASS ORGANIZATION

The thirties were years of labor turmoil, tradition-rupturing, and great union growth. Until the New Deal emerged in 1933, organized labor seemed too demoralized and hidebound to take advantage of worker disillusionment and resentment at management favoritism and arbitrary actions during the economic downswing. But with a sympathetic Federal administration and favorable legislation, the wave of social discontent and worker protest began to find effective outlets.

Workers flocked into unions, demanding a new and better deal in industry. Total membership rose about a million between 1933 and 1935, and soared 3.5 million more from 1935 to 1937 (see Table 8). At times, plant employees took matters in their own hands, even staging "sit-down" strikes, during which they occupied the factory, refusing to permit nonstrikers to enter.[8] Insistence on objectivity in lay-offs and in employment allocation caused the seniority principle to be embedded deep in the governmental practices of American industry. Schism over the issue of craft *vs.* industry basis of organization led to intense rivalry and a civil war in organized labor. In short, it was a period of rank-and-file effervescence and epidemic-like growth of organized labor, of crusading idealism and aggressive union tactics, of interunion warfare and last-ditch resistance on the part of many large employers.

The Rise of Industrial Unionism

The AFL was not well situated to capitalize on the organizing opportunities presented to it in the mass-production industries—autos, rubber, steel, electrical equipment, aluminum, and so forth. Largely controlled by unions of skilled workers, the Federation steadfastly refused to grant charters to industrial workers that would involve abandonment of the jurisdictional claims of the craft unions in those industries. At first the AFL offered only charters as "federal labor unions"—a transitional arrangement prior to parceling out the new recruits among its national union affiliates.

---

[8] About half a million workers were involved in the rash of sit-down strikes in 1936 and 1937.

TABLE 8

Total Union Membership, 1930–1961*

Year	Total	AFL Affiliates	CIO Affiliates	Per Cent of Total Nonagricultural Employment
1930	3,401,000	2,961,000		11.7
1931	3,310,000	2,890,000		12.6
1932	3,050,000	2,532,000		13.1
1933	2,689,000	2,127,000		11.5
1934	3,088,000	2,608,000		12.0
1935	3,584,000	3,045,000		13.4
1936	3,989,000	3,422,000		13.9
1937	7,001,000	2,861,000	3,718,000	33.8
1938	8,034,000	3,623,000	4,038,000	27.8
1939	8,763,000	4,006,000	4,000,000	28.9
1940	8,717,000	4,247,000	3,625,000	27.2
1941	10,201,000	4,569,000	5,000,000	28.2
1942	10,380,000	5,483,000	4,195,000	26.1
1943	13,213,000	6,564,000	5,285,000	31.4
1944	14,146,000	6,807,000	5,935,000	34.1
1945	14,322,000	6,931,000	6,000,000	35.8
1946	14,395,000	7,152,000	6,000,000	34.9
1947	14,787,000	7,578,000	6,000,000	34.0
1948	14,319,000	7,221,000	n.a.†	32.2
1949	14,282,000	7,241,000	n.a.	33.0
1950	14,267,000	7,143,000	n.a.	31.9
1951	15,946,000	7,846,000	n.a.	33.7
1952	15,892,000	8,098,000	n.a.	32.9
1953	16,948,000	8,655,000	n.a.	34.1
1954	17,022,000	9,604,000	n.a.	35.1
1955	17,749,000	10,900,000	5,200,000	33.6
1956	18,477,000	16,392,000	(AFL-CIO)	33.8
1957	18,430,590	16,379,000		33.3
1958	18,080,000	14,770,000		33.7
1959	18,169,000	14,657,000		32.8
1960	18,117,000	14,884,000		32.1
1961	17,456,000	14,103,000		31.1

* Figures include Canadian membership of national unions with headquarters in the United States; in 1960 such Canadian members amounted to about one million.

† Figures are not available for the CIO for years noted "n.a."

Sources: For membership figures up to 1951: *Handbook of Labor Statistics*, United States Department of Labor, 1950 edition, p. 139 and 1951 Supplement, p. 47; for recent figures: *Directory of National and International Unions in the United States*, 1961, Bulletin No. 1320, United States Bureau of Labor Statistics, 1962, p. 45; and Bulletin No. 1267, 1960, p. 8, and Bulletins No. 1222 and 1185; and *Monthly Labor Review*, LXXXV (September 1962), p. 975. For employees in nonagricultural establishments, see *Employment and Earnings*, Annual Supplement Issue, vol. 5, No. 11 (May 1959), United States Department of Labor, Table A–1, p. 1.

The issue of craft *vs.* industrial organization in manufacturing came to a head in the 1935 convention of the Federation. In the preceding convention a compromise resolution had authorized the issuance of charters for national unions in automobiles, cement, aluminum, and other mass-production industries. However, the only two charters issued for autos and rubber excluded certain craftsmen and maintenance employees from the restricted jurisdiction. Also the Federation officials deemed an organization campaign in steel not then advisable. The consequence of such actions, including an attempt by President Green to appoint the presidents of the two newly chartered auto and rubber organizations, was growing demoralization among the new labor leadership in the mass-production industries. When the 1935 convention rejected a resolution favoring straight industrial organization and adopted one endorsing the industrial principle but providing protection for the jurisdictions of the craft unions, revolt occurred within the AFL. Six affiliated national unions and the presidents of the printers and hatters formed a "Committee for Industrial Organization," whose stated purpose was to promote unionization in the mass-production industries. The AFL authorities demanded that the Committee disband as a "dual" outfit. When it refused to do so, the offending unions (by then increased to ten) were expelled from the Federation in November 1936.

CIO Challenge and AFL Response

The Committee for Industrial Organization (the CIO) brought to the labor movement new viewpoints, a new militancy, new methods of organization, and, along with John L. Lewis and Sidney Hillman, a new group of young leaders, who were unhampered by respect for inherited traditions. Compared with the AFL, the CIO leaders were more willing to resort to political action and welcome to full membership the unskilled, women, Negroes, and other minority groups. As part of their kit of organizing techniques, the CIO unions used publicity experts, research studies, downtown offices, conferences with opinion leaders and civic groups, and various inducements to win over the leaders of company unions. Large sums were spent on organizing campaigns. Even the services of organizers with Communist leanings were utilized, thus allowing them to become entrenched in a number of CIO unions.[9]

The timing of CIO's formation proved excellent. In the 1936 election, Roosevelt swept the country. The CIO gained prestige from its part in his landslide victory. In February 1937, General Motors capitulated, after a two-month sit-down strike, and signed an agreement with the CIO Auto Workers. The next month, U.S. Steel, an arch foe of unionism, signed with the union following a most effective organizing program. In April 1937, the constitutionality of the Wagner Act was upheld by the Supreme Court. Those four victories had a bandwagon effect. In the Summer of 1937 a number of AFL affiliates began to shift to the CIO as the more progressive outfit. By the Fall of 1937 (as suggested by Table 8), the membership of CIO affiliates exceeded that of AFL units by almost 30 per cent. Earlier, in May 1937, the organizing committee had been transformed into a regular union center, with a constitution and set of officers. Preserving the magic initials (CIO), the Congress of Industrial Organizations practically paralleled the AFL in structure and functions.

That the CIO gains were won in the face of strongly organized opposition was indicated by the hearings on labor espionage and employers' associations, conducted by the Senate Committee on Education and Labor in 1937. Reports of the Committee revealed that over 1,400 firms and fifty employers' associations had used the services of detective agencies for labor spying and strikebreaking between 1933 and 1936.[10] Also during 1936 and 1937, citizens' committees were formed in a number of cities for strikebreaking purposes. They aided in the defeat of the steel union in the "Little Steel Strike" of 1937 (against Bethlehem, Inland, Republic, and Youngstown Sheet and Tube). It was only in 1941 that those holdout steel firms and others like the Ford Motor Company were required to comply with the Wagner Act and deal with unions.

The CIO challenge shook the AFL from its complacency. The

---

[9] In justification of the use of Communist-line followers as CIO staff, President John L. Lewis is reputed to have said: "Who gets the bird, the dog or the hunter?"

[10] *Industrial Espionage*, Report of the Committee on Education and Labor Pursuant to S. Res. 266, Senate Report No. 46, Part 3, Seventy-fifth Congress, 2nd session, 1937, pp. 89–121.

competition of the CIO forced the AFL to modify its traditional views regarding state assistance, to expand existing craft unions to include semiskilled and unskilled workers, and to engage in aggressive organizing campaigns. In jealous rivalry, the AFL chartered industrial unions, and the CIO set up craft unions. As a consequence, charges of union raiding, scabbing, and mutual betrayal filled the air. The bitterness of this interunion warfare damaged the cause of unionism in the eyes of the public.

Nevertheless, labor organization continued to expand. It spread from metropolitan centers and the mass-production industries into middle-sized and smaller manufacturing communities and even into retail and service lines, as the two rival groups strove to outdo each other. Consequently, total union membership in 1941 was three times the 1934 figure, with over half in industrial or quasiindustrial unions.[11] In terms of nonagricultural employment (a rough measure of eligible workers), total union membership jumped from 12 per cent in 1934 to around 28 per cent in the years 1938–41 (see Table 8).

Wartime Gains

During World War II, union membership increased over four million, or about 40 per cent. The conditions were favorable for further expansion. As in World War I, the cost of living rose, labor shortages occurred, the government was sympathetic to organized labor, labor leaders occupied high positions in war agencies, and employers were in no position to resist strenuously or to engage in antiunion campaigns. During the war, interunion conflict lessened, and the tripartite War Labor Board freely granted unions "maintenance of membership," along with the "check off" of union dues by the employer. Under that compromise formula for union security, members at the time a new agreement was signed had to continue their membership for the duration of the agreement— usually a year. The Board served as a substitute for collective bargaining in the settlement of labor disputes. Although wage-rate

---

[11] In contrast, over three-fourths of all union members were in craft or compound-craft unions in 1930.

increases were held in check by the Government's stabilization policy, the Board granted approval of "fringe benefits" (paid vacations and holidays, insurance and pension plans, etc.) rather freely. That liberality helped to promote such benefits and had a lasting effect on the pattern of employment practices.

During the war, organized labor declined somewhat in public favor, even though it expanded greatly in membership. In spite of a no-strike pledge by union leaders right after Pearl Harbor, numerous short work stoppages occurred in 1943, 1944, and 1945. Mostly they were local outbreaks, disapproved by the leaders of national unions. However, strikes in coal, called by the audacious John L. Lewis, were more serious, even necessitating "brown-outs" to conserve coal and government seizure of the mines to stop the strike. The result was a notable cooling of public sentiment. Public opinion polls in 1944 showed a 67 per cent majority in favor of further curbs on unions. Public concern about abuse of union power was reflected in the Smith-Connally Act of 1943, passed over a Presidential veto. It empowered the President to take over plants closed by labor disputes, and provided for a government-conducted strike vote prior to any work stoppage. The vote provision proved completely ineffective, a result somewhat frustrating for proponents of the measure.

On the other hand, business management during the war regained much of the prestige that it had lost in the Great Depression. And business was fearful that wartime practices strengthening labor's position would become entrenched and hamper management's operations in peacetime.

POSTWAR PLATEAU AND THE MERGER

The postwar years (1946–63) have been characterized by membership stability, considerable public disenchantment with organized labor, and a shift in legislative policy from union encouragement to restriction. Notable developments were: the great strike wave in 1946, passage of the Taft-Hartley Act in 1947, merger of the AFL and CIO in 1955, and enactment of the Landrum-Griffin Act in 1959.

Reaction and Taft-Hartley

At the end of hostilities, labor and management pressed for abolition of wartime controls in the industrial relations area. Although both sides favored return to collective bargaining, the Labor-Management Conference late in 1945 showed that they agreed on little else.

Reconversion of industry gave rise to a great epidemic of strikes. Unions demanded large wage increases to offset the sharp reduction in weekly hours on peacetime production. They sought to maintain and improve total take-home pay. Also, a sharply rising price level contributed to large wage demands and difficulties of settlement without governmental intervention. In the twelve-month period following the surrender of Japan, a total of 120 million man-days of idleness occurred as a result of work stoppages. At one time almost two million—an unprecedented total—were on strike, and many of them were out for four or five months. Nevertheless, for the first time during a critical strike period, there was practically no violence or bloodshed. The employers did not attempt to open the struck plants. However, the Federal Government seized and operated the coal mines and the railroads on the grounds that strikes in those industries threatened to create a national emergency.

This great strike wave, along with shortages of goods and price inflation, aroused public ill-will. Popular demand for restraints on union power and leaders was reflected in Congress and public opinion polls. The drive to curb unions gathered momentum when the Republicans gained control of both Houses of Congress in the 1946 elections. The Southern organizing campaigns of the AFL and CIO in 1946 and 1947 met with slight success. Nevertheless, it is significant that no national campaign to eliminate unions occurred after World War II, as was the case following World War I.

Public pressure to curb unions culminated in the Taft-Hartley Act, passed over President Truman's veto in 1947. During that same year, restrictive labor legislation was also enacted in many states, including "right to work" (or antiunion shop) laws encouraged by Section 14 (b) of the Taft-Hartley Act. To the Wagner Act, the new law attached a series of "unfair practices" that were illegal for unions to engage in, and established an emergency strike procedure based on a 75- to 80-day court injunction against striking. President Truman's unexpected victory with labor support in the 1948 election helped to halt the legislative attack on unions and caused Republicans in Congress to express a willingness to modify the severity of Taft-Hartley in a number of respects. However, organized labor and the Democratic Administration insisted unsuccessfully on outright repeal.

As the figures in Table 8 indicate, during the decade following enactment of the Taft-Hartley Act, the labor movement failed to expand in terms of total eligible workers. No new territory was conquered. The increase in absolute numbers came mainly from employment expansion in plants previously organized.

Passage of Taft-Hartley probably did hamper new organization somewhat (mainly by lowering the prestige of the labor movement), but its retarding effects can easily be exaggerated. In effect, the law said to workers: You are free to join or not to join just as you wish, and protection will be provided for either decision. In addition, the act, as interpreted, permitted greater freedom for employer oral attacks on unions, prevented the use of some pressure-type organizing tactics (the closed shop, secondary boycotts, mass picketing), and encouraged State "right-to-work" laws, which forbid any requirement of union membership for getting or holding a job. Those laws, passed in twenty (mostly Southern and Midwest agricultural) States, were partly disregarded and unenforced.[12] They were, however, indicative of public sentiment and, therefore, helped to blunt the union appeal. Nevertheless, it is doubtful whether organized labor would have enlarged its total membership much beyond the figures in Table 8 even if Taft-Hartley had not been passed. Union expansion apparently continued in "right-to-work" States at about the same pace as in other comparable areas.[13] The AFL and CIO Southern organizing campaigns, aimed at

---

[12] See, for example, Thomas J. Luck, "Effects of the Taft-Hartley Act on Labor Agreements, 1947–1952," *Southern Economic Journal*, XX (October 1953), pp. 145–55.

[13] See, for example, Frederic Meyers, "Effects of 'Right-to-Work' Laws: A Study of the Texas Act," *Industrial and Labor Relations Review*, IX (October 1955), pp. 77–84; and *Right to Work in Practice* (New York: Fund for the Republic, 1959).

penetrating areas unconquered in the depression or the war, were largely foredoomed before Taft-Hartley was enacted.

Internal friction in the CIO, centering around the Communist issue, also probably was an expansion-checking influence. Between 1939 and 1949 the leadership in eleven CIO unions had wiggled with each turn in the Russian Communist line. With the Nazi-Soviet Pact in August 1939, President Roosevelt became a "warmonger," and seemingly Communist-inspired strikes occurred in a few war plants (e.g., North American Aviation in California). After the Nazi invasion of Russia in June 1941, Roosevelt's halo was restored in the left-wing press, and Communist-line followers in the labor movement became zealous spokesmen for complete dedication to the war effort, even brashly advocating piecework in automobile plants. After the war, Russia's aggressive program was supported. When, however, in 1948 leaders in those eleven unions opposed the Marshall Plan and supported Henry Wallace for President, that was just too much for Philip Murray, the head of the CIO. In the 1949 convention the CIO constitution was revised to make Communists ineligible for any executive office in that organization and to provide that a national union following the Communist line could be expelled from the CIO by a two-thirds vote of a convention. In 1949 and 1950, the eleven unions, then representing perhaps a million members, left or were expelled from that union center. In some cases, the CIO established new rival unions; in others, it sought to capture members of the purged unions through existing affiliates such as the Auto Workers and Steelworkers.

Less rivalry between the AFL and CIO after the war also may have helped to level off the total membership figures. Leaders in the two federations had cooperated in the war agencies, and had come to recognize the disadvantages of internecine strife from a public relations viewpoint. The CIO had largely completed its "historic mission" to organize the mass-production industries, and AFL affiliates had expanded sufficiently so that numerically it held a comfortable lead over the CIO.

Either singly or in combination, these three factors (Taft-Hartley, the CIO purge, and reduced AFL-CIO rivalry) are not too effective in explaining the failure of unionism to penetrate new areas during the decade from 1945 to 1955. This failure, and the lack of any greater expansion following the AFL-CIO merger in 1955, would seem to indicate that general upsurges in membership are abnormal and require the stimulus of society-shaking forces. We will return to this question in the final section of the chapter.

The AFL-CIO Merger

Efforts toward consolidation of the two national federations occurred repeatedly in the late thirties, the forties, and the early fifties. However, unity was achieved only with a conjuncture of favorable circumstances, following a period of gradual reduction of differences.

First, the craft *vs.* industrial issue largely disappeared as AFL unions (e.g., the Machinists, Electricians, Carpenters, Butchers) acquired large numbers of factory workers.

Second, the CIO purge of Communist-dominated unions removed an important obstacle to reunion, in view of the marked aversion of many AFL leaders toward Communism. The two federations cooperated in founding the anti-Communist International Confederation of Free Trade Unions in 1949.

Third, enactment of Taft-Hartley and right-to-work laws showed the need for unified efforts in the political sphere. The unfavorable climate of the postwar period indicated the desirability of more cooperation and fewer interunion contests having adverse public consequences.

Fourth, the threat existed that a third union center might be established, which would include the Mineworkers, the unions purged from the CIO, and the International Longshoremen's Association expelled from the AFL in 1953 for corruption.

Fifth, President Green of the AFL and President Murray of the CIO both died in November 1953. The struggle for succession in the CIO left its presidency a position of doubtful power, partly also because of the reduced total membership now represented by CIO affiliates. Consequently, in the merger negotiations, the CIO leaders were willing to allow the new AFL incumbents to be president and secretary-treasurer of the merged federation.

Sixth, the two federations cooperated in negotiating a no-raiding pact in 1953, subsequently signed by most of their affiliates. The pact worked well in preventing interunion invasion of established bargaining relationships.

Actual merger was facilitated by an agreement to take all affiliated national unions into the new federation without alteration, thus preserving the integrity of each of them. An Industrial Union Department was established to include most of the former CIO unions and some AFL unions with significant numbers in plant-wide locals.

The merger was consummated in December 1955 under the jointed, unwieldy title: American Federation of Labor—Congress of Industrial Organizations. As the outstanding innovation in organized labor during the postwar period, the restoration of "organic unity" aroused great expectations. Actually, the fears of conservative business and the hopes of ardent unionists both proved excessive.

The merger did not mean a great "labor monopoly" or a "political powerhouse." The AFL-CIO itself is, economically speaking, rather impotent. As a federation of autonomous national unions, it does not call strikes or engage in collective bargaining over wages, hours, and working conditions. Rather, its functions are principally in the areas of publicity, political and international activities, new organization, and research.

Even as a political agency, a national federation of unions has serious weaknesses. The leaders of the affiliated national unions have had diverse political views and party alignments. The political independence of rank-and-file members and their families has been repeatedly demonstrated. Also, under Taft-Hartley, dues money cannot be used for financing campaigns for Federal office; unions must raise voluntary contributions for that purpose. Although many labor-supported candidates were elected to Congress in 1958, the Landrum-Griffin Act was passed over the vigorous opposition of the AFL-CIO leadership, which worked hard for a less stringent bill.

With respect to organization, the AFL-CIO proved rather ineffective during its first eight years. Its organizers, fearing insecurity from a cut in their employment, actually organized themselves into a union in 1957 to bargain with the AFL-CIO itself.

Demand for Union Reform

The constitution of the AFL-CIO provided that affiliated unions should be free of corrupt, Communist, or fascist influences. Soon the issue of corruption and unethical practices became the merged federation's number one problem.

Investigations by Congressional committees from 1954 on, revealed that leaders of some half-dozen unions had manipulated union funds for personal gain, betrayed the trust placed in them, and maintained themselves in office by tyrannical methods. The most prominent of those unions was the Teamsters, headed by Dave Beck and his successor, James Hoffa. However, leaders in other former AFL unions (e.g., the Bakers, the Laundry Workers, and the Operating Engineers) were also guilty of similar misconduct. Positions of power were misused for self-enrichment, and opposition was suppressed by strong-arm tactics. The trusteeship device was employed to maintain machine control and even to provide graft for officials. In the Teamsters, hoodlums and racketeers had been appointed to staff positions.

As the story of shady dealings and corruption began to unfold in Congressional hearings, the AFL-CIO Committee on Ethical Practices drafted in 1956 and 1957 a series of codes of ethical conduct of union affairs. In its 1957 convention, not only were the codes adopted by the AFL-CIO, but the Teamsters, Bakery Workers, and Laundry Workers (with a combined membership of 1.6 million) were expelled from the federation for malpractices and misuse of union funds. Such vigorous action in ousting over one-tenth of its affiliated membership required considerable courage on the part of the new AFL-CIO.

Despite that evidence of fortitude, front-page publicity for the shocking revelations of the Special Senate (McClellan) Committee created an unsavory image of the union movement in the mind of the public. The climate of opinion grew less favorable for unionism as labor leaders in significant numbers pled the Fifth Amendment and refused to answer charges of misconduct, betrayal of trust, embezzlement, or assault and battery, and later as many of them were convicted and fined and imprisoned.

The issue of internal corruption and undemocratic practices

placed the labor movement on the defensive. Along with the claim of wage-propelled inflation, it tended to alienate large sections of the public. Many intellectuals became somewhat disenchanted with the labor movement. The result was the enactment of a union reform law (the Landrum-Griffin Act) in 1959 over the strong opposition of the AFL-CIO, especially to the nonreform provisions dealing with picketing and secondary boycotts. The prestige of the labor movement thereby suffered another setback.

In the meantime, changes in the structure of employment were significantly restricting the growth of industrial unionism, and employer attitudes toward unions were toughening in certain industries (particularly electrical equipment and steel). As explained in Chapter 1 (see Table 3), blue-collar employment contracted relatively during the fifties. In some mass-production industries like autos and steel, plant employment actually declined after 1956. Automation was a factor in such absolute reductions. As a consequence, membership in some industrial unions began to fall off. Reduced dues income forced the Auto Workers (UAW) in 1958–59 to cut the staff by one-fifth and institute an across-the-board salary reduction. In the midst of the 1958 recession the Auto Workers settled for a wage increase about the yearly equivalent of the increase negotiated in 1955. However, the steel companies in 1959 insisted that the new contract in that industry contain no wage rise because that would be inflationary. The hardening attitudes in steel resulted in prolonged negotiations and the long steel strike of 1959, which lasted 116 days. In 1962 and 1963, on the other hand, settlements were negotiated in steel without even an overt threat of a strike.

ANALYSIS OF UNION DEVELOPMENT

Broadly speaking, the 180 years of union history in America divide themselves into three periods: (1) a century of fluctuation before a stable organizational pattern was achieved (up to, say, 1890); (2) some 45 years in which craft unionism with a Gompers philosophy predominated (1890–1935), and (3) the era of industrial unionism under regulating legislation (1935–63). By the twenties, craft unionism had lost its momentum and was being undermined by secular economic changes. By the late fifties, broad economic and political shifts also seemed to be reducing the potency of industrial unionism, as plant employment began to contract in mass-production industries and as public sentiment pressed for union restraint and reform.

This final section will be devoted to further analysis of the historical material in this and the preceding chapter. In seeking answers to some of the questions posed at the beginning of Chapter 3, it is necessary to examine carefully patterns of union development and the factors influencing them. Why, for example, did the great transformation of unionism in the thirties prove to be but one phase in an evolutionary cycle? Answers to questions about the historical unfolding of unionism will also provide a basis for the discussion of the theory of American unionism in Chapter 6.

Factors in Secular Change and Cycles

Looking back one is impressed with the obstacles to collective action by labor during the nineteenth century. They included: immigration and great labor mobility, an individualistic philosophy embedded in the law, political dominance by agricultural and middle-class interests, and employer opposition fortified by a battery of antiunion devices. Yet, despite frequent defeats and frustration, the idea of self-protection through labor organization persisted and revived after each collapse. Continuing organization was, however, largely confined to skilled and strategically placed workers who were in a position to form effective combinations to defend themselves against the harsh rule of market forces and managements. Unionization was their way of attempting to modify the commodity concept of labor.

Gradually, however, secular changes were altering the setting. Immigration declined to a trickle, the nation became more industrialized and urbanized, government grew more friendly to the concept of collective action by labor, and as firms expanded, managements became more impersonal and their chain of command developed new links. Such factors were favorable to the growth of labor organization.

Nevertheless, it is worth noting that, despite secular changes, the labor movement still proceeded in a wavelike fashion, with

spurts of organization followed by fairly long periods of decelera-
tion or slowdown in momentum. What light does historical experience shed on this pattern of upswing and level off?

Since the achievement of a stable form of unionism in the
1890's, general membership upswings have developed out of periods of disturbance and ferment. Severe depressions and wars have
provided the generating forces for rapid expansion in the ranks of
organized labor. As worker-protective and -protest agencies, unions
tend to gain recruits during unsettled periods. Organized labor
generally has lost impetus during more normal times. Then membership expansion may slow down to the pace of employment
growth in areas previously unionized.

During prosperous periods the appeal of unionism and its crusading zeal seem to be reduced by a number of factors. Living
standards are generally rising, so that workers are inclined to be
less dissatisfied and discontented. An intellectual climate of middle-
class moderation is likely to prevail. Most union leaders, lacking a
doctrinaire philosophy (such as Socialism) or a class-conscious
clientele (as in Europe), are prone to succumb to the comforts
of institutional security and American materialism. The increasing
size and administrative complexity of unions has helped to make
labor leaders more organization- and management-minded. Another
secular factor serving to blunt the union appeal has been increased
enlightenment of business management, as industry has been shifting from a callous commodity to a humane welfare concept of
employment.

Unions have both innovating and conservative aspects. As
worker representatives, they press for new rights and economic
breakthroughs during periods of general stress and social upheaval.
At other times, they are likely to pursue traditional patterns and
ideologies.

The founders' philosophy may be adhered to long after changes
have reduced its potency. The Gompers' program of "business"
unionism on a craft base was, by the late 1920's and early 1930's,
clearly inadequate to meet the organizing and economic needs of
the time. But it took the Great Depression and a civil war in labor
to burst the bonds of tradition and to force a revision of orthodox
views. The new CIO creed included not only industrial unionism
but also stress on gains through government intervention and the

use of modern methods of organization and political action. The Gompers' ideology, of course, was not completely displaced. Unions such as the building trades and the Teamsters continued to follow it to a large extent.

The CIO or New Deal orientation of industrial unionism has not changed much since the 1930's. By the 1950's its effectiveness had, however, become somewhat reduced by two developments. One was the changed political and intellectual climate. The other was the metamorphosis that had taken place in the industrial unions as they matured.

Implications for the Theory of Unionism

Study of the rise and decline of labor organizations and ideologies encourages an evolutionary or historical interpretation of the labor movement. During a particular period a certain philosophy may flourish and then begin to fade. Change in the environment is an important factor, serving to foster or frustrate a particular orientation or structural pattern in organized labor. But environmental change alone does not explain the meteoric existence of the Knights of Labor or the less spectacular rise and fall of the I.W.W. (Industrial Workers of the World). Their ideology and structure lacked staying power against hostile elements, which, of course, included employer reaction.

Labor organization represents a method, a way of decision-making that utilizes primarily negotiation and collective action. As a means of adjustment and a protest outlet, it serves as an alternative or a supplement to the market mechanism. It is adaptable to changed conditions because, as a method, American unionism has not been bound by fixed objectives.

Therefore, the emphasis and orientation of organized labor in this country have tended to shift with the times. During the nineteenth century, for example, the importance of immigration led to stress on craft exclusiveness. Faced with a large increase in labor supply, skilled workers sought to protect themselves by means of craft protective devices—insistence on apprenticeship, jurisdictional claims, the closed shop. With the great waves of immigration during the decades prior to World War I, craft unionism had drawing and staying power broadly enough based to dominate the labor movement. But as a general philosophy of the movement, it became much less apt as circumstances changed—as immigration contracted, educational levels rose, production techniques advanced, and widespread worker discontent was generated by economic collapse.

Given an evolutionary view of unionism as an adaptive mechanism subject to cultural lag, some diversity in union orientation is likely to exist. Unions are founded at different times, have different constituencies, face a variety of industrial circumstances, and are in various stages of development. Merger into a single federation can do little to diminish historical, institutional, and environmental differences among national and local unions. Labor organizations have a life of their own. Each has its special traditions, loyalties, vested interests, and quality of leadership.

Secular trends and general conditions do, however, affect all unions, although in differing degrees. In normally prosperous periods, union policies are prone to follow traditional patterns. There are, of course, pressures for imitation, pattern following, and uniformity among unions. That is especially the case where their jurisdictions overlap or where significant elements in their memberships work for the same firms or live in the same communities. Consequently, in the labor movement, unifying and diversifying influences are operating concurrently.

The history of unionism in America is a story of variation, adaptation, shifts in orientation, and survival of the strong. It indicates the difficulties that confront any attempt to explain our labor movement in terms of a single factor or a universal theory. The theory of union behavior is examined in more detail in Chapter 6.

SUMMARY

During the three decades from 1933 to 1963, unionism in America experienced great expansion and gradual reaction. Factors in that development were both cyclical and secular.

1. The Great Depression and World War II largely accounted for the cyclical elements in the phenomenal upswing of organized labor between 1933 and 1945. Those elements included: (a) governmental promotion of labor organization, collective bargaining,

and labor standards; (b) the upsurge of industrial unionism that involved organizational innovations and a crusading spirit; (c) the resulting shock to AFL complacency, which set off a period of intense rivalry and interunion warfare; and (d) the substitution of friendly government policies for collective bargaining during the war, with employers largely forced to comply.

2. The reaction that set in after the war had both cyclical and secular aspects. They included: (a) strikes during the war and especially the great strike wave of 1945–46; (b) the postwar wage-price spirals, for which unions were partly blamed; (c) the malpractices and corruption engaged in by union leaders and exposed by Congressional committees; (d) the extension of management privileges to wage-earners, with the shift toward a welfare concept of factory employment; and (e) the decline in physical violence and sympathy for strikers, as employers stopped trying to operate their plants during strikes.

3. Some concrete results of public pressure for union restraint and reform were: the Taft-Hartley Act, State right-to-work laws, and the Landrum-Griffin law.

4. The shift from Gomperism to New Deal unionism increased labor's effectiveness for a decade, but after the war the new philosophy lost some of its potency, as the climate of opinion changed and former union sympathizers became lukewarm.

5. Organized labor made a strong effort through the AFL-CIO merger to stem the tide and to improve its organizing and political powers. However, the great expectations and great fears that "organic unity" aroused were not realized.

DISCUSSION QUESTIONS

1. Explain and critically discuss the notion that there has been a shift from a commodity to a welfare concept of employment.
2. How did the New Deal enhance the possibilities of labor organization? Did any New Deal legislation adversely affect organizing possibilities?
3. Why was the great expansion in industrial unionism delayed until after 1934? Why did it not continue after 1945?
4. Contrast the background influences and philosophy of the Wagner Act and the Taft-Hartley Act.

5. Explain the elements in the shift of public sentiment toward organized labor after World War II.
6. Discuss the future of industrial unionism, indicating the main factors that have been and are likely to be significant in its development.
7. Drawing on union history, discuss the claim that organized labor has been a conservative force in the American economy.
8. Explain the broad changes in the American labor movement since the 1890's.

SELECTED READINGS

Ching, Cyrus S., *Review and Reflection, A Half Century of Labor Relations* (New York: Forbes, 1953).

Derber, Milton, and Edwin Young, *Labor and the New Deal* (Madison: University of Wisconsin Press, 1957).

Dulles, Foster Rhea, *Labor in America: A History* (New York: Crowell, 1955).

Dunlop, John T., "The Development of Labor Organization: A Theoretical Framework" in R. A. Lester and J. Shister (eds.), *Insights Into Labor Issues* (New York: Macmillan, 1948).

Lester, Richard A., "Revolution in Industrial Employment" in *Labor Law Journal*, IX (June 1958), pp. 439–46.

Millis, Harry A., and Emily C. Brown, *From the Wagner Act to Taft-Hartley* (Chicago: University of Chicago Press, 1950).

———, and Royal E. Montgomery, *Organized Labor* (New York: McGraw-Hill, 1945).

Perlman, Mark, *Labor Union Theories in America: Background and Development* (Evanston, Ill.: Row, Peterson, 1958).

Schlesinger, Arthur M., Jr., *The Coming of the New Deal* (Boston: Houghton Mifflin, 1959).

Ulman, Lloyd, "The Development of Trades and Labor Unions" and "Unionism and Collective Bargaining in the Modern Period," Chapters 13 and 14 in Seymour E. Harris (ed.), *American Economic History* (New York: McGraw-Hill, 1961), pp. 366–482.

United States Department of Labor, *Brief History of the American Labor Movement*, Bureau of Labor Statistics, Bulletin No. 1000, 1957 Revision (Washington: United States Government Printing Office, 1957).

5.
Evolution of Management's
Views and Policies

THE EMPLOYER VIEW of labor and the policies of management toward unions have experienced decided changes during the past century and a half. The transformation has been especially marked since the twenties.

During the nineteenth century, management conceived the factory worker as an inferior breed, who needed to be bossed and disciplined by a severe system of rewards and penalties. By the 1940's, the image of the manual worker had altered radically. Then, particularly in large firms, he was thought of as a complex human being, whose morale is important and who responds best to understanding and self-respecting treatment.

Hostility toward unionism was characteristic of much of American industry during the nineteenth century and the first three decades of the twentieth century. Generally speaking, however, during the forties and fifties, basic opposition in principle had given way to tolerance or accommodation in practice; militant combat had been replaced by experienced negotiation and sophisticated preservation of management rights.

In recent decades, the alteration in management attitudes has been particularly pronounced in big corporations. Since World

War I, increasing stress has been placed on human and social skills in the handling of industrial relations. Not only has management in the large firm been humanized and professionalized, but employee well-being and work satisfaction have tended at times to take precedence over maximum profits for the stockholders or lower prices for consumers. Indeed, so much stress is being placed on employee interests that in some economists' thinking the notion of consumer sovereignty is giving way to a predominance of worker interest as the guiding or controlling force in our economy. That is another facet of the claim that ours is becoming a "laboristic economy."

This chapter examines various stages in the development of the labor philosophy of American management. It includes a historical sketch of the labor policies of employers and employers' associations, along with a review of the great antiunion campaigns. The chapter closes with an examination of the succession of systematic approaches that have influenced management thinking and practice in the labor field.

TRADITIONAL IDEOLOGY AND TACTICS

Employer policies and programs with respect to labor and labor organization must be interpreted in light of the ethos of the time. For the most part, a ruggedly individualistic, freedom-for-management type of economic philosophy permeated the nineteenth century. A survey of employer countermeasures against unions should, therefore, take account of conventional opinion concerning management and labor. With that in mind, our survey of employer reactions to labor organization is preceded by a brief consideration of the accepted business creed and antiunion tactics during that century.

The Traditional Management Creed

On the labor side, management is the government of men. Employment is the utmost in administered relationships in economic affairs. The worker accepts a subordinate position in an authoritarian and hierarchical organization. He works on the premises of the employer, performing under orders. In the absence of a union, the management lays down the rules and enforces them with sanctions—suspension, demotion, discharge. The employer enjoys sovereignty in his plant and resents any attempt to interfere with his "right to run his own business." In the employment process, issues of government—prerogatives, rights, justice, and penalties—assume a large and expanding role.

The first article of faith in the old-fashioned employer creed was, therefore, freedom of management to exercise absolute authority in the plant. This position was clearly expressed by the stove manufacturers when they announced the formation in 1866 of the first national employers' association "especially for the purpose of resisting any and all actions of the Molders' Union, which shall in any manner interfere with our right to control our own workshops, and to manage our own business" and, in addition, "Resolved, . . . that we will in every way possible free our shops of all dictation or interference on the part of our employees."[1]

The second article of faith was the determination of wages by "natural" or competitive forces. Reliance on market solutions may seem inconsistent with the first article, namely, administrative discretion and absolute authority, including the practice under which management quoted its wage scales on a take-it-or-leave-it basis. However, in the first part of the nineteenth century, faith in laissez faire and the "natural laws" of economics predominated. Attempts by labor organizations to enforce a scale of minimum wages were considered an "artificial means" of raising "the price of wages" above its "natural level."[2] Employers insisted that labor organization was "unnecessary, because labour, like every other commodity, will seek its own level, and its true value, in an open and unfettered market."[3] Competition would serve as labor's

---

[1] From the announcement of the formation of the American National Stove Manufacturers' and Iron Founders' Association, published in the *Boston Evening Voice*, March 13, 16, 17, 20, 23 in 1866 as quoted in Philip S. Foner, *History of the Labor Movement in the United States, From Colonial Times to the Founding of the American Federation of Labor* (New York: International Publishers, 1947), p. 353.

[2] Those were the concepts used by the Supreme Court of Pennsylvania in a "conspiracy case" in 1821.

[3] Quoted from the Preamble and resolutions adopted at a meeting of the employers, Curriers and Leather Dealers, of the City of New York and Brooklyn, on March 24, 1836, reproduced in John R. Commons, *et al.* (eds.), *A Documentary History of American Industrial Society* (Cleveland: Clark, 1910, Vol. 5), p. 310.

protector. Little attention was paid to statements like one by a Massachusetts legislative committee in 1850 which, while fully favoring laissez faire under normal circumstances, pointed out that the legislature had "destroyed the natural relations" between employer and employee by passing incorporation acts, which "created immense artificial persons [business corporations], with far larger powers than are possessed by individuals."[4]

The third article of faith assumed that a harmony of interests existed between employer and employee. Not only was a sale between independent contractors considered mutually advantageous, but employers were thought to be buying loyal and faithful service. That kind of service was required because both would suffer if the employer lost out in competition with rival manufacturers located elsewhere in this country or abroad. That, for example, explains why President Monroe, in an annual message in the 1820's, congratulated businessmen on the "fall in the price of labor, apparently so favorable to the success of domestic manufactures." To employers, unions were trouble-making agencies that sought to interject themselves into and to disrupt a mutually beneficial relationship.

Given the tenets of this creed, it is understandable that employers often attacked labor unions as injurious, monopolistic, un-American, and illegal. And the practices that management used to combat and destroy labor organization prior to the Wagner Act of 1935 were in keeping with the stern, struggle-for-survival doctrines of the day.

Pre-New Deal Tactics

To combat and eliminate labor organizations, the employers resorted to a variety of legal and economic measures. On the legal side, they brought law suits against unions as criminal conspiracies or agencies using illegal methods, got court injunctions forbidding certain union actions, enlisted the aid and protection of local police and State militia in strike situations, and sought legislation to restrict union activities.

In the economic sphere, the employers used a number of effec-

---

[4] S. M. Kingsbury, *Labor Laws and Their Enforcement with Special Reference to Massachusetts* (New York: Longmans Green, 1911), pp. 79–80.

tive weapons. One of them applied at an early date was the "yellow dog" (or "iron clad") contract, under which the employee agreed as a condition of employment not to join a union (sometimes contracting to forfeit all pay due him at the time if he did join). Discrimination against union members in hiring and employment was another potent tactic. It included not only the discharge of any employee discovered to be a union member, but also the requirement that a job applicant provide a "clean" or "honorable" discharge from his previous employer, and the systematic blacklisting of "union agitators." Information serving as the basis for such discrimination against unionists might be supplied by workers secretly employed as espionage agents for the employer or an employers' association. More unusual was the employer threat to close the plant in a lockout of employees or to move his operations to a nonunion location.

Not infrequently, employers combined temporarily (later permanently) in employers' associations. Their purpose was to strengthen the use of some weapons (e.g., the blacklisting of unionists, labor espionage, importation of strikebreakers, and operation of an employer-controlled job agency), or to gain the active cooperation and financial participation of fellow employers in antiunion programs. Pressures were sometimes brought to bear upon employers to enlist in such campaigns. Financial pressure might be exercised by the threat of an employer boycott of firms continuing to deal with a union, or by such means as the member firms posting a bond or making a cash contribution to a fund, which would be forfeited if the employer did not continue to operate nonunion. Cooperating firms might also arrange to perform work for a shop struck by a union and thus to supply that employer's customers for him.

Public opinion and community action against labor organization were enlisted in some cities by publicity programs pointing to the potential loss of local business or to the added cost to consumers resulting from union activities. Such efforts, at times, led to the formation of *citizens' committees* designed to maintain "law and order" during strikes or aimed at the elimination of labor organization from industry in the community.

With respect to employer actions against unions, the Wagner Act of 1935 constituted a great divide. Most of the antiunion tactics discussed above were outlawed by that piece of Federal legislation. Previously, in 1932, the issuance of court injunctions in labor disputes was severely restricted by the Norris-La Guardia Act.

THE STORY OF EMPLOYER COUNTERACTION

In view of the economic philosophy of the time, strong employer opposition to unions was to be expected as soon as they began to appear. Not only were the law and courts used against labor organizations, but employers' organizations to combat unions, "to break them up altogether, root and branch," were formed as early as 1798 by employer-shoemakers in Philadelphia.[5]

The Doctrine of Criminal Conspiracy

Employers in this country, as in England, turned to the courts to attack the new "evil." From 1806 to 1815, shoemakers' organizations were prosecuted in six cases under the English common-law doctrine of conspiracy, which the courts ruled was also the law in this country. In four of these first six cases, the journeymen shoemakers were found guilty and were given slight fines, but they were not imprisoned as in England. In the first decision of 1806, the defendant shoemakers were held to have been "guilty of a combination to raise wages." This decision called forth a vigorous protest, with the Jeffersonian Democrats attacking both the Federalist judges and the English common law, while the workers complained that other groups, including employers and merchants, had their associations and meetings to affect wages and the prices of goods. In the succeeding conspiracy cases, judges changed the emphasis in their decisions or charges to the jury. They declared that combinations to raise wages were illegal only when unlawful means (such as coercion or intimidation) were used, or when the workers conspired to injure a third person (such as a nonmember, by trying to secure a closed shop). Two of these early conspiracy cases centered on the closed shop.

---

[5] John R. Commons, *et al.*, *History of Labour in the United States* (New York: Macmillan, 1918), vol. 1, p. 133.

From 1821 to 1827, there were four more conspiracy cases. In one, the shoemakers tried unsuccessfully to prosecute employers for conspiring to reduce wages. The court held that it was lawful for masters, if forced by employees to raise wages, to combine in order to restore the wages to their "natural level"; but that "it would have been criminal" if the employers had combined to depress the wages below what they would be in the absence of resort to "artificial means" by either side.[6] In the other cases, two against tailors and one against hatters, the workers were found guilty of conspiracy in restraint of trade. From 1828 to 1842, there were eight more prosecutions for conspiracy but only two convictions. In one of them the New York Supreme Court held a shoemakers' union guilty of the charge of conspiring to raise wages and thereby injuring trade and commerce.

Finally, in the famous case of *Commonwealth vs. Hunt* in 1842, Chief Justice Shaw of Massachusetts ruled that the objective of a closed shop was legal and that combined action to achieve a lawful purpose was not necessarily a criminal conspiracy; legality depended on whether the means used to accomplish the aim were lawful. This decision proved a landmark. It provided a firm basis for the legality of labor unions and ended effective court prosecution of labor organizations for a number of decades —until injunctions were issued against strikes in the 1880's and conspiracy charges against unions occurred under the Sherman Act of 1890.

Early Employers' Organizations[7]

During the years 1809 to 1830, employers' associations were formed and operated in an informal and secretive fashion. Among their common practices were: agreements on wages, understandings not to employ union members, contributions to a fund to finance conspiracy prosecutions, and the farming out of work of struck shops to be done in other shops. In the 1830's, employers' associations became more numerous and cohesive. Many of them

---

[6] *Ibid.*, p. 163.

[7] This discussion of employers' associations is based on Clarence E. Bonnett, *History of Employers' Associations in the United States* (New York: Vantage Press, 1956).

were formed to combat the movement for a ten-hour day. The growth of such organizations was also stimulated by the numerous strikes that occurred—over 160 between 1833 and 1837. By then, employers were also using yellow-dog contracts; when strikes threatened to break into riots, armed forces (the militia) were used in some cities to help break the strike.[8]

In the 1850's, another wave of employer organization occurred. Singly and in combination, employers blacklisted union members, forced through wage reductions, and imported European labor, especially to break strikes over wages. Mass picketing, violence, and injury to property characterized certain strikes, some of which lasted ten to twenty weeks.

Employers also organized extensively in the mid-sixties. Many employers' associations in 1866 and 1867 were actively hostile toward unions, some using the "honorable discharge" system for new employees and refusing to hire union members. On the other hand, the Pittsburgh iron manufacturers in 1865 negotiated with the iron puddlers' union a sliding pay scale based on the price of iron. This local agreement established an industry pattern for similar scales throughout the West, and was an early example of "pattern bargaining."

The Antiunion Drive of the 1870's

Adverse economic conditions during the 1870's gave rise to a succession of wage cuts, mass meetings of unemployed workers in a number of cities, and a series of vigorous and violent struggles between industry and labor. Among employers in a variety of industries—shoes, coal, railroads—an open-shop movement was conducted between 1872 and 1877. Employers sought to eliminate unions by such means as blacklists, labor espionage, "ironclad" oaths not to join a labor organization, use of Pinkerton detectives, legal prosecution, and lockouts of employees until nonunion conditions were accepted.

Beginning with the Panic of 1873 the big issue was wage reductions. Strikes against pay cuts were widespread and usually unsuccessful. In 1873, the boot and shoe manufacturers' association in Massachusetts refused to deal further with the union and com-

---

[8] *Ibid.,* pp. 45, 53, and 54.

pletely crushed that formidable labor organization in the State. In anthracite coal, the union lost a bitterly fought strike in 1875, in which the "Molly Maguires" (a secret miners' organization that terrorized the coal fields) was destroyed. The Great Railroad Strike of 1877 developed from a drive to smash the railroad unions; workers on the Philadelphia and Reading Railroad were asked to withdraw from unions, and nearly every railroad announced a ten per cent cut in wages. The resulting strike extended from the Atlantic seaboard to the Mississippi River and involved 60,000 railroad workers. It was characterized by rioting, the destruction of millions of dollars of property, and the killing of forty persons in Pittsburgh alone. Citizens' committees were formed, the regular army and militia were called out, court injunctions were issued, and, after the strike was broken, strikers were blacklisted by all the railroads.

With the violence of the railroad strike, the business community became thoroughly aroused and belligerent. Workers were pressured not to join unions, yellow-dog contracts were imposed, strikebreakers were imported from abroad, and antiunion organizations mushroomed.

Interestingly, this period of union-management militancy produced an employers' association which, during its short-lived existence in 1872, advanced a program containing modern industrial relations ideas. The "Employers Central Executive Committee" of New York City was an open-shop association, which sought to "discourage trade unions by every fair means," and opposed the eight-hour day because the increased costs would take business away from New York. Yet the committee was also interested in "industrial-betterment activities" and "welfare work." It proposed that employers concern themselves with the nonwage interests of their men "by providing a room, for instance, where they could read or enjoy light amusements, and by establishing a more general intimacy with them."[9] Increased wages would not always satisfy discontented workmen, and a test of brute force was not the answer. Among the committee's recommendations were: "It would be well to take a kindly interest in the welfare of their employees, by seeing that their individual efforts were appreciated," and "It would be wise for employers to encourage by their example everything that tends to perpetuate the dignity of labor by training their

---

[9] See *ibid.*, pp. 107–108.

children in such a manner that each may become the master of some trade."[10] Such enlightened suggestions "for the government of employers," however, fell on deaf ears during the ensuing years of storm and strife in industrial relations.

Employer Reaction to the Knights of Labor

In 1886 "law and order leagues" were established in many cities. They were a counteraction to increasing labor strikes, boycotts, and violence, especially the Haymarket Square Riot in Chicago. These secret citizens' committees were designed to prevent lawless actions and to exert influence on public officials to protect employers and individual workers in labor disputes. Especially they were formed to oppose the Knights of Labor.

Along with the leagues, many new employers' associations were organized for "mutual protection." In 1886, the brass-goods manufacturers nationally, and the textile manufacturers in New England, formed associations with strike benefits' features "to protect the trade against the unreasonable demands of organized labor."[11] In the same year, the Stove Founders' National Defense Association was established to assist a struck member by having other members manufacture for him. The lockout of employees by groups of firms was frequently used to break strikes or to exclude members of the Knights from shops. By 1890, employers' associations were likewise operating against "the tyranny of [AFL] trades unions."[12]

During the period from 1886 to 1892, collective bargaining was also expanding. Written agreements between unions and employers or employers' associations became more common. In addition, the use of arbitration to settle wage disputes was fairly frequent.

Association Bargaining and Conflict (1892–1902)

During the 1890's, collective bargaining was extensively practiced. In industries like building, coal, and foundries, uniform wage scales negotiated by a union and an employer association came to serve as a means of helping to stabilize the industry. The 1890's were mostly depression years, and some claimed that employers on occa-

[10] *Ibid.*
[11] *Ibid.*, p. 255.
[12] *Ibid.*, p. 322.

sion welcomed industry-wide strikes as a means of restricting supply and maintaining prices. So prevalent was union-association bargaining that it was charged that some "joint combinations" were raising profits and wages at the consumers' expense.[13]

Sometimes unions tried to break up the employers' solid front by striking them one at a time. Sympathetic strikes were also common. In response, employers as a group might threaten to lock out all their employees unless the union ceased those tactics. So strong had some unions become that they began to be attacked as monopolistic "trusts" and agencies for extortion.[14]

With economic depression, increasing unemployment, and wage cuts, labor relations in some industries became more strained. Strikes were likely to be lost and erupt in violence, if strikers could be easily replaced by jobless workers. Consequently, some strikes were characterized by lawlessness, and government intervention for the purpose of settling labor disputes became more common. However, after a number of violent strikes, the soft-coal operators' association and the miners' union were able to negotiate an interstate agreement in 1898, covering the Central Competitive Field, which accounted for most of the country's output.

In some instances, strikes against large companies culminated in private warfare. In 1892 at the Carnegie Steel Company at Homestead, Pennsylvania, a pitched battle between company-imported Pinkerton detectives and the strikers resulted in ten deaths. In the strike against the Pullman Car Company in 1894 (which provoked sympathetic walkouts and a boycott of Pullman cars on many railroads), both Federal and State troops were used, court injunctions were issued, and a total of 25 persons were killed. Thereafter, the strikers were blacklisted by the railroads and the American Railway Union was destroyed. These two great strikes, growing out of the industrial unrest of the time, foretold stiffening employer opposition to the growing strength of trade unionism.

The Great Open-Shop Movement (1902–1914)

With a fourfold expansion in union membership between 1898 and 1904 and a number of union successes in strikes, employer opposition to unions increased and became more highly organized.

---

[13] See *ibid.*, pp. 350, 358, 360, 407, 413, and 417.
[14] See *ibid.*, pp. 322, 353, and 427.

Hostility largely took the form of an open-shop drive, spearheaded by employer associations.

Between 1901 and 1903, many employers' organizations, including the National Metal Trades Association and the National Association of Manufacturers, made strong statements in favor of the open shop and absolute employer control of industry. As an illustration of some employer sentiment, the president of the NAM in his annual report for 1903 spoke of the association's success in defeating antiinjunction bills and the "socialistic" eight-hour day, noted the need for strong counterorganization to combat the "encroachments" of organized labor, and added: "Once thoroughly alive to the true nature of this un-American institution, the people, I firmly believe, will place their stamp of disapproval upon it, and it will dwindle in power faster than it grew. . . .

"Composed as it is of men of muscle rather than men of intelligence, and commanded by leaders who are at heart disciples of revolution, it is not strange that organized labor stands for principles that are in direct conflict with the natural laws of economics."[15]

In 1903, employer counterorganization reached a peak. Some employer organizations formed a federation for collective action on a national scale in order to prevent labor organization and collective bargaining by employers. The National Founders Association and the National Metal Trades Association began a systematic antistrike program. It consisted of issuing certificates of loyal workers to nonstrikers, paying bonuses to strikebreakers, and obligating the associations' members to give employment preference and leaves of absence for strikebreaking—thus creating a body of skilled and efficient strikebreakers. The settlement of a strike against any member employer was left in the hands of the association.[16]

Antiunion feeling was so strong among employers before World War I that another president of the National Association of Manufacturers declared in 1911: "The American Federation of Labor is engaged in an open warfare against Jesus Christ and His Cause."[17] Employers' associations agreed that all employers should

[15] *Proceedings of the Eighth Annual Convention of the National Association of Manufacturers of the United States of America*, April 1903, pp. 17 and 20.

[16] *Ibid.*, pp. 451–52.

[17] *Labor Policies of Employers' Associations, Part 3, The National Association of Manufacturers*, Senate Committee on Education and Labor, Senate Report No. 6, Part 6, Seventy-sixth Congress, 1st session, 1939, p. 19.

join and help defray the cost of combating strikes because "in defending a fellow manufacturer, no matter where located, you are defending yourself, and postponing just so much longer the time when you will be attacked."[18] Citizens' committees and vigilante groups were active in driving unions from localities so that the community would not suffer "untold loss from being unionized"; employers dealing with unions were called "traitors."[19]

The upsurge in union membership also stimulated the beginnings of a management philosophy of industrial relations. Companies began to grope for methods of promoting more work interest among employees and a more personal atmosphere in the plant. Among the welfare techniques commencing to be used by companies were: recreational facilities, lunchrooms, employee picnics and outings, employee clubs, profit-sharing and stock-ownership plans, pensions, and (just before World War I) group life insurance. These early attempts at company welfare were rather paternalistic and often antiunion in intent, but they represented the first stage of programs that expanded after the war.

In addition, the idea of "scientific management" had taken root by 1910. It represented the application of measurement (time and motion study), of careful analysis (job specification, evaluation, and training), and of wage incentives (with production standards based on measured performance). Scientific management, which left no role for collective bargaining, came to have a marked impact on industrial relations in the second and third decades of this century. As a distinct philosophy of industrial relations, it is considered more fully at a later point in the chapter.

World War I Influences

Changes in management thinking about industrial relations were stimulated by labor shortages and labor turnover during World War I. Shortages were due to the withdrawal of men into military service, cessation of immigration, and increased demand with the pressure for military production. In such a tight labor situation,

---

[18] *Labor Policies of Employers' Associations, Part 1, The National Metal Trades Association,* Senate Committee on Education and Labor, Report No. 6, Part 4, Seventy-sixth Congress, 1st session, 1939, p. 23.

[19] *Labor Policies of Employers' Associations, Part 3, The National Association of Manufacturers, op. cit.,* p. 10.

workers had no need to worry about job security, and the resulting rise in the quit rate brought home forcefully to employers the high cost of heavy labor turnover.

As a consequence, firms began to hire "employment managers" or "personnel managers" in order to provide orderly arrangements for employee recruiting, selection, testing, training, and record-keeping. Increased use was made of systematic classification of jobs and the methods of scientific management. Also, significant expansion occurred in profit-sharing and pension plans.

During the war, employers generally cooperated with the government's labor policies. Not wishing to be labeled "obstructionists," the employer antiunion campaign was put in storage. A period of friendly attitudes between management and organized labor set in. Top management people came to know many union leaders through common efforts and membership in a number of war agencies. In the patriotic atmosphere, the decisions of the tripartite War Labor Board were generally accepted. The Board's principles included the right of workers to bargain collectively through representatives of their own choosing.

The device of employee representation under a plan instituted by the employer (later dubbed "company unions") got its start during the war. The Federal labor boards, in over 125 awards affecting plants where no union existed, called for the establishment of some form of worker-representation or works-council plan.[20] In addition, many firms adopted such plans without any award of the war labor agencies. Consequently, by 1919 over 400,000 workers were covered by arrangements for employee representation.

Employers in significant numbers were coming to see the need for more labor-management understanding and for some kind of organization or representation arrangements for dealing with large work groups. As early as January 1915, John D. Rockefeller, Jr. expressed this more reflective and conciliatory point of view before the United States Commission on Industrial Relations in the following words: "I believe it to be just as proper and advantageous for labor to associate itself in organized groups for the advancement of its legitimate interests as for capital to combine for the same object. Such associations of labor manifest themselves in pro-

---

[20] See *Collective Bargaining through Employee Representation* (New York: National Industrial Conference Board, 1933), p. 8.

moting collective bargaining in an effort to secure better working
conditions, in providing machinery whereby grievances may easily
and without prejudice to the individual be taken up with management."[21]

The "American Plan" Offensive and "Welfare Capitalism"

After the war, the "open shop" drive was renewed. Federal protection of labor's right to organize was withdrawn, and a wave of
strikes broke out in 1919 and again in opposition to general wage
cutting in the 1921 recession.

The antiunion campaign in the twenties was called "the American Plan." In 1921, an official of the National Association of Manufacturers stated that more than five hundred organizations in two
hundred and fifty cities had endorsed the plan, and an American
Plan Conference, attended by representatives of some one hundred
employers' associations, met semiannually during the twenties. In
certain cities like Chicago, San Francisco, and Cleveland, various
financial and merchant groups raised million-dollar funds in the
early twenties in order to weaken the building-trades unions and
to introduce the open shop in local construction. Building unions
were charged with monopoly, corruption, and extortion. In the
metal-working industries, the employers' organization (the National Metal Trades Association) pursued a vigorous nonunion
shop drive from 1920 to 1924, using such antiunion practices as
labor espionage, blacklisting, mobilization of strikebreakers, and the
accumulation of a common defense fund. Yellow-dog contracts
were effectively used to check union organizing efforts in a number of industries.

The twenties was the period of so-called "welfare capitalism."
In industry, departments of personnel administration multiplied. A
survey in 1928 showed that 34 per cent of the firms with 250
or more employees had personnel departments.[22] In the larger firms,
a number of personnel techniques were used. Employees were

---

[21] *Industrial Relations, Final Report and Testimony Submitted to Congress
by the Commission on Industrial Relations*, Vol. VIII (Washington: United States
Government Printing Office, 1916), p. 7764.
[22] *Industrial Relations in Small Plants* (New York: National Industrial Conference Board, 1929), p. 20.

favored with benefit and recreation programs, employee magazines, health and safety programs, group life insurance, and profit-sharing and employee stock-ownership plans. Through centralized control of hiring, discharge, and employee rating and promotion, workers in an increasing number of companies were given some (if slight) protection against unfair and arbitrary treatment by a foreman. Large firms in such industries as metals, oil, rubber, railroads, and gas and electric utilities adopted employee representation plans. Under them, mostly minor complaints were handled, but employees were provided a limited channel for the expression of their views to management. To that extent, they might have been considered an alternative to independent unionism, which in the twenties had little possibility of organizing those firms. By 1928 the coverage of employee representation plans exceeded 1,500,000 workers.[23] Because formal membership and dues were not part of such plans, their coverage was not comparable with union membership figures.

Reaction to Industrial Unionism and the New Deal

The stock-market crash in 1929 and the ensuing depression played havoc with the program of welfare capitalism. In the economic pinch, the personnel management movement suffered a temporary setback. Some benefit programs were slashed or abandoned. Employee stock-ownership and profit-sharing for plant workers backfired as stock prices skidded and profits disappeared. The relative impotence of employee representation was revealed in the arbitrariness and favoritism that occurred with large-scale lay-offs.

With the coming of the New Deal, employers were impelled to alter their employment and personnel policies. The thirties were years of labor unrest and of friendly attitudes toward labor organization on the part of the middle-class and the government. It will be recalled that Section 7(a) of the Recovery Act stipulated that employees should have the right of self-organization, free from employer interference or restraint, and should not be required to join a company union. The introduction of employer-dominated labor organizations was not, however, prevented and, therefore, many more employers adopted employee representation plans. Be-

---

[23] *Collective Bargaining through Employee Representation, op. cit.,* p. 16.

tween 1932 and 1935, the coverage of such plans doubled to 2.5 million.[24]

In the mid-thirties many firms in manufacturing were determined to prevent or destroy unionization in their plants. Between 1933 and 1937, labor espionage and "professional" strikebreaking reached a peak. An incomplete list, compiled by a subcommittee of the United States Senate from its investigations into industrial espionage, contained the names of some 1,420 firms and fifty employers' associations that had used detective agencies for such services as espionage and strikebreaking during the period from 1933 through 1936.[25] The list contained many of the country's best-known firms. One detective agency alone had at least 330 of its operatives in ninety different national unions, of whom one was a national vice-president, fourteen were presidents of locals, thirty-eight were secretaries of locals, and six were business agents or organizers.[26] General Motors paid approximately a million dollars for spy services from 1933 to 1936; at times G.M. had as many as two hundred labor spies in its plants, with the spies of one hired agency spying upon the spies of another G.M. agency.[27] In 1935, 1936, and 1937, citizens' committees were used in many communities as a strikebreaking device.

The labor policies of most large firms had to be altered significantly when the Supreme Court upheld the Wagner Act in 1937. From then on, labor espionage and employee representation plans (supported or dominated by the employer) were clearly unlawful. Other traditional management weapons (such as discrimination against unionists in hiring or employment, blacklists, antiunion statements intended to discourage unionization, and refusal to recognize and negotiate with a union representing a majority of the employers) were also illegal. In short, management was deprived of its customary implements for antiunion offensives or campaigns. In addition, seniority as an employment rule and

---

[24] A. L. Bernheim *et al.*, *Labor and the Government* (New York: Twentieth Century Fund, 1935), p. 24.

[25] See *Industrial Espionage*, Report of the Committee on Education and Labor Pursuant to S. Res. 266, Senate Report No. 46, Part 3, Seventy-fifth Congress, 2nd session, 1937, pp. 80–89.

[26] *Ibid.*, pp. 26–28, 75–79.

[27] *Ibid.*, p. 23.

grievance procedures ending in arbitration, spread once unionization became established.

The combination of these legal and regulatory developments caused many managements to react bitterly against the New Deal. They felt that now their hands were tied; they no longer had adequate disciplinary authority or ability to reward employee loyalty to the firm and the management. Management authority over a wide area was open to union challenge and outside review.

Management's response to the spread of unionism was to expand its efforts to improve employee loyalty by other means. They included the development of two-way (management-employee) communication, training of foremen in human relations techniques, and employee counseling and other devices for increasing satisfaction on the job. The result was expansion of personnel or industrial relations departments, not only for the purpose of expert dealing with unions but also to limit and offset their effectiveness with employees.

By the late thirties, the "human relations" movement had begun to have an evident effect on management thinking and practice. Managements, shocked by the upsurge of unionism, were ripe for a new orientation. An approach that could be applied with complete disregard of unionism and that had manipulative possibilities, appealed to the paternalistic proclivities traditionally strong in American management. Focused on the shop level and the individual, the human-relations orientation stressed interpersonal relations and the application of industrial psychology to "humanize" employment.

That and other management approaches are more fully analyzed in the final section of this chapter. Here it is only necessary to recognize the relationship of this development to the management situation in the late thirties, and to point out that the human relations approach has played a significant role in the changing concept of employment.

Government Control in World War II

Business management joined in the great spirit of national unity generated by Japan's attack on Pearl Harbor. During the war, labor relations were subject to Federal controls and determinations, particularly to the decisions of the National War Labor Board. With few exceptions, management accepted Federal regulations and awards. The prestige of industry rose, while strikes were injuring organized labor in the eyes of the public and were causing Congress to pass the Smith-Connally (strike-vote) Act over a presidential veto.

Significant elements in management did object to some of the War Labor Board's policies, especially the practically automatic award of maintenance-of-membership, along with the check-off of union dues, and the board's generosity in granting some "fringe" benefits (i.e., vacations and shift differentials). There was concern that reforms adopted during the war might establish precedents that would restrict management in the postwar period (i.e., widespread use of arbitration, industry-wide uniformity of employment terms, pattern-spreading). Experience on government boards did provide management representatives with valuable (and for some, a liberalizing) training.

Postwar Accommodation and Legislative Gains

In the Labor-Management Conference in November 1945, management representatives urged limits on the scope of collective bargaining. Unsuccessfully, they sought agreement on a specific and restricted list of negotiable subjects. Also the managements of large firms traditionally have opposed multiple-employer and industry-wide bargaining. They almost succeeded in having a ban on such association bargaining written into the Taft-Hartley Act. A dozen years later, however, management was less worried about union invasion of its "prerogatives," and much more tolerant of employer combinations in collective bargaining.

No organized open-shop campaign occurred after World War II. The prohibitions of the Wagner Act forestalled any such drive. Although the severity of postwar strikes surprised management, no significant attempts were made forcibly to open struck plants. In some cases, amenities like coffee, doughnuts, and heat were provided pickets by the management.

By and large, management learned to live with and deal with organized labor. In the postwar period, management won back some of the industrial relations initiative that it lost in the thirties and during the war. The practice of long-term (three to five years) agreements, with automatic-increase provisions, was originated by General Motors. General Electric developed a union-frustrating program, based on company announced increases designed to forestall the need for bargaining.[28] Wage-price inflation enabled management to place blame for price rises on unionism and collective bargaining, and the antiinflation exhortations of the Eisenhower Administration led to some toughening of management attitudes toward unions. A case in point was the adamant no-increase position of the steel companies that led to the 116-day strike in that industry in 1959.

The postwar period did not give birth to a new movement (like scientific management, personnel management, or the "human relations" approach) or even to a widely accepted systematic philosophy of union-management relations. Rather, the picture on the management side was one of some diversity in actual policies and concentration on further development and application of established approaches and philosophies. By the late fifties some disillusionment with extreme forms of the human-relations approach had resulted in a mild stiffening in management's attitudes in grievance handling, in collective bargaining, and in personnel programs in many companies. This moderate shift undoubtedly was influenced by slack in the economy after the recession of 1957–58 as well as the altered political atmosphere.

In the legislative field, conservative managements made a number of gains. The Taft-Hartley Act, with its "balancing" prohibitions on union activities, contained most of the labor provisions for which the National Association of Manufacturers had campaigned. The right-to-work laws enacted by twenty States were also strongly supported by the NAM and the United States Chamber of Commerce. The Landrum-Griffin Act, in addition to union reform provisions, contained further prohibitions on secondary boycotts and picketing. From 1952 to 1960, business had the advantage of the Eisenhower Republican Administration. That not only helped to achieve management-desired statutory restrictions on unions, but business could be sure that its interests in the labor relations

---

[28] See Herbert R. Northrup, "Management's 'New Look' in Labor Relations," *Industrial Relations*, I (October 1961), pp. 9–24; and Northrup, "The Case for Boulwarism," *Harvard Business Review*, XLI (September–October 1963), pp. 86–97.

area were accorded sympathetic consideration (by such means as management-understanding appointees to the National Labor Relations Board and the Labor Department, use of Taft-Hartley procedures in labor disputes, and exhortations concerning restraint in wage developments).

With the Kennedy Administration a change occurred. As a senator and in the 1960 campaign, President Kennedy had had the support of many labor leaders. The new appointees to the National Labor Relations Board were more sympathetic to the problems and views of labor representatives. Although the procedures of the Taft-Hartley Act were employed at times, the new Administration also used fact-finding boards which made recommendations for settlement.

PHILOSOPHIES OF INDUSTRIAL RELATIONS

As the story of management policies and programs has indicated, business executives' views toward labor and employment have experienced an interesting evolution since the nineteenth century. Management's image of the manual worker has shifted with alterations in industry (e.g., changes in the work force and production techniques and the rise of industrial unionism) and with new discoveries in psychology and sociology. Notions about management prerogatives and the proper administration of industry have been modified with the development of the view that supervision is the government of men. Stress on training, turnover costs, and employee security has lengthened the employment horizons of management and led to policies based on work-career patterns within a firm.

This final section examines the successive management philosophies of labor and industrial relations. The discussion explains some management influences on the changing concept of industrial employment.

The Market Ideology Plus Absolute Authority

As has been observed, all during the nineteenth century American management stressed the competitive struggle and the supreme authority and wisdom of management. Industrial employment was considered purely a market matter. Competitive forces supplied the "natural" answers, and individual self-interest provided the proper assignment of personnel. Work life was thought of as a dog-eat-dog struggle for survival and advancement, with manual workers constituting the more ignorant and lower forms of economic life. Labor was viewed as one factor of production—a kind of cross between economic man and a piece of equipment, who needed to be driven and prodded by financial incentives and sanctions.

As market-selected superiors and plant owners, employers were endowed with full authority in the workshop. Obviously, they knew what was best to provide workers with employment, and the interest of business should determine work issues, such as the correct length of the work week. Rightly conceived, employment was a transaction of economic advantage to both parties, so that worker-manager relations basically rested on a harmony of interests. Such views easily led to a paternalistic attitude by employers toward their employees.

The Scientific Management Movement

Prior to World War I, industrial engineering studies of jobs commenced to have an impact on management thinking, especially with the publication of Frederick W. Taylor's books.[29] Taylorism, or scientific management, involved the systematic analysis of jobs. Its instruments were the stopwatch and other devices for measuring time and motion in order to fix the proper interval for a worker to complete a particular operation. Scientific management involved the accumulation of data and experimentation to determine the one best way to perform a task. Then workers were to be selected and trained to fit the job requirements and instructed to follow a uniform, or standard, method for performing the work. Under incentive schemes, the worker's pay was geared to the time or speed of his performance.

Initially, union leaders opposed Taylor's program as a brand of "speed-up," applying techniques that were too mechanical. Not

---

[29] Although he published books in 1903 and 1906, his principal work was *The Principles of Scientific Management* (New York: Harper, 1911).

only did it disregard historical, institutional, and human factors, but also it left no place for labor organization. It concentrated on technical production matters and assumed that all the answers to labor problems could be supplied by measurements and objective methods. One consequence of labor opposition was a Congressional investigation of scientific management in 1912. In 1914, a rider was attached to a military appropriations bill, prohibiting the use of the funds for any "time study with a stop watch or other time-measuring device." This ban was repeatedly reenacted.[30]

After 1915, leaders in the scientific management movement became less doctrinaire. In World War I they were thrown together with labor officials and came to recognize that human elements affect productivity and that wage scales are subject to some negotiation. In the twenties, the AFL even advanced a program of union-management cooperation, under which industrial engineers might make studies to determine proper production standards subject to joint acceptance.[31]

Scientific management also met some hostility from business executives. They objected to the substitution of studies and measurement for the old-fashioned dictatorial methods of exercising an employer's authority. The new movement was concerned with the efficiency of workers *and* management. Therefore, it tended to cast doubt on the efficacy of competition and the fitness of some managements. Indeed, Taylor and his followers came to the conclusion that a high percentage of labor and material was wasted through inefficient organization and supervision of work.

Although the scientific management movement has the limitations of its focus and techniques, it has made a permanent contribution to management thinking and practice. Systematic study increased management's understanding of job elements, led to more skillful selection and placement of workers, resulted in more intelligent job training and job pricing, and provided a sounder basis for wage incentives than the former hit-and-miss methods. These improvements make scientific management a valuable instrument of modern management.

---

[30] See A. Lepawsky, *Administration* (New York: Knopf, 1949), p. 121.

[31] For the changes in scientific management's orientation see Milton J. Nadworny, *Scientific Management and the Unions* (Cambridge: Harvard University Press, 1955).

Personnel Management and Welfare Capitalism

As already explained, experience in World War I caused managements to be more conscious of labor turnover and the need for employment management and employee organization. As a consequence, many large companies adopted rather elaborate programs of personnel management and employee benefits in the twenties.

This personnel administration movement headed by big firms consisted of a battery of devices and a sort of benevolent paternalism. In addition to the use of scientific management methods in employment matters, the personnel techniques included: employee representation (plant committees or councils largely for exchange of information and views), employee suggestion systems with monetary rewards for ideas adopted by management, employee magazines, employee savings plans and credit unions, athletic teams, employee stock-ownership and profit-sharing, and a battery of benefit plans (e.g., group life insurance, sickness benefits, pensions, dismissal compensation). The number and variety of devices adopted caused this era of personnel administration to be dubbed the "gimmick period" in industrial relations.

With this movement the image of the manual worker shifted a bit further away from economic man. Management was beginning to be interested in the worker's wants on the job itself. Undoubtedly, the curtailment of immigration was a factor in this change. However, the shift in the image of the manual worker was not great. Only a limited amount of employee self-expression and self-determination was permitted. And a "benevolent paternalism" tends to increase the employee's dependence on the company—not only for wages but also for investment of savings and for benefits of various kinds.

The company, of course, is no Santa Claus. Such personnel programs had to be sold to boards of directors as paying for themselves in terms of employee morale and attachment and the avoidance of unionization. Therefore, strings were sometimes attached to the benefits. Under some plans, they could be granted or withheld at the discretion of management. A number of pension plans permitted withdrawal of benefits if an employee was not loyal in case of a strike or if he participated in "demonstrations detrimental to the company's best interest."[32] Consequently, personnel administration in the twenties sometimes had an odor of charity and an expectation of gratitude attached to it.

As previously explained, personnel administration and welfare capitalism suffered a setback in the depression years of the early thirties. Like scientific management, the personnel management movement had no place in its philosophy for independent labor unions. It was, therefore, unprepared to cope with the upsurge of industrial unionism in the mid-thirties. Not only were some representation plans ("company unions") captured by the CIO, but interpretation of the Wagner Act to require that companies bargain concerning benefit plans led to their incorporation in negotiated labor agreements whenever companies became unionized. Thus, any aroma of paternalism was eliminated.

In the late thirties, personnel management regained its position as corporate managements sought to deal directly with the employee as an individual in contrast to group dealing through the union. The new human-relations movement also added to the importance that management placed on personnel administration.

The Human Relations Approach

The labor turmoil of the thirties gave rise to a new image of the worker and a new approach in industrial relations. The basis for this new orientation was provided by the million-dollar study discussed in Chapter 2, which was conducted by a group of Harvard Business School professors in the Hawthorne plant of the Western Electric Company between 1927 and 1932.[33]

This new human-relations approach represented the joint contribution of applied psychology and industrial sociology. Dubbed "plant sociology," it stressed the social structure in the factory, the interpersonal relations among small and informal work groups (in

---

[32] See Mary Conyngton, "Industrial Pensions for Old Age and Disability," *Monthly Labor Review*, XXII (January 1926), p. 53; and *Industrial Pensions in the United States* (New York: National Industrial Conference Board, 1925), p. 64.

[33] Reported most fully in F. J. Roethlisberger and W. J. Dickson, *Management and the Worker* (Cambridge: Harvard University Press, 1939).

contrast to the formal company organization and lines of author-ity), communication between supervision and workers, and the therapeutic uses of confidential interviews and employee counseling as personnel techniques. Ideally, the foreman was conceived as a friend and confidant, who relieves workers' frustrations by listen-ing sympathetically and offering advice. The manipulative possi-bilities of this new notion of human relations in industry led some to consider it a new kind of Freudian paternalism.[34]

Top management's interest in the psychological problems and social relations of workers was aroused by this new theory of hu-man behavior in industry. Stress was placed on two-way communi-cation and on learning to work with small groups as a means of securing worker participation in company decisions. The result was almost as much money devoted to discovering the attitudes and desires of employees and to training foremen in human-relations skills as was being spent on market research. Elaborate programs were devised to satisfy the worker's wants while at work (rather than as a consumer).

Because employee morale and job satisfaction (and hence pro-ductivity) were assumed to be related to supervisors' personal skills, managers as well as workers were the subject of analysis and remedial programs. Companies selected and trained first-line super-visors (foremen) so that they would be "employee-centered" rather than "production-centered." The foreman's leadership was to be "permissive" and not "authoritarian." The successful manager was visualized as a sort of professional, who had acquired the "human-social skills" necessary to lead complex organizations.

One reason for the wide acceptance of the human-relations approach was that it provided no real role for unions. Indeed, in the early writings of this school, organized labor was completely disregarded; the Hawthorne Works operated nonunion. Inherent was an assumption that, with proper human relations in the work-shop, a union would have little excuse for existence.

Such a conclusion reveals some of the weaknesses of the human-relations approach and programs. The focus is too narrowly on in-

---

[34] For a union attack on management's "humanistic" approach, see Solomon Barkin, "A Trade Unionist Appraises Management Personnel Philosophy," *Har-vard Business Review*, XXVIII (September 1950), pp. 59–64.

ternal plant relationships; extraplant considerations are neglected. As a result, the economic, or market, dimension is largely ignored. Conflicts of economic interest are glossed over and group economic interests are disregarded. Furthermore, insufficient attention is paid to institutional developments and institutional relations among organized groups. In other words, problems and answers that are more broadly based than the plant or company are overlooked by this particular management philosophy.[35]

It is interesting to observe that each of the three management philosophies (scientific management, which blossomed in the tens, personnel management in the twenties, and human relations in the thirties) found no role for unionism within its orientation.[36] And during the forties, fifties, and sixties, when industrial relations problems have been heavily concerned with union dealings and collective bargaining, no new movement or systematic philosophy of industrial relations has developed. That has been true despite great expansion in the study of management and all the money spent on social science research.

The welfare concept of employment has, however, grown and spread since World War II. Employee interests have been more and more ministered and catered to as corporate management has become increasingly "humane" and "employee-centered." Both companies and unions seek to make employees contented on the job. But their methods are different. Unions rely on collective determinations, negotiated standards, and individual protection through the grievance procedure. Industry seeks to reduce personal frictions and impediments to production and to build up the company as the institutional source of employee gains and satisfactions. In the contest for credit and institutional loyalty, employee interests are not likely to be neglected but they will be differently interpreted. Even management's interpretation of the worker's interest has undergone a marked evolution during the past half century.

---

[35] Most of these criticisms are forcefully presented in K. M. Thompson, "Human Relations in Collective Bargaining," *Harvard Business Review*, XXXI, (March–April 1953), pp. 116–26.

[36] This point is made by Peter Drucker in *The Practice of Management* (New York: Harper, 1954), Chapter 21.

SUMMARY

The evolution of the labor policies of American management is a story of advance—from the practical equivalent of commodity treatment to enlightened (even soulful) management, utilizing some of the findings of social science research.

1. In the nintenth century, employers and employers' associations resorted to a variety of legal, economic, and community measures to combat unionism and to retain management's authority over the terms and conditions of employment. The employer creed of that period had the puritanical appeal of simplicity and self-righteousness.

2. During the twentieth century, dominant employer views have altered with regard to some aspects of unionism and collective bargaining (e.g., long-term agreements and grievance procedures ending in arbitration). In other respects, employer opinion generally has been rather unchanging (e.g., criticism of unions as monopolistic and stress on individual employee relations with management).

3. The twentieth century witnessed a succession of hostile and tolerant phases in employer attitudes toward unions (the open-shop campaigns after 1900 and 1920, and the years of truce and acceptance during World Wars I and II). More stability and less violence characterized the late forties, the fifties, and the early sixties, which could be considered an era of accommodation to industrial unionism and acceptance of collective bargaining.

4. Management thinking on industrial relations has been influenced not only by such hostility-accommodation cycles but also by secular economic changes, statutory and other governmental developments, the rise of industrial unionism, and the discoveries of social science. The Wagner Act constituted a sort of watershed in industrial relations because it made illegal many of management's most effective antiunion measures.

5. Each decade from 1910 to 1940 saw a new management philosophy—scientific management, personnel management, and human relations. None of the three had a role for unions within its approach and intellectual framework.

6. Drawing heavily on applied psychology and industrial sociology the human relations movement contributed significantly to the trend toward a welfare or humanistic view of employment. That conception shifted the emphasis from employment as a means of living to employment as a way of life, and from workers as human equipment to workers as human beings having constructive ideas and deserving self-respecting treatment on the job.

7. The fact that no new management ideology was developed during the forties, fifties, and early sixties, raises the question whether most of the possible approaches have already been tried, or whether industrial unionism has made it difficult to develop a new approach that disregards organized labor and collective bargaining.

8. In addition to academic research, a number of large firms have spent considerable sums on extensive studies of industrial relations subjects. This is all a part of the professionalization of American management. Also it is tied up with a desire to supervise contented workforces and to forestall the unionization of white-collar employees.

DISCUSSION QUESTIONS

1. Explain the industrial relations creed of American management during the nineteenth century, indicating its ideological foundations and the environmental factors contributing to its general acceptance.
2. Explain the effectiveness of the antiunion tactics of management prior to the Wagner Act of 1935.
3. In the first half of the nineteenth century, it was claimed that unions constituted monopolistic combinations. Could a similar claim have been made against management in the industrial relations fields during that period? Explain.
4. It is claimed that American management has tended to be paternalistic. Explain the extent to which such a claim is justified by the historical evidence.
5. Contrast the industrial relations programs and philosophies of American management in the decades after World War I and World War II. What factors explain the difference?

6. Explain the program of personnel management and "welfare capitalism" in the 1920's. Did it carry the seeds of its own destruction as some have claimed? Support with reasons your view on that issue.

7. Explain why the scientific management movement first began to develop and gain acceptance in the early years of the twentieth century.

8. Contrast the images of the worker in scientific management (Taylorism) and in the human-relations approach.

9. Critically discuss the human-relations approach, indicating its weaknesses as well as its merits. Do you think that approach will develop further in the kind of industrial relations situation you expect during the next decade? Explain.

SELECTED READINGS

Bendix, Reinhard, *Work and Authority in Industry: Ideologies of Management in the Course of Industrialization* (New York: Wiley, 1956).

Bernstein, Irving, *The Lean Years, A History of the American Worker, 1920–1933* (Boston: Houghton Mifflin, 1960), Chapter 3, "The Employer: Concord or Discord."

Bonnett, Clarence E., *History of Employers' Associations in the United States* (New York: Vantage Press, 1956).

Brown, Douglas V., and Charles A. Myers, "The Changing Industrial Relations Philosophy of American Management," *Proceedings of the Ninth Annual Meeting of the Industrial Relations Association*, December 1956, pp. 84–99.

Hicks, Clarence J., *My Life in Industrial Relations* (New York: Harper, 1941).

Landsberger, Henry A., *Hawthorne Revisited: Management and the Worker, its Critics, and Developments in Human Relations in Industry* (Ithaca: Cornell University, 1958).

Stewart, Bryce M., *Development of Industrial Relations in the United States*, Industrial Relations Counselors, Inc., New York, 1952 (mimeographed).

Sutton, Francis X., *et al.*, *The American Business Creed* (Cambridge: Harvard University Press, 1956), esp. Chapter 6.

Wilcock, Richard C., "Industrial Management's Policies Toward Unionism" in Milton Derber and Edwin Young (eds.), *Labor and the New Deal* (Madison: University of Wisconsin Press, 1957), pp. 275–315.

Part *TWO*
ECONOMICS OF
COLLECTIVE ACTION

6.
Analysis of
Union Behavior

THIS PART OF the book deals with the economics of collective action. To a considerable extent, ours is an organizational economy. Collective units (business corporations, labor unions, governments, and agricultural cooperatives and associations) tend to dominate or control economic processes. The focus in this part is on unions, management, and negotiations between them. The analysis concentrates on the characteristics of the collective actors, the principles governing their actions, and the consequences of collective determinations. This and the next two chapters supply the analysis and theory basic for the rest of the book. Public policies with respect to industrial relations are treated in Part III.

The subject matter of the present chapter is union behavior, government, and evolution. The chapter begins with a discussion of the essence of unionism in the American setting. It examines the obstacles that beset any unitary (single-purpose) explanation of complex and dynamic institutions like labor unions. An eclectic type of model is presented that combines political and economic interpretations. It is supplemented by a development analysis, indicating the institutional changes that have taken place in American unions and the resulting adaptations that have occurred in union behavior and programs.

Union theory, union government, and union development are all intricately interconnected. A politicoeconomic explanation of American unionism obviously involves an understanding of union political processes and must elucidate the long-run trends and adaptations of unions. Consequently, the final two sections of the chapter contain an examination of the structure and government of unions and an analysis of the evolution of labor organizations.

MODELS OF UNIONISM

A theory of union behavior seeks to explain the factors or principles that guide organized labor. The purpose is to provide a basis for interpreting and understanding union policies and programs. The theory of union behavior is not far advanced. Systematic analysis of unionism (including model building) is still in a rather elementary stage. Theoretical constructs and systems of logic developed and refined to explain business and consumer behavior have not unlocked many secrets of trade unionism.

Before embarking on a discussion of union theory it may be well, therefore, to examine some of the difficulties that confront attempts to generalize about American unionism. Recognition of the obstacles to a simple, universal explanation of the labor movement helps one to appreciate why any theory must draw on more than one approach and be qualified by time and circumstance. The material in Chapters 3 and 4 on the historical development of unionism in this country serves as a background for the analysis in this chapter. A section at the end of Chapter 4 pointed out some of the implications of a century and a half of adaptive experience for the theory of American unions.

Difficulties for a Unitary Explanation

A number of considerations render it hazardous to adopt any single-principle or single-factor interpretation of the behavior of the labor movement.

In the first place, the theorist trying to uncover a unifying principle for union behavior is confronted with the question: What kind of union and what kind of behavior? There are local unions (confined to a plant or community), national unions (composed of locals within the nationwide jurisdiction), and a national Federation (the AFL-CIO). In addition (and usually less significant), there are intermediate forms (district or regional units between locals and nationals) and city and state federations of locals. Unions differ in their basis of organization, ranging from craft and multicraft to industrial and multiindustry unions. Also, unions may be conservatively led or Communist led. A monolithic theory may not be equally valid for explaining the character and actions of the different types of labor organization in this country.

Union behavior covers a multitude of activities. Among them are: the organization of new members, the formulation of bargaining demands, the ratification of new agreements, striking and picketing, grievance presentation and settlement, convention resolutions and decisions, political activities, educational and publicity programs, labor solidarity actions (e.g., sympathetic strikes and financial gifts to other unions on strike), union disciplinary measures, the administration of benefit plans.[1] Especially in their early stages, unions may be considered as part of a cause, as a vehicle for social change through the pursuit of certain ethical, social, and political aims, in which case union organizing becomes almost equivalent to religious conversion of the heathen. Is it possible for all these various forms of behavior to be controlled by a common aim or principle?

Second, in achieving their goals, unions must, for the most part, work with and through employers. They attempt to persuade or force the employer to agree to numerous terms and conditions of employment. Thus, employer behavior can be an important variable in union behavior. It has even been said that employers get the kind of union that corresponds to or is encouraged by their policies. Must any union theory be integrated, therefore, with a theory of management?

Third, there seems to be no single, definite test of union

---

[1] The participants in a particular type of union behavior may be leaders, delegates, individual members, or some combination of the three.

success. This obstacle breaks down into three parts. The first part is the claim that unions in this country have no fixed objective or program—"no ultimate ends" to use Samuel Gompers' words. Except possibly Communist-dominated unions, they have only conditional goals, subject to revision with developments. A series of revisions and adaptations to circumstances hardly provides a good standard or measure of success. The second part is that union aims constitute a bundle of incommensurables. They range from wages and fringe benefits with dollar dimensions to individual rights and protections (shop rules, seniority, production standards, the grievance procedure) and institutionally oriented demands (the union shop, the check-off of union dues, the privileges and rights of shop stewards, etc.).[2] The only common denominator of such dissimilar items seems to be the political one of group acceptance by the membership (and also by the management). The third part is that some suggested measures of success are so general and vague as to have no operative or heuristic value. They are unenlightening because practically any and all behavior can be rationalized to comply with their ambiguous criteria. That is the case, for example, with such guides as "the feelings of the members," the "welfare of the membership," the "well-being of the union as an institution," and "maximum money and psychic income for the membership." The relevant membership (whether the total present membership, the total potential membership, or the dominant elements in the present membership) is even unclear. In part, the promotion of the union as an institution depends on the membership's aims as well as the leadership's aspirations.[3] And most unions have a heterogeneous membership; different elements and levels of the organization may have divergent views on the proper objectives for the union and the proper distribution of gains from collective bargaining. Furthermore, efficiency and economy of union operation are hard to define. As in politics, much union work is performed *gratis* by unpaid activists. Unionism, in part, is a "cause"

---

[2] For a somewhat similiar presentation of the "incommensurables" problem see Arthur M. Ross, *Trade Union Wage Policy* (Berkeley: University of California Press, 1948), pp. 27–28.

[3] For a discussion of this point see Melvin W. Reder, "The Theory of Union Wage Policy," *Review of Economics and Statistics*, XXXIV (February 1952), pp. 34–36.

and a movement with even international ties. Therefore, union values are not just market values. The success of causes is usually difficult to calculate.

Fourth, conclusions concerning labor unions often are limited by time and country qualifications. Evolutionary change means that a union today is different in a number of respects from the same union, say, forty or fifty years ago. As was indicated in Chapters 3 and 4, much union development is irreversible. At various times, new characteristics and dimensions have been added that cannot be subtracted now. Furthermore, unions show significant international variation, arising from historical, environmental, and other factors. American unions differ notably from (say) English, German, or Egyptian unions. Such time and national differentiation adds to the problems of any unitary hypothesis.

Identity of Method and Approach

Despite diversity in behavior and even in policy, unions in this country have common procedures for decision-making, use the same kit of techniques, and share viewpoints and habits of thought. It is through similarity in operations and approach that our labor movement achieves a measure of unity.

American unions utilize two methods of arriving at decisions, one for internal affairs and the other for dealing with employers. In organized labor, the democratic tradition is strong; balloting is the accepted means of making final decisions. Although in practice democratic procedures are sometimes honored in the breach, union constitutions generally are highly democratic, and, theoretically, acceptance by the constituents (the membership in the unit) is the ultimate authority. All unions, whether led by supporters of the Communist line, the New Frontier, or rock-ribbed Republicanism, profess to adhere to the democratic determination of their internal affairs.

Likewise all unions, whatever the ideological shadings of their officials, use the method of collective bargaining and negotiated agreements for fixing the terms and conditions of employment. In connection with collective bargaining, the strike and picketing are techniques common to practically all unions (exceptions are where the strike is prohibited by law as in public service). Other common techniques of unions include: a set of demands served on the employer, the use of a bipartisan grievance procedure, a written constitution and periodic conventions, and the same dues for all members regardless of unequal individual use of union services.

Unions stress solidarity. They emphasize strength through combined action. Their methods of decision-making and their techniques provide group expression and aim at a united front. Actually, the union usually is not so solid in opinion as outward appearances might seem to indicate, especially when a decision has been made around which the leaders and members feel compelled to rally. Such compulsion may stem not only from loyalty to *their* institution and from social pressures by the membership, but also from a common approach to industrial relations problems.

Just as management has its own creed, so manual workers tend to develop common habits of thought from a similarity of work status and conditions. The union viewpoint represents the like-mindedness of supervised employees.[4] It is an interest-group outlook that also pretends, as part of a movement with international ties, to transcend sectional interests. (Incidentally, such a broad ethical outlook widens the range of action that can be interpreted to be in the union's interest.) The influence of a common training and common work interests among a fairly homogeneous group is especially evident in some craft unions. In fact, the craftsman's outlook is often so occupationally centered that it results in a variety of forms of cohesiveness and exclusiveness (e.g., insistence on apprenticeship rules, observance of jurisdictional lines, and the closed shop).

The union viewpoint must, of course, be interpreted by the leadership, and top union officials generally enjoy some latitude of construction. They can play up or play down particular demands or policies. Even a respected leader may, however, hesitate to stray far from accepted thinking and norms. The area of discretion of a union's leadership is constricted by the fact that the leaders are elected officials, politicians with a definite constituency.

---

[4] In viewing trade unionism, Robert F. Hoxie stressed the work group's likeness of outlook induced by common experience, needs, and aims. As he explained, "workers similarly situated economically and socially, closely associated and not too divergent in temperament and training, will tend to develop a common interpretation of the social situation, and a common solution to the problem of living." *Trade Unionism in the United States* (New York: Appleton, 1924), p. 58.

To be reelected they must satisfy a majority of the voting members or convention delegates. Any threat to their security in office, whether from internal factionalism or left-wing competition, serves as a constraining force. The greater is the control of the administration's political machine, the more can the leadership indulge in policies for its own convenience or aims, and the less is it forced to be guided solely by the interests of the membership. Studies show that leadership interests and objectives in unions are likely to extend beyond those of the membership; especially is that true of politics and international affairs.[5] For some purposes, therefore, it may be necessary to distinguish between the outlook and approach of the union hierarchy and that of the rank and file members.

A Politicoeconomic Model

The theory of the union presented here is built around the elements that American unions have in common. These similar features constitute the essence of American unionism. The theoretical formulation is eclectic in that it draws on both political and economic interpretations. The term "model" as used here means a mental construct (or synthesis) representing the common characteristics or core of American unionism. The model is designed to aid in understanding and interpreting the union as an institution, especially the operations of the national union. Further refinement of the model would be required to convert it into a specific set of propositions formulated with sufficient rigor to permit mathematical manipulation or experimental verification.

Consideration of the respective roles of political and economic factors will serve to sharpen some aspects of our model. That is desirable because statements are often encountered to the effect that unions are political instruments for economic ends, or are political organizations whose policies are largely economic, or are political agencies operating in an economic environment. The

---

[5] See Joel Seidman, *et al.*, *The Worker Views His Union* (Chicago: University of Chicago Press, 1958), pp. 181 and 227–36; H. Rosen and R. A. H. Rosen, *The Union Member Speaks* (Minneapolis: University of Minnesota Press, 1955), pp. 36–42, 85–7, and 100; and Arthur Kornhauser, *et al.*, *When Labor Votes, A Study of Auto Workers* (New York: University Books, 1956), pp. 115–18.

discussion will be divided into two parts: (1) the decision-making processes and (2) policies and objectives. As the analysis under each heading will indicate, some elements cannot be clearly classified in an "economic" or a "political" pigeonhole.

1. THE DECISION-MAKING PROCESSES.   As already explained, the internal decision-making process in unions is essentially political and ideally democratic. Union leaders think and act in political terms. Patronage, in the form of staff appointments, helps to build up a loyal political machine. A leader's reelection partly hinges on his success in developing compromises that are politically acceptable to a majority among a membership with differentiated interests. The leadership has negotiated a valid collective agreement with an employer only when the proposed agreement has the approval of the membership concerned, usually through ratification by a majority vote. Both the fact that union leaders think politically and the fact that the test of an agreement's validity is political acceptance are responsible for the employer view of the union as essentially a political agency. With voting so often the basis for decisions, the union member also is prone to think of the internal processes of the union as political. Even the organizing of new members is now mostly by electioneering and balloting rather than by a test of economic strength as was so often the case prior to the Wagner Act.[6]

Collective bargaining is a decision-making process in which a political (democratic?) union and an economic (authoritarian?) firm participate. It consists of (a) the negotiation of a new contract and (b) the administration and interpretation of the contract under a bipartisan grievance procedure, usually providing for final appeal to outside arbitration. The more collective are the determinations on each side (e.g., bargaining between an employers' association and a group of unions), the more likely are political considerations to enter the picture.

---

[6] In a number of respects, the internal operations of national and local unions resemble those of a political party. Both local unions and local political clubs rely on majority votes, have regular (monthly?) meetings, and membership dues. At the national level, periodic conventions are the supreme legislative and judicial unit. They draft programs or platforms, dealing heavily with economic subjects. Of course, the two organizations also differ in a number of important respects.

In aiming at a theory of union behavior, our concern with collective bargaining is from the union angle. From that viewpoint the process consists of the formulation of demands and the negotiation and acceptance of the agreement, plus its administration and interpretation. The formulation of demands is, as already explained, political. The negotiation and acceptance of an agreement are also mainly political in character. The leadership must decide, chiefly on political grounds, how far particular demands can be compromised or sacrificed and still remain an acceptable "package." Generally it is the bundle (the whole agreement), and not separate parts, that must receive membership approval. In this respect, collective bargaining differs significantly from the market process of piecemeal choice and purchase by the individual. It is collective goal determination through political compromise, with balloting as the ultimate method of decision-making. Various echelons and elements of the union may have different viewpoints and interests; political leadership in the union seeks to reconcile them into an acceptable package.

From the union viewpoint, the leadership largely has to decide the allocation problems involved in "package" negotiations. It has to take some position on the distribution of money items among the various elements in the membership (the spread of any wage increase among different occupations, the allocation of any gain between wages and benefits, and the relative stress on particular benefit programs—pensions, hospitalization, unemployment benefits). The appeal that particular benefit programs have for various parts of the membership depends on their age, health, and seniority,[7] which determines the order of lay-off.

Package bargaining also involves determination by the union leadership of the relative stress to be placed on demands concerned with job rights for the individual and on demands to establish rights for the union as an institution. The personal rights, which involve limits to management's authority, include such items as shop rules, lay-offs according to seniority, and restrictions on disciplinary measures and discharge. Provisions with respect to a union's institutional rights or status under an agreement include the union shop and check-off of union dues, preferential seniority

---

[7] Seniority is discussed in Chapter 12.

for shop stewards, and the union's role in the grievance procedure and in the administration of negotiated benefit plans.

Clearly, union decisions with respect to the specific contents of a package settlement are likely to be political compromises. Of course, economic forces, operating on the employer, limit the concessions that management can make to union demands. Economic constraints also affect union demands. In making wage demands, market forces cannot be disregarded. Nonunion competition may cause the union to be highly conscious of the employment effects of increased labor costs in the union sector. But, for the most part, economic forces should be stressed in the employer model rather than in the union model. The union's job is to satisfy the member's interests and institutional requirements.

It is true, of course, that unions seek through collective bargaining to limit the influence of market forces or to modify their impact. Usually labor organizations try, to some extent, to "take labor out of competition." Also economic arguments are freely used in supporting wage and other demands. But that is what one would expect. Economic reasons are respectable; political reasons usually are not. No union leader would be likely to admit publicly that he was making a particular set of demands in order to remain in office, or that he had to have a certain settlement because of the distribution of political power within his union. Also, employers are presumed to be economically oriented, and reply to union demands with economic arguments. Consequently, justifications of union demands are generally couched in economic terms. But mediators, arbitrators, and experienced management negotiators look for the political realities behind the economic case worked up by the union's research department.

The interpretation and application of an agreement by means of a bipartisan grievance procedure is really a continuation of collective bargaining under other circumstances. Especially in the early stages of collective bargaining, unions may achieve almost as much in membership-desired gains through negotiated interpretations as through bargaining for a new agreement. Membership interest in grievance application and work rules may approach that in wage settlements.[8] Actually, the full- and part-time staffs

---

[8] See, for instance, Joel Seidman, *et al.*, *The Worker Views His Union* (Chicago: University of Chicago Press, 1958), pp. 80–81, 89, 100–101, 104–105, 120–21, 196.

of some unions spend more than 50 per cent of their time on grievances. From a union point of view, the administration of agreements and adjudication of individual rights are primarily political.

To sum up, both agreement-making and agreement-administering seem to be mainly governmental activities, and union behavior in those respects rests heavily on political considerations.

2. POLICIES AND OBJECTIVES. Many union aims and policies are too pragmatic and multifaceted to permit any labeling of them by academic disciplines. The political and financial, the economic and noneconomic, the psychological and sociological may be so blended as to defy the skills of the classifier.

Mixtures of purpose and policy are understandable in agencies with an interest-group base and the idealistic pretensions of a reformist movement. They are to be expected in institutions that use a variety of techniques and appeals (political and economic, emotional and idealistic), and seek to serve the needs and aspirations of workers outside as well as inside the workshop. It is not surprising, therefore, to find unions stressing nonmarket values and the human side of work problems, yet, at the same time, ostensibly striking for (say) a ten-cent increase in wages instead of accepting nine cents (as one element in a package).

Because union policies are multifaceted, they can be variously interpreted. Policies aimed at promoting the union as an institution (union shop, check-off of dues, stewards' seniority, etc.) may be considered sociological (institutional development and status), or they may be viewed as enhancing the economic and political power of unions and, therefore, increasing their potential gains from collective bargaining or political action. Policies designed to provide workers with job rights and employment tenure may be regarded as governmental (the rules and grievance procedure constituting "industrial jurisprudence"[9]), or they may be looked upon as sociological (part of an effort to eliminate an inferior status in industry). Policies that involve governmental action (e.g., full employment, minimum wages, social security) may seem political, yet they are also economic in that they serve to increase labor demand, to protect union wage standards, or to increase the income security

[9] This phrase was coined by the late Professor Sumner Slichter of Harvard University.

of workers. Union policies on wages may be influenced by notions of fairness, equity, and union solidarity, and benefit policies may serve to strengthen the union as an institution. A good example of union behavior requiring multiple explanation is the strike. Strikes may involve not only economic issues but also personality conflicts, emotionalism, group psychology, social pressures of various sorts, and local politics and law enforcement.

As a group, economic issues usually are the most important ones in negotiations for a new agreement. And single and associated craft unions are generally more economically, and less politically, oriented than are large industrial unions. Nevertheless, policies that seem to be primarily economic usually have political aspects or implications. And unions carry on a variety of political activities (e.g., lobbying, election campaigns, political education), although rank-and-file members customarily have less faith and less interest in union political activity than in collective bargaining.

Union leaders are circumscribed in their demands and the settlements they can achieve by both political and economic influences. Nevertheless, the leadership usually has some area of discretion, some freedom of variation. It is for that reason that Nathan Goldfinger and Everett Kassalow of the AFL-CIO say of unions in collective bargaining that "The outer limits are probed and alternative choices are weighed in the light of institutional factors, membership pressures, and personal predilections of leadership, as well as economic factors," and "From the union's side of the bargaining table, each bargain is determined by institutional and leadership factors quite as much as by economic factors."[10] The point is that political and economic constraints form an elastic framework within which a number of combinations or "package" settlements are possible. It is one function of union leadership in collective bargaining to probe the possibilities.

In summary, American unions use common methods in their internal politics and in dealing with employers. They have common viewpoints arising out of the worker's position in industry. They stress human costs of production and protections to workers against competitive forces.

Unions are negotiating institutions designed to achieve both

---

[10] N. Goldfinger and E. Kassalow, "Trade Union Behavior in Wage Bargaining," in G. W. Taylor and F. C. Pierson, *New Concepts in Wage Determination* (New York: McGraw-Hill, 1957), pp. 51 and 69.

income goals and industrial and social rights. Generally, in this country their aims are short run and pragmatic. The union leadership seeks (a) to promote the common interests of the bulk of the present membership and (b) to hold the loyalty and interest of individual members by various (economic, political, educational, and social) programs and by grievance protection. The leadership maintains itself in office through compromise, persuasion, and patronage, taking into account any actual or potential threat of rival leadership.

Union leadership and union policies are circumscribed by both political and economic constraints. The latitude that union leadership enjoys partly depends on how potent is the threat of rival leadership from within or rival unionism from without. Its range of latitude is also limited by economic (market) constraints. Usually, the employer in negotiations represents such market constraints, so that the need for the union to live with the employer is part of the economic constraint.[11]

Because union leadership generally pursues both economic and political objectives and is subject to both economic and political constraints, the general conception of the union here presented is a politicoeconomic model.

Other Interpretations

Comparison with some other interpretations of union behavior may serve to sharpen the outlines of the concept set forth above. The abbreviated statements of the particular theories presented here lose, of course, much of the richness of each author's full treatment.

Writing near the end of the last century in England, Sidney and Beatrice Webb presented a combined economic and political view of the labor movement. They pictured unions as organized to promote and protect the economic interests of the members by reducing competitive pressures on wages and to bring representative government to industry.[12] According to their theory, trade

---

[11] Under the Taft-Hartley Act, the employer must deal only with the certified union with respect to wages, hours, and working conditions, and that union is required to bargain in good faith for all employees in the bargaining unit.

[12] The Webbs' theory is to be found in *Industrial Democracy* (London: Longmans Green, 1920 edition), esp. the final chapter; and *The History of Trade Unionism* (London: Longmans Green, 1920 edition), Chapter XI.

unions are motivated by a desire to elevate both the economic and political status of workers in industry. The means of economic elevation were greater economic power through collective bargaining and adherence to "common rules" (union wage scales, hours, and craft regulations) designed to "take the worker out of competition." The political objective of "industrial democracy" was also to be achieved by negotiation. Believing in class conflict, the Webbs in addition favored political action by unions and socialization of heavy industry.

Although they broke much new ground by their detailed studies of British unionism, the Webbs did not develop a systematic theory of union behavior. Nor did they attempt to analyze the constraints on union policies and accomplishments.

An essentially economic interpretation of American unionism was presented by Selig Perlman in 1928.[13] Drawing largely on experience with craft unionism in this country during the preceding decades, Perlman stressed manual workers' consciousness of the scarcity of employment opportunity. This consciousness caused unions, in Perlman's view, to concentrate on the control and allocation of jobs under collective bargaining and union rules. Under the American capitalist and political environment, Perlman considered that a pragmatic, business-type of negotiating unionism, interested in job control and distrustful of political programs, was the appropriate and natural result. Consequently, he did not predict, and was surprised by, some union behavior and policies during the New Deal period of the thirties. Perlman's theory is not very effective in explaining the political and social activities of large industrial unions or even certain aspects (e.g., membership lethargy or upsurges in growth) of craft unions.[14]

Although his view of American unionism was basically economic, Perlman did not attempt to relate his theory to market analysis or traditional economic theory. Consequently, he did not analyze the process of decision-making in unions or the economic limitations on union policies or collective bargaining.[15]

---

[13] Perlman, *A Theory of the Labor Movement* (New York: Macmillan, 1928).

[14] See Mark Perlman, *Labor Union Theories in America, Background and Development* (Evanston, Ill.: Row, Peterson, 1958), p. 238.

[15] For an elaborate criticism of Perlman's theory from a different viewpoint see C. A. Gulick and M. Beers, "Insight and Illusion in Perlman's Theory of the Labor Movement," *Industrial and Labor Relations Review*, VI (July 1953), pp. 510–31.

In 1944, John T. Dunlop offered an economic model of the union as "a seller" of labor services in the market.[16] Union leaders were assumed to know the employer's demand curve for labor and to take account of the employment effects of their wage demands. The most suitable union objective for analytical purposes was stated to be the maximization of the total wage income (wage scale × employment) for the current membership of the union. As critics have pointed out, with a sufficiently elastic demand curve, that objective might require the union leaders to request small wage cuts in order to increase the total income of the membership.

Clearly this model leaves out the nonincome aims of unions. It seeks to isolate money items from a set of demands. Empirical studies of wage and benefit improvements indicate that unions, especially in mass-production lines, are not generally guided by assumed elasticity of the employer's demand for labor at various possible wage levels. Studies of the automobile and steel industries reveal that unions will permit wage increases less than the "pattern" settlement in order to avoid complete shut-down of the plant, with total loss of all jobs.[17] Where survival of the operation is threatened, workers are reluctant to strike and union leaders are likely to allow a deviation or differential from the pattern that they insist the better situated companies follow.

Some local unions do tend to tailor their wage policy to the presumed effects on total employment in the plant. That is particularly the case in soft-goods lines where a firm is under pressure from nonunion or other wage competition in bidding on private contract work.[18] A prime example is the shoe industry in which standard machines are rented, variable costs (machine rent, materials, and labor) are a large percentage of total costs, and the geographically dispersed plants are either nonunion or are organized by one among a number of small unions.

---

[16] Dunlop, *Wage Determination under Trade Unions* (New York: Macmillan, 1944), esp. pp. 31 and 44.

[17] See H. M. Levinson, "Pattern Bargaining: A Case Study of the Automobile Workers," *Quarterly Journal of Economics*, LXXIV (May 1960), pp. 307–17; and G. Seltzer, "Pattern Bargaining and the United Steelworkers," *Journal of Political Economy*, LIX (August 1951), pp. 329–31.

[18] See G. P. Shultz and C. A. Myers, "Union Wage Decisions and Employment," *American Economic Review*, XL (June 1950), pp. 362–88; and G. P. Shultz, *Pressures on Wage Decisions* (New York: Wiley, 1951).

A contrasting approach to union behavior was presented by Arthur M. Ross in 1948.[19] Criticizing Dunlop's economic model, Ross contended that unions generally are not well suited to a strictly economic analysis, that many interesting aspects of union behavior cannot be explained by the logic of traditional economic theory. The union is not a seller of labor, it is not trying to maximize any particular economic quantity, and a collective agreement covers a "congeries of discrete things." Normally, Ross claims, unions do not take demand elasticity into account in making wage or other money demands, because the volume of employment associated with a particular wage scale in a firm is unpredictable in advance and undecipherable after a wage change. Ross insists that the links between a wage increase, any resulting increase in total unit costs, prices of the products, and manual employment in the plant are loose and uncertain in most industries. However, he admits that, in some soft-goods lines with the piece-rate method of payment like the manufacture of clothing and shoes, the connections between wages and employment in the individual firm are relatively clear and predictable.

In Ross' opinion, the central aim of unions is the political one of survival and growth of the organization. Union leadership has the problem of reconciling political pressures of various sorts. Some of those pressures arise from notions of equity in the minds of the members and their wives, influenced by the size of settlements in other firms and by other unions. A pattern settlement may be established and spread by imitation and "orbits of compulsory comparison."[20] Political pressures also are generated by economic forces. Consequently, Ross considers a purely political model of the union to be too narrow and improper. The union may, for example, need to take economic factors into account for the political purpose of enhancing the union's security by avoiding actions that would cause great hostility on the part of the employer.

Ross draws a distinction between a union's leadership and its membership, and between union-oriented demands like the union shop or superseniority for union shop stewards and member-orien-

---

[19] Arthur M. Ross, *Trade Union Wage Policy* (Berkeley: University of California Press, 1948).

[20] Pattern setting and spreading were especially common from 1945 to 1948 when Ross was writing his book.

ted demands such as wages and benefits. He points out that the formulation of wage and other demands is a leadership function. Since most unions of any size have a rather heterogeneous membership, it is the task of the leadership to reconcile conflicts of interest within the union. Ross tends to minimize the effects of unemployment on the leader's wage demands because he stresses the need, on institutional grounds, for unions to appeal to potential recruits as well as to different sections (especially the dominant elements) in the existing membership, some of whom (such as maintenance crews) may be largely unaffected by fluctuations in employment.

Quite a controversy has developed from the contrasting views of Dunlop and Ross.[21] It has centered largely on the extent to which unions in negotiations take account of the possible employment effects of various wage scales. The discussion and studies are, however, unclear as to which union purpose is presumed to be operating when, in an individual case, a union differentiates among firms with respect to wage and benefit increases by settling with one or more employers below the general pattern of increases in the industry. The union's aim could be any one of the following: (1) to make employers pay wages and benefits according to their financial ability; (2) to maximize the wage income of the present membership; (3) to expand the employment and wage income of the total membership; (4) to expand employment so as to increase the union's membership and dues income; (5) to keep the plant from closing; (6) to maintain a certain type of relationship with the employer; (7) to avoid a strike to which the membership would not give strong support; or (8) to permit more emphasis on employee or union security. In view of the range of possible purposes, it is risky to generalize in the absence of a carefully designed study or experiment which would clearly differentiate and verify the presence and influence of each possible purpose.

The theory of union behavior developed in the preceding

[21] See for example M. W. Reder, "The Theory of Union Wage Policy," *The Review of Economics and Statistics,* XXXIV, February 1952, pp. 34–45; G. P. Shultz and C. A. Myers, *op. cit.;* H. M. Levinson, *op. cit.;* G. Seltzer, *op. cit.;* I. L. Herrnstadt, "The Reaction of Three Local Unions to Economic Adversity," *Journal of Political Economy,* LXII (October 1954), pp. 425–39; and Albert Rees, "Union Wage Policies," in G. W. Brooks, *et al., Interpreting the Labor Movement* (New York: Industrial Relations Research Association, 1952), pp. 130–48.

section is similar in many respects to Ross' model. Like Ross' concept, our theory assumes unions have both income and non-economic aims. The latter seem to be of increasing importance as the interests of large unions expand both domestically (e.g., stressing equal rights regardless of race or sex, housing, and fiscal policy) and internationally.

Compared with Ross' theory, however, our model puts somewhat more emphasis on economic constraints. The union may not make market calculations but the employer often does, and thus living with the employer may involve an economic constraint on the union. Also our model is drawn in terms of the political and economic constraints that determine how wide or narrow is the latitude for union leadership. The area of maneuver that a union's leadership enjoys will vary with the economic and political circumstances. Economic constraints significantly restrict the latitude of union leadership in many soft-goods lines. Differences in past experience and internal political pressures may explain why some local unions favor job evaluation and others oppose it, why some local unions accept wage incentive schemes and others do not, and why some unions favor percentage increases in wages and others prefer uniform increases in cents per hour across the board. The position of some locals on such matters may differ markedly from the position of other locals in the same national union.

In some situations, the political factors may provide more constraint in the short run, whereas the economic factors may exert a more controlling influence on long-run trends. Over long periods of time, however, economic constraints can become rather elastic. In their extensive study of experience under collective bargaining, Slichter, Healy, and Livernash point out how plants or companies that were about ready to close because of economic pressures were able, through improved labor relations and production methods, to become more efficient and profitable. They report that "Instances of improvement in labor efficiency of as much as 50 per cent have not been uncommon in our study."[22]

Consequently, in theorizing about unions, one needs to think in terms of evolutionary change and trends. This was indicated in Chapters 3 and 4, and a theory of union development will be pre-

_____
[22] S. H. Slichter, J. J. Healy, and E. R. Livernash, *The Impact of Collective Bargaining on Management* (Washington: Brookings Institution, 1960), p. 550.

sented in the last section of this chapter. Here it is only necessary to point out that the models of a union summarized above are assumed to be timeless in their applicability, although Perlman's theory clearly applies best to the period of domination by AFL craft unionism (1886–1933). The evolutionary development of American unions can be discussed more effectively after an analysis of union government. The next section deals with that subject.

THE GOVERNMENT OF UNIONS

Union structure and government have been influenced by economic and political considerations. The function of collective bargaining favors units of union government and union policy determinations along employer, occupational, and industry lines. Political activity stresses organization by political levels—city, State, and nation. The resulting structure of government is one of sovereign national unions drawn largely on economic lines, and federations of those unions (or their local branches) operating along political lines.

Union government differs from our political government largely because unions seek to achieve most of their objectives through negotiations with and pressure on, another organization (the company or employers' association). With the employer providing the opposition, stress is placed on union solidarity and effective action. Consequently, union government has no separation of powers (executive, legislative, and judicial), has few governmental checks and balances, and, at the national-union level, tends to be one-party government.

On the other hand, unions are also representational agencies. Effective representation presumably involves the free expression of views, popular control of policies, and the membership as the ultimate source of union authority. This representational aspect helps to account for the use of such democratic procedures as popular election of officers, strike votes and balloting on issues, and decisions by delegate votes in a national convention.

In practice, union government tends to be a compromise between effective representation and administrative efficiency, between democratic unionism and "responsible" unionism that can negotiate with management on its own grounds and can live up to the agreements it signs.[23] Where the line is drawn between those two purposes in a particular union depends, of course, on many historical, economic, political, and personal factors.

Union government can perhaps be best comprehended by starting with a discussion of the national union, then proceeding to the subordinate local unions, and finally considering the federations. In the structure of organized labor in America, the national union is the basic governmental unit and the major influence, since it has almost exclusive dominion over the collective bargaining function.

The National Union

Like each nation, the national union is a self-governing and independently financed center of power. It operates under a written constitution, normally of 25 to 50 printed pages. Individual workers are members of national unions, which exercise supreme power over members in relation to the union, over affiliated local unions, and over the other subordinate units in the government structure of the national union.

There are about two hundred national unions varying in size from a few hundred members in some small, craft unions to more than a million members in the Auto Workers, the Steelworkers, and the Teamsters. Because over a hundred national unions have locals and members in Canada, they are commonly referred to as "international" unions.

The functions performed by national unions vary somewhat with their size and programs. Generally the national headquarters promotes organizing activities, charters and supervises locals, bargains directly with employers (as in the Steelworkers) or provides (economic, legal, and technical) services for locals which do the bargaining (in local-market industries), publishes the union's official paper or journal, administers the union's benefit and strike funds, aids or supervises strikes, conducts education and training programs, and carries on political and lobbying activities. For

---

[23] For a discussion of anti-democratic tendencies in unions see S. M. Lipset, "The Political Process in Trade Unions: A Theoretical Statement," in Morroe Berger, *et al.*, *Freedom and Control in Modern Society* (New York: Van Nostrand, 1954), pp. 82–124.

such purposes, national unions of any size have a staff of specialists, such as economists, lawyers, and journalists, and a staff of "international representatives," who help to service the local unions.

The constitution of the national union is the basic law of the organization. It sets forth the duties of the union's officers, defines limits of authority, and allocates legislative, executive, and judicial powers. The typical constitution states the union's purposes and jurisdiction, outlines its governmental structure and the procedures for conducting union meetings, specifies the functions and powers of the affiliated locals, establishes the requirements for membership, and contains provisions with respect to dues and the disciplining of members. Generally, union constitutions lack a specific bill of rights to protect members from arbitrary or unfair action by union officials or by the national convention. As is explained subsequently, some such protections are contained in the Labor-Management Reporting and Disclosure Act (popularly known as the Landrum-Griffin Act).

1. THE CONVENTION.   Under union constitutions, the national convention is the supreme governing power in the union. The only exception is where issues are submitted to referendum vote of the total membership or officers are elected by that means. In over two-thirds of the national unions the convention elects the national officers. The convention combines the functions of a constitutional assembly, a legislature, and a supreme court. It approves officers' reports, passes resolutions, amends the constitution, and hears appeals from decisions in locals or by national officials.

Most unions hold a convention annually or biennially. In some of the larger unions, the total number of delegates from the locals runs between a thousand and three thousand, so that the expense of holding a week-long convention is a significant sum. The voting power of the delegates is according to the paid-up membership they each represent for the local.

As is the case in conventions of the major political parties, much of the important work of union conventions is performed in committees or in informal meetings off the convention floor. In most unions, the president appoints the convention committees,[24] and he presides over the sessions of the convention. To a considerable

---

[24] See Leo Bromwich, *Union Constitutions*, A Report to the Fund for the Republic, New York, N.Y., 1959, p. 13.

extent, union conventions are "stage managed" by the administration of the national union. The programs and actions of the administration are generally approved, although not infrequently the recommendation of a dues' increase is rejected.

2. THE PRESIDENT.   Between conventions, the union's executive board or council has theoretical authority over the president, since his acts are subject to the board's approval and it can modify or reverse his decisions or even suspend him from office on proven charges. However, in most unions the executive board meets only two to four times a year and is usually under the president's influence.

In his extensive study of union government, the late William M. Leiserson found a distinct trend toward giving the president unrestricted appointive powers and making him principal judicial officer. "The rank and file," he concluded, "admire and rather prefer strong leaders who win victories."[25] Authority to appoint organizers, international representatives, and the headquarters staff, plus control over the union's newspaper or journal, places the president in a strong political position.

Concentration of authority and power in the hands of the chief officer in American unions is in contrast to the situation in British unions, where the executive boards or councils are primarily responsible for policy determination and general supervision of the national union, with a "general secretary" to carry out the decisions of the council. Lack of strong political constraint through executive-board control helps to explain some of the latitude enjoyed by entrenched leadership in many national unions in this country.

The Local Union

The policies and programs of the national union are implemented by the local unions. They are the immediate point of contact of the average union member. The local union hall is where he meets with the other members.

Generally, local unions administer collective agreements, proc-

---

[25] *American Trade Union Democracy* (New York: Columbia University Press, 1959), pp. 63 and 67.

ess members' grievances, collect their dues, formulate bargaining demands and participate in negotiations with the employer, vote to call a strike or to ratify an agreement, conduct strikes, elect local officials and delegates to the national's convention, and perform a variety of other administrative functions. The local has a charter from the national and its own constitution and bylaws, which must conform to those of the parent union.

In industrial unions, locals are usually organized on a plant basis; in craft unions, locals generally are on an area basis including a number of employers. The extent of the authority that a local union exercises normally varies with the nature of the industry. A local union in one of many plants in a mass-production industry manufacturing for a nationwide market will usually have less control over bargaining policy than a craft local in community-market types of industry such as entertainment or building construction.

There are some 78,000 local unions in the United States. They range in size from a handful of members to over 60,000 at Local 600 of the United Automobile Workers at the River Rouge Plant of the Ford Motor Company. The average local contains about two hundred members.

In theory, the authority at the local level stems from the membership meeting, held regularly or called for a special purpose. All official action must either be authorized or ratified by vote at such a membership meeting. In practice, the "actives"—the officers, the executive committee (officers and several elected members), the bargaining committee, the shop stewards, and members who regularly participate in meetings—tend to run the local. That is usually the case because most of the membership does not attend union meeting except when a strike vote is to be taken, an agreement is to be submitted for ratification, or a vote is to be taken in a strongly contested election.

The elected officers of a local include the president, the secretary-treasurer, and a business agent or manager if the local has one. They usually must run for election each year. In contrast to the national union, the presidency in local unions is frequently contested and subject to fairly high turnover. Except in large locals, the president and secretary-treasurer are usually men at the bench who take time off their regular jobs in order to conduct union business or do it outside of work hours. Large locals often have one or more full-time officials, who may be the president, a business agent, or the secretary-treasurer, depending on local practice and personalities.

In a speech before the 1958 convention of the Amalgamated Clothing Workers of America, then Senator John F. Kennedy stated: "There are roughly half a million local union officials in this country, another half a million business agents, lawyers and other paid officials, and another 750,000 shop stewards and others employed in serving the labor movement."[26]

1. BUSINESS AGENTS AND SHOP STEWARDS. Typically local unions have business agents where members are employed under non-factory conditions (small-scale service lines) and by several firms (as is often true for craft-based unions). The business agent is a full-time, paid official, who is a key figure in the operation of the local. Among his duties are negotiating with employers concerning new contracts or members' complaints, signing up new members, serving as an employment office, and calling or settling strikes, which he can do on his own authority.[27] The concentration of power in the hands of the business agent (e.g., in some construction unions) has invited abuse of power, bribe-taking, and other forms of corruption.

In the locals of an industrial union, whose members are all employed by one firm, there is little need for the special functions of a business agent, traveling from employer to employer. In industrial plants, the management has an employment office, the union has a negotiating committee, the members vote on striking, and grievances are handled by shop stewards and a shop committee.

Shop stewards represent the union in its daily contact with the members. Stewards perform the important function of investigating members' grievances, presenting the member's complaint in bipartisan grievance hearings, and negotiating settlements of griev-

---

[26] *Twenty-first Biennial Convention, GEB Report and Proceedings,* Amalgamated Clothing Workers, Atlantic City, New Jersey, May 12–16, 1958, pp. 187–188.

For a discussion of the internal politics of local unions see Jack Barbash, *Labor's Grass Roots: A Study of the Local Union* (New York: Harper, 1961).

[27] For a study of the business agent at work, see George Strauss, "Business Agents in the Building Trades: A Case Study in a Community," *Industrial and Labor Relations Review,* X (January 1957), pp. 237–51.

ances with the foreman under the terms of the agreement. As already explained, much of the time of unions is likely to be spent on handling the grievances of members.

In large plants, a steward is elected by and responsible to a particular work unit or department, consisting of ten to twenty or more employees. Usually, the stewards in a plant form a grievance or shop committee under a chief steward to negotiate concerning grievances appealed from the steward-foreman level to the second step in the grievance procedure. "The grievance committee is the focal point of shop government."[28]

As representatives of the union in the day-to-day administration of the agreement, shop stewards can exert a significant influence on the character of union-management relations. The fair and prompt settlement of grievances helps to reveal and correct trouble spots. That is one reason why managements in some industries have agreed to pay for time spent by union stewards in investigating and adjusting grievances, up to a certain number of hours per week.

2. INTERMEDIATE BODIES.   With the increase in size and complexity of unions, governmental units have been established between the locals and the national headquarters. Such intermediate bodies may be on a regional, industry-subdivision, major-firm, or craft basis. They serve to coordinate local union activities or as a vehicle for joint action by a group of locals in dealing with management.

There has been a tendency for such district councils, trade conferences, or joint boards to increase in importance as the area of bargaining has expanded beyond the individual firm. Recent expansion in such units explains why, generally speaking, in the constitutions of national unions their functions are only loosely defined where they are mentioned at all.

The Federations

The national AFL-CIO and the State and city federations composed of local unions parallel the Federal, State, and city political units. Strictly speaking, the federations are not unions but agen-

---

[28] Joseph Kovner and Herbert J. Lahne, "Shop Society and the Union," *Industrial and Labor Relations Review*, VII (October 1953), p. 7.

cies of their affiliated unions. They do not engage directly in collective bargaining, strikes, and grievance handling, and, except for newly organized and transitional units, they do not have any persons as members.[29] Rather they pursue the interests of organized labor through nonbargaining means.

Although the AFL-CIO performs a variety of functions at the national level, it operates mainly in five areas: (1) engaging in and coordinating all sorts of political activity including legislative lobbying and candidate support in elections; (2) promoting the interests of American labor in international affairs, including representation in the International Confederation of Free Trade Unions and the International Labour Office; (3) coordinating and supplementing the organizing work of the national unions; (4) attempting to resolve jurisdictional disputes between affiliated unions; and (5) providing a variety of staff services such as economic research, labor education, legal aid, and public relations material including publications.

In dealing with its affiliated national unions, the AFL-CIO depends largely on persuasion and moral sanctions. It has, for example, sought to enforce codes of ethics. For violation of its constitution or the ethical codes, the only sanction is expulsion from the AFL-CIO. Such action has been taken against the Teamsters and a few smaller unions. However, expulsion from "the house of labor" has proved to be rather ineffective as a sanction in the case of the powerful Teamsters union.

Final authority in the AFL-CIO rests in its biennial convention. The delegates' voting power varies according to a formula based on the monthly per capita tax (four cents) paid by the national union. Consequently, a dozen large unions can control AFL-CIO policy. Between conventions, policy-making authority rests in the Executive Council, which is composed of the president, the secretary-treasurer, and 27 vice-presidents elected at the convention from the affiliated national unions. The Executive Council meets at least three times a year. From among its membership, six vice-presidents are selected to form, with the president and secretary-treasurer, the Executive Committee, which meets bimonthly to advise on policy.

---

[29] The AFL-CIO does administer a few hundred locals that are directly affiliated with it until they can be attached to an existing or newly-chartered national union.

As president of the AFL-CIO, George Meany has been a dominant figure. He has exterted considerable personal and moral influence throughout the labor movement. And the influence of the central federation has increased with the extension of the Federal Government further into economic and social affairs. Nevertheless it remains true that the AFL-CIO has less authority and influence than is possessed by the top union federations in most European countries.

To promote the mutual interests of unions in certain sections of industry, the AFL-CIO has six departments—Building and Construction Trades, Metal Trades, Maritime Employees, Railway Employees, Union Label, and Industrial Union. The Industrial Union Department, headed by Walter Reuther, is composed of seventy-odd unions and is dominated by the former CIO unions in the mass-production industries. It has its own staff and publications and holds a biennial convention.

The State and city federations, although part of the AFL-CIO structure, are not dominated by the national federation. In turn they have little power in the top federation, having only one vote each in the AFL-CIO convention, or the voting equivalent of four thousand paid-up members in a national union.

The State and city federations have their own conventions and policy committees. Their operations are largely in the areas of legislation, political activity, community services, and public relations. Locals of the national unions can join the appropriate State and city federation at their own discretion; some do not, either because they wish to operate independently or do not consider the services received of sufficient importance to them to justify the expense.

Finances

From an examination of union revenues and expenditures one can learn much about the operation of unions. The size and complexity of their operations are indicated by the payrolls that unions meet and the variety of uses of their funds.

The annual income of American unions from all sources amounts to about two billion dollars a year. Most of that sum is derived from regular monthly dues paid by each member. In addition, unions receive initiation fees from new members, assessments on members for special purposes, and earnings from investments.

Union dues average less than four dollars a month. However, they are much higher than that in some craft unions with their own benefit or insurance programs, in which case part of the dues represent an insurance premium. Total income from dues alone amounts to about one and a half billion dollars a year.[30]

The most common initiation fee is five dollars, but for predominantly craft unions the most prevalent charge is twenty-five dollars. Some local unions in the amusement industry and building construction charge initiation fees of $100.00 or more as a means of forcing newcomers to pay for past gains or of excluding them from employment in jobs under the union's control. The Taft-Hartley Act makes it an unfair labor practice for a union to charge "excessive or discriminatory" fees, and a few cases have been brought up under that provision of the act.

Special assessments are generally for extraordinary purposes. Frequently, they are to help finance a strike, or to build up a fund in anticipation of a strike, or to support an organizing campaign. Under union constitutions, such assessments normally must be approved by a vote of the membership.

On the average, 60 per cent of the dues income is retained by the local unions,[31] which usually collect it. The remaining 40 per cent is remitted to the international unions. The national union's share has tended to increase as its functions have expanded.

At the local level, expenditures are largely for rent, compensation to officers for lost work time, strike costs, education, and general administrative expenses. Salaries are not as large a proportion of the total as they are for national unions. In addition to the salary item, the national union has such outlays as cost of publications, strike expenses, benefits, organizing expenses, legal proceedings, AFL-CIO per capita tax, and travel.

While the salary of the average union employee ranged from

[30] For material on union dues, fees, assessments, and strike funds see "AFL-CIO Finds Increasing Number of Affiliates Setting Up Strike Funds," *Daily Labor Report,* November 18, 1959, pp. B-1 to B-14.

[31] Bambrick, James J., Jr., and Marie P. Dorbandt, "Union Membership and Revenue," *Management Record,* XIX (December 1957), pp. 414–17ff. See also *Union Dues, Initiation Fees, Per Capita Taxes, Per Capita Revenue and Membership Reported by 150 Unions in 1961,* National Industrial Conference Board, 1961.

$5,000 to $10,000 in 1962, the presidents of twelve unions had salaries between $30,000 and $75,000. Generally, presidential salaries tended to be higher the older the union and the higher the income level of members. Little correlation seems to exist between size of the union and size of the president's salary.

Broadly speaking, union salaries approximate those for other nonprofit organizations and are well below those of the top officers in corporations with which the union bargains. The president of a national union of 100,000 members or more is managing a large and fairly complex enterprise. With salaries in national unions tending to be adjusted to the top, there may, of course, be considerable pressure from the staff to have the president's salary increased so that "middle" and "lower" levels of management in the union can get a raise. Top salaries in European unions are much closer to the earnings of the men at the bench than is true in this country. That is partly because of a difference in philosophy and much more class feeling in Europe. Union leaders there and their families remain part of the working class both in mode of life and in type of residence. In this country, trade union leaders and their families generally aspire to middle-class and even upper-class standards of living.

The Labor-Management Reporting and Disclosure (Landrum-Griffin) Act regulates union financial practices. It requires that all national unions and intermediate and local unions, engaged in an industry "affecting" interstate commerce, file annually a report showing all assets and liabilities, receipts and disbursements including salaries over $10,000, expense allowances and reimbursements, and direct and indirect loans over $250 to any officer or member. Officers or employees of a union must report business transactions and investment holdings that may involve any conflict of interest with the union. Such financial reports are public documents. Publicity and public scrutiny are relied upon as deterrents to improper financial dealings.

THE ISSUE OF UNION DEMOCRACY

American unions have a democratic tradition. Their constitutions establish voting as the ultimate means of decision-making. In 1957, the AFL-CIO adopted a code of democratic practices to apply to its affiliated unions.[32] The code provides for honest elections, the free expression of opinion in union meetings, and a fair trial for disciplined members. And the Labor-Management Reporting and Disclosure Act of 1959 contains many provisions designed to protect the democratic rights of union members.

Clearly, unions are affected with the public interest and have an obligation to represent all the workers in the voting unit. Not only is representation their business, but under the Taft-Hartley Act the Federal Government certifies a union as the *exclusive* bargaining agent for the employees in that "bargaining unit," required by the law to present the grievance of any one of them. In other words, each worker in the unit has a right to representation in the process of government in the plant. In addition, under a union shop, all employees covered by the agreement must be members of the union and pay dues to support it. In unions with broad social welfare aims, the dues money is used, not just to obtain on-the-job improvements within the "bargaining unit," but for all sorts of labor, social, and even international purposes. Presumably, the membership should have some say in how the dues money is used beyond the area of collective bargaining.

In spite of public sentiment and legislation favoring democratically operated unions, there remains a question concerning how much control can or should actually rest in the hands of the membership as a whole. That is particularly true with respect to the national union, which does not hold membership meetings and may have hundreds of thousands of members. In most national unions, ultimate authority (as already explained) is lodged in a convention of delegates from the locals. In view of the way many national conventions are run, one may question how much control the membership can exert upon the union's top officials through an annual or biennial convention. And even in the case of local unions which (except for the very large ones) do hold regular membership meetings, the actual control that the general membership can exercise over important policy decisions and their administration may be only loose or indirect. That may be especially true where bargaining policy tends to be determined at the national-

---

[32] See *AFL-CIO Codes of Ethical Practices*, American Federation of Labor and Congress of Industrial Organizations, June 1957, Ethical Practices Code VI, pp. 41–45.

union or intermediate-body level, or where a fairly large local is "run" by a business agent.

Questioning of the possibility or feasibility of democratic control of unions, however, goes deeper than such matters as delegate representatives to a convention or the structural distribution of union functions. It is argued that other values—effective negotiation, continuity and expertness of administration, and responsible adherence to agreements—conflict with completely democratic decision-making. Unions negotiate with (nondemocratically administered) companies, against which they threaten and conduct strikes. It is claimed that effective negotiation and pursuit of their objectives requires union solidarity and the delegation of authority because of the nature of negotiating tactics and the complexity of industrial relations. Most unions have "one-party" government without the checks and balances of separate legislative, executive, and judicial branches.[33] Democracy, it is said, weakens the union by encouraging factionalism and discouraging union discipline and responsibility. With a union subject to frequent voting on policy and administrative decisions, it is claimed that the officers would feel compelled to press vigorously even invalid grievances, would hesitate to punish members who led wildcat stoppages in violation of a collective agreement, and might even be reluctant to negotiate an agreement, for fear that subsequently a majority vote might repudiate their actions, injure their prestige, and lead to their loss of office.

This conflict of values is not as sharp and complete as some statements of the issue might seem to indicate.[34] Nevertheless, it may be difficult in practice to reconcile effective union discipline and effective union democracy, a high degree of union responsibility and union responsiveness to shifts in membership opinion,

---

[33] The International Typographical Union is unique in that for over half a century it has had a stable two-party system, each with its own organization, means of communication, and nucleus of trained leaders. Historical and occupational factors help to explain this exceptional case. For a discussion of this union situation see S. M. Lipset, M. A. Trow, and J. S. Coleman, *Union Democracy: The Internal Politics of the International Typographical Union* (Glencoe: The Free Press, 1956).

[34] For a skeptical view see C. P. Magrath, "Democracy in Overalls: The Futile Quest for Union Democracy," *Industrial and Labor Relations Review*, XII (July 1959), pp. 503–25.

the members' positive demand for leadership and membership control over the actions of officers.

Such possible differences do raise a question concerning the opportunities for expression of membership views, the amount of membership participation in union affairs, and the kinds of protections of membership rights that are essential for the government of unions to be representative of the wishes and interests of a majority of the membership. What is necessary for proper membership participation? Must there be facilities for the free flow of union information, a guarantee of free and honest elections, constitutional protections for opposing views and opposition candidates,[35] and perhaps some right of appeal to an independent tribunal from union disciplinary actions?[36]

Apparently, the Congress thought so when, in 1959, it passed the Labor-Management Reporting and Disclosure Act, which is analyzed in Chapter 14. That act contains provisions (1) assuring union members adequate information about the conduct of the union's financial affairs, (2) guaranteeing freedom of speech inside and outside union meetings, subject to rules of order and prohibitions on irresponsible conduct toward the organization or its legal or contractual obligations, (3) requiring the election of officers by secret ballot with full opportunity to nominate and other safeguards to ensure free and honest elections, and (4) affording a member a full and fair hearing following service on him of specific charges of offense in writing and a reasonable time to prepare his defense. The Act contains no provision with respect to the independence of any union tribunal for ruling on disciplinary actions against members.

---

[35] Many union constitutions contain a number of vaguely worded prohibitions such as acting against the interests of the union, discussing union business, circulating printed material among members without the permission of officers, participating in unofficial meetings where union business is discussed, or disobeying the orders of officers. In practice, a charge of violation would be accompanied by a bill of particulars. For a study of disciplinary actions and appeals see Philip Taft, *The Structure and Government of Labor Unions* (Cambridge: Harvard University Press, 1954), Chapter 4 and Supplement to Chapter 4.

[36] The United Automobile Workers has had such an independent tribunal since 1957. For a review of its activities see Jack Stieber, Walter E. Oberer, and Michael Harrington, *Democracy and Public Review, An Analysis of the U.A.W. Public Review Board*, Center for the Study of Democratic Institutions, Santa Barbara, California, 1960.

Membership Participation

Union democracy, it is said, cannot be forced or even promoted by law; it must grow within the union and depends on members' attitudes, their interest in the meetings, the type of leadership in the union, and other factors affecting the distribution of power. The law can provide a moral force and legal safeguards, but it cannot open channels of communication, develop critics, or create a democratic "climate." Also it is pointed out that members do not need to attend the regular meetings of the local union in order to affect union decisions and change union policies or even the leadership. On the other hand, members of a union who do regularly attend meetings may have little influence on the union's policy because that is controlled by the leadership and the meetings serve only to rubber-stamp the officers' programs and actions.

As is true of most other political and social organizations, a small minority of "active" union members tends to exercise the dominant political influence. As unions grow in size and settle down, a shift generally occurs from a high level of active participation by the rank and file in the early years to a low percentage of membership participation in the management of union affairs as the union matures. In the absence of an election contest, a strike vote, ratification of an agreement, an organizational crisis, or some other major conflict, usually only 2 to 10 per cent of the membership of a local with five hundred or more members will be in attendance at a local union meeting.[37] In elections or strike votes as many as 60 to 80 per cent of the membership may participate.[38] Close election contests and policy disagreements at the local level help to explain the high turnover in the presidency of many local unions.

Members can, of course, exert their influence on union policies

---

[37] See Joel Seidman, *et al., The Worker Views His Union* (Chicago: University of Chicago Press, 1958), p. 182. The percentages seem to be about the same in British unions. See B. C. Roberts, *Trade Union Government and Administration in Great Britain* (Cambridge: Harvard University Press, 1958), pp. 95–99.

[38] Seidman, *et al., op. cit.,* p. 192; and Herbert S. Parnes, *Union Strike Votes, Current Practice and Proposed Controls,* Industrial Relations Section, Princeton University, Princeton, N.J., 1956, pp. 50–51 and 85–86.

outside of formal meetings. Their views can be made known to the leadership in various ways, and it is part of skillful leadership to keep its ear to the ground. One means is by informal discussion in the shop or at lunch. Daily contact with the shop steward may serve to keep members informed and participating in decisions.[39] Members of craft unions are generally in contact with the business agent and, in addition, tend to form a kind of cohesive occupational group with close social relations.[40] Another means of communicating with the leadership is through complaints and grievance sessions. In addition, campaigns for election or ratification of an agreement and ballot results are often good indications of membership sentiment.

The responsiveness of union leadership to the desires of a majority of the membership varies, of course, from union to union. Leadership contact with membership thinking is likely to be close at the local level. However, there has been a tendency for a gap to develop between the top national officials and the rank-and-file in some unions, as they grow further apart in their daily work and in their way of life. Consequently, loose connections tend to develop in the ability of the rank and file to give directions to the union's leadership. That, of course, is part of the latitude enjoyed by union leadership in pursuing its purposes.

Strike Votes

Strikes and strike votes bring out some of the problems of determining leadership or membership control of unions. Preparations for a strike and the conduct of a strike are largely leadership functions, yet rank-and-file support and participation are vital elements in successful strike operations.

As already explained, membership participation in strike votes is high. Based on sample studies, it averages between two-thirds and three-quarters of the eligible membership, and most unions vote by secret ballot.[41] The vote is usually taken during negoti-

---

39 See Robert L. Kahn and Arnold S. Tannenbaum, *Participation in Union Locals* (Evanston, Ill.: Row, Peterson, 1958), esp. Chapters 9 and 10.

40 See George Strauss, "Control by the Membership in Building Trades Unions," *American Journal of Sociology*, LXI (May 1956), pp. 527–35.

41 See Parnes, *op. cit.*, pp. 42, 50, and 85.

ations, often when they are stalemated. In most cases, the vote simply vests in the leaders the discretion to call a strike or not as they determine. They are authorized to strike "if necessary" or "if satisfactory settlement cannot be reached."

What purposes, then, do strike votes serve? Obviously they are a means of ascertaining rank-and-file sentiment. But, in addition, they serve a number of leadership objectives. They represent a vote of confidence in the negotiators. They may be a bargaining tactic by which the leadership both demonstrates to the management the membership's support for the union's demands and tries to get the management to improve its offer. They may be a means of having the membership share responsibility if a strike does occur, thus helping to protect the leadership from the threat of rivals.

Do strike votes enhance rank-and-file control or strengthen leadership control of unions? On the basis of particular cases, one can argue either way. But, in general, the leadership has come to exercise more and more control over strikes, and that control has gradually tended to become more centralized in the hands of the national union, partly because of the comparative size of its strike funds.

Of course, strikes represent a risk for union leadership—the risk of defeat and encouragement of rival leadership. Such uncertainties and risks, along with the financial costs, may make the leadership less strike-prone and more conciliatory than the "actives" among the membership. Often the absence of strikes increases the latitude and range of flexibility of the top leadership.

THE THEORY OF UNION EVOLUTION[42]

As explained in Chapter 4, the thirties were a period of union rejuvenation and mushroom growth. New organizing methods and a fresh economic philosophy were developed under the youthful

---

[42] This section draws heavily from the author's book, *As Unions Mature, An Analysis of the Evolution of American Unionism* (Princeton: Princeton University Press, 1958). For a discussion of the "lassitude" that has developed in the trade union movement by a trade unionist, see Solomon Barkin, *The Decline of the Labor Movement and What Can Be Done About It,* Center for the Study of Democratic Institutions, Santa Barbara, California, 1961.

leadership in the CIO unions. The upsurge in union morale and membership continued during the war.

However, in the years since 1945, most unions have matured. With stability in top leadership and total membership, and with the spread of middle-class modes of living, the militancy and missionary zeal of the New Deal years have given way to emphasis on orderly arrangements, effective administration, and broadened perspectives. Union presidents now are managers of large and complex organizations; they have community and international interests as well as union responsibilities. It is not surprising, therefore, that while unions through collective bargaining have narrowed the gap between plant and office employment, union leaders have been more closely approaching corporation executives in their daily activities, in their concerns with management problems, and in their levels of living.

Although it is generally recognized that unions change as they settle down to the problems of administration after their formative years, few studies have focussed on the factors or stages in union evolution. It is, of course, important for the theory of union behavior to know whether there is some pattern in the transformation of unions as they become more secure, as their growth curves level off, and as they succeed in achieving some of their goals.

In this section the long-run factors in union change are discussed. They will be analyzed first in terms of the change in the operations within unions (internal developments) and then in terms of union adaptation to the community (external integration).

Internal Developments

Probably the greatest change that occurs in unions as they mature is a tendency toward the centralization of functions and authority. The result is a weakening of the influence and control of locals.

A number of factors have been instrumental in shifting some functions, decisions, and power from the local level to the national headquarters of unions. In the first place, expansion in the area of bargaining and enlargement of the scope of bargaining have contributed to central determination of union policies. The national seeks a common program for the whole industry or area of competitive production. Bargaining strategy necessitates some central control of demands, along with headquarters' approval of settlements negotiated by locals and of strikes proposed by locals. In short, unionwide programs, stimulated by uniformity of policy in large firms, increase the influence and authority of the national headquarters.

Second, a change in the character and subject matter of negotiations has added to the dependence of the locals on the top echelon of the union. Collective bargaining has become increasingly technical, statistical, and full of economic reasoning, so that the amateur negotiator feels himself at a disadvantage and increasingly dependent on the national administration and staff. Subjects like job evaluation, time-and-motion study, pensions, medical and hospital care, and supplemental unemployment benefits, are generally beyond the training of persons at the local level, who must rely on the advice of staff experts on the national's payroll.

Third, national labor legislation, intervention in industrial relations by Federal agencies, and increased use of arbitration enhance union dependence on experts, especially lawyers and economists attached to the national headquarters and appointed by the top officials. The Taft-Hartley and Landrum-Griffin Acts are complicated pieces of legislation, on many aspects of which legal advice may be necessary before a local union can take action.

Fourth, with expansion in the size of the national union and more central pooling of strike and other funds, the possibilities of control of the union by a political machine increase and emphasis tends to be placed on effective management. Not only does the national's administration have more patronage to dispense but it can also more easily control communication within the union. As the union settles down, the top administration is prone to take a longer-run view and to be concerned about its reputation. This means not only stress on living up to agreements but the appointment of trustees by the president to take over and run the affairs of a local accused of financial looseness, of a strike in violation of an agreement, or of control by Communist or corrupt influences.

Another change that tends to occur within unions as their growth slows down is a reduction in militancy and in rivalry for leadership. Spread of organization invigorates a union with the fervor of new recruits; lack of new organizational conquests means the absence of such new blood. Failure to grow also slows down promotion to higher union positions and encourages conformity in the union hierarchy. Under institutional stability, advancement to high office is not only slow but usually goes to the organization-type person who is willing to work up through the political machine and await the death or long delayed retirement of top officers.[43]

External Integration

When unions achieve some of their most immediate aims (e.g., the union shop, seniority in lay-offs, and a good grievance procedure), their interests tend to broaden and their activities enlarge. Local unions participate in community services and in sport contests; their leaders serve on school boards and in local political office. National union leaders become both respectable and respected as they meet with Federal cabinet officers and the President and are appointed on Federal advisory boards and international agencies or missions.

Once unions no longer have to fight for their existence and bargaining rights, they become more closely integrated into industry and the community. Achievement of sole bargaining rights by winning a majority vote in a National Labor Relations Board election is certainly a moderating factor. It avoids the necessity of striking for union recognition and for bargaining authority. In organizing, the union leader sees himself almost as a director of a political campaign. In administering and enforcing agreements he practically becomes a part of management's system of government.

As unions accumulate funds and spread into the administration of benefit plans, they are desired as customers by banks and insurance companies. They also begin to hold sizable investments in companies, in housing and real estate developments, and in hospitals and medical centers. Indeed, top union leaders are almost as likely to be found reading the *Wall Street Journal* as the *AFL-CIO News*.

All this is a marked change in the status and activities of

---

[43] For an analysis of internal developments in local unions in Buffalo, see George Strauss, "The Shifting Power Balance in the Plant," *Industrial Relations*, I (May 1962), pp. 65–80.

unions from the pre-World War II days. Unions and union leaders have become rather fully integrated into American industry and community life.

What do these long-term trends, which seem definitely irreversible, signify for the theory of union behavior? They mean that many top union officials come to visualize themselves as community and national leaders and are, therefore, particularly conscious of public opinion. Also, as union members move into the middle class and as unions become better integrated into the community, they are more subject to the influence of general public attitudes and views. As a result, union behavior is less likely to offend community mores or values, which have, of course, been affected to some extent by unions themselves.

Therefore, insofar as union leaders have some latitude of discretion in policy making and in compromise settlements, they may be less extreme and more moderate in both their views and their decisions. The range of difference may be only slight but in the long run it can be significant.

SUMMARY

1. Despite considerable diversity in policies and behavior, all unions in the United States use collective bargaining to fix the terms and conditions of employment, and they presume to use democratic political processes for internal decision-making.

2. In view of union internal methods and the fact that employers conscious of market forces are partners in collective bargaining, a politicoeconomic model of union behavior seems the most appropriate one.

3. Union leadership generally enjoys a varying amount of latitude. Its range of discretion is limited by both political pressures and economic constraints.

4. The basic aim of most unions appears to be the security and growth of the institution. Although a union's leadership may take account of the employment consequences of its money demands, in large-scale industry any such consideration seems to be largely in terms of plant or company survival and, therefore, survival of the local union.

5. Unions bargain for a package settlement containing a variety

of cost and nonfinancial items. An economic theory of the union or the concept of job-conscious unionism (especially applicable to craft unionism) is too narrow to explain significant parts of the behavior of large industrial unions.

6. In the structure of organized labor, the national union is the key unit. Authority has tended to concentrate in the hands of the top officers of the national, without the separate legislative and judicial checks that exist in our national government.

7. The AFL-CIO performs largely nonbargaining, political functions. Its influence within organized labor, although relatively weak, has been increasing.

8. Unions are financed by membership dues and fees. Union expenditures, which run to about two billion dollars a year, support a sizable bureaucracy and a variety of economic, political, and social purposes.

9. The demand for union democracy raises the question of how to reconcile membership control with effective administration. Although the rate of participation in union meetings may be low, membership views can find effective expression in various ways.

10. Strike votes serve a variety of purposes, only one of which is to ascertain membership support for a strike.

11. As unions settle down, they become less militant and more administrative. Central authority expands under machine control, and, at the same time, the union becomes more fully integrated into the industry and the community.

DISCUSSION QUESTIONS

1. Samuel Gompers said that the AFL was a "rope of sand," by which he meant that it had no power. Others have said that, over time, central federations of unions gradually accumulate power. Would you expect the AFL-CIO to gain much authority over its affiliated national unions during the next decade, and, if so, by what means and in what areas?

2. Analyze the factors that have led to increased centralization of unions. Is greater decentralization of union functions likely or possible? Explain.

3. Discuss the Dunlop-Ross controversy, explaining which model of union behavior you consider more appropriate and why.

4. To what extent does union democracy conflict with union effectiveness? Explain.
5. To what extent are the following necessary to assure the existence of union democracy: a two-party system; an independent judiciary; a free press? Explain.
6. It is said that secret-ballot votes on striking are absolutely essential in order to curb the excesses of "strike-happy, union bosses." Discuss.
7. It is claimed that "success has been spoiling trade unions," that unions have gained most of their objectives and, therefore, we are witnessing the beginning of the end of the union movement. Discuss.

SELECTED READINGS

Barbash, Jack, *Labor's Grass Roots: A Study of the Local Union* (New York: Harper, 1961).
————, *The Practice of Unionism* (New York: Harper, 1956).
Barkin, Solomon, and Albert A. Blum, *The Crisis in the American Labor Movement*, 15 articles in *The Annals of the American Academy of Political and Social Science*, CCCL (November 1963).
Brooks, George W., *The Sources of Vitality in the American Labor Movement*, Bulletin No. 41, New York School of Industrial and Labor Relations, Cornell, July 1960.
Herberg, Will, "Bureaucracy and Democracy in Labor Unions," *Antioch Review*, III (Fall 1943), pp. 405–17.
Kahn, Robert L., and Arnold S. Tannenbaum, *Participation in Union Locals* (Evanston, Ill.: Row, Peterson, 1958).
Leiserson, William, *American Trade Union Democracy* (New York: Columbia University Press, 1959).
Lester, Richard A., *As Unions Mature, An Analysis of the Evolution of American Unionism* (Princeton: Princeton University Press, 1958).
Lipset, S. M., "The Political Process in Trade Unions: A Theoretical Statement," in Morroe Berger, *et al.*, *Freedom and Control in Modern Society* (New York: Van Nostrand, 1954), pp. 82–124.
Perlman, Mark, *Labor Union Theories in America, Background and Development* (Evanston, Ill.: Row, Peterson, 1958).
Perlman, Selig, *A Theory of the Labor Movement* (New York: Macmillan, 1928).
Roberts, Ben C., *Trade Unions in a Free Society, Studies in the Organisation of Labour in Britain and the U.S.A.*, The Institute of Economic Affairs (London: Hutchinson of London, 1962).

Ross, Arthur M., *Trade Union Wage Policy* (Berkeley: University of California Press, 1948).

Seidman, Joel, *et al.*, *The Worker Views His Union* (Chicago: University of Chicago Press, 1958).

Sultan, Paul E., *The Disenchanted Unionist* (New York: Harper and Row, 1963).

7.
Theory of
Management

THE CHANGES IN the industrial relations philosophy of American management were outlined in Chapter 5. The shift away from a commodity (or pure market) concept of manual employment represented growing recognition of the importance to workers of decent treatment within the plant and of other non-market values. Unions, of course, seek some sharing of in-plant government and some protection for workers from competitive pressures.

The management of an industrial firm tends to be market-conscious. Purchases and sales, prices and costs, are its daily concern. In industrial relations, management stresses the market constraints on liberal labor policies, on the welfare concept of employment.

Understandably, the traditional theory of the firm centered on the market behavior of business organizations. In the late nineteenth century, economists could assume, without too much questioning, that firms of all sizes operated like single enterprises bent on maximizing their profits, and that all markets, including those for labor, were fully competitive and, therefore, controlled by the forces of demand and supply. Under such assumptions, the economist could explain and predict the behavior of firms without studying the process of decision-making within the business organization.

Concentration on the market and the profit motive, and disregard of the firm's internal operations, permitted the theory to be quite simple. No attention was given to such matters as the design and marketing of new products, the development of an effective work force, or the complexities of group behavior and collective decision-making. Indeed, the traditional theory of the firm omitted much of modern industrial management; it left, for example, no particular role for an industrial relations department.

Much economic analysis in the labor field is based, at least in part, on the orthodox theory of the firm. That is true, for instance, of many conclusions regarding the economic consequences of minimum-wage legislation, of settlements under collective bargaining, and of other actions that affect labor cost. The traditional theory of the firm has even been called upon to deny the need for labor organization, or for laws against race discrimination in employment, or for hours and plant-safety legislation.

Because a satisfactory theory of management is so important for determining the economic effects of collective bargaining and of labor legislation, it will be necessary in this chapter first to examine the traditional theory of the firm and then to consider a general theory of management that seems more appropriate for modern industry. That management theory will provide a foundation for the next section on industrial relations programs.

THEORY OF THE FIRM

The classical theory of the firm is elegant in its simplicity and the precision of its predictions. It rests on two assumptions: (1) that the single motive of maximum profits over the long run governs the behavior of the firm and usually profit maximization occurs by the rational method of marginal analysis (comparison of incremental costs and income), and (2) that either competition rules all markets, permitting the firm to take prices and demand and supply as given (as parameters so that the management of a firm has no reason to consider its influence on any market in planning its actions) or that the firm has some monopoly power, in which case it takes demand as given and fixes either prices or supply so as to maximize profits. By the selection of a single goal, a single method, and a given set of conditions it is possible to arrive at a simple explanation and an exact result. And the test of the theory, it is argued, is not the accuracy of its assumptions but the validity of its predictions.

One advantage of the traditional model of the firm is that it furnishes the basis for the entire structure of the classical theory of production and distribution. This simple model of firm behavior is used to explain the particular combination of productive factors that the firm will use, the income returns that will be received by each factor, the firm's total output and capital investment, the movement of firms into and out of industries, and many other economic phenomena. And the sum of all employment, output, and investment of the individual firms is the total for the private economy as a whole. If the assumptions of the traditional doctrine of the firm hold true, presumably every one (workers, landlords, investors, entrepreneurs, etc.) would be paid exactly according to his contribution to the economy.

Understandably, the classical theory of the firm has great intellectual appeal to economists. To abandon it, or to admit that it has serious defects, would mean an undermining of the entire structure of orthodox economic theory. Consequently, economists are likely to continue to rely to some extent on the traditional theory of the firm despite its deficiencies, unless and until an alternative is developed that is equally effective in supporting the superstructure of economic theory.

It is desirable, therefore, to examine the traditional theory in some detail, considering possible modifications and alternatives. To that end the discussion will proceed under the following headings: goals, decision-making methods, extramarket pressures, and adjustment possibilities.

Goals

Basic to any discussion of business behavior is the question: What guides or motivates business management? Is a single institutional motive or an exclusive goal sufficient to explain the variety of conduct of business firms? Or are companies, especially large corporations, multimotivated, with their operations influenced by a number of goals? Noteworthy perhaps is the fact that business managements seldom formulate and stress a single objective for the firm, any more than they establish and insist upon an exclusive aim for all industrial relations activities.

As already explained, the traditional theory of the firm assumes single motivation of a special sort, namely, the optimum or largest possible profits for the collective unit over a long-run period. That goal is not as precise as it sounds. "The long run" is ambiguous. Presumably, it depends on the horizon of the firm. And the maximum supposedly is in terms of current value, calculated by discounting the intended profits plus expected capital gains, distributed over the appropriate time period. Of course, speculators, traders, and fly-by-night concerns are likely to aim for maximum profits in the immediate future.

The goal of "satisfactory profits" or a "good profits record" should be distinguished from "maximum profits."[1] Such a standard, based either on the firm's past achievements or the current accomplishments of competitors, is a less rigorous and precise goal than optimum profits. It is argued that comparative, not absolute, profits are generally used as a test of successful management.

More definite perhaps is a target rate of profit on investment. The rate-of-return target used by managements in deciding whether to make a capital investment usually is a figure within the range of 10 to 20 per cent. A Brookings study of pricing policy objectives in twenty well-known corporations[2] found that seven of them aimed at a certain return on investment, four sought to maintain or improve their market share or position, four priced to meet competition, and the remaining five had other pricing objectives. The authors concluded that profits-maximizing was

---

[1] R. A. Gordon, "Short-Period Price Determination in Theory and Practice," *American Economic Review*, XXXVIII (June 1948), pp. 265–88; and E. E. Hoogstraat, "Attacks on the Value of the Profit Motive in Theories of Business Behavior," in J. W. McGuire (ed.), *Interdisciplinary Studies in Business Behavior* (Cincinnati: South-Western Publishing Co., 1962), p. 28.

[2] See A. D. H. Kaplan, J. B. Dirlam, and R. F. Lanzillotti, *Pricing in Big Business: A Case Approach* (Washington: Brookings Institution, 1958), pp. 127–219; and R. F. Lanzillotti, "Pricing Objectives in Large Companies," *American Economic Review*, XLVIII (December 1958), pp. 921–40.

"operationally a less useful" working hypothesis than target return or market share, because it did not provide a satisfactory basis for predicting the actual price behavior of large firms.[3]

The objective of maintaining or improving a firm's market position, measured in percentage of total sales in its product lines, is both definite and meaningful. Managements generally know, watch, and base decisions on that figure. Developments in a company's market share indicate its current competitive position and customer reaction to its products. Subject perhaps to the achievement of a minimum profit goal, desired market position may be the main target, especially of firms in industries where model changes and new products are important competitive elements. And the firm may be forced by the expansion of competing companies to undertake new investment in order to retain its market position, even though the additional expenditure itself may yield less than would the investment of the funds elsewhere. Business executives normally do not willingly give up sales volume in order to eliminate relatively unprofitable product lines or sales territory. Such a retreat would not be in accordance with their psychology, because sales are considered a measure of customer satisfaction and the business ability of management. Thus the objective goals of sales volume and market share are related to other aims, such as survival and growth of the firm and reputation and prestige of the management.

So significant are sales as a criterion of the state of a business enterprise that William J. Baumol has developed a theory that large corporations seek to maximize total sales revenue, subject to the constraint of a minimum necessary level of profits.[4] The profits constraint may be in the form of a certain yearly total, or a minimum return on sales or on investment, sufficient to enable the firm to finance current expansion plans through retained

---

[3] Kaplan, *et al.*, *Pricing in Big Business, op. cit.*, p. 129; and R. F. Lanzillotti, "Pricing Objectives in Large Companies: Reply," *American Economic Review*, XLIX (September 1959), pp. 938–39.

[4] William J. Baumol, "On the Theory of Oligopoly," *Economica*, XXV (August 1958), pp. 187–98 and *Business Behavior, Value and Growth* (New York: Macmillan, 1959), esp. Chapters 6–8. See also Baumol's subsequent stress on the rate of growth of sales in contrast to the static concept of the current level of sales ("On the Theory of Expansion of the Firm," *American Economic Review* LII [December 1962], pp. 1078–87).

earnings or by the sale of its own securities. Therefore, maximum product sales rather than profits are presumed to be the ultimate objective.

Business managements may pursue, simultaneously or successively, two or more goals, which may be interrelated. Indeed, a certain level or rate of profits may be necessary for the attainment of a number of the assumed objectives of business firms. At the same time, pursuit of one of these other goals may be partly at the expense of maximum possible profits. Consequently, where there is a conflict of goals, a question may arise concerning the relative priorities and balance among them. The balance may, of course, shift as firms adjust their sights with changing circumstances.

Other suggested goals of business firms include: (1) institutional growth and development, (2) financial security, (3) convenience and prestige of the management, and (4) general reputation of the firm. The top executives in a firm may gain considerable personal satisfaction from being known in the community as leaders in good industrial relations and community benefits.

Growth usually means larger salaries for top management and better promotion possibilities for the lower levels of management. Financial security increases the independence of management and enhances its ability to take advantage of developing opportunities. It is convenient to supervise a satisfied and well-trained work force and to have a good labor-relations reputation. Managements also like to be considered professionally competent and technically advanced. Growth, technical progress, and the firm's labor-relations record are measures of achievement just as profits are.

The general reputation of the firm as a management goal brings up the fact that a large corporation is a collective, combining various specialized elements. It cannot be viewed as having the same singleness of purpose and action as an individual enterpriser. Furthermore, professional managers of large corporations may have interests and motives distinct from those of the bulk of the stockholders. Subject to some profit constraint, such managements may be able to make corporate donations, adopt employee programs, and promote the welfare of management, in ways and to an extent that would be difficult to justify in terms of maximizing the firm's profits or even making a normal return on those expenditures over the long run.

The influence of nonprofit motives in some corporation activities is explained by Chester I. Barnard as follows: "In the broad sense that no business can escape its balance sheet, it is true that the economic or money motive governs the administration of business. Nevertheless my observation in several different well-managed businesses convinces me that business decisions are constantly being made that are not based upon economic motives. This is something that business men seldom admit, and of which they are frequently unaware. Prestige, competitive reputation, social philosophy, social standing, philanthropic interests, combativeness, love of intrigue, dislike of friction, technical interest, Napoleonic dreams, love of accomplishing useful things, desire for regard of employees, love of publicity, fear of publicity—a long catalogue of non-economic motives actually condition the management of business, and nothing but the balance sheet keeps these non-economic motives from running wild."[5] In a similar vein, James C. Worthy, vice-president of Sears, Roebuck and Company points out that business executives usually give a profit explanation for actions arising from noneconomic motives and adds by way of illustration: "Modern corporate philanthropy, for example, is typically explained as a means of promoting good will, although the real motivation may well be simply a sense of corporate responsibility. Employee benefit plans are usually justified on the basis of their presumed effect on productivity, although anyone experienced in personnel management can testify that genuine concern for employee welfare is often the compelling factor."[6]

Tested knowledge of the motives and mental processes of business management is rather limited. Nevertheless it seems evident that salaried management in large corporate enterprises frequently enjoys sufficient latitude to promote different objectives, that competition and stockholder pressures do not force such management persistently and consistently to pursue the goal of

---

[5] Chester I. Barnard, *Organization and Management, Selected Papers* (Cambridge: Harvard University Press, 1948), pp. 14–15. For over two decades Mr. Barnard was president of the New Jersey Bell Telephone Company.

[6] James C. Worthy, *Big Business and Free Men* (New York: Harper, 1959), p. 28.

maximum profit.[7] And, while management may need "satisfactory" profits in order to be free to consider other objectives, sales volume and market share (which are closely tied in with institutional survival and growth as well as reputation of the management and the firm) are often considered such significant measures of success for well-established companies that they may be given priority— be pursued even though the possible result is a somewhat lower rate of profit in the long run.

Decision-making Methods

The second assumption of the traditional theory of the firm is that business managements, consciously or unconsciously, use a kind of marginal analysis in making decisions with respect to prices, output, employment, and capital investment. Marginal analysis is the means by which profits are supposed to be maximized. It consists of a mental comparison of the additional cost and the additional income from successive units of potential employment or output and then expanding or contracting actual operations of the firm to the point where marginal (the extra unit) cost approximately equals marginal revenue (the income yielded by that extra unit of output). Up to that scale of operations, each unit is returning a profit. Thus, marginal analysis assumes that business management has for each item or product at least a rough idea of its unit cost schedule and its unit revenue schedule.[8]

The application of marginal analysis is appropriate in agriculture and other industries where it is possible to vary labor, land, and materials (e.g., seed and fertilizer) over a wide range without

---

[7] From an analysis of published material and personal interviews in about thirty companies, Robert A. Gordon came to the conclusion that "the traditional reward of the business leader—the profits arising from business ownership—is not a primary incentive to the majority of top executives in our largest corporations" and that "in terms of the personal desires which motivate businessmen, the non-financial attractions offered by the large corporation also frequently outrank profits as an incentive for the salaried business leader." See Gordon, *Business Leadership in the Large Corporation* (Washington: Brookings Institution, 1945), pp. 312–13.

[8] Under pure competition (numerous small firms producing a standard product for the same market), the management of any one would assume it could not affect the price and, therefore, its average and marginal revenue would be the same at all output quantities.

changing the techniques of production. This is so because, as Robert Dorfman points out, "marginal analysis depends on being able to differentiate the production revenue and cost factors independently with respect to each input and output."[9] In manufacturing processes having a high interrelationship between productive factors (e.g., the use of a particular piece of equipment predetermining the amount of labor, materials, and electricity required), it is not possible to think in terms of independent variation of the factors.

Marginal analysis is not too appropriate where productive operations are complex and where demand and cost are interrelated, changing, and uncertain. The more complicated the situation, the less valid is reasoning on the basis of equilibrium models limited to a two-dimensional scheme of variables.[10] An elaborate study of automobile demand in 1938, for example, showed that probable variation in sales at lower or higher prices was difficult to determine within a wide range because income and other factors apparently had more effect on sales than any feasible price variation would have.[11]

For marginal analysis, time is a particularly troublesome problem. Over an extended period, changes can be expected to take place in the important variables—prices, costs, and demand—but just how they will change is uncertain. The likelihood yet unpredictability of significant changes in those and other pertinent variables makes demand elasticity for marginal estimates seem not too significant for long-range decisions. If demand is expanding and expected to continue to rise, a management is likely to enlarge its plant capacity despite any question-raising because of the assumed elasticity of demand at any one point of time.

In pricing products, managements generally seem to follow full-cost or some other formula rather than marginal analysis. That may be the case because they favor stability of prices, because short- and long-run unit cost curves appear to be fairly horizontal

---

[9] Robert Dorfman, *Application of Linear Programming to the Theory of the Firm* (Berkeley: University of California Press, 1951), p. 10.

[10] See J. M. Clark, *Competition as a Dynamic Process* (Washington: Brookings Institution, 1961), pp. 39 and 43–44.

[11] C. F. Roos and Victor von Szeliski, "Factors Governing Changes in Domestic Automobile Demand," in *The Dynamics of Automobile Demand* (New York: General Motors Corp., 1939), esp. pp. 94–95.

(unit variable costs approximately constant) over most of their length,[12] and because accounting methods do not lend themselves to marginal cost and marginal revenue calculations. If cost curves are rather flat and really should be represented by a band rather than a single line,[13] then the effects on unit costs of a proposed change in plant capacity would seem too small to be a controlling factor. The calculation of marginal costs is difficult in many cases, since accounting data generally provide figures for average, but not marginal, costs. The Brookings study of pricing policies in twenty large corporations found that "Even in companies where the most detailed cost data are available to pricing officials, the typical practice is to base prices on 'standard cost' at some long-run 'normal' output rate."[14]

Partly because of uncertainty, long-term capital investment may not be well adapted for marginal analysis. John R. Meyer and Edwin Kuh examined the available studies of investment behavior and could only find a 1951 public utility study that seemed to support the validity of the profit-maximization, marginal-analysis theory. In addition they analyzed published data on investment for 750 firms during a five-year period and found "nothing to justify any claim to unique superiority for any one theory above all other alternatives."[15] Certainly, maintenance of a firm's market position is often a motivating factor in investment decisions of business management.

One factor contributing to uncertainty is that demand and cost curves are not fixed by physical law but are subject to modification by management programs. Demand for trade-marked products is influenced by advertising and other sales programs. Costs can

---

[12] Clark, *op. cit.*, p. 60; P. J. D. Wiles, *Price, Cost and Output* (Oxford: Blackwell, 1956), Chapter 12; and W. J. Eiteman and J. E. Guthrie, "The Shape of the Average Cost Curve," *American Economic Review*, XLII (December 1952), pp. 832–38.

[13] Clark, *op. cit.*, p. 126; and Wiles, *op. cit.*, p. 52.

[14] Lanzillotti, *op. cit.*, p. 685. Use of "normal" output eliminates overhead cost as a variable and narrows marginal and full-cost differences to variable costs.

[15] John R. Meyer and Edwin Kuh, *The Investment Decision, An Empirical Study* (Cambridge: Harvard University Press, 1957), p. 204. The authors themselves advocate for the short run a residual-funds theory of investment for large corporations, under which whatever cash inflow is left over after conventional dividend payments is invested; and find that, in the long run, the profit motive for such a corporation is closely linked to a desire to retain market shares.

be cut by improved managerial techniques and other methods used in cost-cutting campaigns. For example, Ray R. Eppert, president of Burroughs Corporation, explained to the Annual Meeting of the stockholders on May 8, 1958 that the management had taken "a long hard look at the cost factors affecting our revenue picture" and had acted as follows: "In a systematic approach to the problem, we have established a corporate-wide profit improvement program. Profit-improvement committees have been set up at divisional levels to scrutinize our operations. Their objective is to reduce costs and expenses without reducing the quality of our products, and without eliminating those activities or programs which would hurt our long-range potential. We have had substantial success in resisting the downward trend of earnings through acceleration of deliveries, vigorous promotion of products that are readily available and by reduction of general operating costs and expenses."[16] Additional evidence that waste elimination can be accomplished under pressure is provided by a study of large corporations during the depression of the Thirties. From that study, which included interviews with some 250 executives in thirty companies, the authors concluded: "Theoretically, management should seek constantly to maximize profits, and should never be satisfied merely because they appear adequate. But the urgency of the depression revealed how far from the truth that assumption is, because it reckoned without human laziness. The biggest companies felt the pinch and responded with increased attention to economies."[17]

Some management decisions involve broad, long-range questions such as a shift in product lines, a new market strategy, or a significant change in industrial relations policies. Initially, the problem may be surrounded by so much uncertainty and be so unstructured as to cause management to decide to feel its way in the form of a series of tentative moves rather than to try to make a definite choice among alternatives, based on marginalist principles. Analysis of the results of the first steps provides partial

---

[16] *Report to Stockholders*, Burroughs Corporation, sent to stockholders July 21, 1958, with checks covering the 234th consecutive dividend.

[17] Marshall E. Dimock and Howard K. Hyde, *Bureaucracy and Trusteeship in Large Corporations*, Monograph 11, Temporary National Economic Committee (Washington: United States Government Printing Office, 1940), p. 66.

information that reduces uncertainty and permits revisions in the program in the light of early experience. Thus, the management is better able to develop workable compromises that may satisfy more than one goal.

It seems clear that marginal analysis is distinctly limited in its application to the problems facing managements, especially in large companies where decision-making may be widely diffused within the organization. Uncertainty, cost flexibility, and management's need to balance different goals mean that the method of a sequence of decisions, guided by analysis of the effects of each move, may have practical advantages in many cases over the more rational but restricted method of comparison of marginal quantities.

Extramarket Pressures

To the extent that market forces completely rule all employer actions, it is possible, of course, to reason as though no other circumstances make any difference. Insofar, however, as managements have some latitude of decision or some flexibility policy-wise, then personal, institutional, and political influences may make a difference in the firm's behavior.

In a sense, business management in the large firm is in the middle of pressures from various functional groups. The corporation consists of production workers, staff and clerical employees, salesmen, dealers, stockholders, and various elements within management itself. In addition, there are distributors, customers, suppliers, bankers, other creditors, and the general public, to all of whose opinions the management of the large public corporation may be sensitive.

The management's task is to develop an adequate demand for its pool of resources and to keep all parties sufficiently satisfied to maintain their interest in the firm and its products. That requires leadership and innovation in production methods and sales; markets provide only part of the framework and constraints within which the management maneuvers.

Wage-paid employees supply one important source of pressure on management, especially if they are represented by a union. Managements generally desire good union-management relations and seek to avoid an interruption of the firm's operations by a strike. The labor agreement contains regulations or constraints on the freedom and policies of management. By such means as wage guarantees, company unemployment benefits, and seniority protections, unions seek to constrict or alter the channels through which management might apply policies that would require wage employees to bear the brunt of adjustments. The union constantly presses upon management the importance of human values, and seeks to make it costly for management to disregard the needs and desires of production workers.

Large firms have sizable investments in employee training and good will. With production resting on willing cooperation, management wants to maintain a satisfied as well as a competent workforce. If wage employees were all on salary, management would have less freedom to lay off employees or to vary widely their hours of work. Unions, in seeking to increase job and benefit security, are striving to make labor more like a fixed or overhead cost.

Management actions are likewise influenced by laws, governmental policies, and the climate of public opinion in which companies operate. Government establishes legal and moral constraints through legislation, administrative actions, investigations, and pronouncements. In the labor field, for example, management is required to bargain in good faith with the certified union on a number of specific items including benefits, and discrimination in private employment on the basis of race is banned by law in a number of States and cities and by presidential executive order in the case of private employment on Federal contracts.

Generally, the managements of well-established firms are concerned about their reputations both in management circles and in society at large. Businessmen seek to exert leadership in business organizations and in the community. Many firms spend sizable sums each year in contributions to community chests and hospitals, in specific and general grants to colleges and universities, and on programs of "economic education" and "political education" for their employees.

Through the board of directors, stockholders press for high earnings and large dividends; salesmen push for a wide line of up-to-date and well-advertised products; distributors object to price fluctuations and other changes that may result in inventory losses; customers demand good products and repair service on them, and so it goes. Different interest groups within and outside the company stress and press for attention to their problems and interests. For instance, specialist and functional groups in the company strive to expand their share of the company's budget.

In responding to these various pressures, top management is likely to take account of the personal, political, and economic (market) power each can exert within the company and outside it. Thus, even though a particular management may not be severely limited by *market* constraints, it may not enjoy as much latitude of discretion as that fact alone might imply. Extramarket constraints of varying potency may also limit or channel the actions of the management.

Adjustment Possibilities

We have discussed the latitude that management may enjoy where market constraints are not so severe that all avenues of adjustment are blocked except those postulated by the traditional theory of the firm.[18] And we have noted that some extramarket constraints may be as restrictive on management as are market compulsions.

Despite both types of constraint, the managements of large firms are often likely to have some latitude in decision-making—some scope for experimentation, for the pursuit of relatively unprofitable ventures, and for the indulgence of personal preferences. This has already been indicated by the quotations from Chester Barnard, James Worthy, and Ray Eppert.[19] Anyone who has engaged in the pulling and cutting process of budget-making knows that wasteful expenditures are ever present in large organizations. This is one reason why union-pressured, labor-cost increases can, under certain conditions, stimulate management to make additional improvements in its products, sales methods, and operating efficiency.[20]

---

[18] Based on the assumption of a single institutional goal, a single method of decision-making, maximum level of managerial efficiency, and one channel of reaction that disregards extramarket constraints.

[19] See pp. 197 and 201 above.

[20] Such possibilities are further evidence that corporations do not single-mindedly and relentlessly pursue a goal of maximum profit but rather are more likely to have multiple goals which include market-share and satisfactory-profits targets. For a discussion of "inefficiencies" in business see F. H. Harbison, "Entrepreneurial Organization as a Factor in Economic Development," *Quarterly Journal of Economics,* LXX (August 1956), pp. 371–78.

Many factors may influence the extent to which a management can or does enjoy a range of discretion in the type and timing of the adjustments it makes to, say, an increase in wage rates or employee benefits.[21] Among them are: (1) the firm's present and prospective position in its product markets; (2) its current and anticipated financial position; (3) the size and suddenness of the labor cost change (which may determine the degree of "shock" stimulus to managerial innovation and the management's time span of adjustment); (4) the restrictions on management actions that are contained in any labor agreements; (5) the firm's cost structure and, therefore, the degree of looseness in cost-price relationships; (6) the feasibility, for cost reasons, of altering labor-equipment ratios in the firm's production operations; (7) the possibilities of changing the quality of the firm's work force; and (8) the place of the firm's wage scale in the community's and industry's wage structures. To the extent that the firm has enjoyed a labor-cost advantage, the wage or benefit increase may mean reduction or elimination of that favorable factor.

A study of company adjustments to labor shortages indicates that local differences in wage scales among comparable firms amounting to 10 or even 15 per cent may exist without causing noticeable effects on labor mobility, labor supply to the firm, or employee morale within the firm.[22] In other words, in some localities a sort of no-response area may prevail within which companies have wage latitude. Beyond such a "10 per cent" range, perceptible consequences do or would occur, taking such forms as poor employee morale, loss of skilled maintenance workers, high turnover among recently hired employees, or even difficulties in union-management relations.

Effective management seeks to create a range of discretion for itself. This a dynamic management may accomplish by innovations

---

[21] Much of the material in this and the following paragraphs is drawn from R. A. Lester, "Economic Adjustments to Changes in Wage Differentials," in G. W. Taylor and F. C. Pierson (eds.), *New Concepts in Wage Determination* (New York: McGraw-Hill, 1957), pp. 206–235.

[22] See R. A. Lester, *Hiring Practices and Labor Competition*, Industrial Relations Section, Princeton University, Princeton, 1954, pp. 84–85; and R. A. Lester, *Adjustments to Labor Shortages, Management Practices and Institutional Controls in an Area of Expanding Employment*, Industrial Relations Section, Princeton University, Princeton, 1955, pp. 56–64.

in products or selling and production methods, so as to reduce the restrictive power of market forces. It may make some extramarket constraints more elastic, as, for example, by means of the skill with which a particular program is "sold" to the employees and subsequently administered. Firms have industrial relations departments in order to influence labor cost and to help the workforce adapt to changes. Thus managements may be able to influence the way that a particular wage change affects employee attitudes and labor productivity. One of the reasons that business management may prefer the trial-and-error method of a sequence of decisions, guided by analysis of the results of earlier actions, is that it permits more flexibility and latitude of decision than a single-type, timeless method like marginal analysis, even if it assumes the use of successive approximations to equilibrium.

The adjustment to labor-cost increase stressed by the traditional theory of the firm (i.e., curtailment of employment or less employment expansion than would otherwise occur) may conflict with the psychology of management and such goals as company growth and market position. Especially is that true if labor-equipment ratios cannot be altered much. Operating costs per unit of output[23] seem generally to be constant or slightly decreasing until operations approach full plant capacity. By maintaining output near capacity, the management has the advantages that accompany stability of employment as well as reduced overhead costs per unit of product.[24]

An important element in the dynamics of company growth is the fact that stockholders, workers, dealers, lower management, and top management all have an interest in increased volume. Expansion tends to result in higher incomes, advancement, or both. Some of the forces behind company growth are briefly explained by A. D. H. Kaplan and A. E. Kahn as follows: "A big business represents an immense investment that presses for full and productive utilization. Not only must its factories and machines be used fully if it is to beat the breakeven point, but the fact

---

[23] Technically, marginal variable cost.

[24] In addition to savings in labor transfer under seniority, there are the savings from longer production runs, lower unemployment compensation taxes, and efficient use of transport and other services. Additional overtime employment is one possible offset.

is that its whole costly organization is geared for expansion."[25]

The theory of management that emerges from our analysis is a rather complex one. It might be called the multipurpose, multi-adjustment theory of management. It assumes that business management may have a number of goals, with priority among them subject to change as the circumstances of the firm alter. Management is subject to a variety of pressures and constraints, yet it normally enjoys some latitude in formulating policy and in making adjustments to internal and external changes. In part, the latitude that a management has depends on its ability to create for itself strong market positions, to develop a well-functioning organization, and to open up different channels of adjustment. And the process of adjustment itself provides experience for improving tentative decisions and policies.

This is a dynamic view of business management. It is in contrast to the static concept of timeless adjustment by means of a mechanistic enforcement of market equilibrium. Although the traditional theory of the firm is severely limited in its application (because it postulates one goal and one method of operation and adjustment), nevertheless it is useful for understanding the behavior of business management, particularly under certain circumstances. Its application seems most likely to be appropriate where the firm is small and operates on narrow profit margins, sells and buys in highly competitive markets, manufactures a product by relatively simple techniques that permit ready variation in labor-capital ratios, and has a high ratio of labor to total costs. For the large corporation with specialized management, including an industrial relations department, a more general, development type of theory, postulating some range of discretion, seems more suitable.

THE RATIONALE OF INDUSTRIAL RELATIONS PROGRAMS

Although the industrial relations activities of a firm may not have one exclusive goal, the general purposes of such activities are evident. With the process of production resting on the willing cooperation of employees, managements of well-established firms

---

[25] A. D. H. Kaplan and A. E. Kahn, "Big Business in a Competitive Society," insert in *Fortune*, XLVII (February, 1953), p. 3.

seek: (1) to recruit and maintain an effective work group that contains enough promotable material for the company's supervisory needs; and (2) to supervise a satisfied and loyal workforce so as to avoid the wastes of high labor turnover; and (3) if unionized, to maintain a good labor-relations record so that losses from strikes are minimized. Of course, management also wishes to avoid being unduly hampered in its managerial functions by the clauses of a labor agreement.

Such a statement of purposes does not provide a simple guide, with clear-cut limits, to different types of industrial relations expenditures. Presumably, most investments in industrial relations programs are made on the assumption that ultimately they will pay off in the form of a compensating gain in labor productivity. That, however, is a somewhat ambiguous and immeasurable criterion. It is difficult to determine, either in advance or after the fact, just how much the labor productivity of a workforce is affected by differing amounts of expenditure on particular programs made at various times.

Despite considerable study, industrial relations is still more of an art than a science, with too many variables to permit prediction of the productivity effects of particular expenditures for, say, employee benefits, employee counseling, or employee stock-purchase plans. That is especially true where a company employs its workforce on the basis of a work-life career with the firm, so that the pay-off period could extend over forty years or more. In the meantime, the composition of the workforce and the supervisory staff and many other conditions in the company would be experiencing numerous changes.

New industrial relations programs are, therefore, likely to be venturesome, long-term investments. They are subject to considerable uncertainty of results and generally are "sunk" in the sense that once adopted they may be difficult to curtail, to terminate, or to shift to another purpose. The uncertainty and unmeasurability of results make it almost impossible to determine the amount of expenditures on new industrial relations programs by means of marginal analysis, although presumably some rough expectations concerning results are involved in making up budgets or in negotiating with a union. Under those conditions, new employee programs may be started largely on faith. Introduced in a small way and enlarged a step at a time, they would be open to revision in line with sequence analysis. Also such a method of decision-making fits better the pattern of periodic union negotiations to revise the collective agreement.

The objectives of industrial relations programs often extend beyond labor productivity. The statements of business executives quoted above indicate that some elements of industrial relations programs (i.e., employee benefits and recreational facilities) are adopted by certain managements because of their concern for employee welfare, their sense of social responsibility, the paternalistic propensities of top management, or some other nonprofit reason.[26] Private benefit programs may, for example, be extended by some managements in order to forestall the adoption or expansion of government social security programs. In some instances, managements introduce new industrial relations programs because they wish to maintain a reputation for being progressive or they follow the lead of progressive firms. In still other cases, industrial relations programs may be started or expanded in order to help avoid unionization of the firm. Should unionization occur nevertheless, the investment could be considered a failure, but seldom would that lead to a reduction or elimination of the industrial relations department.

The variety of possible motives or goals behind industrial relations programs makes it difficult to generalize about the factors that control such programs or to assess the extent of their success. Industrial relations departments, therefore, lack clear guidelines with which to determine how they should allocate their resources among different activities and how large a total effort is economically justified. Consequently, it seems even more difficult to construct a separate theory of management's industrial relations

---

[26] J. C. Worthy, *op. cit.*, p. 28; and C. I. Barnard, *op. cit.*, pp. 14–15. Barnard explains that if you observe the business man in practice "you will find he is taking care of poor old John who couldn't be placed anywhere else, that he is risking both profit and failure rather than cut wages, that he continues an unprofitable venture on nothing but hope rather than throw his men out of work. Much of this is unsound. It would be better if economic motives did operate more effectively, but the point is that it is impossible to get to the root of personnel relations or understand labor troubles or successes on the unrealistic assumption that economic motives exclusively govern. They merely limit and guide."

activities than it is to fashion a theory of management as a whole. A systematic theory of the industrial relations activities of business management has still to be developed. Presumably, such a theory would need to take account of (1) management's different objectives in industrial relations and (2) pressures by labor and pattern-spreading by imitation, both subject to the constraint of satisfactory profits.

Particularly for large firms, industrial relations programs may be visualized by management as investment in the company's workforce. That investment has two facets—the good will and welfare of the individual employee and the effectiveness of the organization as a productive unit.[27] Managements of well-established firms have a fairly long horizon so that they are concerned with results over the long pull as well as in the short run.

Whether investments in industrial relations activities pay off depends partly on (1) the industrial relations goals of management and (2) the intelligence and skill with which policies are formulated and administered. Employment, it is well to bear in mind, is one of the most administered relationships in economic life. Management, in its industrial relations aspects, is largely the government of men while they are at work. Consequently, determination of the "pay-off" (results) encounters the serious difficulties already discussed.

Management of the Workforce

Chapter 5 explained the shift from a commodity to a welfare concept of employment, partly due to educational levels, curtailed immigration, larger capital investment per worker, and advances in industrial psychology. As management's perspective on employment has lengthened, production workers are hired at the bottom rung of the job ladder with the expectation of a work-life career with the company. The management selects workers not so much for their qualifications to perform the hiring-in job (i.e., yard labor), as their potentialities for development and advancement under its supervision. Selection according to work-life potential, with emphasis on development and advancement during employ-

---

[27] See Frederick H. Harbison and John R. Coleman, *Goals and Strategy in Collective Bargaining* (New York: Harper, 1951), p. 8.

ment, means that the company is investing in the worker from the start, for it suffers a financial loss in case he leaves during the first year or two. That loss is measured by the cost of putting him on the payroll (record keeping, interviewing, test giving, indoctrination, any initial training, etc.) and the difference between his productivity at the outset and his initial compensation.

A management's thinking on labor-supply matters, therefore, is influenced by the quality of workforce that the management seeks. The type of labor desired is, in turn, related to the kinds of jobs in the plant and the management's perspective—how much stress it puts on the immediate, intermediate, and distant future. If the jobs in a plant require little training or responsibility and offer few promotion possibilities, the management may not be too concerned with its employees' capacity for development and is less likely to discriminate against the "restless" worker with a short-run view of employment. On the other hand, in firms whose operations require considerable investment in employee training and where stress is placed on promotion possibilities and ample benefits, management is interested in hiring dependable workers, say, in their late twenties, with family responsibilities and ready to settle down. The more a management plans for the long pull, the greater will be the care exercised in selecting and developing the workforce. A firm can be severely handicapped by a poorly disciplined, low-grade, and unreliable labor force. Such a handicap is difficult to overcome because the existing workforce generally attracts and indoctrinates new recruits after its own image.

A firm's workforce objectives have a bearing on its methods of employee recruitment, its selection practices, its training programs, its wage and benefit policies, and other aspects of its industrial relations program. The effectiveness of the different parts depends, of course, on coordination within the whole program.

1. RECRUITMENT AND SELECTION.[28] Companies recruit new production workers in various ways. The most common recruitment channels are unsolicited applications at the employment office ("at the gate") and referral by someone already in the workforce. In addition, companies may use the State employment agency,

---

[28] This subsection draws on the author's study, *Hiring Practices and Labor Competition, op. cit.*

schools, unions, private employment agencies, and advertising in the newspapers or on the air.

The particular methods that a company uses at any one time and over a period of time will depend on its job openings and the circumstances confronting the management. Well-established firms that are hiring mostly for replacement of retirees and normal attrition may be able to rely on the informal means of gate-hiring and employee referrals. In contrast, new firms and those that must expand rapidly usually have to resort to more aggressive methods that involve a financial cost such as advertising, direct mail inquiries, or sending recruiters to other localities. A firm seeking to improve the quality of its workforce would not stress employee referrals and may use "blind" advertisements to conceal its identity before the receipt of an application. Also, advertising is more likely to be used for special skills than for unskilled workers. The more restrictive a company's selection policy is in terms of race, nationality, or social status, the less likely it is to utilize a State employment service that finds it difficult to discriminate on such grounds in making referrals.

Most managements seem to prefer to obtain the bulk of their new hires through direct application at the gate or through internal recruitment by employee referrals. Direct application shows that the worker had sufficient interest in the company to seek employment there, and permits prescreening at that time. Candidates referred and recommended by present employees are likely to be the type of worker that the management wants. These two methods enable the management to keep intimately in touch with labor-supply currents and opinions, and to screen applicants without any implied commitments or the embarrassment of rejecting an applicant who was prescreened and selected as fit by an employment agency.

Many firms normally use no other recruitment measures. Their reputations and reserve drawing power are sufficient so that word to employees about the existence of openings or the rumor in the community that the company is hiring are sufficient to bring the needed number of qualified applicants. In fact, many firms report that their reputations are such that they are swamped with applicants as soon as it is known they are hiring, and they find that the flow of applications almost ceases as soon as they start laying off employees.

Experience indicates that a firm's reserve drawing power (ability to recruit by costless means when expansion is necessary) may be much more important than the number of applications on file at any one time. Many persons may file an application at a company's employment office as a means of gathering job information, or of satisfying the requirement of active search for work under unemployment compensation, or of putting pressure on their present employer to improve wages or working conditions. When offered employment immediately after the application is completed or somewhat later, a high proportion of the applicants may reject the bid. Consequently, job applications do not express a willingness to accept a starting or other job at a particular wage, and, therefore, do not, strictly speaking, constitute part of the supply of labor to that firm.

Managements generally have a definite conception of the type of worker they prefer to hire from among their applicants. In selecting new employees, well-established firms are prone to choose workers with a long-term approach so that the management can, with confidence, invest in their training. In their selection policies, the managements of such firms generally discriminate against "job hoppers" or restless dollar-chasers who have only short-range work interests. The same may be true of workers on lay-off from another firm to which they would be likely to return upon recall. Usually interviews with applicants are used to determine which of them are "our type of employee" or "the kind of man who will fit into our organization."[29]

Standards of selection are, of course, somewhat flexible in most companies. If the firm has to expand its workforce rapidly, especially during a period of labor stringency, it may be forced to hire applicants who, under normal conditions, would be rejected. Once such employees have worked beyond the probationary period (thirty or sixty days), they enjoy seniority and the protection of the grievance procedure and cannot be dismissed without good cause.

A reputation as a good place to work not only gives the

---

[29] See E. William Noland and E. Wight Bakke, *Workers Wanted, A Study of Employers' Hiring Policies, Preferences, and Practices in New Haven and Charlotte* (New York: Harper, 1949), pp. 7–11. See also Alexander R. Heron, *Beyond Collective Bargaining* (Stanford: Stanford University Press, 1948), Chapters 10 and 11.

management reserve drawing power but also contributes to flexibility in hiring and stability in personnel policies. In companies enjoying such a reputation, personnel officers have more leeway to pick and choose among applicants, and there are likely to be fewer pressures on management to change wages or other job attributes as minor fluctuations occur in labor demand and supply in the locality. Also, relatively good wage scales, benefits, and other employment conditions strengthen a policy of a work-life career with the firm, by reducing the stress on the pay for a particular job, especially the hiring-in job at the bottom of the occupational hierarchy.

2. TRAINING AND DEVELOPMENT.   Programs of induction, training, and economic education aim to develop a constructive attitude on the part of the employee toward his job and the company. Orienting new employees so that they know the company organization and policies helps the worker understand the significance of his task and its relation to other jobs and the company's total program.

On-the-job training is designed not only to increase the worker's proficiency on a particular job but to prepare him for promotion. Including the full costs of formal and informal methods, private industry spends perhaps five billion dollars a year for on-the-job training.[30] Such training, including the training of foremen, helps to improve employee morale. The more skilled that foremen and supervisors are in the art of managing men—in human relations, including grievance handling—the more effectively do work units function.

As already explained, in selecting new production employees, management seeks not only certain physical, skill, and intellectual qualifications but also less measurable characteristics such as motivation and social accommodation to the company's existing workforce. Training is part of the adaptive and development process, extending all the way up to executive development. For effective operations, the growth of an employee under the company's supervision may be as important as his qualities at the time of selection.

It has been pointed out that recruitment and on-the-job training costs constitute fixed investment by the firm in its labor force,

---

[30] See Jacob Mincer, "On the Job Training: Costs, Returns, and Some Implications," *Journal of Political Economy* (October 1962: Supplement), LXX, p. 62.

amortization of which drives a wedge between a worker's value productivity (marginal value product) and his wage rate, and which could account for a range of indeterminacy in wage scales.[31] Actually the fixed cost elements in employment include much more of a firm's industrial relations program than merely recruitment and training costs. Also, some of the investment costs of a firm's industrial relations program cannot be broken down and allocated separately to particular employees. And, as explained in the next chapter, the range of latitude or of indeterminacy in wage rates rests on a number of factors and not just the fixed cost involved in recruitment and on-the-job training expenditures.

3. COMPANY ATTACHMENT.   Both management and employees have an interest in developing a workforce tied to the company. For management, company attachment saves the costs of labor turnover (including training), develops company loyalty, and aids morale through reliance on in-plant promotion to fill jobs up the occupational ladder. For employees, ties to a company afford protection to their investment in employment with that firm.

A variety of management practices and negotiated arrangements help to link employees to a company. The seniority principle gears employee job rights, promotion opportunities, and vacation and other benefit rights, to length of continuous service in the plant or company. Promotion from within, coupled with seniority, discourages interfirm transfer by making every change of employer a compulsory slide to the bottom job on the least desirable shift, with no job protections during the probationary period and usually some loss of benefit rights (all loss of vacation and perhaps pension rights). Thus, company benefit programs are considered much more effective in retaining employees with the firm than in attracting new recruits.[32] Except for benefits, new plants do provide strong attractions, since jobs all up and down the line are available with groundfloor seniority.

In part, company personnel programs are designed to attach employees to the firm. Studies indicate that perhaps four-fifths of the employees in established manufacturing concerns have

---

[31] Walter Y. Oi, "Labor as a Quasi-fixed Factor," *Journal of Political Economy*, LXX (December 1962), pp. 542, 554–55.

[32] See Lester, *Hiring Practices and Labor Competition, op. cit.*, Chapter 7.

sufficient seniority, promotional gains, benefit rights, and other ties to be firmly attached to a company.[33]

In general, managements do not try to compete with each other for labor already attached to a firm. In fact, in many cities, either by informal practice or as part of a personnel association program, managements will follow a "gentlemen's agreement" or code of hiring ethics not to "pirate" labor from one another. Such a nonpirating rule of management conduct aims to avoid unnecessary turnover and training costs and to afford companies some protection against "raiding." Under the code, a management will not hire a worker employed elsewhere until it notifies his employer of his application and ascertains whether the company would be seriously inconvenienced by the loss after a two weeks' notice period. Some managements will not hire the employee of another firm if it objects to releasing him.[34]

With strong company ties, a considerable part of the community's labor is compartmentalized by individual firms. Also, employee grumbling on the job may be a more effective form of pressure for improved terms of employment than is labor mobility (the threat to quit or actual movement to another firm).

Company attachment of labor and management attitudes toward labor competition do, of course, have an effect on the supply of labor to the firm and on company wage policies. This discussion of workforce policies provides, therefore, background material for subsequent chapters on wages and company benefits. It is well to bear in mind that the focus has been on manual or production workers and not white-collar, professional, or managerial employees. Company recruiting on college campuses is, of course, quite a different process, and professional or management personnel can transfer between firms without being restricted or penalized by some of the practices discussed above.

---

[33] *Ibid.*, p. 59; and Lloyd G. Reynolds, *The Structure of Labor Markets* (New York: Harper, 1951), p. 83. Managements usually believe workers to be fairly well attached to the company after a year of employment, but the time period of attachment does, of course, vary somewhat with the circumstances.

[34] For a discussion of the operation of "anti-pirating" arrangements in a period of labor stringency in Trenton, New Jersey, see R. A. Lester, *Hiring Practices and Labor Competition, op. cit.*, pp. 62–66; and *Adjustments to Labor Shortages, op. cit.*, pp. 46–49.

Modern Personnel Management

The historical material in Chapter 5 explained the development of industrial relations activities and discussed the three philosophies that lie behind modern personnel administration, namely, scientific management, welfare capitalism, and the human relations approach. Management's philosophical attitude shifted toward humanizing employment with the changing image of the worker and with accumulating knowledge in the social sciences.

Despite widespread unionization, modern management finds a need for personnel management, not only to handle the recruitment, selection, and training of employees but also to maintain and develop a relationship with them apart from collective bargaining.

To counteract the impersonal qualities of employment in large units, modern personnel management stresses the management's interest in each employee as an individual. In doing so it seeks to separate a company's "employee relations" from its collective bargaining relationships. Collective bargaining generally centers on the common interests of employees—their demands as a group—although the grievance machinery is designed to take up the complaints of individual employees who feel aggrieved by management action that they consider to have violated the letter or spirit of the negotiated agreement.

Personnel administration uses a variety of techniques to cultivate the company's interest in the individual employee. Many of them were mentioned in Chapter 5. They include: employee counseling, employee rating plans, suggestion systems, employee savings and stock-ownership plans, and safety and recreational programs.

Important elements in an "employee relations" program are communications and benefits. The management needs to maintain and use its own channels of communication in order to keep close contact with employee views and to get management's messages or positions clearly explained to the worker and his family. In such a two-way communication program, the foreman is a key element, for he is in daily contact with the men he supervises. In addition, there are written channels such as the company magazine, special announcements, and letters from the president sent to the worker at home. Benefits include not only sick pay and hospital and medical care for the worker and his dependents but also educational support and social facilities for the employee and his children. The idea of the welfare corporation, which assumes personal and social responsibilities, is an outgrowth of modern personnel management.

Of course, unionism and collective bargaining have affected management in a variety of ways. Some of its programs have become a part of collective bargaining. That is true of most benefit programs. Indeed, under the Taft-Hartley Act, managements are legally required to bargain with the union on such matters as pension and health and welfare plans or employee bonuses and profit-sharing.

Collective bargaining has tended to cause management to centralize its policy-making in industrial relations and to curtail the authority and disciplinary powers of the foreman. Top management may consider central determination of policies and procedures necessary in order to maintain uniformity of interpretation of the labor agreement. Otherwise, the union may spread a favorable grievance settlement at one plant to other locations of a multiplant company. Under the circumstances, foremen may hesitate to make personnel decisions or to take disciplinary action without checking with higher supervision. Also, negotiations and the grievance procedure permit the union to take cases over the head of the foreman.

Centralization of industrial relations policies and decisions is, of course, in conflict with the management philosophy of trying to settle industrial relations problems at the plant level, close to the individual workers. Many managements preach decentralization yet practice company-wide uniformity, insisting that benefit plans or job evaluation should be the identical throughout all of a company's operations.[35] Because many industrial relations plans or actions can be costly, top management is reluctant to run the risk of inexpert local determination. Therefore, the industrial rela-

---

[35] See Helen Baker and Robert R. France, *Centralization and Decentralization in Industrial Relations,* Industrial Relations Section, Princeton University, Princeton, N.J., 1954.

tions staff is constantly advising line management on personnel matters, especially those that may be subject to collective bargaining.

Because a large part of industrial relations expenditures are in the nature of a long-term investment it is understandable that managements wish to exercise considerable central control over such expenditures. The lack of a clear-cut goal for industrial relations activities and the pressures exerted by unions may make central control seem all the more necessary.

SUMMARY

This chapter has attempted to explain the aims of management in employing and supervising a workforce. It provides a necessary background for the analysis in subsequent chapters such as those dealing with collective bargaining, wage theory, company benefits, management adjustments to minimum wages, and public policy with respect to manpower.

The first part of the chapter indicated the limitations of the traditional theory of the firm for employment analysis and for industrial relations practice, and it explained the elements in a multipurpose, multiadjustment theory of management. The grounds for considering such a theory to be the more appropriate one for analytical and practical purposes include:

1. The large modern firm seems to have a number of objectives, including maintenance of its market position, growth of the company, and a satisfactory and satisfied workforce.

2. In pursuing its objectives, a management must balance various pressures, including union demands and internal pressures for full use of its resources.

3. In adjusting to changes in labor cost, managements of corporations generally enjoy a range of discretion. They may avoid certain channels of adjustment for such reasons as the provisions of the labor agreement or labor legislation and the protection of the firm's past investment in its workforce or in good labor relations.

Such a theory of management makes industrial relations programs of companies much more meaningful than is possible with the traditional theory of the firm.

On the basis of that theoretical foundation, industrial relations programs were considered in terms of their objectives and the problem of determining their success. Any theoretical explanation of industrial relations activities and programs ought to include the following elements:

1. Objectives in addition to profits often underlie such programs. As they are venturesome, long-term investments in a continuing workforce, the profit pay-out of programs for employees is difficult to determine. Therefore, industrial relations programs tend to move by steps and a sequence of decisions.

2. Industrial relations activities involve planning and developing the firm's workforce. Effective accomplishment of the objectives of a program depends on coordination of its different parts.

3. In their industrial relations policies, managements seek to attach employees firmly to the company because of the high costs of labor turnover and the desire to have a loyal workforce. The various elements in an industrial relations operation are a means to that end.

Modern personnel management seeks to recognize the individuality of the employee and to indicate the management's interest in his welfare. Unions have tended to cause managements to centralize the determination of labor policy, which may lead to some conflict between their industrial relations philosophy and actual practice.

DISCUSSION QUESTIONS

1. What are the assumptions of the traditional theory of the firm? How do they square with the assumptions underlying the industrial relations programs of modern industry?
2. How do the goals of a firm's management affect its industrial relations policies and program?

3. What are the advantages and drawbacks of the multipurpose, multiadjustment theory of management set forth in the text?

4. What factors should management take into account in deciding whether to adopt a particular industrial relations activity and the amount of funds to be allocated to it? What difference does union pressure make in a management's decision on such a matter?

5. How and why would the objectives and parts of an industrial relations program of a large oil or chemical concern differ from those of a large construction company or a large marine shipping firm?

6. Explain the various means by which managements seek to reduce labor turnover and tie workers to the company? Is there a point beyond which such company attachment ceases to be socially desirable? Explain.

SELECTED READINGS

Baumol, William J., *Business Behavior, Value and Growth* (New York: Macmillan, 1959).

Clark, John Maurice, *Competition as a Dynamic Process* (Washington: Brookings Institution, 1961).

Gordon, Robert A., *Business Leadership in the Large Corporation* (Washington: Brookings Institution, 1945).

Lester, Richard A., "Economic Adjustments to Changes in Wage Differentials" in G. W. Taylor and F. C. Pierson (eds.), *New Concepts in Wage Determination* (New York: McGraw-Hill, 1957).

————, *Hiring Practices and Labor Competition*, Industrial Relations Section, Princeton University, Princeton, N.J., 1954.

McGuire, Joseph W. (ed.), *Interdisciplinary Studies in Business Behavior* (Cincinnati: South-Western Publishing Co., 1962).

Pigors, Paul, and Charles A. Myers, *Personnel Administration: A Point of View and a Method* (New York: McGraw-Hill, 1961, 4th ed.).

Strauss, George, and Leonard R. Sayles, *Personnel: The Human Problems of Management* (Englewood Cliffs, N.J.: Prentice-Hall, 1960).

8.

The Collective
Bargaining Process

MUCH HAS BEEN written about collective bargaining. However, the theory of collective bargaining is not well developed. Most of the literature consists of historical and institutional descriptions or of highly abstract bargaining theory that is non-operational and has little relation to reality.[1] The parties themselves have developed little systematic theory; they seem to consider the process largely an art. Game theory has not been applicable, because a form suitable to the complex nature of collective bargaining has not been constructed.

This chapter analyzes the significant elements in the process known as collective bargaining. Perhaps, as it has evolved in this country, the process might more appropriately be termed collective dealing, because it involves an intricate, continuing relationship and the administration and enforcement of agreements as well as their negotiation. Following a discussion of the nature of the process or relationship, the different approaches of unions and

---

[1] For a criticism that bargaining theory has been too abstract see Jan Pen, "Wage Determination Revisited," *Kyklos*, XI (No. 1, 1958), pp. 1–25.

management to collective bargaining are considered. Then some aspects of bargaining experience are examined for the light they may shed on the theory of the relationship. Finally, an analytical framework is constructed as a basis for understanding the range of settlements under union-management negotiations.

NATURE OF THE PROCESS

Any theory of collective bargaining must explain the significant features of the process as it has evolved in American industry. Since the union and management are the negotiators, bargaining theory involves some theory of union behavior and some notions about management's goals and decision-making methods.

Among the important elements in the bargaining process are the following:

1. Collective bargaining is not a discrete event or one bargain, but a continuing, legal relationship. It consists of a series of contract negotiations and of day-to-day negotiations under the grievance procedure. The negotiations are conducted by representatives of the parties, backed up by their collective power.

Upon certification of a labor organization by the National Labor Relations Board, the union and the management must deal with each other on a continuous basis. They have no alternatives to their relationship. Under the Taft-Hartley Act, the employer is required to bargain in good faith with the union about wages, hours, and working conditions and the settlement of grievances, and the union must likewise negotiate with the management as the sole bargaining agent for the employees. Even in the absence of NLRB certification, the two organizations may be equally dependent on continuing relations with each other.

Such a monogamous relationship is bound to change with experience and with different circumstances and personalities. It has a history which influences the current attitudes of the parties and may limit the alternatives open to them. In some cases it is unfortunate that the parties cannot forget their past history.

2. Collective bargaining is a process of adjustment or mutual accommodation between two institutions, in which acceptance is an important ingredient. As the two preceding chapters have

indicated, union leaders and management have different viewpoints, goals, and methods of decision-making. Management is concerned with its competitive position and adequate profits for dividends and expansion; union leadership seeks to satisfy its constituents and to be reelected to office. Both, however, have a mutual interest in developing workable compromises in order to arrive at a satisfactory agreement. Consequently, collective bargaining is a mixture of conflict and cooperation, of rivalry and mutuality, of problem-accentuation and problem-solving. The relative emphasis on conflict and problem-solving will vary with the dynamics of the relationship.

The bargainers do not represent themselves. They are spokesmen for their institutions. Generally their tentative understandings must be ratified by the union membership and by top management.

In arriving at agreement under collective bargaining, persuasion plays a significant role. With industry resting on the willing cooperation of workers, accent is on consent and voluntary acceptance. Persuasion may involve both argument and the threat of economic loss. Hence collective bargaining is a system of communication and mutual education as well as a power relationship.

3. The collective bargaining relationship has many dimensions, some economic and some governmental. Certainly, it is not just a means of price determination. In addition to the various aspects of wages and benefits, negotiations deal with the making and enforcement of all kinds of work rules and plant practices. To a significant degree, therefore, the negotiation of new contracts and of grievance settlements is part of a system of industrial government and industrial jurisprudence. Like most government, it is concerned with many incommensurables that cannot be priced in a market, ranging from seniority and the grievance procedure to the union shop and the no-strike clause.

Bargaining for a new contract may involve twenty or more proposed changes or demands. The task of the negotiators is to arrive at a combination or package of items that will be mutually acceptable, which may mean ratification by the employees. Joint acceptance may, of course, require the negotiators to compromise in various ways and to trade some items off against others. Even nuances of wording may make a difference, because of the way that the language will be interpreted by management and perhaps an arbitrator.

Not only is a negotiated settlement usually a "package deal" but it applies to the future. With many variables and uncertainties, its consequences are often highly unpredictable, especially if the agreement runs for three years or more. But with negotiations continuing under the grievance procedure as to the interpretation and application of the contract and with the union and management able to influence some of the variables (especially those affecting productivity), the risks from unpredictability may be somewhat reduced.

4. Collective bargaining involves a variety of short-run pressures and tactics, but with experience the perspective of the parties tends to lengthen. It is evident that both sides suffer some economic loss with a strike. Generally speaking, under collective bargaining one party does not necessarily gain at the expense of the other; both may profit from a constructive compromise.

Nevertheless, each side may seek to obtain an advantage in negotiations by maneuver, bluff, and threat to use its bargaining power. Bargaining power may be defined as the ability to force the other party to move toward your position, to concede in whole or in part. Organized labor may exert bargaining power without a strike through such means as a slowdown, absenteeism, filing many grievances, and grumbling and discontent on the job, all of which may affect productive performance. That management is concerned about employee opinion is indicated by its use of attitude surveys. In addition, employee opinion may affect the public image of the company and stimulate community and government pressures on the management. A strike, of course, not only may reduce profits but also, where customer continuity or attachment are important, may injure the market position of the firm over a considerable period of time.

The bargaining power of management takes other forms. Management determines employment and can threaten to curtail it, shift operations to a different location, or contract the work out to another concern. Disciplinary measures may be taken against slowdowns or absenteeism. It is well to bear in mind that management has the power of initiative; it applies the agreement. In case of a strike, the company may have longer staying powers than the union, particularly if it has a large inventory.

This brief discussion of bargaining power does not mean that collective bargaining is an endless tussle, with each side seeking the maximum concession from the other. Where employment is on a work-life basis, management wishes to avoid antagonizing its employees, and union leaders are generally interested in achieving satisfactory settlements without offending the management. In any particular dispute, both sides know that sooner or later they must reach an agreement that is mutually acceptable. Economic force is only one means of persuasion. As George W. Taylor has explained, "The factor of consent involves much more than an economic power relationship."[2] That is one of the reasons why bilateral monopoly theory cannot be appropriately applied without modification to the complex relationship of collective bargaining.

5. To a significant extent, collective bargaining is noncompetitive or anticompetitive in its methods and its effects on the employment relationship. Seniority, wage policies "to take labor out of competition," and other protections and benefits written into collective agreements are designed to block or blunt the operation of competitive forces with respect to industrial relations.

When the Federal Government adopted a policy of supporting collective bargaining by requiring that method of settling the terms and conditions of employment where a union is certified,[3] it established a partial alternative to the market. In essence the government said, whenever a union is certified as the bargaining agent, the purchase and sale of labor (wages, hours, benefits, and working conditions) can no longer be determined simply by employer decision, constrained by market forces. Those items must be settled by union-management negotiation and joint acceptance, constrained by market forces. However, one of the negotiating parties is a representative agency, with political motivations and, in part, anticompetitive viewpoints. And with a work-life, welfare concept of employment, management's policies with respect to

---

[2] "Wage Determination Processes" in G. W. Taylor and F. C. Pierson (eds.), *New Concepts in Wage Determination, op. cit.*, p. 85.

[3] For the railroads, with enactment of the Railway Labor Act of 1926, and for industry generally, with the passage of the Wagner Act in 1935.

employment have become less competitive, at least on a short-run basis. Consequently, collective bargaining has developed a process of decision-making (dispute settlement) and a "web of rules" that restrict and, to some extent, replace competitive forces.

APPROACHES TO COLLECTIVE BARGAINING

There is no standard pattern of collective bargaining. Managements and unions have their particular practices, problems, and ways of solving them. And the problems and tactics change with the circumstances. Collective bargaining is dynamic. Each union-management relationship may not proceed with regularity through a series of stages from militancy to maturity, but the relationship does alter and evolve over time.

To understand why the parties take certain positions, why they may modify their positions, and why they will endure the hardships of a lengthy strike in defense of a position, it is necessary to appreciate the basic objectives of the parties in labor relations matters. The collective bargaining approaches of business management and labor unions are bound to be somewhat different. They are, however, subject to change with experience.

Management

Despite diversity of practice, management's basic approach to collective bargaining is founded on three elements: (1) the goals of the firm, which, as explained in the preceding chapter, include some combination of survival and growth, market position, and profits; (2) the rights of management (which include freedom to take necessary action to cut costs and to maintain efficient operations), so that the management has some latitude; and (3) a satisfactory workforce, which involves both a productive body of employees and responsibility on the part of their representatives.

Industrial managements in most large firms also wish to have collective bargaining tailored to their own circumstances, including the conditions in particular plants. That is one reason many of them object to bargaining through an employer association or on an industry-wide basis. Given the importance of investment in the workforce and of employee attachment, managements in many corporations desire to preserve their own industrial relations policies and departments. By that means they maintain independence of decision and the standing of the company in industrial relations matters. Some managements wish to assert leadership, although, under collective bargaining, leadership may have the disadvantage that the union uses negotiations with that company to establish settlement patterns. Managements are also likely to have ethical views concerning fair and decent treatment of their employees. Such factors help to explain their willingness to agree to benefit payments "only vaguely related either to current or future production."[4]

The extent to which a management will make compromises that it believes encroach upon its industrial relations objectives depends upon its assessment of the union, the attitude of the employees and customers, and the firm's market position. Some companies may be particularly vulnerable to a strike. That is true not only of those that are financially weak but also of some that are financially strong. A company may have persistent compulsions to maintain production either because its industrial customers stress the importance of a dependable supply or because the firm's market position can be injured by failure to maintain continued retail sales.[5] Nevertheless, the management of such a company may reach a point beyond which it believes further compromise would seriously jeopardize its basic position and, therefore, it will take a strike rather than concede any further on an issue. Of the limits to compromise in collective bargaining negotiations, Edward L. Cushman, vice-president of American Motors, has written: "Obviously the area of compromise varies with the issue involved. On certain issues, such as management's right to operate the company efficiently, there is little ground for compromise. . . . In other areas, such as wages and employee benefits, there is more room for compromise."[6]

Although they may have the same basic position or objectives,

---

[4] Leland Hazard, "Wage Theory: A Management View," in G. W. Taylor and F. C. Pierson (eds.), *op. cit.*, p. 38.

[5] See *ibid.*, pp. 40–49; and Edward L. Cushman, "Management Objectives in Collective Bargaining," in Arnold R. Weber (ed.), *The Structure of Collective Bargaining: Problems and Perspectives* (New York: Free Press, 1961), p. 66.

[6] *Ibid.*, p. 67.

the collective bargaining policies or approaches of companies will vary. Managements have different attitudes toward unionism and the unions with which they deal. Some may wish to limit the effectiveness of the union by circumventing it as much as possible and by trying to contain its activities within a narrow, legalistic view of collective bargaining. Other managements may use the union as one of the company's channels of communication with the employees and, through consultation with the union on advance planning, encourage its participation in solving industrial relations problems.

A systematic program of challenge and containment is that followed by the General Electric Company in the fifties and early sixties. Called "Boulwarism" after Lemuel R. Boulware, a former vice-president, it involves vigorous competition with the union for the loyalty of the employees and the practical elimination of old-fashioned bargaining so that the union can claim little, if any, credit in the way of winning concessions. By means of a long-range program of communications to the employees, the management presents its views in advance of negotiations in order to "correct" union assertions and shake employee confidence in "extreme" union claims. At the time of negotiations, the company counters the union's demands with a single package proposal, based on a careful study of employee needs and attitudes. The proposal embodies the full amount that the management believes is justified, and the management insists that it will adhere to its package offer unless it can be convinced that the proposal is not supported by the facts. This one-offer approach precludes the conventional pattern of bargaining and concession, under the pressure of a strike deadline set by the union. The union can choose to strike, but the company warns that it will put into effect its proposal and adhere to it. Thus, the "Boulware" approach deprives the union of the opportunity to maneuver and to claim responsibility for improvements in wages and working conditions.[7]

At the other extreme are managements that have leaned over

---

[7] For a further discussion of the Boulware approach see Monroe Berkowitz and Allan Weisenfeld, "A New Look in Collective Bargaining," *Labor Law Journal*, VI (August 1955), pp. 561–66; the exchange between Philip D. Moore and George Strauss under "Criticism and Comment" in *Industrial Relations*, II (October 1962), pp. 101–103; and Herbert R. Northrup, "The Case for Boulwarism," *Harvard Business Review*, XLI (September–October 1963), pp. 86–97.

backward in an effort to appease the union. Under such a policy, managements often grant unreasonable demands that the union leadership had to submit for political reasons. The result is likely to be an accumulation of inefficiencies and excessive costs that will culminate in a crisis, a change in management policy, and a basic revision of the agreement, usually accompanied by a severe strike.

Union

The policies and practices of unions were considered in Chapter 6. It was pointed out that unions pursue no single principle or purpose, and that there are both institutional goals and membership goals.

In their approach to collective bargaining, union leaders generally hold certain basic beliefs. Three key elements in union bargaining philosophy are: (1) a strong faith in collective bargaining as a method of decision-making, (2) a belief that the union and collective bargaining are necessary in order to protect and promote the interests of the membership, and (3) a desire to enhance the security and strength of the union as a collective bargaining institution.

The business of unions is representation. Collective bargaining is their chief function. Therefore, it is natural for their leaders to seek to gain a strong bargaining position for the union and to include as much as possible within the scope of collective bargaining. In trying to expand the subjects covered by collective bargaining, unions exert pressures for change, for innovations in the terms of employment and in the treatment of employees.

Faith in collective bargaining carries with it the conviction that the results of the process will be more satisfactory and acceptable to workers and the public than either unilateral management determination or reliance on market forces. Such a conclusion may be difficult for some managements to accept, especially those that consider themselves stewards of employee welfare and, therefore, question the need for any "interference by an outside agency." But faith in bargaining has a wider perspective than the individual firm. It focusses on the occupation (in the case of a craft union), the industry, and the whole economy. An important aim of most unions is to spread collective bargaining to the whole area of competitive production or work in order "to take labor out of competition." One of the strongest reasons for central determination of bargaining policy in unions is to prevent a local union from undercutting national standards.[8]

The belief in collective bargaining as a vehicle for protecting and promoting the interest of the membership has both economic and governmental aspects. On the economic side, union philosophy stresses not only individual living standards but also the national need for increased purchasing power and consumer spending by workers in order to provide adequate demand for the products of industry. On the governmental side, there is a strongly held view in union circles that a collective bargaining agreement is required to force foremen and supervisors to treat workers with respect. In the absence of a union and collective bargaining, it is assumed that manual workers would be subject to arbitrary discipline, unreasonable demands, and other oppressive actions by the management.[9]

The desire to strengthen the union as a bargaining agency leads to stress on investment in the union as an institution. So that the union will command the respect of management, strike funds are accumulated, impressive union buildings are constructed, and the union disciplines members who violate the collective agreement. Also to increase the security and strength of the organization, industrial union leaders generally favor company-wide and multicompany bargaining over plant-by-plant bargaining.[10]

This general system of beliefs lies behind the bargaining approach of most unions. However, the bargaining policies and tactics of individual unions will vary, largely depending on the conditions and problems that they face. Some craft unions, for example, are less interested than industrial unions in negotiating lengthy agreements containing detailed provisions that regulate or restrict management, such as seniority, on-the-job rules, and grievance procedures. That is because craft unions, such as the

---

[8] See Robert R. France, *Union Decisions in Collective Bargaining*, Industrial Relations Section, Princeton University, Princeton, N.J., 1955, p. 47.

[9] See Joel Seidman, *et al.*, *The Worker Views His Union* (Chicago: University of Chicago Press, 1958), pp. 80, 82, 89, 104 and 120.

[10] France, *op. cit.*, pp. 10–16. As explained in Chapter 14, there are some notable exceptions.

building trades, exercise their influence and control in other ways. Because their members generally are not firmly attached to one employer and are not closely supervised at work, building unions are not so concerned about on-the-job rights and disciplinary actions.

To satisfy the membership that the union achieved all that was possible in a particular negotiation, it may be necessary for the leadership to assume a militant pose, press unreasonable demands, and otherwise seek to impress the constituents with its aggressiveness in their behalf. In the meantime, a tentative understanding may have been reached in a private meeting, so that continued negotiations are stage-playing for the effect on the membership. Short-circuiting collective bargaining by a secret deal, however, aborts the process of sincere search for acceptable solutions by two parties with differing outlooks and constraints.

An extreme form of short-circuiting is the case where union leaders deprive employers of an opportunity to participate in the bargaining process. In some instances a local Teamsters union, for example, has placed a prepared document before a small employer and demanded that he sign it forthwith or suffer some suggested consequences. Such a practice is in violation of the Taft-Hartley Act's requirement of "good faith" bargaining but a small employer may not care to contest the matter.

As this discussion has indicated, management and union leaders approach collective bargaining with differing objectives and different systems of belief. And within both management and organized labor, significant variations exist with respect to both purposes and tactics in collective bargaining. Nevertheless, as the parties gain experience, they come to understand and make allowances for the necessary differences in their respective positions.

BARGAINING EXPERIENCE

The process of collective bargaining is adaptable to the circumstances. Partly because of differing circumstances, experience with the process varies widely from firm to firm and industry to industry. For example, marked contrasts exist in collective bargaining in steel, autos, soft coal, railroads, the airlines, building, textiles, and men's and women's clothing, all of which have had a fairly long experience with negotiating and administering agreements.

Patterns and Trends

Widely divergent industrial conditions and experience result in notably different patterns of collective bargaining. In autos and the airlines, bargaining is on a company-by-company basis. In building construction and women's clothing, negotiations have been with employers' associations, mostly city by city. In coal the multiemployer bargaining has been on a regional basis, whereas in railroads, steel, and men's clothing the key negotiations have been nationwide. The textile industry has had both multiemployer regional bargaining and single company negotiations. The contrast is not only in employer and geographic coverage but also in occupational inclusion. In building, railroads, and the airlines the bargaining is craft by craft, or by groups of crafts in some railroad negotiations. On the other hand, in coal, clothing, textiles, steel, and autos, a single negotiation covers all mine or plant workers.

Once bargaining has been established on a particular (employer, occupation, and geographic) basis, the participation coverage is not likely to change. Since World War II there has been a slight tendency for multiemployer bargaining to expand relatively, but steel is the only new case that comes to mind of a shift to multiple-employer bargaining on a national level during the past two decades.

The subject matter of bargaining is influenced by the type of problems confronting the parties and the need for the union to help stabilize the industry. In coal and men's and women's clothing, the union has served to help regulate competition and perform functions that normally are management activities. Declining employment in the auto and steel industries caused the unions to demand guaranteed employment and led to the negotiation of joint programs of supplemental unemployment benefits. Declining employment on the flight deck with the widespread use of jet airplanes has resulted in a jurisdictional contest between the Air Line Pilots and the Flight Engineers, with the companies finding it difficult to settle the crew complement problem through collective bargaining. A sticky problem for collective bargaining on the railroads has been "work rules" in train operations, under which railroad managements have sought to reduce the size of crews, claiming that firemen are unnecessary in yard and freight operations.

The pattern of wage increases and other gains has been quite different in the soft-goods industries from that in hard goods. Men's and women's clothing and textiles have had periods of two and three years without a wage increase while autos, steel, electrical equipment, and other mass-production lines were experiencing an increase every year. Collective bargaining in soft-goods, and especially in cotton textiles, is influenced by the competition of nonunion firms and also by foreign competition.

Particularly in mass-production industries the pattern of yearly negotiations has since 1950 given way to longer-term agreements running two, three and (at times) five years. The five-year contract negotiated in May 1950 between General Motors and the United Automobile Workers stimulated longer-term agreements. The Bureau of Labor Statistics found that in 1951 about 70 per cent of the 1,000-odd major agreements examined had a duration of one year whereas by 1956 around 65 per cent of them ran for two years or more.[11] A sample of 400 agreements in mid-1960 revealed that 82 per cent had a term of two or three years.[12] With collective bargaining involving all aspects of an agreement including benefits, many managements and unions have found the negotiation of a new contract too complex and too upsetting to engage in the task as frequently as every year.

The emphasis given to major negotiations tends to conceal the fact that there are over 125,000 separate collective bargaining relationships and the same number of agreements. Less than 2,000 of the agreements cover 1,000 or more workers, but these large agreements account for half of all workers under collective contracts.

The size of a single negotiation affects not only the amount

---

[11] "Characteristics of Major Union Contracts," *Monthly Labor Review*, LXXIX (July 1956), p. 810.

[12] *Daily Labor Report*, No. 140 (July 20, 1960), p. B-1.

of publicity it receives but also the professional or amateur character of the proceedings. With an increase in the size of particular negotiations, the amount of central influence and control has tended to expand both for the union and the management.

As the parties have gained increased experience with collective bargaining it has, in some instances, almost become a method of joint formulation of labor policies and joint administration and enforcement of those policies. As workable compromises are hammered out and each side's security no longer seems threatened, the parties tend to take a longer view of their collective bargaining relationship. Long-term agreements are one result of a change in perspective. Another result is the changed nature of strikes in firms and industries with considerable experience with collective bargaining. Generally, strikes are much more orderly and less militant than they were before World War II. In some cases they seem almost to be friendly differences, with the management supplying coffee and doughnuts for the pickets.

Some Comparisons

Experience with collective bargaining in four industries is briefly explained and compared in this section. Such comparisons emphasize the diversity that characterizes collective bargaining in particular industries. Much of the diversity springs from differences in the economic, technological, and environmental problems that the parties have faced. But, in addition, each union-management relationship has its particular history, its particular atmosphere, and its particular leadership.[13]

The first comparison of bargaining experience is between the basic steel industry and the automobile assembly industry. In a number of respects the difference of experience between the two industries has been surprising.

In terms of strikes the contrast has been particularly sharp. From 1945 to 1960 there were ten negotiations in steel in which

---

[13] The elements of individuality in each collective bargaining situation are emphasized in Sumner H. Slichter, James J. Healy, and E. Robert Livernash, *The Impact of Collective Bargaining on Management* (Washington: Brookings Institution, 1960), pp. 954–57.

the Steelworkers had the right to strike. In connection with five of the negotiations, major strikes occurred: 1946 (a 26 days' strike), 1949 (45 days), 1952 (59 days), 1956 (36 days), and 1959 (116 days). During the same fifteen years, the Automobile Workers had eight general negotiations with General Motors, Ford, and Chrysler, in which disagreement over new terms could have resulted in a strike. The only major automobile strikes were the General Motors stoppage in 1946 lasting 113 days and a 100-day strike at Chrysler in 1950. Thereafter, new agreements were negotiated with no more than a day of company-wide work stoppage at Chrysler in 1955 and at General Motors in 1958, and with some strikes at local plants of General Motors, Ford, and Chrysler, especially in 1953 and 1958.

Two major steel strikes occurred over issues "of principle" that bargaining in the auto industry had settled a year or two earlier without a strike, yet the auto industry has been steel's largest customer. The principal issue in the 1949 steel strike was the companies' insistence on employee contributions to pensions, which the auto companies had conceded to the Automobile Workers a year before. In 1952 the chief point of basic conflict was the union shop, which General Motors had granted to the UAW two years earlier. In steel, the Federal Government intervened directly in four of the major disputes (Presidential fact-finding boards in 1946 and 1949, the Wage Stabilization Board in 1952, and a Board of Inquiry under the Taft-Hartley Act in 1959), and cabinet members worked behind the scenes during the 1956 strike as well as in 1959. Only in 1946, when a fact-finding board was appointed in the General Motors' strike, did the Federal Government intervene directly in negotiations in autos.

Steel and autos also differ in the pattern of negotiations, although both are industrial unions dealing with large firms. Until 1956, steel negotiations were on a company-by-company basis, but the companies were closely coordinated in their positions and policies through the American Iron and Steel Institute. In the year 1956, a committee of four persons was authorized to bargain on major issues for the twelve major companies. By the 1959 negotiations, the four-man committee had power to negotiate a complete agreement, and it was clear that the companies favored a form of industry-wide bargaining. This seems to have been the industry's response to the union's industry-wide strike strategy that frequently brought about Government intervention.[14]

In autos, on the other hand, separate company bargaining has continued under skillful company and union leadership. Since World War II, the UAW and General Motors have been unalterably opposed to industry-wide bargaining. Auto manufacturers have been vigorous rivals, but in 1958 the three large firms did present and support identical proposals. However, the union has successfully used a divide and conquer strategy, threatening to strike one at a time. Unlike steel companies which sell a standard product to other employers, auto concerns and their dealers compete with one another in new models, carry the product all the way to the ultimate consumer, and service it as the consumer uses it. A firm's dealers put great pressure on it to avoid a strike, which would not only reduce car sales but the dealers' prospects for car servicing business far into the future. Also, there is little need for government intervention in an auto strike since it is a durable consumer product, new purchases of which can be postponed for a considerable period of time with little inconvenience to the public or serious damage to other parts of the economy.

In the automobile industry, individualism and a propensity to pioneer on the part of both management and the union have resulted in a number of pathbreaking settlements, as the union has stimulated different auto firms to take the lead. Among the pioneering settlements are: the long-term agreement with an escalator and annual improvement factor (General Motors, 1948 and 1950), pensions and supplemental unemployment compensation (Ford, 1949 and 1955), and profit-sharing as a means of meeting increased benefit costs (American Motors, 1961). In contrast to steel where in some years little bargaining has taken place before government intervention, serious bargaining and most settlements have occurred in autos prior to the expirations of agreements or a strike deadline. Auto bargaining has not been restrained by the anticipation of government intervention.

In steel the most troublesome bargaining issues in addition to contributory pensions and the union shop have been wage-price

---

[14] See *Collective Bargaining in the Basic Steel Industry: A Study of the Public Interest and the Role of Government*, U.S. Department of Labor (Washington: United States Government Printing Office, January 1961), pp. 89–90.

inflation and work rules, especially the size of work crews. The marked rise in steel prices from 1953 to 1959, the relatively large increases in wages in steel (where average hourly earnings rose from five cents below autos in 1952 to 38 cents above in 1959[15]), and government pressures against steel price rises, led steel management to charge the union and collective bargaining with responsibility for steel price increases. The union, citing its productivity figures and pressing the consumer purchasing power explanation for economic slack, argued that the industry's price policy was at fault. Basic conflicts in economic analysis resulted in extended argument in the press. Although similar differences in economic philosophy existed in autos, the above-average increases in productivity and the relatively smaller wage increases in that industry were sufficient to permit the auto companies to hold down their price increases to not much more than half the percentage rise in steel from 1950 to 1960. And, although a shrinking workforce raised problems for collective bargaining in both industries, work rules or manning issues never became the source of conflict in autos that they were in the 1959 steel negotiations.

In steel in the midfifties, the top leadership of the union was rather insecure. Not only did Steelworker's President David McDonald have to worry about the support of his district leaders, but, following widespread criticism of the leadership in the union's 1956 convention, a local leader of no prominence ran against McDonald for the union's presidency and received one-third of the vote. By contrast, Walter Reuther, president of the UAW, enjoyed wide and firm support in the union hierarchy and in the membership; therefore, the UAW's leadership could be more flexible in its negotiations and somewhat less insistent on the exact size of a wage gain in any one negotiation.

In the settlement of the prolonged 1959 steel strike, provision was made for a standing joint Human Relations Research Committee. In recognition of the fact that many collective bargaining issues have become so complex and technical as to require extended analysis, the committee is charged with the duty to plan and oversee studies and recommend solutions to problems in such areas as job classification, wage incentives, medical care, seniority,

---

[15] On a wages-only basis, the steel settlement in 1955 was about double the size of the automobile settlement.

and protection of long-service employees. The committee appears
to have aided in the achievement of a negotiated settlement in
1962 three months in advance of the contract's expiration date,
and to have paved the way for the "extended vacation," no-wage-
increase settlement in June 1963, which occurred after five and a
half months of discussion in the committee without any hint of a
strike threat.[16] That achievement represented a dramatic change in
bargaining relationships in steel.

In mid-1963, joint study committees were also established by
the big three auto firms and the UAW. They were set up to investigate and report on common problems in anticipation of negotiation in 1964. Thus, collective bargaining in both steel and autos
seems to have reached a point where crisis bargaining against a
strike deadline has given way to year-around analysis and negotiation, with joint study and, hopefully, joint recommendations
prior to, and as aid to, negotiations for a new contract.

Collective bargaining in the other two industries to be compared—soft coal and the railroads—has also tended to move from
crisis bargaining to serious investigation of long-range problems
of the industry in advance of negotiations.

Until 1950, collective bargaining in soft coal was characterized by a series of nationwide strikes that helped to bring about
the Taft-Hartley Act. Between January 1943 and June 1949, the
coal industry experienced eleven strikes, representing a combined
total of some two hundred days of idleness, and on four separate
occasions the Federal Government seized the mines, itself negotiating two labor agreements with the union during periods of
seizure. Boards of Inquiry under the Taft-Hartley Act were appointed in connection with a six-week coal strike in 1947 and a
series of strikes in 1949–50.

The four years of industrial warfare that culminated in 1950
caused the coal industry to lose business to competing fuels and
stimulated the management and union leaders to seek a new

---

[16] Under this program the upper half of each company's seniority list will
be eligible for a special thirteen-week vacation (including that year's regular
vacation) once every five years. This form of employee gain was negotiated
rather than a wage increase in order to spread available work and thus expand
the new job opportunities by an estimated 10,000 to 20,000 to meet vacationers'
absences. The annual cost is estimated at about nine cents per hour over the
twenty-one months that the revised contract will run—to May 1, 1965.

approach with accent on dependability of delivery to the large coal-using utilities. A Bituminous Coal Operators' Association was established in 1950, aimed at working with the union to solve mutual problems in a businesslike way and to avoid strikes and government intervention.[17]

Beginning with the 1951 modification of the basic National Wage Agreement of 1950, instead of a definite termination date, the contract has been open-ended, terminable on sixty days' notice. This permits relaxed consideration and negotiation, without the threat of a strike deadline. In 1955, 1957, and 1958, amendments to the agreement were negotiated without the union even serving advance notice of a desire to reopen the contract.

The union has joined with the operators in promoting markets for coal and in lobbying against rival fuels, such as imports of low-cost residual oil from Latin America. Coal prices averaged $4.61 a ton in 1961 compared with $4.88 a decade earlier, and a postwar peak of $5.08 in 1957. Hourly earnings in coal averaged $3.14 in 1961, up 55 per cent from 1950, an increase slightly less than the average rise for all production workers in manufacturing for that period. Labor costs were kept down because between 1950 and 1960 the output per man in coal doubled to fourteen tons a day. Mechanization of the mines, which John L. Lewis as union president strongly supported to assure competitive survival of the industry, has meant that employment in coal mining in this country dropped from some 500,000 right after World War II to less than a third of that number in 1962.

It was Lewis' autocratic domination of the union that enabled the industry to automate without strong worker resistance.[18] Since 1950 the negotiations for new terms have been carried on for the union and the association in secret between the presidents of both organizations. The union's membership becomes aware that negotiations have been taking place only when the settlement is announced. The new technique of two-man "rational" bargaining was praised by President Lewis at the union's 1956 convention

---

[17] See "The New Look in Industry—UMWA Relations: Fox of BCOA Reports on Bargaining in Coal," *United Mine Workers Journal*, LXVIII (February 15, 1957), pp. 10–12.

[18] See A. H. Raskin, "John L. Lewis and the Mine Workers," *Atlantic Monthly*, CCXI (May 1963), pp. 53–58.

as auguring well for the future "providing the leaders of the industry on both sides continue to exercise that discretion and judgment which they have now exhibited that they possess."[19] During the five-year period from 1958 to 1963 the union's leadership did not reopen the agreement for any wage changes; a big problem had become the volume of coal mined nonunion (over a quarter of the total) in order to avoid the union wage scale and the royalty of forty cents a ton for the union's welfare and retirement fund operations. The growing need relative to fund income forced a reduction in pension payments from $100 to $75 a month, tighter eligibility rules for medical and hospital care, and the closing of some of the union's ten hospitals.

Although collective bargaining in the railroad industry has not had to contend with nonunion competition, it has been faced with a reduction in employment nearly as drastic as in coal. The decline was from an average of 1,439,000 employees in 1945, to 1,071,000 in 1955, to 793,000 in 1960. As in coal mining, much of the work is peculiar to the industry. But, in contrast to a single union in coal, there are some twenty-one standard (craft) unions in railroading, plus thirty-odd other unions.[20] Also, by way of contrast, prices (freight rates and passenger rates) are regulated by the Federal Government, which has provided special railroad labor legislation and social insurance programs for the industry. The Railway Labor Act of 1926, which the parties themselves developed, specifically places a "duty" on both sides "to exert every reasonable effort to make and maintain agreements," and establishes for serious disputes an emergency board procedure that provides for Presidentially appointed fact-finding boards, which make recommendations for settlement. By 1963, a total of 154 such emergency boards had been appointed (an average of over four a year), and beginning in 1941 the unions had developed a practice of rejecting emergency board recommendations and gaining more by various pressures and tactics. In 1946, 1948, and 1950 the Federal Government seized the railroads to head off a

---

[19] *Proceedings of the Forty-second Consecutive Constitutional Convention of the United Mine Workers of America*, 1956, Vol. 1, p. 309.

[20] By way of comparison, there is one railroad union in Sweden and three in England (a general railroad union and separate ones for locomotive engineers and for clerks).

strike—a two-day nationwide railroad strike did nevertheless occur following seizure in 1946. Prior to 1951 the collective agreements on the railroads had no terminal dates, but thereafter they have had fixed terms.

Since 1931, the railroads have negotiated with the fifty-odd unions singly or in combination—usually most of the nonoperating unions negotiate together. Collective bargaining for the running trade unions (Engineers, Firemen, Conductors, Trainmen, and Switchmen) has been complicated by the existence of elaborate work rules that have a marked influence on earnings. Such rules stem in large part from a wage incentive system that was generally established before the outbreak of World War I, with mileage standards of pay based on the speed of trains at that time and not revised for half a century.[21] The result has been a wage structure with all sorts of inequities, and demand by both the carriers and the unions for rule changes.[22] Dealing with so many different unions, the railroads have sought to avoid whipsawing by making all wage increases uniform in cents per hour (especially from 1937 to 1959) and providing equal or equivalent treatment in fringe benefits. The result was a marked compression in the wage structure.[23]

Because the emergency-board procedure had proved incapable of achieving a basic overhaul of the pay structure and work rules, the carriers and the five operating unions finally agreed to an extraordinary procedure—the appointment of a fifteen-man Presidential Commission, composed of an equal number of union, carrier, and public representatives, to make a report and recommendations on the issues in dispute with respect to manning, employee assignments, and compensation. Railroad management had claimed that rules required inflated and unnecessary employment (popularly referred to as "featherbedding"), to the extent of a needless

---

[21] The complicated methods of compensation of railroad operating employees are fully explained in Part IV of *Report of the Presidential Railroad Commission,* February 1962.

[22] In 1945–46, the emergency board had before it in addition to the unions' wage demands, 44 union proposals for rules changes and 29 carrier proposals for changes in working rules.

[23] In December 1959, for example, office boys and messengers averaged $2.20 an hour, compared with $2.61 for gang or section foremen and $2.79 for machinists.

yearly expense of $600,000,000. After thirteen months during which some 35,625 pages of testimony and exhibits were accumulated, the Commission issued its report with dissents by union representatives in February 1963. Although objecting to certain recommendations, the carriers accepted the report in its entirety. By rejecting the Commission's recommendations which labor claimed would eliminate 20,000 firemen's jobs in a year, the unions forced the appointment of an emergency board. That board's recommendations stressed procedures for arriving at a negotiated settlement. A month after the emergency board's recommendations had been issued, the Secretary of Labor stated that until then there had been "no real bargaining" in this work rule dispute, which had extended over a four-year period.

In order to avoid a nationwide strike on August 29, 1963, Congress passed legislation providing for "temporary" compulsory arbitration of two of the issues in dispute (elimination of firemen's jobs and the size of train crews). Under the law, the decision of the 7-man arbitration board was to take effect on January 25, 1964 and remain in force for two years unless revised by a negotiated agreement. The two labor members of the board dissented from its award, and the unions contested in the Federal courts both the law and the decision. Meanwhile, collective bargaining in the railroad industry remained completely ineffective. Negotiations on other issues in the Presidential Commission's report (e.g., revision of the wage structure, lengthening train runs, and combination of road and yard work) were deadlocked, and those issues promise to be before the Congress under another threat of a nationwide railroad strike in the spring of 1964.

The combination of entrenched practices, numerous competing craft unions, the likelihood of government intervention, and sharply declining employment has tended to prevent effective operation of collective bargaining on the railroads. The Firemen's union could hardly be expected voluntarily to agree to the elimination of firemen from trains in yard and freight service, even though their services as firemen may not really be required; any such action would shrink the union to one-seventh of its size in 1963. And it is difficult for the Locomotive Engineers' union to accept a revision of the wage structure that would sharply reduce the earnings of senior passenger engineers on "red apple" runs, on which they can earn three days' pay for six hours' work. That would be true even though the revised wage structure would result in slightly higher earnings for locomotive engineers as a group, because the high-seniority engineers tend to exert disproportionate influence in the union.

Comparing collective bargaining in coal and railroads over the past decade, it is evident that the experience in those two declining industries has differed significantly. The single (industrial) union in coal was dominated by one man who assumed full power of negotiation. He was not hampered by the existence of rival unions and factions as in the railroads, nor was the bargaining in coal obstructed by elaborate work rules and narrow seniority districts. Unless it could eliminate threats of work stoppage, the coal industry was confronted with loss of its utility and other markets. Collective bargaining in the railroad industry, on the other hand, has had a different set of hurdles. Not only could it not avoid government intervention under the provisions of the Railway Labor Act, but it seemed unable to solve the problems of manning and pay structure that had been getting worse and worse in the forties, fifties, and early sixties.

This comparison of collective bargaining in four industries indicates the different ways that each industry sought to meet the problem of job insecurity arising from technological change and shifts in consumer demand. In coal, the union and management joined in promoting the product, in improving efficiency, and in efforts to avoid work stoppages. In steel, bargaining led to arrangements for supplemental unemployment benefits and a long strike involving work rules, followed by efforts to avoid crisis bargaining and the negotiation of extended vacations to help spread work. In autos, the bargaining has not restricted mechanization or led to overmanning but has resulted in a program of supplemental unemployment compensation and demands for a more flexible work week. In railroads, as we have just observed, collective bargaining, aided by study and recommendations of a Presidential Commission, was unable to remedy most of the problem of excess manning and inequitable pay structures.

Clearly in all four relationships, efforts are being made to study and discuss problems and their solution in advance of formal negotiations. Continuing machinery for that purpose has been established in steel and autos. In coal and steel the parties have sought to avoid government intervention and crisis bargaining against a strike deadline.

RANGE OF ACCEPTABILITY

The introductory discussion of the nature of collective bargaining explained that it was a mixture of a number of elements. Not only is it a continuing relationship between two institutions with conflicting viewpoints, which resort to various pressures and tactics in support of their views, but it involves the compulsion to work out mutually acceptable compromises which, in the case of a new contract, means an acceptable "package" settlement.

Because the relationship has many dimensions, a variety of different combinations of money and noneconomic items may result in acceptable terms for a new contract. In the case of grievance negotiation, sometimes the personal considerations or questions of authority outweigh any money cost involved in a settlement. Therefore, in examining the economic limits within which negotiated settlements take place, it is necessary to bear in mind that the collective bargaining relationship is a continuing one which includes grievance handling as well as new contract negotiations.

Latitude and Limits

The analysis in this section rests on the theory of union behavior in Chapter 6 and the theory of management in Chapter 7. Chapter 6 contained a discussion of the economic and political constraints on union leaders and the latitude that they may have for maneuver and for developing acceptable settlements. It was pointed out that increasing centralization of control in the hands of an entrenched leadership in many national unions reduces the political constraints upon such leaders' decisions. The economic constraints on the union largely operate through the company, but the union leadership may be able to modify such constraints by its influence on management efficiency and on workers' attitudes and productivity.

As explained in Chapter 7, the latitude of management in

policy-making and in adjustment to economic pressures is influenced by various factors, both market and extramarket. The leeway of corporate management undoubtedly is greater to the extent that the company has multiple goals, multiple channels of adjustment, and a long perspective on the workforce, including a company-welfare concept of employment. Management's latitude is constricted not only by market forces but also by extramarket pressures from within the firm and from stockholders, suppliers, unions, dealers, and customers. Creative management seeks to maintain a significant margin of discretion for itself by such means as skill in product design, marketing, cost-cutting efficiencies, and industrial relations.

Within such a framework of limits and latitude, union and management leaders try to develop acceptable settlements. In negotiating an agreement, the leaders on each side have their special problems and pressures.

The concerns of union leadership are likely to be mainly political. In collective bargaining negotiations, union officials worry about (1) acceptance by the membership, (2) any threat of rival leadership, (3) the prestige of the leaders and the union in the labor movement and the community, and (4) the reaction of the management. Union leaders have to think in terms of achieving an agreement that will be acceptable to the membership, particularly to the "active" elements in the local union. The "actives" are the source of potential opposition and rival leadership. The support of most of them is necessary for rank-and-file ratification and for effective enforcement of the agreement until its expiration. For prestige purposes, comparison of negotiated settlements must be largely in terms of wages, benefits, and union security. Most of the governmental items like seniority, shop rules, and the grievance procedure are tailored to local conditions and are difficult to rate in relative terms. Management's reaction is of concern to union leaders because employer hostility can create difficulties in grievance negotiations and future contract negotiations, and also may influence the amount of employment provided in the plant. In cases of differences of opinion in the management, union leadership may seek, through negotiations, to aid the favored elements in the management hierarchy.

In their analysis of union behavior in collective bargaining Nathaniel Goldfinger and Everett Kassalow of the AFL-CIO point out that institutional and leadership factors modify and "often overshadow" economic forces. They write: "The union possesses considerable discretionary powers in collective bargaining. The framework within which bargaining takes place is usually far from rigid; it contains potentialities as well as limitations. Alternative choices among monetary and nonmonetary issues must be made in bargaining demands. Likewise, alternatives must be selected in the final decisions."[24]

The management negotiators have a different set of concerns. In bargaining, they must bear in mind (1) the approval of top management, (2) the reaction of line management in the plant, (3) the opinion of other employers and the public, (4) the basic interests of the employees as management sees them, and (5) support for the elements in the union that management favors. Top management wants to avoid costly competitive handicaps or undue restrictions on management initiative (sometimes referred to as the preservation of management prerogatives). Much of line management's concern is with plant rules, the effectiveness of discipline, and the practicability of agreement provisions. In union-management negotiations and settlements, management wishes to enjoy the good opinion of other managements and the public. In view of a company's investment in the workforce, its management obviously desires to be certain that the money expenditures required by a negotiated settlement are used in the best long-run interest of the employees. Finally, management favors the responsible elements in the union and its leadership, partly because management needs the support of the union in enforcement of the agreement.

In negotiations the parties may use various tactics to exert pressure or otherwise persuade the opposite side to compromise or concede. As the preceding section indicated, the nature of negotiations varies considerably from industry to industry, depending on past practice, internal politics within the union and the management, and economic circumstances. Each side may seek to

---

[24] Nathaniel Goldfinger and Everett Kassalow, "Trade Union Behavior in Wage Bargaining," in G. W. Taylor and F. C. Pierson (eds.), *New Concepts in Wage Determination, op. cit.*, p. 51.

impress the other with the firmness of its position and the support for it. In part, negotiations and informal conversations in connection therewith, are for the purpose of discovering the real facts behind the formal demands and contentions—the relative priorities and support for different demands.

The consequence of nonagreement is usually a strike.[25] In well-established union-management relationships, strikes result not so much from miscalculation[26] as from inability to work out an acceptable set of compromises. Sometimes the negotiators' hands are tied by rigid positions of the parties. Sometimes one side concludes that a work stoppage is necessary for it to command respect or to "teach a lesson."

Usually there is not just one and only one combination that will lead to a settlement. A part of skill in negotiations is to explore the range of acceptability in terms of different "package" solutions that might be approved. That involves taking account of the needs and fears of the other side, stressing elements of possible mutual gain, and trying to minimize the loss or expense to the other side. Creative bargaining may thus serve to expand the area within which mutually acceptable terms can be negotiated. As experience accumulates and the relationship stabilizes, greater stress tends to be placed on mutual exploration of complex issues and less on forced gains by threats in a crisis situation.

In analyzing collective bargaining, focus on a single negotiation runs the risk of excessive concentration on current incidentals. The result may be loss of perspective, disregard of the elements of investment to enhance respect, and neglect of threads of continuity in a long-range relationship. Each negotiation of a new contract is, in a sense, part of a sequence.

Probably it is true that over the long run economic constraints are more limiting than they may appear to the observer of the details—the give and take—in any one negotiation. A union or a management may gain from the particular circumstances, includ-

---

[25] The alternatives are arbitration or continuation of operations during disagreement.

[26] For a theory of industrial disputes based on miscalculation see J. R. Hicks, *The Theory of Wages* (London: Macmillan, 1935), Chapter 7 on "The Theory of Industrial Disputes," pp. 136–58.

ing economic conditions, at the time of a negotiation, or the management may have made a generous settlement for some reason at that time. However, over time the forces of comparison and competition are likely to prevent intercompany differences from growing.

Function of the Strike

Basically, a strike puts economic pressure on both sides to reach a settlement, to search for a mutually acceptable "package." As the strike deadline approaches, the pressures for compromise increase. The burden of loss from a strike, of course, may be much greater for one of the parties than for the other, and may vary over the course of a strike.

The range of acceptable compromises may expand as the strike deadline nears, since both sides may wish to avoid strike losses. Work stoppages are generally unpredictable in length and cost. Therefore, the parties' limits to compromise may stretch somewhat when the alternative clearly is a strike whose course is most uncertain.

A long strike may reduce the intransigence of the parties, but also it may serve to restrict the latitude of management and the union leadership. With reduced profits or a sizable loss to recover, management may have less freedom to indulge in liberal industrial relations policies. Also, union leaders may feel less secure and be more governed by membership opinion, because the hardship of the strike has resulted in criticism of the leadership, and the strike has tended to develop rival leaders.

Many strikes do not seem to make sense from an economic standpoint. The workers' monetary losses during the strike may be much greater than any additional monetary gain as a result of strike action. A work stoppage encouraged by management may result in large losses for the company without offsetting gains. That, for example, was the case with the Republic Steel Corporation, which in 1937 refused to sign an agreement with the Steelworkers (CIO) involving no increase in wages, as had U.S. Steel and fifty other companies employing half the workers in the industry. The strike, which the Chairman of Republic's Board characterized as "a tremendous waste of everything," cost the stockholders of Republic Steel about four million dollars in direct expenses plus millions of dollars of lost business.[27]

Although the parties usually support their positions in strikes by economic arguments, their main motivation in calling or accepting a strike may lie elsewhere. Unions may strike to solidify or sober their membership, or to try to teach management to respect the union. As explained in the discussion of union behavior in Chapter 6, labor organizations seek security and growth as institutions. The strike losses of members may be considered as an investment in the union itself, or as an investment in better day-to-day treatment of workers by a chastened management. The return on such an investment cannot be translated into money terms and is not confined to the life of the contract to be negotiated.

In the face of a strike threat, corporate management may sacrifice profits to adhere to "principles." That, as already mentioned, was the case in steel in 1949 and 1952. In 1949, the large steel firms invited a strike by refusing to accept the principle of non-contributory pensions, recommended by a Presidential fact-finding board, which simultaneously turned down the union's request for a wage increase. In 1952, the steel companies took a strike in opposing the union shop, which they had granted in their captive coal mines and other parts of their operations and which a majority of the Wage Stabilization Board had recommended in this steel case.

When a management thus decides to adhere to a principle despite the losses involved, it seems evident that the goal of maximum profits, even in the long run, may not be predominant in such management decisions. Profits may, however, be a major factor when management accepts a strike in order to "teach the union a lesson," namely, that it cannot expect to force management to accept unreasonable demands by strike harassment or by the strategy of all-out commitment to a position.

As experience with collective bargaining accumulates, the parties are apt to take a longer view of their continuing relation-

---

[27] See *Hearings on S. Res. 266*, Seventy-fifth Congress, 3rd session, 1939, p. 13888.

ship. They may not only worry about precedents but also think in terms of investment in constructive relations. They may come to recognize that through their relationship they have the power to influence costs and profits and, thus, to create additional "play" or scope for improvements in the terms and conditions of employment by means of collective bargaining. They may also come to realize that, for serious problems of employment security, study and mutually acceptable solutions are more advantageous to both sides in the long run than is an answer forced upon one of the parties by economic threats or strong pressures exerted when circumstances are temporarily quite unfavorable for that side.

SUMMARY

1. Collective bargaining involves a continuing relationship, with conflict and cooperation mixed in varying proportions, but generally the end purpose is an acceptable settlement that establishes the framework for the relationship for a period of time in the future.

2. Collective bargaining is not only a process for fixing the terms of employment but it is also a method of industrial government.

3. Particular collective bargaining relationships differ from one another and change in the course of time. There is no simple approach to collective bargaining and no one pattern for its evolution.

4. As collective bargaining has dealt with increasingly complex matters and has gained in experience, the perspective of the parties has tended to lengthen and so has the period or term of agreements.

5. As experience has accumulated and problems have become more knotty, there has been a far greater use of study and discussion in advance of negotiations and apart from the pressures of a strike deadline.

6. The range within which acceptable "package" settlements are possible depends on various factors and constraints, and the parties themselves can influence the range. In some cases, the possibility of government intervention and public opinion may be influential elements.

7. The function of a strike is to cause economic losses in order to stimulate the parties to seek a settlement. Strikes, however, may serve institutional and political needs as well as economic purposes. Especially with employment on a work-career basis, employees and union leaders can exert pressures on employers without resort to striking. Also, for some issues, substitutes for the strike have been developed.

Such comments on various aspects of collective bargaining experience do not, of course, add up to a theory of bargaining. The few bargaining models that economists and psychologists have offered are at such a high level of abstraction that they omit many important elements and have little explanatory or predictive value for labor negotiations.

From this analysis of union-management negotiations it seems evident that any theory of collective bargaining must involve what in Chapter 2 was called "development analysis." Collective bargaining is a dynamic process, evolving as it adapts to a changing environment. It takes place between two institutions that have a continuing relationship and institutional goals and needs. Any theory of collective bargaining must, therefore, take account of important noneconomic variables. It must also be integrated with wage theory, which is the subject of the next chapter.

DISCUSSION QUESTIONS

1. It is claimed that labor organization is necessary in a modern industrial society composed of large business units. Critically discuss that claim.

2. What factors do you consider the most important ones in determining the character of collective bargaining in an industry? Explain.

3. How do you account for the sharp contrast in strike experience in the steel and automobile industries during the period from 1946 to 1960?

4. Why has the union response to technological change been so different in the coal and railroad industries?

5. Can one make any generalizations about the factors that pro-

mote constructive collective bargaining? To what extent does it depend on favorable economic factors—good profits, expanding employment, little technological change? To what extent does constructive collective bargaining depend on the character of union and management leadership, the absence of union insecurity and rivalry, the size and coverage of a single negotiation?

6. What functions do strikes perform? Can those functions be achieved by other means than a strike?

7. What purposes would a theory of collective bargaining serve? How general or abstract can a theory of collective bargaining be and still serve such purposes?

SELECTED READINGS

Chamberlain, Neil W., *Collective Bargaining* (New York: McGraw-Hill, 1951).

Davey, Harold W., *Contemporary Collective Bargaining* (Englewood Cliffs, N.J.: Prentice-Hall, 1959, 2nd ed.).

Davey, Harold W., Howard S. Kaltenborn, and Stanley S. Ruttenberg (eds.), *New Dimensions in Collective Bargaining* (New York: Harper, 1959).

Dunlop, John T., and James J. Healy, *Collective Bargaining: Principles and Cases* (Homewood, Ill.: Irwin, 1953, 2nd ed.).

Harbison, Frederick H., and John R. Coleman, *Goals and Strategy in Collective Bargaining* (New York: Harper, 1951).

Pen, Jan, "Wage Determination Revisited," *Kyklos*, XI (No. 1, 1958), pp. 1–25.

Raskin, A. H., "The Newspaper Strike: A Step-by-Step Account of How and Why It Happened," *New York Times*, April 1, 1963, pp. 1, 22, 23, and 24.

Rothschild, K. W., "Approaches to the Theory of Bargaining" and G. L. S. Shackle, "The Nature of the Bargaining Process," in John T. Dunlop (ed.), *The Theory of Wage Determination* (New York: St Martin's Press, 1957), Chapters 18 and 19, pp. 281–314.

Selekman, B. M., S. K. Selekman, and S. H. Fuller, *Problems in Labor Relations* (New York: McGraw-Hill, 1958, 2nd ed.).

Slichter, Sumner H., James J. Healy, and E. Robert Livernash, *The Impact of Collective Bargaining on Management* (Washington: Brookings Institution, 1960).

Stevens, Carl M., *Strategy and Collective Bargaining Negotiation* (New York: McGraw-Hill, 1963).

United States Department of Labor, *Collective Bargaining in the Basic Steel Industry: A Study of the Public Interest and the Role of Government* (Washington: United States Government Printing Office, January 1961).

Weber, Arnold R. (ed.), *The Structure of Collective Bargaining* (New York: The Free Press of Glencoe, 1961).

9.
Wage Theory and
Labor Markets

THIS CHAPTER EXAMINES wage determination under collective bargaining, and develops an analytical basis for understanding negotiated wages. Money wages are viewed as the chief element in a total employment complex.

Some economists insist that wages must be explained in terms of market demand and supply. Traditional wage theory is based on the market mechanism. Such an analytical framework is appropriate for explaining wage determination under simple, commodity-like conditions of employment. It is, however, too narrow a base where a welfare concept of employment prevails and where wages are negotiated as part of a "package" settlement. Our discussion of union behavior, management in large firms, and collective bargaining indicated the importance of political factors and extra-market pressures as well as market forces. The investigation of wages under collective bargaining in this chapter draws on the analysis in Chapters 6, 7, and 8. This and succeeding chapters apply that general analysis to the main subject areas of collective bargaining.

In considering wages as part of a negotiated package, it will be necessary to discuss relations between wage rates and labor mobility in order to see how market forces operate or do not operate in particular situations. Therefore, after clearing away some terminological difficulties, so-called "labor markets" will be examined to find out how fruitful the market concept is for different types of employment and particularly for manual work in manufacturing. On the basis of that examination, the usefulness and limitations of traditional wage theory will be considered. The chapter ends with a section discussing the elements of a theory of negotiated wages.

TERMINOLOGICAL DIFFICULTIES

To some economists, wages are just another price, and the market for labor functions like other markets. Actually, it may be quite misleading to apply to employment under union-management agreement the apparatus of reasoning that has been developed for analyzing commodity and security transactions. As employment has become a complex process, the intellectual equipment for understanding it should be adjusted to take account of its current characteristics.

Wages

As a monetary income for the worker and a cost to the firm, wages would seem to be a rather simple concept. However, under company industrial relations programs and union-management agreements, compensation for employment has become an elaborate set of premiums, perquisites, guarantees, and protections. The question arises whether the term wages includes the following: overtime rates, shift differentials, bonuses, other incentive pay arrangements, reporting pay, profit-sharing, free lunches, discounts on company products, vacation rights, income guarantees such as sick pay and supplemental unemployment benefits, dismissal compensation, and other company benefits. In a sense they could all be considered part of a bundle of compensation for employment. In addition, there are other items that might be viewed as part of compensation if one thinks of employment in long-run terms. They are automatic or merit pay increases, training that leads to advancement, and the opportunity for promotion into higher-paying positions.

To the worker, of course, employment has many other dimensions. Since he has to deliver his services on the property and under the supervision of the employer, the worker is interested in plant conditions, work speeds and rules, the quality of supervision, and protections from sanctions and arbitrary actions by management as well as in his potential work-life earnings with that company. The longer the employment horizon of the worker, the less emphasis he puts on the money pay for the hiring-in job and the more he is interested in promotion possibilities, pay scales up the line, benefits, and other aspects of the employment relationship.

To the management, employment involves not only wage payments to the worker but a large number of other costs. They include such items as recruitment and placement expenses, training costs, accumulating obligations under company benefit programs, social insurance taxes, and the cost of supervision. Economists are prone to overlook the fact that generally labor requires supervisory costs. And in employing a manual worker, the management is buying not only his current contribution to output but also the opportunity to attach him to the firm and develop him under its supervision. Does the price of labor include some of these costs such as recruitment, social insurance contributions, and required supervision?

Under collective bargaining the various items in an agreement are negotiated together, although in intercompany or interindustry comparisons, money wages, employee benefits, and work rules may be considered separately. Within limits, wages and benefits may be substituted for one another to arrive at an acceptable package settlement. Obviously, benefits are a form of income to employees and an element of cost to the employer; clearly, therefore, they are part of the price of labor. Wages alone are the price of labor only where the employer has no other costs in connection with employment, as is often the case, say, with harvest labor that is paid by piece rates, is unorganized and unsupervised, and is not covered by social security taxes.

Thus, the extent to which wages can be isolated depends on the employment relationship. In so far as employment is a casual, cash-nexus type of transaction with the employer assuming no continuing obligations, wages are the price of labor and the traditional market analysis may be appropriate.[1] Where wages are part of a negotiated bundle, any separate analysis of wages should bear in mind that the money wage is only part of a total compensation complex.

Labor Markets

The term "labor markets" has come into widespread usage but its exact meaning and significance remain ambiguous. Practitioners usually think of the labor market as the geographic territory within which people reside and commonly commute to work. Normally, it is centered in a city and includes the metropolitan area.

Economists seem to mean by the labor market the area over which the market forces of demand and supply operate to determine price. That would include not only the commuting range, but also the reach of the wage-determining factors, and specifically the area of collective bargaining influences.

If a labor market is thought of as the location where labor is bought and sold, it is generally the actual place of work. Public employment exchanges and other agencies may match job seekers and job vacancies, but the actual hiring normally occurs only after the worker appears at the plant. Especially with seniority, promotion from within, and other company attachments, some writers think that each plant should be considered a separate labor market.[2] With multiplant firms, that would mean more labor markets than there are employers.

Still others would define the labor market in occupational terms. It is said, for example, that there is a separate market for unskilled labor, for skilled craftsmen like plumbers or printers, for stenographers, for actors, for engineers, and for university pro-

---

[1] As employment approaches conditions of pure competition it tends to become a matter of indifference to employees whether they are discharged or not. Some of the employment in building construction is so short term that it approaches such a condition of indifference as to employer attachment.

[2] See, for example, Lloyd G. Reynolds, *The Structure of Labor Markets* (New York: Harper, 1951), pp. 42 and 45.

fessors. They constitute distinct labor supplies and demands which are not substitutable and, therefore, do not compete with one another. In addition, they have widely different mobility areas. Unskilled workers, stenographers, and plumbers seek jobs and are recruited mostly within the community. Printers may travel between cities for work. To a considerable extent, aircraft engineers and university professors seek jobs and are recruited by employers on a nationwide basis. Movie stars frequently move internationally in their patterns of employment. Thus, a single employer may be thought to be operating in a large number of occupational labor markets—a separate one for each occupation that requires a considerable amount of specialized preemployment training. For types of work peculiar to the company that necessitate on-the-job training, the company itself may seem to be a separate labor market in terms of an occupational delineation.

In summary, the term "labor market" may mean: (1) the work commuting area, (2) the area of wage-determining forces, (3) the place where labor purchase and sale occurs, or (4) an occupation and its labor mobility area. The boundaries of the "market" and the character of "market forces" are likely to differ significantly from one of these four concepts to another. The appropriate concept may depend on the question asked. Much confusion has arisen because authors have not been clear as to which concept they had in mind, and have been using the term to mean quite different things.

THE ADMINISTERED MARKET

The discussion in this section deals primarily with plant employment in manufacturing. It will assume the existence of collective bargaining, which covers perhaps two-thirds of all manual employment in factories.[3] The focus will be on wages and on labor supply and demand. Some significant differences in the case of

---

[3] A study in 1958 showed that 66.6 per cent of production workers in manufacturing were in establishments with a majority of the workers under collective bargaining agreements and 33.4 per cent were establishments with none or a minority of the workers under agreement. See H. M. Douty, "Collective Bargaining in Factory Employment, 1958," *Monthly Labor Review*, LXXXIII (April 1960), p. 347.

white-collar and agricultural employment will be indicated after manufacturing employment has been analyzed.

The term "administered market" is used to indicate the extent to which factory employment and wages are managed under company policies and collective bargaining. As has been noted, such employment is subject to various rules, protections, and attachments developed by management or in negotiations. And, under collective bargaining, wages become administered prices, fixed or foreordained for periods of a year, two years, or even longer.

Mobility and Company Attachment

Both management and workers generally seem to support employee attachment to a particular firm. They have developed many rules and practices to discourage or penalize intercompany movement of factory workers.

1. Perhaps the most binding is seniority. It makes length of continuous service with the company[4] the governing factor in the order of avoidance of lay-off when employment is reduced, and the criterion for determining the order of priority to qualify for promotion to a vacancy. The widespread existence of seniority means that a worker, upon leaving a company, loses all his accumulated protection against lay-off and all his promotions. It usually means, in addition, that at another company he must start at the bottom of the occupational ladder and pay structure as a probationary employee, without any protection against lay-off or dismissal until after he has served the probationary period, usually thirty to sixty days. A new plant is an exception to that abrupt drop because there jobs are open all up and down the job hierarchy and the first persons hired have top seniority.

2. In addition to giving up job security for insecurity and sliding to the bottom job grade, the worker who changes employers loses his accumulated benefit rights. The number of weeks of paid vacation usually varies with the employee's length of continuous service with the company. However, cancellation of company

---

[4] Seniority may be by department or other unit within a plant or company. The seniority area that is controlling may vary with the type of lay-off, being wider for long-term than for brief lay-offs. See Chapter 12 for an extended discussion of seniority.

pension rights is the greatest loss for employees with a number of years of service.[5] In addition, there may be a gap in the worker's protection under hospital, medical, and other welfare programs, amounting to the length of the probationary period or even longer.

3. Manufacturing firms discourage change of employer in other ways. In hiring, managements tend to discriminate against the mobile worker, particularly one with a record of job changes after, say, twenty-five years of age. Under antipirating codes, as explained in Chapter 7, they attempt to control or eliminate competition between firms for workers already on a company's payroll. And they make company comparisons and job shopping difficult by (a) favoring informal, personal canvass of job opportunities as against a central employment exchange, which would increase job knowledge and facilitate comparison; (b) hiring workers not for one job at one wage but on a work-life basis—"for a roughly envisioned sequence of jobs at an equally roughly estimated sequence of wage rates";[6] and (c) generally requiring that applicants decide to accept or reject a job offer at the time it is made.

The consequence of these factors of attachment and discouragement is that around four-fifths of all manufacturing employees seem more or less firmly tied to a particular firm.[7] They are the employees with one to three years of seniority, depending on the company's stability of employment. Such company-attached employees can be considered "out of the labor market" or, preferably, as a continuing supply of labor to the employer, unaffected by intercompany differences in terms and conditions of employment—at least within some kind of tolerance zone. Those workers rely on collective bargaining rather than mobility to achieve improvements in their terms and conditions of employment. And through the grievance procedure, they can air their personal

---

[5] The loss may be reduced by vesting, which permits the employee to take some of the accumulated funds with him, but normally vesting takes effect only after at least fifteen years of employment.

[6] Martin Bronfenbrenner, "Potential Monopsony in Labor Markets," *Industrial and Labor Relations Review*, IX (July 1956), p. 586.

[7] See Reynolds, *op. cit.*, pp. 81–83; Herbert S. Parnes, *Research on Labor Mobility* (New York: Social Science Research Council, 1954), pp. 80 and 106; R. A. Lester, *Hiring Practices and Labor Competition*, *op. cit.*, pp. 60–62; and Eva Mueller and Jay Schmiedeskamp, *Persistent Unemployment, 1957–1961*, W. E. Upjohn Institute for Employment Research, Kalamazoo, Michigan, November 1962, p. 21.

complaints without any need to threaten to quit and lose their job rights.

The one-fifth of the manufacturing workforce that is not rather firmly attached to a company is composed largely of new or recent entrants into the labor force, unmarried youths with only a few years of work experience, seasonal and casual workers, and older workers unfortunate enough to have been repeatedly laid off or severed from a job so that they have accumulated no significant seniority with a firm.

Studies indicate that unskilled manual workers are likely to be poorly informed about alternative job opportunities and only infrequently are faced with a choice between two or more job offers.[8] A 1946–48 study of workers in New Haven, Connecticut, showed that they knew little about their first job before they entered it, that they obtained that job rather haphazardly without making any deliberate choice, and that in two-thirds of the cases the first job was a blind alley one.[9] The same study revealed that about as many workers in low-wage plants considered their wages were fair and relatively high as was the case in high-wage plants.[10] The unemployed on jobless benefits must accept the first offer of a suitable job, usually chosen by the employment service, or they lose their eligibility for benefits. These are some of the reasons why a wage theory resting on personal job choices is of limited

---

[8] In contrast, youths graduating from high school or college and going into secretarial, technical, professional, or other white-collar occupations often enjoy such choice opportunities. The school serves as an employment exchange, the placement people at the school can provide significant job data and experience, and single graduation time permits a concentration of offers in a particular period.

[9] Reynolds, *op. cit.*, pp. 130–31. Other labor-market studies made in smaller communities indicate somewhat less, although considerable, worker ignorance about jobs and pay in other plants. See R. C. Wilcock and I. Sobel, *Small City Job Markets* (University of Illinois, Urbana: Institute of Labor and Industrial Relations, 1958), pp. 63–65 and 99–100; and C. A. Myers and G. P. Shultz, *The Dynamics of a Labor Market* (New York: Prentice-Hall, 1951), pp. 58, 60, and 119 footnote 5. Myers and Shultz conclude that, although manual workers do not usually weigh job alternatives, they have a fair knowledge of the job characteristics of other available jobs, yet their figures show that only one-sixth of the 195 workers interviewed knew about wages on their present job before they applied for it, and one-third of them knew nothing about their jobs before employment except that the company was hiring (see Table 11, p. 58).

[10] *Ibid.*, p. 213.

usefulness for explaining wage behavior in manufacturing employment.

During the fifties the quit rate in manufacturing declined from a monthly average of about 2.7 per 100 workers to a figure of 1.5 per 100 workers.[11] In the early 1960's with higher unemployment, the quit rate was 1.3, which is about two-fifths of the average in the twenties.[12] Undoubtedly, the immobility influences discussed above have contributed significantly to that decline, but the contribution of each to the drop in the manufacturing quit rate is impossible to determine. Arthur M. Ross has pointed out that other factors help to explain that drop.[13] They include a rise in the average age of the nation's workforce (quit rates decline with age), and an even greater increase in the average age of the workforce in manufacturing because manufacturing employment has been relatively stable. However, such age factors, plus the higher unemployment rates which discourage quits, are hardly adequate to explain most of the increase in labor immobility in manufacturing since the twenties or since World War II. Seniority, company benefits,[14] and other management and union policies undoubtedly have played an important part in the reduced rate of job quitting, particularly among semiskilled workers from twenty-five to forty years of age.

Labor Supply and Wages

Economists like to think in terms of demand and supply schedules. Assuming no other changes (a static analysis), they stress that a

---

[11] Figures for quits are given in the "Labor Turnover" section of the *Monthly Labor Review*. The averages in the text are the averages for 1950–53 and 1956–59.

[12] The twenties is the best base for comparing with the fifties and sixties because no war or severe depression affected the figures and labor organization in manufacturing was relatively insignificant outside of a few industries like printing and clothing. The annual average for 1926–28 was 2.86 per 100 workers, as calculated from figures in the *Monthly Labor Review*, XXVI (January 1928), p. 43 and *Handbook of Labor Statistics, 1947 Edition*, Bulletin No. 916, United States Department of Labor, Washington, D.C., 1948, p. 686.

[13] See Arthur M. Ross, "Do We Have A New Industrial Feudalism?" *American Economic Review*, XLVIII (December 1958), pp. 903–20.

[14] For employer comments on the retention power of company benefits see R. A. Lester, *Hiring Practices and Labor Competition, op. cit.*, pp. 89–92. See also the discussion in Chapter 11 below, pp. 350–51.

rise in the price of one commodity will result in a smaller quantity demanded and a larger quantity supplied, and that a drop in price will cause people to demand more and suppliers to curtail their offerings. Putting such a simple relationship in the form of a price-quantity curve on a graph may be helpful for illustrative purposes.

Unfortunately, the factors that influence labor supply in manufacturing cannot be well explained by such a simple wage-quantity relationship, constructed on the assumption that all other factors or influences remain unchanged when a change occurs in the wage or in the labor supply. Often the other factors do not remain unchanged. Changes in them may have more influence on supply than do changes in the wage itself. Or, as in the case of seniority, the other factors may render the supply unresponsive to modest wage changes. With respect to employment in a modern factory, not only must one think in terms of a total complex of employment advantages and disadvantages instead of wages alone, but the company attachments and the barriers to intercompany movement may make any relationship between labor supply and the "employment complex" loose and ineffective within a range or zone. Furthermore, one must often think, not in terms of one job, but the rough relationship between labor supply and the employment complex for the expected sequence of jobs that persons may be expected to occupy during their work-life with the company. In addition, under collective bargaining wage rates for all jobs are fixed for a year or two at a time, and any influence of labor supply on wages would have to work through the union-management negotiations.

With those qualifications, let us examine more closely the manual labor supply of a manufacturing firm. As previously explained, company ties and mobility barriers mean that perhaps four-fifths of the workforce of a representative firm have sufficient attachment so that few of them could be attracted to another employer except under most unusual terms or conditions. For all practical purposes, they can be considered the firm's *regular* labor force, providing it with a continuously available labor supply. In supply-curve terms, they represent an inelastic labor supply, that would be unaffected by a *relative* decline in the company's wage scale or (preferably) its employment complex—at least a relative decline within any realistic range.

The remaining labor supply to the firm consists of recent hires (say within a year), plus the potential supply from job applications on file and from the firm's reserve recruiting power. The recent hires do not have strong attachments to the company, and it is possible that a short-term, relative decline in a firm's terms of employment might cause some (particularly workers in their early twenties) to quit. Much might depend on the reasons for the relative decline and the expected trend of employment in the industry and the firm. However, even recent hires face mobility barriers and risks in any employment transfer. In most States, for example, voluntary quits lose their rights to unemployment compensation for a specified period or entirely. Whether a relative decline in a firm's employment terms would, therefore, cause its labor turnover among recent hires to rise would depend on many factors, including the current demand for labor in the area.

Most job applications cannot be considered part of the labor supply to a firm. Applications are not an offer to work and generally are not related to a specific job. They are more in the nature of an inquiry, and often a person will have applications on file at a number of firms. Usually only a fraction of the recent applicants would accept a specific offer, which normally would be an unskilled job at the bottom rate. The volume of job applications rises when a firm is hiring and drops off sharply or ceases when the firm stops hiring or starts to lay off employees.[15] The New Haven study found little evidence that a high wage level brings more applicants to the plant; low-wage firms were able, even in a condition of "more than full employment," to hire and retain enough labor to meet their production schedules. Little relationship was found between the firm's wage scale and its quit rate or between its wage scale and the apparent quality of its labor, except for firms at the extreme top and bottom of the community wage hierarchy.[16] Other studies tend to confirm those conclusions.[17]

---

[15] For a discussion of the significance and usefulness of job applications see Lester, *Hiring Practices and Labor Competition, op. cit.*, pp. 39–41 and 47–53.

[16] Reynolds, *op. cit.*, pp. 11, 161, 217–18, and 219.

[17] See, for example, Lester, *Hiring Practices and Labor Competition, op. cit.*, pp. 49–51 and 74–75; and Lester, *Adjustments to Labor Shortages, op. cit.*, pp. 63–64.

More important to most firms than the volume of applications on file is their reserve or potential drawing power. That is measured by the management's ability to recruit by informing existing employees and the union of job openings. A good reputation as an employer, including stability of employment, helps a firm in expanding its labor supply by the costless means of regular employees referring friends and relatives for a job. Not only for a firm but for the community as a whole, increased demand tends to stimulate increased supply, particularly of second workers in a family, without any change in wage scales.[18]

Whether a firm's labor-supply curve for new plant workers is a horizontal line (or more likely a horizontal band) over a wide stretch depends not only on its reserve drawing power but also on (a) the relative amount of unemployment in the area and (b) the rate and amount of employment expansion that the firm requires. The larger the volume of unemployment, the easier it is for a firm to recruit new employees of the regular quality. However, if with manual labor in short supply a relatively large plant must (say) double its workforce within a short period (such as six months or even a year), the management may exhaust its reserve strength. In that case, it may be forced (a) to resort to aggressive methods of recruitment that cost money (i.e., advertising, recruiting teams, payments for new recruits), or (b) to hire in at a wage rate above the normal starting rate,[19] or (c) to lower its standards of employee selection and accept what it considers to be poorer quality. Any of those measures means that new hires are more costly to the firm than ordinarily is the case, and therefore, the labor-supply curve begins to tip upward from its normal horizontal position at the point of supply where such measures are necessary.

No mechanism exists by which workers desiring employment in a particular firm can successfully bid for a job by undercutting the current wage rate for it. In most manufacturing firms wages

---

[18] Wilcock and Sobel, *op. cit.*, pp. 103–23 and 125.

[19] The wage scale itself has, of course, been fixed by collective bargaining. It is the practice in the United States to negotiate a "standard" scale. In contrast in England and Sweden the nationally negotiated rates are minima which individual firms are free to exceed and frequently do.

have been established by a collective agreement, by a systematic program of job evaluation, or by both means, and, therefore, in the short run, they cannot be reduced in a particular occupation by labor-supply pressures. With seniority permitting only one person at a time to qualify for promotion into a vacancy and with on-the-job training to qualify for the work, it is difficult to say just what the supply of labor for a particular opening is. Certainly the concept of an oversupply for a particular job in the middle of a regular line of promotion makes no sense under such administered employment conditions.[20]

Basically, it appears that there is a labor recruitment process and a wage determining process, each influenced by its own set of factors and usually without strong connections between the two, at least in the short run. The supply of labor to the firm normally appears to be a horizontal line or band, which means that over the relevant range an adequate supply can be developed without a change in the terms of employment or an increase in the cost of recruitment.[21] An exception to such a short-run supply schedule may occur if a firm must expand its employment rapidly under conditions of local labor shortage.

A horizontal labor supply for the firm is an important element in the model of a community wage structure in which individual company wage scales differ by as much as 10 or 15 per cent. The model postulates such a 10 per cent, wage-tolerance zone for essentially the same quality of labor at recruitment, assuming the same type of work, and no compensating differences in the non-wage aspects of the employment complex. In other words, this range-of-rates model postulates that genuine interfirm wage differentials of 10 per cent or even 15 per cent will continue to exist in a locality over a long period of time that includes both recession and boom years. It is based on empirical studies, including a New Haven investigation that showed no long-run narrowing of the

---

[20] For such reasons, proposals to judge and adjust company wage scales by means of labor-supply tests are impractical. They are based on a misconception of the employment process under a "web of rules." For a discussion of this matter and a criticism of some of the proposals see Lester, *Hiring Practices and Labor Competition, op. cit.*, pp. 98–101.

[21] For a similar conclusion see Reynolds, *op. cit.*, pp. 225–29; and Wilcock and Sobel, *op. cit.*, pp. 12 and 125.

band of interfirm differentials between 1940 and 1948[22] and studies based on employer conclusions from experience during periods of labor stringency.[23]

The labor-demand aspects of this model are considered below. From the labor-supply side it seems clear that there is a lack of wage-equalizing effects within a band of rates, which for operational purposes may be termed a 10 per cent range or wage differential.

Labor Demand and Wages

A schedule of demand for a company's product is based on the same reasoning as supply schedules. There is assumed to be a clear, inverse relation between price and quantity such that, all else remaining constant, a smaller quantity will be demanded at a higher price and a larger quantity will be demanded at a lower price.

The demand for a factor of production like labor is derived from the demand for the product manufactured by labor in combination with other productive factors. It is assumed that, over the long run at least, the management can vary the factor mix and will strive to conserve on the use of labor as its relative cost rises. The extent to which the labor-equipment ratio can be varied by management is a crucial question in the demand for labor. With a fixed ratio, the demand for the product would directly determine the firm's demand for the labor to make it.

Again, as in the case of supply, any relationship is presumably

---

[22] Reynolds, *op. cit.*, pp. 190, 233–35, and 246–48.

[23] Lester, *Hiring Practices and Labor Competition, op. cit.*, pp. 84–86; and *Company Wage Policy, A Survey of Patterns and Experience,* Industrial Relations Section, Princeton University, Princeton, New Jersey, 1948, pp. 32–34 and 44–45.

From a study of 144 job offers from corporations to 44 prospective graduates of the Graduate School of Business of the University of Chicago and from data on corporate offers to college graduates, George J. Stigler concluded: "These fragments illustrate rather than prove the existence of substantial dispersion in hiring rates for homogeneous labor. This dispersion cannot be measured precisely, but is of the order of magnitude of 5–10 per cent even in so well organized a market as that of college graduates at a single university." See "Information in the Labor Market," *Journal of Political Economy,* LXX (October 1962, Supplement), p. 96.

between the firm's labor demand and the total cost of employing that quantity of labor and not just money wages alone. The total labor cost would include the imputed costs of supervision and of provisions of the collective agreement. Also, a labor-demand schedule for a firm with a long view of its workforce should be conceived in terms, not of one particular job and its cost complex, but in terms of expected worklife productivity in a series of jobs. A management expects to have an employee cost it more than it can gain from his employment during the early weeks that he is on the payroll.[24]

Conceptually, the short-run demand schedule is distinguished from the long-run schedule. The long-run is the time required for a change in production techniques and for new investment, so that the combination of productive factors can be altered in order to economize on the factor or factors whose relative costs have increased. For most modern factories with large-scale production, the equipment would be engineered for a certain work crew at a particular rate of operations. Therefore, the labor-equipment ratio could not be changed significantly in the short run. Consequently, the short-run demand schedule for labor in a modern plant is likely to be determined by the management's decision with respect to total output. Its output decision, in turn, is generally based on expected demand for the product. Sales volume controls output decisions, which control the size of the workforce. In other words, the short-run demand for labor varies directly with changes in the demand for the product. The labor-cost effect on a management's demand for labor exerts its influence more in the long run. Cost considerations may affect the intensity of the use of labor-saving equipment. However, cost-cutting methods may be used that involve no reduction in the firm's demand for factory labor.

The management of a well-established manufacturing concern is under a number of pressures or constraints to keep its workforce employed—to maintain its labor demand in the short run. Normal labor turnover including employee retirements would permit some reduction in labor demand in the long run without lay-offs or dismissals.

---

[24] Martin Bronfenbrenner even attempts to diagram the differences between a worker's expected cost and productivity over a work career. See "Potential Monopsony in Labor Markets," *op. cit.*, p. 586.

The pressures to maintain the short-run demand for labor are generated by management goals and the cost advantages of employment stability. As explained in Chapter 7, managements seek to maintain and improve the firm's product-market position. They may adjust to increased wages by such means as increased sales efforts, better product design, or elimination of wastes in management. As Kaplan and Kahn point out, a firm has a large investment in plant, machines, and organization that presses for full utilization.[25] Normally, the lowest unit costs of production are achieved at or near plant capacity. Moreover, management has a significant investment in the training and development of its workforce. Generally, it wishes to protect and enhance that investment, and not have it deteriorate with disuse or become dissipated while on layoff. And, as indicated in the preceding subsection, a firm's reserve drawing power in recruitment rests, in part, on its record of stability in employment.

Additional incentives for a management to maintain labor demand include experience rating under unemployment compensation, company costs of "supplemental unemployment benefits" or dismissal compensation where they exist, and the costs of transferring employees when workforces have to be reduced and restored according to seniority. Under unemployment compensation, a firm's taxes vary with the benefits drawn by its laid-off employees, so that maintenance of labor demand assures the firm of the lowest tax rate. The savings from employment stability under s.u.b. and dismissal compensation are obvious. With lay-off by seniority, a series of "bumpings" occur that result in many more transfers of personnel from job to job than the number of lay-offs, all of which is costly because of the resulting training costs and inefficiencies. These considerations make it costly for a firm not to continue steady use of its workforce.

Even a firm's long-run demand for labor has some inflexibility or constraints. A reduction in labor costs would not be likely to lead to replacement of modern equipment with old-fashioned techniques of production that are more labor-consuming. For such reasons as resale value and worker training problems, a management would hesitate so to design and equip a new plant. A marked

---

[25] See page 206 above.

North-South differential in wages in some industries apparently has not led to higher labor-to-equipment ratios in modern factories in the South than in the North.[26]

Our analysis leads to the conclusion that a firm's demand for labor in modern manufacturing is generally quite inelastic to realistic wage changes in the short run. It varies with actual and expected demand for the product, subject to pressures for a high and stable employment of the firm's workforce. That, of course, does not preclude general cost-cutting campaigns (including labor economies) that are stimulated by reduced profits.

Over the long run, a firm's demand for labor is more flexible. The management can decide whether or not to expand the scope of the firm's operations. Relatively higher wages may increase the pressure for capital investment in labor-saving equipment, while at the same time perhaps making such investment more difficult to finance to the extent that the higher labor costs have reduced the firm's current and prospective profits. Nonlabor considerations, including management's desire for technical progress, may limit the possibilities of labor substitution for capital equipment if, relatively, labor costs should decline.[27]

Any analysis of the possible effects of a shift in an employer's labor demand upon negotiated wage scales should take account of certain aspects of wage determination under collective bargaining. Among them are the following: (a) collective bargaining fixes wages and any wage increases for a year or more regardless of changes in demand during the life of the agreement, (b) wage increases under collective bargaining do not vary with the total or occupational demand of a single employer, and (c) the wage orientation of many firms is much broader than the local labor market area.[28]

In discussing labor supply to the firm, a model of a community wage structure having genuine intercompany wage differentials of 10 or 15 per cent was postulated. It was pointed out that a

---

[26] See R. A. Lester, "Effectiveness of Factory Labor: South-North Comparisions," *Journal of Political Economy*, LIV (February 1946), pp. 69–70.

[27] Lloyd Reynolds concluded from his study that a sloping demand curve for labor (higher wage, less demanded) is valid but that it holds true only for substantial wage increases and only after a sufficient period of time for management to make adjustments. See Reynolds, *op. cit.*, p. 182.

[28] See Lester, *Company Wage Policies, op. cit.*, p. 13.

horizontal labor supply to the firm would not serve to compress such wage differentials. The labor-demand policies of established firms also would not seem to have significant equalizing effects upon the wage structure of the model. Managements of nearby firms, even in the same industry, are not conscious of competing with each other for labor, nor do high-wage firms draw labor especially from low-wage firms—not at least within the 10 to 15 per cent range.[29] Partly to avoid stimulating labor turnover, managements may follow an antipirating code. A 1951–53 study of company adjustments to labor stringency showed no close coordination between a firm's position in the community's wage hierarchy and its turnover or recruitment problems.[30]

Different Types of Employment

Studies have been made of labor-market practices in certain non-manufacturing lines. Some of them show more competition for labor, less company attachment, and shorter management perspectives on the workforce than in factory employment.

One of the studies dealt with the hiring by thirteen Boston banks and insurance companies of girls trained in school as clerks and stenographers.[31] Covering the period 1948–56, this study showed that, compared with factory workers, these girls (a) were better informed about wages and working conditions (half of them got their jobs through school guidance counselors or employment agencies), (b) were frequently able to choose between two or more job offers (because they were graduating and, therefore, the hiring was concentrated in time for persons whose date of availability was known well in advance), and (c) had short perspectives on employment with emphasis on wages because they hoped to marry and withdraw from gainful employment within a few years. In addition, the companies were not unionized, the practice of seniority did not prevail, and the companies cooperated

[29] See Lester, *Hiring Practices and Labor Competition, op. cit.,* pp. 65–68.

[30] Lester, *Adjustments to Labor Shortages, op. cit.,* pp. 63–64.

[31] G. P. Shultz, I. L. Herrnstadt, and E. S. Puckett, "Wage Determination in a Non-Union Labor Market," *Proceedings of the Tenth Annual Meeting of the Industrial Relations Research Association,* September 5–7, 1957, p. 194–206; and G. P. Shultz, "A Non-union Market for White Collar Labor," in *Aspects of Labor Economics, A Conference of the Universities-National Bureau Committee for Economic Research* (Princeton: Princeton University Press, 1962), pp. 107–55.

to the extent of sharing wage and hiring information and in agreeing not to bid up wages against themselves. Also, the school placement counselors channeled the best qualified girls to the firms that they considered from past experience to have the best openings. It is not surprising, therefore, that the authors conclude that a 10 per cent differential in wages generally meant some difference in quality of worker.[32]

Examination of the employment practices for agricultural labor hired to harvest crops in California revealed a different set of circumstances.[33] They include (a) a horizontal supply of labor to the growers as a group (no wage increase within reason would expand the supply and higher wages might even contract it by causing some in the family to withdraw from work), (b) a fixed demand for labor (as long as the piecerate for picking is below the selling price for the fruit or vegetable, the grower wishes to harvest the whole crop), (c) combined action by the growers to keep a lid on wages, and (d) a pure commodity concept of employment with no labor organization.[34]

These two studies show that the nature of employment, hiring practices, and opportunities for rational job choice vary widely. College students should be careful not to generalize without qualification from their own experience or that of their fellow students to other sections of the economy.

TRADITIONAL WAGE THEORY

Wage theories have changed with employment practices and issues of public policy. There has, however, been some tendency for wage thinking to lag in the march of intellectual progress.

In the late eighteenth and early nineteenth centuries, when workers in England hardly earned enough to live on, the subsistence theory of wages held sway. It assumed that a rise in wages above subsistence would lead to an increase in population, which would enhance the labor supply, thus driving wages back toward the norm of subsistence. This was a theory of the level of wages

---

[32] Shultz, Herrnstadt, and Puckett, *op. cit.*, p. 204.
[33] Lloyd Fisher, "The Harvest Labor Market in California," *Quarterly Journal of Economics,* LXV (November 1951), pp. 463–91.
[34] *Ibid.*, pp. 469–70, 472–74, and 488–89.

based on long-run changes in labor supply. Population pressures in Africa, India, and the Far East might seem to provide a basis for present-day application of this theory.

In England, the subsistence theory was replaced by the wages fund theory, which rested on both demand and supply. It assumed that the demand for wage-paid labor was a fixed amount consisting of the fund (whether money or a store of consumer goods was not too clear), set aside each year by employers for wage payments to labor. With demand fixed in the short run by the fund, variations in the total labor supply would determine the level of wages for the whole country. The wages fund theory was dominant until about 1870 when some of its strange assumptions were clearly proved invalid.

Since then the marginal productivity theory has been the most widely held wage theory, although it has been subject to increasing criticism by labor economists. A distinct advantage of this theory of wages was that it constituted part of the all-embracing theory of marginalism. Consequently, there was no need for a separate or special theory of wages apart from general price theory. Furthermore, the marginal productivity theory presumed to explain not only the general level of wages but occupational, geographic, and other wage differentials as well. This it did in terms of demand. As a theory of employment for the firm, it assumed labor supply to be given and did not attempt to explain variations in supply.

Despite marked changes in the concept of employment during the past half century, the marginal productivity theory has not yet been eclipsed by another widely held wage theory. Labor economists, although increasingly aware of the limitations of marginal productivity as an explanation of wage determination in modern industry under collective bargaining, have not developed a substitute theory with the same intellectual appeal but greater explanatory and predictive properties. Skillful attempts have been made to force the new features into the old analytical framework.

The Marginal Productivity Theory

As a demand explanation the marginal productivity theory is based on two propositions: (1) individual employers will continue to hire labor as long as they can profit from doing so (up to the point where the cost per unit of labor equals or exceeds the net contribution of that labor to the firm's revenue), and (2) competition among employers seeking to maximize their profits assures that they will bid wages up to the value of the marginal contribution of that class of workers to the firm's output.

The marginal productivity theory assumes that wages are market determined—by demand and supply. Neither the total market supply nor labor supply to the firm is explained by this theory. Under competitive conditions, presumably the labor supply to the firm would be a horizontal line at the "market" wage. With market imperfections or monopoly elements, an individual firm's labor-supply schedule is assumed to slope gradually upward, because increased supply involves higher wages, greater recruitment costs, or lower quality of labor.[35] The upward sloping supply curve for the firm, plus diminishing returns (if more labor is added without proportional increases in other factors)[36] and diseconomies of scale (greater problems of coordination and management as firms grow in size) are used to explain why the firm faces increasing costs with expansion in output and employment beyond a certain point.

Total market demand for labor is assumed to be a downward sloping schedule—more labor will be employed only at a lower wage. Individual firms in purely competitive markets think in terms of a horizontal demand schedule for their products because they can sell all of the standard commodity they are producing without affecting the selling price of that commodity. By contrast, under monopolistic competition (firms producing differentiated, brand-name items) it is assumed that the management can sell larger amounts only at lower prices (or lower net revenue per unit if larger selling costs are required). Therefore, the demand curve for the firm's product is downward sloping, and the demand curve for productive factors slopes downward more steeply. The summation of the labor demand curves of the individual firms gives the market demand curve for labor.

Labor demand and supply in a market area can be illustrated, according to the theory, by Figure 4. The supply curve (SZ) slopes gradually upward. The demand curve (DB) slopes

---

[35] See, for example, Allan M. Cartter, *Theory of Wages and Employment* (Homewood, Ill.: Irwin, 1959), pp. 54–55.

[36] This idea arose in agriculture where land was considered the fixed factor and the crop results of added doses of labor or fertilizer were evident.

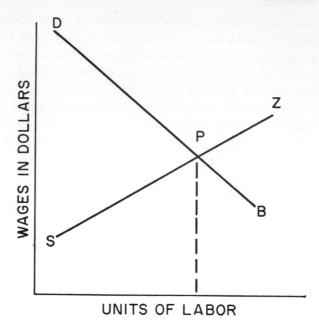

LABOR DEMAND AND SUPPLY

FIG. 4

downward. Where they meet (*P*) is considered to be "the equilibrium rate" or "the competitive wage." Figure 4 can also be used to illustrate labor demand and labor cost for a firm under monopolistic competition. For such a firm, the curve *DB* is both a demand curve and a marginal revenue schedule; the *SZ* curve is a marginal cost curve, indicating that increase in total labor cost from hiring an additional unit of labor.[37] Where the two marginal curves meet (*P*) is an equilibrium point. The firm employs the amount of labor indicated by the dotted line at *P*, because up to that point it makes the profit indicated by the space between the two lines (*DPS*). Employment greater than *P* would, according to our assumptions, cost more than its marginal contribution to the firm's revenue.

Thus, under perfect competition, marginal productivity is a

---

[37] It should be noted, however, that the price of labor for the firm cannot be read from the graph. It would be given by the average cost curve which is not shown in Figure 4.

theory of employment from the standpoint of the individual firm and a theory of wages viewed from the market as a whole. Where the market is imperfect and individual firms have some monopoly powers which permit them to exercise a measure of discretion in fixing their wage scales, marginal productivity becomes a theory of wages and of employment from the viewpoint of the individual firm. With collective bargaining, however, the firm enjoying some discretion in wage-setting no longer has sole wage authority. That authority is shared with the union. Then marginal productivity cannot be considered an adequate explanation of wage determination for those firms and it becomes, for them, mainly a theory of employment.

The proponents of the marginal productivity theory recognize that, although it is precise in its analytical apparatus, it can only be rough and approximate in its application in particular cases. In practice, demand and supply schedules may not be smooth and continuous.[38] Expansion may occur in "chunks" of capital and labor. Labor is not completely homogeneous, not even unskilled labor, as is usually assumed for strict application of the principle of marginalism to that labor. Demand and supply are not completely independent of each other; increased demand may call forth additional supply. Institutional frictions may impede the operation of market forces. A firm's management may not expand and contract employment by little increments with each shift in marginal cost or marginal revenue. In the short run it may be unable to substitute one factor for another. However, the theory's supporters insist that the basic tendencies are always present and will assert themselves, particularly over the long run when management makes decisions with respect to the purchase of new equipment or the expansion or contraction of other capital investment.

Application and Limitations

Basically, the marginal productivity theory of wages rests on the traditional theory of the firm and competition between firms

---

[38] A special case is that of oligopoly (a few large suppliers of an item) in which it is assumed that any price reduction by a firm would be immediately followed by its competitors but any price rise by the firm would not be matched by them. Under such circumstances, there would be a corner in the firm's demand curve at the existing price, and the curve marginal to that "kinked" demand curve would have a gap or discontinuity in it.

for labor. Chapter 7 discussed the modern shortcomings of both notions. It is evident that, for short-run purposes the marginal productivity theory is most appropriately applied to small-scale operations producing a standard item by means of simple techniques that permit independent variation of productive factors. Farming, logging, and simple types of mining provide good examples. In farming the amount of labor for cultivation, land, seed, and fertilizer can be varied widely. However, in hiring labor for harvesting purposes, the demand may be for complete harvesting, with little variation possible in labor-equipment ratios in picking fruit or vegetables. From his study of the "harvest labor market" in California, Lloyd Fisher concluded that (a) both labor demand and labor supply are fixed and (b) there is no intersection of marginal revenue and marginal cost at any point short of the whole harvest demand for labor, and even at that point marginal revenue and marginal cost may be a distance apart.[39]

From the discussion in Chapter 7 it is clear that modern, large-scale industry may not pursue maximum profits as the marginal productivity theory postulates. Market position or maximum sales subject to a minimum profits' constraint may be more appropriate goals to assume in analyzing the behavior of big business. Factories with assembly lines and automated equipment may, for technical reasons, have fixed labor requirements. Consequently, modern plants in the deep South where low wages prevail have the same labor-equipment ratios as do similar factories in high-wage Detroit or Seattle.

Managements do not compete for labor as the theory assumes. On the contrary, they erect all sorts of company attachments and barriers to intercompany movement, including antipirating codes and arrangements. The theory assumes that management has a short-run commodity concept of employment. In fact, with work-career hiring and the welfare concept of employment, only the hiring-in jobs at the bottom of the company's wage structure may have any direct market ties. With on-the-job training and promotion from within, the internal wage structure of a large firm is, in the absence of collective bargaining, likely to be administered by a scheme of job evaluation, because of the lack of appropriate market indicators or mechanisms.

---

[39] "The Harvest Labor Market in California," *op. cit.*, pp. 473, 474, and 489.

Although the marginal productivity theory is silent with respect to supply, it does assume labor mobility. Workers are supposed to be motivated to change employment to take advantage of 10 or 15 per cent wage differentials without offsetting differences in other terms and conditions of employment, whereas studies indicate that workers with any length of service want to improve their incomes and employment conditions without changing employers. A theory of wages that relies on market forces assumes that a high rate of unemployment (surplus labor) will depress individual wage scales, whereas studies show that non-unionized firms of any size and permanency will not, for temporary labor-supply reasons, lower one job rate in the firm's wage structure or even lower the whole structure with a sharp cyclical rise in unemployment. Such firms are generally interested in maintaining a reputation as fair-minded employers of labor.

If the marginal productivity theory were effectively operating, there would not be wage differentials between firms based on their differing ability to pay high wages. Actually significant inter-firm differentials based on ability prevailed rather generally before widespread unionization in the thirties. Likewise, if marginal productivity were controlling there would be no wage differentials simply on the basis of race,[40] unless all employers were discriminating against Negroes to the same extent. Otherwise, one or more employers who did not discriminate could, by definition, buy labor cheaper than competing firms and, through competition, compel them not to discriminate or force them out of business.

In the preceding section, a model of a community wage structure was postulated with intercompany wage differentials amounting to as much as 10 or 15 per cent. Presumably if the marginal productivity theory were operating as assumed, genuine differentials of such size could not persist over any length of time. Actually, as noted, studies show their existence over as long a period as eight or ten years with no evident compression as a result of cyclical fluctuations in employment.

Collective bargaining adds greatly to the limitations of marginal productivity as an explanation of wage determination and wage differentials. It introduces a new set of variables and a new concept of employment. With wage fixing by negotiations, political

---

[40] Assuming, of course, that quality of labor was the same.

factors within the union become important in the determination of wage structures. Collective bargaining alters employment by adding a web of rules and barriers, both financial and administrative, that restrict or impede treatment of workers as the theory implies. The possibility of a strike and of various package settlements enlarges the range of short-term wage decisions. The next section considers in some detail how collective bargaining has affected the structure and movement of wages. Here it is only necessary to point out that, although collective bargaining is subject to economic pressures, it makes wages an administered part of a continuing union-management relationship.

Although the marginal productivity theory has severe limitations as an explanation of short-run wage determination in modern industry, it is valuable for understanding wage differences over long periods of time and under significantly different economic conditions. For example, it supplies a good basis for explaining why real wages increased as much as they did in the past half century in this country, or why real wages are so much higher in the United States than they are in Italy or India, or why they are higher for unskilled labor in the oil industry than for migratory farm labor. For such gross comparisons, average productivity would usually serve the purpose and certainly be easier for the layman to comprehend. However, marginal productivity provides a more rigorous and elegant type of analysis.

The Monopsony Case

Marginal productivity theory is used as a basis for trying to explain the behavior of large firms that employ a significant proportion of a particular type of labor in a labor market area. Where an employer is such a large buyer of a certain class of labor that his demand may affect its wage in the area, he is termed a "monopsonist"—a monopolistic buyer. It is assumed that the management of such a firm will realize that it is faced with an upward sloping supply curve—that in order to buy more of that labor the management will have to raise wages enough to attract qualified workers into the area, or out of other occupations in the area, or into gainful employment from retirement or semiretirement. Such an increase in wages for that type of labor would mean that the firm would have to pay its regular force the higher wage as well as the new hires, thus adding greatly to its costs. It is assumed, therefore, that the management will keep down its employment and, thus, avoid a wage increase. If it paid the firm to do so because of the sloping supply curve, the management would reduce its employment and thus depress the wage rate.

The difficulty with this explanation is obvious from the discussion of the theory of management in Chapter 7. The managements of large firms generally do not think and act in those terms. Usually the large, dominant firms pay the highest wages in the community or the industry. Where the managements of large units cooperate in antipirating codes or engage in other noncompetitive practices, they do so usually in order to avoid labor turnover costs and not to influence wages. Actually their labor-supply schedules are, or can be made, horizontal over the relevant range, unless a large, sudden expansion is involved. A collective bargaining agreement serves to enforce such a horizontal supply curve. Therefore, the manipulation of wages by the purchase of labor according to monopsonistic calculations seems to be misguided academic speculation.

The monopsonistic logic may help to explain why an employer will seek to expand his labor supply by means of increased recruitment efforts or by lowering his selection standards rather than by raising his wage scale. Such "discrimination" permits the firm to confine the increased cost of labor to the new recruits, whereas a wage-scale increase would also raise the firm's labor costs for all existing employees as well. However, other factors may explain the use of nonwage methods for increasing a firm's labor supply. They include the assumption that such other methods of recruitment are more effective and a management desires not to offend other firms in the community by a wage increase that would spread to them through the pressure of employee comment and comparison.

THE THEORY OF NEGOTIATED WAGES

Collective bargaining shifts wage fixing from unilateral to union-management determination and administration. Instead of one party, three groups are involved—the management, union leadership, and the union's membership which must approve a new agreement. As already noted, the membership of all except narrow craft unions is heterogeneous in its interests.

New Dimensions and Variation

New considerations and elements are, therefore, added to wage determination by collective bargaining. Bargained wage scales are not the same as management-fixed rates offered to workers on a take-it-or-leave-it basis. Under collective wage determination, compensation issues and criteria are jointly explored, any solution must be mutually acceptable, and applications of the wage sections of an agreement are subject to the joint grievance procedure.

Basic to an analysis of bargained wages is an understanding of the aims and methods of unions and managements. Chapter 6 explained that unions have both leadership and membership objectives, and the leadership has the problem of reconciling the differing interests among the membership—skilled *vs.* unskilled, young *vs.* old, male *vs.* female, and so forth. Chapter 7 pointed out that industrial management is likely to have multiple goals, is subject to various pressures, and may be able to create a number of channels of adjustment.

In bargaining for a new agreement, the parties bring their separate interests and orientations to bear on a bundle of issues. Usually, the union makes most of the demands, but managements have tended to increase the number of counterdemands as the relationship has matured. In addition to various wage issues, the bargaining may involve changes in a medical and surgical plan, in the pension plan, in group life insurance, in the paid vacation program, in the seniority provisions, and in a dozen or more other sections of the agreement. In such "package bargaining," wages cannot be isolated from benefits and other parts of the employment complex.

As mentioned in Chapter 8, there are over 125,000 collective agreements covering about twenty million workers. Each one deals with wages and a multitude of other topics. With the various goals, interests, pressures, constraints, and experience combined in different ways in particular negotiations, it is understandable that no single model, no one unifying principle, has been uncovered as the key to all collective bargaining or to wage determination under union-management negotiations.

One advantage of collective bargaining is its flexibility and its adaptability to different circumstances. The consequence is wide variation in patterns and agreements. The size and coverage of the unit of bargaining ranges from part of a factory to national, multiple-employer and multiple-union bargaining as in the railroad industry. Both multiemployer and multiunion negotiations present special problems of accommodation of diverse interests and varying company abilities to pay. Differences also exist in the length of time over which the agreement extends. The term of agreements may vary from six months to five years. Fixing wages and wage increases by formula for a period of three or five years into the future involves considerations that are not present under unilateral determination of wage scales by management, subject to change at any time.

Compulsions and Limitations

Generally, collective bargaining makes a firm's wages subject to a wider range of considerations and pressures than is the case under unilateral management determination. Union leadership is likely to be influenced by wide-reaching comparisons and the drive to extend union wage standards. The "orbit of compulsory comparison"[41] for a union leadership may be interindustry, interunion, or even nationwide, especially if the government has a wage policy or may intervene if negotiations reach an impasse. With widespread publicity for key negotiations, collective bargaining accomplishments may be a basis for leadership rivalry and for prestige in the labor movement.

Union leaders bring to the bargaining table strong notions about equal pay for equal work, about taking labor out of competition, and about a single, standard rate for journeymen in a craft. Thus, pressures exist on the union side for wage uniformity within an industry, within the jurisdiction of a union, or within a skilled occupation. The force of compulsory comparison is especially strong for uniformity of wage increases within certain

---

[41] This is Arthur M. Ross' well-known phrase.

industries and industry groupings, such as steel and autos. Nevertheless, the unions in both of those industries will make special wage concessions (below pattern increases) to keep a plant from closing or a firm from going out of business.[42]

The element of leadership prestige is a factor in union efforts to make a breakthrough in the form of a new type of benefit or to set a high-increase pattern in a key bargain. Sometimes it is done by threatening to strike an exposed firm and using the continuing operations of its competitors as strong pressure for bargaining concessions. Then that "key bargain" is spread to other firms in the industry by similar threat of strike exposure. In the spread of patterns, compelling forces to maintain customary wage relationships are also a factor.

Areas of common wage influence arise under collective bargaining because of similarity of industrial characteristics, plant location in the same areas, and organization by unions that have been closely associated. Thus the so-called hard-goods industries (steel, autos, farm equipment, aircraft, electrical equipment, rubber, and flat glass) form a sort of interrelated wage complex. Certain soft-goods industries (textiles, clothing, blankets, and carpets) constitute a similar interconnected wage group. Wage movements in these two groupings have varied significantly.[43] For periods of as much as three years, the soft-goods industries have had no wage increase while the hard-goods lines were experiencing an increase every year.

Negotiated wages are administered wages, but there are limits to the range of administrative latitude. True, the economic constraints may have some short-run elasticity; the dynamics of a union-management relationship affect costs and adjustment possibilities. Nevertheless, the technical and economic facts of industrial life may allow only quite restricted manipulation. Although collective bargaining can significantly modify the structure of wages

[42] See H. M. Levinson, "Pattern Bargaining: A Case Study of the Automobile Workers," *Quarterly Journal of Economics*, LXXIV (May 1960), pp. 296–317; and George Seltzer, "Pattern Bargaining and the United Steelworkers," *Journal of Political Economy*, LIX (August 1951), pp. 319–31.

[43] See Arthur M. Ross, "The External Wage Structure" in G. W. Taylor and F. C. Pierson, *New Concepts in Wage Determination, op. cit.*, pp. 192–94.

in some industries, the basic wage profile of the country may remain largely unchanged. That is because differences in product markets, profit margins, labor-equipment ratios, labor-cost ratios, and similar factors affect a firm's or an industry's ability to pay relatively high wages.[44] The extent to which collective bargaining has actually affected wage structures and wage levels in particular industries is discussed in the next chapter.

Development of a theory of negotiated wages has been hampered by the great variation in union-management relationships and the difficulty of selecting a few primary variables from which to construct a model. As noted in the preceding chapter, abstract bargaining theory and game theory have not, as yet, helped to illuminate the process or to provide new meaningful insights.

Significant elements that would need to be incorporated in a theory of negotiated wages are, however, clear from the discussion in this and the preceding chapter. They include the following factors or considerations: (1) Collective bargaining brings into wage determination the influence of union politics and ethical notions, the question of mutual acceptability, and comparisons that may extend over wide areas. The result is a wage structure less market-oriented and containing new differentials and dimensions (i.e., wage guarantees, shift differentials, and premium pay for overtime and for work on holidays, etc.). (2) Collective bargaining makes wages part of a package, with possible substitutions of benefits or other demands for some of the potential wage increase. Negotiated wages cannot, therefore, be considered apart from the total negotiated package. (3) Union pressures including the strike can serve to increase the range of possible wage settlements. As experience in the steel industry from 1955 to 1959 indicates, a particular union may, in a few years under certain circumstances, raise the level of wages of its members by 10 per cent more than the increase experienced in similar industries or than seems to be supported by economic factors.[45] (4) Under collective bargaining, wages are

---

[44] See *ibid.;* and R. A. Lester, "Economic Adjustments to Changes in Wage Differentials," *ibid.,* pp. 223–25.

[45] See *Collective Bargaining in the Basic Steel Industry, A Study of the Public Interest and the Role of Government,* United States Department of Labor, January 1961, Chapter 9, pp. 133–53.

fixed for considerable periods of time and are especially resistant to any reduction either in individual rates or in the wage level of a firm.

The Role of Wage Criteria

In the negotiation of a general wage increase, economic arguments are employed by the parties in support of their positions. Labor leaders use economic criteria in order to explain the size of a particular wage demand, and managements reply with counterarguments formulated in similar terms. Although the wage criteria and arguments are couched in economic jargon they often carry strong ethical overtones.

The principal wage criteria used in collective bargaining are: (1) wage scales for comparable work in other plants or industries; (2) the change in the cost of living; (3) the change in "labor productivity" (output per work hour) in the plant, firm, or industry; and (4) the company's or industry's ability to pay wages, usually measured by profits. Since bargaining is for future wages, economic prospects as well as past developments enter into the discussion.

In negotiations, the parties cast their reasoning in terms of one or more of these wage criteria in the absence of a single, practical standard by which to determine the proper wage change. Marginal productivity does not furnish such an operational yardstick for fixing the future course of wages. Unions seldom argue for a general wage increase on grounds of shortage in labor supply to the firm or industry. Nor do they base a wage increase claim on increased demand for labor, although that may be a factor in the final result. Managements do not generally use heavy unemployment as grounds for insisting on a wage cut, although they may argue that a large increase will force them to close the plant or reduce employment in the firm or the industry. And both union leaders and managements have notions about "fair wages," which play a role in negotiations.

No one of the wage criteria can be consistently and rigidly applied for any length of time on a company or industry basis. Certainly that is true of the cost of living (which would permit no increase in real wages and would frequently require wage decreases), or labor productivity (which varies from job to job and industry to industry with the incidence of technological advance), or ability to pay (which fluctuates widely up and down in some industries).

Therefore, the parties will not infrequently reverse positions with respect to wage criteria from one negotiation to another. One year the union negotiators may emphasize cost of living (because it has been rising) and ability to pay (because profits have been increasing). Management may counter with cogent arguments to the effect that conformity with wage scales in the community, industry, or selected firms is the only proper basis for determining the amount of any wage increase. The next year with profits and the cost of living declining, the union may shift to another criterion which is increasing, such as labor productivity, while management may now reverse its position, insisting that ability to pay should be the controlling test of any change in wages.

Does such a performance mean that the parties are hypocrites and that wage criteria are useless? Not at all. True, arguments couched in economic terms may mask the real political reason why union leaders believe that they need to obtain a wage increase of a certain size. A management may likewise be influenced by general management opinion or the personal views of particular members of the company's board of directors. In shifting ground the parties, lacking a generally accepted guide, may be opportunistic but usually they are sincere.

Wage criteria serve a number of useful purposes. They represent the main reasons that workers and their wives believe a wage increase of a certain amount is justified and is, therefore, due them. Examination of the arguments in terms of each criterion means that consideration is given to rank-and-file opinion. The process of applying the criteria to wage claims and counterclaims may serve to narrow the possible range of wage increase. Furthermore, application of wage criteria helps to rationalize the wage increase that is actually negotiated and to gain acceptance for it by the parties and the public. If the wage issue is submitted to arbitration or comes before a government tribunal, the wage criteria provide a structure for the presentations of the parties and a basis for the arbitration decision or the tribunal's recommendation.[46] The marginal productivity theory is of little value for those purposes.

Widespread use of various wage criteria, either singly or in combination, indicates that there is some latitude in wage determination. The problem for a theory of negotiated wages is to explain the chief factors that determine where, within a range of possibilities, wages will tend to be fixed by collective bargaining. That involves some systematic explanation of the way that economic and political influences operate through unions and managements, especially in the key, pattern-setting bargains.

A satisfactory model of union-management negotiations has not yet been developed. Consequently, we lack a good generalized explanation of the wage content of negotiations and the principles that determine the allocation of gains between wages and fringe benefits. A theory must not only explain the main features of past developments but also help to predict the general character of future wage change. It should, for example, have enabled one to predict that, in the steel industry in 1962, the negotiated settlement would consist of no increase in wage rates but fringe-benefit improvements, and that the 1963 settlement in steel also would contain no wage increase but instead an extended vacation program and further benefit improvements.

Analysis of negotiated wages is handicapped by the lack of a systematic theory. However, the material developed in the preceding three chapters (analysis of union behavior, theory of management, and the bargaining process) provides a good background for understanding wages as the most significant element in a continuing union-management relationship. Also the discussion of labor supply and demand and of some important elements in a negotiated wage theory offers both guidelines and insights into the wage negotiation process. It has pointed to the influential factors and considerations that operate below the surface.

The chief task is to work out a normal pattern of relationships upon which to base predictions. First, however, it is necessary to sort out the numerous variables, to determine their relative signifi-

---

[46] See Irving Bernstein, *Arbitration of Wages* (Berkeley and Los Angeles: University of California Press, 1954).

cance and the ways in which they operate. That is required before the primary elements can be selected and fitted into a general theory, with the necessary qualifications for special circumstances. This is a real challenge to the student of wage determination under collective bargaining.

SUMMARY

This chapter has explained that wage theory is in the process of reformulation. Two major developments—the great expansion of collective bargaining and the shift to a welfare concept of employment—have still to be incorporated in the main body of economic analysis. Our discussion has indicated the need for new concepts, the present-day difficulties with traditional theory, and the path to a theory of negotiated wages.

In review, the main points of the chapter may be outlined as follows:

1. Wages have taken on new dimensions and must be viewed in a "package" setting. The "price of labor" is no longer simple to define.

2. The "labor market" is a fuzzy concept, open to numerous interpretations and misunderstandings.

3. For factory workers, various company ties and policies promote immobility by penalizing worker transfer from one employer to another. Consequently, perhaps four-fifths of all manufacturing employees are either not interested in changing employers or cannot afford to consider such a move.

4. For a variety of reasons, including seniority and company benefits, the quit rate in manufacturing has evidenced a downward trend since World War II.

5. In the absence of severe labor stringency or rapid company expansion, most well-established firms with collective bargaining seem to have horizontal labor-supply curves or bands. Thus, labor-supply factors normally do not exert pressure for increased wages in such firms.

6. Particularly in the short run, manufacturing firms have various pressures to maintain their demand for labor. Even in the

long run, alteration in labor-equipment ratios for reasons of labor cost may be impractical for certain operations or industries.

7. Given the labor supply-demand situation and various institutional practices, a model of a community wage structure with genuine intercompany wage differentials of 10 or 15 per cent seems to be appropriate for urban areas. The model is a viable one in the sense that, under modern conditions, such a wage structure does not generate forces that would diminish the wage spread.

8. The marginal productivity theory is limited in its application. For short-run purposes, it is most appropriate where production techniques are simple and a commodity concept of labor prevails. It is useful for explaining long-run trends and gross differences in real wages. The monopsony case illustrates the difficulties of attempting to apply the theory to large firms with advanced industrial relations policies and collective agreements.

9. A theory of negotiated wages must include a number of factors neglected by the marginal productivity theory. Among them are union and company goals and practices, wages as part of a package settlement fixing terms for two or more years, and pattern-spreading by compulsory comparison.

10. Pending the development of a systematic theory of negotiated wages, it is important to bear in mind that the parties often enjoy some latitude and alternatives, because wages under collective bargaining are part of a continuing, long-run relationship.

DISCUSSION QUESTIONS

1. What items should be included in a definition of wages?
2. How would you define and delineate a "labor market"?
3. It is claimed that company policies and collective agreements have reduced labor mobility. To what extent do you think that claim is true? From a national viewpoint, how much labor mobility is desirable and when is labor mobility excessive?
4. Discuss the nature of labor supply to the firm.
5. How would you explain the continued existence of significant interfirm wage differentials in a locality?
6. What changes in management policies and in market mechanisms would be necessary in order to make the purchase and sale of labor more competitive?

7. Explain the marginal productivity theory of wages. What are its virtues? Its limitations?
8. What factors do you consider to be most important in the determination of wage increases in the key negotiations in the hard-goods industries? In the soft-goods industries? Explain the differences.

SELECTED READINGS

Bachman, Jules, *Wage Determination* (Princeton: Van Nostrand, New Jersey, 1959).

Bronfenbrenner, Martin, "Potential Monopsony in Labor Markets," *Industrial and Labor Relations Review*, IX (July 1956), pp. 577–88.

Cartter, Allan M., *Theory of Wages and Employment* (Homewood, Ill.: Irwin, 1959).

Dunlop, John T. (ed.), *The Theory of Wage Determination* (New York: St Martin's Press, 1957).

Fisher, Lloyd, "The Harvest Labor Market in California," *Quarterly Journal of Economics*, LXV (November 1951), pp. 463–91.

Lester, Richard A., *Hiring Practices and Labor Competition*, Industrial Relations Section, Princeton University, Princeton, New Jersey, 1954.

————, *Adjustments to Labor Shortages*, Industrial Relations Section, Princeton University, Princeton, New Jersey, 1955.

————, *Company Wage Policies*, Industrial Relations Section, Princeton University, Princeton, New Jersey, 1948.

Myers, Charles A., and George P. Shultz, *The Dynamics of a Labor Market* (New York: Prentice-Hall, 1951).

Parnes, Herbert S., *Research on Labor Mobility, An Appraisal of Research Findings in the United States*, Social Science Research Council, New York, Bulletin 55, 1954.

Reynolds, Lloyd G., *The Structure of Labor Markets* (New York: Harper, 1951).

Rothschild, K. W., *The Theory of Wages* (Oxford: Blackwell, 1954).

Shultz, George P., "A Nonunion Market for White Collar Labor," in *Aspects of Labor Economics: A Conference of the Universities— National Bureau Committee for Economic Research* (Princeton: Princeton University Press, 1962), pp. 107–55.

Taylor, George W., and Frank C. Pierson (eds.), *New Concepts in Wage Determination* (New York: McGraw-Hill, 1957).

Wilcock, Richard C., and Irving Sobel, *Small City Job Markets*, Institute of Labor and Industrial Relations, University of Illinois, Urbana, 1958.

IO.
Wage Structure and
Wage Changes

ALMOST EVERYONE SOME time works for a wage or a salary. Usually, employees compare their rates of pay and have opinions as to whether a particular rate is too low, too high, or just right for the job. Employers likewise have views on the wage scales they are paying. In the absence of a union, particular workers may ask "the boss" for a raise, which could mean either more money for the same work or promotion to a higher job grade. Demands for a wage increase raise questions concerning the rationality of the price tags on particular jobs and concerning the circumstances under which a rise in the level of wages in a plant or an industry is justified.

This chapter first discusses some of the conceptual and statistical problems that confront attempts to compare wages and to isolate union influences on wages. Guided by that orientation, the nation's wage *structure* is analyzed; the various types of wage differentials are examined and an attempt is made to assess the effects that collective bargaining has had on such differentials. Next, attention is directed to changes in the *level* of wages in sections of the economy and in the economy as a whole. The influence of both collective bargaining and unemployment upon the changes in the wage level is analyzed in order to try to assess the impact of unions on wage levels and, through labor costs, on the general price level.

Before turning to the technical problems of wage analysis, however, a brief glance at wage structures and wage changes in the 1930's, prior to the great spread of collective bargaining, may provide a useful perspective. It will help to indicate the wage situation that existed during a period when nonunion conditions were rather general.[1]

Wage structures in the absence of collective bargaining were unsystematic and irregular. C. Canby Balderston, a careful student of wage structures, wrote of the situation in the thirties:

> The majority of American companies have no definite program of wage and salary administration, and as a consequence their wage structures are replete with inconsistencies. Differing rates are paid to employees performing the same work through the operation of such factors as consideration of length of service, transfers of workers without rate adjustments, the absence of standard hiring rates, favoritism, and the frequent practice of allowing foremen to judge the value of each employee to the company. Often there is no logical relationship between rates for different occupations; with every flat percentage advance in wage the differentials are increased and the discriminations are emphasized.[2]

Nor were economic forces sufficient, even in the Great Depression, to force a considerable measure of uniformity in the pattern of wage decreases. A detailed study of wage change and profits for 95 individual pulp and paper companies between 1929 and 1939 showed "surprising diversity" in wage-rate changes for an industry so uniform in character.[3] A considerable number of companies cut wages several times while around one-seventh did not cut them

---

[1] For figures on the extent of unionization at various times see Figure 3, p. 85.

[2] *Wage Setting Based on Job Analysis and Evaluation* (New York: Industrial Relations Counselors, 1940), p. 3.

[3] For the data in this paragraph see W. Rupert Maclaurin, "Wages and Profits in the Paper Industry," *Quarterly Journal of Economics*, LX (February 1944), pp. 196–228. Few of the companies were organized in the 1929–33 downswing period; by the 1937–38 recession about two-fifths of the mills in the sample were unionized but the same proportion of union as nonunion mills cut wages in that recession.

at all. In a number of cases, the timing of the first wage reduction after 1929 differed by as much as two years for competing firms operating in the same town. Companies that maintained their wages at predepression levels apparently did so out of a sense of community responsibility and at considerable loss to their accumulated surplus from past profits.

Since the thirties, of course, expansion in the welfare concept of employment and the spread of collective bargaining have further reduced the effectiveness of market factors in determining wage structures and wage changes. We shall return to the question of the respective roles of market forces and institutional factors in shaping both wage differentials and wage changes after dealing with the difficulties of wage measurement.

PROBLEMS OF WAGE ANALYSIS

In any attempt to explain the wage structure and the effects unions have had on it, one is concerned with both wage differentials and wage equalities. And in investigating the influence of collective bargaining on wage movements one is interested in determining precisely the amount of wage change. For both purposes it is necessary to make careful statistical comparisons between occupations, firms, and industries. In attempting to do so one immediately encounters serious problems of definition and measurement. Those problems are particularly difficult because, with the shift to a long-term welfare basis of employment, the price of labor has become such a complex concept.

The many dimensions of employment make it troublesome to determine just what the employee is receiving for his work and what the employer's full costs of employment are. In addition to money income, the worker receives a variety of benefits and perquisites, including on-the-job training, insurance protections, deferred forms of pay such as pension rights, job rights through seniority, provisions for safety and physical comfort, employer subsidies for lunches, and the quality of immediate supervision on the job. The employer, of course, pays for all of those items in addition to the dollars in the pay envelope. However, in the analysis in this chapter these nonwage forms of employee income and employer cost will be largely disregarded. They are treated in detail in the next chapter.

Measurement Questions

Even with the analysis confined to money wages, real problems of comparability arise in examining wage differences between firms or industries at any one point of time, and between firms or industries on two different dates. Jobs with the same title may have significantly different duties and skill requirements in different firms and in the same firm on different dates.

In addition, the available wage statistics are largely in the form of average hourly earnings and average weekly earnings and not in the form of wage *rates*. As a calculated figure, average earnings have the disadvantage that they are affected by a variety of factors that change over time (i.e., composition of the work force, production methods and skill-mix, geographic shifts of industry,[4] opportunities for incentive earnings, automatic wage increases with length of service, and opportunities for overtime).

Devices exist for estimating and deducting premium pay for overtime and holidays and for shift differentials in order to arrive at a calculated figure for straight-time earnings. However, it is not possible to make statistical estimates for most of the other factors and, therefore, average earnings remain a conglomerate kind of a figure. For the most part, wage rates and average hourly earnings do tend to move together, though the linkage between them is rather loose. Therefore, despite the statistical difficulties, practical considerations make it necessary to use average hourly earnings' figures as the basis for much of our analysis.

Because that is the case, perhaps the differences between the time method of payment and incentive methods should be

---

[4] In a significant wage arbitration, Bureau of Labor Statistics figures for average hourly earnings of skilled and unskilled occupations in building construction were offered by the union's economist in proof of a spread in the skilled-unskilled differential between two dates. The employers' economist, however, demolished the proof by pointing out that the inference drawn from the statistics was invalid because by the second date the average included many more Southern cities which had an especially large skilled-unskilled wage differential in construction.

indicated. The hourly earnings' averages include both, and over a period of time there may be some divergence. Incentive methods base wages on output. The simplest method is piecerate—so much pay for each unit of output. More complicated incentive systems vary the relationship between output and pay; they may also combine payment by results with a guaranteed minimum hourly earnings or a time rate when the worker for some reason is "off incentive." A survey showed that in 1958 some 27 per cent of the production and related workers in manufacturing were paid on an incentive basis.[5] The proportion on incentive varied from 71 per cent in men's clothing and 66 per cent in cigar making to 3 per cent in cigarette and 2 per cent in hydraulic cement production. Comparison with corresponding figures for 1945–46 showed that during the twelve-year interval there had been no change in the over-all percentage of workers on incentive and little, if any, change in the ratios for most of the 56 industries.

Although the proportion of workers on incentive may remain stable, there is a tendency for incentive earnings to rise relative to time-rate earnings over a period of years. That occurs because incentive rates or production standards for incentives are not always adjusted to take account of minor improvements in the techniques of production or in the materials used, so that workers can turn out more with no greater effort.

Another issue on which opinion is divided is whether wage differentials should be measured in absolute or relative terms—in cents per hour or percentages. The difference in results can be indicated by an illustration. Suppose in the base year the average hourly wage for unskilled workers was $1.00 and for skilled workers was $2.00, and that ten years later the averages were $2.00 and $3.00 respectively. Has the skilled-unskilled differential narrowed or not over the ten-year interval? In absolute terms it remains the same, namely, a $1.00 difference, but in relative terms it has shrunk sharply. The skilled average, which in the base year was 100 per cent above the unskilled, is only 50 per cent above 10 years later.

For comparative purposes, a percentage standard might seem

---

[5] See L. Earl Lewis, "Extent of Incentive Pay in Manufacturing," *Monthly Labor Review*, LXXXIII (May 1960), pp. 460–63.

more appropriate. Equal percentage changes leave a person in the same relative position and seem a better measure of the relative attractiveness of jobs. Also, many other basic economic measurements are indexes expressed in relative terms.

On the other hand, workers and union leaders during some periods tend to think in terms of maintaining a differential in cents per hour or tend to measure their wage gains in absolute terms. That was especially true during World War II when the Government's wage stabilization policies fixed a maximum increase in percentage terms for each firm, which the parties translated and applied in the form of an equal increase in cents per hour across the board. Also from 1946 until 1950, uniform cents-per-hour increases were the prevalent pattern of wage change. In the fifties and early sixties, however, it became a widespread practice to grant percentage increases, or additional cents-per-hour increases for higher-paying jobs in order to maintain roughly the same percentage difference. Consequently, a cents-per-hour measure might be considered appropriate for the period 1941–50 but not thereafter. In our analysis, wage differentials will, however, be measured in percentage terms unless otherwise specified. For percentage comparisons of averages, the base period should be fairly typical or representative if the percentage changes are not to give a mistaken impression.

Analytical Approaches

In general, there are two approaches or ways of focussing one's thinking about a wage structure. One stems from the concept of a purely competitive labor market and visualizes wages as the resultant of market forces tending to bring about an equilibrium of demand and supply at "*the* competitive wage." That wage rate, according to this "competitive market approach," is the norm from which deviations or differentials should be measured and the standard on which judgments about the appropriateness of wage scales should be based.

An alternative framework of analysis may be called "the differential-range approach." It starts with the assumption that genuine wage differentials between firms within a zone or range are the normal situation in the absence of unions or intercompany collusion. This approach, therefore, considers differentials within a 10 or 15 per cent range to be natural. It postulates that pressures do not generally exist to enforce a single rate or even a central tendency within the range, partly because companies have different wage-paying ability and wage policies, their managements enjoy varying amounts of wage discretion, and most factory workers have a degree of attachment to the company.[6]

It is evident that the competitive market approach rests heavily on the traditional theory of the firm, the marginal productivity theory of wages, and the commodity concept of employment. The differential-range approach relies largely on a different set of concepts. They include the multipurpose, multiadjustment theory of management (Chapter 7), the notion of an administered labor market (Chapter 9), and the welfare concept of employment.

The competitive market approach would deny that genuine interfirm or interindustry wage differentials could exist in a locality over the long run. It would insist that any such differentials either are transitory or represent interfirm differences in quality of workforce.

A significant limitation of the competitive market approach is the difficulty of verifying it by operational or statistical testing. Its concepts of labor demand and supply schedules cannot be quantified in particular cases.[7] Even differences in quality of workforce between firms are hard to measure.[8]

The differential-range approach has the advantage that it takes account of the individualistic character of much company wage policy,[9] and allows for the variety of wage differentials revealed

---

[6] For an early version of this approach see Richard A. Lester, "A Range Theory of Wages," *Industrial and Labor Relations Review*, V (July 1952), pp. 483–500.

[7] See the discussion between Simon Rottenberg and Robert J. Lampman concerning the problem of empirical testing of classical wage theory and the "verifiable predictions" of empiricists in "On Choice in Labor Markets," *Industrial and Labor Relations Review*, IX (July 1956), pp. 629–41. See also Lloyd G. Reynolds and Cynthia H. Taft, *The Evolution of Wage Structures* (New Haven: Yale University Press, 1956), p. 169.

[8] See Robert Evans, Jr., "Worker Quality and Wage Dispersion: An Analysis of a Clerical Labor Market in Boston" and "Discussion," *Proceedings of Fourteenth Annual Meeting of Industrial Relations Research Association* (Gerald G. Somers, ed.), December 28–29, 1961, Industrial Relations Research Association, 1962, pp. 246–59 and 289–98.

[9] See Richard A. Lester, *Company Wage Policies: A Survey of Patterns and Experience*, Industrial Relations Section, Princeton University, Princeton, N.J., 1948.

in the statistics, including not only interindustry differentials but also wage differentials based on race and sex and a tendency for size-of-firm differentials. With that approach one is not surprised by Professor Balderston's comments on the haphazard character of company wage structures,[10] or by the markedly divergent wage policies pursued by the pulp and paper companies in the thirties.[11] And one can readily understand the need of company managements for job-evaluation programs[12] so as to bring some semblance of order out of chaotic wage conditions.

Indeed, the existence of job evaluation is evidence that wage differentials within an industrial plant are largely administratively (not market) determined. With work-life attachment and promotion from within, it is difficult even to conceive of a separate demand and supply schedule for each particular job in a line of promotion or in a job hierarchy.[13]

The differential-range approach also has its limitations. It too is troubled by the problem of measurement of labor quality and the determination of job comparability. But its chief difficulty is that so many different factors (including historical accidents) can affect both a firm's location in the range and the width of the range that it is difficult to develop an uncomplicated theory that would explain and predict both firm location and the width of the range.[14] Clearly, certain institutional arrangements, such as agreements on wage levels and wage change among employers and

---

[10] See p. 293.

[11] See pp. 293–94.

[12] Job evaluation or "job rating" is a way of pricing the jobs within a plant by a systematic scheme. Formal methods usually involve ranking the jobs according to the composite figure arrived at by weighting each job for certain selected attributes (such as skill and education required, degree of responsibility, physical effort involved, and disagreeableness of work conditions). Then the graduated series is priced by establishing the wage for a few particular jobs in the series as "peg points" and pricing the others according to their ranking relative to the peg jobs. Hiring-in jobs, such as unskilled labor and maintenance crafts, are usually used as peg jobs because they are common to many companies and a local wage survey will provide a picture of such rates in the locality. Where in the scatter of rates for a job in the locality the company wishes to establish its wage for that job under its evaluation program is a matter of judgment and would depend on the management's objectives.

[13] For a discussion of this point see E. Robert Livernash, "The Internal Wage Structure" in G. W. Taylor and F. C. Pierson (eds.), *New Concepts in Wage Determination* (New York: McGraw-Hill, 1957), pp. 140–47.

[14] For a discussion of these matters see R. A. Lester, "A Range Theory of Wage Differentials," *op. cit.*

the guidance of new labor supplies by experienced counselors, can serve to narrow the wage range for an occupation in a community.[15]

As each type of differential is analyzed, the usefulness of one approach or the other in illuminating the facts will be indicated. In general, it can be said that the competitive wage approach is better for long-run analysis than for short-run analysis, and that the differential-range approach is better for analyzing community wage structures than it is for interregional or international wage differences.

Determination of Union Influence

Any attempt to measure the influence of unions on wage structures and wage levels encounters basic methodological problems.[16] As has already been observed, wage rates are influenced by many factors of which unionism may be one. The problem is to isolate the *independent* influence of a union from all other factors operating at the same time. Unions, of course, affect wages through bargaining negotiations and agreements with employers.

One might think that a comparison of wages (wage scales or average earnings) in union plants with those in nonunion plants would provide an answer, that the differences would be due to the union. Unfortunately, it is not that simple. As the differential-range approach indicates, such a difference may be caused by many factors. In addition, unions often organize first the larger plants, so that unionized plants as a group might have higher wages without any collective bargaining.

For conclusions regarding the effects of particular unions on wage structures, one can also study changes within the unionized sector itself. Where unions have policies with respect to wage

---

[15] See the author's comments on a study of clerical employees of banks and insurance companies in *Aspects of Labor Economics, A Conference of the Universities-National Bureau Committee for Economic Research* (Princeton: Princeton University Press, 1962), pp. 152–53.

[16] For more detailed discussions of these problems see William G. Bowen, *The Wage-Price Issue: A Theoretical Analysis* (Princeton: Princeton University Press, 1960), pp. 163–66; and Robert Ozanne, "Impact of Unions on Wage Levels and Income Distribution," *Quarterly Journal of Economics*, LXXIII (May 1959), pp. 180–83.

differentials and seek to achieve them through negotiations with employers, the settlements may give some indication of union influence. However, one cannot be sure that a change of the same sort would not have occurred in the absence of the union.

The interrelatedness of wage change makes it especially difficult to determine union influence on movements in the wage level for an area, industry, or the whole economy. Wage changes in unionized firms may spread to nonunion companies because of customary relationships or a management's efforts to avoid unionization.

Consideration of the effect of wage increases in the unionized sectors of the economy upon wages in the nonunionized sectors illustrates how the competitive market approach and the differential-range approach often lead to opposite conclusions. The competitive approach assumes that higher wages in the unionized sectors would reduce the amount of labor that companies there will employ, forcing the disemployed labor to seek employment in the nonunion sectors. The increased supply of labor in the nonunion sectors "would tend to lower wage rates [there] because of the increased competition of workers for jobs."[17] Thus, the assumption of the competitive market approach would be that collective bargaining, by raising wages above "the competitive level" in unionized lines depresses "the competitive wage" in nonunion lines, thereby serving to widen wage differentials between union and nonunion industries.

Actual experience, however, indicates that reasoning on company wage policy in terms of pattern-spreading and imitation to avoid organization (a differential-range type of reasoning) is more correct, at least in the short run, than the chain of analysis in terms of labor supply and labor competition.[18]

---

[17] See Milton Friedman, "Some Comments on the Significance of Labor Unions for Economic Policy," in David McCord Wright (ed.), *The Impact of the Union* (New York: Harcourt, Brace, 1951), p. 216 (footnote), and Milton Friedman, "Comment" in *Review of Economics and Statistics*, XXXVII (November 1955), p. 404.

[18] For a discussion of company policies aimed at maintaining a fixed relationship to community or industry wage levels see Richard A. Lester, *Company Wage Policies, op. cit.*, pp. 13–18. For a discussion of the effects of unions on nonunion wages see Lloyd Ulman, "Marshall and Friedman on Union Strength," *Review of Economics and Statistics*, XXXVII (November 1955), pp. 394–98.

An additional difficulty with the use of direct comparisons of wage change to measure union impact is that the unionized sectors of the economy are, generally speaking, dominated by large firms enjoying a considerable degree of control over their markets. Consequently, they may react differently than small-scale industries with respect to changes in product prices, and they may differ in terms of profitableness of operations, increases in labor productivity, skill composition of the work force, and distribution of employee gains between wages and employee benefits. As a result, short-run comparisons of wage change in union and nonunion sectors may be measuring, to a significant extent, the influences of differences in type of firm and in management policies.

Chapter 2 discussed the pitfall of single causation. The problems of wage analysis richly illustrate the risks one runs in drawing single-causation inferences from statistical comparisons. Significant wage-determining factors often appear together and operate in combination, so that the analyst must guard against assuming that one factor alone is responsible for joint-factor results.

PATTERN AND BEHAVIOR OF DIFFERENTIALS

The notion of a wage structure composed of a variety of differentials is, of course, an abstraction. Wage statistics can be grouped (classified) and summarized (averaged) in various ways. For analytical purposes, some of the most meaningful groupings are by occupation, industry, and geographic location (urban-rural and region). Workers and managements tend to think about wages along those lines.

Where there are distinct occupations or crafts cutting across industries, the wage orientation tends to be occupational. Where a national industry is a rather cohesive unit, for such reasons as common markets, production methods, or special employment characteristics, the wage focus is likely to be industrial. Notable examples are railroads, coal, steel, automobile assembly, airframe manufacture, glass, pulp and paper, meat packing, oil, and rubber tires. For many types of work, especially unskilled labor and jobs in firms catering to local or regional markets, the wage orientation tends to be geographical (the locality or the region).

There are, of course, additional classifications of wage data from which differentials can be derived. Some wage differences stem from personal characteristics—race, sex, and inexperience (learners or apprenticeship rates). Others, like local interplant differences in the same industry or for the same occupation, may be the result of a mixture of factors, including the so-called size-of-firm differential and product-market differences that affect a firm's wage-paying ability.

Our analysis will concentrate on four types of wage differentials: occupational, interindustry, local interplant, and geographical.

Occupational Differentials

In examining the statistics of hourly earnings for an industry over a long period, one is struck by (a) the persistence of a pattern of occupational differentials and (b) a tendency during certain periods (especially wars) for the percentage difference between unskilled and skilled rates to narrow (although the cents-per-hour differences continue to increase). During such inflationary periods the whole wage structure tends to be compressed.

Once a ladder of occupational rates becomes established in an industry, each job tends to maintain its position in that ranking.[19] Workers and managements develop a notion of where a particular occupation belongs in the company's wage structure. Tradition, patterns of promotion, workers' efforts to maintain status, and many other influences operate against changing the rank of the job, despite significant alterations in job content or in the number of available trained personnel for it.

Over the past century, the skilled-unskilled differential in most industries has tended to narrow in percentage terms. During some decades, however, skill differentials have even widened somewhat. For example, a careful study by Clarence D. Long indicates that, generally speaking, the percentage differential between the daily wages of unskilled and skilled occupations increased slightly (perhaps 4 per cent on the average) during the three decades from 1860 to 1890.[20]

---

[19] For a statistical study indicating over a forty-year period no essential change in the structure of occupational wage rates in seven industries, see Stanley Lebergott, "Wage Structures," *Review of Economics and Statistics*, XXIX (November 1947), pp. 283–84.

[20] See Long, *Wages and Earnings in the United States, 1860–1890* (Princeton: Princeton University Press, 1960), pp. 98–104.

The long-run trend toward compression of skill differentials is indicated by comparisons of occupational differentials in the early 1960's with those for the same occupations in the 1840's and 1850's.[21] Such comparisons show, for example, that in cotton textiles, loom-fixers changed relatively from three times the pay for female drawing-frame tenders to only about one and a third times as much, printing pressmen's wages from over three times the wages of press feeders to but one and a fifth as much, and bricklayer's wages from double hodcarrier's pay to one and a third as much.[22] Interestingly, in view of their use in a study discussed below, wages for skilled occupations in the metal trades (machinists, millwrights, and pattern makers) in the middle of the last century were only 40 to 50 per cent above the pay for laborers,[23] which is not much larger than the present-day percentage.

A well-known study by Harry Ober indicates that between 1907 and 1947 the skilled-unskilled differential declined from skilled hourly earnings running about double unskilled earnings to a figure of only around 50 per cent above unskilled wages.[24] The bulk of that compression occurred during and after World War I and World War II (1916–20 and 1941–50). Rising living costs in war periods tend to stimulate wage increases in the form of uniform cents-per-hour across the board; also, in war booms unskilled

---

[21] Of course, content of the occupations changed somewhat but they still represented skilled and unskilled types of work and, therefore, were near the top and bottom of the plant wage hierarchy.

[22] For the wage statistics for these occupations in the 1840's and 1850's see *History of Wages in the United States from Colonial Times to 1928*, Bureau of Labor Statistics Bulletin No. 604 (Washington: United States Government Printing Office, 1934), pp. 154, 178, 340, 355, 437, and 441. For the 1960 figures see *Wage Structure: Cotton Textiles, 1960*, United States Bureau of Labor Statistics Report No. 184, May 1961, pp. 19 and 20; *Union Wages and Hours: Building Trades, July 1, 1961 and Trend 1907–61*, United States Bureau of Labor Statistics, Bulletin No. 1316, p. 9; and *Union Wages and Hours: Printing Industry, July 1, 1961 and Trend 1907–61*, United States Bureau of Labor Statistics, Bulletin No. 1315, May 1962, p. 10.

[23] *History of Wages in the United States from Colonial Times to 1928*, pp. 253, 298, 308, and 318.

[24] See Ober, "Occupational Wage Differentials in Industry," in W. S. Woytinsky and Associates, *Employment and Wages in the United States* (New York: Twentieth Century Fund, 1953), pp. 466–74; and Ober, "Occupational Wage Differentials, 1907–1947," *Monthly Labor Review*, LXVII (August 1948), pp. 127–34.

labor becomes relatively scarce and its turnover rates rise significantly.

From an intensive study of wages at the McCormick Works of International Harvester Company over the century from 1858 to 1959, Robert Ozanne concluded that no long-run narrowing trend in occupational differentials was evident.[25] For skilled wages over most of the period he used an average of hourly rates for pattern-shop craftsmen, which, as observed above, were only about 50 per cent higher than unskilled wages in the 1850's.

Ozanne's study does, however, throw doubt on some widely held views concerning wage behavior. He found that, contrary to labor-supply reasoning, skill differentials at the McCormick Works tended to widen in prosperity and narrow in depression, primarily because of the management's reluctance to cut the low wages of common labor. Significant short-run changes occurred in the skill differential as a result of pressures (labor unrest, organization, and strikes), which were brought to bear by skilled employees and unskilled employees at separate time intervals, and which influenced the management's attitude and wage policies. Ozanne concluded from his study that (a) unionization had a substantial effect on skill differentials (craft unionism widening and industrial unionism narrowing them), and (b) skill differentials were influenced as much by internal pressures (union policies and management and worker notions of equity) as they were by external conditions of labor supply.[26]

An extreme illustration of the influence of union policies on wage structure is the railroad industry. From 1937 to 1956, it consistently followed a system of uniform pattern settlements for all classes of employees. That was done to meet the problem of intense rivalry for membership, jurisdiction, and prestige among the 51 unions holding representation rights on railroads, with employees free to move from one union to another and with many of the unions seeking to represent the same classes of employees. Under uniform, cents-per-hour increases across the board, the cumulative total of general wage increases between August 1937 and December 1955 was $1.09 for the road operating

---

[25] Robert Ozanne, "A Century of Occupational Differentials in Manufacturing," *Review of Economics and Statistics*, XLIV (August 1962), pp. 292–99.

[26] *Ibid.*, p. 299.

occupations and $1.094 for the nonoperating employees. The consequence was that by 1960, the hourly earnings of boiler makers and machinists in railroad shops were less than 20 per cent above those for common labor.[27]

In the steel industry, the United Steelworkers and the managements have pursued the opposite kind of a policy. Although between 1907 and 1938, most skill differentials in steel experienced much the same general contraction that occurred in most other industries, beginning with the industry job-evaluation program negotiated in 1947, the wage differences between the job classes maintained almost the same percentage throughout the period from 1947 to 1960—the base rates for the 32 labor grades or classifications just about doubled in those thirteen years.[28]

The union had a considerable influence in maintaining those percentage differentials, especially between 1947 and 1952 when most other industries were experiencing a significant narrowing of differentials between skilled and unskilled jobs. This was done with management support by allocating part of the wage increase to widening increments between the 32 job classes in seven of the nine negotiated settlements from 1947 to 1960.[29] The work force in basic steel has a higher proportion in the upper skill categories than is true for most industries organized by industrial unions, and the skilled workers in steel are especially influential with the union's leadership.[30]

Undoubtedly, the new industrial unions exerted some influence on reduction in the percentage wage differentials by favoring uniform cents-per-hour increases in the forties and in the fifties under the cost-of-living escalator clauses. The resulting compression in the wage structure caused protests by skilled workers, some of

---

[27] The average earnings per hour worked as reported by the railroads to the Interstate Commerce Commission for December 1959 were: boiler makers $2.81, machinists $2.79, common laborers $2.37, office boys and messengers $2.20.

[28] See Jack Stieber, *The Steel Industry Wage Structure: A Study of the Joint Union-Management Job Evaluation Program in the Basic Steel Industry* (Cambridge: Harvard University Press, 1959), pp. 238–43; and *Agreement between U. S. Steel Corporation and the United Steelworkers of America, Production and Maintenance Employees,* January 4, 1960, Appendix A, pp. 88. The 1963 agreement continues the same wage scales to 1965.

[29] In contrast to the railroad situation, the rate for machinists in steel in 1960 was about 48 per cent above the hourly rate for common labor.

[30] See Stieber, *op. cit.,* pp. 247–49.

whom threatened to withdraw from industrial unions as in autos. Special additional increases for skilled workers and more wage increases in percentage form caused percentage differentials to become fairly stabilized in the fifties.

Probably, the railroads and steel represent the extreme cases of union influence resulting in the narrowing and the maintenance of skilled-unskilled wage differentials. In general, however, industrial unions in the thirties and forties seem to have had somewhat more influence on the structure of occupational wage differentials than Reynolds and Taft conclude from their extensive study, namely, that "the effect of unionism on occupational differentials appears to have been slight" and not "very strong relative to the influence of market forces."[31]

Interindustry Differentials

The occupations that generally cut across industry lines are the skilled maintenance crafts at the top of plant wage scales and the unskilled or common labor jobs at the bottom. Some industries pay much higher wage scales than others for those "hiring-in" jobs as well as for the jobs in between to which employees are promoted. The following are high-wage industries not only in this country but in Canada, Great Britain, and other countries: petroleum refining, aircraft and automobile assembly, chemicals, printing, rubber tires and tubes, and steel. On the other hand, wage scales are relatively low in industries like cotton textiles and clothing, tobacco, leather and leather products, food preparation and canning, furniture, and fertilizer.[32] Most of these low-wage industries are close to agriculture, from which they attract labor and whose wages generally are at the bottom of the wage hierarchy.

With significant interindustry differentials, diversified firms may be unable to follow consistent company-wide wage standards or policies. Such multiindustry companies often find it necessary to follow different wage scales and separate patterns of wage

---

[31] Lloyd G. Reynolds and Cynthia H. Taft, *op. cit.*, pp. 185–186.

[32] See Stanley Lebergott, *op. cit.*, pp. 275–76; and Sumner H. Slichter, "Notes on the Structure of Wages," *Review of Economics and Statistics*, XXXII (February 1950), p. 83.

change in their textile, fertilizer, or plastics operations from those in their rubber tire, oil, or chemical plants. Over a decade the amounts and timing of wage increases in soft-goods industries may be significantly different from those in hard goods.

Nevertheless, studies show that the industry wage hierarchy has persisted over a half century with little change in the relative position of industries and little long-run tendency toward compression of percentage wage differences between industries.[33]

Interindustry differentials seem to be largely determined by economic factors. In general, an industry tends to rank high in terms of hiring rates for male common labor[34] when it has most of the following characteristics: value added by manufacturing per wage-earner hour is a large figure, labor costs are a low percentage of total costs, profit margins are high, and the industry tends to be dominated by a few large firms.[35] Low-wage industries generally have the opposite conditions with respect to labor productivity, labor-cost percentage, profit margins, and product market competition.

Evidence indicates that managerial policy plays a role in determining interindustry wage differentials.[36] Where economic conditions are favorable, managements tend to follow a high-wage policy. Henry Ford, by boldly establishing a five dollar minimum wage for an eight-hour day in all Ford operations in 1914, influenced the auto industry wage level far into the future.[37] The early policy of the Standard Oil Company of paying "at least the

---

[33] See Donald E. Cullen, "The Interindustry Wage Structure, 1899–1950," *American Economic Review*, XLVI (June 1956), pp. 353–69.

[34] Of course, industries may hire somewhat different quality of labor. The newly hired steel worker is different from the new textile worker, both of whom are entering the bottom jobs.

[35] See Slichter, *op. cit.*, pp. 83–91; Joseph W. Garbarino, "A Theory of Interindustry Wage Structure Variation," *Quarterly Journal of Economics*, LXIV (May 1950), pp. 282–305; and Arthur M. Ross and William Goldner, "Forces Affecting the Interindustry Wage Structure," *Quarterly Journal of Economics*, LXIV (May 1950), pp. 254–61.

[36] Slichter, *op. cit.*, pp. 89–90.

[37] Before going to a five dollar minimum Ford stated that his wages already averaged "about 15 per cent above the usual market rate," and the large increase to bring workers up to five dollars was thought of as a form of profit-sharing by Ford. See Henry Ford in collaboration with Samuel Crowther, *My Life and Work* (New York: Doubleday, Page, 1922), pp. 126–28.

prevailing scale of wages for similar work in the community" helped to establish a high wage rank for the oil industry.[38]

Unions have had some impact on interindustry wage differentials. Just how much industrial unions have themselves been responsible for bringing about a relative increase in an industry's wage level is, however, subject to dispute. The influence of a union in promoting a significant increase in an industry's wage rank appears to be confined to particular periods of time or stages in union development. One such time is during and right after the unionization of an industry.[39] Also long-term agreements with automatic annual wage increases and cost-of-living adjustments tended to raise the wage levels of certain industries during recession periods in the fifties.

On the basis of some industry studies, Albert Rees estimates that strong unions may have been responsible for raising wages in some mass production industries by as much as 10 to 15 per cent.[40] The 1953–59 experience in the steel industry is often cited as an example. Total negotiated wage increases in steel for those years were some twelve to eighteen cents per hour above the increases negotiated by the other mass production industries, thus advancing steel by 5 to 8 per cent.[41] Between 1954 and 1959 average hourly earnings in steel rose 40 per cent, whereas in other mass production industries they rose 23 to 29 per cent and in all manufacturing by 23 per cent.[42] Increases in steel during those years brought the average hourly earnings of skilled craftsmen in the steel industry well above those for similar jobs in other industries

---

[38] See Clarence J. Hicks, *My Life in Industrial Relations, Fifty Years in the Growth of a Profession* (New York: Harper, 1941), p. 56.

[39] Ross and Goldner, *op. cit.*, p. 267 conclude that "New unionism (that is, unionization) has been a source of relative wage advantage during the 1933–46 period, whereas continuing unionism has not." Paul H. Douglas drew a similar conclusion from his study of real wages over a 36-year period [*Real Wages in the United States, 1890–1926* (Boston: Houghton Mifflin, 1930), p. 562].

[40] Albert Rees, *The Economics of Trade Unions* (Chicago: University of Chicago Press, 1962), p. 78.

[41] *Collective Bargaining in the Basic Steel Industry, A Study of the Public Interest and the Role of Government,* United States Department of Labor, January 1961, p. 142.

[42] *Ibid.*, p. 137. For that period the increases in average hourly earnings ranged from only 13 to 17 per cent for the following soft-goods industries: textile mill products, apparel, furniture, and leather and leather goods.

in steel producing cities.[43] Thus, market forces could hardly account for the larger increases in steel. However, the influence of market forces may help to account for the more modest wage increases in steel from 1961 to 1963 and the absence of any increase in wages in the agreement for 1963–65.[44]

If company contributions to benefit plans were added to wages as part of compensation, the interindustry differentials would probably be widened somewhat. High-wage firms generally have more benefit programs and more liberal benefit provisions than low-wage firms. Steel, for example, made significant increases in company benefits during 1953–59.

One consequence of widespread unionism and collective bargaining on interindustry differentials seems to have been a reduction in the effect that employment changes have on such differentials, particularly during business recessions.[45] For the period from 1952 to 1960, some of the industries whose employment declined significantly (such as steel, autos, railroads, and coal) were among those with the largest percentage increases in average hourly earnings.

Local Differentials

One of the most significant facts about wages is that sizable differences often exist in the rates of pay for essentially the same work within one community. As was explained in the preceding chapter, usually there is a marked differential between the highest-paying and the lowest-paying firm using comparable labor in a

---

[43] Jack Stieber, *op. cit.*, pp. 245–47.

[44] As explained in the next chapter, in the 1963 steel negotiations the stress of the union was on employment and benefit protections, the added costs of which were well below the annual wage increases in 1953–59.

[45] A statistical study by William G. Bowen found a high correlation between an industry's rate of increase in wages and in employment during two of the postwar boom periods but no correlation during the other boom and the three recession periods. (See Bowen, *Wage Behavior in the Postwar Period, An Empirical Analysis,* Industrial Relations Section, Princeton University, Princeton, N.J. 1960, pp. 64–67 and Appendix C.) Statistical analyses of 27 and 61 industries using annual percentage changes in hourly earnings and annual percentage changes in employment in each industry found no significant relationship between them. (See *Staff Report on Employment, Growth, and Price Levels,* prepared for consideration of the Joint Economic Committee, Congress of the United States, December 24, 1959, pp. 147–49.)

particular locality. Furthermore, the high-wage firms generally have more favorable nonwage terms and conditions of employment (employee benefit plans, physical working arrangements, safety programs, and employment security).

Partly, local wage differentials are a reflection of interindustry differentials. At the extremes of the community wage range, they undoubtedly reflect differences in type, sex, experience, or quality of labor. But studies indicate that, in part, local wage differentials are due to differences in such factors as the past company developments, the company's ability to pay, management attitudes and policies, and the particular union organization and its policies in case the company is organized.[46]

Various methods can be used to try to eliminate from local wage comparisons the factors of interindustry differentials, differences in worker quality, and union differences. One way is to make local wage comparisons only for firms in the same industry or even to confine them to one branch of an industry. Another is to compare local wage rates for one occupation that is common to many firms and is under the jurisdiction of a single "craft" union.

The first method was applied to all the cotton textile mills in six southern textile communities in the spring of 1945. The number of mills ranged from seven to sixteen per community. The occupations selected for comparative purposes had considerable homogeneity because the equipment being used was standard. All of the mills were nonunion except for one in each of four communities, and none of the union mills was the highest paying one in its locality for any occupation. Nevertheless for the six communities the average occupational spread (expressed as the per cent that the highest paying firm was above the lowest paying

---

[46] Apparently interfirm comparisons are not affected much by personal dispersion of wages within occupational categories in particular manufacturing establishments. A study of seven plant occupations in thirteen labor market areas found that 91 to 96 per cent of the variation in rates was due to interestablishment rate differences and only 4 to 9 per cent was due to intraestablishment variations in rates. The author concluded that "the major factor in occupational wage dispersion within labor markets is, in fact, differences in wage levels among establishments." See H. M. Douty, "Sources of Occupational Wage and Salary Dispersion within Labor Markets," *Industrial and Labor Relations Review*, XV (October 1961), p. 72 and Table 3, p. 71.

firm for that occupation) was as follows: 9, 13, 14, 17, 19, and 41 per cent.[47] Those figures would seem to indicate that a model that assumes genuine interfirm differentials within 10 to 15 per cent range in a locality is not extreme.

Similarly, as part of another study, the bottom or starting rates for males in twelve rubber companies and four tableware companies in Trenton, New Jersey, were compared in the early months of 1952. For the twelve rubber companies, the top firm's starting rate of $1.44 was 37 per cent above the rate of $1.05 for the lowest paying firm.[48] Among the twelve rubber companies were four rubber hose manufacturers and four hard rubber manufacturers; the corresponding spread for them was thirteen and fourteen per cent respectively. For the four tableware firms the spread in starting rates was from 85 cents to $1.225, or 44 per cent. In each case, inspection of the plant and an interview with the management failed to reveal significant differences in quality of the workforce in the rubber hose, hard rubber, and tableware factories.

Using the method of a single occupation and a single union, John T. Dunlop compared union rates for motor-truck drivers in various types of service in Boston in July 1953.[49] The rates were negotiated between the Teamsters' union and an association or group of local employers for each branch of truck transportation. The relative ranking for the various branches in Boston was similar to that in most other cities.

The figures showed a wide disparity in rates. At the top of the twenty-two-rate hierarchy were: $2.49 an hour for magazine hauling, $2.393 for newspaper trucking, $2.215 for oil trucks after

---

[47] For full details see Richard A. Lester, "Wage Diversity and Its Theoretical Implications," *Review of Economics and Statistics*, XXVIII (August 1946), pp. 154–57.

[48] See Richard A. Lester, *Hiring Practices and Labor Competition*, Industrial Relations Section, Princeton University, Princeton, N.J., 1954, pp. 75–77. In the first half of 1953 the 12 rubber companies were restudied and at that time the starting-rate spread was from $1.20 to $1.51 or 26 per cent. (See Lester, *Adjustments to Labor Shortages, Management Practices and Institutional Controls in an Area of Expanding Employment*, Industrial Relations Section, Princeton University, Princeton, N.J., 1955, p. 60.)

[49] John T. Dunlop, "The Task of Contemporary Wage Theory," in G. W. Taylor and F. C. Pierson, *New Concepts in Wage Determination, op. cit.*, pp. 134–36.

thirty months on the job, $2.062 for paperhandlers' hauling, and $1.90 to $2.00 for large building construction trucks and tractors. At the bottom of the array were wholesale laundry trucking at $1.28, and scrap iron and metal trucking at $1.27. Thus, the top rate was 96 per cent above the bottom rate.[50]

Dunlop points out that the truckdrivers who worked at those different rates were essentially similar in qualifications and were substitutable for one another even though "some small part of the differences in wages may be attributable to variations in skill or work performed; some may be related to differences in length of the work week and the timing of contract expiration during a year, and some may arise from differences in method of wage payment."[51] To cite what might seem to be rather comparable jobs, beer trucks paid hourly rates 24 per cent above trucks carrying Coca-Cola.

A number of factors help explain such intraoccupational wage disparities. Part of the explanation is that interindustry wage differentials affect the trucking wage structure through direct contact of truck drivers with, say, high-paid oil and building construction workers and low-paid laundry and scrap metal employees. Partly, it is a matter of differences in the ability of the various branches of trucking to pay high wages. To some extent such truckdriver differences are a result of historical developments that occurred prior to unionization, and a pattern once established cannot be rapidly altered.

Generally, unions seek to take wages out of competition through a policy of equal pay for equal work—the same scale for competing firms, a standard rate for all journeymen trained in the craft. In many instances such a policy of wage uniformity has led, by collective bargaining, to the elimination of local differentials among firms in the same industry or organized by the same union. In fact, wage uniformity among firms in a locality or an industry generally is the result, not of market forces, but of collective bargaining or employer cooperation on wage scales and

---

[50] Nine years later (July 1962) the spread between the extreme rates had declined to 48 per cent. See *Union Wages and Hours: Motortruck Drivers and Helpers, July 1, 1962 and Trend 1936–62*, United States Bureau of Labor Statistics Bulletin No. 1356, May 1963, pp. 8–9.

[51] *Op. cit.*, p. 134.

wage changes. Through collective bargaining, unions have also tended to spread standard rates or wage uniformity from the center of a city to operations on the outskirts or in the surrounding area.

In some cases, however, interfirm differences are so embedded or are so unimportant competitively that union leaders may decide that intercompany wage uniformity is not worth the struggle it would require. That seems to be the situation with the Auto Workers in Detroit. Minor differences in the wage structure of General Motors, Ford, and Chrysler have not been "ironed out" by any union campaign for wage uniformity in the automobile industry's center of production.

Geographical Differentials

Wage levels tend to vary with population density and the region. Generally speaking, pay scales are higher in cities than in rural areas and are higher, the larger the city. Also wage levels are generally lower in the South than in the North (Northeast and Midwest), and are higher in the West (Mountain States and Pacific Coast) than in the North. Such geographic differences in wages usually are larger for unskilled occupations than for skilled jobs.

Of course, industries with a national market and a definite wage structure may disregard geographic wage differences and pay the same scale wherever their plants are located. That is largely true of the following industries: automobile assembly, aircraft assembly, bituminous coal, glass, railroads, rayon, and basic steel.

The influence of high-wage industries and the degree of labor organization on community wage levels is indicated by a study of 82 metropolitan areas in 1960–61.[52] It revealed that Detroit had the highest wage level for office and skilled maintenance workers, and that for unskilled plant workers the highest-paying areas were in this order: San Francisco, Akron, and Detroit and South Bend (Indiana), the latter the location of the Studebaker plant. The lowest-wage metropolitan areas among those with a population of a quarter of a million or more were: for unskilled workers, San Antonio (Texas) and New Orleans; for skilled workers, Portland

---

[52] T. P. Kanninen, "Wage Differences among Labor Markets," *Monthly Labor Review*, LXXXV (June 1962), pp. 614–20.

(Maine), New Haven (Connecticut), and Providence (Rhode Island). The best known geographic wage difference is the so-called "North-South differential." The amount of that differential is, however, difficult to determine. Partly the reason is that regional differences in wages vary so much from industry to industry and from occupation to occupation and for different areas in each region. Also allowance has to be made for the fact that the South has a higher proportion of low-wage types of industry (mostly soft goods), and that its manufacturing plants are generally more scattered in small communities.[53]

The average North-South differential is now probably around 10 per cent. Over the past seventy years it has declined for some industries but not for others. From the midtwenties to the midforties the North-South differential narrowed considerably in such industries as cotton textiles, hosiery, pulp and paper, and fertilizer. In bituminous coal the North-South differential was eliminated for day work by collective bargaining in 1941. In basic steel a North-South differential, which amounted to 17.5 cents an hour for U.S. Steel in 1945, was practically eliminated through constant pressure on the part of the union.[54] On the other hand, the ratio of Southern to Northern wage scales appears to have experienced little long-run change in other industries like lumber, furniture, building construction, and agriculture.[55]

A study covering manufacturing industries for the period 1947 to 1954 showed that the North-South wage differential narrowed for 62 per cent of the industries having 73 per cent of the employees.[56] Separate calculations revealed that this regional differential declined for 70 per cent of the industries dominated by multiplant concerns and producing for national markets, whereas it narrowed for only 40 per cent of the industries producing for

[53] For an indication of the magnitude of average size-of-city differentials see *ibid.*, p. 620.

[54] See Jack Stieber, *op. cit.*, pp. 250–52. A 17.5-cent differential was equivalent to about 12 per cent of the average hourly earnings in steel in 1947.

[55] For calculations prior to 1945, see Richard A. Lester, "Trends in Southern Wage Differentials since 1890," in *Southern Economic Journal*, XI (April 1945), pp. 317–44; and for a general review see Lester, "Southern Wage Differentials: Developments, Analysis and Implications," *Southern Economic Journal*, XIII (April 1947), pp. 386–94.

[56] Martin Segal, "Regional Wage Differences in Manufacturing in the Postwar Period," *Review of Economics and Statistics*, XLIII (May 1961), pp. 148–55.

local or regional markets. The study concluded that collective bargaining exerted a distinct influence on the course of regional differentials, helping to account for the high proportion of multi-plant concerns that experienced some narrowing of the differential, but that its influence varied considerably between different sectors of manufacturing and among individual industries.

Various economic reasons have been offered for the relatively lower level of wages in the South. They include: the rapid growth of population and thus the supply of labor there, the lower productivity in Southern agriculture, a lower cost of living, a claimed lower efficiency of workers, and an alleged lower ratio of capital to labor in manufacturing.

All of those factors, it is worth noting, should presumably affect all industries and can, therefore, hardly explain why some industries have no North-South differential and others have southern wage scales averaging 20 to 30 per cent below those of competing northern firms.[57] Furthermore, some of these reasons do not hold up well under examination. Studies show that regional differences in the cost of the same standard of living in the same type of community average no more than 3 to 4 per cent. Experience of multiplant firms in both regions shows that southern labor can be just as efficient as northern labor. With respect to capital-labor ratios, many plants in the South have more capital per employee than comparable northern plants, because southern plants tend to be relatively newer and more modern. Census data show that the electric energy used per man-hour in southern manufacturing has generally averaged well above the comparable average for the North.

Many significant aspects of wage differentials cannot be elucidated by one factor alone or just by the operation of economic principles. It is easy to exaggerate the importance of a particular factor—whether market forces, managerial policy, or union pressures—when wages are actually affected by so many variables, some of which operate in conjunction with others. Under collective bargaining, of course, management has to agree with the negotiated settlements, so that union wage policies affect geographic differentials through company managements.

---

[57] These reasons can hardly explain why the average differential between the two regions has been three or four times as great for rubber tire production as it has for such related industries as autos, aircraft, and oil.

WAGE LEVEL CHANGES

Normally, the level of wages rises from decade to decade. That is true of money wages and also of real wages (the purchasing power of the money wages). As Tables 9 and 10 show, average earnings in manufacturing rose from 9.5 cents an hour in 1860 to $2.26 an hour in 1960, and the increase in real hourly earnings per decade averaged 24 per cent for the century from 1860 to 1960.

TABLE 9

Average Hourly Earnings in Manufacturing, 1860 to 1960

Year	Cents per Hour
1860	9.5
1870	14.5
1880	13.0
1890	14.4
1900	15.1
1910	19.8
1920	54.9
1930	54.6
1940	65.5
1950	144.4
1960	226.0

Sources: Clarence D. Long, *Wages and Earnings in the United States, 1860–1890* (Princeton: Princeton University Press, 1960), Table A-11, p. 153; Albert Rees, *Real Wages in Manufacturing, 1890–1914* (Princeton: Princeton University Press, 1961), p. 4; and *Employment and Earnings Statistics for the United States, 1909–60,* United States Bureau of Labor Statistics Bulletin No. 1312, 1961, p. 32.

There are various reasons why the wage level has been and should be an inclined plane. The chief explanation is that the output per worker tends to increase from decade to decade. That occurs largely because of increased capital equipment per worker, improvements in technology and management, and progress in the level of education and training of the work force (more investment in human resources per worker). The rate of increase in output per unit of labor input apparently averaged 1.6 per cent per year from 1889 to 1919, and 2.3 per cent a year from 1919 to 1957.[58]

---

[58] See John W. Kendrick, *Productivity Trends in the United States* (Princeton: Princeton University Press, 1961), p. 60.

TABLE 10

Per Cent Change in Real Hourly Earnings in Manufacturing, by Decades, 1860–1960

Decade	Per Cent Change
1860–1870	8.6
1870–1880	14.9
1880–1890	31.2
1890–1900	13.3
1900–1910	16.8
1910–1920	33.4
1920–1930	19.3
1930–1940	42.9
1940–1950	29.1
1950–1960	27.6

Sources: Calculated from Long, *op. cit.,* Table A–11, p. 153; Rees, *op. cit.,* pp. 4 and 38–39; and for 1910 to 1960 the figures in Table 8 adjusted for changes in the cost of living for 1914 on by the Consumer Price Index in *Handbook of Labor Statistics,* 1950 edition, United States Bureau of Labor Statistics, Bulletin No. 1016, 1951, p. 100 and for subsequent years from the *Monthly Labor Review.*

Additional factors help to give the wage level an upward trend. One is that the earnings of workers on incentive tend to creep up with minor advances in production methods or materials; reduction of incentive rates with every minor improvement in work arrangements would stimulate worker resistance to change and tend to rob incentive methods of any virtue they might have. A third reason is that since 1954 one-third or more of the workers covered by major collective bargaining agreements have been under long-term contracts providing for fixed installment wage increases.[59]

This section has dealt primarily with the general level of wages. The wage level of the whole economy is, however, made up of all the individual rates. Conceptually it is a sort of representative average of them. Because wage movements in one part of the economy tend to spread to others, changes in the wage structure affect the general level. The interdependence between structure and level may be particularly evident as the economy approaches near-full employment.

---

[59] See George Ruben, "Deferred Increases Due in 1963 and Wage Escalation," *Monthly Labor Review,* LXXXV (December 1962), p. 1343.

Collective Bargaining and Prices

During the decade after the Korean War, it was strongly debated whether demand-pull, cost-push, or some combination of the two was responsible for the rise in the price level, which averaged about 1.5 per cent a year from 1952 to 1962. The most rapid increase occurred between the spring of 1956 and the spring of 1958.

Those who claimed that cost-push was largely responsible for "the price inflation"[60] argued (a) that collective bargaining forced wage scales up faster than productivity (output per man hour) increased, (b) that such "excessive" wage increases, by raising labor cost per unit of output, led to an increase in total cost and thus exerted pressure on prices, and (c) that the monetary authorities then were faced with a dilemma: they had to choose between having stable employment but price inflation or having a stable price level but increased unemployment. Either the monetary authorities could permit the upward cost push to be converted into higher prices through monetary expansion, or they could prevent a rise in the price level through a restrictive monetary policy which, however, would cause increased unemployment.[61]

Those who argue that the price level was pushed up by wage costs face the difficult problem of disentangling and isolating causes in a mixed-up situation. Many factors contribute to wage change and to price change. The spontaneous and independent influence of unions alone on prices is not easy to determine and measure. Not only are there loose links between money wages and prices in many industries (especially in industries with rather stable "administered" prices), but also it is most difficult convincingly to conjecture (and that is all one can do) what wage scales would have been in the absence of a union in the industry, and, in the more general case, in the absence of all unionism in the economy.

---

[60] Defined as a sustained upward movement in the Consumer Price Index, which includes, in addition to the retail prices of consumer goods, the cost of services (housing, medical care, personal care, etc.).

[61] William G. Bowen explores the questions raised by that "dilemma model" in *The Wage-Price Issue: A Theoretical Analysis* (Princeton: Princeton University Press, 1960). The discussion that follows in the text draws on Bowen's analysis.

Further analysis indicates the elements included in the thesis of general price increase through independently generated union pressure. Supporters of that thesis rest their case on the following arguments:[62] (1) Unions are in the business of making (wage, benefit, and other) gains for their members; the unions in the strongest bargaining positions make the largest gains; and their gains exceed, by a considerable margin, the average increase for the economy. (2) The largest gainers tend to serve as wage leaders; other unions generally are under pressure through "coercive comparison" to achieve settlements equal to or not far below the leaders. (3) Nonunion firms in industries or communities directly affected by (1) and (2) are under pressure to follow the pattern set by the leaders, because otherwise there would be an adverse effect on employee morale and a threat of unionization. (4) By such pattern-spreading of the gains in "key bargains," labor costs for the whole economy exceed the margin that productivity increases create, and prices, which are largely cost-determined, generally rise. (5) Correction of the situation through smaller gains or no gains during business recessions does not occur, because the pattern-setting unions in industries with fairly inflexible prices continue to negotiate sizable gains, or obtain them automatically as the result of instalment increases under a previously negotiated long-term agreement, and the spread of such gains continues to occur through "coercive comparison." (6) The monetary authorities have to validate the price level rise because it is not politically feasible for them to try to prevent a general price increase (or to cancel one) by creating tight money and more unemployment. Pattern-spreading is helped by another practice. Management generally gives the firm's unorganized white-collar workers wage increases equivalent to those negotiated for its production workers; there is what has come to be called a "tandem relationship" between them. Such pressures to maintain wage structures—to preserve or restore differentials—explain how the effects of union action can be far

---

[62] This is a synthesis; no author states his case in just this manner. For statements of this position see Sumner H. Slichter, "Do the Wage-Fixing Arrangements in the American Labor Market Have an Inflationary Bias?" *American Economic Review,* XLIV (May 1954), pp. 322–46 and "Discussion" by Albert Rees, pp. 363–65; and Lloyd Ulman, "Marshall and Friedman on Union Strength," *Review of Economics and Statistics,* XXXVII (November 1955), pp. 384–401.

more widespread than figures for total union membership might imply.[63]

Supporters of the thesis of cost-push through independent union pressure point to the "wage-price spiral" in the steel industry from 1953 to 1959. A study for the Joint Economic Committee of the Congress concluded that steel accounted for half of the 5 per cent rise in the wholesale price index during that period, and that "The wage and price behavior of the steel industry represents an important instance of inflation caused to a substantial degree by the exercise of market power."[64]

Economists who claim that price-level increases stem basically from expansion of demand and who, therefore, minimize the influence of cost-push by unions as an independent causal factor, make the following points:[65] (1) Although, under collective bargaining, wages and prices often rise at the same time, that fact does not explain the cause or causes for their rise; during all well known inflations, wages rose faster than productivity but that is what one would expect with "excessive" demand. (2) It would require a progressive increase in union power in order to explain a continued rise in prices as a result of union pressures. (3) Pattern-spreading is not so widespread and inflexible as the supporters of the cost-push theory imply; building construction and many local-market industries seem to have considerable wage autonomy. (4) Union impact is mainly on the wage structure and not on the general level; that is partly because a wage-price spiral in an industry like

---

[63] In this country, as Table 8 indicates, about one-third of all employees are organized; in manufacturing, two-thirds are in unions. See H. M. Douty, "Collective Bargaining Coverage in Factory Employment, 1958," *Monthly Labor Review*, LXXXIII (April 1960), pp. 345–49.

[64] Otto Eckstein and Gary Fromm, *Steel and the Postwar Inflation*, Study Paper No. 2, materials prepared in connection with the *Study of Employment, Growth, and Price Levels*, Joint Economic Committee, Congress of the United States (Washington: United States Government Printing Office, 1959), p. 34; see also Chapter 5 on "The Postwar Inflation," in *Staff Report on Employment, Growth, and Price Levels*, Joint Economic Committee, dated December 24, 1959 (Washington: United States Government Printing Office, 1960), pp. 103–60. For a different analysis and interpretation see Chapters 10 and 11 of *Collective Bargaining in the Basic Steel Industry, op. cit.*, pp. 155–96.

[65] For a clear statement of this viewpoint see Albert Rees, *The Economics of Trade Unions* (Chicago: University of Chicago Press, 1962), Chapter 5, pp. 100–120.

steel decreases the volume of employment there and increases the number of job seekers in other industries, thereby tending to spread the wage differential between (say) steel and those other industries. (5) To have an effective impact on the price level, the wage increases would need to expand total wage payments (i.e., not discourage business spending by higher costs); the supporters of the cost-push thesis have not yet supplied the satisfactory national-income type of analysis[66] that would explain not only the rise in the price level but how it is supported.

The critics of cost-push theorizing point out that if money wages normally are an inclined plane, collective bargaining may just be a means of reaching a foreordained result by negotiating the rise in steps. And, since collective bargaining affects wages through employers, any theory about the price impact of collective bargaining should take into account economic conditions and the employers' ability to pass on cost increases through higher prices.

Certainly cost-push inflation is more difficult to achieve and less continuous than one might offhand assume. Undoubtedly, collective bargaining had some effect on the price level in the 1953–58 period, but just how much effect is debatable and is quite difficult to determine for reasons already explained.

Both the Eisenhower and Kennedy Administrations seem to have accepted the cost-push thesis as having some validity. In his 1958 Economic Report, President Eisenhower said: "The leadership of labor must recognize that wage increases that go beyond over-all productivity gains are inconsistent with stable prices, and that the resumption of economic growth can be slowed by wage increases that involve either higher prices or a further narrowing of the margin between prices and costs."[67] This theme was repeated in the 1959 Report in the following words: "Labor leaders have a particularly critical role to play, in view of the great power lodged in their hands. . . . Increases in money wages and other compensation not justified by the productivity performance of the economy are inevitably inflationary."[68]

---

[66] Discussed in Chapter 2 (see pp. 32–33).

[67] *Economic Report of the President, Transmitted to the Congress January 20, 1958* (Washington: United States Government Printing Office, 1958), p. V.

[68] *Economic Report of the President, Transmitted to the Congress January 20, 1959* (Washington: United States Government Printing Office, 1959), p. VI.

In his 1962 Economic Report, President Kennedy cautioned that "when both companies and unions possess substantial market power, the interplay of price and wage decisions could set off a movement toward a higher price level," and he asked that labor leaders in the major industries "accept the productivity benchmark as a guide to wage objectives" and that managements in those industries "practice equivalent restraint in their price decisions."[69]

For discussion purposes the Council of Economic Advisers explained some of the practical implications of the President's policy by setting forth "guideposts for noninflationary wage and price behavior." Parts of the discussion are more pertinent to later chapters on public policy, but the following statements of the Council are significant for the analysis here:

> Individual wage and price decisions assume national importance when they involve large numbers of workers and large amounts of output directly, or when they are regarded by large segments of the economy as setting a pattern.[70]
>
> The general guide for noninflationary wage behavior is that the rate of increase in wage rates (including fringe benefits) in each industry be equal to the trend rate of over-all productivity increase.
>
> Wage rate increases would exceed the general guide rate in an industry which would otherwise be unable to attract sufficient labor; or in which wage rates are exceptionally low compared with the range of rates earned elsewhere by similar labor, because the bargaining position of workers has been weak in particular local labor markets.
>
> Wage rate increases would fall short of the general guide rate in an industry which could not provide jobs for its entire labor force even in times of general full employment; or in which wage rates are exceptionally high compared with the range of wages earned elsewhere by similar labor, because the bargaining position of workers has been especially strong.[71]

The anticipated cost-push in 1962, however, failed to develop, partly because the economy lacked sufficient buoyancy, and the "guideposts" proved to be generally rather ineffective either as discussion stimulators or as practical restraints on wage increases.

---

[69] *Economic Report of the President, Transmitted to the Congress January 1962*, together with the Annual Report of the Council of Economic Advisers (Washington: United States Government Printing Office, 1962), pp. 16–17.

[70] *Ibid.*, p. 185.

[71] *Ibid.*, p. 189.

Some economists thought that the widespread unemployment in 1962 and 1963 made any wage guideposts by the Government rather superfluous.

Unemployment and Wage Change

Assuming that demand and supply determine price, economists might expect that increasing unemployment would put downward pressures on wage scales and that, therefore, a rather close and consistent relationship would exist between the *level* of unemployment and the *rate* of change in wages. Low unemployment would be expected to cause relatively large wage increases, and high unemployment would generate pressures that would bring about relatively small wage increases, no wage increases, or even wage decreases. Such a wage-unemployment relationship might be expected to exist both on a national basis and for local labor market areas.

Actually, statistical studies covering the years since 1900 indicate that, nationally, any relationship between the level of unemployment and the rate of increase in average hourly earnings is loose and not too consistent.[72] The national average of wages does tend to rise faster when unemployment is relatively low; pronounced and persistent differences in unemployment levels do seem to affect the size of wage increases, but the relationship is too weak and unstable for reliable wage predictions on the basis of unemployment figures. There is some indication that, at a given level of unemployment, wages have tended to rise more rapidly since World War II than was true before World War I, but that tendency is not strong and clear.[73] Any such tendency might seem to be the result of widespread unionism and long-term agreements.

---

[72] See William G. Bowen, *Wage Behavior in the Postwar Period, An Empirical Analysis,* Industrial Relations Section, Princeton University, Princeton, N. J., 1960, pp. 85–86; and William G. Bowen and R. Albert Berry, "Unemployment Conditions and Movements of the Money Wage Level," *Review of Economics and Statistics,* XLV (May 1963), pp. 164–66.

[73] Bowen and Berry, *ibid.,* pp. 165–66. Presumably the inclusion of fringe benefits would add to the upward shift in the unemployment-wage relation in the postwar years since such benefits have expanded relative to wages in the postwar period.

A somewhat closer relationship appears to have existed between *changes* in the level of unemployment and the size of wage increases. That has been especially true in post-World War II recessions, when, at a given level of unemployment, average hourly earnings increased much less rapidly during the downswing than in the subsequent upswing. The direction of change in unemployment (and, of course, sales as well) presumably affects the economic outlook of management and labor and, thus, the size of negotiated increases.[74]

At the local level, it is difficult to find any consistent relationship between the size of unemployed labor supply and the size of wage increases. A study of 84 labor market areas from 1954 to 1960 showed no significant inverse correlation between either the level or the rate of change of unemployment and the rate of change in average hourly earnings in each area from year to year.[75] Violent changes in the level and rate of change of unemployment were not associated with any consistent response in the behavior of average hourly earnings.

Presumably, collective bargaining and management policies have helped to blunt the wage effectiveness of local labor-supply factors. Pattern-spreading by unions is not generally adjusted for labor-supply conditions in particular communities.[76] The influences determining wage increases in multiplant companies and in industry-oriented firms are largely outside the boundaries of a single locality. The same may be true for certain occupations, especially some organized by national craft unions. This is but another illustration of the fact that market forces in a locality may not be the main wage-changing influences, and that reasoning about wages in terms of *the* competitive wage (microeconomic theory) may be unrealistic and inappropriate.

---

[74] See *ibid.*, p. 167.

[75] See Philip Ross, "Labor Market Behavior and the Relationship between Unemployment and Wages," *Proceedings of the Fourteenth Annual Meeting of the Industrial Relations Research Association*, G. G. Somers (ed.), Industrial Relations Research Association, 1962, pp. 275–88.

[76] Robert R. France concludes that wage increases under trade unions were less sensitive to labor-market conditions, especially in post-World War II recessions, than was the case under nonunion conditions in the pre-1932 era. See France, "Wages, Unemployment, and Prices in the United States, 1890–1932, 1947–1957," *Industrial and Labor Relations Review*, XV (January 1962), pp. 187, 190.

Labor's Share in the National Income

It might be assumed that the expansion and increased strength of organized labor from the midthirties on would have resulted in a sufficient upthrust on employee compensation[77] to increase labor's share in the national income. Actually, the statistics do not seem to support that presupposition.

Allowing for the relative expansion of employees in the labor force, the share of labor income in the total income has been remarkably stable for the whole period since 1935. In corporate businesses or in manufacturing as a whole, employee compensation remained about 75 per cent of total income produced in the forties and fifties. Furthermore, labor's share of income receipts has generally fared no better in highly unionized industries than in industries subject to little labor organization.[78]

Labor's share has risen temporarily, especially in depressions or recessions, when profits were subject to some "squeeze." But over the longer run, unions seem to have been frustrated in attempts to increase labor's share in the national income, because they could not control product prices and production methods. Management was able by such means to protect or restore profit margins.

Thus, the statistics appear to lend little support to the proposition that unions have obtained gains for labor at the expense of other forms of income (profits, interest, and rent).[79] For purposes of testing that thesis, however, the available statistics have some weaknesses. Wage and salary income are lumped together. Union strength is measured by percentages of an industry's work force who are organized in any kind of a union or are under any kind of collective agreement. It is possible that more refined statistics and other analytical methods might enable an investigator to uncover some union influence on the functional distribution of in-

---

[77] This includes employee benefits as well as wages.

[78] See Clark Kerr, "Labor's Income Share and the Labor Movement," in G. W. Taylor and F. C. Pierson (eds.), *New Concepts in Wage Determination* (New York: McGraw-Hill, 1957), pp. 283 and 285; and Paul E. Sultan, "Unionism and Wage-Income Ratios: 1929–51," *Review of Economics and Statistics*, XXXVI (February 1954), p. 73.

[79] See Joseph D. Phillips, "Labor's Share and 'Wage Parity,'" *Review of Economics and Statistics*, XLII (May 1960), p. 174.

come. But sufficient studies have been made to indicate that union-ism itself is not likely to cause much redistribution of income between labor and property shares.

SUMMARY

This chapter has dealt with a complex and pervasive subject. It has not been possible to provide unqualified answers to many important wage questions. But pertinent facts have been discussed, different approaches have been examined, and some tentative con-clusions have been reached. The results can be summed up as follows:

1. In the twenties and early thirties, when most of American industry was unorganized, the wage structure was rather hap-hazard, if not chaotic, in the nonunion sections of the economy.

2. The competitive wage approach and the differential-range approach to wage questions start from different premises, visualize different channels of adjustment, and predict different conse-quences will flow from genuine wage differentials within a 10 to 15 per cent range. Each approach has its limitations. The compet-itive wage approach may be helpful for long-run explanations of differentials. The differential-range approach is especially suited for analyzing community wage structures.

3. Occupational wage differentials have generally narrowed in percentage terms over the past century. Many factors have oper-ated to compress occupational differentials, including management and union policies. Extreme illustrations of union-management in-fluences on occupational differentials are the railroads (1937–56) where differentials of the same cents per hour were maintained with every general wage increase, and the steel industry (1947–63), where the spreads between occupations were expanded with al-most every general wage increase in order to maintain the same percentage differentials.

4. Interindustry differentials seem to be largely governed by economic factors. Unions may succeed in improving the relative wage position of an industry for a period of time, after which they may experience difficulties in holding to the new position.

5. A variety of economic and institutional factors help to explain genuine wage differentials between establishments in a locality; studies show that a model with a range of 10 to 15 per cent for differentials in an industry or occupation is not abnormal where unions or management cooperation have not forced uniformity. The influence of unions generally has been to reduce and eliminate such local interplant differentials in the same industry or occupation.

6. Labor supply and demand are part of the explanation of some geographical wage differentials. However, the North-South differential (averaging perhaps 10 per cent) varies between firms and industries so widely and with such seeming irrationality as to require an explanation that recognizes the importance of historical, managerial, and union influences. Many of the popular economic reasons given for the North-South differential do not hold up well under careful examination.

7. The relation between unemployment conditions and wage changes nationally has been loose and rather unpredictable. On a local basis, any wage-unemployment relationship is difficult to discover.

8. Studies indicate that labor unions have not succeeded in making any significant change in the distribution of income between labor and property shares.

Perhaps one can conclude that wage behavior is too complex and incongruous to be adequately explained by orthodox partial analysis and that, though unions do influence wage structure and levels in some industries, their independent influence does not expand over the long run and is not sufficiently strong or inclusive to have much effect on their members' share in the total national income.

DISCUSSION QUESTIONS

1. How do you explain the unsystematic nature of company wage scales and the wide disparity in wage structures, prior to unionization in the thirties and forties?
2. Explain some of the circumstances that make it difficult to com-

pare wage scales between firms, industries, and regions at any one time and to compare changes in wage structures or levels over an extended period of time.

3. What are the essential differences between "the competitive wage" and "the differential-range" approaches? How would they lead to different recommendations with respect to public policy regarding wages and union power?

4. How do you account for the high degree of stability in the relative positions of industries in the nation's wage structure? How much influence can unions have in changing the relative wage position of an industry during a five-year period? Over a quarter of a century? Explain.

5. What factors explain local wage differentials? What factors limit the range of variation in such differentials within an industry or within an occupation?

6. What explains the varied pattern of regional wage differentials? What are the weaknesses of some economic explanations for the North-South differential?

7. Why does unemployment not have more effect on wages on a national basis and especially on a local basis?

8. How would you explain the apparent stability in labor's share of the national income?

SELECTED READINGS

Bowen, William G., *The Wage-Price Issue, A Theoretical Analysis* (Princeton: Princeton University Press, 1960).

————, *Wage Behavior in the Postwar Period, An Empirical Analysis*, Industrial Relations Section, Princeton University, 1960.

Garbarino, Joseph W., *Wage Policy and Long-Term Contracts*, (Washington: Brookings Institution, 1962).

Lester, Richard A., "Southern Wage Differentials: Developments, Analysis, and Implications," *Southern Economic Journal*, XII (April 1947), pp. 386–94.

————, "A Range Theory of Wages," *Industrial and Labor Relations Review*, V (July 1952), pp. 483–500.

Ozanne, Robert, "A Century of Occupational Differentials in Manufacturing," *Review of Economics and Statistics*, XLIV (August 1962), pp. 292–99.

Rees, Albert, *The Economics of Trade Unions* (Chicago: University of Chicago Press, 1962).

Reynolds, Lloyd G. and Cynthia Taft, *The Evolution of the Wage Structure* (New Haven: Yale University Press, 1956).

Taylor, George W. and Frank C. Pierson (eds.), *New Concepts in Wage Determination* (New York: McGraw-Hill, 1957).

II.

Employee Benefits and Work Hours

ONE OF THE most remarkable developments in collective bargaining in this country has been the rapid expansion in employee benefit programs since World War II. Wage-earners have been receiving a larger and larger proportion of their total compensation in the form of negotiated benefits of various kinds.

This chapter examines the facts about the marked expansion in nonwage benefits and the factors behind that development. It analyzes the role that collective bargaining has played and discusses the implications that a great expansion in nonwage compensation has for economic theory and for public policy.

The second part of the chapter deals with another major issue in collective bargaining, namely, the hours of work. If allowance is made for increased vacations and holidays, the scheduled work time per year continued to decline after World War II as it has every decade since 1850. What would be the economic consequences of further reductions in work hours? The normal work day and work week have been determined by a combination of hours' legislation, collective bargaining, and market forces. What should public policy be with respect to this matter? How much reliance should be placed on collective bargaining to fix satisfactory working hours? Those are some of the questions that will be considered after the discussion of employee benefits.

Three other important issues in collective bargaining are reserved for the next chapter. They are: the use of seniority for job rationing and advancement, the problem of adjustment to rapid technological change (automation) under collective bargaining, and the question of union security or the union shop.

NONWAGE BENEFITS

Companies make a variety of contributions aimed at enhancing employee welfare. They range all the way from subsidies for meals and for recreational activities to various social and private insurance programs. Popularly all such items are lumped together under the term "fringe benefits."

The result has been considerable confusion and misunderstanding. Total figures for "fringe benefits" vary significantly with the items brought under that heading. In some cases, for example, premiums for overtime, night shifts, and holiday work as well as suggestion and service awards are included under this catch-all term.

For purposes of clarity, the phrase "nonwage benefits" will be used instead of "fringe benefits." It will include both social insurance programs and private insurance-like programs such as pensions, life insurance, disability, sickness and accident, hospitalization, medical care, supplemental unemployment compensation, and dismissal compensation. Thus, nonwage benefits are separate and distinct from cash payments for a worker's presence at work or for activity on the job. They do not include vacation pay, holiday pay, or miscellaneous bonuses and subsidies. The private benefit programs may, of course, be the result of collective bargaining or unilateral action by the employer.

Developments and Trends

The sharp upward trend in nonwage benefits commenced in World War II. Between 1932 to 1942 there was no increase in employer contributions to private employee benefit plans as a percentage of all wages and salaries. In mid-1942, however, the National War Labor Board imposed definite limits on wage increases (under the so-called Little Steel formula), but no such restraints were placed on reasonable contributions to employee benefit programs. Such contributions were viewed as less inflationary than wage increases, and were favored by some managements to help attract and hold employees. As a result, employer contributions to private pension and other benefit programs rose from .55 to 1.27 per cent of total wages and salaries.[1]

Another sharp rise in benefits occurred after the Supreme Court ruled in the Inland Steel case in 1949 that employers were required under the Wagner Act to bargain with a certified union on pensions. Spurred by that decision and the results of the auto and steel negotiations in 1948 and 1949, the coverage of negotiated pension plans increased some 3.4 million workers between 1948 and 1950, and the coverage of negotiated health and other insurance plans expanded by about 4.4 million during the same period.

Throughout the period from 1942 on, the trend in private benefit programs has been definitely upward, measured by employer contributions to such plans compared with total payroll or by the proportion of the workforce included under coverage of the plans. Table 11 indicates the trend of employer contributions as a percentage of all wages and salaries for the country as a whole. Table 12 gives similar figures for 91 identical companies, generally large, well-established firms so that the percentages are higher. In 1961 the cost of nonwage benefits to employers averaged about twenty cents per hour worked for the country as a whole and around thirty cents per payroll hour (or $612 a year) for the 1,120 firms included in the United States Chamber of Commerce survey.[2]

Expansion in the coverage of different types of benefit plans since 1954 is indicated in Table 13. From the table it is evident that the rate of growth in coverage was generally more rapid from 1954 to 1958 than from 1958 to 1961. The slackening in the rate of increase seems to have been partly due to the recession of 1958 and the

---

[1] The source for these figures is indicated in Table 11.

[2] *Fringe Benefits, 1961*, Economic Research Department, Chamber of Commerce of the United States, Washington, D.C., 1962, pp. 14–15.

TABLE 11

Nonwage Benefits as Per Cent of Wages and Salaries, 1929–62

Year	Employer Contributions to Private Pension and Welfare Funds	Total, Including Employer Contributions for Social Insurance
1929	.3	1.3
1935	.5	1.8
1940	.6	4.6
1945	.9	4.8
1950	1.9	5.3
1955	2.6	6.1
1960	3.2	8.2
1961	3.2	8.4
1962	3.2	8.7

Sources: Calculated from data in C. F. Schwartz and G. Jaszi, *U.S. Income and Output, A Supplement to the Survey of Current Business,* United States Department of Commerce, 1959, pp. 126–27; and *Survey of Current Business, National Income Number,* July 1963, p. 12.

short-lived recession of 1960–61.[3] Those recessions, by putting some squeeze on profits, seem to have had a dampening effect on expansion of benefit plans. During the 1954–61 period, the coverage of temporary disability plans and supplemental unemployment benefit plans remained practically unchanged. The latter plans have been largely confined to the auto, steel, and rubber industries. The combination of employer opposition and workers' (especially skilled workers') preferences for other types of benefit has meant even a slight decline in coverage for s.u.b. plans as plant employment in those three industries has contracted.

Coverage of dependents is not included in the figures in Table 13. For hospital and various medical benefits, dependents' coverage increased at a more rapid rate than employee coverage in 1954–61. By 1961, about one and a half dependents were covered in those programs for every employee included. In that year employee coverage was 46 million for life insurance and death, 42 million for hospitalization, 39 million for surgical, and 23 million for retire-

---

[3] Nevertheless in 1958, gains in insurance plans were won by unions in about one-third of all negotiated settlements, and new and improved pension benefits in 14 per cent of all settlements.

TABLE 12

Nonwage Benefits for 91 Firms as Per Cent of Total Payroll, 1947–61

Year	Private Pension and Other Agreed-Upon Payments*	Employer Contributions to Social Insurances	Total
1947	4.1	2.9	7.0
1949	4.8	2.8	7.6
1951	5.7	2.9	8.6
1953	6.6	2.7	9.3
1955	7.2	3.0	10.2
1957	7.8	3.6	11.4
1959	8.1	3.8	11.9
1961	8.7	4.5	13.2

* In addition to insurance-type benefit programs, the figure includes meals furnished by the company and payments to needy employees.

Source: *Fringe Benefits, 1961*, Economic Research Department, Chamber of Commerce of the United States, Washington, D.C., 1962, p. 28.

ment. Including dependents, hospitalization and surgical plans covered over 100 million persons.[4]

The relative importance of benefit plans varies considerably by size of firm, by wage level of the firm, and by industry. The differentials in benefits are greater than corresponding differentials in wages.

For the year 1959 the United States Bureau of Labor Statistics made a study of employer expenditures on private benefit plans for production workers in manufacturing.[5] The study covered 4,400 establishments with 3.5 million employees; 92 per cent of the establishments had private benefit plans. Table 14 indicates some of the interesting results. The variation by size of firm is quite pronounced. Pensions are the greatest differentiating factor. Relatively few companies with less than one hundred employees have their own pension plans.[6]

---

[4] See Alfred M. Skolnik, *op. cit.*, p. 5.

[5] *Employer Expenditures for Selected Supplementary Remuneration Practices for Production Workers in Manufacturing Industries, 1959*, Bulletin No. 1308, United States Bureau of Labor Statistics, January 1962.

[6] The lack of more pronounced size-of-firm differences in the United States Chamber of Commerce surveys is because of some selectivity in the respondents and the smallest category is under five hundred employees. See *Fringe Benefits, 1961, op. cit.*, p. 17.

TABLE 13

Covered Employees as Per Cent of All Wage and Salary Workers, by Type of Employee Benefit Plan, 1954–61*

Year	Life Insurance and Death	Accidental Death and Dismemberment	Hospitalization	Surgical	Regular Medical	Major Medical Expense	Temporary Disability, Including Formal Sick Leave	Supplemental Unemployment	Retirement
1954	56	26	59	53	32	2	50	—	31
1956	63	30	63	59	40	6	51	4.1	34
1957	66	32	65	61	44	9	52	3.6	37
1958	70	33	67	63	46	11	52	3.6	40
1959	73	34	66	64	49	14	51	3.8	41
1960	74	36	69	66	51	17	51	3.4	43
1961	78	36	70	67	53	20	52	3.6	45

* For temporary disability, supplemental unemployment, and retirement the percentages are of wage and salary workers in private industry.

Source: Alfred M. Skolnik, "Growth of Employee-Benefit Plans, 1954–61," Social Security Bulletin, XXVI (April 1963), Table 2, p. 7.

TABLE 14

Employer Expenditures on Private Benefit Plans by Size of Establishment, Wage Level of Establishment, and Union Agreement Coverage, 1959

Establishment Characteristic	Per Cent of Gross Payroll	Cents per Hour Paid for
Establishments with:		
Under 100 employees	2.7	5.3
100 to 499 employees	4.1	8.1
500 employees and over	6.2	15.5
Establishments with average hourly earnings:		
Under $1.60	2.1	2.8
$1.60 but under $2.20	3.6	7.0
$2.20 and over	5.9	16.2
Establishments with:		
A majority of employees covered by collective bargaining agreements	5.6	13.5
None or a minority covered	3.2	6.0

Source: *Employer Expenditures for Selected Supplementary Remuneration Practices for Production Workers in Manufacturing Industries, 1959, op. cit.,* pp. 93–95. Year-end and Christmas bonuses have been eliminated from the total figures

The variation by hourly earnings' level is even more pronounced than that by size of plant. Again pensions are the greatest spread-producing factor. It is clear from Table 14 that benefit differences are much greater than wage level differences between firms.

The influence of collective bargaining on employer benefit expenditures is discussed more fully subsequently. The figures in Table 14, broken down into two categories of unionization, are presented here to indicate that size-of-firm and wage-level differences are factors in the benefit differences revealed according to degree of organization, since unionized firms generally are larger and higher-paying ones.

That high-wage industries generally have a much higher ratio of benefit expenditures to wages is indicated by Table 15. Petroleum refining, primary metals (chiefly steel), rubber, military ordnance, and transportation equipment (mainly autos) are high-paying industries. Furniture, leather, clothing, textiles, and lumber and wood products generally rank in the lower section of the wage hierarchy for manufacturing industries. The oil industry stands

TABLE 15

Average Expenditures for Private Benefit Plans (1959) and Unionization Ratios (1958), by Industry Groups

| | Benefit Expenditures | | |
Industry Group	Per Cent of Gross Payroll	Cents per Hour Paid for	Unionization Ratios
Petroleum refining and related industries	12.2	37.0	89.5
Primary metal industries	6.8	19.2	88.6
Rubber and miscellaneous plastic products	6.4	15.2	80.6
Ordnance and accessories	6.1	16.7	83.9
Transportation equipment	6.0	16.0	86.8
Machinery, except electrical	5.9	15.2	67.9
Tobacco manufactures	5.6	9.1	62.6
Stone, clay, and glass products	5.3	11.8	77.9
Food and kindred products	5.2	10.8	68.1
Paper and allied products	5.0	11.1	75.5
Furniture and fixtures	3.8	7.2	49.6
Leather and leather products	3.4	5.6	49.3
Apparel and related products	3.2	5.1	59.7
Textile mill products	3.0	4.9	30.1
Lumber and wood products, except furniture	2.4	4.3	43.8

Sources: *Employer Expenditures for Selected Supplementary Remuneration Practices for Production Workers in Manufacturing Industries, 1959, op. cit.,* p. 9; and H. M. Douty, "Collective Bargaining Coverage in Factory Employment, 1958," *Monthly Labor Review,* LXXXIII (April 1960), p. 347.

out by itself both in relative and absolute terms. Benefits as a percentage of payroll are about twice as high for the high-wage industries as they are for the low-wage ones, and around three times as large in terms of cents per hour. The United States Chamber of Commerce survey shows that in public utilities, banks and trust companies, insurance companies, and the chemical industry, private benefit expenditures by employers are about as high in percentage of payroll or in cents per hour as they are for primary metal industries.[7]

In Table 15, the "unionization ratios" are fairly well correlated

---

[7] See *Fringe Benefits, 1961, op. cit.,* pp. 13 and 14. The proper comparative figures are those for "Pension and other agreed-upon payments" minus items e, f, and g in *ibid.*

with benefit expenditures relative to payroll in the first column. Correlation, however, says nothing about cause. Some of the same economic factors that contribute to high wages in an industry also help to account for relatively high benefit levels. Furthermore, the "unionization ratios" are not a good measure of union strength or union pressure for benefits. For each industry they are the proportion of that industry's workers who are in establishments where a majority of the employees are covered by collective bargaining agreements.

Reasons for Relative Expansion

A number of considerations and factors help to explain the rapid expansion in employee benefits compared with wages. Union pressure is only a part of the explanation.

1. MANAGEMENT. From the viewpoint of management, increased expenditures for benefits may have some advantages over an equivalent sum spent on wage increases. Benefits help to tie employees to the firm and preserve company investment in the workforce through reduced labor turnover.[8] Certain benefit rights, such as pensions, may be forfeited if the employee leaves the company, and coverage under others may be lost for a time with any shift of employers.

Benefit programs may permit employer savings in ways that cannot be achieved by a wage increase. Pension and disability programs help management eliminate inefficient employees. For some plans, the net premiums are lower than the gross premiums, and savings are also possible through premium reductions with a favorable experience record. Unlike wages, benefits involve no social insurance taxes, no added pension contributions, no increase in vacation or holiday pay, and no extra cost for overtime hours. Some companies figure that every wage increase of $1.00 entails 30 to 40 cents of "fringe" costs of various kinds. That is not true of $1.00

---

[8] Benefits seem to be much more effective in retaining than in recruiting new employees. Job applicants seem to have little interest in a company's benefit programs as such. See Richard A. Lester, *Hiring Practices and Labor Competition*, Industrial Relations Section, Princeton University, Princeton, N.J., 1954, pp. 88–92.

in benefit costs. However, an increase of benefits *now* tends to raise the future costs of wage increases.

Another advantage of benefits is that management can use them often for company differentiation with less complaint about upsetting local standards than would be true of an equivalent wage increase. As part of a personnel program they help to distinguish the company, build employee loyalty, and give the impression of management's humanitarian interest in employees as individuals. They fit in well with the human relations approach of concern with the worries of the workers. And they give the company a good "public image."

Some managements take the position that worker demand for security is bound to be met through public or private plans. They would prefer to have the programs under private control, tailor-made for the company, rather than paying for the employee benefits through taxes to a uniform, government program.

2. EMPLOYEES. For workers, company benefit programs also have advantages over a wage increase. Group purchase of insurance protection is much cheaper than individual purchase. Furthermore, benefits paid by the company enable the worker to make large savings in personal taxes. Workers pay no taxes on employer contributions to benefit plans like life insurance and hospitalization and medical care. In contrast, if they purchased such protection through a wage increase they would have the income tax on the increase and have to pay higher premiums for individual purchase. And when employer contributions to a pension plan are received later (with accumulated interest) in the form of benefits, they are taxed at a lower rate because then the recipient on retirement is in a lower income bracket.

The significance of the tax-saving aspect of benefits was indicated by James R. Hoffa, president of the Brotherhood of Teamsters, in a statement in June 1963. He explained: "Our guys are going home with $200 a week in their pockets and it might be better to put most of any increase we negotiate into fringes instead of wages."[9] Hoffa said that, since his trucker members were moving into higher tax brackets, the stress on benefits in the wage-benefit package he would seek from employers might depend on what

9 *The New York Times*, June 25, 1963, p. 20.

Congress did about the Kennedy Administration's proposal for an income tax cut.

As workers' incomes have risen, stress has been placed on job security. Wives have tended to favor hospital and medical care insurance and better pensions. Surveys among steelworkers in the spring of 1959 and again at the beginning of 1962 showed that they generally preferred more generous pensions and earlier retirement, additional hospital and medical insurance, and longer vacations and shorter hours, to a raise in pay.[10] The workers interviewed claimed that pay increases were practically eaten up by the additional income taxes and by the increases in store prices and in rents that soon followed pay increases in steel towns.

Benefits may be favored by some workers because they tend to have a leveling effect on real incomes within an industry or company. That is true, for example, of hospital and medical-care programs; usually all employees have the same protection regardless of wage income. Other company benefits may also have a bias in favor of the lower wage-earners and, therefore, be more egalitarian than a wage increase, particularly a percentage increase.

In most companies, individual employees do not have a choice as to the extent that they will participate in a pension or hospitalization program or as to the particular kind of pension or hospitalization program they can select. In large firms, like du Pont, General Electric, or General Motors, usually there is a single pension plan for all plant employees. They have no choice. The economies of uniformity and company insistence on a single program preclude any catering to individual needs and desires.

Clearly company-wide or even plant-wide benefit programs cannot meet individual workers' preferences for wages *vs.* particular benefit programs or for one benefit program as opposed to another. Studies show that such preferences vary widely among workers according to their age, sex, size of family, annual income, and attitude toward the job.[10a] However, any analysis must be in terms of collective, compulsory participation.

---

[10] *See U. S. News and World Report*, XLVI (May 18, 1959), pp. 44–46; *Time*, LXXIII (May 4, 1959), p. 12, and (June 15, 1959), p. 88; and *Business Week*, 1961 (January 27, 1962), p. 121.

[10a] See, for example, Stanley M. Nealey, "Pay and Benefit Preference," *Industrial Relations*, III (October 1963), pp. 17–28.

3. UNION. Labor leaders may favor benefits over wage increases for other reasons. The negotiation of a new benefit program for production workers is an achievement for which the union can claim institutional credit more clearly than for a wage increase. That is true even though it involved only spreading to plant employees protections that the office employees already enjoyed. Unions can take special credit for a new program like supplemental unemployment benefits, severance pay, or special thirteen-week vacations, which the company's office employees have not had.

Benefit programs help to strengthen the institutional security of the union in other ways. The union may have a part to play in their administration. Members may be dependent on the union officials to represent them in their benefit claims.

Union leaders have even pressed benefits against an apparent preference of members for a wage increase. They have done so sometimes on the grounds that such programs are in the long-run interests of the membership. Usually, union leaders do not present the membership with a choice between a wage increase or an equivalent benefit gain, or between different mixtures of wages and benefits.[11] Instead, the leadership presents a particular negotiated wage-benefit package to the membership for ratification or rejection. Some union leaders strongly believe that, by presenting employers with a variety of demands and negotiating in terms of a package, it is easier to reach a mutually acceptable settlement and that the total gains for the employees are likely to be larger that way.

4. MARKET FORCES. How much of the relative expansion in employee benefits can be explained by market forces or pressures? Surely some can. The cost of hospital care has risen relatively and, consequently, an expanded share of all benefit costs has been devoted to that purpose. Management's desire to avoid the costs of labor turnover presumably is partly motivated by a long-run profit objective. Workers' desire for job security and for low-cost insurance protection (through group purchase and tax savings by employer purchase) certainly would find some market-influencing

---

[11] For a discussion of the absence of choice and union leaders' favoritism for benefits against members' desire for wage increases at various times, see A. I. Mendelson, "Fringe Benefits Today and Tomorrow," *Labor Law Journal*, VII (June 1956), pp. 325–28 and 379–84.

expression, if not through job shifting (because of company ties), then perhaps through employee dissatisfaction on the job resulting in difficulties for supervision and reductions in labor productivity.

5. UNION INFLUENCES.   Certainly, there is evidence that unions have been an important force in the marked growth of company expenditures for employee benefits. The independent influence of unions in the expansion of benefits relative to wages is, however, difficult to determine.

The rapid spread of private benefit plans under collective bargaining is indicated in Table 16, in terms of the absolute number of workers covered and in the percentage of workers under collective agreements who are covered by pension plans and by health and other insurance plans. In 1960, almost four-fifths of all workers under collective agreements were covered by a health and insurance plan and three-fifths of them were covered by a pension plan. Between 1950 and 1960, the coverage of negotiated pension plans expanded percentage-wise no faster than the coverage of nonbargained plans. That fact alone, however, does not mean that union leadership failed to play a significant role in expanding coverage, in eliminating employee contributions, and in improving benefits.

Between 1950 and 1960, the negotiated health and other insurance coverage did expand proportionately more than nonnegotiated

TABLE 16

Estimated Coverage of Health and Insurance and Pension Plans under Collective Bargaining, 1945–60

	Health and Insurance Plans		Pension Plans	
Year	Number of Workers (millions)	Per Cent of all Workers under Agreements	Number of Workers (millions)	Per Cent of all Workers under Agreements
1945	.6	4	—	—
1948	2.7	18	1.7	11
1950	7.1	47	5.1	34
1954	11.1	60	7.1	38
1960	14.5	78	11.1	60

Source: Dorothy R. Kittner, "Health, Insurance, and Pension Plan Coverage in Union Contracts," *Monthly Labor Review*, LXXXV (March 1962), p. 275. The figures include workers outside the United States (mainly Canadian) who are covered by agreements of unions having their headquarters in the United States.

coverage did.[12] In addition, unions provided leadership in raising benefit amounts, in extending coverage to the dependents of employees and to retired workers and their dependents, and in adding new types of benefit.

In 1960, about one-half of all workers under private pension plans were under collectively bargained ones, and bargained plans covered approximately a third of all workers under private health and other insurance plans. In the midfifties both pension plans and health and insurance plans spread rapidly in the building construction and trucking industries, under multiemployer arrangements. In 1950, only one-tenth of all workers covered by pension plans were under multiemployer plans; by 1960, the proportion was almost one-sixth.[13]

Coal is perhaps the prime example of the influence of a union on benefit expansion. Through union pressure, a royalty of forty cents on every ton mined under negotiated agreements, has been set aside for pensions and hospital and medical benefits since 1952. Without the union's (really John L. Lewis') insistence, the amount for employee benefits in the coal industry would have been much smaller. And surely the Automobile Workers and the Steelworkers are largely responsible for the existence of plans for supplementary unemployment benefits. On the other hand, unions may claim little credit for the very high ratio of benefits to wages in the petroleum industry. Oil companies were known for their generous benefit policies as early as the twenties.

Effects on Negotiations

The great expansion in negotiated benefit programs has exercised a variety of influences on union-management negotiations. Benefit programs have brought a number of new issues into labor negotiations, including insurance and medical practices and the investment of pension reserves. Indeed, negotiated benefit plans have developed an organized consumer interest in the costs of hospitalization and

---

[12] See Dorothy R. Kittner, "Health, Insurance, and Pension Plan Coverage in Union Contracts," *Monthly Labor Review*, LXXXV (March 1962), p. 274.

[13] Alfred M. Skolnik, *op. cit.*, pp. 11–12. See also Dorothy R. Kittner, *op. cit.*, p. 274.

medical care. In negotiations with respect to such benefit programs, the experts tend to play an increasingly important role. And the need for advance study, for consideration of actuarial estimates, and for careful weighing of alternatives means that joint discussion and analysis should precede the formal negotiation of a new agreement.

The complexity of details of a pension or even a medical-care program serves to discourage frequent change and to promote longer term agreements. The parties do not wish to face the negotiation of revisions in benefit programs every year or two. Thus, benefit programs not only add to the size of collective agreements, they also help to alter the character of the negotiations.

Implications for Theory

The market analysis of demand and supply is not well suited for explaining the introduction and expansion of particular types of employee benefit plans. How can one visualize labor demand and supply schedules for different cost levels of a pension plan or a medical-care plan? An employee benefit plan is a form of collective, compulsory purchase, for which marginal analysis based on individual consumer choice lacks direct applicability. Even under a unilateral employer decision, the programs are compulsory in the sense that the employer contributes a certain sum for that purpose even though many individual employees might prefer to receive their share in cash rather than the benefit protection that the employer has bought for them.

A management's decision concerning how much to devote to a particular benefit program may depend on a number of factors. Among them are speculation about the effectiveness of the plan at various expenditure levels: (1) in helping to recruit high quality labor, reducing labor turnover, and serving to increase labor productivity; (2) in promoting satisfactory union-management relations; and (3) in easing the problems of supervision, promoting good public relations for the firm, and relieving the conscience of management.

A number of writers have pointed out that benefit programs may be "only vaguely related either to current or future production."[14] How, on grounds of marginal revenue and marginal cost, can one explain the inclusion of retired employees and their dependents in company hospitalization and medical-care plans, or company-financed increases in pensions for former employees long since retired from the company? That the motivation for the expansion of some benefit programs extends far beyond economic calculation is indicated by statements of company executives quoted in Chapter 7. It will be recalled that James C. Worthy said: "Employee benefit plans are usually justified on the basis of their presumed effect on productivity, although anyone experienced in personnel management can testify that genuine concern for employee welfare is often the compelling factor."[15]

The multipurpose, multiadjustment theory of management explained in Chapter 7 finds support in the facts of employee benefits —their rapid expansion relative to wages and the marked interindustry variation in benefit-wage ratios. Relative benefit levels seem closely correlated with company and industry ability to pay. Compared to wages, the differentials in benefits are much larger between the heavy industries dominated by large firms and the soft-goods lines that have the traditional type of competition.

The combination of ability to pay plus union pressures in some cases, appears to have more influence on intercompany and interindustry benefit differences than labor-supply factors do. That is because, as already explained, benefits are not effective as a means of recruiting labor for a firm,[16] and companies do not lose employees to other firms for benefit reasons.[17] So far as labor supply is concerned, company benefits are chiefly effective as one of the factors helping to tie the employee to the company.

The behavior of unions in the benefit field is what one might expect on the basis of the politicoeconomic model presented in Chapter 6. Benefit plans do help to meet the institutional needs of unions, and the uneven expansion of such benefits and the occa-

---

[14] Leland Hazard, "Wage Theory: A Management View," in G. W. Taylor and F. C. Pierson, *New Concepts in Wage Determination* (New York: McGraw-Hill, 1957), p. 38.

[15] James C. Worthy, *Big Business and Free Men* (New York: Harper, 1959), p. 28.

[16] See footnote 8, page 339.

[17] Based on exit interviews by management and interviews in labor-market studies.

sional breakthroughs of a new program indicate that union leadership enjoys some discretion. That discretion may be enhanced by negotiations for a whole wage-benefit-rules package, so that benefits are not presented for separate vote of the membership. Union policy does generally seem to reflect the views of the bulk of the membership or at least of the "actives" among the members. However, the leadership may be able to "sell" the membership on a plan, as Walter Reuther and his staff in the midfifties sold the Automobile Workers on the "guaranteed annual wage" (which ended up as supplemental unemployment benefits) rather than demanding shorter hours or the equivalent amount in wages, which the Patternmakers insisted upon in auto plants where they had representation rights.

Public Policy Questions

The great growth in employee benefits and the prospect for continued relative expansion[18] raise three important issues of public policy. They are: (a) the equity issue of expensive benefits for high-wage employees in administered-price (oligopolistic) industries and firms, (b) the issue of tax evasion through nontaxable benefits, and (c) the issue of labor immobility through benefit ties to a single company.

1. EQUITY. This issue is simply that some managements and unions enjoy too much leeway in fixing benefits, largely because of product-market conditions. Through administered pricing, the low-wage and low-benefit workers along with the self-employed, are required to help pay for an elaborate and expensive structure of company benefits for workers receiving high wages. The situation presumably could be corrected if the market mechanism operated more effectively so that employers' ability to pay benefits and their actual programs varied in a less extreme fashion. Or it could be remedied by having the government provide a larger proportion of all benefits under social insurance programs, which do not vary benefits according to a company's ability to pay.

The second solution would be in line with European methods.

---

[18] Projection of the trend in Tables 11 and 17 over, say, the next two or three decades is cause for some serious analysis of the issues that such expansion raises.

Statistical studies show that employers in Europe have a considerably higher ratio of benefit costs to wages than is the case in the United States. For example, in Austria, Belgium, France, Germany, and Italy in 1955, nonwage benefits generally amounted to 20 to 30 per cent as much as wages.[19] However, in those countries employers' contributions to public social insurances usually constitute over 90 per cent of all their employee benefit costs; company programs customarily represent less than 10 per cent of the total.[20] That is because European companies have few benefit programs of their own for medical care, hospitalization, supplemental unemployment compensation, and pensions. European unions, with a strong social viewpoint, generally believe that such benefits should be provided under public social insurance in order to assure uniformity of treatment and to avoid barriers to labor mobility.

In the United States since 1951, employer contributions to private benefit programs have ranged from 42 to 49 per cent of total employer contributions to all benefit plans. Table 17 gives the dollar figures in five-year intervals. With private programs such a large share of the total and so influenced by company ability to pay and union pressures, the possibilities for inequity are wide indeed.

2. TAX.   The figures in Table 17 also show the amount of personal income that has been escaping (or in the case of pensions, partially escaping[21]) the Federal and State income taxes.[22] Permitting employer-paid benefits to be tax free for the recipients in essence represents a government subsidy for such contributions, and thus

---

[19] The figure for the United Kingdom, however, was only about 5 per cent.

[20] See *Labour Costs in European Industry*, Studies and Reports, New Series, No. 52, International Labour Office, Geneva, 1959, Table 4, p. 24 and the breakdowns between "social insurance contributions" and "direct benefits and subsidies" for individual industries in the ten European countries represented in the study.

[21] Because the worker's lower annual income during retirement is taxed at lower rates and he has also had the advantage of accumulated interest.

[22] For some indication of the tax loss to the Federal Government from private pension plans alone see Daniel M. Holland, "Some Characteristics of Private Pension Plans," in *Tax Revision Compendium: Papers on Broadening the Tax Base*, submitted to the House Committee on Ways and Means, Eighty-sixth Congress, November 16, 1959, Vol. II, pp. 1324–25; and John W. McConnell, "Treatment of Pension Plans," *ibid.*, p. 1348.

TABLE 17

**Employer Contributions for Social Insurance and to Private
Pension and Welfare Funds, 1930–62, in Millions of Dollars**

Year	Social Insurance Contributions	Private Fund Contributions
1930	$ 160	$ 106
1935	180	171
1940	1,624	282
1945	3,805	1,132
1950	3,976	2,743
1955	5,814	5,523
1960	11,346	8,629
1962	13,685	9,473

Source: Same as Table 11.

penalizes, by the absence of subsidy, employee contributions to such benefit programs.

The fact that private company-paid benefits are a form of untaxed income would not be so troublesome if such benefits were spread rather evenly over the whole tax-paying population. But, as we have observed, they tend to be heavily concentrated in certain industries. Thus, tax exemption compounds the inequity arising from unequal company ability to provide generous benefit programs.[23]

3. LABOR IMMOBILITY. It is claimed that company benefits, by tying labor to particular firms, cause an uneconomic distribution of the labor force. The contention is that if workers are perfectly free to move without high transfer costs to the best jobs available to them, regardless of employer, both worker satisfaction and the Gross National Product are enhanced. Loss of large benefits, or a gap in benefits, with shift of employers, means high transfer costs for workers.

The validity of this argument partly depends on the proper concept of employment. The case for a fluid labor supply rests heavily on the notion of a competitive labor market, a commodity

---

[23] For a brief discussion of this point see Michael Reagan, "Fringe Benefits," *New Republic*, CXLI (June 15, 1963), pp. 7–8.

concept of labor, and full employment so that one does not have to allow for the uncertainties and wastes of unemployment. The optimum amount of labor mobility and the test for socially desirable mobility are more difficult to determine where companies have considerable investments in their work forces (e.g., recruiting costs, orientation costs, on-the-job training costs), workers have some investment in employment with a particular firm (e.g., housing, work record, investment in the union), and the existence of widespread unemployment increases the risk of loss of some employment with transfer. Certainly from a social viewpoint, losses to employers from labor turnover should be deducted from any economic gains achieved through such turnover. Therefore, even though it may seem advantageous to the worker to move, from the point of view of the national economy his transfer might mean a net loss—his gain would not offset the additional cost of recruiting and training two persons in new jobs (himself and his replacement) rather than one if the job had been filled from the ranks of the unemployed or new entrants into the labor force.

The extent to which company benefits themselves significantly restrict labor mobility is open to question. Most of the barrier to transfer may consist of loss of seniority and benefit rights and loss of occupational advancement because of the management practice of hiring in at the bottom jobs and promoting from within. The retention power of company benefits seems to increase with age, but age alone is a mobility-reducing factor. The conclusions from studies as to the mobility-reducing effect of pension programs are mixed. From an analysis of two companies fairly comparable except that one had a pension plan and the other did not, Herbert S. Parnes concluded that private pension plans make little difference in the degree to which manual workers are tied to their employers.[24] A statistical analysis indicates that, although firms with pensions generally have lower turnover

---

[24] See "Workers' Attitudes to Job Changing: The Effect of Private Pension Plans," in Gladys L. Palmer, *et al.*, *The Reluctant Job Changer, Studies in Work Attachments and Aspirations* (Philadelphia: University of Pennsylvania Press, 1962), pp. 45–80, esp. the conclusions, pp. 76–80. Arthur M. Ross arrived at a similar conclusion with respect to benefits in general by a more deductive route. See his article, "Do We Have a New Industrial Feudalism?" *American Economic Review*, XLVIII (December 1958), pp. 903–19.

and quit rates, other immobilizing influences may be more important than pensions.[25]

Of course, to the extent that company benefit plans are ineffective in recruiting and retaining employees, the economic justification for management spending such large sums on them is reduced. It then becomes limited to any increase in labor productivity on the job that actually results from such programs.

From a public policy viewpoint, a combination of the inequity and tax-evasion criticisms seems more valid and substantial than the mobility criticism. In addition, it would seem easier to reduce or eliminate the tax loophole than to try to reduce or eliminate any labor immobility effects of benefit programs. A system of full vesting of pension contributions, such as most professors have, permits a shift of employees with no reduction in pension rights, but such vesting is expensive.

HOURS OF WORK

The length of the work week and work year is a basic factor in the nation's total output of goods and services. With labor by far the largest productive element, time spent on the job has serious implications for the whole economy. Work time, of course, affects not only the productivity of labor but also the use time of capital equipment as well.

The productivity of labor may be calculated in terms of an average per hour, per week, or per year and the total for a person's whole work career. Longer schooling and early retirement reduce the total work time on a career basis. Increases in paid vacations and holidays reduce the total hours worked in a year. The work week is composed of the number of days worked times the average hours at work each day.

In line with the three-prong treatment of this book, we will discuss first historical developments in work hours, then the economics of the shorter work hours, and finally the public policy aspects of the work week question.

---

[25] See Hugh Folk, "Effects of Private Pension Plans on Labor Mobility," *Monthly Labor Review,* LXXXVI (March 1963), pp. 285–88.

Historical Developments

Work hours have had a downward trend since 1850, as workers have taken part of the increased productivity in the form of more leisure.

The methods by which reductions in work time are accomplished have, however, altered somewhat from period to period. First the work day was shortened. In 1850, average weekly hours for all persons employed in industry were around 68, or roughly eleven hours a day, six days a week. In agriculture they were 72, or twelve hours a day (see Table 18). During the next half century, through adoption of the ten-hour day in many industries and the eight-hour day in a few, the average hours worked per week in nonagricultural employment fell to around 56 in 1900 and under 40 by the mid-thirties. In the twenties a work week of five and one half days began to become rather common, and by the mid-thirties the five-day, forty-hour week had become the standard practice in most of American industry.[26] Since 1940, the reduction in work hours in manufacturing has largely taken the form of longer paid vacations and more paid holidays. Thus, as work hours have contracted, the emphasis has tended to shift from the shorter work day, to the shorter work week, to the shorter work year.

In discussing historical developments in work hours, a distinction should be drawn between the standard, basic, or full-time work week and the actual hours worked in any week. The forty-hour week is a standard work week or full-time norm. The actual hours worked may fall below that standard because of absenteeism, holidays, part-time employment, or short work weeks. In the other direction, the actual hours may exceed the standard week by the amount of overtime hours worked and the amount of "moonlighting" (holding two or more jobs).

Generally, actual hours of work have declined along with cuts in the standard work week. However, considerable divergence between the standard and the actual work week occurred with the

---

[26] The historical parts of this section draw heavily on Milton Derber, *The History of Basic Work Hours and Related Benefit Payments in the United States*, in *Studies Relating to Collective Bargaining Agreements and Practices Outside the Railroad Industry*, Appendix Volume IV to *Report of the Presidential Railroad Commission* (Washington: United States Government Printing Office, February 1962), pp. 265–305.

TABLE 18

Estimated Average Actual Hours Worked per Week, 1850–1963

Year	Weighted average	Nonagriculture	Agriculture
1850	69.8	65.7	72.0
1860	68.0	63.3	71.0
1870	65.4	60.0	70.0
1880	64.0	58.8	69.0
1890	61.9	57.1	68.0
1900	60.2	55.9	67.0
1910	55.1	50.3	65.0
1920	49.7	45.5	60.0
1930	45.9	43.2	55.0
1940	44.0	41.1	54.6
1950	42.5	41.3	50.1
1960	40.8	40.1	48.0
1963	40.7	40.2	46.9

Source: For 1850–1940, J. Frederick Dewhurst and Associates, *America's Needs and Resources, A New Survey* (New York: Twentieth Century Fund, 1955), Appendix 20–4, p. 1073; for 1950–63, United States Bureau of the Census and Bureau of Labor Statistics in *Hours of Work, Hearings on H.R. 355, H.R. 3102, and H.R. 3320,* Select Subcommittee on Labor, Committee on Education and Labor, House of Representatives, Eighty-eighth Congress, 1st session, Part I, June 1963, p. 76.

share-the-work movement in the thirties; actual hours worked in manufacturing in 1934 averaged more than five hours a week below the average standard week. Again, during World War II there was marked divergence, when actual hours worked in manufacturing exceeded the standard by as much as an average of five hours a week in 1944.

The decline in average hours on a yearly full-time basis is indicated in Table 19. Those estimates show that the reduction in the standard work years in the fifties was at an annual rate at least as high as from 1910 to 1930, although well below the rate of reduction from 1930 to 1940. While in the forties, fifties, and early sixties, the standard work week in manufacturing was relatively stable, the long-term decline in nonmanufacturing industries toward the standard forty-hour week continued, and the annual figures were reduced by expansion in types of paid time off, chiefly, vacations and holidays. For the whole period from 1850 to 1960, the reduction in the work time has averaged about three hours a week each decade, but in the fifties and early sixties the average was no more than two hours a week per decade.

TABLE 19

Average Standard Hours a Year per Employee, 1910–58

Year	Annual Hours
1910	2,700
1920	2,630
1930	2,507
1940	2,286
1945	2,206
1950	2,138
1955	2,086
1958	2,060

Source: Edward F. Denison, *The Sources of Economic Growth in the United States and the Alternatives Before Us* (New York: Committee for Economic Development, 1962), Table 5, p. 37.

It has been estimated that the increase in leisure time in 1960 compared with 1940 consisted of the following reductions in hours of work throughout the economy: an average reduction of 1.5 hours in the work week, six additional days of paid vacation, and four additional days of paid holidays a year. On an annual basis those hours' reductions represented respectively, 75, 48, and 32 hours per full-time employed person. That is a total of 155 hours or almost four weeks of employment.[27]

With that general picture in mind, let us examine more closely particular developments in work time since 1850.

1. MOVEMENTS FOR A SHORTER WORK DAY.   The movement for shorter hours can be traced as far back as a strike by the Philadelphia carpenters for a basic ten-hour day in 1791. During the 1820's and 1830's through strikes in some cities, the skilled craftsmen (building, printing, and mechanical trades) succeeded in establishing the ten-hour day for men. In 1842, Massachusetts enacted a ten-hour law for children under twelve in manufacturing, and a ten-hour law for women workers in 1874. In 1840, by Presidential Executive Order "the ten-hour system" was established for manual workers on Federal public works.

The drive for the eight-hour day began after the Civil War.

---

[27] See reproduction of a speech on shorter hours by Ewan Clague in *John Herling's Labor Letter*, June 8, 1963, p. 3.

From a heavily political movement, it shifted in the 1880's to economic action by skilled tradesmen, particularly in the building trades. In the 1890's, the Carpenters' and Printers' unions had won the eight-hour day in many of the nation's leading cities, and the Mine Workers achieved it after a big strike in 1897. Between 1910 and 1920, the newly formed unions in men's and women's garments were able through collective bargaining to establish nine- and eight-hour days in urban production centers in those industries. In 1916, a Federal eight-hour law was enacted for the railroads; by then public sentiment seemed generally to support the eight-hour day. However, it was only in 1923 that the steel industry, strongly upholding two twelve-hour shifts for its continuous operations, yielded to unprecedented public pressure and adopted an eight-hour day with three shifts.

It is evident that the skilled unions in local market lines like building and newspaper printing tended to spearhead the movement for the eight-hour day. Generally, employers' organizations and large employers, with some notable exceptions, opposed each new movement for shorter hours. Therefore, work hours in strongly unionized industries were considerably shorter than those in unorganized or weakly organized industries from 1890 to 1930. Even in manufacturing it is estimated that in both 1890 and 1920, unionized factory workers averaged almost eight hours less per week than nonunion factory workers.[28] The decline in union membership between 1919 and 1929 also resulted in a slight reduction in the estimated percentage of all factory workers on the eight-hour system from 48.7 per cent to 45.5 per cent.[29]

It was in the Great Depression of the thirties that the basic eight-hour day became firmly established in American industry, first under the industry codes of the National Industrial Recovery Act and then in 1937 with the enactment of the Fair Labor Standards Act. That act did not regulate daily hours directly but, by providing for a standard forty-hour week, it really signified national acceptance of the basic eight-hour day and five-day week for industrial wage-earners.

---

[28] See Harry A. Millis and Royal E. Montgomery, *Labor's Progress and Some Basic Labor Problems* (New York: McGraw-Hill, 1938), Table 79, p. 470 and pp. 471–72.

[29] *Ibid.*, Table 81, p. 473.

By 1963, most of the women's garment trades, about a quarter of the printers, and the building trades in New York City, were on a 35-hour week. Indeed, in that year the New York local of the Brotherhood of Electrical Workers won through a strike a basic 25-hour week, with an hour a day of regularly scheduled overtime.[30] It is frequently charged that union demands for shorter work days and weeks are primarily aimed at increasing wages through more premium-paid overtime. The claim is that male workers generally do not want shorter daily or weekly hours, as is indicated by the strong demand for (and grievance cases about) overtime work[31] and the extent of "moonlighting" or multiple-job holding (in 1962 amounting to some 3.3 million workers, or 5 per cent of the work force, averaging 52 hours a week).[32] Actually, from 1948 to 1963 there was an exception to the general pattern in that a slight rise occurred in the percentage of nonfarm wage and salary employees working over 48 hours a week. The biggest such rise was for professional and technical employees, but there was also some increase in the percentage of sales and skilled trades employees working more than 48 hours per week.

2. THE FIVE-DAY WORK WEEK.   The 44-hour week with a half day off on Saturday was first achieved by some building tradesmen in a few cities in the 1890's, and by 1915 generally prevailed in building construction in the organized centers. By 1919, through collective bargaining and brief strikes, the Amalgamated Clothing Workers had won the 5.5-day, 44-hour week in every major garment-producing center.

The American Federation of Labor, which had called for a 44-hour week in 1919, set the five-day week as its goal in 1926. In that same year Henry Ford adopted the forty-hour week for his

---

[30] For an explanation of how Local 3 officials, and particularly President Harry Van Arsdale, are trying to prevent a decline in output with the shift from a basic 30-hour to a basic 25-hour week, see A. H. Raskin, "Labor's Welfare State, The New York Electrical Workers," *Atlantic Monthly*, CCXI (April 1963), pp. 40–41.

[31] For a presentation of this view see George W. Brooks, "History of Union Efforts to Reduce Working Hours," *Monthly Labor Review*, LXXIX (November 1956), p. 1273.

[32] Jacob Schiffman, "Multiple Jobholders in May 1962," *Monthly Labor Review*, LXXXVI (May 1963), pp. 516–23.

company on the ground that it would help to promote a high-consumption economy. In 1930, less than 6 per cent of the workers in manufacturing had attained the five-day standard.

As already mentioned, it was governmental action in the Great Depression of the thirties (following a privately promoted spread-the-work movement) that permanently established the five-day standard in American industry.

3. SPREAD OF PAID VACATIONS AND HOLIDAYS. Vacations with pay for wage-earners were practically nonexistent in industry before World War I. Substantial seasonal and other lay-offs in industries where unions were strong, such as construction, mining, and clothing, discouraged any demand for regular paid vacations. In industry, generally, relatively few firms had paid vacation plans for manual workers before 1940. In 1931, a survey by the National Industrial Conference Board found only 281 then in effect.

The significant expansion in paid vacations and paid holidays for wage-earners began in the midthirties with the great spread of unionism into mass production industries. In 1940, one quarter of all union members were receiving annual vacations with pay under collective bargaining agreements, and by 1944, approximately 85 per cent were under agreements providing paid vacations.

Paid vacations and holidays had been established much earlier for office employees in large firms. Vacations and holidays for plant workers were generally without pay. An analysis of 12,000 union agreements in January 1943 found that the majority merely provided for time off on holidays without compensation. Thus, annual vacations with pay and holidays off with pay became a status issue as well as a claim of an earned right. Limits on wage increases and War Labor Board policies helped to spread such plans during World War II. A report by the National Industrial Conference Board showed that, whereas only 9.6 per cent of its cooperating companies had paid holiday arrangements for wage-earners in 1940, some 42 per cent had them in 1946 and 77 per cent in 1948.[33]

Once well established, the unions pressed for liberalization, especially up to three and four weeks of paid vacation for employees with long seniority. The United States Chamber of

[33] *Holiday Practices* (New York: National Industrial Conference Board, 1948), p. 8.

Commerce estimates that by 1961, paid vacations and holidays for the country as a whole amounted to 6.2 per cent of wages and salaries compared with 0.6 per cent in 1929.[34] From 1929 to 1961, the work year was thus reduced by approximately three weeks.

In 1962, the Steelworkers negotiated a two-year agreement with the large firms manufacturing metal cans, which provided for a thirteen weeks' paid vacation every five years for employees with fifteen years or more of service. This breakthrough in the form of a "sabbatical" every five years helps to spread jobs by reducing total work hours per employee. The program was adopted by basic steel in 1963 under a twenty-one-month agreement, also with no wage increase. The adoption of "sabbatical" programs for long-tenure employees was explained on the grounds that the high-paid steelworkers were more "security conscious" than "wage conscious" as a result of reduced employment in steel plants.

4. FACTORS IN THE CONTRACTION OF WORK HOURS. Unlike wages, changes in work hours in each industry occur by jumps, usually with rather long plateaus between each breakthrough. Also unlike wage changes, movements in hours before the thirties varied widely between industries in amount and especially in timing (e.g., some industries had the eight-hour day two or three decades before others did; for some years, steel was on a 72-hour week, while construction and clothing were on a 40-hour week), and gains in shorter hours were seldom lost through reversals in a depression[35] as wages were cut during economic downswings prior to the mid-thirties.

Often the work week was considerably shorter in the unionized than the unorganized parts of the same industry, especially in local-market lines. For example, a survey in building construction in 1936 showed that less than 4 per cent of the union workers had a normal work week exceeding forty hours, whereas the full-time hours of half the nonunion workers were above forty a week, 8 per cent of them having scheduled weeks over 48 hours.[36]

---

[34] *Fringe Benefits,* 1961, *op. cit.,* p. 31.

[35] One exception was the suspension or discontinuance of some two-fifths of the relatively small number of paid vacation plans for manual workers during the depression of the thirties.

[36] "Hours of Labor in the Building Trades, 1936," *Monthly Labor Review,* XLV (October 1937), p. 798.

Historical evidence bears out the conclusion that the market mechanism is not well adapted for determining the length of the work week or the issue of paid vacations and holidays. In factory employment, hours generally have to be uniform for all employees. Individual workers can hardly be permitted to negotiate separate work schedules. In addition, experimentation is discouraged not only because the effects of a change in hours or vacation on worker productivity may be impossible to isolate, but also because a reduction in the standard work week or a paid vacation once granted may be practically irreversible.

There is some evidence that employers at times in the past have insisted on longer hours for factory employees than would provide the maximum output per week over a period of time.[37] In other words, market forces could not be relied upon to determine optimum hours of work from the employer's own self-interest viewpoint.[38]

Over the past century the main factors leading to shorter hours appear to have been collective bargaining and action by the

---

[37] For example, Robert Owen testified in 1818 that a reduction from fourteen to twelve hours a day in his factory at New Lanark in England had actually resulted in an increase in output, and evidence from studies by factory inspectors after hours legislation was passed in 1844 in England showed that the output of eleven hours' work might be as great or greater than that of twelve or fourteen hours, and that long hours, far from being productive, resulted in spoiled work, inefficiency, and breakdowns. [See B. L. Hutchins and A. Harrison, *A History of Factory Legislation*, 3rd ed. (London: 1926), pp. 21–23 and 122–26.]

When the work day was reduced from ten to eight hours in the bituminous coal industry in this country in 1897, the average output per worker per day increased, even in States where the proportion of coal mined by machine decreased. (See Report of the United States Industrial Commission, *Final Report*, vol. 19, 1902, pp. 767–72.) A study of a number of paper mills by the United States Tariff Board showed that the labor costs per ton of output decreased almost 15 per cent with the change from a twelve-hour to an eight-hour work day in 1909. (See United States Tariff Board, *Report on Pulp and News Print Industry*, 1911.) In a National Industrial Conference Board survey in 1929, some 68 per cent of the responding companies reported no reduction in output, and 18 per cent reported an increase in output, with a change from 5.5 or six days to a five-day work week. [See *The Five-Day Week in Manufacturing Industries* (New York: National Industrial Conference Board, 1929), p. 41.]

[38] The classical economist, A. C. Pigou came to the same conclusion. He stated that "a large volume of experience" contradicted the "optimistic view" that employers' and workers' self-interest would prevent unduly long hours and indicated that "private self-interest has often seriously failed in this matter." [See *The Economics of Welfare* (London: Macmillan, 1920), p. 414.]

government. In the nineteenth century and early twentieth century, much of the leadership in most general reductions was provided by the craft unions in local-market lines like construction and newspaper printing. They were able, through economic pressure and strikes, to secure considerable control over jobs and working conditions. Unions in coal mining and clothing were also able to exert similar control and pressures to gain shorter hours. However, the unions in the mass-production industries appear to have had little influence on daily or weekly hours because the forty-hour week was well established before unions had organized those industries. The Steelworkers, Automobile Workers, and other large industrial unions have, however, provided leadership in the post-World War II move for liberalization of paid vacations, holidays, and employee benefits.

Government has influenced work hours by means of legislation, administrative policy, and example. State hours laws for women in the nineteenth century were the first legislation. Later in 1916, the Federal Government by law set an eight-hour standard for the railroads. In the thirties, the forty-hour week was established under the Fair Labor Standards Act, and the eight-hour day and forty-hour week on government contracts by the Walsh-Healey Act. The Federal Government set an example by its hours' policies with respect to Federal employees. Federal action in favor of the standard eight-hour day for private industry was pressed in World War I, and the basic forty-hour week and paid vacations had the support of Federal boards in World War II and the Korean conflict.

Thus, the relative influence on work hours of union pressures (economic and political) varied from period to period. Private employers, with a few notable exceptions like Henry Ford, did not provide much leadership in changes in the standard work day and work week except during the depression of the thirties. Then they promoted the share-the-work movement and the five-day week.

As the work week shortened, the arguments for hours' reductions shifted. When wage earners worked over ten hours a day for six days a week, advocates of shorter hours stressed arguments based on workers' health and safety and pointed out that such hours stunted workers' growth as citizens by failing to permit sufficient time for social, cultural, and political activities. Some also argued that a shorter day would actually lead to greater output.

As hours were reduced to ten a day and later eight, the case for shorter hours was based more and more on the question of unemployment. It was tied up with the fear that mechanization would reduce employment opportunities. Shorter hours, it was assumed, would both spread the available work and raise the total income of the workers by curtailing the supply of labor, and, thus, permitting an increase in wage scales to compensate for the hours' reduction. In that way, it was claimed, consumer purchasing power would be increased. Of course, employers answered with stress on the adverse effects of higher hourly pay on employment.

Economics of Shorter Hours

Union leaders frequently point out errors in the past predictions of economists with respect to the economic consequences of shortening work hours. Mistakes in analysis were made by some of the classical economists in England who opposed a ten-hour law for female workers on the ground that output would decline in proportion to any hours' reduction. Those economists failed to take account of the dynamics of productivity increase and to distinguish between the short-run and long-run effects of reductions in working hours.[39] The relationship between hours and output was much more complex and more significantly influenced by circumstances than they thought.

1. HOURS AND OUTPUT. Studies of variation in worker output with changes in work hours have mostly examined experience during World War I and World War II, when hours were temporarily increased.[40] Few careful studies, therefore, have been made

---

[39] For a discussion of the bases for the opposition of many classical English economists to hours' legislation see Mark Blaug, "The Classical Economist and the Factory Acts—A Re-examination," *Quarterly Journal of Economics*, LXXIII (May 1958), pp. 211–26.

[40] The discussion in this section draws heavily on *Hours of Work and Output*, United States Bureau of Labor Statistics Bulletin No. 917 (Washington: United States Government Printing Office, 1947). It covers the experience of some fifty firms and their workers, most of whom were on some form of wage incentive.

on which to base predictions of the productivity consequences of reducing the standard work week to 35 and 30 hours.

The influence of work hours on output is not a simple matter. Many factors have a bearing on output results, and there are different ways of measuring the effects. The productivity consequences of increasing (or decreasing) weekly hours may vary with such factors as the work schedule adopted (hours per day, lunch and rest periods, etc.), the physical demands of the job, the age and health of the workers and their interest in the work, and the length of time over which the change is sustained. It may require as much as a year for an hours' change to have its full effects on a worker and thus on his output. During such a long interval, other changes that affect workers' productivity are likely to occur, thus complicating the problem of isolating the effects of the alteration in work hours.

Changes in worker output can be measured in terms of the average per hour or the total per day, per week, per year, or per work career. Shorter hours may increase the worker's average output per hour but reduce his total output per day, week, and year. On the other hand, a shorter work day and week may permit married women to work more continuously during the year and allow workers to remain on their jobs for more years before retirement.

In addition to the worker's own output, work hours may affect the total output of the plant by their influence on the amount of absenteeism and equipment breakage. Long hours may necessitate more absence from the job for health and personal reasons (shopping, dentist appointments, etc.). The length of the work day and of the work week may also affect total costs of output through their influence on the number and severity of work accidents and the incidence of defective product.

The hours-output relationship is further complicated by the fact that it is not proportional. Work injuries rise progressively as hours are increased above eight a day and forty a week, and especially sharply if the work week is 54 hours or more.[41] The evidence indicates that for hours above eight a day and forty-eight per

---

[41] *Ibid.*, p. 5.

week, it usually requires three additional work hours to produce two additional hours of output if the work is light, and with heavy work two more hours of work produce only one hour of added output.[42] As a rule, the factor lowering output effectiveness of longer hours over an extended period is fatigue.

On the other hand, work hours can be too short for efficient operation. There seems to be no clear tendency for the incidence of industrial accidents, machine breakdowns, defective output, or even male absenteeism to decline when the work day is progressively reduced below seven or eight hours a day. With reductions in hours below seven or eight a day and thirty-five or forty a week there is a possibility of an absolute decrease in the worker's average output per hour. That is because the first and last hours of a work shift (and to some extent the time directly before and after lunch) tend to be relatively inefficient hours, since they involve "set-up" time (preparing for work and achieving the normal pace) and "knockdown" time (slowing down and preparing to stop work). The shorter is the work day, the higher is the percentage of such less productive hours in the total time on the job.

Reductions in work hours may also cause an increase in capital costs per unit of output and in recruitment and training costs if a shortage of skilled labor is thereby created. The effect on unit capital costs depends on whether or not the shorter work day results in a change from single-shift to double-shift operation. If so, capital equipment will be used more hours per week; if not, reduced hours create more unemployment for machinery. The idleness time of capital equipment is increased, and capital costs per unit of output tend to rise. As a consequence of the change to a double shift, less equipment and more employees would be required for a certain volume of output. Thus, the demand for capital goods would tend to decrease and the demand for labor to increase.

2. WORK HOURS AND TOTAL EMPLOYMENT. During periods of widespread unemployment, elements in organized labor have argued for shorter hours as a means of meeting the problems of joblessness. Relatively high rates of unemployment, partly as a result

---

[42] *Ibid.*

of job elimination by automation, led the AFL-CIO in 1962 to adopt, as a major goal, a reduction of the standard work week to 35 hours without a cut in weekly wages.

It is evident that work sharing through short work weeks enables more workers to have jobs. Some unemployed can be given part of the total employment that way. Even with no increase in hourly wages accompanying a cut in the standard work week, employers would have the higher costs of adding workers to the payroll. These include recruitment and training costs if new employees are added, and also larger social insurance and benefit costs.

Indeed, so large have the costs of fringe benefits and other non-wage items become that it sometimes is cheaper for employers to work men overtime at a penalty rate of 150 per cent rather than to add new workers to the payroll. That may be particularly true for short periods. Such a result arises because the costs of private benefit plans, paid vacations and holidays, and, to a considerable extent, social insurance taxes, are tied to the individual and usually do not vary with the length of time he actually works in a week or in a year above a certain minimum.[43] By 1962, fringe and other costs were counterbalancing the premium rate of time and a half for overtime to such an extent that some labor leaders were urging an increase in the overtime penalty rate under the Fair Labor Standards Act to double time.

Usually, organized labor insists that any shortening of the work week be accomplished without a reduction in the worker's weekly pay check. In other words, hours cuts are to be offset by a corresponding pay increase. Reduction from 40 to 35 hours in that way would require a 14 per cent increase in wage rates.

The claim that a shorter standard work week would increase the total hours of employment rests on much the same reasoning

<hr>

[43] The tax on employers for unemployment compensation in most States is on the first $3,000 of wages earned in a year, and for the Federal Old-Age, Survivors', and Disability Insurance program the employer tax is on the first $5,200 of wages. For a comment on this situation see Leonard Woodcock, "New Problems for Collective Bargaining," in Gerald G. Somers (ed.), *Proceedings of the Fifteenth Annual Conference of the Industrial Relations Association*, Madison, Wisconsin, 1963, p. 203.

that supports a wage increase for that purpose.[44] There are, however, some possible differences as follows: (1) To a greater extent than wage increases, the hours' reduction method might result in larger output per manhour. Although that has been the case in the past, in most industries such a result seems unlikely to be caused by reductions below forty hours, for reasons already explained. Especially is such a result questionable when one takes account of development costs and lower output for the new, less experienced employees. (2) Unlike wage increases, hours' reductions, by absorbing employees on lay-off, might result in some savings in an employer's unemployment costs under experience rating in unemployment compensation. However, any such savings would probably be outweighed by the additional costs for social insurance taxes and fringe benefits for the added employees. (3) The existing employees with no weekly pay increase and the added employees combined would be likely to spend their wage income even more fully and rapidly than the average employed worker would spend a wage increase that raised his weekly earnings proportionately. This seems to be a valid argument under most circumstances. (4) Compared with wage increases, hours' reductions come in larger chunks and are likely to be more varied in amount and timing unless accomplished by national legislative enactment. (5) Hours' reduction may create shortages in certain occupations and scheduling problems especially in multiple-shift industries. (6) Above all, reductions in the standard work week below forty hours are likely, in most industries, to result in a permanent curtailment of the nation's productive potential or capacity.

Assessment of those six differences would hardly seem to tip the scales in favor of shortened standard hours as an employment-stimulating device, unless stress is placed on absorption of the unemployed into industry even at the expense of some decline in output potential. Pessimists might argue that, with the levels of unemployment existing in the early sixties, that potential was not being used and not likely to be used. That, of course, assumes that

---

[44] For a statement of the AFL-CIO case for shorter hours as a means of stimulating demand and generating additional employment see *American Federationist*, LXIX (November 1962), pp. 20 and 21; and also "Reducing Hours: Choices and Costs," *ibid.* (October 1962), p. 20.

monetary, fiscal, and other measures would not succeed in reducing unemployment to normal, frictional levels.

On the grounds of inflationary pressures, a reduction in the standard work week is potentially likely to raise prices more than an equivalent increase in wage rates. That is largely because it tends to create shortages of qualified labor in certain lines.

The case for the shorter work week as a recovery measure, thus, rests heavily on the proposition that it is an effective means to increase total spending for consumption and capital investment. Often the proponents stress the income aspects and neglect cost questions and the probable effects on investment spending. For one-shift operations, a reduction in the standard work week would make necessary more equipment to produce the same total output.

Whether a measure serves to increase total spending for consumption and investment hinges on the reaction of different groups in the economy. That, in turn depends somewhat on how the measure is put into effect, its coverage, and the circumstances at the time. The achievements of lower hours' standards by means of decentralized bargaining, firm by firm and industry by industry, is not likely to provide much over-all stimulus to the economy. Reasoning about the effects of such piecemeal action would presumably have to be on the basis of collective partial analysis rather than national-income analysis. The latter would be more applicable to an hours' reduction by national legislation.

Of course, in the dynamics of a situation where employees and not machines pace the work, the drop in potential output with a sharp cut in standard hours may be partly forestalled for the time being. That seems to have been accomplished by the Electrical Workers in building construction in New York City after they struck and won a change from a standard thirty-hour week to a standard twenty-five-hour week in 1962.[45]

Public Policy on Hours

In 1961 and 1962, the Kennedy Administration clearly expressed its opposition to a reduction in the standard work week as a means of meeting the unemployment problem. A reduction in the basic

---

[45] A. H. Raskin, *op. cit.*

work week that would raise production costs and lower the nation's growth potential seemed most inappropriate to a government concerned about possible price inflation, a deficit in the country's balance of payments with more intense foreign competition, and the country's low rate of economic growth. In view of the nation's needs in the cold war and at home, monetary and tax reduction measures to overcome unemployment seemed more fitting.

The Administration, however, had no power to prevent local unions like the New York electricians from using their economic muscle to win significant reductions in standard working hours. As has been observed, labor market forces are not effective in establishing or enforcing the correct standard for the work week. Competition in product markets does, of course, stiffen employer opposition to increased costs through hours' reduction with no cut in take-home pay. But is it sufficient to rely on the opposition of employers in each collective bargaining negotiation?

One difficulty may be that the union's hours' demands may not fully reflect the wishes of a majority of its membership, to say nothing of the wishes of the members' wives and the public in general. Partly this is because hours' changes usually involve wage changes. But also it is because there may be a difference between workers' interests as a group and their desires as individuals. As a group they may be interested in raising the price of their labor and providing employment for more of the union's members. The group gains by a common restrictive policy. As individuals, however, they may gain and satisfy their desires more fully if they can work longer hours than the shortened standard work week. Individually, they want to be "overtime hogs."

Changes in standard work hours are an issue much broader than the effect of reduced hours on a worker's output, or on the employer's costs, or even on the level of prices. The length of the work day and the work week affect such matters as the participation of married women and others in the labor force, the duration of the average total work life, the use of transportation and recreation facilities, patterns of family life, and the operation of the nation's economy, ranging from potential Gross National Product to the balance of payments.

In some respects, the thirteen-week "sabbatical" every five years for long-service employees has distinct advantages over a blanket reduction in the basic work week. It allows time to plan for, and train, the additional workers needed. And the worker can personally select his period of extended time off.

Given the wide ramifications and national significance of work hours, changes in the standard work week should be part of a program of over-all manpower planning. Walter Reuther, president of the UAW, stressed the planning aspects of the work-week issue in a speech in February 1963, when he said:[46]

> The UAW does not share the view of a 35-hour work week, although labor generally does. We are committed to try to achieve a flexible full employment work week because we share the view that neither labor nor management nor government should arbitrarily dictate the number of hours that should be worked. That ought to be a rational and responsible decision that flows out of what a society wants to do with its manpower resources, with its economic resources; how much more material wealth do you want to enjoy balanced against the measure of human leisure you would like to enjoy. And that decision should be the result of that kind of rational process rather than a negative move against unemployment.

Presumably, the Federal Government would need to provide the framework for the broad, rational consideration of work hours that Reuther envisages. The place of work hours in a program of national manpower planning and institutional arrangements for such a program are discussed in Chapter 18.

SUMMARY

1. Since World War II, expenditures for nonwage benefit plans have been expanding rapidly compared with total wages. Company benefit costs per employee are much greater in large, high-wage firms in oligopolistic industries than they are under the opposite conditions.

2. Managements, workers, and unions may each have good reasons (e.g., savings to the company, savings to employees in insur-

---

[46] "Labor-Management Relations—Responsibilities, Problems, and Opportunities Ahead," a talk before the Economics Club of Detroit, February 4, 1963, printed in *Daily Labor Report*, No. 29, February 11, 1963, E-3.

ance costs and taxes, and special credit and increased security for the union) for preferring a bigger benefit component in any wage-benefit-rules package.

3. Although managements have economic justifications for parts of most benefit programs, noneconomic motives also seem to be influential, and company ability to pay helps to explain wide intercompany and interindustry differences in benefit levels. Demand and supply analysis is not very useful in explaining amounts spent by a company on each type of benefit.

4. Unions have played a significant role in enlarging the items covered and the persons eligible under company benefit plans. Breakthroughs in one negotiation have been spread.

5. Company-financed benefits for employees raise important questions of (a) equity as between employees of firms with widely differing ability to pay such benefits, (b) tax exemption for employees in relation to company ability to pay benefits, and (c) labor immobility through ties resulting from company-related benefits. Of these, tax exemption seems to be most in need of remedying.

6. For a century or more the trend in work hours has been downward, the drop averaging three hours per decade.

7. Reductions in the standard work day, in the work week, and in the work year through paid vacations and holidays were spearheaded by organized labor and were accomplished partly through legislation and government policy. Generally, market forces were less effective in such hours' reduction than were collective bargaining and governmental action.

8. Although the relation between workers' hours and output is complex and varies with the circumstances, hours' reductions below seven or eight a day and forty a week usually do not seem to result in a long-run increase in average hourly output.

9. Reduction of the standard work week to 35 or fewer hours has a number of drawbacks as a measure to stimulate the economy; it has serious implications for the nation's output potential and economic growth.

10. The length of the standard work week is so important to the nation that it should be a part of national manpower planning.

DISCUSSION QUESTIONS

1. How do you explain the rapid expansion in private nonwage benefits since 1942?
2. As an industrial relations executive, how would you justify an extension of the coverage of a noncontributory hospital and medical-care plan to the dependents of present employees and to retired employees and their dependents?
3. To what extent do you favor the present exemption in the Federal income tax for company-financed benefit protection for employees? Justify your answer on economic grounds.
4. Do company benefits serve as a significant restraint on labor mobility? Explain.
5. What factors caused a shift in the form of hours' reductions from a shorter work day, to fewer days per week, to paid vacations and holidays?
6. Why were market forces not more influential in determining changes in standard working hours? Explain.
7. Discuss the economic arguments for and the economic arguments against the AFL-CIO's goal for a 35-hour week.
8. Critically discuss Walter Reuther's position with respect to "rational" determination of work hours. What are its implications for collective bargaining?

SELECTED READINGS

A Shorter Workweek? An Information Manual on Key Questions, Chamber of Commerce of the United States, Washington, D.C., 1962, 113 pp.

Brooks, George W., "History of Union Efforts to Reduce Working Hours," *Monthly Labor Review*, LXXIX (November 1956), pp. 1271–73.

Denison, Edward F., *The Sources of Economic Growth in the United States and the Alternatives Before Us*, Supplementary Paper No. 13, Committee for Economic Development, New York, 1962, Chapters 5 and 6 on Employment and Hours of Work, pp. 35–66.

Derber, Milton, *The History of Basic Work Hours and Related Benefit Payments in the United States*, in *Studies Relating to Collective Bargaining Agreements and Practices Outside the Railroad In-*

dustry, Appendix Volume IV to *Report of the Presidential Rail-road Commission* (Washington: United States Government Printing Office, February 1962), pp. 265–305.

Greenbaum, Marcia L., *The Shorter Workweek*, Bulletin 50, New York School of Industrial and Labor Relations, Cornell University, Ithaca, New York, June 1963.

Mendelson, A. I., "Fringe Benefits Today and Tomorrow," *Labor Law Journal*, VII (June 1956), pp. 325–28 and 379–84.

"Repercussions of a Reduction in Hours of Work," *International Labour Review*, LXXIV (July 1956), pp. 23–45.

Skolnik, Alfred M., "Growth of Employee-Benefit Plans, 1954–61," *Social Security Bulletin*, XXVI (April 1963), pp. 4–17.

Slichter, Sumner H., James J. Healy, and E. Robert Livernash, *The Impact of Collective Bargaining on Management* (Washington: Brookings Institution, 1960) Chapters 13–16 on benefit plans, pp. 372–489.

"The Long Trend to Shorter Hours," *The American Federationist*, LXIX (August 1962), pp. 5–10.

United States Congress, *Hours of Work, Hearings before a Special Subcommittee of the Committee on Education and Labor*, House of Representatives, Eighty-eighth Congress, 1st session, Part 1 and Part 2 (Washington: United States Printing Office, 1963 and 1964).

12.
Seniority, Technological Change, and Union Security

THIS CHAPTER DEALS with certain aspects of employee security and union security. Two of the most troublesome non-wage issues in collective bargaining have been seniority and the union shop. Improvements in production techniques have been affecting both. Fast-changing technology has caused widespread employee concern about job security and worry among labor leaders about the future of unions because of the effects on membership totals and on strike effectiveness.

The welfare concept of employment accentuates the problems arising from worker displacement by new machines. With work-life ties to a firm, disemployment constitutes a great personal loss. Not only does the worker's wage income cease but also he forfeits his benefit rights, his seniority protection against future lay-offs, his preference rights to recall from lay-off, and his priority to opportunities for promotion to a higher level job. Under a commodity concept of employment (such as still prevails in casual employment like crop harvesting), job rights and expectations are not built up, and loss of a job only severs a payroll connection.

Basically, therefore, this chapter is concerned with the conflict between the forces of economic change and the structures of employee and institutional security, largely developed through collective bargaining. Competition and market forces lie behind economic change. The savings from mechanization partly come from the elimination of workers' jobs; sometimes the change involves obsolescence of a whole occupation (such as navigator or flight engineer on the airlines or firemen on the railroads).

Collective bargaining has designed nonmarket systems of job allocation, either in the form of a system of priorities based on seniority (in manufacturing and rail and air transportation) or assignment from a union hiring hall (in the building trades and the maritime industry). In addition, negotiated work rules may stipulate the manning requirements for particular operations. But revolutionary changes in industry, such as the introduction of automated equipment, may render the seniority and work-rule protections in collective agreements largely ineffective. Such changes have presented a great challenge to collective bargaining in many industries in recent years.

In this analysis of problems of worker and union security amid marked technological change, first the concept and practice of seniority will be examined. Then the impact of mechanization upon employment and seniority, and attempts to meet the problem through collective bargaining, will be discussed. Finally, the question of union security will be considered, including both the economic and the legal aspects of compulsory union membership.

SENIORITY

A strong union demand for control of lay-offs arose in the mass-production industries during the 1930's. Many workers joined unions then because they believed that the widespread lay-offs had been conducted without proper regard for workers' job equities and with foreman favoritism too often the deciding factor. With employers free to conduct antiunion campaigns before the United States Supreme Court validated the Wagner Act in 1937, and in the absence of a union-shop contract, labor organizations needed protection against discriminatory lay-off or transfer of union members and officials to undesirable jobs.[1] The result was that one of the first demands of the new unions was an objective system for distributing curtailed employment. Seniority, which until the early thirties had been largely confined to the railroads, was written into new agreements and became a widespread practice.

The Principle and Its Application

Seniority is based on the employee's length of continuous service with the company. Generally, a seniority roster is kept showing the hiring date for all who have been employed beyond the probationary period (usually no more than sixty days).

Often there is a distinction between seniority for job rights and seniority for benefit rights. For job rights the worker should be qualified, or be able soon to qualify, for the work performed in the unit or area where seniority applies. Therefore, job seniority may be confined to a single craft, a single line of promotion, or a single department in a plant. That is not true of benefit rights including vacation, which normally are determined by the worker's hiring date regardless of where he has been working.

For job rights, the worker's relative position on the seniority roster determines one or more of the following, depending on the provisions of the particular agreement: (1) the order of lay-off, the last worker entering the unit being the first one to be furloughed; (2) the order in which workers are recalled to work from among those on furlough, the one with the longest seniority being the first to be recalled; (3) the order in which management transfers workers temporarily to less desirable or more desirable jobs or work shifts, with seniority providing priority of protection or choice; and (4) the order in which a job opening must be offered to employees to qualify, with the employee with the highest seniority having the first refusal and so on down the roster. Actually, the area over which an employee can exercise his seniority may vary with the purpose; for lay-offs the area of application may be broader than for promotions.

For lay-off and recall to work, seniority operates in a mechani-

---

[1] Freedom to lay off and keep a worker furloughed is equivalent to unrestricted right of discharge; freedom to transfer him to another job is tantamount to unlimited power to demote an employee.

cal fashion and is the only factor considered in agreements covering about half the workers under contracts with seniority provisions.[2] For the other half, seniority is qualified by the requirement that the employee must be capable of doing the work, or that length of service will apply where the ability and fitness of employees for the job are approximately equal. In actual practice under such qualified seniority, length of service may be applied in practically all cases, especially in large lay-offs.

Lay-offs and recalls are governed by seniority in perhaps nine-tenths of all agreements in manufacturing and half of the agreements in nonmanufacturing industries.[3] The exceptions consist largely of industries where workers regularly shift employers (e.g., building and maritime) or there are regular seasonal fluctuations in employment (e.g., clothing manufacture). Those industries generally have a system of work-sharing or rotation of job assignment from a union hiring hall.

Although length of service within the seniority unit may determine which employees are eliminated first, such employees may avoid actual lay-off if they have the privilege of displacing or bumping employees with lesser service in another seniority unit. About half of the agreements with lay-off procedures contain bumping provisions, often qualified by length or type of lay-off.[4] The wider the application of bumping rights, the greater the dislocation of employees from jobs in a sort of chain reaction. In rather extreme cases, contraction of the work force by 10 per cent may, through bumping, necessitate the reassignment of as much as 40 or 50 per cent of the firm's work force.[5] The reverse process occurs with expansion. Widespread bumping can have adverse effects on operating efficiency.

Use of the seniority principle in connection with promotions is less prevalent than in lay-offs. For promotions it can hardly be

---

[2] See *Analysis of Layoff, Recall, and Work-Sharing Procedures in Union Contracts*, Bulletin No. 1209, United States Bureau of Labor Statistics, (Washington: United States Government Printing Office, 1957), pp. 21–22. The data in this paragraph are from that source.

[3] *Ibid.*, pp. 3–5 and 20–22.

[4] *Ibid.*, p. 27.

[5] See George W. Taylor, "Seniority Concepts," in Jean T. McKelvey (ed.), *Arbitration Today, Proceedings of the Eighth Annual Meeting of the National Academy of Arbitrators* (Washington: BNA Incorporated, 1955), p. 130.

supported on grounds of job security. Where seniority is one of the factors considered in promotion, it is usually secondary to skill and ability. If ability and fitness are approximately equal or applicants have "sufficient fitness," the one with the most seniority generally is given the first opportunity to qualify for a higher level vacancy. Too much emphasis on seniority in promotions may seriously weaken incentives to superior performance, but some companies have found that where significant differences between jobs are lacking, where group incentives prevail, and where the union is "reasonable," such weakening has not occurred.[6]

Some Problems

Seniority, of course, reduces the authority of management to grade the work force and to use nonmonetary rewards (e.g., employment security) for incentive purposes. It places employee security as determined by length of service above the freedom of management to manipulate individuals in the work force, just as a grievance procedure ending in arbitration limits management's right to discharge or threaten discharge as a disciplinary force. Indeed, the existence of seniority provisions in an agreement may themselves serve to limit the effectiveness of the discharge instrument, because arbitrators are often reluctant to uphold or award outright discharge since it terminates the worker's seniority, with the resulting loss of accumulated job and benefit rights. In order to achieve a measure of flexibility and to maintain essential operations and training, seniority provisions may be waived for key or exceptional personnel (e.g., set-up men, maintenance experts, emergency squadrons, management trainees, students, and handicapped employees). Approximately one-fifth of the workers under agreements with lay-off provisions contain an exemption for a small number or percentage of the work force to cover such cases.[7]

For unions, seniority can create serious internal conflicts. It places the burden of job loss on the young, short-service employees,

---

[6] See for example, Frederick H. Harbison and King Carr, *The Libbey-Owens-Ford Glass Company and the Federation of Glass, Ceramic and Silica Sand Workers of America*, Case Study No. 2 in Causes of Industrial Peace under Collective Bargaining (Washington: National Planning Association, October 1948), pp. 27–28.

[7] See *Analysis of Layoff, Recall, and Work-Sharing Procedures in Union Contracts, op. cit.*, pp. 23–24.

and thus may tend to split the union into contending interest groups. Dynamic changes may wrench a delicate balance developed over a long period of time. Corporate mergers may give rise to knotty problems of integrating separate seniority lists.

Seniority does not guarantee employment; it simply determines the allocation of work curtailment. Rapid technological change may require radical revision of seniority units if long-service employees are not to be laid off while short-service workers continue in employment. Generally, unions have sought fairly wide seniority units to protect long-service workers as automation has wiped out many jobs in a particular seniority area. Management, on the other hand, tends to favor rather narrowly defined seniority units because they necessitate much less interjob transfer and consequent cost of training and displacement. A wider seniority unit, although providing more work security to senior employees, also increases job uncertainty because it enlarges the number of persons who may displace a particular worker from his job.

If local union officers and shop stewards do not enjoy special retention privileges or superseniority, lay-offs could jeopardize the union's representation function by the temporary elimination of experienced representatives from the plant. Therefore, in agreements covering half the employees who are subject to lay-off provisions, such superseniority is granted to certain union representatives.[8] That exemption from seniority may serve as an incentive to members to accept such union responsibilities. In some agreements, the number of union representatives with superseniority is balanced by an equal number of key or special employees with extra seniority or exemption from the seniority restrictions.

Generally speaking, seniority is not considered by the courts as a property right in the sense that an individual's privileges once established cannot be changed without his consent by subsequent union-management negotiations. The parties may, for example, reduce the job security of some employees by revising the seniority system to permit plantwide bumping. Some recent cases have, however, left the question of court enforcement of seniority rights in a rather confused state.[9]

---

[8] *Ibid*, pp. 23–24.
[9] See Benjamin Aaron, "Reflections on the Legal Nature and Enforceability of Seniority Rights," *Harvard Law Review*, LXXV (June 1962), pp. 1532–64.

Economic Consequences

Studies sufficient to support firm conclusions about the economic impact of seniority are lacking. The effects are, of course, different in a rigid and outmoded seniority district system such as exists on the railroads[10] and the more flexible arrangements in some of the mass-production industries.

The net effect of seniority on efficiency within a plant appears to vary with the circumstances. In some respects, seniority for lay-off and recall has favorable effects on plant operations. It tends to make management more careful in selection, in training, and in weeding out new employees during the probationary period. It reduces labor turnover, thus saving on the cost of recruiting and preparing new employees. It also has beneficial effects on worker morale by providing employees greater security and by promoting the feeling that management is treating workers impartially and equitably. From a social point of view, seniority helps to provide employment security for men over forty-five or fifty years of age who, if they lost their present jobs, would be likely to become long-term unemployed.

On the other hand, seniority may have adverse effects on labor productivity. To the extent that bumping results in a high number of job displacements relative to total lay-offs, work teams are disrupted and training costs are increased. Straight seniority for lay-off and recall eliminates management's ability to use the allocation of employment as an incentive and reward. The management cannot weed out less efficient employees in recessions; it must live with mistakes in the selection and retention of employees until they retire or are discharged for cause. The claim is made that the elimination of competition among employees as a factor in employment allocation, and especially as a factor in promotion, blunts worker incentive to excel. Such an anticompetitive device may either dampen the ambition of able young people or discourage them from applying at, or continuing employment in, a firm where seniority threatens to restrict severely their chances of steady employment or advancement.

---

[10] See Jules Backman, "Rigid Railroad Seniority System," *Labor Law Journal*, XIII (February 1962), pp. 117–29.

Seniority may be criticized from a social viewpoint as an obstruction to labor mobility that hampers the operation of market forces. Extreme reliance on seniority would mean that all employment openings would be at the bottom of each firm's job hierarchy. Thus, seniority places a severe loss barrier to transfer from one employer to another.

However, even from a national viewpoint there can be too much interfirm labor mobility. Reasoning on the basis of worker choice tends to overlook that fact. In the absence of seniority, interemployer job shifts may involve significant real costs of transfer and training, which employers correctly stress. Therefore, optimum labor mobility for a nation may be difficult to define, and it could perhaps best be achieved with sufficient mobility among new entrants into the labor force. Seniority, however, tends to obstruct the national allocation and advancement of new entrants.

On balance, the advantages of seniority for lay-off and recall in terms of plant efficiency and even social benefit may at least offset the adverse effects. In any event, seniority has become too entrenched to be uprooted even by radical changes as a result of automation. The practice builds up strong vested interests in its continuation.

Economic theory has not fully reckoned with the anticompetitive effects of seniority. And an analysis of employee compensation should take account of the seniority barrier to any matching of an individual's total gains from work (wage rate, benefits, and job security advantages) with his productivity.

THE IMPACT OF MECHANIZATION

The fear of job displacement through mechanization appears to have increased among factory workers since World War II. Partly, this has been because automated equipment has brought about dramatic reductions in semiskilled and unskilled work in some mass-production lines. Partly also workers are more conscious of the disappearance of jobs when they have the expectation of work-career employment under seniority. An additional factor has been the difficulty of reemployment with chronic underemployment of the economy.

The Pace of Mechanization and Job Effects

Substitution of machines for men is an old story. For more than a century, worker productivity has been increased by the replacement of muscle power with mechanical power. Thus, machines have cut labor costs largely by reducing the number of manual jobs immediately involved in a production operation, and generally, markets have been found for the increased output at lower cost.

Labeling mechanization, "automation," has, however, conjured up the image of a job-destroying Frankenstein. Factory automation is mechanization that uses automatic control and regulation of industrial processes (assembly operations, material handling, product inspection and testing). Such control and self-regulation may be achieved by electronic computers, integrated control systems, and numerical control systems using tapes to direct the operation of machinery.

Whether the rate of technological innovation and change has increased since World War II is uncertain. In 1963, the late President Kennedy said that there was not "yet convincing evidence that the over-all pace of such change has accelerated recently."[11] Since 1950, output per man hour in the private economy has been somewhat above the long-run average (1909–61).

That might seem to indicate a relatively high rate of technological change in the postwar period.[12] However, labor productivity is affected by factors (e.g., education, management, capital investment) other than technological progress. Another indication that technological improvements may be accelerating is the very rapid expansion that has occurred in total expenditures for research and development. In the eight years from 1953–54 to 1961–62, such expenditures more than doubled in private industry and more than tripled for the Federal Government, reaching a total of almost fifteen billion dollars in 1961–62.[13]

---

[11] "Special Message to Congress on the Railroad Work-Rules Dispute," *The New York Times*, July 23, 1963, p. 12.

[12] See Ewan Clague and Leon Greenberg, "Employment," in John T. Dunlop (ed.), *Automation and Technological Change, The American Assembly* (Englewood Cliffs, N.J.: Prentice-Hall, 1961), pp. 116–17.

[13] *Manpower Report of the President and A Report on Manpower Requirements, Resources, Utilization, and Training by the United States Department of Labor,* transmitted to the Congress March 1963 (Washington: United States Government Printing Office, 1963), p. 75.

Technological change upsets job security in two ways. It eliminates jobs in the factory and it changes their content. Either effect tends to result in occupational displacement. As explained in Chapter 1, unskilled and semiskilled factory jobs have been decreasing both relatively and absolutely. Automation helps to explain that development. It favors skilled maintenance workers relative to assembly and other production workers. On production jobs, automation may require workers with a better educational background than those being displaced actually have, but whether ultimately automated machine-tending requires more skill is questionable.[14]

The unemployment-creating effects of mechanization are not possible to isolate or estimate. Unemployment attributable to automation cannot be separated from joblessness caused by fluctuations in the business cycle, by shifts in population and consumer tastes, by the development of substitute materials, and by other dynamic factors. The job-reducing impact of technological change will depend on how fast and extensively such change occurs and how buoyant the economy is at the time.

Union Policies

The views and policies of individual unions with respect to technological change have varied with the circumstances. The official AFL-CIO position has been to welcome technological improvements as a basis for higher real wages and to propose programs through collective bargaining and government action for the purpose of minimizing job dislocation, providing income security for displaced workers, and increasing wages to counterbalance the increased capacity to produce.

Individual unions will resist technological change or block its labor-saving effects by restrictive work rules or rigid manning requirements if the security or survival of the union is threatened. That is likely to be the case where a single craft constitutes the total membership of a union and both are confined to one industry. Good examples are the firemen on the railroads and the flight engineers on the airlines. Under those circumstances, the unions may insist on "featherbedding" (unnecessary employment) as a means

---

[14] See Charles C. Killingsworth, "Industrial Relations and Automation," *Annals of the American Academy of Political and Social Science*, CCCXL (March 1962), p. 76.

of preventing their sharp decline or extinction. By contrast, although boilermakers' employment on the railroads fell over four-fifths (from 13,128 in 1947 to 2,341 in 1960),[15] the Boilermakers' union did not seek, by make-work rules, to maintain superfluous jobs for the fraction of its members in railroad shops. That union's security was not threatened by the employment decline in railroading, and its railroad members could seek employment in other higher-wage industries such as building construction and shipyards.

Craft unions may also exclude minor labor-saving devices in order to maintain the demand for the members' services. Some locals of the Painters' union have forbidden the use of paint spray machines or wide paint brushes; locals of the Electricians and Plumbers have prevented the installation of factory-assembled units. The building unions are in a good position to enforce such make-work policies because they are sheltered from outside competition, the employers must continue to use workers possessing those skills, and the unions cooperate in enforcing each others' work rules through mutual strike support.

By contrast, industrial unions are less likely to resist new labor-saving devices by opposition or imposition of make-work rules. Generally, technological change affects only a small fraction of an industrial union's membership at any one time, and those displaced usually obtain work in another part of the company, so that the union's security is not threatened. In addition, locals of an industrial union are not likely to be sheltered from outside competition including that of substitute products.[16]

Unions that accept change seek to ease its impact by programs that protect the job and income security of their members. Among the union policies embodied in collective agreements designed to help preserve job opportunities for members are: (a) early notice of projected changes so that, by joint planning, dislocations can be minimized; (b) introduction of the changes so that any job displacement can be absorbed by attrition resulting from normal

---

[15] Bernard Yabroff and W. J. Kelly, "Employment Changes in Railroad Occupations, 1947–60," *Monthly Labor Review*, LXXXVI (October 1962), p. 1131.

[16] For a more extended treatment of the reaction of individual unions to technological changes, see Sumner H. Slichter, James J. Healy, and E. Robert Livernash, *The Impact of Collective Bargaining on Management* (Washington: Brookings Institution, 1960), pp. 343–70.

turnover and retirements; (c) enlargement of seniority units and transfer rights so that senior employees can "bump" over a wider area; (d) provision for preferential hiring of any laid-off employees at other plants of the company, including company financing of moving expenses; (e) a shorter work week or work year in order to spread the work, with no decrease in weekly pay; (f) a share in the savings from technological change for workers, and no pay reductions for incumbents if jobs are downgraded; and (g) training or retraining at company expense, so that displaced workers are in a position to obtain equivalent or better employment elsewhere. Unions have stressed the shorter work week as a practical answer to the threat of technological unemployment. They have coupled the hours' demand with the statement that wage income must be increased if our ability to consume is to keep pace with our capacity to produce.[17]

Unions also seek through collective bargaining to provide income protection for workers who actually are displaced. The techniques for that purpose include supplemental unemployment benefits, severance pay or dismissal compensation, retraining benefits, and early retirement on pension.[18] Organized labor also has looked to the Federal Government for a variety of actions and financial assistance in helping to meet the problem of the technological displacement of workers and their reabsorption into productive employment.

Collectively Bargained Programs

Automation has put a special strain on union-management relations and has led to a new type of study approach in collective bargaining. In a number of industries there has been a recognition that the human problems of automation are too complex to settle by an economic power struggle in the crisis atmosphere of bargaining against a strike deadline. Therefore in 1959 and the early sixties, joint study committees were established in industries like

---

[17] See, for example, Albert J. Hayes, "Automation and Our Democratic Institutions," in *A Report to the President of the United States by the American Foundation on Automation and Employment, Inc.*, New York, April 1963, p. 16.

[18] For a statement of union proposals see Edward B. Shils, *Automation and Industrial Relations* (New York: Holt, Rinehart and Winston, 1963), pp. 128–32.

meatpacking, steel, autos, and electrical equipment in order to engage in year-long or continuous exploration of major issues, particularly those connected with technological advance. For the railroads,
a tripartite Presidential Commission was established late in 1960 to
review work rules in train operations and to make recommendations for adjusting the "web of rules" to economic and technological changes that had occurred in that industry since World War I
when some of those operating work rules became firmly embedded.

The first formal study committee was established by collective
agreement in 1959 between Armour and Company and the two
meatpacking unions.[19] Its main function was to investigate "the
problems resulting from the modernization program" and to make
"recommendations for their solution." With a $500,000 fund
financed by company contributions, a pilot training and transfer
program was conducted, and as a result of its studies and experience the committee concluded: "Only through a coordinated
approach in which public policy and private action mutually rein-
force one another can the employment problems of technological
change be met."[20] The 1961 agreement between the company and
the two unions included a program of protections and benefits for
displaced employees.

After a year of experience and study, in 1960 the Pacific Maritime Association and the International Longshoremen's and Ware-
housemen's Union established for longshore operations on the West
Coast a Mechanization and Modernization Fund, financed by employer contributions of five million dollars a year for 5.5 years.
From the Fund three types of benefits are payable to all fully
attached, registered (class A) longshoremen: (1) a guaranteed
minimum weekly wage income regardless of time worked, if the
decrease in work hours is due to increased productivity; (2) a
lump-sum payment at retirement, disability, or death; and (3)
monthly benefits for early voluntary retirement between ages
sixty-two and sixty-five. In return for that protection, the employers were given free hand to mechanize and to change restrictive
work practices including those regulating crew sizes.

---

[19] This and the next paragraph draw on Thomas Kennedy, *Automation Funds
and Displaced Workers*, Graduate School of Business Administration, Harvard
University, Boston, 1962, Chapters 4 and 6.

[20] *Ibid.*, p. 152.

The Human Relations Committee established at the end of the 116-day steel strike did the spadework for the 1962 and 1963 settlements in steel, including the thirteen-week extended vacation to help in reducing unemployment. Under the two-year agreement running to May 1965, it will study the operation of experimental clauses in that contract and seek improved programs for job training and wage incentives.

Through a committee established in the settlement of the 1959 strike, Kaiser Steel and the Steelworkers worked out a plan for giving employees part of the savings from efficiency, with a guarantee that no worker would lose either his job or his wage income because of technological changes. The average employee bonus from increased efficiency under the plan was the equivalent of about fifty cents per hour in first monthly payments in 1963.[20a]

Competitive pressures have been forcing managements to seek the elimination of old work rules in collective bargaining so that full advantage can be taken of technological improvements. Written agreements in this country are much more detailed with respect to work practices and rules governing the manning and operation of equipment than is true abroad. It is understandable that union leaders should seek to defend present manning requirements and to add new ones. A few unions, as at Kaiser Steel, have even negotiated absolute protection against lay-offs by reason of technological change. Strict preservation of jobs (and not just protection of men) can impede mechanization, adding to its cost by preventing savings in manpower.

Usually, however, there are distinct limits to collective bargaining as a means of meeting and solving the disemployment problems arising from marked technological change. Although savings may occur from the introduction of new techniques, competitive pressures can severely limit the possibilities of preserving employment or compensating workers adequately for loss of employment and benefits. Market forces may restrict the discretion of management to determine how much of any savings from technological change will go to stockholders, employees, and customers.

With respect to employees, distribution of gains from technological improvements should not be just job focused. If the savings

---

[20a] See A. H. Raskin, "Approach to Automation: The Kaiser Plan," *The New York Times Magazine*, November 3, 1963, pp. 20–21 and 115–16.

going to labor do largely take the form of earnings increases in proportion to the resulting rise in productivity on particular jobs, the result will be growing disparities in the pay structure when the incidence of technological change is concentrated on certain jobs. On the other hand, a measure of relaxation from strict enforcement of job-evaluation criteria may be necessary in order to encourage workers on rapidly changing jobs to cooperate in the introduction and trial operation of new techniques.

Given the limitations of company-by-company or even industry-wide collective bargaining as a means of meeting the problems of widespread changes in production techniques, aid of the government in labor adjustments to such change may be required in order to help meet both individual and social costs. Those costs take such forms as joblessness, the need for geographic transfer and vocational retraining for the disemployed, and community efforts to break the vicious spiral of unemployment costs in a locality rising and thus tending to create more joblessness there by discouraging local business with heavy taxes.

Collective bargaining does provide an agreement-making mechanism that can help to allay fears that cause worker resistance to technological change. An orderly and effective procedure for introducing change may sufficiently facilitate efficiency so as to offset the cost of "buying" such cooperation. One must bear in mind that make work and resistance to change have also been widely practiced by unorganized workers.[21]

If there is an added cost of introducing technological change under collective bargaining,[22] it may be justified in terms of protection of producer interests at the expense of consumer interests, which are predominant in a purely competitive society. From a national viewpoint, it is desirable that such cost be met in a way that does not curtail the nation's productive capacity, but instead facilitates worker transfer and protects worker income. One reason for concern and action by the Federal Government is to help achieve that goal.

---

[21] See S. B. Mathewson, *Restriction of Output among Unorganized Workers* (New York: Viking Press, 1931).

[22] This seems to be implied in Sumner H. Slichter, James J. Healy and E. Robert Livernash, *op. cit.*, p. 371.

Role of Government

That the "achievement of technological progress without sacrifice of human values requires a combination of private and governmental action" was stressed in a report on "Benefits and Problems Incident to Automation and Other Technological Advances" by the President's Advisory Committee on Labor-Management Policy.[23] Areas of public responsibility include: (1) gathering the facts about automation and communicating them to aid companies, unions, and the public to plan intelligently; (2) providing, for displaced workers, job retraining, additional education where necessary, and relocation assistance; (3) operating a free employment service for job placement of the disemployed and for career counseling in the light of changing technology; (4) providing income protection through adequate unemployment compensation and influencing retirement policies by such means as the Federal Old-Age, Survivors', and Disability Insurance program; and (5) stimulating high levels of employment through monetary-fiscal policies so as to reduce the fear of chronic unemployment that generates resistance to technological progress.[24]

Under the Employment Act of 1946 and the Manpower Development and Training Act of 1962, the Federal Government has the function of planning to assure effective utilization of manpower resources on a national basis. It can lighten the burden of economic change on the individual and on particular firms or industries by having society share some of it through government training programs and the taxing power. The limitations to attempts to meet the problem completely by collective bargaining have been evident in such experience as the Armour Fund experiments. Persistent, abnormally high unemployment encourages demands for work-sharing by shorter-work-week and work-rule impediments to expansion of productive capacity. This was recognized by President Kennedy when in 1963 he appointed a President's Commission on Automation to develop a comprehensive, long-range program that

---

[23] *The New York Times*, January 12, 1962, p. 1.
[24] For a discussion of these points see Arthur J. Goldberg, "The Role of Government," in *Annals of the American Academy of Political and Social Science*, CCCIL (March 1962), pp. 110–16.

would encourage private action while protecting the public interest.

The problem of unemployment is considered more fully in Chapter 17. Manpower planning under the Manpower Development and Training Act constitutes the subject matter of Chapter 18.

Threat to Union Security

Radical technological change may threaten the security of unions in two ways. By eliminating blue-collar jobs, it tends to curtail the growth and even reduce the size of unions. By making it much easier for supervisory workers to keep operations going during a strike, automation can weaken the economic power of unions.

As automation spreads, an increasing proportion of the labor force falls outside the traditional bargaining units. Blue-collar workers engaged in repetitive tasks have constituted the bulk of the membership of unions in the mass-production industries. Shifts in the job structure toward more technical, clerical, and professional types of work has meant erosion in centers of union power and job expansion in areas that historically have been hard to organize.

In widely automated industries like oil refining, dial telephone service, and some public utilities, strike experience in the fifties and early sixties showed that even extended strikes often did not reduce operations much below normal. Supervisors were able to keep equipment functioning. Clearly, in a number of industries, automation has diminished the effectiveness of the strike weapon, and labor leaders are forced to take that fact into account in their planning.[25]

UNION SECURITY

As Chapters 3 and 4 have indicated, a big problem for unions in this country has been survival and growth as organizations. From the outset, a strong effort was made to achieve 100 per cent membership—to be completely collective on the workers' side. In the

---

[25] For a discussion of resulting adjustment in the thinking of the leadership of the Communications Workers of America, see Joseph A. Beirne, *New Horizons for American Labor* (Washington: Public Affairs Press, 1962), pp. 59–63.

early 1800's perhaps as vigorous an attempt was made to achieve the closed shop as at any time since then.

The drive for union security through signed employer agreements is largely peculiar to American unionism. It arose out of the hostile environment confronting labor organization during most of its history in this country. The main elements threatening to undermine unionism were: (1) employer opposition, (2) the individualistic background and heterogeneous character of the labor force, and (3) the importance of nonunion competition and rival organizations.

Employer opposition, as explained in Chapters 3, 4, and 5, has taken such forms as discrimination in employment against union members, union espionage by employer agents, the requirement that employees sign "yellow-dog contracts" not to join a union, open-shop campaigns in communities, drives for right-to-work laws, and legal attacks on union activities. Labor-force handicaps have consisted mainly of a lack of class consciousness and a diversity of cultures, tongues, and races as a result of immigration. Many factory workers have been recruited from rural areas where individualism is rife, or have been women who lacked interest in labor organization because they considered their jobs to be temporary.

In a large country with communities competing for industry, labor organizations have been threatened with displacement by nonunion competition and the movement of industry away from centers of organization. Another form of competition has come from rival organizations (at times, company unions) seeking to enroll the same workers.

However, a number of those threats to union security have disappeared or at least been largely eliminated. As is explained more fully in the next two chapters, in the 1930's the various antiunion tactics of employers were declared illegal or made ineffective (by the Wagner and Norris-LaGuardia Acts), and employers were required to bargain in good faith with certified unions. Since World War I, immigration has been greatly restricted. In 1955, the AFL and CIO merged, thus sharply reducing the threat of rival unionism. And before that, the Taft-Hartley Act made it illegal for a union to use its strike or boycott power to try to replace another union certified as a bargaining agent. Why then have unions continued to press so strongly for union security in collective bargaining negotiations, and why has the union shop continued to be the source of so much controversy between management and unions? We should be in a position to answer that question after consideration of the types of union security arrangements and their prevalence since World War II, and an examination of experience with legal restrictions on union security.

Types of Union Security

Union security clauses in agreements require employer support in recruiting and retaining union membership and in collecting its revenue. Under the closed shop or the union shop, union membership is a condition for continued employment in the plant; membership and employment are tied together. The check-off makes the company the collection agency for the union.

Union-security arrangements provide different degrees of compulsion and union disciplinary power over individual members. Under the *closed shop* the employer agrees to hire and employ only members of the union, so union membership is required in advance of employment. The closed shop has been typical of skilled trades (i.e., printing and building) and the maritime industry where workers are assigned from a hiring hall and employees change employers frequently. Under the Taft-Hartley Act the closed shop is illegal for business in interstate commerce, but that provision of the act has been disregarded or evaded in various ways (i.e., by hiring through the union, giving preference to union members).

Under the *union shop*, membership in the union is required of all employees in the bargaining unit after an initial period of employment, usually thirty to sixty days. Some union-shop agreements exempt from this requirement workers who were not union members on a specific date, or who are members of religious groups with prohibitions on joining a labor organization. Under the Taft-Hartley Act (as modified by the Landrum-Griffin Act), a union-shop agreement cannot require membership sooner than thirty days after hiring except for building construction where the period is seven days.

The device of *maintenance of membership* is an arrangement whereby no worker is forced to join the union as a condition of continued employment, but having voluntarily joined he must maintain his membership for the duration of the agreement in order to continue employment. There may be an escape period of fifteen days at the end of each agreement when he can withdraw from the union without jeopardizing his employment rights. This was a solution worked out by the National War Labor Board to meet demands by unions for a closed or union shop during World War II.

In the *agency shop*, no one in the bargaining unit is required to join the union, but a nonunion employee must, as a condition of employment, pay to the union a sum equivalent to the union's dues for the service of the union in acting as his agent in negotiations, including the grievance procedure. This arrangement is designed to circumvent State "right-to-work" laws that prohibit conditioning employment on union membership.[26]

The *check-off* is a procedure whereby the employer deducts union dues (and often fees and assessments) from the employee's pay for transmittal to the union. Under the Taft-Hartley Act the employee must specifically authorize such deduction. The check-off does not compel union membership; where a union shop prevails, it avoids the problem of discharge from employment because of union dues' delinquency. However, a one-year irrevocable check-off can in practice have the same effect as maintenance of membership.

The prevalence of different types of union security is indicated in Table 20. The data in the table are for major collective bargaining agreements, each covering one thousand or more workers, exclusive of the railroads and airlines which were forbidden to have such agreements before 1951. The figures for 1958–59 are based on 1,631 agreements covering 7.5 million workers.

In 1947, the Taft-Hartley Act was passed forbidding the closed shop in interstate commerce, which explains the lack of figures under that heading after 1946.[27] The percentage of workers required to join unions (closed and union shops) under these major

---

[26] Some State laws forbid conditioning employment on the payment of dues, which would outlaw the agency shop.

[27] The closed-shop agreements, principally in local trade and service, were included in the union-shop category after 1946. In 1958–59 they amounted to about 4 per cent of all agreements.

TABLE 20

Union-Security Provisions in Major Collective Bargaining Agreements, 1946 to 1958–1959

Type of Union Security	Per Cent of Workers Covered			
	1946	1949–50	1954	1958–59
Closed shop	33	—	—	—
Union shop	17	49	64	74
Maintenance of membership	25	20	17	7
No formal provision	25	31	19	19
Total	100	100	100	100

Source: *Union Security and Check off Provisions in Major Union Contracts, 1958–59,* United States Bureau of Labor Statistics, Bulletin No. 1272, March 1960, p. 2.

agreements rose from 50 per cent in 1946 and 49 per cent in 1949–50 to 74 per cent in 1958–59. Although the category, "no formal provision" rose temporarily from 25 to 31 per cent right after passage of the Taft-Hartley Act, it declined and stabilized at 19 per cent during the decade after enactment of that law. That percentage may give a slightly erroneous impression because about one out of the 19 per cent includes coverage under preferential hiring or agency-shop agreements.[28]

Interestingly, in 1958–59 the check-off was more prevalent where no formal union membership requirement existed. Of the workers covered by agreements with no formal provision, 80 per cent were under check-off arrangements as against 76 per cent where provision was made for the union shop or maintenance of membership.[29] In the three Southern regions (South Atlantic, East South Central, and West South Central), 80 per cent of the workers covered by major agreements were under check-off arrangements, compared with less than 40 per cent on the West Coast. In right-to-work States (none of which prohibited the check-off),

[28] See *Union Security and Checkoff Provisions in Major Union Agreements, 1958–59,* United States Bureau of Labor Statistics, Bulletin No. 1272, March 1960, p. 3, footnote 2. About 1 per cent of the agreements provided for the agency shop, mostly in combination with the union shop or maintenance of membership (*ibid.,* table 2, p. 4). About a third of the agreements not requiring membership were in right-to-work States.

[29] Data in this paragraph are based on *ibid.,* pp. 13–14.

85 per cent of the workers were under agreements providing for the check-off compared to 68 per cent in States without right-to-work laws.

Experience with Legal Curbs

The first statutory curb on union-security provisions was contained in the Railway Labor Act of 1926. Its purpose then was to prevent the carriers from fostering or favoring company unions. From 1926 to 1951, both union-security and check-off provisions were illegal in agreements in that industry. Yet the railroad unions experienced no special difficulty in recruiting members or in maintaining their institutional security. There was no real need to amend the Railway Labor Act in 1951 to allow the union shop on the railroads, unless one contends that the pride of the railroad unions required that they have at least the equivalent of other unions.[30]

Although the Wagner Act specifically exempted union-security arrangements from its restrictions on employers, the Taft-Hartley Act contained a number of limitations. Among other provisions, it specified that, before a union could make a union-shop demand, a majority of all employees in the unit (not just a majority of those voting) must have signified in a secret ballot election their approval of the negotiation of a union-shop contract. In addition, union membership could be required no sooner than thirty days after employment, and the only reason for which loss of membership in the union could entail loss of employment was if union expulsion occurred because of the member's failure to pay dues. The Taft-Hartley Act thus in essence restricted the union shop to a compulsory-payment-of-dues shop. The linkage of employment and union membership is only a dues link, for workers are barred from continued employment only if they fail to pay union dues.

The union-shop vote was written into the act on the assumption that workers, if given an opportunity in secret ballot, would vote in large numbers against compulsory union membership. Actually, the employees voted overwhelmingly for the union shop in the 46,119 union-shop elections conducted by the National

---

[30] Actually they got more, since their union-security arrangements are exempt by Federal statute from curtailment by any State right-to-work law.

Labor Relations Board between 1947 and 1961. In those elections, almost 85 per cent of the 6.5 million eligible workers voted. Of those voting, 91.4 per cent voted in favor of the union shop, and the negotiation of union-shop provisions was authorized in 97 per cent of the cases.[31] Those results led to the only amendment to the Taft-Hartley Act between 1947 and 1959; in 1951, the special election requirement for negotiation of a union shop was removed from the act.

Right-to-work laws banning compulsory unionism have been enacted in twenty-three States, beginning with a constitutional amendment in Florida in 1944. Such laws were adopted in eleven States in 1947, following the rash of strikes that led to passage of the Taft-Hartley Act. Section 14(b) of Taft-Hartley provides that where State laws are more restrictive or prohibitive than its union-shop provisions, such State laws shall supersede the Federal act. Four States have repealed their right-to-work laws.[32] Of the remaining nineteen States[33] with laws in effect, all except Indiana are either southern States or agricultural States in the Midwest or Rocky Mountain regions. Political pressure for such laws in the States has come mainly from nonunionized sections—from small business and agriculture organizations—although nationally the National Association of Manufacturers, the United States Chamber of Commerce, and the National Right to Work Committee have been urging the enactment of laws forbidding compulsory union membership.

A drive in the 1958 political campaign to have right-to-work laws adopted in six States[34] by ballot resulted in defeat in all except Kansas and contributed to the defeat of two prominent Republican senators from California and Ohio. On the other hand, an employee vote on the union shop in three aerospace firms (General Dynamics, North American Aviation, and Ryan Aeronautical), conducted by a Presidential fact-finding board late in 1962, resulted in votes for the union shop by 54 to 60 per cent of those

---

[31] *Sixteenth Annual Report of the National Labor Relations Board,* Washington, D.C., 1952, p. 54.

[32] Delaware, Louisiana, Maine, and New Hampshire.

[33] Alabama, Arizona, Arkansas, Florida, Georgia, Indiana, Iowa, Kansas, Mississippi, Nebraska, Nevada, North Carolina, North Dakota, South Carolina, South Dakota, Tennessee, Texas, Utah, Virginia.

[34] California, Colorado, Idaho, Kansas, Ohio, and Washington.

casting ballots. Since the board had set a two-thirds majority for company acceptance, the vote represented a defeat for the union shop in all three firms, and was interpreted as a reaction against compulsion and union domination of the individual.

A survey by *Fortune* magazine of employers and union leaders in eighteen right-to-work States in 1957 disclosed that few States had any effective enforcement apparatus,[35] and that right-to-work laws did not mean much in practice except as a political symbol of the weakness of organized labor. *Fortune* reported that very few of the largest corporations had taken a position for or against State right-to-work laws, and that the big companies in mass-production industries like autos, steel, and rubber had long since given up on the union-shop fight.

Studies of experience in particular States reveal that right-to-work laws have been largely ineffective in preventing closed shops or providing individual protection against forced membership. In the traditional areas of the closed shop, the law has been generally violated.[36] Most employers, in a State like Texas, even those violating the law, seem to favor the legislation as a symbol of the political power of management and as a factor making labor organization more difficult in some industries. In addition, union leaders, in bargaining and grievance prosecution, were required to be more responsive to the more extreme demands of vocal minorities in order to try to hold their membership on a voluntary basis.[37]

State right-to-work laws have also been used to try to attract industry. The General Electric Company has stated that it prefers right-to-work States as locations for new plants. Letters to northern

---

[35] In most States, "a worker who feels he is being pressured into joining a union can only resort to expensive injunction proceedings." *Fortune*, LVI (September 1957), pp. 235–41.

[36] A study of Florida experience found seven years after the constitutional prohibition on union security was adopted (and four years after enactment of Taft-Hartley), 11 per cent of the agreements had closed-shop provisions and 5 per cent retained union-shop clauses. (See T. J. Luck, *Union Security Provisions in Florida's Collective Bargaining Agreements*, Bureau of Business Research, University of Florida, November 1951.) A study of twelve years of experience in Texas showed that there was a generally willing conspiracy between employers and unions to disregard the law in construction and other traditionally closed-shop industries. [See Frederick Meyers, *"Right to Work" in Practice* (New York: The Fund for the Republic, 1959), pp. 13–20.]

[37] See Meyers, *ibid*. pp. 37–42.

and western firms soliciting industry for southern States have emphasized that union shops are in violation of the State's right-to-work law and that local labor "works together joyously with management for the success of both," and that it is "unspoiled native labor eager to give a full day's work for a moderate wage."[38]

Conflict of Economic Philosophies

Basically, the clash of views on union security stems from a fundamental difference in concepts of employment. Those who oppose any form of required membership in collective agreements really want to promote competition among employees and some division on the labor side of the employment process. In the name of freedom and individualism, they oppose disciplined collective action and monopoly of bargaining rights for one union. Instead, they favor competitive supply and some rivalry in employee representation. Their views do, therefore, constitute a challenge to the security of unions.

The proponents of required union membership, on the other hand, stress strength through collective action, group discipline, and the service the union provides as bargaining agent for all the employees in the bargaining unit. To them, stress on individual rights appears to be a form of attack on the concept of collective bargaining and to be designed to weaken the union's organizing potential and its bargaining strength. Employees encouraged by law not to join or to pay dues not only get a "free ride" but also are less dependable in case of a strike. Weak unions cannot be responsible, well-disciplined organizations.

It is worth noting that strong views against union-security clauses in collective agreements are found chiefly in unorganized areas, among small businessmen and farmers. The managements of most large firms are not trying to introduce more competition into employment or seeking more rivalry in labor relations. Generally, they are promoting a welfare concept of employment and stability and responsibility in labor relations.

Given our long history of employer hostility toward unions,

---

[38] See *Subsidized Industrial Migration, The Luring of Plants to New Locations,* A Report by the AF of L Department of Research, American Federation of Labor, Washington, D.C., 1955, pp. 63–65.

the political defeats of organized labor since World War II (i.e., the Taft-Hartley and Landrum-Griffin Acts and the State right-to-work laws), and the decline in union membership resulting from mechanization, it is understandable that many union leaders are concerned about the institutional security of organized labor in this country and press for union-shop provisions in agreements. Whether the union shop serves to strengthen or weaken unions in the long run is a nice question. By assuring certain union revenue and guaranteeing certain membership, it can lull the leadership into lethargy and a false sense of security. For unions, some challenge and opposition to overcome may be invigorating.[39]

SUMMARY

This chapter has dealt with worker and union security in a changing economy.

1. Seniority as a noncompetitive principle for employment allocation can affect management's system of incentives and rewards. However, the economic consequences of lay-off according to seniority depend largely on the particular circumstances so that it is difficult to say whether, on balance, seniority serves to enlarge or reduce the Gross National Product.

2. In terms of public policy, seniority provisions in collective agreements may be criticized for reducing labor mobility. Optimum labor mobility is, however, difficult to define; reasoning on the basis of worker choices tends to neglect significant real costs to employers from worker transfers between firms.

3. While unions may nominally welcome technological change, they can through restrictive work rules reduce its labor-saving advantages. Craft unions in local market lines are more likely than industrial unions to prevent or delay the introduction of new techniques.

4. In accepting technological change, unions have devloped programs to modify or avoid the impact on the jobs of employees with significant seniority and on their pay. In recent years, some

---

[39] For an expression of this view see George W. Brooks, "The Security of Worker Institutions," *Monthly Labor Review*, LXXXVI (June 1963), p. 655.

industrial unions and managements have developed a new study approach to the problem of job displacement from automation.

5. To aid in the effective and efficient use of the nation's human resources, government has a significant role to play in meeting the problem of employment displacement resulting from technological progress. That is specifically recognized in the Manpower Development and Training Act of 1962 and the appointment of a President's Committee on Automation in 1963.

6. Union security remains an important issue despite the existence of the union shop in major bargaining agreements covering three-quarters of workers under such agreements. Now it is mainly a political rather than an economic or a collective bargaining issue. State right-to-work laws have had little practical effect on employment practices or union security.

7. The conflict over union security grows out of a basic difference between the competitive view of labor supply and employee representation and the concept of collective bargaining as the effective and responsible means for reconciling divergent interests in modern industry.

DISCUSSION QUESTIONS

1. Suppose you were assigned to make a case for straight seniority in lay-offs. What economic arguments would you present?
2. Explain how seniority may serve to disrupt the unity of a union.
3. What kinds of union structure and economic conditions promote union restriction of technological change? Why?
4. Explain the advantages and limitations of collective bargaining as a means of meeting the job effects of automation.
5. What should be the role of government in meeting the employment problems resulting from technological advance? What economic limits should be placed on government's activities for this purpose?
6. Explain why the issue of union security is still such an important problem in this country.
7. In what ways may there be a conflict between worker security and union security? Explain.

8. How do you explain the great debate over right-to-work laws in view of the fact that they appear to have been rather ineffective?
9. Is there a conflict between worker freedom under right-to-work laws and effective and responsible collective bargaining? Explain.

SELECTED REFERENCES

Analysis of Layoff, Recall, and Work-sharing Procedures in Union Contracts, United States Bureau of Labor Statistics Bulletin No. 1209 (Washington: United States Government Printing Office, 1957).

Background Information on Impact of Automation and Technological Change on Employment and Unemployment, Bureau of Employment Security, United States Department of Labor, September 1961.

Kennedy, Thomas, *Automation Funds and Displaced Workers,* Graduate School of Business Administration, Harvard University, Boston, 1962.

Killingsworth, Charles C. (ed.), *Automation, The Annals of the American Academy of Political and Social Science,* CCCIL (March 1962), fourteen articles by various authors.

Meyers, Frederic, *"Right to Work" in Practice* (New York: The Fund for the Republic, 1959).

Shils, Edward B., *Automation and Industrial Relations* (New York: Holt, Rinehart and Winston, 1963).

Slichter, Sumner H., James J. Healy, and E. Robert Livernash, *The Impact of Collective Bargaining on Management* (Washington: Brookings Institution, 1960), Chapters 5, 6, 7, and 12.

Sultan, Paul, *Right-to-Work Laws: A Study in Conflict,* Institute of Industrial Relations, University of California at Los Angeles, 1958.

Union Security and Checkoff Provisions in Major Union Contracts, 1958–59, United States Bureau of Labor Statistics, Bulletin No. 1272, March 1960.

Part THREE

PUBLIC POLICY

13.
Bases and Evolution of
Public Policy

THIS PART OF the book examines governmental policies with respect to labor problems. Largely, it deals with labor legislation and with public employment and unemployment programs.

To provide a framework for the subsequent discussion of particular programs, this chapter first analyzes the economic grounds on which government action in the labor field is based. Those grounds, of course, vary somewhat from program to program. That is the case not only because the problems to be solved are not the same but also because economic conditions and the climate of opinion were different when the individual programs were adopted, and the early years of a program are likely to have a strong formative influence.

Because it has moved with events, government policy in the labor area has been pragmatic rather than part of a grand design or the fruit of a body of well-formulated theory. Nevertheless, it is possible to discern some rationality in the division of responsibility among the three major methods of solving labor problems: market forces, collective bargaining, and governmental determination. It is that underlying rationale that we shall first try to analyze.

Following such an analysis, the general developments in governmental labor policy over the past century and a half will be discussed. Such a historical background is helpful in understanding shifts in policy and in relating particular programs to one another.

GROUNDS FOR PUBLIC ACTION

The Federal and State governments have a variety of labor programs. Their large scope and diversity are indicated by the following list: labor-relations and strike-restricting laws (Taft-Hartley Act, Railway Labor Act, State labor relations acts, State right-to-work laws); antistrikebreaker laws (Byrnes Act and State laws); laws against labor racketeering (Hobbs Act and State laws); laws regulating the internal operations of unions (Landrum-Griffin Act and State laws); the Federal and State mediation services; wage and hour laws (Fair Labor Standards Act, Walsh-Healey Act, Davis-Bacon Act, Federal and State equal pay laws, State minimum wage laws, State hours laws); State fair employment practices laws and Federal antidiscrimination activities under the President's Committee on Equal Employment Opportunities; laws regulating private employee benefit programs (Welfare and Pension Plans Disclosure Act); Federal and State social insurance legislation (Federal Old-Age, Survivors', and Disability Insurance, Railroad Retirement Act, Federal-State unemployment compensation, State workmen's compensation, temporary disability insurance in four States); Federal and State manpower legislation and activities (Manpower Development and Training Act, Federal-State Employment Services, vocational education); and general employment legislation (the Employment Act of 1946, popularly termed the full-employment law).

In reviewing such a list, the question arises, what justification is there for all that government intervention? Is there any unity of thought underlying such apparent diversity?

Three Philosophies of Public Policy

Ideological positions with respect to public policy can be stated as (1) reliance on market forces to solve all labor problems, (2) reliance on collective bargaining to solve all labor problems, and (3) reliance on government to solve all labor problems (through legislation, mediation, compulsory arbitration, manpower and economic planning, etc.).

These three positions, of course, are not mutually exclusive. Government action presumably would be required either to enforce a "competitive market" in labor or to promote and protect collective bargaining.

They do, however, constitute three distinct philosophical approaches to labor problems. Each has its own set of values, its own scale of priorities, and its own type of remedies.

There are few pure or doctrinaire supporters of one of these three logical absolutes as a means of meeting all labor problems. Most of us have a labor philosophy that represents some combination or mixture of all three. But the proportions and emphases differ. Management is prone to stress market forces; labor leaders tend to favor as much reliance as possible on "free" collective bargaining. Each may agree that some problems are not suited to a market solution or are beyond the reach of collective bargaining, so that government action of some sort may be required. But within the area of government action the range of alternatives is wide, and choice among them will tend to turn on one's general economic predilections.

For present purposes, it is not necessary to judge the merits of different philosophical positions. In the concluding chapter, after the government programs have been examined, some definite policy positions will be taken. Obviously, the market mechanism has the advantage that it operates in an impersonal, nonpolitical manner; price (wages) serves as the guide and, assuming ideal conditions, labor resources would be distributed in an optimum fashion. Collective bargaining has the advantage that the parties directly involved participate and work out solutions adapted to their situation; ideally, the negotiating process has educational values and enhances the dignity of the worker. Both methods help to preserve a pluralistic society, with independent centers of thought and action.

Limitations of the Market

That market forces operate only imperfectly in the employment area has been explained in preceding chapters. Generally, the managements of large firms, the manual workers in those firms, and the unions representing them, all seek to eliminate outside competition. Despite shifts in labor supply or demand, wage rates remain fixed for considerable periods, with significant differentials that reflect ability or willingness to pay. The model of genuine wage differentials within a range of 10 to 15 per cent in a locality seems valid unless the range has been narrowed by cooperative wage action among employers or by collective bargaining.

Thus, the wage structure is prone to have a ragged lower section. Competition does not eliminate the raggedness by enforcing wage standards. There may, for example, be two different wage scales, one for Negro or white female janitors and the other for white males, regardless of their respective productivity. That sort of inequity and lack of standards leads to a demand for minimum-wage laws and equal pay laws.

As explained in Chapter 11, the market is even less effective in establishing proper hours of work and employee benefits. Also it is rather ineffective in protecting employees from arbitrary discharge or unfair treatment on the job. For such purposes collective bargaining may seem necessary.

Collective Bargaining to Equalize Power

As Chapters 3 and 4 have indicated, labor organization began in the skilled trades and, until the thirties, throve mainly in small-firm types of industry like building, coal mining, clothing, and printing. Before the New Deal, large nonunion firms dominated employment in the prominent mass-production industries.

As early as 1850, it was recognized in a legislative document in Massachusetts that the States by passing incorporation acts had "created immense artificial persons" with power "to fix inexorably, without consultation with the laboring class, all terms and conditions of labor." The state, "by interference in the form of incorporation laws," had "destroyed the natural relations" between employer and employee and had made necessary legislative action to "protect the interest and welfare of the laborers" in the form of factory codes and hours legislation for women.[1]

In 1935, the Congress supported a policy of promoting collective bargaining in order to restore "equality of bargaining power between employers and employees" and thus, to help stabilize, if not increase, wages. The "Findings and Policy" section of the National Labor Relations (Wagner) Act explains the need to redress "the inequality of bargaining power between employees who do not possess full freedom of association or actual liberty of contract, and employers who are organized in the corporate or other forms of ownership association." That inequality, it is claimed, "tends to aggravate recurrent business depressions, by depressing wage rates and the purchasing power of wage earners in industry and by preventing the stabilization of competitive wage rates and working conditions within and between industries."[2] For workers in firms where collective bargaining was not available to support and enhance purchasing power, the "Wage and Hour Law" (Fair Labor Standards Act of 1937) was designed to do so.

After World War II it was agreed that some unions had become "too powerful," that the power of unions and union leaders ought to be curbed by law to restore "equality in bargaining power."[3] That belief among the public supplied part of the political pressure for the enactment of the Taft-Hartley Act, the Landrum-Griffin Act, and State right-to-work laws.

Unemployment and War

Both widespread unemployment and major wars cause less reliance to be placed on the market and more on government action. As explained in Chapter 4, the Great Depression of the Thirties brought widespread intervention of the government in the employment relationship as a component of the New Deal. Partly, that

---

[1] Susan M. Kingsbury (ed.), *Labor Laws and Their Enforcement with Special Reference to Massachusetts* (Boston: Longmans, Green, 1911), pp. 79–80.

[2] Quoted from Public Law 101, Eightieth Congress, 1st session, H. R. 3020.

[3] J. Kenneth Galbraith has developed a theory that power stimulates countervailing power, which develops, if necessary, by political help. The theory provides some insights but is weak as a vehicle for explaining a good part of labor history. See *American Capitalism: The Concept of Countervailing Power* (Boston: Houghton Mifflin 1952).

intervention was based on a theory of economic recovery through increased purchasing power for wage-earners; partly, it was grounded on reasons of human welfare and the dignity of workers. The latter reasoning lay behind the Social Security Act establishing both old-age insurance and the framework for a system of unemployment insurance.

World War II gave rise to labor problems of an opposite sort. Concern then was to limit wage increases for antiinflationary reasons, and to restrict the freedom of collective bargaining in order to prevent strikes that would injure the war effort. Under the National War Labor Board, a ceiling was put on wage increases, and labor disputes were decided by the board and its regional boards under conditions that were, in the end, almost the equivalent of compulsory arbitration.

In the late fifties and early sixties, persistent unemployment of 5 to 7 per cent of the labor force and cold war competition resulted in a more mixed labor policy by the Federal Government. The combination of military spending and high unemployment raised for government policy problems of consistency, coordination, and balance. On the one hand, because of a deficit in the nation's balance of payments and some loss of advantages in international product competition, the Kennedy Administration was requesting restraint in wage increases under the "guidelines" policy mentioned in Chapter 10. On the other hand, as a means of stimulating our lagging economic growth and reducing unemployment, the Administration not only was promoting tax reduction and relatively easy money but also was favoring measures that would tend to raise wage rates or wage income, such as higher minimums under the Fair Labor Standards Act, higher unemployment compensation benefits, equal pay for women, and antidiscrimination in employment.

The complicated economic position of the country seemed to call for a sophisticated and rather mixed sort of economic program, including strong efforts to minimize interruption of military programs or the economy by strikes. A tripartite President's Committee on Labor-Management Policy was established in 1961 to wrestle with problems of public policy. It soon got into monetary and tax policy as well as wage guidelines and legislation with respect to emergency disputes.

Despite the committee's efforts, there remain problems of co-ordination between collective bargaining and government policy. In our kind of mixed political economy, with most labor matters still left to private decision, public policy cannot be a monolithic concept. It rests on the compromises (yes, even the inconsistencies) of a pluralistic society. The problems of coordination and reconciliation are all the greater with 50 States to differ among themselves and with the Federal Government, and with a system of checks and balances at the national level.

Public Policy Views of Labor and Management

Generally speaking, organized labor and management leaders hold fundamentally different views on most issues of public policy in the labor field. On a few matters they ostensibly agree, such as the maintenance of collective bargaining negotiations free from government control.

The full range of policy views of neither organized labor nor industrial management has been set forth in any one document.[4] Indeed, in view of a lack of unanimity, there may be a question as to who has the authority to speak for each group. In the case of organized labor, its public policy views are chiefly represented by the AFL-CIO, and one can, therefore, draw on its convention resolutions, statements of its president, statements of position on legislation in Congressional hearings, and unsigned articles in the *American Federationist*. Management's views have to be assembled from more scattered sources. They are available in the publications of the United States Chamber of Commerce, the National Association of Manufacturers, and the Committee for Economic Development, and in Congressional hearings and statements by management members of advisory committees to government (such as the President's Advisory Committee on Labor-Management Policy). That material provides the basis for the subjective conclusions about labor and management positions presented here.

---

[4] The Swedish Federation of Trade Unions comes close to having such a comprehensive document. See T. L. Johnson (editor and translator), *Economic Expansion and Structural Change: A Trade Union Manifesto*, Report submitted to the Sixteenth Congress of the Swedish Confederation of Trade Unions (London: Allen and Unwin, 1963).

1. LABOR. For the most part, organized labor places little confidence in market solutions to labor problems. Instead of competition with respect to labor, it stresses the method of collective bargaining, and believes that government should protect and promote the free exercise of collective bargaining.

The AFL-CIO has placed great emphasis on the achievement of full employment under the Employment Act of 1946. It insists that the way to accomplish that objective is through increased consumption stimulated by an increase in workers' purchasing power. For that purpose, the AFL-CIO has generally favored increased public expenditures (especially for housing and public works), tax cuts (particularly for low-income groups), improvements in social insurance coverage and benefits, hospital care for the aged under social security, and higher minimum wages. It has been opposed to sales taxes, to tax programs aimed at increasing profits and stimulating capital investment (e.g., investment credits against taxes), and to the Federal Reserve policy of raising interest rates for antiinflationary reasons, at least when unemployment is above (say) 5 per cent of the labor force.

Other policies favored by the AFL-CIO in the labor field include Federal legislation against discrimination in employment or pay, legislation for area redevelopment, a Federal retraining program for disemployed workers, and adequate appropriations for the Federal-State employment service. The AFL-CIO is, of course, vigorously opposed to "right-to-work" laws and to parts of the Taft-Hartley and Landrum-Griffin Acts.

The labor federation usually favors Federal legislation over State action, largely it seems for three reasons: Federal programs are not constrained by interstate competition for industry in terms of relatively low labor standards, a higher proportion of the Federal Government's expenditures is financed from the progressive income tax and a lower percentage from sales taxes than is generally true of the States, and organized labor seems to have more influence in the Congress than in most State legislatures.

Thus, the official position of organized labor appears to be much the same as the New Deal in the thirties and the Kennedy-Johnson Administration in the early sixties. The AFL-CIO differed with the Kennedy Administration on some specific issues like the 35-hour week, wage "guidelines," the tax investment credit, and the distribution of a tax cut between the corporate and personal income tax and among income-level classifications.

In its public policy views, organized labor has been open to the charge of inconsistency in at least two respects. It has supported national planning for full employment, while insisting that wages should remain outside government economic and manpower programming and be subject only to "free collective bargaining." Wage and salary compensation (including employer contributions to public and private benefit plans) constitutes over 70 per cent of total national income. It is difficult to see how such an item can be left outside plans for the allocation and utilization of the nation's manpower resources. The issue will be considered further in Chapter 20.

It may also seem inconsistent for organized labor to advocate increased competition and strict enforcement of the antitrust laws in product markets and oppose such a program for "labor markets." Differences between the character of employment in large firms and the purchase and sale of commodities have already been discussed. The proposal to apply the antitrust laws to labor is considered in the next chapter.

2. MANAGEMENT. As already mentioned, often the public policy views of management are opposite to those of organized labor. In contrast to the AFL-CIO, management spokesmen are philosophically opposed to government regulation of the employment relationship in such forms as minimum-wage laws, maximum-hours laws, and fair employment practices legislation. Of course there are exceptions, but management leaders are prone to stress both market competition as an objective guide for labor allocation and freedom of industry and management from the restraint of "bureaucratic" regulation. Also, management emphasizes the integrity of the firm and is generally against planning for an industry or the whole economy under government auspices. Leaders of management are, therefore, concerned whenever it is proposed to appoint national advisory committees with labor and management representatives. They are apprehensive about further government intervention in the affairs of industry.

If there is to be government action, management generally favors State over Federal legislation, partly for the reasons that organized labor takes the opposite position but also because management fears government power and prefers decentralized government. One exception to the preference for State rather than Federal action is the area of union reform and control. With respect to restraints on the exercise of union power, management generally favors Federal action because it is likely to be more effective, for such reasons as the use of the Federal Bureau of Investigation for detection of violations and the independence of the Federal judiciary under life-time appointment.

Management, of course, stresses the cost aspects of any governmental program, and the problems that added costs create in domestic and international competition. To management, profits are a key element in the economy, and cost pushes from tax or wage increases may both "squeeze" profits and boost prices. Management prefers private employee benefit plans to public benefits under social insurance, because they are more subject to company control and because they emphasize the integrity of the firm. Although there are some dissents for practical reasons, managements generally are philosophically opposed to forms of compulsory unionism and to compulsory arbitration; they favor strictly limiting secondary boycotts and organizational picketing, and many of them object to industry-wide bargaining. In recent years, a number of management leaders have favored placing unions under the Federal antitrust laws, under which injured parties can collect triple damages.

Elements in management and organized labor tend to think in terms of stereotypes and outmoded concepts—whether a commodity theory of employment or a tycoon theory of management. And they are prone to favor government controls for the other side, despite a strong philosophical position in support of freedom of association, freedom of enterprise, and freedom for collective bargaining.

Generally, labor and management recognize that there are distinct limits to what government action can accomplish in the field of union-management relations. Laws cannot establish and administer shop rules, solve production problems, or even eliminate some well-entrenched practices in hundreds of thousands of organized shops and among eighteen million unionized workers. Both sides profess to want to keep most labor relations matters out of partisan politics, but interest groups are prone to ask for a law to protect their interests.

Labor relations legislation has tended to be passed by Congress at the extremes in swings of public opinion—the Wagner Act in 1935 when management was "in the doghouse" as a result of the depression and revelations of the La Follette Committee, the Taft-Hartley Act in 1946 in the midst of reaction against the rash of war and post-war strikes, and the Landrum-Griffin Act in 1959 following the revelations of the McClellan Committee. Later on, when court interpretations extend the power of the government and the long-run implications of the law become more evident, serious doubts begin to arise even in quarters that originally pressed for a law. People begin to wonder how much government intervention and control are compatible with our kind of economic and political system, and whether government regulation of management, unions, and collective bargaining may not curtail their initiative, independence, and responsibility for self-settlement. But when one of the parties poignantly feels the need for legal protections or innocent third parties are hurt by a boycott or a strike, the pressures for statutory assistance mount.

STAGES IN POLICY DEVELOPMENT

Chapters 3 and 4 dealt with the history of labor organization, and Chapter 5 analyzed the evolution of management's labor policies. The remainder of this chapter focusses on changes in the labor policy and action by the government since 1800. It deals not only with collective bargaining law but also with public policy and legislation in such subject areas as work hours, minimum wages, social insurance, and conditions of work in government employment and on government contracts. And it considers the actions of all three branches of government—the executive, legislative, and judicial.[5]

The shifting path of governmental labor policy in this country

---

[5] For a review of public policy confined to union activities and collective bargaining, see Douglass V. Brown and Charles A. Myers, "Historical Evolution," in Joseph Shister, Benjamin Aaron, and Clyde W. Summers (eds.), *Public Policy and Collective Bargaining* (New York: Harper, 1962), pp. 1–27.

over the past century and a half raises a number of interesting questions. Through what stages have governmental attitudes toward unions and labor protective legislation moved? How different were the role and policies of the three branches of government at various times and what explained such differences? What factors influenced public policy changes? To what extent has government policy shifted with prevailing ideologies and concepts of employment? With changes in public opinion? With alterations in the economic and political power of management and labor? As the evolution of public policy is examined, we shall be looking for answers to those questions.

Judicial Regulation

In the absence of any statutory law covering union activities during most of the nineteenth century, decisions in court cases were based on common law (the accumulated decisions of judges). Our common law was, of course, greatly influenced by British precedent and the economic philosophy dominant at the time.

1. CONSPIRACY CASES. As explained in Chapter 5, when the early unions sought to enforce a high level of wages through a closed shop and strikes, the employers began to use the courts against such workers' organizations. Beginning in 1806, shoemakers' unions were prosecuted in six court cases under the English common-law doctrine of conspiracy. In four of the cases, the shoemakers were held to be guilty and were fined a few dollars. As soon as a jury in the first case held eight Philadelphia shoemakers "guilty of a combination to raise wages," a wave of protest arose. The Jeffersonian Democrats attacked both the use of English common law and Federalists judges who contended that a "combination" of workmen "interferes with the 'natural' regulation of wages by supply and demand."[6] In subsequent conspiracy cases, the judges shifted somewhat in their interpretation of the common law, declaring that combinations to raise wages were illegal only when unlawful means, such as coercion or intimidation,

---

[6] For an account of the case, see Elias Lieberman, *Unions Before the Bar, Historic Trials Showing the Evolution of Labor Rights in the United States* (New York: Harper, 1950), pp. 1–15.

were used or when the workers sought to achieve an unlawful end, such as injury to a nonmember through efforts to secure a closed shop.

Between 1821 and 1842, there were twelve additional prosecutions of unions for conspiracy, five of which resulted in convictions. In 1821, a group of shoemakers tried unsuccessfully to prosecute employers for conspiring to reduce wages.[7] Stress on property rights and the need to protect local manufacturing were important factors influencing the outcome in these conspiracy cases.

A decision in 1842 by Chief Justice Shaw of the Supreme Court of Massachusetts was destined to have a far-reaching influence on the development of labor rights and served to discourage subsequent use of the criminal conspiracy doctrine to prosecute unions. The case had been argued by Massachusetts leaders of the two contending political parties (the Whigs and the Democrats). In setting aside the conviction on appeal, Justice Shaw, who enjoyed great prestige in his profession, agreed that, if the intended objective of the union (such as raising wages) was lawful and the means (e.g., noncoercive action) were lawful, a labor combination was not a criminal conspiracy.[8] After this decision rejecting the idea that labor combinations are illegal *per se*, the employers tended to shift from lawsuits based on the conspiracy doctrine to the use of court injunctions forbidding union actions. From 1842 to 1880, however, a total of twenty-one additional conspiracy cases were reported. Between 1869 and 1884, six States enacted statutes to nullify the conspiracy doctrine, but those laws, subject to court interpretation, proved rather ineffective.[9]

Injunctions

In the 1880's, the first court injunctions were issued in labor disputes, and thereafter in labor cases the injunction practically displaced the conspiracy trial. Injunctions are orders issued by courts

---

[7] John R. Commons, *et al.*, *History of Labour in the United States* (New York: Macmillan, Vol. III, 1918), p. 163.

[8] The case, *Commonwealth (Mass.)* v. *Hunt*, is discussed in Lieberman, *op. cit.*, pp. 16–28.

[9] See Edwin E. Witte, "Early American Labor Cases," *Yale Law Journal*, XXXV (May 1926), pp. 830–31.

of equity directing that a person or persons do, or refrain from doing, certain acts. The theory behind injunctions is that they are relief necessary in certain instances in order to prevent irreparable damage to property, damage that could not or would not be fully repaired by the payment of compensation following a successful damage suit. As the courts broadened the concept of property to include market relationships and the right to do business, the pressure activities of unions were made subject to judicial control and prohibition. On the grounds of protecting an employer's established relations with customers and employees, labor injunctions enjoined strikes, boycotts, and peaceful picketing.

For employers, the injunction has many advantages over a law suit. It can be obtained quickly. It forestalls injuries so that damage suits, with the attendant ill effects on labor relations, are avoided. An injunction gives the public the impression that the would-be strikers are running afoul of the law, and any failure to comply with an injunction is punishable as contempt of court. The issue becomes one between the union and the court. Because of these advantages, the number of injunctions increased rapidly each decade from the 1880's until the passage of the Norris-LaGuardia Act (1932) and similar State acts, limiting court issuance of such restraining orders in labor disputes. Up to May 1931, a total of 1,845 labor injunctions were known to have been issued at the request of employers, compared with 43 issued at labor's instance.[10]

Labor objections to the use of court injunctions in industrial disputes have been directed primarily against (a) the procedure of issuing temporary injunctions without a fair hearing for both sides or an opportunity for prompt appeal, (b) the sweeping character of such "judge-made" law, and (c) the denial of a fair trial for those accused of violating the injunction. In almost half of the labor-injunction cases prior to 1932, temporary restraining orders were issued *ex parte*, simply on the basis of the employer's complaint and allegations, without an opportunity for the workers to present their side of the case or to question the employer's assertions.[11] Such temporary injunctions often forbade action that was

---

[10] Edwin E. Witte, *The Government in Labor Disputes* (New York: McGraw-Hill, 1934), pp. 84 and 234.

[11] *Ibid.*, p. 90.

perfectly lawful, including discussions and meetings. Many labor injunctions issued before enactment of the Norris-LaGuardia Act were dragnet decrees with "blanket" clauses extending broad and vague prohibitions to "all persons whomsoever." Failure to obey such an injunction anywhere constituted contempt of court, and the accused violator was usually tried before the judge who had issued the injunction, without the benefit of the jury or specified limits on the penalty. Thus, many labor injunctions were, in effect, judicial legislation enacted, interpreted, and enforced by a single judge.

One result of the experience with labor injunctions was a strong union reaction against the courts. Judges were accused of a promanagement, proproperty bias. Throughout the injunction period, organized labor sought, through political activity, to obtain legislation curbing the injunctive powers of courts in labor disputes and to influence the election or appointment of judges.

Protective Legislation

In 1840, President Van Buren issued an order directing that the "ten-hour system" be observed on Federal public works. But this unprecedented action carried no procedure for enforcement, and both the Executive and Congress paid little attention to labor pleas for Federal hours legislation between 1840 and 1861. Work hours on Federal projects were decidedly less favorable than in comparable private employment, when in 1861 the navy yards were directed to adopt the hours prevalent in private shipyards.[12] In 1868, a law was passed establishing the eight-hour day for all blue-collar workers in Federal employment and all work on Federal contracts. However, interpretations by attorneys general and the courts weakened the effectiveness of the law.[13]

In the meantime, the States had begun in the 1840's to enact child-labor laws and legislation limiting the hours of work of women. Much of that early State legislation, however, was limited

---

[12] See Matthew A. Kelly, "Early Federal Regulation of Hours of Labor in the United States," *Industrial and Labor Relations Review*, III (April 1950), pp. 362–74.

[13] *Ibid.*, p. 370–71.

in applicability or failed to provide for effective enforcement. Nevertheless, loopholes in the legislation were gradually closed and enforcement made effective in some of the eastern States.

The big wave of State labor legislation occurred between 1907 and 1917. Most States enacted their first laws restricting work hours for women during that decade. The AFL supported such legislation for women and children only, on the ground that they were largely unorganized. By 1908 the United States Supreme Court had upheld the constitutionality of State legislation stipulating an eight-hour day for women. The grounds the Court gave would not have applied in the case of men. In 1916, in order to avert a nationwide railroad strike, the Congress passed the Adamson Act establishing an eight-hour standard as an interim measure, and the Supreme Court upheld such Congressional action in view of the nature of the railroad industry.

State minimum-wage legislation for women was enacted by twelve States during the years 1912–17. In a case in 1917, the constitutionality of such legislation was barely upheld by an evenly divided Supreme Court. In 1923, however, the Court held a District of Columbia law unconstitutional, and during the ensuing decade other State laws were either invalidated by the courts or remained unenforced. The individualistic philosophy of judges and the probusiness predilections of most of them[14] strengthened the AFL's official view that, for men, collective bargaining was the appropriate way to achieve economic gains and the legislative route should not be used for that purpose.

The Great Depression of the thirties gave new impetus to minimum-wage legislation, and seven States passed new laws in 1933. Despite the new basis for these statutes, a Supreme Court decision in 1936 invalidating the New York law also brought their constitutionality into question. The next year, however, the Court reversed its 1923 and 1936 decisions, following which a new wave of such legislation occurred.

By his vigorous messages to Congress urging legislation that would require compensation to workers for accidents sustained on the job, President Theodore Roosevelt was instrumental in the enactment of such "workmen's compensation" laws by Congress

---

[14] Federal and high State judges were mostly prominent lawyers, who were likely to be investors and to have social ties with management.

for Federal employment in 1908 and by thirty States from 1910 to 1915. The first laws compelling employers to provide insurance covering industrial accidents were declared unconstitutional by the State Supreme Courts, but were upheld as constitutional by the United States Supreme Court in 1917.

Labor-Relations Acts

Between 1870 and 1925, the legislatures of some twenty-odd States adopted laws which outlawed the use by union members of force or intimidation, and, in some States, boycotts or even peaceful picketing were legally banned. Such laws were, however, of little practical significance; the Federal and State courts afforded employers injunctive relief and generally levied civil penalties based on the common law.

From 1890 to 1925, a total of 33 States enacted legislation designed to accomplish one or more of the following prolabor objectives: limit the issuance of injunctions in labor disputes, exempt unions from State antitrust laws, legalize picketing, outlaw "yellow-dog contracts"[15] or make them unenforceable in the State's courts, and forbid the blacklisting of workers. These early State laws favorable to labor were also largely ineffective, because they were either declared unconstitutional or were made innocuous by court interpretation.[16]

Before World War I, Congress passed a series of laws providing for mediation and voluntary arbitration of labor disputes in the railroad industry—the Act of 1888, the Erdman Act of 1898, and the Newlands Act of 1913. The Erdman Act also prohibited yellow-dog contracts on the railroads, but that part of the law was declared unconstitutional by the Supreme Court. Provisions for mediation and arrangements for arbitration for railroad operating

---

[15] Employment contracts under which, as a condition requisite for employment, the worker agrees not to join a union. Enforcement of such contracts in the Federal courts ceased with the Norris-LaGuardia Act of 1932.

[16] See Charles C. Killingsworth, *State Labor Relations Acts, A Study of Public Policy* (Chicago: University of Chicago Press, 1948), pp. 10–11. In 1917 the United States Supreme Court in *Adair* v. *United States* ruled that yellow-dog contracts might be protected by injunction, thus subjecting union organizers to the possibility of being found in contempt of court if they sought to organize workers who had signed such contracts.

employees in these laws, after functioning successfully in many cases, proved incapable of resolving the controversy over the eight-hour day for such employees. Therefore, Congress had to pass the Adamson Act in 1916.

Presidential Intervention

Presidents and State governors frequently intervened in labor disputes before the New Deal. In the great railroad strikes of 1877, President Hayes sent Federal troops into ten States to stop strike disorders and the interruption of railroad operations. In the Pullman strike of 1894, President Cleveland dispatched Federal troops into a number of States in support of court injunctions obtained by the Federal Government to suppress violence and obstruction of mail transportation. In 1902, President Theodore Roosevelt intervened in an anthracite coal strike and forced the acceptance of an arbitration commission to decide the issues in dispute between the operators and the union.[17]

Between 1894 and 1923, this nation's presidents entered personally into 30 different strike situations.[18] President Franklin D. Roosevelt during his four terms of office (1932–45) intervened personally, sometimes decisively, in over one hundred labor disputes.[19]

Antitrust Cases

Although it is questionable whether Congress in enacting the Sherman Anti-Trust Act of 1890 intended to have it apply to labor

---

[17] It was in this strike that George F. Baer, leader of the operators made his famous statement that "The rights and interests of the laboring men will be protected and cared for—not by labor agitators, but by the Christian men to whom God in his infinite wisdom has given control of the property interests of this country." Also in appointing the seven-man commission, President Roosevelt got around the proviso that no representative of labor would sit on the commission by naming Edgar E. Clark of the Order of Railway Conductors as an "Eminent Sociologist."

[18] See Edward Berman, *Labor Disputes and the President of the United States* (New York: Longmans Green, 1924).

[19] Robert B. Dishman, *The President and Labor Disputes: A Case History of Executive Intervention in Railway Labor Relations*, 1947, p. ii (an unpublished Ph.D. thesis in the Library of Princeton University).

organizations, some of the most important decisions against unions in this country have been under the Federal antitrust laws.[20]

The first case in which the United States Supreme Court ruled that unions could be declared combinations in restraint of interstate commerce under the Sherman Act was the Danbury Hatters case. The United Hatters (AFL), enjoying closed-shop agreements with 70 out of 82 hat manufacturers, called a strike in 1902 against a hat-manufacturing firm in Danbury, Connecticut, that had rejected a demand for a union agreement. In support of the strike, the national Hatters Union promoted a widely publicized boycott of the company's product at retail shops throughout the country. The union's members and their friends sought, as consumers, to bring pressure on firms not to handle hats produced by the Danbury firm against which the union was striking. The company, with financial support promised by sympathetic employers, brought suit for triple damages, as is provided in the Sherman Act. The United States Supreme Court in 1908 and on reappeal in 1911 declared this "secondary boycott"[21] a conspiracy to restrain the company's interstate trade and concluded that 248 members of the union residing in Connecticut were all liable and could each be sued for damages.[22] Their homes and savings had been attached during the long years of litigation. This, of course, was a real blow to the unions and a discouragement to labor organization. The company finally collected approximately $234,000, most of which was raised by the AFL.

The economic weapon of the boycott in industrial disputes was further blunted by a United States Supreme Court decision in 1911 upholding an injunction against the AFL in connection with a nationwide boycott of stoves manufactured by the Bucks Stove and Range Company. A strike was called when in 1907 the company, then under collective agreement with the Metal Polishers' union, unilaterally changed from a nine-hour to a ten-hour day.

---

[20] See Edward Berman, *op. cit.*, for a study concluding that the Sherman Act was not intended to apply to labor organizations. For the opposite view see A. T. Mason, *Organized Labor and the Law* (Durham, N.C.: Duke University Press, 1925).

[21] A "secondary boycott" is a "billiard shot"—action against a third party to influence his dealings with the offending employer. It involves spreading the strike action to make it more effective.

[22] *Loewe* v. *Lawlor*, 208 U.S. 274 (1908) and 235 U.S. 522 (1915).

At the time, the company's head was also president of the National Association of Manufacturers and, in his fight against the strike, had the support of an antiunion employers' group (the American Anti-Boycott Association), which was reported to have paid the entire expenses of litigation for the company.[23] The AFL had urged all workers not to buy the company's products and had put the company on the "We Don't Patronize" list, published in the *American Federationist*, official monthly journal of the AFL. The Supreme Court of the District of Columbia in 1907 issued an injunction that included instructions to the top leaders of the AFL to cease publishing or distributing any copies of the *American Federationist* containing the name of the company or its products on a "We Don't Patronize" or "Unfair" list.

For disregarding that injunction, President Gompers, Secretary-Treasurer Morrison, and Vice-President John Mitchell[24] of the AFL were sentenced to twelve months, nine months, and six months, respectively, in the District of Columbia jail. The injunction and the punishment were upheld by the United States Supreme Court in 1911,[25] but the three were saved from imprisonment by the three-year statute of limitations. That decision clearly meant the outlawing of labor's boycott weapon as a conspiracy in restraint of interstate trade, and convinced the leadership of organized labor that the courts were hostile to the effective use of its economic strength.

The consternation that the Danbury Hatters and Bucks Stove cases caused in labor circles led to a campaign by organized labor to obtain relief from the Sherman Act. In 1914, Congress passed the Clayton Act which provided "that the labor of a human being is not a commodity or article of commerce," and that labor organizations shall not "be held or construed to be illegal combinations or conspiracies in restraint of trade under the anti-trust laws." Although the Clayton Act was hailed as "Labor's Magna Carta," and some labor leaders contended that it excluded unions from the antitrust laws, succeeding court decisions showed that the

---

[23] Elias Lieberman, *op. cit.*, p. 79.

[24] Mitchell was president of the United Mine Workers, which in its 1908 convention had put the company on its "Unfair" list and had stipulated a fine of five dollars for any member who bought a Bucks stove or range.

[25] *Gompers* v. *Bucks Stove and Range Co.*, 221 U.S. 418 (1911).

judges were unable to perceive that this Act made necessary any change in the application of the antitrust laws to labor.

In three cases in the twenties, the United States Supreme Court upheld the continued application of the Federal antitrust laws in labor disputes. In 1921, the Court granted an injunction against the Machinists' union, restraining its New York members from carrying on a boycott to stop the sale and installation of newspaper printing presses produced by the nonunion Duplex Company in Michigan operating on a ten-hour day at less than union rates.[26] In this case, the "boycott" consisted primarily of a concerted refusal to work on the company's presses. It was in support of a strike called by the union because the company had refused to meet terms of employment accepted by the other three producers of printing-press machinery who were unionized, were operating on an eight-hour day, and were paying the union scale. The Court held that the union's efforts to prevent the sale, installation, and use of the company's presses was a conspiracy in restraint of trade under the Sherman Act and that an injunction against the union, denied by two lower courts, should be issued. That decision showed that the Court had interpreted the Clayton Act in such a way as to make it of no consequence in protecting labor from injunctions or prosecution under the Sherman Act.

In the Coronado Coal Company case,[27] finally decided in 1925, the Supreme Court held that members of the United Mine Workers in Arkansas had intentionally interfered with interstate commerce in order to prevent nonunion coal from displacing union-mined coal. After many years under union agreement, the company broke its contract and attempted, with strikebreakers and detective-agency guards, to operate nonunion. In the attempt, violence broke out and mining property was destroyed. When the case first reached the Supreme Court it ruled that the matter was a local dispute having no direct relation to interstate commerce that would bring it under the Sherman Act. After a second trial with "new evidence," the Supreme Court upheld the charge of direct violation of the Sherman Antitrust Act, reversing the Circuit Court of Appeals. In the third trial, the jury disagreed, and the company settled out of court, collecting $27,500 in damages from District 21

---

[26] *Duplex Printing Co.* v. *Deering*, 254 U.S. 443 (1921).

[27] *Coronado Coal Co.* v. *United Mine Workers*, 268 U.S. 295 (1925).

of the union. In the Coronado case, the economic action was not spread to third parties. Therefore, the Court's decision threatened to make any sizable strike a violation of the Sherman Act if the Court interpreted the intent to be in restraint of interstate commerce.

In a third case, the Supreme Court in 1927 upheld an injunction against the Stone Cutters' union for a concerted refusal by the union's members to work on the products of twenty-four limestone quarries in the Bedford-Bloomington District of Indiana.[28] These companies, after years of friendly dealing with the union, combined in refusing to renew agreements with it and established their own company unions of which employees had to become members. The union did not picket or organize a boycott. All that happened was that its members, in line with the union's constitutional requirement, would not work on stone quarried by nonmembers, in this case the product of employers who had combined to eliminate the union from their operations. Although the Court had recently held that only "unreasonable restraints" of trade by business combinations were in violation of the Sherman Act, it ruled the union to be an unlawful monopoly and ordered the granting of an injunction, which in effect would compel the union stonecutters to help the employer combination undermine the union and union work standards.

Thus, by 1927 the Supreme Court had made subject to injunctions and placed under threat of triple damages for Sherman Act violation not only (a) boycotts using the combined purchasing power of organized labor and (b) sympathetic refusal to work on or transport struck materials by allied unions whose economic power was enlisted by the striking union, but also (c) use by a single national union of its own economic power (with no violence, no picketing, no appeal for help to other elements of organized labor) by refusing to work on materials rough cut by firms that combined to eliminate that union from their operations. Understandably, organized labor believed that the courts treated business more favorably than labor and that legislation was needed that would effectively prevent the judiciary from threatening to make most significant strikes violations of the antitrust laws.

---

[28] *Bedford Cut Stone Co., et al.* v. *Journeyman Stone Cutters Association,* 274 U.S. 37 (1927)

Signs of Change Prior to 1933

Before the New Deal, the dominant economic philosophy favored business and opposed government intervention as a general proposition. The courts, especially, protected the right of individuals to enter into contracts and developed the expanded concept of property which included business relationships. Labor unions were under a legal cloud from the start by court interpretation of the common law and were not able to acquire any special rights by statute. The Supreme Court refused to prevent the enforcement of "yellow-dog contracts" or, despite the Clayton Act, to exempt unions from the antitrust laws.

However, in the period from 1908 to 1917, the Supreme Court upheld as constitutional under the police power of a State a considerable body of State labor legislation. That included hours legislation for women and a ten-hour law applying also to men. It likewise included State workmen's compensation laws. As already mentioned, with respect to State minimum-wage legislation for women the record was mixed; the court's position shifted with its personnel. Furthermore, the standard eight-hour day for the railroads by Federal Act was upheld as constitutional.

In addition to early labor-relations legislation for the railroads, Congress passed the Clayton Act (1914), the Railway Labor Act of 1926 which in effect forbade company unions and was upheld by the Supreme Court in 1930, the Davis-Bacon Act of 1931 (providing for the payment of prevailing wages on Federal construction projects), and the Norris-LaGuardia Anti-Injunction Act (1932).

The last act relieved labor from a number of legal difficulties. Commencing with a statement of public policy affirming the right of workers to engage in collective bargaining through unions of their own choosing, the Norris-LaGuardia statute prohibits the Federal courts from issuing injunctions against paying strike benefits or giving publicity to the facts of a labor dispute. Except in unusual circumstances, when temporary restraining orders may be issued for five days upon sufficient testimony under oath, the Federal courts are forbidden to issue temporary or permanent injunctions in labor disputes without a hearing and an opportunity for cross-examination in open court. Before requesting an injunction, an employer must make every reasonable effort to settle the dispute. Prompt appeal to higher courts is provided in labor injunction cases, as well as public trial by jury before another judge in cases of contempt of court occurring outside the courtroom. In addition, "yellow-dog contracts" were made unenforceable in the Federal courts. This law prevented the Federal courts from interfering in labor disputes, and became a vital element in the Supreme Court's reversal in 1940 and 1941 that granted unions wide immunity from the antitrust laws.

The New Deal Period (1933–1940)

During the first two administrations of Franklin D. Roosevelt a marked change occurred in the legal position of organized labor. Under the National Labor Relations (Wagner) Act of 1935 the Federal Government positively encouraged union organization and deprived employers of the right to use many antiunion tactics. The United States Supreme Court, although hostile toward much New Deal legislation prior to President Roosevelt's court-packing proposal in 1936, thereafter became more liberal in its interpretations of the Constitution and upheld the constitutionality of the new labor legislation. The Court went even further. In two cases in 1940, it overruled its earlier decisions on labor and the Sherman Act and granted labor extensive immunity from the antitrust laws. The thirties were thus a period of great shift in public opinion and court attitudes toward organized labor.

1. THE WAGNER ACT.   The National Labor Relations Act of 1935 grew out of experience with employer resistance to Section 7(a) of the National Industrial Recovery Act of 1933. That Act provided for "codes of fair competition" embodying minimum wages and maximum hours, and in addition included a section stating that employees "shall have the right to organize and bargain collectively through representatives of their own choosing," "free from the interference, restraint or coercion of employers of labor or their agents," and that no worker "shall be required as a condition of employment to join any company union or to refrain from joining, organizing, or assisting a labor organization of his own choosing."

To interpret Section 7(a) and to settle disputes arising under it, various labor boards were set up by the President. The main one, the National Labor Board chaired by Senator Robert Wagner and its successor, the National Labor Relations Board established by a joint Congressional resolution, gradually came to interpret Section 7(a) in line with the Railway Labor Act of 1926. That meant that the employer had to negotiate in good faith with representatives of the majority of his employees as determined by elections held by the board. However, employer resistance to the conduct of elections and enforcement of the board's decisions created problems. Without statutory authority, the board had to rely upon its prestige, or upon the Recovery Administration and the Department of Justice for support in the enforcement of its orders. Some firms brought successful injunction suits against the board's attempts to hold elections or to enforce its decisions.

When the National Industrial Recovery Act was declared unconstitutional by the Supreme Court in 1935, Congress enacted as the National Labor Relations Act a bill that was pending in Congress to incorporate Section 7(a) and the board interpretations into a permanent statute.

Provisions of the act dealing with unfair labor practices, elections, and enforcement are discussed in the next chapter. The economic philosophy of the act, as indicated by its preamble, aimed at overcoming inequality of bargaining power, stabilizing wages, and increasing purchasing power. Those objectives were to be accomplished by protecting and fostering labor organization and collective bargaining.

The Federal law was followed by a number of State acts modeled more or less after it. In addition, in the thirties some sixteen States enacted antiinjunction laws of the Norris-LaGuardia type, curbing the power of State courts to issue injunctions in labor disputes.

By 1939, a public reaction had developed against some union activities. In 1937, the number of strikes exceeded 4,700. The sitdown strikes of that year, the disputes and boycotts between rival AFL and CIO unions, and the "radicalism" of the new unions caused opinion in small towns and among middle-class groups to become increasingly critical of organized labor and to demand restrictive legislation.[29] That demand found some expression in

[29] See Charles C. Killingsworth, *State Labor Relations Acts, A Study of Public Policy* (Chicago: University of Chicago Press, 1948), pp. 16–23.

State labor relations acts passed or amended in the late thirties or early forties.

2. PROTECTIVE LEGISLATION. The thirties also witnessed the entrance of the Federal Government forcefully into the field of social insurance and into minimum-wage legislation.

The Social Security Act of 1935 established a Federal old-age insurance system and the basis for a Federal-State system of unemployment compensation. The Walsh-Healey Act of 1936 provided that Federal contractors should pay prevailing minimum wages for the industry and conform to an eight-hour day and a forty-hour week in calculating overtime. The Fair Labor Standards Act of 1938 fixed Federal minimum-wage standards and forty hours as the basic work week for men as well as women.

All of the States enacted unemployment compensation laws. After the United States Supreme Court in 1937 reversed itself to uphold the minimum-wage law of the State of Washington, many more States enacted minimum-wage legislation.

3. IMMUNITY FROM ANTITRUST PROSECUTION. In a series of cases beginning in 1940, the United States Supreme Court reversed earlier decisions and granted unions wide immunity from the antitrust laws. The court did so by reasoning that the Norris-LaGuardia and Clayton Acts together showed a Congressional intent to change the statutory law and to make labor-union conduct as described in the Clayton Act not only nonenjoinable but absolutely lawful under the Sherman Act. That position was set forth in the Court's decision in the Hutcheson case.[30] Like the Danbury Hatters case, it involved a nationwide boycott of Anheuser-Busch beer in support of a strike at the company's St. Louis plant over a jurisdictional dispute with the Machinists' union. Subsequently in two other cases,[31] the Court extended its doctrine to permit unions to restrain interstate trade as long as they did not combine with nonlabor groups (such as employers) to restrain competition or fix prices.

---

[30] United States v. Hutcheson, 312 U.S. 219 (1941).

[31] United States v. American Federation of Musicians, 318 U.S. 741 (1943), and Allen Bradley v. Local 3, International Brotherhood of Electrical Workers, 325 U.S. 797 (1945).

These decisions came at a time when unions had grown much stronger and when refusal to work on or transport either non-union materials or goods produced by members of a rival union was being used as an organizing device, often in a way that interfered with workers' freedom to have unions of their own choosing. Public reaction to the Supreme Court's rulings that boycotts by unions without employer connivance were immune from the antitrust laws helps explain the demand for restrictions on boycotts by unions embodied in the Taft-Hartley Act of 1947.

Wartime Regulation

As mentioned in Chapter 4, a tripartite National War Labor Board was established after the Pearl Harbor attack in December 1941. Its purpose was the peaceful settlement of all labor disputes. Congress also gave it the function of wage stabilization.

The board developed a number of policies that had lasting influence on labor practices. Among them were the granting of maintenance of membership and the check-off of union dues where the union acted responsibly, the use of a range of occupational rates in a locality as a guide for the elimination of "wage inequities," and the granting of joint requests for "fringe benefits," which served as a partial substitute for wage increases. In some 38 cases, it was necessary for the President to seize the properties and have the government operate them because the managements of those firms refused to comply with the board's "directive orders."

On the whole, the War Labor Board was successful in minimizing time lost as a result of labor disputes. However, stoppages of work by the United Mine Workers in 1943 helped to bring about passage, over the President's veto, of the War Labor Disputes Act. This Smith-Connally Act, as it was called, marked the end of a decade of Federal legislation favorable to labor. Among other provisions, the Act required a thirty-day notice and a majority vote in a secret strike ballot before a strike could be called, and prohibited contributions by labor organizations in elections of Federal officials. The provision for a strike vote was incompatible with labor's no-strike pledge given at a labor and industry conference right after the Pearl Harbor attack. Violations of those provisions were widespread but were not prosecuted. Indeed, so unsuccessful did the strike-vote provision prove to be as a strike-reducing measure that Congress stopped such votes by refusing to appropriate funds for that purpose. The Act expired six months after the end of hostilities.

The year 1943 also saw six southern and northwestern States adopt union-regulating and "antiviolence" laws. Between 1944 and 1946, a total of five industrial States adopted constitutional amendments banning the closed shop.[32] The reaction against union power and policies was growing.

Postwar reaction

Legislation passed by a Democratic Congress in 1946 revealed the changing attitude toward organized labor. That year saw the enactment of the Lea Act prohibiting royalty payments to the Musicians' union in the making of phonograph records and the Hobbs Act (directed at the Teamsters' union), which removed labor-union exemption from the Federal Antiracketeering Act. Congress also approved, but failed to pass over the President's veto, the Case bill which contained many features similar to the Taft-Hartley Act.[33]

The large-scale strikes in 1946 set the stage for the enactment of a flood of union-restricting laws in the States in 1947. Campaigns by the National Association of Manufacturers and the United States Chamber of Commerce resulted in such legislation being passed by at least thirty States in that year. Most numerous were laws prohibiting union-security clauses, limiting picketing or other strike activity, and outlawing secondary boycotts.[34]

In the 1946 elections, the Republicans for the first time in twenty years gained control of both houses of Congress. The new Eightieth Congress proceeded to enact over President Truman's veto the Labor Management Relations Act of 1947, commonly known as the Taft-Hartley Act. Its provisions are discussed in

---

[32] See Harry A. Millis and E. C. Brown, *From the Wagner Act to Taft-Hartley, A Study of National Labor Policy and Labor Relations* (Chicago: University of Chicago Press, 1950), pp. 322–27.

[33] See *ibid.*, pp. 360–62.

[34] *Ibid.*, pp. 328–29.

detail in the next chapter. It should be mentioned, however, that the act's secondary boycott provisions placed new legal limits on union actions against third parties that approached those imposed by the Supreme Court under the antitrust laws from 1908 to 1940.

Although organized labor and the Truman Administration sought repeal of the Taft-Hartley Act, public and Congressional opinion were too strongly in favor of restrictions on union power and activities. The Eisenhower Administration in 1954 proposed a series of amendments to the act, but the political situation was too mixed for successful Congressional action.

The Taft-Hartley Act was adopted twelve years after the Wagner Act. It was another twelve years before the Taft-Hartley Act was revised by passage of the Labor-Management Reporting and Disclosure Act of 1959—the Landrum-Griffin Law. Federal legislation with respect to the power and the relations of unions and management has tended to be enacted at the extremes of shifts in public opinion toward organized labor and business management.

The background and pressure for the Landrum-Griffin Act were built up by the disclosures in the hearings of the Senate Select Committee on Improper Activities in the Labor or Management Field. Established in 1957 under the chairmanship of Senator John L. McClellan, the committee found corruption, dictatorial control, and other abuses and undemocratic methods in a number of unions, especially the Teamsters, the Bakery and Confectionery Workers, the Operating Engineers, and the Laundry Workers. As explained in Chapter 4, the revelations of the committee created an unsavory image of the union movement for the public. Political errors by organized labor[35] also helped to lead to the enactment of a union reform law that likewise stiffened the Taft-Hartley Act provisions with respect to secondary boycotts and organizational picketing. The Landrum-Griffin Act is examined in detail in the next chapter. Basically, it assumes that evils exposed by the McClellan Committee can be solved by self-correction with the elimination of undemocratic practices within unions. It was necessary, therefore, to protect the worker from oppression by union officials.

During the postwar period, there was also a growth of State

---

[35] See Sar Levitan, "Union Lobbyists' Contributions to Tough Labor Legislation," *Labor Law Journal*, X (October 1959), pp. 675–82.

legislation restricting and regulating unions, patterned after aspects of the Taft-Hartley and Landrum-Griffin Acts. In addition, nineteen States enacted right-to-work laws.

Labor was helped politically by the election of President Kennedy in 1960. For example, the new appointments to the National Labor Relations Board resulted in Board decisions more favorable for unions.

That the postwar reaction was against union power and its abuse and not against government intervention to help labor generally was indicated by other Federal and State actions. The coverage of the Fair Labor Standards Act and Federal Old-Age, Survivors' and Disability Insurance was expanded. The Manpower Development and Training Act was passed in 1962, providing for retraining and an annual Manpower Report by the President.

In addition, laws providing pay for women equal to that for men were enacted by twenty-two states and by the Federal Government in 1963. During World War II and the Korean Conflict, the President by executive order established Fair Employment Practices Committees to help eliminate discrimination in employment based on race. Beginning in 1945, a total of twenty States had enacted fair employment practice laws by 1963.

The Pattern of Evolution

Clearly, the postwar trend was toward more, and not less, government control of unions, union-management relations, and the employment process.

Public policy with respect to unions has gone through three stages. Until the thirties, the major role was played by the courts, which stressed property rights and freedom of contract. Favorable legislation was rendered largely ineffective by court nullification and interpretation. The result was a century of hostility toward union activities.

The thirties and early forties brought a complete change. The Wagner Act embodied a Federal policy of promoting unions, in part for recovery reasons. The Norris-LaGuardia Act and the Supreme Court's reversal that largely exempted union activities from the antitrust laws relieved organized labor from a century of judicial restraint. No longer were unions considered by the courts to be conspiracies in restraint of trade.

As unions used their increased legal freedom and economic power in ways threatening to jeopardize the rights of individual members and the public, a reaction set in. New restraints were placed on unions by Federal and State statutes, of which the most prominent were the Taft-Hartley and Landrum-Griffin Acts and State right-to-work laws.

The development of labor legislation with respect to wages, hours, social insurance, and employment rights has followed a somewhat different pattern. There have been periods of rapid advance with sympathetic Federal Administrations such as 1907–17 under Presidents Theodore Roosevelt and Woodrow Wilson and the New Deal period of the thirties. In other periods, the prevailing philosophy, economic prosperity, and adverse court decisions discouraged such legislation or restricted its effectiveness. Since the more liberal interpretation by the United States Supreme Court of Federal and State powers in the thirties, this type of labor legislation has experienced rather steady progress in terms of coverage. In the postwar period the most significant expansion has been in the form of fair employment practices laws and executive orders against racial discrimination in employment.

Enactment of the Manpower Development and Training Act of 1962 opened up a potentially broad area of Federal labor activity. Manpower programming under the Act includes not only worker training, occupational counseling, and job placement activities but also national planning for the more effective use of the nation's manpower resources and for adequate supplies to meet developing manpower requirements. As explained in Chapter 18, the provision for an annual manpower report by the President to the Congress places the function of manpower planning on a new level of importance for the whole economy.

Federal executive and administrative action in the labor area has also expanded greatly since the thirties. Each new law has required an administrative agency to administer it. In addition, Presidents by executive order have established agencies like the President's Advisory Committee on Labor-Management Policy and the President's Committee on Equal Employment Opportunity.

SUMMARY

This chapter has examined the bases for government intervention in the labor area, the positions of organized labor and management on public policy, and the actual policy in practice as indicated by actions of the three branches of government.

1. The three logical absolutes of public policy are complete reliance on market forces, on collective bargaining, and on government action. Management generally stresses the first, labor the second, and some elements in the public at times seem to favor the third.

2. For some labor issues, market forces have serious limitations. Government intervention in the market was justified in part in order to equalize bargaining power between labor and management, but after World War II legislative efforts were made to curb the power of elements in organized labor.

3. Both heavy unemployment and major wars encourage government direction and control of wages, manpower resources, and labor relations. The complicated economic conditions in early sixties required a mixed sort of government program of aggregative stimulation and selective limitations without discouraging collective bargaining.

4. The AFL-CIO has pressed for New Deal types of programs, whereas organized management has tended to preach a laissez faire philosophy and to favor State rather than Federal action as potentially less restricting. Labor stresses purchasing power; management emphasizes cost. However, neither is completely consistent; each seems to want more Federal control for the other.

5. During the nineteenth century, the judiciary exercised control over unions, first under the conspiracy doctrine and then through the labor injunction based upon a claim of irreparable damage to private property in the form of business relationships. From 1908 to 1940, the United States Supreme Court placed severe limits on the legality of union activity under the antitrust laws, but in the early forties the Court reversed its position and practically eliminated application of those laws to unions.

6. Under the New Deal, a great change occurred in public

policy. Labor organization and collective bargaining were encouraged by the Wagner Act; the Federal Government began to regulate minimum wages and work hours and established a whole new program of social insurance.

7. Beginning in World II, a reaction set in against the use of their power by some unions, which led to the enactment of the Taft-Hartley Act in 1947. Disclosures of corruption and abuses of power within unions led to passage of the Landrum-Griffin Act in 1959. Both events clearly marked the change in the attitude of Congress and the public toward unions.

8. Other types of New Deal labor legislation have been expanded in coverage and some new areas (e.g., racial discrimination and equal pay for women) have been brought under governmental control. A notable new program was opened up by the Manpower Development and Training Act of 1962.

9. The trend since World War II seems to be toward more government control of unions, of union-management relations, and of the area of manpower and employment practices.

DISCUSSION QUESTIONS

1. To what extent do you think Federal or State legislation with respect to work hours and social insurance protection against work injuries and unemployment are justified by the character of the employment "market" in modern industry? Explain.
2. Criticize the "equalization of bargaining power" between management and labor as a goal of government labor policy. How can it be accomplished for different industries through Federal legislation?
3. Why should unemployment cause an increase in government intervention in the employment relationship?
4. Why should the public policy views of the AFL-CIO and the leading employers' associations be so diametrically opposed on many issues when both groups claim to aim at making American capitalism function successfully?
5. How were judges able to suppress union activities in the nineteenth century? What do the conspiracy cases indicate about the dominant economic views at the time such cases occurred?

6. What was the theory on which labor injunctions were issued? How did they affect union bargaining power?
7. How would you explain the general character of the Supreme Court's decisions in labor cases under the antitrust laws and the Court's reversal in the 1940's?
8. What forces led to the enactment of the Wagner Act? What forces led to its amendment by the Taft-Hartley Act in 1947?
9. How do you explain the broad changes that have occurred in public policy as indicated by labor legislation enacted since 1930 by the Congress?

SELECTED READINGS

American Federationist, official monthly publication of the AFL-CIO.

Galbraith, John Kenneth, *American Capitalism: The Concept of Countervailing Power* (Boston: Houghton Mifflin, 1952).

Gregory, Charles O., *Labor and the Law* (New York: Norton, 2nd rev. ed., 1958).

Killingsworth, Charles C., *State Labor Relations Acts, A Study of Public Policy* (Chicago: University of Chicago Press, 1948).

Lieberman, Elias, *Unions Before the Bar, Historic Trials Showing the Evolution of Labor Rights in the United States* (New York: Harper, 1950).

Millis, Harry A., and E. C. Brown, *From the Wagner Act to Taft-Hartley, A Study of National Labor Policy and Labor Relations* (Chicago: University of Chicago Press, 1950).

Nation's Business, official monthly publication of the Chamber of Commerce of the United States.

Northrup, Herbert R., and Gordon F. Bloom, *Government and Labor, The Role of Government in Union-Management Relations* (Homewood, Ill.: Irwin, 1963).

Sufrin, Sidney C., and Robert C. Sedgwick, *Labor Law: Development–Administration–Cases* (New York: Crowell, 1954).

14.

Government Regulation of
Management and Unions

IN THIS COUNTRY, we tend to seek to cure every evil by passing a law. We are less prone to stop to consider the limits to solution by legal action and whether different pieces of legislation or parts of the same law are logically consistent and support the same basic philosophy.

One result has been the multiplication of statutory and judicial controls over management actions, union activities, and collective bargaining and its results. Persons who profess to want less government interference in union-management affairs, press for more and more governmental controls, particularly on the other party. The National Labor Relations (Wagner) Act was a fairly simple piece of legislation of nine pages, but court interpretations extended its reach and complexity. The Labor Management Relations (Taft-Hartley) Act is a much more complicated law of 28 pages, and the Labor-Management Reporting and Disclosure (Landrum-Griffin) Act is an omnibus law, also running 28 pages. Today, management, unions, and union-management relations are more closely regulated by government in this country than in other industrialized, democratic country, with the possible exceptions of France, Australia, and New Zealand.

This chapter discusses government regulation of managements, unions, and collective bargaining under the Taft-Hartley Act and the Landrum-Griffin Act, along with the proposal to bring union activities again under the Federal antitrust laws. Strikes, government intervention in strikes, and the subject of strike controls are treated in the next chapter. Thus, legislation with respect to "unfair labor practices," including the Wagner Act, is considered in this chapter. Treatment of "emergency disputes," including the Railway Labor Act, is reserved for Chapter 15.

A general analysis of the purposes, methods, and problems of labor relations legislation serves as an introductory framework for discussion of the specific statutory provisions. It indicates some of the economic implications of the laws.

AIMS AND METHODS

Much controversy and considerable difference of opinion have existed concerning the Wagner Act, the Taft-Hartley Act, and the Landrum-Griffin Act. Immediately after the enactment of each law, industrial management and organized labor tended to take extreme positions with respect to it, modified somewhat by experience.

It may be well, therefore, to consider the aims of those three laws and the relation of such aims to the economic power of management and labor. How much restriction have they placed on management? How have they limited unions? How far should the Federal Government intervene in union-management relations and the internal operations of unions? How effective can such Federal intervention be? These are some of the questions explored in this introductory section.

Economic Objectives

It was claimed that the Wagner Act was one-sided because all its proscriptions were placed on management. Most of the antiunion measures mentioned in Chapter 5 as traditional management weapons were ruled to be "unfair labor practices" under the Wagner Act. The actions thus made illegal included: labor espionage, the formation and support of company unions, refusal to recognize and bargain in good faith with a union representing a majority of the employees, the blacklisting of union members or leaders, discriminating against union members or leaders in employment or promotion, closing or moving a plant to avoid dealing with a certified union, and promotion of antiunion campaigns, including speeches that promise economic gain or threaten economic reprisal in order to influence employees in their relation with labor organizations.

Such prohibitions obviously reduced the economic power of management to thwart labor organization and weaken the economic power of labor. A stated purpose of the law was to equalize bargaining power and to promote collective bargaining as a means of reducing strikes and other forms of industrial strife and unrest. Some issues over which strikes had frequently occurred were to be settled by election, by certification of the union, and by the duty to bargain, namely, whether the union really did represent the employees, whether the employer would recognize the union or not, and whether or not he would deal with the union and put in writing and sign any agreement that was reached.

One of the main purposes of the Taft-Hartley Act was to equalize bargaining power between management and labor by limiting the economic strength of unions, if not by weakening them. Union power was to be curbed (1) by making illegal the use of secondary boycotts, coercion to force workers to join unions, and certain forms of union security in agreements; (2) by the provision of various types of secret-ballot votes on the assumption that a union's membership would thereby restrict the leadership; (3) temporary prohibition on the right to strike in national emergency disputes; and (4) proscription on the use of union dues for political contributions or expenditures in elections for Federal office. In addition, the act aimed at protection of innocent third parties and the general public by such means as the boycott prohibition, the emergency disputes provisions, and the outlawing of jurisdictional strikes. By constraints on the use of union power, small employers and individual employees were to be protected from economic coercion by strong unions.

The Landrum-Griffin Act aims mainly at the use of power within unions. It is concerned more with union politics and ethics and the rights of individual members than it is with economic power. But that law also contains amendments to the Taft-Hartley Act. Those amendments close some loopholes with respect to boycotts and organizational picketing, and prohibit "hot cargo" agreements, chiefly demanded by the Teamsters, under which an employer agrees not to handle, use, sell, or transport the products of another employer to whose labor policies the union objects.

Questions about Government Control

Legislation restricting the use of power and certain practices of management and unions raises a number of serious questions. What can and what cannot be accomplished by national labor relations legislation? What labor-management issues require national legislative treatment and, therefore, become issues in national political campaigns? What are the problems of enforcement of such legislation? How can the tendency for government regulation to expand be curbed? What types of labor relations legislation are compatible with our kind of economic and political system? Let us briefly consider each of those questions.

National legislation may declare certain management and union practices illegal. It can attempt to prohibit actions. But attitudes cannot be legislated. Laws may do little to promote good practices and constructive labor-management relations. National legislation is not well suited for in-plant problems such as work standards, the size of work crews, and other shop rules. Furthermore, uniform or blanket provisions in Federal laws run up against the fact that great diversity in practices and conditions prevails in different industries and parts of the country. Detailed legislation implies a homogeneity and unity that do not exist. Laws aimed at curbing strong unions may in fact serve mostly to hamper labor organizations already weak.

National statutes to regulate managements and unions bring labor-relations issues into *national* party platforms and Presidential and Congressional campaigns. Obviously, big corporations and big unions transcend State boundaries. The States, from the viewpoint of markets and other economic aspects, have become increasingly artificial entities. Politically, however, expanding Federal regulation creates problems for a Federal-State system. Strong States'-rights advocates may favor Federal regulation as more effective because the Federal Bureau of Investigation participates in the detection of violations and the Federal courts, with lifetime appointment, are more independent of political pressures than State courts generally are. On the other hand, most State legislatures are more likely than Congress to favor restrictions on union activities because of the great overrepresentation of rural areas in State legislatures.

Any Federal or State legislation to regulate management and union practices confronts serious problems of enforcement. Chapter 12 indicated the existence of widespread violation of right-to-work laws by unions and managements. It may prove quite difficult to change entrenched practices among seventeen million workers in 77,000 local unions under 125,000 collective agreements. Individuals are reluctant to press a formal complaint that the law is being violated by a union or by a union and a management, and the Congress is reluctant to give the Secretary of Labor the authority to conduct investigations in the absence of a complaint.

Appropriate penalties against a union, say, for a strike in violation of an agreement or for insistence on maintaining a closed shop, may be difficult to devise. The employer may not wish to institute a damage suit because of the consequent ill effects on employee relations and labor productivity. Depriving the union of its rights under the law, which the Taft-Hartley Act has used as a penalty, seems inappropriate because it withdraws from innocent workers the protections of the law and permits employers to engage in all sorts of antiunion actions with impunity.

Government regulation of unions, of management's labor practices, and of union-management relations and agreements, inevitably tends to expand. Initially, the law is drafted in rather broad terms, leaving it to the administrative agency and the courts to fill in the specific prohibitions. Experience exposes loopholes and needs for additional regulation. Improper behavior by a few unions or managements stimulates additional regulation that applies to all unions and managements. Such a seemingly simple legal requirement as the duty to bargain in good faith on "wages, hours, and other terms and conditions of employment" under the Wagner and Taft-Hartley Acts has led to detailed regulation of bargaining procedures and even the substance of bargaining. Does good-faith bargaining require the employer (or the union) to give reasons and make counterproposals when rejecting demands (or offers) and to provide available statistics in support of positions? The legislation has been so interpreted by the National Labor Relations Board and the courts. The list of subjects about which the employer or union must bargain has been expanding under interpretation of the law to include pensions, severance pay, the elimination of jobs, Christmas bonuses, the rental of company-owned houses, the price of meals furnished by the employer, and the amount of time for coffee breaks.[1]

Considerable difference of opinion exists concerning the type and extent of government regulation that is most compatible with our kind of politicoeconomic system, which rests on the initiative of management, the willing cooperation of workers, and the existence of independent centers of thought and self-expression. Many fear that the "heavy hand" of government may restrict too sharply the freedom to manage a business, may tend to make unions too much creatures of the state, and may rob collective bargaining of some of its virtues. As explained in Chapter 8, one of the advantages of collective bargaining is that it constitutes self-government, under which mutually acceptable solutions are worked out, which the parties shape to their needs and the circumstances. If the Federal Government specifies in detail the permissible union-security clauses or the permissible pension and welfare arrangements in an agreement, collective bargaining loses some of its flexibility and self-settlement features. To the extent that decisions on the substantive contents of union-management agreements are made by the central government, some measure of freedom of choice and the pluralistic character of our society are sacrificed.

Regulation under the Wagner Act was confined to the preliminary stages of labor relations—to the certification of unions as bargaining agents, to prohibitions on employer actions designed to prevent the existence of unions, and to the positive duty to bargain

---

[1] See Robben W. Fleming, "The Changing Duty to Bargain," *Labor Law Journal*, XIV (April 1963), pp. 297–304.

in good faith. The Taft-Hartley Act is a much more comprehensive labor code. It regulates the allowable area of economic conflict (through prohibitions on secondary boycotts, jurisdictional disputes, etc.) and the contents of collective agreements. The Landrum-Griffin Act extends government regulation to the internal life and government of unions. Such detailed regulation may reduce private initiative, institutional responsibility, and acceptance of the results by the parties.

THE TAFT-HARTLEY ACT

Officially known as the Labor Management Relations Act of 1947, the Taft-Hartley Act was passed by the Republican Eightieth Congress over President Truman's veto. The Wagner Act, with some modifications, was incorporated into the Taft-Hartley Act. Therefore, this discussion of Taft-Hartley will include the Wagner Act as amended, plus the amendments to the Taft-Hartley Act embodied in the Landrum-Griffin Act of 1959.

The Wagner Act aimed at removing employer obstructions that were hampering labor organization and collective bargaining. It was silent with respect to the contents of collective agreements or a procedure in case the parties could not agree. The parties were left free to negotiate what they wished and to strike or lockout when they wanted. The Wagner Act did establish the principle of majority rule, under which the employer is required to bargain with the union winning a majority vote as the exclusive agent of the employees in the electoral (or bargaining) unit.

Coverage and Administration

The Taft-Hartley Act covers any business "affecting" interstate commerce except the railroads and the airlines. Because of restricted appropriations, however, the National Labor Relations Board has administratively narrowed its jurisdiction by various size-of-firm limitations based on dollar revenue.

The Board is a quasijudicial body, consisting of five Presidential appointees, one of whom is designated chairman. The Board's main functions are to hold representation elections and to decide complaints that employers and unions have violated the law by committing one or more of a list of unfair labor practices.

In representation cases, the Board decides "the appropriate bargaining unit" (really electoral unit) and conducts a secret ballot. The act requires separate bargaining units for plant guards and for professional workers unless a majority of them wishes to be combined with nonprofessional workers. The ballot in a representation election contains the name of the union or unions seeking certification as sole bargaining agent, along with an opportunity to vote for "No Union." If a union receives a majority of the votes cast, the Board certifies it as the exclusive representative of the employees in that unit. After a year has elapsed the Board can, upon request, hold a decertification election.

With respect to unfair labor practices, a charge is filed by the aggrieved employee, union, or employer with the office of the Board in that region. The General Counsel, who is independent of the Board, has a staff which conducts an investigation of charges. The General Counsel has sole authority to dismiss a complaint or prosecute it. Most complaints are settled during investigation of the charges. If a case is not informally adjusted then and the General Counsel's office believes the charge has merit, a formal complaint is filed, and the case is scheduled before a trial examiner on the staff of the Board. The role of the trial examiner is similar to that of a lower court judge. The General Counsel and the defending party argue the case. Then the trial examiner issues his findings and decision which is subject to appeal to the Board itself.

On the basis of the evidence before the trial examiner, the Board makes its own decision, and may issue an order calling on the offending employer or union to cease violating the act and to make amends for violations already committed. There is no punishment for refusal to obey the Board's orders before they are validated or modified by a Federal court. Some 95 per cent of the cases are settled at one of the various stages prior to appeal to a court. Once a court, however, issues its own order, refusal to obey it is contempt of court, subject to fine or imprisonment. The procedure is similar to that used by other Federal regulatory agencies. It uses the services of experts for screening charges, collecting evidence, and the initial decision, thus saving complainants the costs of legal expense and the courts from being cluttered with cases, most of which can be settled before they reach a court.

Employer Unfair Labor Practices

The Wagner Act made it an unfair labor practice for an employer:

1. To interfere with, restrain, or coerce employees in the exercise of their rights of self-organization and collective bargaining.

2. To dominate or interfere with the formation or administration of any labor organization or contribute financial or other support to it.

3. To encourage or discourage union membership by discrimination in regard to hire or tenure of employment or condition of work, except such discrimination as may be involved in a closed shop agreement with a bona fide union enjoying majority status.

4. To discharge or otherwise discriminate against an employee for filing charges or testifying under the act.

5. To refuse to bargain collectively with the representatives of his employees certified by the National Labor Board as representing the majority and having exclusive bargaining rights.

Under interpretations by the National Labor Relations Board and the courts, a variety of employer actions have been considered in violation of those broad provisions. The first unfair labor practice is an all-inclusive provision, which clearly forbids such action as spying, blacklisting, and questioning employees about union affiliation or union activities. The second one forbids company-supported unions. The third prohibition against discrimination in employment accounted for some 30,000 (or two-thirds) of all the charges of unfair labor practice filed during the twelve years of the unamended Wagner Act. Where an employer is found guilty of discriminatory discharge, he is required to make restitution in the form of reinstatement in the job, with back pay covering the net loss to the employee during the period he was away from the job. Item 5 is the requirement to bargain in good faith, which has already been discussed.

While retaining these five unfair labor practices, the Taft-Hartley Act added provisions that gave employers some freedoms or exemptions from Board or court interpretations under the Wagner Act. Employers were given the right to express any views, arguments, or opinions about unions or labor organization as long as they did not contain a threat of reprisal or force or a promise of benefit. Thus the employer need not remain neutral in a representation election. In addition, he can petition for a representation election if an individual or union claims representation rights.

Union Unfair Labor Practices

A number of union actions were banned as unfair labor practices by the Taft-Hartley Act. Some union unfair practices paralleled the employer ones, such as placing on unions a duty to bargain in good faith, forbidding them to interfere with the employer's free choice of representatives, and requiring them to respect Board certifications. However, others had no employer counterpart, and were designed primarily to curb the power of organized labor.

The Taft-Hartley Act declares it to be an unfair labor practice for a union or its agents:

1. To restrain or coerce employees in their right to join or assist labor organizations or to refrain from joining or assisting a union.

2. To restrain or coerce an employer in the selection of his representatives for purposes of collective bargaining or the adjustment of grievances.

3. To cause or attempt to cause an employer to discriminate against an employee in violation of the union-shop provisions of the act.

4. To require, under a valid union shop, an initiation fee for new members that "the Board finds excessive or discriminatory under all circumstances."

5. To refuse to bargain collectively with an employer where the union involved is the certified bargaining agent.

6. To cause or attempt to cause an employer to pay a sum, "in the nature of an exaction, for services which are not performed or not to be performed."

7. To engage in or to induce or encourage any individual employee to engage in, a strike or refusal to use, manufacture, transport, or handle or work on any goods or commodities or to perform services, or to threaten, coerce, or restrain any person, where the object is to force or require:

    a. any employer or self-employed person to join any labor or employee organization or to enter into a "hot cargo" agreement,[2]

    b. any person to cease using, selling, transporting, or otherwise dealing in the products of any other producer or to cease doing business with any person,

    c. any employer to violate a Board certification,

    d. any employer to assign particular work to employees in a particular union or trade unless that employer is failing to conform to an order or certification of the Board.

8. To picket or cause to be picketed or threaten to picket any employer with the object of forcing or requiring him to recognize or bargain with a labor organization or to require the employees to accept or select such labor organization as their collective bargaining representative where another union is certified, or where a valid representation election was held in the preceding twelve months, or where the union has failed to file an election petition within a reasonable period of time not to exceed thirty days from the commencement of such picketing.

As already mentioned, items 2, 5, and 7(c) parallel the corresponding employer unfair practices. Item 1 is aimed at mass picketing and the use of strong-arm tactics or threats of physical violence to force individual employees into or out of unions. Such actions are generally in violation of State and local laws, but making them an unfair labor practice in the Federal law gives added strength to the prohibition.

UNION SHOP. Item 3 proscribes illegal demands for union security. As already explained in Chapter 12, the closed shop is prohibited and union shops are illegal unless they conform to the

---

[2] This provision was aimed at the trucking industry. The construction and the apparel and clothing industries are exempt from it because of special circumstances with respect to subcontracting.

following requirements: (a) the union has filed the required financial and other reports; (b) the union has been certified as exclusive bargaining agent; (c) evidence has been offered to show that at least 30 per cent of the employees wish to authorize a union shop; (d) the employees cannot be required to join the union until thirty days after they are hired (seven days in the building industry); (e) the union shop can lead to the discharge of an employee only if he fails to pay his periodic dues or initiation fee; (f) the plant is not located in a State that has a right-to-work law or other legislation more restrictive with respect to union security than the Federal act.

As explained in Chapter 12, this set of restrictions on union security has been widely violated by certain craft unions. Section 14(b) of Taft-Hartley, which permits State right-to-work laws to supersede the Federal law, runs counter to the usual principle that Federal legislation is preeminent with respect to interstate commerce. Also it is a one-way proposition; State laws that are more favorable to union security than the Taft-Hartley Act do not supersede that part of it.

The provision that separates union membership and employment except for nonpayment of dues and initiation fees has the advantage of avoiding government investigation of other reasons for loss of union membership. By preventing a threat of membership expulsion from placing a member's job in jeopardy, it also reduces the power that union officials may exert in order to intimidate members into conformity with the leadership's policies. The corresponding disadvantage is that the disciplinary effectiveness of the union is weakened, which may make it a less responsible institution.

The fourth and sixth unfair labor practices have been of little significance. Only a few initiation fees have been ruled excessive or discriminatory. The so-called "antifeatherbedding" or "anti-make-work" provision has been rendered almost ineffective by court rulings that standby orchestras and the setting of unused "bogus" type in newspaper plants does involve "performing" some work.

BOYCOTTS. Item 7 prohibits secondary boycotts and jurisdictional disputes. Boycotts can involve either a refusal to handle or a refusal to buy or patronize. Item 8 was added by the Landrum-Griffin Act in order to plug a loophole in provisions 1 and 7(c). Picketing is usually part of any meaningful boycott program.[3]

Obviously, the purpose of a boycott is to shut off at least part of the employer's labor supply or to reduce his sales, or both The aim is to put economic pressure on the employer to force him to comply with the union's wishes. Such pressure by the employer's own employees is a primary boycott and is not illegal. In the case of a secondary boycott, against which the Taft-Hartley Act is aimed, an attempt is made to mobilize the help of others (customers, retailers, transportation firms, etc.) in supportive action. In a secondary boycott there is a refusal to have dealings with an employer who has dealings with the offending employer—the "billiard shot." The union and its members exert economic pressure on the "secondary" employer in order to induce him to put economic pressure on the "primary" employer. Opposition to a secondary boycott arises from a desire to limit the arena of economic struggle so as to keep down economic injury to the community and to protect neutrals from damage.

Whether other employers really are in a neutral position becomes a question when firms are linked by common ownership or when the "primary" employer, crippled by a strike, farms his "struck work" to a "secondary" employer. For those cases, the courts have developed the "economic ally" doctrine, which cancels the legal protection of such a "secondary" employer.

Items 7(a) and 7(c) make illegal any strikes or boycotts to coerce employers or their employees to accept and deal with an uncertified, minority union. Item 8 makes organizational picketing under certain circumstances also illegal. Such picketing had been conducted by unions like the Teamsters, in hopes that it would sufficiently hurt the business so that either the employer would capitulate regardless of his employees' wishes or his employees would apply for membership to avoid being laid off.

---

[3] This discussion of boycotts and picketing draws on Donald H. Wollett, "The Weapons of Conflict: Picketing and Boycotts," in Joseph Shister, *et al.*, *Public Policy and Collective Bargaining* (New York: Harper and Row, 1962), pp. 121–51; and Archibald Cox, *Law and the National Labor Policy*, Institute of Industrial Relations, University of California at Los Angeles, 1960, Chapter 2, pp. 20–47.

Given the employer unfair labor practices and speedy representation elections by the National Labor Relations Board, little excuse would seem to exist for the use of economic weapons as organizational methods. Such coercion violates the employees' right of self-organization and free choice of representation. Also, with procedures for orderly settlement available, it is argued that the interests of the community are best served if costly economic conflict is curtailed.

It is on such grounds that jurisdictional strikes are outlawed by item 7(d). If unions do not solve work assignment disputes themselves, the act requires the Board to decide work assignments as a means of avoiding the economic loss resulting from jurisdictional strikes. The construction industry, which is particularly plagued by jurisdictional disputes, has established machinery in order to adjust conflicting claims to particular types of work among the building trades.

A charge of unfair practices under items 7(a), 7(b), or 7(c) must be given priority of treatment by the Board, and, if it has reasonable cause to believe the charge is true, the Board must ask the appropriate district court for an injunction to prevent the union's action until the Board decides the matter. This is the so-called mandatory injunction provision. In addition, the Board is empowered to petition for a court injunction against any unfair labor practice. Unfair labor practices involving violation of the union-security provisions of the act are given next priority of treatment. Also, the act provides that any person injured in his business or property by reason of any of the unfair labor practices under item 7 may sue in the Federal courts for damages. Suit for breach of contract is also provided.

Picketing

Under item 8 the act seeks to limit organizational picketing. Picketing which is "informational" is exempt from this control,[4]

---

[4] The act states that nothing in the subparagraph dealing with organizational picketing "shall be construed to prohibit any picketing or other publicity for the purpose of truthfully advising the public (including consumers) that an employer does not employ members of, or have a contract with, a labor organization, unless an effect of such picketing is to induce any individual employed by another person in the course of his employment, not to pick up, deliver or transport any goods or not to perform any service."

on the grounds that it is a method of disseminating facts and opinions about a labor dispute and is, therefore, within the area of free speech protected by the Constitution.

The attempt, however, to draw a distinction between different types of picketing—recognitional, organizational, and merely informational—encounters, in practice, great difficulty. Picketing as an essential element in the right to strike is usually not completely free from pressure, either overt or implied. So-called informational picketing often is for the purpose of curtailing the market for nonunion goods in order to protect union standards from lower-wage, nonunion competition. Consumer picketing clearly aims at quarantining an employer by labeling his products "unfair." Even the most peaceful picketing encourages union members and sympathizers to withdraw patronage and service and is likely to involve some pressure on the employer, if not the employees and customers.

Appraisal

The Taft-Hartley Act contains many other detailed provisions. It stipulates required administrative arrangements for negotiated benefit plans. It proscribes political contributions and expenditures by labor organizations in Federal elections, and forbids strikes by Federal employees. Workers in private industry engaged in a strike over "economic" issues (in contrast to a strike involving unfair labor practices), who are replaced by strikebreakers, are ineligible to vote in a representation or decertification election in that bargaining unit after they have been out a year. Indeed, the act introduced six new types of election, including decertification and votes on the union shop (repealed in 1951), partly on the assumption that union leaders often fail to represent the real wishes of the workers. One result was that the Board's workload (cases involving representation and unfair labor practices) piled up, and delays of a year or more before a representation election or a hearing before a trial examiner occurred were not unusual.

Such delays hampered union organizing campaigns and tended to cause aggrieved workers to resort to economic action against unfair labor practices. Recently, the Board has reduced the average lag in resolving contested election decisions from 85 days in

1960 to 43 days in 1963.[5] Some delay is, however, inevitable with a workload of over 12,000 cases a year, resulting in more than 7,000 elections annually.

The Taft-Hartley Act has been improved by amendment and by interpretations by the Board and the courts. Nevertheless, its underlying philosophy remains unaltered. Senator Taft in May 1949 submitted a list of 28 changes that he and his Republican colleagues would accept and recommend. They would have made the union-shop provisions less impractical and have remedied a number of other defects. However, organized labor and the Truman Administration were then demanding repeal of the Taft-Hartley Act, leaving only the Wagner Act in effect.

Whether the Taft-Hartley Act balances the power of management and organized labor, generally speaking, is difficult to determine. Conditions vary too widely for that objective to be achieved in each industry under a blanket Federal law. Passage of the act and the Landrum-Griffin amendments to it lowered the prestige of organized labor, stimulated State right-to-work laws, and hampered organization, particularly in the South and non-urban areas in the North.

To a significant extent, the union unfair labor practices do not parallel the employer unfair labor practices. For example, employers can, through purchases, lend economic aid to or put economic pressure on other employers to influence their labor relations policies without any restrictions in the law. Unions, in using their economic power, must treat employers separately, refraining from following their community of interests to the point of seeking to influence one employer's purchases from another. Undoubtedly, employers and unions are so different that any attempt at parallel legal treatment is both impractical and unsound.

The danger with such detailed government regulation as that embodied in the Taft-Hartley Act is that political and legal decisions are substituted for economic considerations and self-settlement. Thus, politics and the courts come to play a larger and larger role in industrial relations. In government, the pendulum

---

[5] See *Compulsion and Freedom in Collective Bargaining*, An Address by Frank W. McCulloch, chairman of the National Labor Relations Board, before the Shulman Conference on Labor Relations, Yale Law School, New Haven, Conn., March 8, 1963, p. 17 (mimeo.).

swings from left to right and back again, with the attendant uncertainty and encouragement to political and legal contests.

Fortunately, the Taft-Hartley Act has had relatively little
effect on industrial relations where the parties had already had
some experience with collective bargaining. Most employers and
most unions desire to settle their mutual problems outside of the
courts and without the intervention of a Federal regulatory agency.

THE LANDRUM-GRIFFIN ACT

The provisions of the Landrum-Griffin Act were briefly outlined in Chapter 6, which dealt with union government and the
issue of union democracy. As was pointed out there, American
unionism has a democratic tradition, and the statutory grant of
exclusive representation implies some obligation on the part of the
government to assure that individual members have the right to
participate freely in the affairs of certified unions.

Influencing Factors

Many influences brought the issue of internal union reform to a
head in the late fifties. As explained in Chapter 6, unions had been
growing in size and a gap had tended to develop between the
national leadership and the rank and file. In their newly found
comfort and security, union leaders' dedication to the cause
seemed to erode somewhat; the older leaders at the top tended to
become "organization men" with some touches of paternalism.
Undeniable successes in elevating the relative status of the manual
worker sapped the labor movement of some of its zeal. Certification and the union shop meant less need to "sell" the union on
a continuous basis, and the increasing technicality and complexity
of bargaining issues expanded the role of the specialist at the expense of participation by the man at the workbench. All this
served to increase membership apathy and enhance the power
and control of the national headquarters.

For two years prior to the passage of the Landrum-Griffin
Act, newspaper headlines blared forth the tale of corruption,
strong-arm tactics, and dictatorial methods applied in six unions

(especially the Teamsters), as the unsavory story was related before the McClellan Committee.[6] The result was that even labor sympathizers in Congress recognized the need for some corrective legislation.

Interestingly, almost all of the dishonesty and legal violations revealed by the committee were already illegal under State and local laws. The difficulty was largely lack of detection and enforcement of the law. Strong advocates of States' rights supported Federal legislation to regulate union affairs because that would bring in the Federal Bureau of Investigation, the Department of Justice, and the Federal courts, and, in addition, would provide a vehicle for tightening some provisions of the Taft-Hartley Act.

As the McClellan Committee exposures developed, the AFL-CIO in 1956 and 1957 adopted codes of ethical and democratic practice and in 1957 expelled the Teamsters, the Bakery and Confectionery Workers, and the Laundry Workers from the Federation for violations of the codes.[7] Until mid-1958, President George Meany of the AFL-CIO opposed legislation to help achieve union reform, but then he favored a bill requiring disclosure of union finances, making it a crime willfully to misrepresent union affairs, providing for reporting on union trusteeships, assuring honesty in union elections, and proscribing conflict-of-interest activities. The AFL-CIO supported the Kennedy-Ives bill in 1958. However, passage of the Landrum-Griffin bill in the House of Representatives in 1959 was over the vigorous opposition of the AFL-CIO. It came right after the election of a Congress considered generally favorable to labor, which raises serious doubts about the political power of organized labor and especially its political skill in dealing with Congress.[8]

---

[6] See *Hearings* and *Final Report* of the Select Committee on Improper Activities in the Labor or Management Field, United States Senate, Eighty-sixth Congress, Parts 1-4, February 26–March 31, 1960 (Washington: United States Government Printing Office, 1960).

[7] It is interesting to note that at least fifteen attorneys and fifty companies were found by the committee to have engaged in collusive deals or other improper activities in the labor-management field, but no bar association (except that in Tennessee) and no management association took any action to expel or otherwise condemn such improper activities by their members or affiliates.

[8] See Sar A. Levitan, "Union Lobbyists' Contributions to Tough Labor Legislation," *Labor Law Journal*, X (October 1959), pp. 675–82.

Purposes and Methods

Officially, the Landrum-Griffin Act is entitled the Labor-Management Reporting and Disclosure Act of 1959. Actually, it is much more than that. Although considerable reliance is placed on disclosure for deterrence and correction, the internal procedures of both local and international unions are specified in considerable detail, with stiff penalties for violation of some of them. The act gives the Secretary of Labor the power to police the government and financial affairs of even the smallest local union. Indeed, the act is quite comprehensive in both scope and coverage, which also includes railroad and airlines unions.

The philosophy underlying the act seems to be that democracy, if it has the facts to work on, can provide its own correctives for most abuses within unions. It is assumed that democracy in unions will serve to check abuse of power, prevent corruption, maintain the interest of members in union affairs, make union policies responsive to the wishes of the majority, and assure minorities of the right to express their views. The act appears to recognize that democracy may not flourish in the union setting unless the government requires that members receive adequate information about the conduct of the union's financial affairs, guarantees fair and honest elections, and protects individual members from unfair disciplinary action within the union.

1. AIMS. Aside from its Taft-Hartley amendments, the Landrum-Griffin Act seeks to achieve four objectives: (1) to promote democratic procedures in the conduct of internal union affairs, (2) to assure honest handling of union funds, (3) to safeguard the individual's rights as a union member, and (4) to prevent labor-relations consultants from serving as a means of violating employees' rights of self-organization and promoting union-management deals.[9] The act's objectives were heavily influenced by the abuses found to exist in the Teamsters' union.[10]

---

[9] See Daniel Bell, "Nate Shefferman, Union Buster," *Fortune* (February 1958), pp. 120–21 and 204–209.

[10] For a discussion of such abuses see Robert F. Kennedy, *The Enemy Within* (New York: Harper, 1960).

2. MEANS.   To a considerable extent the act relies on the individual members to remove dishonest officials, to correct unfair procedures, and to force the union to take account of the interests of all elements of the membership which it is required to represent in collective bargaining. Enforcement of Title I (the "bill of rights") is by private suit in court.

Under the other titles, however, complaint is made to the Secretary of Labor who investigates and, in most instances, arranges for prosecution in cases of presumed violation. In addition, the Secretary of Labor has broad investigatory powers under Title VI. He is empowered to examine the books and records of labor organizations, if he believes it necessary to do so in order to determine whether any person has violated any provision of the act except Title I and the Taft-Hartley amendments.

The act creates some thirteen new Federal crimes, directed principally at officers of labor unions. The penalties for willful violation of the law range up to $10,000 in fines, or imprisonment up to twenty years, or both. Union office is forbidden to persons for five years after having been convicted of any of a list of crimes or having been a member of the Communist Party.

Bill of Rights

This section of the act guarantees every union member (a) equal rights to nominate candidates for union office, vote in union elections, and attend and participate in membership meetings, and (b) the right of freedom of speech and assembly in and out of union meetings. Both rights are subject to reasonable union rules pertaining to the conduct of meetings. The act also specifies the procedures that have to be followed in increasing union dues and initiation fees. It protects a member's right to sue the union in court, and provides that a member may not be disciplined by a union, unless he is served with specific written charges, given a reasonable time to prepare his defense, and afforded a full and fair hearing.

There are some glaring gaps in this bill of rights. It is silent with respect to nondiscriminatory admission to unions, so that there is no protection of the right to join or no equal right to participate in union membership. Second, there are no substantive protections against union disciplinary actions taken on such grounds as "antiunion action" or "slandering a union officer."

The remedy is by a lawsuit and injunction. However, no criminal penalties are provided except where there is use of force or threat of violence. The complaining union member must stand his own costs of litigation. Since with respect to most matters in Title I the Federal law is not preemptive, conflicts between decisions in Federal and State courts are possible.

Unfortunately, the act contains no encouragement of the establishment of independent tribunals like the Public Review Board of the United Automobile Workers, to which an aggrieved member can appeal at no personal expense.[11]

Financial and Conflict-of-Interest Reports

Every union is required to file annually with the Secretary of Labor a financial report, giving the salary and allowances of each officer and union employee paid over $10,000 a year and reporting on all loans over $250 to an officer, union employee, or member. The information in such reports must be made available to all members.

Every union officer and employee must report to the Secretary of Labor any conflict-of-interest transactions; employers and "middlemen" for employers must also report any loans or payments to union officers or payments to employees or others for the purpose of influencing such employees in exercising their rights to join or not join a union and to participate in union activities.

Trusteeships

The McClellan Committee found that certain presidents of international unions had abused the device of putting local unions under trusteeship (or receivership) because of alleged irregularities or violations of the union constitution. While under the authority of a trustee, normal democratic procedures are suspended

---

[11] This board has ruled against the union's officers' decisions in at least six cases. See Jack Stieber, Walter E. Oberer, and Michael Harrington, *Democracy and Public Review, An Analysis of the UAW Public Review Board*, Center for the Study of Democratic Institutions, Santa Barbara, 1960.

and the trustee has authority to spend the dues money and often to vote on behalf of the local in conventions of the international in order to help perpetuate the administration in power.

At the time of the McClellan Committee hearings in 1957, a total of 113 out of 892 locals of the Teamsters' union were under trusteeship (James Hoffa was trustee for twelve of them); twelve of the locals of the Operating Engineers containing one-fifth of that union's membership were under trusteeships, nine of which had been in effect over ten years and two for 29 years; and over half of the districts of the United Mine Workers had for a long time been run by the personal appointees of the president. The vice-president of the Bakery and Confectionery Workers Union was charged with misuse of $40,000 of dues money as trustee for two Chicago locals, including the purchase of two $6,500 Cadillacs, pearl necklaces, cameras, and the like.

In order to prevent abuse of the trusteeship device, the act specifies that trusteeships can be imposed only for the purpose of "correcting corruption or financial malpractice, assuring the performance of collective bargaining agreements or other duties of a bargaining representative, restoring democratic procedures, or otherwise carrying out the legitimate objects of such labor organizations." During the trusteeship, the national union must file an initial report and one every six months, setting forth the facts about the trusteeship including the financial details. Upon complaint by a member that the trusteeship was wrongfully imposed or not in conformity with the statute, the Secretary of Labor is directed to investigate and, if there is cause to believe a violation has occurred, the Secretary is directed to bring civil action in a district court for appropriate relief including an injunction. Trusteeships are presumed invalid after a period of eighteen months unless clear and convincing proof for their continuation is presented. In the first two years of the act, the number of trusteeships was reduced to about one-third the figure when the act was passed.

Election Provisions

The act sets forth detailed requirements with respect to the election of officers of local and international unions by secret ballot. To guarantee open and honest elections and full opportunity for any opposition elements, the law specifies the procedures to be used in the nomination and election of officers, and the rights and privileges of the respective candidates as well as the maximum terms of office. Union officials are forbidden to use union dues for campaign expenses. In fact, the standards and control asserted over union elections are greater than those for public office.

Upon complaint of a member and after a hearing, the Secretary of Labor can, in cases of serious misconduct, remove an elected officer through another secret-ballot election. One problem is that it requires some time for the Secretary to go through the procedure and in the meantime the incumbent remains in office, although he was elected illegally. During the first three years, 27 local or international unions were charged with violations of the election procedure.

Appraisal

The Landrum-Griffin Act's provisions with respect to union reform are extensive and quite detailed in many areas. They include numerous matters in addition to those discussed above. For example, "fiduciary standards" are established for the officers of labor organizations for the purpose of avoiding misappropriation of funds, individual bonding is required for personnel handling union funds, unions are forbidden to pay the fines of officers convicted of willfully violating the statute, and embezzlement of union funds is made a Federal offense, subject to fines up to $10,000, or imprisonment for up to five years, or both. The Federal statute does not limit authority to prosecute for the same crime under State and local criminal laws covering embezzlement.

Early experience under the law indicates that most of the 75,000 to 80,000 unions apparently covered by the law have been able to comply without too much difficulty. The reporting requirements, although somewhat arduous and of possible benefit to employers opposing unions, provide members with data necessary for democratic control of union affairs. Undoubtedly, the requirement of disclosure has served as a deterrent to wrong doing, and the establishment of standards of proper conduct, as in the case of trusteeships, has corrected abuses. In interpreting the new statute, especially Title I, the courts generally have been rather reluctant to discard the doctrine of noninterference in the internal affairs of "voluntary" organizations.[12] Under the act, only about two dozen private suits a year by union members against unions were reported in the first two years that the act was in effect. Indeed, some have questioned whether the results have been significant enough to justify all the expense of reporting, record-keeping, administration, and court cases.[13]

Reflection on the act and early experience under it raises three questions: Will the law bring about a greater degree of self-government in unions? Will it result in the acceptance and promotion of higher ethical standards of conduct in unions? Will it lead to additional Federal legislation and even more detailed regulation?

It is, of course, too early to attempt answers to those three questions. However, some comments can be made with respect to them.

With regard to self-government, there have been conflicting cross-currents. Election procedures have improved but there is little evidence yet that the results are any different. The act has encouraged more centralization of functions in national unions, with the increased use of legal experts and with more control over dues and assessments moving from the local union to the international. On the other hand, national headquarters control over locals through the trusteeship device has been reduced. Also, balloting alone does not increase democracy. There is no evidence that unions that conduct referendum votes on officers and issues are more democratic, generally speaking, than those that settle such matters in a convention of delegates. Many questions of union policy and strategy are too complex or urgent to handle by written ballot.

With respect to ethical standards, the situation is also rather mixed. After passage of the act, the AFL-CIO largely abandoned its self-correction efforts. Its codes of ethical and democratic practice were hardly mentioned. No new public review boards

---

[12] For a criticism of the courts on that score, see Linda Rosenberg, "Interpretive Problems of Title I of the Labor-Management Reporting and Disclosure Act," *Industrial and Labor Relations Review*, XVI (April 1963), pp. 405–27.

[13] See, for example, David Previant, "Have Titles I–VI of Landrum-Griffin Served the Stated Legislative Purpose?" *Labor Law Journal*, XIV (January 1963), pp. 28–41; and J. Albert Woll, "The Legal Thicket of Landrum-Griffin," *American Federationist*, LXX (September 1963), pp. 19–22.

were established by an international union. On the other hand, union officers were made more conscious of their fiduciary position and were more careful in their use of union monies. Public opinion expressed in the law undoubtedly had some salutary effects. But, basically, union leaders get their ethical views from the society at large, and they are not likely to be elevated much above that source by a single law, even one potentially as far-reaching as the Landrum-Griffin Act.

As already has been stated, this law involves more government regulation of the internal operations of unions than exists in any other democratic country. Always there is the tendency, as loopholes develop, to seek to close them by more detailed and stringent legislation. Whether that tendency will be strongly resisted, with unions apparently not gaining in popularity among the general public, remains to be seen.

LABOR MONOPOLY AND ANTITRUST PROPOSALS

As Chapters 3 and 13 have indicated, unions from the outset have been accused of being criminal conspiracies and monopolies in restraint of trade. The charge of monopoly has been used almost as an epithet. Those who seek further union reform or legal restriction frequently support their proposals as antimonopoly measures.

Meaning of "Labor Monopoly"

Elements of monopoly may occur on either the demand or supply side of the employment process. Employers have always been free to cooperate with one another by such means as antipirating codes, informal understandings on the size of any wage increase or benefit improvement, and meetings of employer organizations.

In Chapter 9, it was argued that the monopsony power of companies with respect to labor is not usually used as a means of keeping wage scales down. It may, however, be used for other purposes. The idea of a "company town" carries the connotation of company domination not only of the employment process but also of the whole community. Such employer domination has not been illegal. The term "labor monopoly" has not, however, generally referred to employer domination.

From the supply side, "labor monopoly" may mean any one of a number of things. It can mean merely collective action by employees through a union—the old criminal conspiracy charge. In that sense, all unions are monopolies.

The complaint of labor monopoly may be directed against certification as exclusive bargaining agent—the grant of a monopoly of bargaining rights. Or the concept may be applied to union activities that cover two or more employers or a whole industry. Unilateral, nationwide action by an international union has been condemned as "clearly monopolistic." A collective agreement establishing the terms of employment for two years or more is considered by some economists to be price-fixing, and consequently, "collusive monopoly."

Sometimes the term is applied to particular union practices or tactics. Thus, the closed shop, make-work practices, and secondary boycotts have been labeled "monopoly." Unfortunately, there is no generally accepted definition or consistency of usage.

Competition as a Model

As explained in Chapter 9, employment in modern industry is an administered relationship with welfare overtones. Neither managements or workers in well-established firms visualize labor in short-run, commodity terms. Both seek stable relations and little turnover.

Labor negotiations differ significantly from the purchase and sale of commodities, securities, or commercial services. As explained in Chapters 8 and 9, collective bargaining and the resulting agreements should be considered as a continuing relationship. Consequently, the competitive model is not an appropriate public policy norm, or standard, for much of the labor field. Indeed, both management and labor have been moving away from it in practice as the shift has occurred from a commodity to a welfare concept of employment. The relation of a union to its members, and of a union to an employer or employers, is basically different from that of producers to each other, or between suppliers and buyers in product markets. That was recognized when collective bargaining was made the national labor policy in 1935 under the Wagner Act.

The limitations of market forces as a means of settling certain labor problems have been illustrated in various sections of this book. Partly that is because a number of important labor issues cannot be solved by individual purchase and sale but require negotiation and collective acceptance. That is the case with work hours and employee benefits, as explained in Chapter 10, and is likewise true of discrimination in pay and employment, as is explained in Chapter 16. It also applies to such matters as work rules, the protections of the grievance procedure, and other aspects of government within the plant.

In addition, rivalry between unions, unlike rivalry between companies in product markets, tends to raise wages, labor costs, and prices. That is because it results in more militancy and employee unrest, as well as the processing of more questionable grievances. Interunion rivalry also promotes jurisdictional strikes and "hot cargo" boycotts. One reason for certification of unions as exclusive bargaining agents and the Taft-Hartley protections for that certification is because experience taught the evils of continuous, interunion rivalry.

As the discussion of the Landrum-Griffin Act indicated, there is a tendency to confuse autocratic control of unions and monopoly. Actually, democratically controlled unions may be able to exert more economic power than a union under one-man control. Similarly, there is a tendency to equate union size with economic muscle. Actually, the relative strength of a union depends on many factors including the countervailing power of employers. Many comparatively small unions, like the printers and the airline pilots, are quite powerful in their industries. And who would wish to say that the Electrical Workers are more powerful than General Electric, the Communications Workers are more powerful than the American Telephone and Telegraph Company, the Automobile Workers are more powerful than General Motors, or the Rubber Workers are more powerful than Goodyear Tire and Rubber? And what kind of a competitive norm for employment is at all practical in the relationship between those companies and unions?

Companies as Union Boundaries

It has been proposed that unions be broken up into separate, independent units, each of which would be no larger than the company with which it deals. The notion behind such a proposal is that, thereby, bargaining power would be balanced and monopoly power would either be eliminated or equalized.

Such a proposal is radical in the extent to which it would alter the character and structure of labor unions as they have existed here and abroad for over 150 years. National unions would presumably become ineffectual federations, leaving the labor movement top-heavy with loose federations. Craft unions would be most severely affected, since they are organized by occupation rather than employer.

Without a thoroughgoing break-up and rationalization of the structure of large companies, this sort of proposal seems neither logical nor defensible. There may be little more reason for unions to be cut up according to the odd assortment of activities in many multiplant companies than there would be for companies to be confined to the jurisdiction of individual national or local unions. Unions would be required to reform whenever companies merged or sold parts of their operations. Such restriction and change might make union structure too inappropriate and distorted for effective action.

In addition, the proposal to compel company independence of union and bargaining policy would be practically impossible to enforce. Presumably, that would necessitate making it illegal for national union officials to make statements on union policy or to print suggestions for union demands, if the granting or withholding of the use of the national union's support, insignia, funds, or favors were implied in any way. Consequently, enforcement would seem to require significant curtailments of freedom of speech and the press as well as a marked degree of government intervention in the internal affairs of unions.

Multiemployer and Industry-Wide Bargaining

Some writers wish to outlaw multiemployer and industry-wide bargaining. Often it is assumed that a wider unit for actual bargaining increases union strength. That is not necessarily so. In many instances, small firms need to band together and bargain collectively through an association in order to increase their bargaining power. Combining forces on the employers' side prevents the union from picking on one company at a time and using the competition of other companies against it. Through association bargaining, small employers are able to have skilled experts bargain for them and to gain the protection of mutual-aid arrangements. Because combined action by employers stops unions from choosing one company to set the pattern for the industry, some unions, like the Airline Pilots and the Automobile Workers, prefer company bargaining and oppose multiemployer negotiations.

Multiemployer bargaining, including industry-wide bargaining, has advantages and corresponding disadvantages. It generally develops where the situation is appropriate for it. For the most part large firms find it unnecessary and oppose such bargaining because it reduces the independence of company policy and subordinates the company's industrial relations department to association determinations.

For a union, industry-wide bargaining increases the union's security, reduces the time spent in negotiations, and makes it easier to achieve union standards—to take wages out of competition. The corresponding disadvantages are that the union has a greater risk if a strike occurs, it loses the opportunity to charge individual firms according to their ability, and must be content largely with terms that meet the lowest common denominator.

For companies there is also the security and strength from collective action. Strikes are likely to be less frequent although perhaps more severe when they do occur; the international union is more likely to be able to exercise some restraint on the locals. Association bargaining tends to subordinate the problems of one company to issues of common concern, and to make it difficult for a company to pioneer in industrial relations policy.[14] If widely different interests and ability to pay develop within the association, however, it may be difficult for employers to hold the group together behind a common program.

It has been argued that industry-wide or market-wide bargaining

---

[14] Some of the restraints on innovation under national bargaining in England and Sweden are discussed in R. A. Lester, "Reflections on Collective Bargaining in Britain and Sweden," *Industrial and Labor Relations Review*, X (April 1957), pp. 375–402.

eliminates the check to increased prices arising from interfirm competition. However, standard wage scales and benefits leave many avenues open for intercompany competition, and little evidence exists that less competition (or more monopoly) prevails in industries with multiemployer bargaining than in those with company bargaining. Proposals to outlaw multiemployer bargaining are generally based on doctrinaire reasoning rather than a careful examination of actual experience.

Reintroduction of Antitrust

The proposal that the Federal antitrust laws be made applicable to labor unions as well as business enterprises has won support by its superficial impartiality and plausibility. However, it overlooks the differences that exist between the determination of employment terms and rights and the purchase and sale of commodities.

The national policy has been to deal with improper or illegitimate union practices in the context of labor relations legislation, specifically tailored to the labor field. The proposal to apply the antitrust laws to labor seeks to deal with the employment relationship as part of a statutory scheme designed to preserve competition in the sale of commodities. The Federal antitrust laws have never been applied to the purchase and sale of labor services as such. Consequently, there are no accepted definitions of competition or monopoly in the field of industrial relations.

Instead of spelling out which practices are improper as the Taft-Hartley Act does, the proposal for antitrust application would leave to the courts the task of deciding which union objectives and actions (and presumably also employer practices and tactics with respect to labor) are unreasonable and in violation of the antitrust laws. It would transfer to the courts the task of determining national labor relations policy in a framework of economic competition. That would mean a return to the pre-New Deal days of court-made labor law, with the courts ruling on what is and what is not a proper union objective or practice.

The Taft-Hartley Act makes secondary boycotts unfair labor practices, subject to mandatory injunction and damage suits in the Federal courts. A number of the famous labor cases under the Sherman Antitrust law involved secondary boycotts (e.g., Danbury Hatters and Bedford Cut Stone). But the Sherman Act allows three-way action—private treble damage suits, privately-initiated court injunctions, and criminal proceedings with fines and imprisonment. Such a strong triple threat would, it is assumed, cause labor leaders to hesitate to take steps that might be actionable under the antitrust laws if they applied in the labor field.

They would not, of course, know until many cases had been decided by the United States Supreme Court, whether such practices as the following are licit or illicit and under what circumstances: the fixing of wages by collective bargaining, multiemployer bargaining, different types of union security, seniority in lay-off and promotion, and work rules of various sorts.

Labor unions are subject to the Federal antitrust laws if they join with employers to regulate prices, production, or commercial practices in ways that restrain trade. They should also be liable under such laws if their actions are primarily designed to control prices in product markets or to restrain commercial competition. Since the Apex Hosiery and Hutcheson cases[15] were decided by the United States Supreme Court, unions have enjoyed exemption from prosecution under the antitrust laws if they act alone in restraining trade in commercial markets. That immunity should be eliminated by legislative action.

SUMMARY

1. In the labor relations field, government regulation has, since 1929, grown in scope and intensity through a series of laws. Use of economic power by companies and unions, for certain purposes and in certain ways, has been forbidden by statute.

2. Some provisions of the Taft-Hartley Act have been effective and constructive; others were based on assumptions with respect to unions that have proved to be naive or incorrect.

3. Although it has lowered the prestige of organized labor and hampered labor organization in some areas, the Taft-Hartley Act has had little effect on labor relations or labor practices in most organized firms and industries.

---

[15] Those cases are: 310 U.S. 490 (1940) and 312 U.S. 219, 236 (1941).

4. The Landrum-Griffin Act attempts to promote internal union democracy and to establish ethical standards of conduct. It remains to be seen whether the act will make much practical difference except in such matters as trusteeships and criminals holding union office.

5. The Wagner Act established a national policy favoring collective bargaining and rejecting competition as a model in the labor field. Subsequent legislation has not reversed that basic policy. The proposal to place unions under the antitrust laws is an effort to return (a) to the competitive model as a public policy norm; (b) to the commodity concept of labor, with legal disregard of the plant-government aspects of labor relations; and (c) to court determination of national labor relations policy.

6. Multiemployer bargaining, including industry-wide bargaining, has advantages and disadvantages to both employers and unions, depending largely on the circumstances. Company boundaries could not be expected to be well suited as union boundaries, and any effort to restructure unions along company lines would involve tremendous practical, legal, and enforcement problems.

DISCUSSION QUESTIONS

1. What in your opinion should be the philosophy and purposes of a national labor relations act? How closely does the Taft-Hartley Act conform to your views?
2. Explain, with reasons, the economic actions that you think unions should be forbidden by law to take.
3. What are the full, long-run implications of the Landrum-Griffin Act for (a) union democracy and (b) government regulation of unions? Explain the reasoning by which you arrive at your conclusions.
4. It is argued that detailed regulation of the internal operations of unions is necessary because they have a "government-sanctioned monopoly" and so much economic power. On the other hand, it is claimed that the Landrum-Griffin Act is too restrictive, hampering the unity of policy and action necessary for effective unionism and threatening the free trade-union movement by the heavy hand of government. Discuss the validity

of these opposing views. Where and how would you draw the balance between them in terms of national policy?

5. It is said that government-enforced competition with respect to the terms of employment under the antitrust laws would mean the end of collective action and that our national labor policy cannot support both collective bargaining and competition in the labor area. Critically discuss that claim.

6. Discuss the contention that because government policy in product markets is to enforce competition the same policy should be applied with respect to "labor markets."

SELECTED REFERENCES

Applicability of Antitrust Legislation to Labor Unions: Selected Excerpts and Bibliography, prepared by the Legislative Reference Service of the Library of Congress, Committee on Education and Labor, Eighty-seventh Congress, 1st session (Washington: United States Government Printing Office, 1961).

Cox, Archibald, *Law and the National Labor Policy*, Institute of Industrial Relations, University of California at Los Angeles, Monograph Series 5, 1960.

Kennedy, Robert F., *The Enemy Within* (New York: Harper, 1960).

Northrup, Herbert R., and Gordon F. Bloom, *Government and Labor, The Role of Government in Union-Management Relations* (Homewood, Ill.: Irwin, 1963).

Slovenko, Ralph, *Symposium on LMRDA, The Labor-Management Reporting and Disclosure Act of 1959* (Baton Rouge, Louisiana: Claitor's Bookstore Publishers, 1961).

The Public Interest in National Labor Policy, A Report by an Independent Study Group (New York: Committee for Economic Development, 1961).

15.
Strikes and the
Government

THE MOST DRAMATIC aspect of labor relations is the strike. It is an accepted form of industrial conflict, an overt means for expressing labor discontent and protest.

A strike is a concerted withholding of labor supply from the employer. The purpose usually is to put economic pressure on an employer so that he will accede to one or more of the union's demands. In practice a strike puts economic pressure on both sides—workers lose wages while employers lose business. Thus, disagreement is made costly to both parties, and they each are under continuing, often increasing, pressure to settle their differences by a compromise solution.

The right to strike is considered a necessary element in collective bargaining. It is said that only if the employer is threatened by economic loss through a strike will he pay serious attention to a union's demands. That contention, however, overlooks other means by which economic, psychological, and political pressures can be exerted by workers and their unions upon business management. Among those other instruments are: slowdown in the

470

pace of work, an increase in grievances, adverse publicity that threatens loss of company investment in public relations, and the threat of some sort of political action. Unions have continued to flourish in countries in which strikes are forbidden or greatly restricted, and the same is true in this country for Federal employment, high-priority defense work, and the railroads, all of which have strong legal or practical restrictions on the right to strike.

Furthermore, the role and significance of the strike have been changing with the development of strike substitutes and the evolution of industrial conflict and cooperation. In most industrial countries, the strike has been falling more and more into disuse, even though collective bargaining continues to function.

In this chapter we shall consider the changing pattern of strikes here and abroad, the pressures for government intervention in serious strikes, and the various methods of such intervention. With that background, emergency strike legislation and experience under it will be examined.

STRIKE BEHAVIOR

Although individual strikes make newspaper headlines, the strike statistics tell a more significant story. They provide the proper perspective and historical framework for the fireworks of a current strike.

The Declining Propensity to Strike

Since the early twenties, the strike figures show a downward trend in practically all industrial countries in the non-Communist world.

One way to measure the propensity to strike is the ratio of the number of persons involved in strikes in a year to the total union membership in the country. For the period 1900 to 1929, this strike-participation ratio was 33 per cent a year for the United States, or one out of every three union members involved in a strike in an average year during those three decades. The United States had the highest average for any of the fourteen countries.

Others with high strike-participation ratios were: Japan, 30 per cent; France and Norway, 27 per cent; Finland, 25 per cent; South Africa, 24 per cent; and Sweden, 23 per cent.[1]

In all fourteen countries except France and Australia, the strike-participation ratios declined between 1920–29 and the post-World War II period of 1948–56. In the United States, the decline was from 33 to 15 per cent. In the United Kingdom, it was from 16 to 6 per cent; in Canada, from 15 to 6 per cent; in Germany, from 14 to 3 per cent; in Norway, from 27 to 1 per cent; and in Sweden, from 27 to only 0.3 per cent.

The intensity of each strike may be measured by its duration. Between 1900–29 and 1948–56, the average duration of strikes declined in all twelve countries for which figures are available. The twelve countries had an average duration of strikes in 1948–56 of 9.7 days, compared with a figure of 25.8 days for 1920–29.[2] For the United States, duration statistics are available only beginning in 1927.

Another way of comparing the relative significance of strikes between countries and over time intervals is the annual work loss from strikes per union member. That method takes account of both the number of strikers and the duration of strikes. On that basis, the eleven countries for which figures are available had an average of 4.7 working days lost per union member per year for the 1900–29 period and less than one day in the 1948–56 period. In the latter postwar era, the loss per union member in the United States was 2.4 days. For most industrial countries in 1948–56 the working-day loss from strikes was remarkably low, amounting to about two-tenths of a day in the United Kingdom, Denmark, Norway, and Germany, and only one-tenth of a day or less in Sweden, Netherlands, and South Africa. Canada had a figure of 1.3 days, and Italy and Australia slightly under one day.[3]

The figures for different countries show that strike activity is generally high in periods of rapid spread of unionism and low

---

[1] Data on these countries are to be found in Arthur M. Ross and Paul T. Hartman, *Changing Patterns of Industrial Conflict* (New York: Wiley, 1960), p. 18. The sources and methods of calculation are indicated in the Appendix.

[2] Calculated from the table in *ibid.* p. 24.

[3] *Ibid.*, p. 31. Compared with the United States, only Finland and India had higher loss figures of 5.8 and 3.2 days respectively.

when union membership figures are relatively stable. Also, industrial conflict seems to decline as the relations between the parties become more extended and advanced. Apparently, national bargaining through employer associations helps keep the strike figures low. In some countries the role of the government appears to have reduced strike activity by two different means. One is an increasing government intervention to stop strikes or to reduce their duration. The other is the use of political activity rather than strikes in order to achieve the goals of organized labor, especially under labor governments.

The declining propensity to strike in the United States is clearly evident in Table 21. The year of greatest severity of strikes in this country, at least since 1900, was 1919, when over 4,100 strikes occurred in which 21 per cent of all employed industrial workers were involved. The next highest year was 1946 when 15 per cent of all industrial workers participated in 4,600 strikes. During both World Wars, organized labor expanded rapidly, and the first postwar year was a time of marked adjustment. Despite such postwar peaks and some tendency for strike activity to rise and fall with the business cycle, a definite and continuing downward trend is evident from the figures in Table 21. The table shows that the average duration of strikes, however, does not evidence a similar downward trend. Since 1927, strikes have, on the average, lasted longer in Sweden and Norway than in the United States. On the other hand, in the United Kingdom, Denmark, France, Italy, Japan, Australia, and South Africa in the post-World War II period, the average strike has lasted no more than one-third the number of days shown for the United States in Table 21.

Various explanations have been offered for the declining trend in strike losses in this country. They include: (a) longer experience with collective bargaining in major industries resulting in more mature relationships, (b) the development of strike substitutes, (c) a reduction of strike effectiveness in some industries with increased automation, (d) the relative stability in union membership since 1946, and (e) greater concentration of strike control in the national union where the leadership is likely to be more stable and financially conservative. Let us briefly examine each of those five factors.

TABLE 21

Trend of Strike Activity in the United States, 1900–1960

Period	Strikers as a Per Cent of all Union Members	Average Duration of Strikes (days)	Average Lost Time per Union Member per Year (days)
1900–29	33.2	n.a.	n.a.
1930–47	20.3	14.6	2.96
1948–60	13.3	15.9	2.14
1948–50	17.4	16.7	2.90
1951–53	16.9	12.9	2.29
1954–56	10.1	14.3	1.63
1957–60	9.8	18.6	1.82

Source: Computed by Arthur M. Ross from data supplied by the United States Bureau of Labor Statistics and adapted from Table 1 of his article, "The Prospects for Industrial Conflict," *Industrial Relations*, I (October 1961), p. 58.

Strike Activity in Major Industries[4]

Since the figures for man-days lost from strikes have been available for the United States beginning in 1927, eight industries have accounted for most of the total lost time from strikes. The industries that have been particularly strike-prone are: coal mining, construction, basic steel, autos, clothing, maritime, lumber, and textiles. In the five-year period of 1927–32, these eight industries accounted for four-fifths of all strike activity, although they employed only one-fifth of all wage and salary earners.

Most of those eight industries show a sharply-declining strike trend. To be specific, the men's and women's clothing industries have experienced practically no strike losses since 1940, and much the same has been true since 1950–53 for autos, coal, lumber, and textiles. In only steel, the maritime industry, and contract construction did strike activity continue at a high level into the early sixties, and indications already discussed suggest a period of industrial peace under collective bargaining in steel following the 116-day strike in 1959–60. As a consequence, in the period 1953–60, the eight industries accounted for only about one-third of all

---

[4] The analysis in this section draws on Arthur M. Ross, "The Prospects for Industrial Conflict," *Industrial Relations*, I (October 1961), pp. 57–74.

time lost from strikes, compared with four-fifths for 1927–32.

If one deducts the statistics for the eight industries from the total man-days lost from strikes, the residual figures appear not to have a downward trend. That evidence seems to confirm the thesis that improving relations in the eight industries (except construction and perhaps steel) largely accounts for the declining trend in our strike figures calculated in terms of union membership.

Strike Substitutes

Since 1927, substitute methods for settling certain labor issues have been developed. Before 1935, many strikes were declared in order to try to force reluctant employers to recognize and deal with a union. Since then union recognition is required by law where the union is certified by the National Labor Relations Board following an election. In a sense the ballot is substituted for the strike for recognition.

A number of strikes also occurred over refusal of employers to sign an agreement with a union setting forth in writing any oral understanding they might have achieved. Now that is required under the Taft-Hartley Act as part of bargaining in good faith.

Prior to the New Deal, only a few industries like men's clothing had grievance arrangements that ended in arbitration. In most cases, where the parties continued to disagree over the interpretation or application of any agreement, there was no substitute for a strike to settle the matter. During World War II, the practice spread of making arbitration by an outsider, who provides a binding decision, the final step in the grievance procedure. In the fifties and sixties, over nine-tenths of all collective agreements have provided for such arbitration of unsettled grievances. On the railroads under the Railway Labor Act amendments of 1934, a form of compulsory arbitration was established for grievances. If the bipartisan divisions of the National Adjustment Board cannot agree on the validity of a grievance, a neutral referee is appointed to break the tie and provide a binding decision.

As explained in the preceding chapter, the Taft-Hartley Act

provides the equivalent of compulsory arbitration for jurisdictional strikes. If they cannot be settled in a brief period by the parties, the National Labor Relations Board is to hand down a decision that is binding. As a result of that provision in the law, the construction unions and contractors established a National Joint Board for Settlement of Jurisdictional Disputes for bipartisan handling and settlement of jurisdictional disputes in that industry.

Prior to Taft-Hartley, many strikes involved the issue of union security. Under that law, union-shop elections were held until provision for them was eliminated by amendment in 1951. By 1954, the union-security issue had been largely settled in the major industries.

In 1963, in order to avoid a nationwide railroad strike, Congress legislated a procedure for compulsory arbitration of two issues in dispute between the railroads and the five operating unions, namely, the need for firemen in yard and freight service and the size and composition of train crews. A number of States adopted compulsory arbitration statutes or other strike control legislation in the late forties, but the United States Supreme Court has ruled such State laws inapplicable to employment affecting interstate commerce, which is preempted by the Taft-Hartley Act provisions for national emergency disputes.

Technological Obsolescence of the Strike

In a number of industries, technological advance has sharply reduced the effectiveness of the strike as a means of putting pressure on management. With most of the operations automatic or largely so, the supervisory staff, technicians, and office workers are able to maintain operations at close to normal levels without the use of strikebreakers.

The dial telephone and associated automatic equipment has greatly diminished the effectiveness of the strike in that industry. In 1955, the Communications Workers of America conducted a ten-week strike against the Southern Bell Telephone system, in which over four-fifths of the 50,000 rank-and-file employees stayed out most of the period. Despite widespread sabotage of equipment, local calls were readily made and long-distance calls, which then required the service of operators, for the most part went through with supervisors manning the equipment. Joseph A. Beirne, president of the Communications Workers, has commented on that strike as follows: "Hopes for deterioration of the service through lack of the maintenance normally provided by the men on strike, never did seriously materialize. In the vernacular of the prize ring, 'We hardly laid a glove on 'em.' "[5] Similar results accompanied the equipment installers' strike against Western Electric's operations in 45 States in 1957. That strike also had little effect on the general public because about nine-tenths of the nation's phones can function with full effectiveness under dialing arrangements.

In most large electric and gas utilities and in the oil refining and chemical processing industries a similar situation exists because so much of the operations is highly automated. The Oil, Chemical and Atomic Workers struck the American Oil Company's refinery at Texas City, Texas, for six months in 1959, and the Sugar Creek, Missouri, refinery of the Standard Oil of Indiana also for 9 months in 1959 and 1960. In both cases, operations were continued, soon reaching 50 to 75 per cent of capacity despite the fact that all or practically all of the hourly rated employees joined the strike. In the end both strikes proved quite ineffective because supervisors working six or seven days a week were able to make the operations almost strike-proof. Additional arresting evidence of the obsolescence of the strike weapon was provided by the year-long strike of 2,200 workers in 1962-63 at the Shell Oil Company refinery and chemical plant in Houston, Texas. Although the oil union's ranks remained unbroken, the company was able to maintain full production by the efforts of its 1,200 supervisors, engineers, and technicians. The final settlement was clearly a management victory.

Strike effectiveness seems to have been maintained in nonautomated operations like truck driving and localized services. But, as explained in Chapter 12, the spread of mechanization in the economy promises to continue, perhaps at an accelerated rate. That is one reason President Beirne of the Communications Workers has concluded: "I am firmly convinced that in most of the country's

---

[5] *New Horizons for American Labor* (Washington: Public Affairs Press, 1962), p. 60.

principal manufacturing industries and in many sectors of the economy involving transportation, communications and various 'vital' services, the use of the strike as a weapon by established unions will continue to decline."[6]

Union Developments

The remaining two factors of union membership stability and concentration of control in the national union will be discussed under this heading.

Stability of membership means that unionism has ceased to spread to new areas, where the early stages of adjustment are prone to give rise to strikes. As explained in Chapter 6, in the process of settling down, union militancy and rivalry for leadership in the national tend to decline, and there is also a tendency toward the centralization of functions and control. Such developments provide the leadership with more latitude. It is not surprising, therefore, to find that a well entrenched national leadership desires to avoid strikes that may develop rival leaders or at least cause a drain on the national union's strike funds.

A study of 102 national unions in 1961 showed that 57 of them provided strike benefits for members who go out on strike with the approval of the national union's top officials.[7] Two-thirds of the unions supplying benefits to strikers pay them as a matter of "right" rather than according to family needs. The strike benefits paid by most national unions fall within the range of $15 to $30 a week. However, the Air Line Pilots pay $11.70 to $18.33 a day and the Mailers and Photoengravers, $50 a week. The Steelworkers national union does not pay strike benefits because it would be too costly with their industry shutdowns.

Although the availability of strike benefits may make individual members somewhat less reluctant to strike, the national union officials know that members may also resist increased dues and assessments in order to replenish a national union's depleted strike funds. As officers of a national union who generally have been in

---

[6] *Ibid.*, p. 59.

[7] Data from "National Union Strike Benefits—1961," *Management Record*, XXIII (July–August 1961), pp. 29–37.

office for a long time, the top leaders usually are anxious to arrive at settlements and to avoid running the unknown risks of a serious strike.

METHODS OF INTERVENTION

Strikes can serve a constructive purpose. They teach the parties the economic cost of rigid positions and adamant disagreement. It is claimed that, in some cases, that lesson can only be learned the hard way—through economic combat without government intervention.

Often, however, the government and the public cannot take the position that any strike is a private dispute of no concern to others. In our interdependent economy, a large strike for any length of time is likely to have an effect on the whole economy—on total employment and the Gross National Product. That is especially true if it involves a basic material or essential parts for a variety of manufacturing operations. The 116-day steel strike of 1959 was charged with some of the blame for the 1960 recession, mainly as a result of the inventory build-up before the strike and the reduction in purchases as a result of the strike.

Often more serious for the public and the government is a strike in transportation services. For example, an East Coast maritime strike shutting down all shipping has a marked effect on foreign relations, foreign aid programs, and the nation's balance of payments as well as the domestic economy. Even a city subway strike causes great inconvenience to the business commuters and shoppers.

Our national safety is dependent, in part, upon the ballistic missile and space programs. Consequently, the frequent strikes that occurred at missile bases in the four-year period before President Kennedy established the Missile Sites Labor Commission in May 1961, were of great public concern.[8]

The health and safety of a city may be jeopardized by a milk

---

[8] See *Work Stoppage at Missile Bases,* Report of the Committee on Government Operations, United States Senate, Eighty-seventh Congress, 2nd session, Senate Report No. 1312, March 29, 1962.

delivery strike, hospital strikes, garbage collectors' strikes, or a utility strike. A citywide newspaper strike, like the 114-day stoppage that shut down New York City's newspapers from December 8, 1962 to March 31, 1963, may hamper the operation of democratic government.[9] In addition, it is estimated that the overall cost to the city's economy may have been as high as a quarter of a billion dollars.[10]

These comments and examples indicate the various facets of the public interest in labor disputes. They include: (a) inconvenience to the public, (b) damage to the local or national economy, (c) threat to public health and safety, (d) injury to the defense program, and (e) ill effects on the country's prestige and its foreign policy. They explain why the public becomes impatient with such strikes and puts pressure on the President, the Governor, and the Mayor to intervene and help to bring about a quick end of the strike if not a settlement of the issues in dispute.

Governments may intervene in labor disputes in a variety of ways. One problem with intervention is to promote or protect the public interest without blocking or injuring the process of self-settlement through collective bargaining. The public may wish a quick end of the stoppage while collective bargaining, which involves mutual acceptance and, therefore, persuasion, may take some time.

Mediation

The intervention method of mediation involves a third party entering the controversy to aid the parties to settle the issues in dispute themselves through collective bargaining. Mediation or conciliation (the terms are commonly used synonymously) is a form of industrial diplomacy without resort to public pressure. The mediator seeks to narrow the issues and to propose solutions that may be acceptable to both sides. To function effectively he must have the confidence and trust of the parties, so that he may serve as a counselor and learn the concessions that each side is willing to

---

[9] For a most interesting chronological account of the New York newspaper strike and attempts to settle it by intervention, see A. H. Raskin, "The Strike, A Step-by-Step Account," *The New York Times*, April 1, 1963, pp. 1, 22–24.

[10] *Ibid.*, p. 21.

make. To enjoy confidence and respect, the mediator must be strictly impartial and be experienced in negotiations. As a neutral, he should not let considerations of equity or justice prejudice the prime objective of finding a solution acceptable to the parties. Thus, mediation is simply an aid to continued collective bargaining. The parties still make their own settlements and accept full responsibility for any agreement.

A Federal Mediation and Conciliation Service has been established by the Federal government as an independent agency. Under the Taft-Hartley Act, labor and management are required to notify one another of a desire to modify a collective agreement sixty days prior to its termination, and to notify the Federal Mediation and Conciliation Service within thirty days thereafter if no agreement has been reached in the meantime. The Service has a staff of about 225 conciliators distributed throughout the country. All except two States have some provision or facilities for mediating labor disputes, as do a number of cities.

Voluntary Arbitration

Where the parties themselves agree to submit their differences to the decision of a third person or board and to accept the arbitration award as final and binding, the procedure is known as voluntary arbitration. It is voluntary in that the parties are free to resort to it or not as they see fit. In agreeing to abide by the decision, the process of arbitration is substituted for collective bargaining. However, the parties negotiate the arbitration conditions and select the arbitrators, who are responsible to the parties and not to the public or the government. In contrast to mediation, arbitration implies an award involving some judgment on the merits of the issue or issues in dispute. Before making an award, arbitrators may try informally to settle the dispute, and some arbitration awards represent understandings that one or both parties cannot openly support.

One difficulty with arbitration of the terms of a new agreement is that no generally accepted principles or standards exist for determining in any particular case the "right" wage rates, the "proper" benefits, the "correct" production standards, or the "appropriate" set of work rules. Some of those matters may be so vital to the continual operation of the company or the union that it will not submit them to decision by an "outsider," preferring the risk of a strike to the risk of an adverse award under arbitration.

Fact-finding

A form of noncompulsory action is the appointment of a board to investigate a dispute and make a report with recommendations for settlement. That procedure permits the parties either to adopt the recommendations or to bargain further. It does not preclude a strike.

As is explained later in detail, fact-finding with recommendations is the procedure under the Railway Labor Act for emergency disputes. It has been used by Presidents at various times. President Truman appointed a number of *ad hoc*, extralegal fact-finding boards during the 1945–46 strike wave and again in the steel strike in 1949, after using the emergency disputes procedure of the Taft-Hartley Act seven times in 1948. Upon agreement of the parties, President Eisenhower appointed such a fact-finding board in 1960 to make recommendations with respect to the work-rules dispute on the railroads. President Kennedy established *ad hoc* fact-finding commissions or boards to make reports and make recommendations in the flight engineers' dispute on six major airlines in 1961, in the aerospace industry on the West Coast in 1962, and in the East Coast longshore dispute in 1963, after the Taft-Hartley procedure had been exhausted without a settlement.

Outside the railroads and airlines, no Federal statute provides for fact-finding with recommendations. Therefore, the parties usually must agree to maintain the status quo for sufficient time for the board to conduct hearings and prepare and present its report. Since 1907, Canada has had statutory provision for fact-finding by a special board appointed to investigate a particular dispute if it occurs in one of the specified industries. The parties are compelled to comply with the procedures of the law but need not accept the board's findings or recommendations.

Certain conditions appear necessary for the success of fact-finding with recommendations. The parties should have confidence in the impartiality and ability of the board. The board must aim at developing a set of recommendations acceptable to both parties, since each side is free to reject any proposed solution. Often it is helpful to have frank informal soundings of the views and positions of leaders on each side and even the submission of off-the-record proposals. Fact-finding may be helpful by serving to save the face of a party who has become prisoner of an extreme position, a bargaining tactic, or the internal politics of his organization. A President may help to marshal support for the recommendations of a fact-finding board appointed by him. But there is only a limited amount that a President can do in that regard, and, if he becomes firmly committed in advance, his position as an instrument of last resort may be impaired. For the most part, the board must seek to develop acceptable recommendations, and to persuade the parties that they form a sound basis for settlement.

Injunction and Seizure

In case of an impasse in negotiations in a vital industry, a court injunction prohibiting action by the union or the employer and temporary seizure of the production facilities by the government are ways of attempting to prevent a strike or lockout.

Injunctions are usually used against union action. They tend to be offensive to labor because of their rather indiscriminate use prior to 1932, but actually they are employed, as indicated in the preceding chapter, to enforce the orders of the National Labor Relations Board against unfair labor practices. The injunction may tend to encourage management to delay settlement because it usually involves maintenance of the status quo, thereby representing a temporary denial of the union's demands with no promise of retroactive application of any settlement. Its use is particularly appropriate in public utilities and transportation, where the employer cannot resort to a lockout without jeopardizing his franchise, where he is unable to build up stock in anticipation of a strike, and where the effect on the public may be severe.

Generally, seizure is preferred by unions because, in contrast to the injunction, it may seem to imply some blame on the employer and because it often involves an incentive to the employer to seek an early settlement in order to restore the property to full private operation. Also under seizure there may be a possibility of direct government negotiation with the union concerning new terms of employment (as was twice the case in bituminous coal in the forties) or a threat of appointment of some board to hand down a decision in the dispute. In actual results, there may be little difference between seizure and injunction. Since President Truman's seizure of the steel industry in the 1952 dispute and the Supreme Court's decision that under the circumstances the seizure was unconstitutional, the Republicans in Congress have generally tended to oppose seizure as a statutory means of halting a strike in a vital industry. Yet Republicans in New Jersey have favored seizure as a method of preventing public utility disputes under a Public Utility Labor Dispute Act, proposed by a Republican Governor and enacted by a Republican legislature. The legislature has refused to repeal the law despite a recommendation for repeal by a Governor's Committee in 1954[11] and the fact that a United States Supreme Court decision in 1951 indicates that such State legislation is unconstitutional because dispute settlement for all industry "affecting" interstate commerce is preempted by the Taft-Hartley Act.[12]

Compulsory Arbitration

Under the legal requirement of compulsory arbitration, an unsettled dispute must be submitted to an arbitrator or arbitration board for final and binding decision. Strikes and lockouts in industries covered by the law are illegal.

One might assume that the threat of compulsory compliance with a decision by an outside party or board would serve as an incentive to the disputants to settle their differences themselves. Actually the existence of compulsory arbitration tends to discourage collective bargaining. The negotiating parties often hesitate to make reasonable demands or offers or to agree to any concessions during negotiations for fear that the other side will be able to use reasonable counteroffers as a springboard for securing a much better decision from an arbitration board that tends to split the difference between the parties just prior to the arbitration hearing.

---

[11] *Report to Governor Robert B. Meyner by the Governor's Committee on Legislation Relating to Public Utility Labor Disputes,* Trenton, New Jersey, 1954.

[12] *Amalgamated Association of Street, Electric Railway and Motor Coach Employees of America,* et al., v. *Wisconsin Employment Relations Board,* 340 U.S. 383.

Consequently, unions tend to make numerous and extreme demands under compulsory arbitration and managements are prone to offer little or nothing. With the parties relieved of the responsibility for reaching agreement and arbitration the last step instead of a strike, negotiating tactics are adjusted accordingly. The weaker side naturally assumes that it can gain more through arbitration than by collective bargaining and, therefore, conducts negotiations with the preparation of its case before the arbitration tribunal in mind.

During World War II, this country virtually had compulsory arbitration even though the courts held that the "directive orders" of the National War Labor Board were "advisory."[13] Compliance with Board orders was obtained largely by threat of government sanctions. The chief sanction was seizure of the facilities and their operation temporarily by the Federal Government. That occurred in 50-odd cases by Presidential order. To employers, such seizure was more troublesome and embarrassing than it was costly. The government turned over all profits to the owners and was responsible for net losses. While under government operation, however, the Board's orders were put into effect, thus tending to establish Board policy by practice. In addition, the sanction of denial of priorities with which to acquire controlled materials or parts, was used against one noncomplying employer. In cases of labor noncompliance, the union was denied a maintenance-of-membership arrangement and the check-off, and local draft boards in a few instances took steps to cancel the draft deferment of strikers.

The difficulties and disadvantages of compulsory arbitration became evident from experience under the National War Labor Board and the Wage Stabilization Board in the Korean War (1950–53). Dispute cases multiplied, and the number of issues in dispute in each case increased, as the parties neglected collective bargaining and mediation on the assumption that a Board decision was going to be necessary in the end. In the three and a half years of its existence, the tripartite National War Labor Board decided some 21,000 dispute cases. In the latter months of the war, the

---

[13] For a discussion of the issue of compulsory arbitration under the National War Labor Board and the Board's experience, see Edwin E. Witte, "Wartime Handling of Labor Disputes," *Harvard Business Review*, XXV (Winter 1947), pp. 169–89.

National Board alone was averaging over one hundred decisions a week. Some cases had as many as twenty or thirty separate issues. In a few instances, panels or regional boards had to draft the entire agreement and make it a directive order. As soon as Japan surrendered, the public members of the Board sought to return the parties to self-settlement under collective bargaining.

In both Australia and New Zealand legislation was passed in the 1890's establishing machinery for fixing wages and hours of work by arbitration awards. Strikes and lockouts have been outlawed in industries covered by the awards of the national court of arbitration. Nevertheless Australia, with numerous short strikes, has had about as great a loss from work stoppages per union member as the United States, and New Zealand, where all strikes are illegal, has had a strike participation ratio approximately equal to that of Great Britain. Governments in Australia and New Zealand have simply declined to prosecute strikers for violating the law.

Strike Votes

Despite the lessons of experience, many employer representatives continue to believe that government-conducted strike votes are an important means of reducing lost time from work stoppages. The proponents of strike-vote legislation assume that union officers are "strike happy" and that the membership through a secret ballot vote would repudiate the leadership.

In Chapter 6, strike votes were explained as part of the bargaining tactics of unions. They usually represent a vote of confidence for the negotiators and a means of putting pressure on the employer to improve his offer. In a sense, a membership vote to authorize a strike "if necessary" or "if satisfactory settlement cannot be reached" is a vote for the best terms of employment that it is practical to negotiate for those voting. No wonder secret votes generally are overwhelmingly in favor of strike authorization.

Despite organized labor's no-strike pledge[14] right after Pearl Harbor and its cooperation under the War Labor Board, the Congress passed in June 1943 over President Roosevelt's veto, the (Smith-Connally) War Labor Disputes Act. It forbade strikes in

---

[14] Except for John L. Lewis, president of the United Mine Workers.

privately owned establishments unless (a) a thirty-day strike notice had been filed in advance, and (b) a secret ballot poll had been conducted among the workers on the question: "Do you wish to permit an interruption of war production in wartime as a result of this dispute?" The issues in dispute were stated briefly on the ballot. After the vote a strike was permitted regardless of the outcome of the ballot.

In 1,571 cases under the act, strike votes were conducted, and in 89 per cent a majority voted to interrupt war production in wartime. In addition there was wholesale violation of the law. Of the strikes in 1944 and 1945, less than 5 per cent in number (representing 15 per cent of all striking workers) were in units that had had a government-conducted strike vote. Even so, in some regions in the latter half of 1945, between half and all of the National Labor Relations Board's personnel was engaged in administering such votes. So unsatisfactory was the experience under the act that in December 1945 the Congress stopped any further strike votes under it before its expiration (six months after official termination of the war), by the simple expedient of prohibiting further expenditure of funds for that purpose.

The Congress, however, forgot this lesson when it enacted the Taft-Hartley Act. That law provides for a vote on the employer's "last offer" in national emergency disputes and directs that, where mediation fails, the Federal Mediation and Conciliation Service seek, among other means, to induce the parties to have a vote on the employer's "last offer." For a year the Service did make such a suggestion but that part of the act has been largely forgotten since then.

Much ambiguity surrounds strike vote proposals. If all employees including nonunionists are eligible to vote what happens to the exclusive bargaining right of the union? The timing of a strike vote may make considerable difference. By and large, a strike actually occurs in only about one-fifth of the cases where a strike is authorized by the membership. Therefore, a vote before the strike would almost always result in approval of it as a means of obtaining the best negotiable terms. If the vote were to be taken long after the strike commenced and the strikers were beginning to be discouraged, it could serve as a strikebreaking device.

Perhaps most ambiguous is the purpose to be achieved by the

proposal. If it is to enhance rank-and-file control of the union, strikes may be increased because the national union officers are usually less militant and unreasonable than the membership. If the purpose is to reduce strikes, experience indicates that result is not likely to be achieved. A favorable vote may seem to lend government sanction to a work stoppage. The balloting itself tends to draw the parties away from settlement efforts into a campaign to affect the vote. And rejection of an employer's "last offer" leaves the parties deadlocked, with no alternatives to the strike since the members have voted down what is supposed to be the best and last offer the management will make.

EMERGENCY DISPUTES

A major strike in a basic industry may, if sufficiently extended, jeopardize the safety or health of millions of people, along with their economic well-being. In our highly interdependent economy, the shutting off of transportation service, or electric power, or fuel, can soon paralyze the significant part of the economy and threaten the food supply, refrigeration, and household heating over wide areas. A nationwide railroad strike, or an extended coastwide shipping stoppage, or a prolonged coal or steel strike, could endanger the health and safety of the nation.

A major strike tends to have international as well as domestic implications. Strikes such as those mentioned above could adversely affect the country's international position, its short-run military strength, the foreign aid program, and our balance of payments. Even a strike in a key defense plant or missile base (as at Cape Kennedy) could temporarily endanger the national safety and thus have an effect on our foreign policy and our relations with other countries.

Except for railroads and coal, national emergency strikes are largely a post-World War II phenomenon. Such major disputes raise a number of difficult problems. One is the practical impossibility of determining in advance which strikes will, and which will not, create a national emergency. The very concept of a national emergency dispute is surrounded by grey areas. In 1952, President Truman said that the war effort in Korea could not stand even a brief steel strike, yet the strike in that year lasted 59 days. After 51 days, the Secretary of Defense stated that the national defense program was coming to a complete halt as a result of the shortage of steel. Did the 59-day steel strike in 1952 create a "national emergency" and, if so, at what point?[15]

A second difficulty is that no two strikes with a national emergency potential are exactly alike. Each dispute has its special features. In no two cases are the issues in dispute, the personalities on each side, the past history of relations, or the relative bargaining power of the parties precisely the same. The internal politics in the union and management, their strategies, the outside pressures for settlement, and the extent of genuine collective bargaining, differ from case to case. The economic and military impact of strikes also varies widely. Therefore, successful intervention by the government is an art that needs to be adapted to the peculiar circumstances of each different situation. Any intervention has to be by executive action, and to confine the executive to a single, rigid procedure is to limit his possibility of achieving a settlement through government intervention.

Another troublesome aspect is that government intervention may impede self-settlement. Stopping a strike is not the same as resolving it. An injunction or seizure may halt a work stoppage and get the men back to work but such action is not, by itself, designed to contribute to settlement of the issues in dispute. The purpose of mediation, fact-finding with recommendations, and arbitration is to help solve the controversy. Some forms of government intervention (such as a vote on the employer's "last" offer) may impede settlement. Some government intervention or procedures may discourage collective bargaining by causing one of the parties (usually the weaker one) to aim at bringing about government intervention. He may hope to gain more that way than through collective bargaining. Consequently, machinery to deal with national emergency disputes should be designed to preserve self-settlement through collective bargaining as much as possible.

Any proposal for dealing with emergency disputes under a

---

[15] For a discussion of the economic and military effects of the 1952 steel strike, see Irving Bernstein, "The Economic Impact of Strikes," in Bernstein, *et al.*, *Emergency Disputes and National Policy* (New York: Harper, 1955), pp. 40–42.

statute has to face up to the three problems just discussed. In brief they are: (a) the method and criteria for determining the existence of an emergency dispute, (b) the adjustment of intervention to take account of the peculiarities of each dispute, and (c) the preservation of collective bargaining despite government intervention. The timing of intervention could be a factor in all three aspects.

Two other aspects of emergency disputes should be mentioned in this introduction to the specific statutes. One is that government intervention raises to three the number of parties interacting and adapting their strategy to the moves of the other parties. This adds to the complexity and is all the more reason why the executive needs to be both flexible and skillful—flexible to create uncertainty, thereby discouraging intervention by making it risky for each party, and skillful in order to take advantage of changing pressures and the inherent powers of the Presidency or a Governorship.

The other aspect that should be recognized is that, although the statutory language of the procedure may remain unchanged, attitudes toward it alter with experience and personnel. Overuse or misuse may injure its "magic." Once any weaknesses have been exposed, the procedure may never again enjoy the same respect.

Such considerations should be borne in mind as we examine each piece of emergency disputes legislation. The procedure in the Railway Labor Act will be considered first. Then the Taft-Hartley Act section on national emergency disputes and experience under it will be analyzed. Finally, the program of providing the executive with a choice of procedures will be discussed.

The Railway Labor Act

Dissatisfaction by management and the unions with the Railroad Labor Board under the Transportation Act of 1926, led them to agree on a bill that became the Railway Labor Act of 1926. The act contains, along with other features, a step-by-step procedure for settling disputes over the terms of a new agreement. In general, the steps embodied in the law were established practice.

1. PROVISIONS.   Under the law, the parties have a positive duty to exert every reasonable effort to make and maintain agreements

and to settle all disputes peacefully. Until the fifties, railroad agreements had no termination date. When one of the parties desires a change (say one of the twenty-one standard railroad unions seeks a wage increase), written notice is served on the other party. If no settlement is achieved through direct bargaining, one of the parties can call for the conciliation services of the National Mediation Board, or the Board can enter the dispute on its own initiative. If the Board's mediatory efforts prove unsuccessful, it must urge the parties to accept voluntary arbitration under arrangements set forth in the law. The parties are free to reject voluntary arbitration, and usually do so, but there has been more voluntary arbitration of new terms in the railroads and airlines under the Railway Labor Act than has been true in industry generally.

After the Board has notified the parties that its mediatory efforts have failed, no change in wages, rules, or working conditions can occur for thirty days except by mutual agreement. If, in the Board's judgment, the dispute threatens to deprive any section of the country of essential transportation service, the Board must so notify the President. At his discretion, the President may appoint an emergency board (usually of three neutrals) to investigate and report to the President within thirty days of its appointment—a time too brief for the proceedings and, therefore, usually extended. For thirty days after the emergency board has made its report *with recommendations* for settling the dispute to the President, the parties are required to continue to maintain the conditions unchanged except for any alteration by mutual agreement. That is to allow time for further negotiations and public pressures toward settlement. Thereafter the parties are legally free to make changes, strike, or take other action.

It is evident that the Railway Labor Act's procedure for new-contract disputes is designed to place reliance on collective bargaining. Without the irritant of a court injunction, it requires both sides to maintain the status quo while attempts are made to settle the dispute. Usually at least four months elapse from the time of notification of a desired change until strike action is permissible under the law.

2. EXPERIENCE. For the first fifteen years (until 1941), the emergency disputes provisions of the Railway Labor Act worked

well and it was considered a "model law." In that year, however, an emergency board recommended a *temporary* wage increase of 7.5 per cent for the operating employees and nine cents an hour for the nonoperating employees. The unions rejected the recommendations and the operating unions scheduled a strike for December 7, 1941, which later became Pearl Harbor Day. President Roosevelt finally took the unprecedented action of reconvening the emergency board, which, after additional hearings, served as a board of mediation. Pressure was put on the managements and, to avoid a strike, they finally granted *permanent* increases of 9.5 cents an hour for the operating employees and ten cents an hour plus paid vacations for the nonoperating employees. Thereafter, the practice of union rejection of board recommendations as a means of gaining additional benefits became common. One consequence was that often serious collective bargaining only took place after a board had made a report.

For successful collective bargaining the railroads have certain handicaps. In contrast to a single railroad union in Sweden and one general railroad union and two craft unions in railroading in England, the United States has twenty-one "standard" railroad unions and some thirty other unions with representation claims in the industry. In engine and train service, obsolete work rules complicate the bargaining process. The incentive system based on miles run or hours worked has train speed standards for pay purposes unrevised from World War I to 1963. As stated in Chapter 8, in 1945–46 an emergency board had before it in dispute, 44 union proposals for rule changes in addition to wage increases and 29 carrier proposals for rule changes plus wage counterdemands.

The emergency-board procedure is not well suited for recommendations with respect to work-rule changes. Generally speaking, the issues are too complicated for brief, *ad hoc* handling. For that reason the railroads and the operating unions finally agreed in October 1960 to a special Presidential study commission to examine carefully the proposed rule changes and to make a set of recommendations. After over a year of study (including 15,500 pages of oral testimony and 20,000 pages of exhibits), the tripartite Presidential Railroad Commission issued a comprehensive 342-page report, with the labor members dissenting.

The railroads accepted the Commission's recommendations in

principle, but the five operating unions rejected them. The threat of a strike was postponed by the appointment of an emergency board, whose recommendations likewise the carriers accepted and the unions rejected. The Secretary of Labor and a special six-man subcommittee of the President's Advisory Committee on Labor-Management Policy tried to assist the negotiations. However, in the end, collective bargaining broke down completely, and the country was faced with the prospect of a crippling strike in August 1963 as the railroads and shippers made preparations for it.

The Council of Economic Advisers estimated that by the thirtieth day of a general railroad strike some 6,000,000 nonrailroad workers would have lost their jobs from such a strike, plus 700,000 railroad workers. Thus, unemployment would reach 15 per cent, and the decline in the Gross National Product would be nearly four times as great as the drop that occurred in the most severe postwar recession.[16]

To avoid such an economic catastrophe, President Kennedy recommended that Congress legislate a procedure that would have been equivalent to compulsory arbitration by the Interstate Commerce Commission. The Congress, however, passed a joint resolution that provided for compulsory arbitration of two of the issues in dispute by an *ad hoc* board appointed by the President. The two issues were whether firemen were needed in diesel locomotives in yard and freight service and what the crew consist or manning of trains should be. It was hoped that a binding arbitration ruling on those two issues would clear the way so that the parties could settle by collective bargaining other issues such as pay structure, arrangements for combined yard and road work, and employment security with technological and other changes. As explained in Chapter 8, the union members of the arbitration board dissented from the board's decision, and early in 1964 the unions were contesting the law and the decision in the courts. In the meantime, little genuine bargaining was occurring on the other issues, so that compulsory arbitration threatened to be necessary also for their settlement.

Experience indicates the need for revision of the emergency

---

[16] See the text of President Kennedy's message to Congress on the work-rules dispute in *The New York Times*, July 23, 1963, p. 12.

disputes procedure of the Railway Labor Act. It has been overused (the superfluous emergency board in the work-rules case was No. 154), and recently the availability and predictability of the procedure has discouraged collective bargaining. Generally, top management on the railroads has favored compulsory arbitration. The railroad unions are opposed to binding decisions by arbitrators, insisting that reliance must be placed on collective bargaining. However, the pattern of their actions in recent years and particularly in the work-rules case extending over four years, has discouraged faith in the bargaining process in the railroad industry.

The Taft-Hartley Act

The emergency disputes provisions of the Taft-Hartley Act were influenced by the experience in the year before its passage when President Truman used fact-finding with recommendation extensively to meet the immediate postwar strike wave. Industry had objected to the use and composition of such boards. Therefore, the act as drafted forbade any recommendations and set forth a rigid procedure from which the President cannot deviate. A new step—employee voting on the employer's last offer—was written into the act on the assumption that it would reveal the membership to be more anxious to settle the strike than the leadership.

Out of experience, Senator Taft became convinced that the last-offer vote was a mistake, and that a board of inquiry should be empowered to offer recommendations for settlement of the dispute. Despite widespread opinion among students of the subject that the emergency disputes provisions of the law are ill-conceived and need revision, they have not been amended. Consensus on an alternative proposal has been lacking.

By stipulating a single procedure with a rigid timetable, the act gives the President only the choice of invoking it or not. The series of steps under the act is predictable, with no variation to meet the special circumstances of a particular dispute. The opposing parties can plan their bargaining strategy with the certainty of those steps in mind.

PROVISIONS. The mandatory sequence of steps under Sections 206 to 210 of the act are as follows:

1. The President may appoint a board of inquiry if he believes that a strike "affecting an entire industry or a substantial part thereof" will imperil the national health and safety.

2. The board makes a report on the dispute, which cannot include recommendations.

3. The President may then direct the Attorney General to seek an injunction to prevent or stop the strike for eighty days, and the Federal district court issues the injunction, providing it believes that the strike does threaten the national health and safety.

4. During the next sixty days the Federal Mediation and Conciliation Service is to attempt to mediate the dispute.

5. Upon the issuance of the injunction, the President reconvenes the board of inquiry, which at the end of the sixty-day period, reports on the current positions of the parties and the employer's last offer of settlement.

6. The National Labor Relations Board conducts a secret ballot among the workers as to whether they wish to accept the employer's last offer; the vote, however, is informational and not, in any way, binding.

7. At the expiration of eighty days from its issuance, the injunction must be dissolved, whether or not the dispute has been settled; the employees are then free to strike.

8. The President submits to Congress a full report of the proceedings, together with any recommendations he may have for appropriate action.

It is evident that the injunction releases the parties from economic pressure during the eighty-day period. The respective roles of the Federal Mediation and Conciliation Service and the board of inquiry during the sixty-day period are unclear in the law. The vote on the employer's "final offer of settlement" substitutes a political campaign for further collective bargaining on the assumption that union officers may not correctly represent their constituents. No similar vote is taken to see whether corporation officers correctly represent their stockholders.

The procedure really ends with the vote. When rejection of the employer's "final" offer occurs, as is probable since workers are not likely to repudiate their representatives in the course of contract negotiations, the union's negotiators naturally consider that they have a mandate from the rank and file to insist on terms more favorable than those rejected in the ballot. The result of the vote, therefore, is to freeze the positions of the disputing parties so as to make settlement more difficult. At a time when they are deadlocked by the vote, the injunction must be lifted. Unlike the practice under the Railway Labor Act, there is no assurance that the terms finally agreed upon will be retroactive to the time when the old agreement expired or notification was given of a desired change in the agreement.

EXPERIENCE.   By the end of 1963, the national emergency disputes section of the act had been invoked on twenty-three different occasions. President Truman applied it ten times in five years, President Eisenhower seven times in eight years, and President Kennedy six times in three years. The industries in which the national emergency disputes provisions of the law have been most frequently utilized are: ocean transportation (East and West Coast longshore and maritime), seven times; atomic energy, five times; bituminous coal, three times in the period 1948–50; and the aerospace industry three times in 1962 and 1963. In some cases (meatpacking, telephones, and one instance in coal and atomic energy) the dispute was settled before an injunction was issued.

In the twelve instances where a "last offer" ballot has occurred, the employees have overwhelmingly voted for rejection, except for the West Coast longshoremen who completely boycotted the vote. Generally, the unions have been able thereafter to negotiate a superior settlement. Strikes of varying length (up to ten weeks) followed the lifting of the injunction in five instances, and in parts of an industry in a few other cases brief strikes resulted because of delays in settlement.

Experience has clearly indicated the weaknesses in the Taft-Hartley provisions for national emergency disputes.[17] A single procedure is ill-suited for the variety of actual cases that have occurred. A predetermined sequence of steps permits the parties

---

[17] For a good discussion of these weaknesses, see Joel Seidman, "National Emergency Strike Legislation" and the discussion of Seidman's paper in Ralph Slovenko (ed.), *Symposium on Labor Law* (Baton Rouge, Louisiana: Claitor's Bookstore Publishers, 1961), pp. 473–514.

to anticipate developments and to plan their strategy accordingly. The party expecting to gain from use of the procedure has an incentive to avoid settlement by collective bargaining before the eighty-day injunction is issued under the act. The function of the board of inquiry is so routine that it lacks the stature needed for effective settlement efforts. The injunction eliminates the incentive to settle by withdrawing the threat of economic loss for that period, and could even promise economic gain by the lack of provision for retroactive settlement. The "last offer" ballot interjects a political campaign into the proceedings and then freezes the position of the two parties just at the time when, with the injunction soon to be lifted, serious bargaining should begin.

The 116-day steel strike in 1959 well illustrates some of the defects in the Taft-Hartley provisions. In anticipation of a strike, the industry built up a large stockpile in the first half of 1959. Prior to the start of the strike on July 15, bargaining had been largely perfunctory. Also little bargaining progress was made during the first two and a half months while the accumulated inventories were used up and the parties sparred with each other and the government.[18] Then economic pressures began to operate, and on October 2 the industry made its first offer involving any increase in wages. The union rejected the offer. A board of inquiry entered the dispute and an injunction was requested; thereupon a legal contest began over the issue of whether the statute was applicable in such a dispute. When the Supreme Court upheld the injunction on November 7, the strike ceased. However, the negotiations returned to their more perfunctory character now that the economic pressures had been withdrawn.

With a vote on the employer's last offer scheduled for January 11–13, the parties turned their attention to that contest. As they did so, new types of pressures began to operate on the industry. Private sample polls showed that the workers would vote 90 to 95 per cent to reject the last offer. Vice-President Nixon indicated that, in case of a resumption of the strike following such a vote, Congressional opinion would be antiindustry and the

---

[18] See *Collective Bargaining in the Basic Steel Industry, A Study of the Public Interest and the Role of Government,* United States Department of Labor, January 1961 (Washington: United States Government Printing Office, 1961), pp. 300–307 for a summary account of the 1959 steel dispute.

Administration would be unable to protect the companies against hostile legislation. In addition, under the escalator clause of the old agreement extended by the injunction, it seemed likely that the employees would automatically get four cents per hour increase in mid-January, which would be outside any settlement. Under those circumstances Vice-President Nixon and Secretary of Labor Mitchell were able to work out a settlement, entirely outside the Taft-Hartley Act, that avoided a last-offer vote. The settlement, based on the Nixon-Mitchell formula, was announced on January 4.

Choice of Procedures

Perhaps more students of the subject favor a "choice of procedures" arrangement for handling emergency disputes than support any other approach. For example, an independent study group of nine experts in 1961 recommended a program that would equip the President with a variety of possible courses of action.[19] In 1955, Arthur J. Goldberg and W. Willard Wirtz, both of whom later became Secretary of Labor, favored the choice-of-procedures approach.[20] Partly as a result of experience under the Slichter law in Massachusetts, John F. Kennedy in the 1960 Presidential campaign advocated a number of possible courses of action as a program for handling national emergency disputes.

Under the choice-of-procedures method, the law would provide the President with the authority to use a variety of possible measures. He would be free to select one or more courses of action that would best fit the circumstances of the particular dispute. The President could determine the timing and sequence of the measures or he could decide not to use any of them. Among the battery of possible courses of action might be mediation, fact-finding with any recommendations released at the President's discretion, a hearing at which the parties would explain why they are

---

[19] See *The Public Interest in National Labor Policy*, Committee for Economic Development, New York, 1961, pp. 97–104.

[20] See Arthur J. Goldberg and Jack Barbash, "Labor Looks at the National Emergency Provisions," and W. Willard Wirtz, "The 'Choice-of-Procedures' Approach to National Emergency Disputes," in Irving Bernstein, *et al.*, *Emergency Disputes and National Policy* (New York: Harper, 1955), pp. 114–18 and 149–65.

not willing to submit the dispute to voluntary arbitration, arrangements for emergency operation of part of the facilities by the government, seizure, injunction, and authority for the President to submit recommendations to the Congress at any stage.

In practice, such selectivity and flexibility could have a number of advantages. The President's action would be unpredictable, thus creating uncertainty and discouraging the parties from relying on any particular government action as a calculated part of their bargaining strategy. The President could tailor-make his intervention to fit the needs of the situation and could change his method of intervention if the situation altered. Alternatives to select from would enable the President to put a greater variety of pressures on the parties to settle their dispute by collective bargaining. It would permit considerable experimentation, and avoid the danger inherent in a single procedure, namely, that it will become discredited with unsatisfactory experience.

Statutory provision for a choice among a number of alternative measures has the possible disadvantage that a President may be too quick to intervene and use his powers, or that he may be able to put too much pressure on one of the parties. Flexibility means latitude of discretion; the President is also the head of a political party. Those who worry about the power of the executive and of the Federal Government may oppose arming the President with what appears to be additional powers.

1. THE MASSACHUSETTS LAW. The prime example of a choice-of-procedures statute is the so-called Slichter law enacted in Massachusetts in 1947. The main provisions of the law were part of the comprehensive recommendations of a nine-man, tripartite committee, with Professor Sumner Slichter as chairman, which the Governor appointed to make a careful study of industrial relations problems in the State. The act covers the production and distribution of food, fuel, water, electric light and power, gas, and hospital and medical services. It makes available four procedures which the Governor may use as alternatives or in series. They are: (1) Require the parties to appear before a skilled moderator to show cause why they should not submit the dispute to arbitration. (2) Request the parties to agree to submit the dispute to a tripartite fact-finding board with power of recommendation. (3) If

steps 1 and 2 fail or are not deemed appropriate, the Governor may arrange with either or both parties for continuing enough of the operations to provide the goods or services necessary for public health and safety. (4) The Governor may seize any facilities of parties to the dispute and have the government operate them. During seizure, various alternatives are provided with respect to the determination of wages and the income from the seized property. While under State operation, it is unlawful to strike or encourage striking. The seizure ends when the parties notify the Governor that they have settled the dispute, or when the Governor decides it is no longer necessary.

The Massachusetts law has been invoked on six occasions, twice in 1948 and four times in 1953.[21] Each procedural step in the law has been used, and in the six cases a wide variety of action was applied. Apparently, the law has not discouraged collective bargaining, although its frequent use in 1953 was beginning to cause concern on that score. Since then Governors have been restrained in its use, and, of course, now supervisors can operate facilities for considerable periods of time. Four of the six disputes were settled by collective bargaining after government intervention, and two were resolved by voluntary arbitration.

2. STATUS OF STATE LAWS.   The Massachusetts law has neither been defied or challenged in the courts. However, other State laws restricting the right to strike have been declared unconstitutional by the United States Supreme Court in so far as they apply to operations "affecting" interstate commerce. As already mentioned, the Court has held that the Taft-Hartley Act preempts such coverage, and, therefore, strike-restricting statutes in Wisconsin, Florida, Indiana, Minnesota, Michigan, and Missouri were declared invalid because they conflicted with the rights and duties conferred by the Taft-Hartley law.

Since the Federal act applies only to national emergency disputes, local emergency strikes are not covered by statute. Also, the present constitutional and statutory restrictions on State legis-

---

[21] The most complete study of experience under the Massachusetts law is George P. Shultz, "The Massachusetts Choice-of-Procedures Approach to Emergency Disputes," *Industrial and Labor Relations Review*, X (April 1957), pp. 359–74.

lation prevent further experimentation by that means. Experience and legal opinion seem to indicate that, in view of recent technological and other developments, the public could be given sufficient protection against crippling local strikes under the powers inherent in the office of Governor.[22]

SUMMARY

1. Since the twenties, strike statistics here and abroad show a downward trend. The declining trend in most of our strike-prone industries is explained by various factors including the settling-down of union-management relations, the development of strike substitutes, and increased central control of strike decisions.

2. Government intervention may aim at stopping the strike, helping to settle the issues in dispute, or both. For those purposes, each method of intervention has its strong and weak points.

3. Experience and analysis indicate that a program of government-conducted strike votes would tend to increase the number and duration of strikes.

4. The problem of national emergency disputes raises many complicated issues. Government intervention in such strikes is an art. A rigid, mandatory procedure may discourage collective bargaining and hamper settlement efforts by the President.

5. The emergency-disputes procedure of the Railway Labor Act worked well for fifteen years but since World War II has often served to postpone collective bargaining and encourage lengthy proceedings before presidentially appointed boards. In the work-rules dispute (1959–63), collective bargaining broke down completely, and the Congress legislated arrangements for compulsory arbitration of two major issues.

6. Experience has demonstrated that the emergency disputes sections of the Taft-Hartley Act badly need revision. The last-offer vote generally impedes settlement of a dispute.

7. Much expert opinion supports a choice-of-procedures statute similar to the Slichter law in place of the present emergency disputes provisions of the Taft-Hartley Act.

---

[22] See *Report to Governor Robert B. Meyner by the Governor's Committee on Legislation Relating to Public Utility Labor Disputes*, Trenton, New Jersey, September 9, 1954.

DISCUSSION QUESTIONS

1. How do you explain the declining trend of strikes in this country since the 1920's? Indicate the weight that you place on various factors in your explanation.
2. Explain the advantages and limitations of the different methods of government intervention in labor disputes.
3. How do you explain that each session of the Congress a number of bills are introduced to require a government-conducted strike vote either before a strike can occur or after it has commenced?
4. How would you determine whether and when a major strike had resulted in a national emergency?
5. Discuss the advantages and disadvantages of a program of compulsory arbitration for the railroad industry.
6. Evaluate the emergency disputes provisions of the Taft-Hartley Act. In what ways would you recommend revision of those sections of the act?
7. Contrast the differences in the emergency disputes provisions of the Railway Labor Act and the Taft-Hartley Act. What justification, if any, is there for such differences?

SELECTED REFERENCES

Bernstein, Irving, Harold L. Enarson, and R. W. Fleming (eds.), *Emergency Disputes and National Policy* (New York: Harper, 1955).

Cole, David L., *The Quest for Industrial Peace* (New York: McGraw-Hill, 1963).

Kornhauser, Arthur, Robert Dubin, and Arthur M. Ross (eds.), *Industrial Conflict* (New York: McGraw-Hill, 1954).

Northrup, Herbert R., and Gordon F. Bloom, *Government and Labor, The Role of Government in Union-Management Relations* (Homewood, Ill.: Irwin, 1963).

Ross, Arthur M., and Paul T. Hartman, *Changing Patterns of Industrial Conflict* (New York: Wiley, 1960).

The Public Interest in National Labor Policy, by an Independent Study Group (New York: Committee for Economic Development, 1961).

16.
Minimum Wage and
Fair Employment Laws

THIS CHAPTER IS concerned with government policy
with respect to inequities in the wage structure and discrimination
in employment. It analyzes legislation and executive action with
respect to minimum wages, equal or nondiscriminatory pay scales,
and fair or equal employment opportunities regardless of race or
other nonmerit factors.

ECONOMIC BACKGROUND

To a considerable extent the analysis in this chapter rests on
two concepts developed in Chapters 7, 9, and 10: (1) the model
of community wage structures that postulates genuine interfirm
wage differentials within a range of 10 to 15 per cent for hiring-in
and other jobs; and (2) a multipurpose, multiadjustment theory of
the firm, which assumes strong pressures to use output capacity
and a variety of channels of adjustment, including improvement in
efficiency through development of the existing work force.

Although the areas of impact of the three types of legislation (minimum wage, equal pay, and fair employment practices) overlap, the universe of significantly affected employment and firms is somewhat different for each. Minimum-wage action affects most extensively female employment in low-paying industries and areas. In the case of equal pay laws, the impact appears to be greater for female employment in office work, including fairly large firms like banks and insurance companies, than it is for female factory employment. The discrimination against which fair employment practices programs are directed is largely racial and is spread throughout the economy; corrective action has been aimed primarily at prominent firms and especially those working on government contracts. The kinds of competition and possibilities of adjustment as well as the social and institutional barriers to correction are, therefore, somewhat different for the bulk of the employment covered by each program.

Common Basis for Legislation

Nevertheless, the three programs have a common economic basis. It is the looseness, or play, in the processes of wage determination and employment allocation that permits discrimination to occur and to continue undiminished within a range of tolerance. Economic factors do not enforce a single wage rate for the same grade of labor in a locality; rather the normal situation is variation within a range.

With respect to discrimination in hiring, training, and promotion on the basis of race, sex, or nationality, economic factors are not sufficiently effective to overcome social barriers and weaknesses in bargaining power. The tolerance factors in employment discrimination are somewhat like those for work hours discussed in Chapter 12. Market forces do not operate with sufficient effectiveness and precision in the labor area to penalize significantly firms that fail to follow a policy of hiring, training, and promotion on the basis of merit alone, any more than they have operated to eliminate firms that worked employees beyond the optimum number of hours a week, or those firms that have been uneconomically affected by seniority provisions. Where a condition is fairly general in the labor area, market forces have not usually been good correctors.

Experience indicates that normally there is enough play, or latitude, to permit some inefficiency or variation in policy. Partly, such play exists because differences in the innate qualities of work forces may not be as important for efficiency over a period of time as the training and supervision that they have on the job. Many investigators have noted wide differences in output in plants having the same equipment and quite similar work forces.

General elimination of social barriers or ancient prejudices may contribute to more efficient operations for all in the long run. However, there may be transitional costs to the individual firm in the short run, which may prove high for firms that attempt to pioneer in breaking barriers. The size of such transitional costs may be greatly reduced by a national program that affects attitudes generally and lowers barriers by law. Then managements may no longer be stymied by the fear of the short-run difficulties and costs they would incur by strict application of merit factors.

Approaches to Governmental Action

Those who support legislation to establish minimum wages, equal pay for both sexes, and equal employment opportunity regardless of race, do so because they lack faith in the efficacy of market forces in these areas. They contend that, given the inherent and growing limitations on competition in the labor field, such legislation can lead, and generally has led, to a more efficient allocation and use of labor resources. They would claim that all race and sex discrimination in employment and pay that is not justified on individual merit grounds has an adverse effect on the nation's Gross National Product.[1] And they would contend that government fixing of minimum-wage standards leads to improvements in management,

---

[1] In 1962, the Council of Economic Advisers made estimates of the economic loss to the United States resulting from racial discrimination on two different bases: (1) failure to use currently in work the existing skills of nonwhites as fully as those of whites with the same education, and (2) failure to develop, through education, potential skills for nonwhites as much as for whites. On the first basis (elimination of discrimination on the basis of current skills and assuming nonwhites had the same labor-force participation and employment rates as whites), the Council estimated that GNP would be increased by about $13 billion. On the second basis, the estimate was an additional $17 billion increase in GNP. See *Economic Costs of Racial Discrimination in Employment*, Council of Economic Advisers, Executive Office of the President, Washington, D.C., September 24, 1962, 9 pp.

in the productivity of the affected workers, and in total consumer spending, all of which have beneficial effects on GNP.
Furthermore, employment discrimination, pay inequities, and substandard wages are an affront to human dignity and help to create
social costs in terms of crime, poor health, and poverty breeding
poverty.

The supporters of such legislation generally favor collective
bargaining also, because of the limitations and ineffectiveness of
competition in the labor area. To a considerable extent, they insist
that legislation is needed because the groups directly affected by
minimum-wage and equal-pay laws are, for the most part, not covered by collective bargaining. In the case of racial discrimination
in employment, collective bargaining has been rather limited in its
effectiveness, especially in some of the skilled trades. Because the
bargaining is between employers and unions, employees excluded
for racial reasons have had no representation in the bargaining
sessions.

The opponents of legislative action, especially at the Federal
level, stress the results of "the normal functioning of a free-market
economy."[2] Generally, they agree with such objectives as equal
pay for equal work, wages equal to the full value of the work
performed, and nondiscrimination in employment on account of
race, sex, or other nonmerit factors. They object, however, to governmental intervention as unnecessary because of the efficacy of
competition and as positively harmful because it introduces political considerations and interposes artificial obstructions to the functioning of a free-market economy. They base their reasoning on
the marginal productivity theory of wages and the traditional
theory of the firm. Thus, they assume that such legislation raises
employer costs by force of law. However, since employers cannot
be compelled to pay workers more than they are worth, the result
is likely to be disemployment of some workers and a less efficient
allocation and use of labor resources, resulting in a lower GNP.

Obviously, there is a basic difference in economic philosophy
and approach between those who would rely on competition and
those who would have the government intervene on the grounds
of market limitations. In between the extreme views, there is plenty

---

[2] See, for example, *The Economics of Minimum Wage Legislation*, A Report
of the Committee on Economic Policy, Chamber of Commerce of the United
States, Washington, D.C., June 1947, p. 5.

of room for more moderate positions. Employers recognize that they have some discretion or flexibility in setting wages and in the selection, training, and promotion of employees.[3] And most supporters of such legislation recognize that government requirements can have injurious effects on costs and employment if carried to an extreme.

LEGAL MINIMUM WAGES

Before analyzing the economics of minimum standards by law for the bottom of the wage structure, it may be desirable to consider the purposes and methods of legal minimum-wage determination and to review the steps that have been taken by the States and the Federal Government. In this complex subject it is necessary to avoid some of the pitfalls discussed in Chapter 2.

Aims and Methods

Minimum-wage laws generally serve a number of purposes. Supporters advocate such legislation in order to (1) establish a floor below which competition cannot depress wages and upset wage standards followed by reputable firms; (2) bring more order into the ragged lower tenth of the rate range by requiring that a few low-paying employers meet the minimum of "going and tested rates" paid by other employers for comparable work in the locality or industry; (3) eliminate "exploitation" of workers with weak bargaining power and thus prevent discrimination or dual pay structures on the basis of race or sex; (4) raise the productivity of low-paid workers by improving their income and living standards, by stimulating management to adopt the more efficient production methods in use elsewhere, or by causing a shift of the work to more efficient plants; and (5) help expand the economy by increasing the purchasing power of low-income workers and thus raise total spending for consumption.

For some of those purposes, a single, statutory minimum is a

---

[3] If market forces fully determined wages and the allocation of employment, there would be little point in employers making periodic wage surveys, introducing and administering job evaluation programs, and relying on subjective interviewing rather than objective tests to select out "our type of employee."

blunt and only partly effective instrument. It is, however, used by the Federal Government for a number of practical reasons.

The alternative utilized in about half of the States is the industry-board method, under which a separate minimum is established for each industry or industry grouping. A tripartite board, with equal industry, labor, and public members, is appointed. It holds hearings, studies a survey of wage rates in the industry, and recommends a minimum or a number of minima (by size of city, branch of industry, etc.) to a State official, who subsequently issues a wage order based on the board's recommendation. In that way the minimum wage is tailored to economic conditions and wage scales in the industry and generally has the support of important elements in industry's management as well as labor. The chief drawbacks of the industry-board method are expense, delay, and restricted coverage. It takes time and appropriations to make a wage survey and to go through all of the procedures, and in the end only a minimum for that one industry is established.

Historical Development

Massachusetts adopted the first minimum-wage law in 1912. By the time the United States Supreme Court ruled a District of Columbia law unconstitutional in 1923,[4] some seventeen States had enacted such legislation. These State laws, because of AFL opposition to coverage of men and constitutional doubts about such coverage, applied only to women and children. In 1937, the Supreme Court reversed itself and declared a Washington State law constitutional.[5] In 1940, twenty-six States and the District of Columbia had minimum-wage laws. By 1963, some thirty-four States had minimum-wage laws on their statute books, but in six States the law is either inoperative or practically ineffective. In fourteen States there is a statutory minimum, and in fifteen the laws now apply to men as well as women.

State laws probably apply to no more than a third of their potential coverage. Wage orders are commonly issued for such industries as retail trade, laundries and dry cleaning, and hotels and

---

[4] *Adkins* v. *Children's Hospital,* 226 U.S. 525 (1923).
[5] *West Coast* v. *Parrish,* 300 U.S. 370 (1937).

restaurants. Some States like New York, Massachusetts, New Jersey, Pennsylvania, Washington, and California have tended to keep their minimums up to date, but in many others the minimums are obsolete and, therefore, ineffective.

Before enactment of the Fair Labor Standards Act of 1938, the Congress passed two minimum-wage laws of a different type. The Davis-Bacon Act, adopted in 1931, provides that the Secretary of Labor shall determine the prevailing minimum-wage rates that must be paid to various crafts by contractors engaged on Federal construction projects. The Walsh-Healey Act, adopted in 1936, stipulates the same sort of procedure for Federal contracts for nonconstruction items in excess of $10,000. The Secretary of Labor has generally adopted as "prevailing" wages the rates in collective agreements where they apply to a considerable portion of the industry. Recently, there has been a strong effort by labor to amend the Walsh-Healey Act to include "prevailing benefits."

The Fair Labor Standards Act was conceived in part as an antidepression measure. Commonly known as the Wage and Hour Law, it aimed at spreading work by a forty-hour week and eliminating child labor, as well as placing a floor under wages in order to prevent any downward spiral in the recession of 1938. In addition, it was designed to eliminate substandard wages "as rapidly as practicable" in covered industries "without substantially curtailing employment."

To achieve those objectives, the act originally established a statutory minimum of twenty-five cents an hour beginning in October 1938 and of thirty cents an hour commencing in October 1939. From then until October 1945, industry committees were to raise minimums, industry by industry, as rapidly as economically feasible to forty cents an hour, which was to be the effective statutory minimum beginning October 24, 1945. The Administrator estimated that, for reasons probably traceable to the initial effect of the act, between 30,000 and 50,000 persons lost their jobs at least temporarily, but he pointed out that from September to November 1938 employment covered by the act rose slightly more than the normal seasonal increase.

World War II soon made the thirty- and forty-cent minimums obsolete. However, the statutory rates of twenty-five and thirty cents created substantial unemployment in Puerto Rico and the

Virgin Islands, especially in the needle trades. Therefore, the act was amended to provide for minimum wages set by industry committees in those two areas, but elsewhere there has been no provision for industry committees since 1945.

Since World War II, the statutory minimum has been changed every five years. In 1949, it was raised to 75 cents, in 1956 to $1.00, and in 1961 to $1.15, with the proviso that it would be increased to $1.25 in September 1963. Noteworthy is the fact that in each of those years the new minimum was just about half of the average hourly earnings in manufacturing. When the minimums were raised in 1956 and 1961, it was estimated that approximately two million of the twenty-four million covered workers (or one-twelfth) were being paid less than the new minimum and, therefore, had their wages raised by it.

The 1961 amendments brought an estimated 3.6 million employees under the law. Coverage was extended to retail and service establishments with sales of one million dollars a year (except hotels, motels, restaurants, and other food-service enterprises) and to firms over a certain size in such lines as construction, gasoline stations, and local transit. It was estimated that 663,000 of those newly covered employees were currently being paid less than $1.00 an hour. In order to permit their employers to adjust without too great an impact on labor costs and employment, the amendments provided that the statutory minimum for new coverage would be $1.00 an hour until September 1963, and would increase to $1.15 in September 1964 and $1.25 in September 1965. The coverage of the act with the 1961 amendments amounted to 27,500,000, with some 17,500,000 of potential coverage expressly excluded.[6] The Administrator can permit learners, apprentices, and handicapped workers to be paid rates below the statutory minimums.

Analysis of Economic Effects

A uniform national minimum-wage law affects significantly only certain low-wage manufacturing industries. Among them are: cotton shirts and cotton hosiery, wooden boxes and wooden furniture, food processing, tobacco stemming, leather footwear, fertilizer,

---

[6] The exclusions include agriculture and the processing of agricultural products, laundry and dry cleaning, auto sales and service, hospitals, employers of less than twelve in logging, and small establishments in industries mentioned in the text.

small-scale logging and sawmill operations, and handmade cigars.

They are highly competitive industries. Operating on a small scale, entrance into the business is relatively easy, and nonunion competition presents a threat to labor standards. Much of the employment is likely to be on a short-term basis, closer to the commodity concept than to the company-welfare notion. Sometimes these low-wage industries are mistakenly referred to as "marginal" (the first ones to contract and disappear with an increase in cost or price). That, however, is misleading. In part, they produce essentials, for which the demand may be very inelastic.

The State laws generally cover service types of industry and types of manufacture not sufficiently in interstate commerce to come under the Fair Labor Standards Act. The services are mostly local-market in character—hotel, restaurant, laundry and dry cleaning, retail stores. For some of those services, the demand may be fairly elastic to price changes, because supply of the service by production in the home (i.e., meals or laundry) is an alternative.

Generally speaking, the low-wage industries come closest to competitive assumptions and high-wage industries are furthest away from them. Firms most affected by minimum-wage laws, therefore, are likely to be relatively small, to operate on narrow profit margins, to stress short-run profits, to be unable to raise selling prices (partly because they often are manufacturing unbranded products), to have little latitude of adjustment, to be nonunion, and to have relatively low investment in equipment per worker, so that the management may not need to be so concerned about retaining a well-trained workforce over a long period of time. The management's employment perspective or horizon may be comparatively short. Thus, the firms most affected by minimum-wage laws should provide quite favorable conditions for testing predictions based on the traditional theory of the firm and the marginal productivity theory of wages.[7]

1. UNEVEN IMPACT. Minimum-wage experience also provides favorable conditions for theory testing, since the impact on each

---

[7] For a further discussion of company conditions restricting or enlarging the possible channels of adjustment to a wage increase, see Richard A. Lester, "Economic Adjustments to Changes in Wage Differentials," in George W. Taylor and Frank C. Pierson. (eds.), *New Concepts in Wage Determination* (New York: McGraw-Hill, 1957.), esp. pp. 223–25.

firm is different and is confined in direct effect to the lowest section of the wage structure. As already explained, wage surveys show that pay scales differ considerably from firm to firm, both in the hiring-in pay for the bottom jobs and the structure of occupational differentials above the minimum. Consequently, an increase in the national legal minimum is equivalent to raising the wage floor by an unequal amount for firms in the same industry or locality and eliminating all interfirm differentials below that minimum. Although designed to indicate how an increase from 75 cents to $1.00 in the national minimum in March 1956 affected the structure of wages in an industry, Table 22 brings out the practical elimination of all pay below $1.00 an hour and the pushing of a whole scatter of rates up to that figure.

The lowest-paid jobs in a firm or an industry are the unskilled occupations—common labor, janitor, sweeper, stacker, hauler, yard labor, floor boys, and the like. Usually, no more than 3 to 5 per cent of the workforce of a firm or industry is paid at the minimum rate. Although jobs such as janitor may involve much the same work in various plants and industries, as explained in Chapter 10, significant interfirm and interindustry differentials exist, often without apparent justification in terms of employee qualifications.[8] A high proportion of the lowest-paid workers are women, whose bargaining power is weak.[9]

In terms of market forces, no good reason would seem to exist for wage rates above the new minimum to be disturbed by an increase in the minimum, say, from 75 cents to $1.00. Presumably, the rise in the wage floor has not reduced the supply of, or increased the demand for, workers in those higher-paying jobs, unless substitution of machinery for unskilled labor should sufficiently expand the demand for more skilled labor to man the new equipment, and that is not likely to occur within a few months.[10] Also,

---

[8] Even in the same firm there may be race or sex differentials unwarranted in terms of worker productivity. Before World War II, it was common to pay Negro janitors in Southern cotton textile mills five cents an hour less than white janitors, even though they did not differ in output.

[9] Only about one-eighth of all women in gainful employment are in unions. The difference that organization may make is indicated by wage scales in the laundry industry in cases where the drivers of laundry trucks are organized by the Teamsters' union. In some instances, the high drivers' wages seem to be partly at the cost of especially low wages for female plant employees.

[10] For a similar view, see Harry M. Douty, "Some Effects of the $1.00 Minimum Wage in the U.S.," *Economica*, XXVII (May 1960), pp. 142–43.

the job rates for skilled craftsmen are frequently occupationally oriented and vary less widely between firms than unskilled rates, often because of the influence of craft unions. Rather than pressure from market forces, the pressures to raise rates above the new minimum generally stem from such factors as workers' insistence on preservation of male-female and occupational wage differentials, management's desire to maintain the integrity of a job-evaluation plan and ladders of promotion, or management's worry about adverse effects on workers' loyalty and susceptibility to unionization.

Because an increase in the legal minimum directly affects only a minor fraction of the labor force, such changes have had a relatively small impact on total costs, total employment, or total income and consumption. According to estimates, the 1956 increase from 75 cents to $1.00 an hour under the Fair Labor Standards Act necessitated an addition of $560,000,000 to the annual wage bill in order to bring low-wage workers up to the $1.00 hourly minimum. That increase represented only 0.7 per cent of the yearly total of wages paid to all workers covered by the Act.[11]

The increase in the national minimum in 1961 from $1.00 to $1.15 was estimated to have required an addition of $336,000,000 in wages for 1.9 million workers out of the twenty-four million already covered. Extending coverage to 3.6 million more workers at $1.00 an hour minimum was estimated to have added $200,000,000 to the wages of 663,000 workers. In terms of percentage of the total annual wage bill, those additions amounted to 0.3 per cent for previously covered workers and 1.5 per cent for the newly covered. Of course, for specific low-wage industries, the increase in the wage bill as a direct result of raising wages to the new minimum was a considerably larger percentage of each industry's yearly payroll; for a few industries, the increase from 75 cents to $1.00 in 1956 required an addition to the industry's total wage bill of 20 to 25 per cent. Of course, for some individual firms in those lowest-wage industries, the percentage was even higher.

2. POSSIBLE EFFECTS ON WAGES. Elaborate studies were made of wage distributions for thirteen low-wage industries and seven

---

[11] The estimates in this and the next paragraph are from Arthur J. Goldberg *Report Submitted to Congress in Accordance with the Requirements of Section 4(d) of the Fair Labor Standards Act,* United States Department of Labor, January 1962, p. 3.

low-wage communities before and after the increase in the minimum from 75 cents to $1.00 in March 1956 under the Fair Labor Standards Act.

The distribution in Table 22 for the men's seamless hosiery industry is typical of the changes that occurred between August 1955 and August 1957, and especially between February and April

TABLE 22

Percentage Distribution by Average Hourly Earnings of Workers in Men's Seamless Hosiery before and after $1 Minimum Wage in March 1956

Average Hourly Earnings	Aug. 1955	Feb. 1956	April 1956	April 1957
Under 75 cents	0.5	0.4	0.1	0.1
75 and under 76	12.2	7.6	—	—
76 and under 80	4.4	2.6	.1	.2
80 and under 85	8.8	7.3	.5	.6
85 and under 90	8.4	6.5	.5	.5
90 and under 95	8.0	7.8	.4	.3
95 and under 100	7.0	7.0	.2	.2
100 and under 101	—	—	26.8	22.7
101 and under 105	8.1	10.8	7.4	7.0
105 and under 110	5.9	7.2	11.3	11.2
110 and under 115	5.7	6.8	9.6	9.5
115 and under 120	4.6	5.2	6.5	7.3
120 and under 125	3.8	4.4	5.4	6.2
125 and under 150	13.1	15.4	18.3	19.6
150 and over	9.5	11.1	12.8	14.8
Total	100.0	100.0	100.0	100.0
Under $1.00	49.3	39.2	1.8	1.9
$1.00 and under $1.01	—	—	26.8	22.7
Over $1.00	50.7	60.8	71.4	75.4
Average	$ 1.06	$ 1.11	$ 1.20	$ 1.22

Source: *Studies of the Economic Effects of the $1 Minimum Wage, Effects in Selected Low Wage Industries and Localities,* Wage and Hour and Public Contracts Divisions, United States Department of Labor, January 1959, Appendix Table F–3.

1956. It is evident from Table 22 that during those two months a marked change occurred in the proportion of the workforce in that industry who were paid less than $1.00 an hour. Some increases also occurred in the percentages in the wage classifications above

$1.00. However, it is evident from the percentage figures and those for average hourly earnings, that workers receiving above $1.00 an hour in February 1956 got increases averaging less than one-third as much in cents as were received by workers paid under $1.00 an hour that month. Clearly, wage increases were generally omitted or tapered off for most workers in the middle and upper wage brackets.

With respect to the minimum-wage increase to $1.15 an hour in September 1961 (and the establishment of $1.00 minimum for the new coverage), the Secretary of Labor reported that "where the increase had maximum impact, only a portion of the work force was affected" and the higher minimum did not generate "any appreciable increase in higher wage industries."[12] Consequently, the increase in average straight-time hourly earnings in nondurable manufacturing industries (the sector most affected by the minimum wage changes) was only four cents per hour from August to December 1961, whereas the August-December rise in the preceding year had been five cents despite a significant decline in industrial production. Secretary Goldberg pointed out that a rise less than that in the corresponding months a year earlier showed "the relatively slight impact of the minimum wage increases on the national wage structure."[13]

Apparently, wage increases up to the minimum in covered industries have little tendency to spread to noncovered industries. Studies of the effects of the $1.00 minimum in seven low-wage communities or cities[14] showed that increases in average hourly earnings in industries subject to the Fair Labor Standards Act were not accompanied by similar increases in industries not covered by the act. In the three communities most affected by the $1.00 minimum, hourly earnings increased 10 to 11 per cent between February and April in the subject industries but only 1.1, 2.4, and minus 1.1 per cent in nonsubject industries. During the next year, earnings in the nonsubject industries rose more rapidly in two of the three communities but, for the whole period from February

---

[12] *Ibid.*, p. 4.

[13] *Ibid.*

[14] Dotham, Alabama; Athens, Georgia: Meridian, Mississippi; Hickory, North Carolina; Sunbury-Shamokin-Mt. Carmel, Pennsylvania; Dalton, Georgia; and Fort Smith, Arkansas, listed in the order of impact of the $1.00 minimum.

1956 to April 1957, the increase in hourly earnings in the three communities combined averaged 13.6 per cent for subject industries and 6.9 per cent for nonsubject industries.[15] However, where the bulk of an industry was covered by the act, the increase in the minimum did tend to bring the noncovered part of the industry up to the $1.00 figure.[16]

On the basis of competitive market reasoning, instead of a spread of the minimum from covered to noncovered industry, one would expect the disemployment from the wage increase in covered industry to intensify "the job-seeking competition" in noncovered industry and to press down wage rates there. So the United States Chamber of Commerce and others have argued.[17] Actually, in the seven low-wage communities studied, the experience was just the reverse. Between February 1956 and April 1957, the four communities experiencing a decline in employment in covered industries (averaging 4.7 per cent) had a combined increase in average hourly earnings of 7.8 per cent in nonsubject employment, whereas the three communities experiencing an increase in covered employment (averaging 9.1 per cent) had a combined increase in average hourly earnings of only 5.4 per cent in non-subject employment.[18]

3. POSSIBLE EFECTS ON PRODUCTIVITY. Because legal minimum wages have a restricted application and an uneven impact firm by

---

[15] See Louis E. Badenhoop, "Effects of the $1 Minimum Wage in Seven Areas," *Monthly Labor Review*, LXXXI (July 1958), p. 739; and *Studies of the Economic Effects of the $1 Minimum Wage, op. cit.*, Appendix M.

[16] For example, about a quarter of the fertilizer workers in the Southeast were in plants selling only intrastate and were, therefore, exempt from the act, yet in those exempt mills between April 1955 and April 1956 the proportion of workers receiving under $1.00 an hour declined from 83 to 27 per cent and their average hourly earnings rose by even a greater percentage than in the covered mills. See *Studies of the Economic Effects of the $1 Minimum Wage, op. cit.*, Appendix D, Table 3.

[17] See *The Economics of Minimum Wage Legislation*, A Report of the Committee on Economic Policy, Chamber of Commerce of the United States, Washington, D.C., June 1947, pp. 12, 14 and 33. For the same type of reasoning applied to union wage increases see Milton Friedman, 'Some Comments on the Significance of Labor Unions for Economic Policy," in David McC. Wright (ed.), *The Impact of the Union* (New York: Harcourt, Brace, 1951), p. 216; and Albert Rees, *The Economics of Trade Unions* (Chicago: University of Chicago Press, 1962), p. 74.

[18] The figures are simple averages of data in *Studies of the Economic Effects of the $1 Minimum Wage, op. cit.*, Appendix M.

firm, they serve to stimulate improvements in management and in worker performance. The lowest-wage firms, faced with an increase in their wages relative to those paid by the bulk of their competitors, are under pressure to improve plant organization and functioning so that their operations approach the efficiency of their unaffected or less affected competitors. Because the wage effects of a change in the legal minimum are differentiated between firms and between occupations in affected companies, they are much more likely to have a "shock" effect, stimulating improvements in management and labor performance, than would a general wage increase affecting an entire industry, a labor market area, or the whole economy.

Denial or neglect of the productivity-improving stimulus of legal minimums has vitiated the analysis and predictions of many critics of minimum wages.[19] As explained in Chapter 7, management's adjustment possibilities range far beyond those envisioned in the traditional theory of the firm. Experience with minimum-wage legislation has demonstrated that managements, even in highly competitive industries, may be inefficient and wasteful in some respects, perhaps partly because low wages permit them to be.

The relative wage impact on a firm from a minimum-wage increase can be offset or partially offset by a variety of improvements in management and in labor utilization. If increased productivity offsets the wage rise, labor costs per unit of output do not increase. Experience with the increase from 75 cents to $1.00 per hour in the Fair Labor Standards minimum in 1956 showed that management could increase productivity by such means as: improvements in plant lay-out and in the quality of line supervision; installation of labor-saving equipment and better use of machines and materials; better selection and training of workers; reduction in waste, such as excessive overtime and labor turnover; increased selling efforts in order to provide longer runs and lower overhead costs per unit of output; and higher production

---

[19] The pamphlet of the U.S. Chamber of Commerce on minimum wages suffers from neglect of the productivity effects of minimum wages. (See *The Economics of Minimum Wage Legislation, op. cit.*, pp. 20–21 and 32–34.) Reasoning on the basis of the traditional theory of the firm, George J. Stigler finds practically no room for a productivity effect. [See "The Economics of Minimum Wage Legislation," *American Economic Review*, XXXVI (June 1946), pp. 359–61.]

standards.[20] Of course, some of the improvements in management would have been made sooner or later without the stimulus of a new floor to wages. However, a rise in the legal minimum provides new pressure and opportunity for instituting cost-cutting actions while demonstrating that competitors have found ways to operate successfully on the new wage standard.[21]

A differentiated wage increase may also increase labor productivity by raising worker morale, improving living standards, and reducing absenteeism and voluntary turnover. Wages are supposed to be an incentive. In addition, such an increase in the wage floor provides management with a basis for insisting on higher standards of worker effort and discipline.

Effects on Employment

Marked differences of opinion have arisen with respect to the specific effects on employment attributable to minimum-wage increases. Some writers interpret the results of statistical studies as supporting the prediction of the traditional theory of the firm and orthodox wage theory that employment and wages are inversely related, that an increase in wages will lead to reduced employment. Other writers point to the same statistical studies as demonstrating that the orthodox competitive model lacks good predictive value within a "moderate" range of wage change (say an increase in the firm's wage costs up to 10 per cent).

Partly, writers draw different conclusions from the data be-

---

[20] See *Studies of the Economic Effects of the $1 Minimum Wage, op. cit.,* pp. 28, 47, 59, 79, 107, 141–42, 168, 254, 260, 277, 283, 288, and 294; Paul A. Brinker, "The $1.00 Minimum Wage Impact on 15 Oklahoma Industries," *Monthly Labor Review,* LXXX (September 1957), pp. 1092–95; and "Plant Adjustments to the $1.00 Minimum Wage," *Monthly Labor Review,* LXXXI (October 1958), pp. 1137–42. See also N. Arnold Tolles, "American Minimum Wage Laws: Their Purposes and Results," in *Proceedings of the Twelfth Annual Meeting of the Industrial Research Association,* published by the Association, Madison, Wisconsin, 1960, p. 130.

[21] In practice, it is difficult to distinguish cuts in labor cost as a result of a "shock" effect, which do not raise nonlabor costs, and cuts in labor costs that involve an increase in nonlabor costs and, therefore, result in some increase in total costs. Conceptually, it is desirable to distinguish between a production improvement that involves no net increase in costs and a change in production methods induced by a change in relative wages which does involve some increase in costs.

cause of the difficulty of isolating and determining the employment effects (or lack of them) caused solely by the minimum-wage change. A variety of factors besides the new wage floor may affect a firm's employment over a period of time. For example, technological change or foreign competition may be reducing employment in its industry, consumer demand for the firm's products may have an upward or downward trend, or the business cycle may cause temporary expansions or contractions in the firm's employment.

For an analysis based on comparisons of employment before and after the increase in the minimum, the time interval to use presents a problem. A relatively brief period has the drawback that it may be affected by an inventory build-up or some other transitory factor. In some industries, firms did expand employment to build up inventory in advance of the new $1.00 minimum, with a corresponding dip in employment right afterwards. On the other hand, a long period, although allowing sufficient time for such adjustments as plant and equipment changes or plant closings, tends to complicate the problem of eliminating the influence of other employment-affecting factors. Usually employment in identical plants is compared over the period, but obviously the new minimum could cause some plants to close and some new plants to open; also shifts of production among existing plants may occur for a variety of reasons. Therefore, the longer the period used for before-after comparisons, the more difficult it is to determine the employment effects attributable only to the change in the legal minimum.[22]

Perhaps the best that one can do is to present employment data for a series of dates and to seek to eliminate all factors that affect the industry as a whole. Such elimination can be practically accomplished by comparing employment of firms in one industry and region, grouped by the degree of impact of the new minimum wage. The degree of impact can be measured by the percentage increase required in a firm's average hourly earnings in order to comply with the new minimum.

---

[22] For a good discussion of the "hazards" of determining the effects of minimum wages on workers see Donald E. Cullen, *Minimum Wage Laws*, Bulletin 43, New York School of Industrial and Labor Relations at Cornell University, Ithaca, N.Y., February 1961.

1. INDUSTRY STUDIES. A comparison using that technique is presented in Table 23. It provides data for the thirteen lowest wage segments of manufacturing, selected by the Department of Labor for special study of the effects of raising the minimum under the Fair Labor Standards Act from 75 cents to $1.00 on March 1, 1956. The employment in the high-impact establishments is given as a percentage of the combined employment of all establishments included in the study. Thus, employment changes in high-impact establishments are being compared with employment changes in lower-impact establishments in the same sections of an industry.[23]

TABLE 23

Per Cent That Establishments Having High Impact from $1 Minimum in March 1956 Were of Total Employment, Identical Firms in Thirteen Industries, 1955–57

Industry and Area	Aug. 1955	Feb. 1956	April 1956	April 1957
1. Tobacco stemming and redrying, South	31.95*	n.a.†	31.64*	28.11*
2. Wood containers, South	32.98	33.12	32.65	32.73
3. Processed waste, South	37.79	36.53	32.59	30.71
4. Sawmills, South	30.35*	n.a.	29.06	27.89
5. Raw sugar, Louisiana	51.07	n.a.	51.15*	51.52*
6. Work shirts, Southeast	48.51	48.89	48.84	49.13
7. Fertilizer, South	16.38	n.a.	14.95	14.13
8. Men's seamless hosiery, Southeast	24.57	24.66	22.76	25.79
9. Children's seamless hosiery, Southeast	32.58	32.03	30.98	29.27
10. Men's dress shirts and nightwear, U.S.	n.a.	39.58	39.09	40.00*
11. Footwear, South and Border States	46.11	44.26	44.19	n.a.
12. Cigars, Southeast	n.a.	18.78	18.53	16.68
13. Citrus canning and freezing, Florida	n.a.	47.11*	46.08*	46.64*

* For tobacco, the time periods are September–January of each year; for sawmills, the first date is October–December 1955; for raw sugar, the time periods are November–December of each year; for men's dress shirts, the last column is for October 1956; for citrus canning and freezing, the time periods are January–February of each year.

† n.a. means data are not available.

Source: Percentages calculated from *Studies of the Economic Effects of the $1 Minimum Wage,* op. cit., Appendix Tables A–6, B–5, C–4, D–4, E–4, F–11, F–24, G–11, H–4, I–4, J–4, K–4, and L–9.

---

[23] The establishments are classified as high impact, middle impact, and low or no impact except in four industries (processed waste, raw sugar, footwear, and citrus canning) where only high- and low-impact categories are used. No regional breakdown is available for the men's dress shirt industry.

The listing in Table 23 is by order of required increase in average hourly earnings to meet the $1.00 minimum.[24]

It is evident from the percentages in Table 23 that experience differed considerably among those thirteen industries. They can perhaps be classified into three groups. The first group consists of industries in which the employment of the high-impact plants was practically constant over the period. That constant group seems to include five industries: wood containers, raw sugar, men's dress shirts, and citrus canning, although, for the last two, an August 1955 figure is not available, and if it were for men's dress shirts that industry might be in the increasing group. A second group consists of industries in which the high-impact establishments constituted a declining percentage of the industry throughout the whole period, for the half year from August 1955 to February 1956 before the minimum wage took effect as well as over the year thereafter. That second group seems to include seven industries: processed waste, children's seamless hosiery, footwear, and presumably also tobacco stemming, sawmills, fertilizer, and cigars, although the conclusion in their cases has to rest on only three figures. The third group includes industries in which the employment of the high-impact establishments represented a noticeably higher figure in August 1957 than the one two years earlier. That group seems to include work shirts and men's seamless hosiery, the figures for the latter in February and April 1956 having been noticeably affected by a building up of inventories prior to the effective date of the $1.00 minimum and a drawing down of inventories immediately thereafter.

With six industries in the constant and increasing groups and seven in the declining group, one can conclude that there is not a very consistent or predictable relationship between minimum-wage increases and the subsequent employment effects. Furthermore, where the employment of the high-impact group was declining during the six months prior to the new minimum (as was the case in the processed waste and footwear industries), the minimum wage may only have accelerated a trend. The high-impact

---

[24] To be included in the high-impact group, an establishment had to meet the standard of a certain percentage increase in average hourly earnings calculated as necessary for compliance with the $1.00 minimum. Those minimum percentages, in order of industry listing in the table, are: 26, 25, 22, 22, 20, 17, 14, 12, 12, 10, 7, 6, 4. The actual average increases required for the high-impact firms by industry in the same order were: 29, 28, 28, 26, 22, 21, 28, 18, 16, 17, 12, 14, and 8 per cent.

firms (which generally are smaller measured by number of employees) may have been a declining part of the industry.

The studies made in connection with the imposition of the $1.00 minimum under the Fair Labor Standards Act in 1956 provide a basis for the different type of comparison by impact groups in Table 24. That comparison is confined to the three industries from among the thirteen in Table 23, in which "high impact" was defined as having the establishment's average hourly earnings directly increased by at least 10 or 12 per cent as a result of the $1.00 minimum.[25] Also, the three industries in Table 24 include a representative of each of the three groupings (constant, decreasing, and increasing) into which the industries in Table 23 were classified.

TABLE 24

Comparison of Percentage Changes in Employment and Earnings (in parenthesis) by Minimum-Wage Impact Categories in Seamless Hosiery and Dress Shirts Industries for Specified Periods, 1955–57

| | Men's Hosiery, Southeast | | |
Period	High Impact	Middle Impact	Low Impact
Feb. 1956–April 1956	−18.7 (+18.3)	−12.5 (+7.4)	−7.8 (+3.3)
Feb. 1956–April 1957	−6.1 (+19.4)	−9.0 (+8.3)	−13.3 (+4.9)
Aug. 1955–April 1957	−4.3 (+24.7)	−9.6 (+13.6)	−10.8 (+8.5)
	Children's Hosiery, Southeast		
Feb. 1956–April 1956	−16.1 (+17.0)	−9.6 (+10.8)	−13.6 (+6.1)
Feb. 1956–April 1957	−19.3 (+19.1)	−2.9 (+11.8)	−11.8 (+5.3)
Aug. 1955–April 1957	−21.8 (+24.4)	−5.1 (+16.3)	−11.3 (+11.1)
	Men's and Boys' Dress Shirts and Nightwear, U.S.		
Feb. 1956–April 1956	−3.4 (+20.2)	−1.9 (+6.3)	−1.0 (+1.5)
Feb. 1956–Oct. 1956	+2.9 (+19.1)	+2.6 (+9.9)	−0.3 (+6.8)

Source: Percentages calculated from *Studies of the Economic Effects of the $1 Minimum Wage,* op. cit., Appendix Tables E–4, F–11, and F–24.

---

[25] In men's and boys' shirts, establishments to be classified as "high impact" had to have their average hourly earnings raised by 10 per cent or more as a consequence of the $1.00 minimum; for men's and for children's seamless hosiery the requirement was 12 per cent or more. The average increases in the wage bills of those establishments required by the $1.00 minimum amounted to 15.7 per cent for the 45 high-impact establishments making children's hosiery, 16.8 per cent for the 188 establishments manufacturing men's and boys' shirts, and 18.3 per cent for the 82 plants making men's seamless hosiery.

Table 24 has been calculated from the Department of Labor study, which divided each of those industries into three roughly equal groups in terms of relative impact of the $1.00 minimum.[26] For each impact group, percentage changes in employment have been paired with figures in parenthesis giving the actual percentage increase in average hourly earnings for establishments in that group over the same period.

It is evident from Table 24 that for one period the relationship between percentage changes in wages and in employment may be the opposite of the relationship in another period that includes the first one, and that the wage-employment relationship may vary unpredictably between impact grades. For men's seamless hosiery, the first relation between percentage increase in wages and percentage decrease in employment is properly ordered by impact grade, but the relationship in the two longer periods is just the reverse of that in the first period (the two months, February to April 1956). Partly, those contradictory results are to be explained by the fact that March and April are low employment months in the normal seasonal pattern, and inventories were built up in February in anticipation of the new minimum.[27]

In children's seamless hosiery in Table 24, the order is consistently irregular for all three periods, with the middle impact group having a considerably smaller decline in employment than the high- or the low-impact establishments.

For men's and boys' dress shirts, statistics are available for only three separate months in 1956. The gradation by impact group is consistent for the two overlapping periods, but the wage-employment relation for the eight-month period is just the opposite to that for the two-month period (February–April).

These divergent and contradictory results seem to indicate that firms adjusted in various ways to the new minimum, and that some firms temporarily absorbed some of the increased wage cost through reduced profits. The statistics in Table 24 do not lend much support to the notion that a forced increase in the minimum

---

[26] For the three industries, the "middle impact" ranges were as follows in order of listing the industry in the table: 6 to 11.9 per cent, 7 to 11.9 per cent, and 2 to 9.9 per cent. The "low impact" classification runs from 0 to the lowest figure of the middle-impact range.

[27] See *Studies of the Economic Effects of the $1.00 Minimum Wage, op. cit.,* pp. 128–29.

wage will soon lead to a reduction in a firm's employment in proportion to the relative size of the wage increase. Of the eight sets of figures, only two (men's hosiery and men's and boys' shirts, for the two-month period of February–April 1956) conform to that hypothesis. For the two-month period, the high-impact group consistently had the largest reduction in employment, but for the longer periods that was true in only two out of five cases.

2. LOCALITY STUDIES. In discussing the influence of new minimums on wage structure, reference was made to studies of the effects of the $1.00 minimum on seven low-wage communities. It is possible to grade those communities by degree of impact of the $1.00 minimum,[28] to compare employment in industries subject to the act with employment not subject to it in the same community, and to compare experience over a longer period of time, since for six of the communities employment data are available for June 1959. However, the employment data are not for identical firms over the whole period, and "are subject to a considerable margin of error," so that "small changes are not significant."[29]

For the communities as a group there was little change in employment in the subject industries from February 1956 to April 1957, while the nonsubject industries apparently had an employment increase of about 5 per cent. However, for the six low-wage industries over the whole period from February 1956 to June 1959, employment in subject industries increased 20 per cent and in nonsubject industries only 14 per cent, and employment in subject industries rose by the largest percentages in the two communities most affected by the impact of the $1.00 minimum.[30] On the other

---

[28] The percentage increase in average hourly earnings required in subject industries to bring all workers up to the $1.00 minimum were the following percentages: 9, 7, 7, 3, 3, 2, 2. It seems evident that a really significant general impact occurred only in the first three, namely, Dotham, Alabama; Athens, Georgia; and Meridian, Mississippi.

[29] See *Report Submitted to Congress in Accordance with the Requirements of Section 4(d) of the Fair Labor Standards Act, 1959,* Wage and Hour and Public Contracts Divisions, United States Department of Labor, Part II, January 1960, p. 11.

[30] *Ibid.,* pp. 10–11. This has been explained in the case of Athens, Georgia, by the fact that two substantial new firms located there at about the time that the $1.00 minimum took effect. See *Minimum Wage–Hour Legislation, Hearings before the Subcommittee on Labor Standards of the Committee on Education and Labor,* House of Representatives, Eighty-sixth Congress, 2nd session, Part 2, April-May 1960, p. 669.

hand, if comparison is confined to identical firms (which restricts it to about half the February 1956 sample), employment in subject industries shows no significant change while employment in non-subject industries increased by 14 per cent.[31] Such somewhat contradictory data do not lend much support to the hypothesis of a consistent wage-employment relationship.

3. STUDIES OF STATE EXPERIENCE. The most extensive studies of the employment effects of State minimum-wage legislation also show rather mixed results. Frequently, employment declined somewhat in the firms most severely affected by a new minimum, but often it did not; employers were able to make other adjustments or absorbed the added costs by reduced profits. In some respects in each study, results were contrary to, or failed significantly to conform to, the hypothesis of a strong inverse relationship between minimum-wage changes and employment of the workers directly affected by the minimum.[32]

A recent study of the effect of the $1.00 minimum for retail stores in New York State found that the 42 small stores investigated (whose payrolls were increased on the average 7.7 per cent directly by the $1.00 minimum) reacted in a variety of ways. Some 60 per cent of the added wage cost was absorbed by the employer. The remainder was offset by such operational changes to improve efficiency as adjusting store hours, revising work assignments, better selection of employees, and more attention to employee training, as well as the laying-off of 4.5 per cent of the workers previously paid less than $1.00 an hour.[33]

State minimum-wage laws apply mostly to local-market services, such as retailing, hotels, restaurants, laundries, and dry cleaning. Labor costs are generally a high proportion of total costs in restaurants, laundries, and dry cleaning, and self-performance of the service in one's home is normally an alternative to purchase

---

[31] *Report Submitted to Congress in Accordance with the Requirements of Section 4(d) of the Fair Labor Standards Act, 1959, op cit.,* p. 11.

[32] For emphasis on contrasting facts and for different interpretations of three State studies, see John M. Peterson, "Employment Effects of State Minimum Wages for Women: Three Historical Cases Re-Examined," *Industrial and Labor Relations Review,* XII (April 1959), pp. 406–22; and comment on that article by your author with reply by Peterson in the *Industrial and Labor Relations Review,* XIII (January 1960), pp. 254–73.

[33] See N. Arnold Tolles, *op. cit.,* pp. 127–32.

from a commercial establishment. Consequently, demand for the service may be highly elastic for price increases, making employment particularly sensitive to increases in costs and prices.

Some Conclusions

The studies of the effects of minimum-wage actions provide good testing material for the theories of management and wages and for the labor-market models presented in Chapters 7 and 9. Unfortunately, they also show some of the real obstacles to such testing.

Despite the limitations of the data and the difficulties of reading cause and effect relationships into statistics, some conclusions can be drawn from minimum-wage experience. The studies show that there is not a consistent and compelling relationship between minimum-wage increases and changes in employment in the affected plants. That, however, is a negative conclusion. It does not provide positive proof for an alternative explanation or other relationships. Some of the evidence does seem to support a conclusion that even in relatively small, low-wage firms, managements have some latitude of adjustment and can, therefore, adapt to a new minimum in a variety of ways, including better utilization of labor and efforts to improve the workforce.

Where the wage impact of a new minimum exceeds the normal range of local wage differentials of 10 to 15 per cent, the minimum-wage effect on employment is likely to be more certain and pronounced. Within that range, the minimum tends to bring wage laggards (say 10 per cent of an industry) up to the standards voluntarily adopted by their competitors and neighboring firms.

In local-market service lines and in extractive industries like logging, a minimum-wage increase that affects, say, over 10 per cent of the supply is likely to increase prices and to contract employment. Because the impact of a national minimum is differentiated by firm, industry, and locality and directly affects only a small fraction of employment in an industry, it stimulates increases in labor productivity and discourages price rises. Indeed, in many low-wage industries the nature of the product market makes impractical, separate price rises by individual firms. And any output reduction in the wage-pressured sections of such an industry would be likely to be balanced by added output in unaffected firms, probably at no increase in unit costs or in prices.

Theoretically, it can be demonstrated that a forced increase in minimum wages will increase employment where there is domination of and control by an employer or group of employers in a labor market area. This is the so-called "monopsony case" discussed in Chapter 9. As explained there, it has little applicability because employment and wage scales are not so closely and rigidly related as such reasoning implies.

The minimum wage needs to be put in proper perspective. Because increases in the minimum under the Fair Labor Standards Act have directly required less than a 1 per cent increase in total payrolls, such increases have had no evident effects on the price level or total consumer spending. Nor could they be expected to have much effect, one way or the other, on GNP. It seems likely that unemployment-creating effects have been more than offset by the minimum-wage stimulus to productivity improvements in the affected plants and by shifts of production to more efficient plants in the industry.[34] Of course, full employment is a more effective force for eliminating substandard wages than minimum-wage legislation could possibly be, because such legislation is bound to be more restricted in its application and it uses legal force rather than economic drawing power.

EQUAL PAY FOR WOMEN

Since World War I, women's and civic organizations have been promoting the principle of equal compensation for women and men when they are working on the same job or on jobs requiring equal qualifications and performance. Discrimination against women by means of dual pay scales in the same establishment, based on sex, is criticized as inequitable, degrading, morale-depressing, and an unfair method of competition.

If competition were fully effective in the labor area, presumably it would eliminate any sex differences in wages and salaries

---

[34] With complete coverage of the law and severe limits on the granting of learner and handicapped exemptions from the minimum, the lowest quality, unskilled labor might be rendered unemployable at that minimum. It now finds some (often part-time or casual) employment in agriculture and work in or around the home. To the extent that a statutory minimum wage eliminates demand for their services, potential GNP is reduced.

that are not based on job performance and employment-related differences. However, as explained below, that has not been the case.

The consequence has been the enactment of legislation. Between 1919 and 1963, some twenty-two States in the North and West[35] adopted equal pay laws, applying mostly to private industry operating within the State. By 1963, a total of thirty-eight countries had ratified the 1951 Convention Concerning Equal Remuneration for Men and Women for Work of Equal Value, adopted by the International Labor Office. Federal action occurred with enactment of the Equal Pay Act of 1963, which amends the Fair Labor Standards Act. That law prohibits wage differentials based on sex and has the same coverage and administration as the minimum-wage provisions of the Fair Labor Standards Act. Employees were given a year in which to make preparatory adjustments or changes in their job classifications and wage structures before the law went into effect.

Prevalence of Sex Discrimination in Pay

The extent of genuine sex discrimination in pay is difficult to determine. Statistical data showing sex differences in pay scales or earnings for an occupation in a factory or an office do not, by themselves, establish the existence of sex discrimination in pay. Male and female employees may differ with respect to quantity or quality of output, costs of particular employee benefits, costs arising from absenteeism and labor turnover, and costs of complying with State labor laws requiring special work hours, rest periods, or working conditions for women. Presumably, any wage comparisons would need to allow for such output or cost differences.

The methods of wage determination in the bulk of factory employment tend to preclude sex differences in pay scales. Under systematic job evaluation, wages are presumably set strictly according to the characteristics and requirements of the job, without regard to the qualifications of particular workers occupying it. Under collective bargaining, unless the contract specifies otherwise, the negotiated rates of pay apply regardless of sex, and any dis-

---

[35] Except for Arkansas.

crimination by management could be taken up as a wage inequity under the grievance procedure. However, dual wage schedules— one for males and the other for females—have existed in plants with job evaluation and in collective bargaining agreements.[36]

Dual pay scales on the basis of sex have been most prevalent in office work and other white-collar employment. One-third of the 1,900 firms included in the 1961 National Office Management Association survey reported that they have a double-standard pay scale for male and female office workers.[37] A survey of public employment offices in five cities in 1961 found about 120 examples of job orders placed by employers, which specified different wage rates for the job depending on the sex of the worker referred by the agency. Most of the hiring orders with wage differentials based on sex were for clerical, service, or sales jobs.[38] A similar study in nine cities in 1963 found 91 job orders offering higher rates for men, although applicants of both sexes were acceptable.[39] About one-third of the orders contained sex differentials of 10 per cent or less below the men's rate, and over half had differentials ranging from 11 to 25 per cent of the men's rate.

The existence of genuine sex differentials would seem to be indicated by the fact that such differences have been eliminated in many plants through collective bargaining. For example, a sex differential averaging 10.5 cents in 1951 in the meatpacking industry had, by 1958, been eliminated entirely in a substantial section

---

[36] For examples of collective agreements that provide either dual pay arrangements or a separate wage increase for men and a smaller increase for women, see *Equal Pay Act, Hearings before the Special Subcommittee on Labor of the Committee on Education and Labor on H.R. 3861 and Related Bills,* House of Representatives, Eighty-eighth Congress, 1st session, Washington, D.C., March 15–27, 1963, pp. 16 and 53. The Equal Pay Act of 1963 allowed two years for collective agreements to be renegotiated to comply with its provisions.

[37] See *Office Executive,* XXXVI (February 1961), pp. 10–13. The questionnaire was sent to 4,000 of the organization's membership of 17,000 in the United States and Canada, and returns were received from over 1,900. Presumably, practically all the employers reporting dual scales were in the United States, since Federal and provincial laws requiring equal pay for equal work covered virtually all Canadian employers in 1961.

[38] See *Economic Indicators Relating to Equal Pay, 1962,* Women's Bureau, United States Department of Labor (Washington: United States Government Printing Office, 1962), pp. 1–2.

[39] *Equal Pay Act, Hearings before the Special Subcommittee on Labor, op. cit.,* p. 32.

of the industry without apparently reducing the proportion of female employment; and a large chemical company recently granted a special wage increase of thirteen cents an hour to females in its New England plant in order to wipe out all existing sex differentials.[40]

Economic Aspects

Sex discrimination in the wage structure may have no more justification than convention, prejudice, and the weak bargaining position of working women, only one-eighth of whom are organized. On the other hand, wage differentiation by sex may be partly or wholly justified on economic grounds.[41]

In considering the economic basis of sex discrimination, it is necessary to distinguish discrimination in pay from discrimination in employment opportunity (selection, training, and promoton). Pay and opportunity may, of course, be connected, particularly with the work-career or welfare concept of employment. Management may wish to pay better those employees whom it hopes and expects to retain. That can be accomplished through promotion. Under job evaluation, the pay is based on the job and not on the personal attributes of individuals occupying it, except where there is a rate range. In that case, pay raises within the range may be based on merit or length of service, but such individual treatment is quite different from separate pay scales based on sex.

Presumably, the pay for a job could be differentiated on the basis of sex, without violating the integrity of job evaluation, if the labor cost per unit of output consistently averaged higher for women than for men. That could be the case because of higher absenteeism and turnover rates among female employees and restrictions or requirements applying only to women under State labor laws. For some jobs, however, such additional costs might be offset by female advantages in dexterity, adaptability to monotony, and acceptance of authority.

---

[40] See *Equal Pay Primer*, Women's Bureau Leaflet 20, Department of Labor (Washington: United States Government Printing Office, rev. January 1963), p. 2.

[41] For a discussion of the economic aspects of a report by a Royal Commission on Equal Pay in England see E. H. Phelps Brown, "Equal Pay for Equal Work," *Economic Journal*, LIX (September 1949), pp. 384–98.

Discrimination Prohibited by Federal Law

The Equal Pay Act of 1963 forbids an employer, within one establishment, from discriminating

between employees on the basis of sex by paying wages to employees of such establishment at a rate less than the rate at which he pays wages to employees of the opposite sex in such establishment for equal work on jobs the performance of which requires equal skill, effort, and responsibility, and which are performed under similar working conditions, except where such payment is made pursuant to (i) a seniority system; (ii) a merit system; (iii) a system which measures earnings by quantity or quality of production; or (iv) a differential based on any other factor other than sex: . . .

The legislative history indicates the significance of that long and complicated part of a sentence. Essentially, it means (a) that, for comparative purposes, jobs considered "equal" must be virtually or substantially identical; (b) that the law does not prevent pay differences based on a worker's seniority status, or a merit system for rating employees, or piecerate or incentive earnings; and (c) that specific and ascertainable costs of employing persons of one sex rather than the other (such as greater absenteeism and turnover or State laws requiring special hours, rest periods, or working conditions for women) can be used to justify wage differences by sex.

It is evident that in administering the law the Secretary of Labor and his agents will need to look at the total situation in an establishment and the willingness of the employer to comply with the purpose of the act. Although most business spokesmen in Congressional hearings opposed a Federal law for equal pay, preferring to rely on collective bargaining and State legislation, industrial management supports the principle of equal pay, and generally follows some system of job evaluation as a means to achieve equity in pay scales.

RACIAL DISCRIMINATION IN EMPLOYMENT

Racial discrimination in employment consists of refusal of an employer to hire, train, or promote available qualified workers because of their race. The employer voluntarily blocks off or restricts that part of his potential labor supply which is nonwhite.

Two questions arise. One is why does management curtail part of its labor supply, and the other is why market forces permit management to follow such a restrictive and seemingly uneconomical practice.

Gary S. Becker has developed a theory that presumes white managements of firms discriminate in employment against Negroes because they prefer, for reasons of personal taste or out of ignorance of the quality of Negro labor, to employ only whites or a restricted group among the whites; skin color is an obvious basis for a "taste for discrimination."[42] That, however, would seem to be only one possible factor in a complex situation.

Empirical studies indicate other important reasons why managements discriminate by refusing to hire or promote qualified Negro workers. One is the tradition in the community and, as part of it, the customary policy of the company. Another factor in some cases has been craft-union exclusion of Negroes from apprenticeship, membership, and the employment-agency functions performed by the union. A third factor has been the costs and difficulties managements assume that they will encounter in the form of white-employee opposition or unfavorable customer reaction to the hiring or promotion of Negroes.[43] As explained in the introductory remarks to this chapter, government programs are partly aimed at reducing the anticipated difficulties and costs to the firm, which might occur because of employee, customer, or community reaction.

Managements have tended to hire Negroes for the first time, or to promote them for the first time, when sufficient qualified white labor is not available or when the government has exerted pressure.[44] Labor stringency during World War II and the Korean

---

[42] See *The Economics of Discrimination* (Chicago: University of Chicago Press, 1957).

[43] For management reasons found in a survey of over 1,200 firms in Pennsylvania, see *Employment Practices in Pennsylvania*, Report of the Governor's Commission on Industrial Race Relations, Commonwealth of Pennsylvania, Harrisburg, February 1953, pp. 6–7. This study is discussed more fully in the next section.

Some firms have reported a reduction in their white labor supply with the employment of many colored workers.

[44] See *ibid.* (pp. 22 and 23) which reveals that, among the 69 establishments that liberalized their hiring practices and gave reasons why they reduced or eliminated discrimination, 56 mentioned governmental influences (negotiations by government agencies, fair employment practices ordinances in the municipality, and

War caused many managements to relax self-imposed barriers to the use of the nonwhite part of the available labor supply. If, faced with continuing labor stringency, a management persists in hiring only whites although better qualified Negroes are available, that would indicate either that the management assumes its costs of breaking racial barriers would exceed the gains from hiring better Negro labor, or that the firm enjoys sufficient latitude of discretion to bear the diseconomies of prejudice, the luxury of a "taste for discrimination," or the wastes of inertia (depending on the management's motivation). As is explained more fully below, the government may exert customer pressure on Federal contractors by threatening to withhold purchases from a firm practicing race discrimination, or it may apply the compulsory powers of law under a Federal, State, or municipal statute.

Extent of Discrimination

Because so much hiring by managements is based on interviews and subjective evaluations and because promotions also involve subjective judgment, it is difficult to determine the extent of discrimination in employment against Negroes. Racial breakdowns of employment statistics by occupation, industry, and area are not too helpful. The statistics show that Negroes are overrepresented in the unemployment figures, in unskilled blue-collar jobs, and in the lowest-level white-collar work such as janitor, elevator operator, messenger, and chauffeur. Negroes are increasingly underrepresented as one moves up the occupational ladder to skilled craftsman and into higher-paying office, managerial, and professional work.

Such disproportions can be due either to differences in qualifications for the higher-level jobs, or they can be due to discrimination, or both. Without an objective measure of relative qualifications, it is difficult to determine the extent to which Negro-white disparities in occupational distribution are due to differences in training and other qualifications, and the extent to which they are due to a lack of equal employment opportunities (discrimination).

United States Government contract regulations) and 43 gave as a reason or an additional reason the tight labor market conditions or dwindling labor supplies in 1952, primarily as a result of the Korean War boom.

Of course, discrimination and the acquisition of qualifications are interrelated. If Negroes are excluded from certain occupations, they are discouraged from training for them. A disparity in qualifications is created if Negroes are barred from apprenticeship programs for skilled crafts or from on-the-job training by segregation in jobs or the equivalent of separate seniority lists. It is well known that, in particular industries or areas, Negroes have been restricted to certain unskilled and semiskilled jobs. For instance, even in a progressive industry like oil, southern refineries in the past have hired Negroes only for work in departments composed of laborers, and promotion from those departments has been almost impossible.

One cannot measure the degree of racial discrimination in individual plants and come up with some total figure showing the extent of lack of equal employment opportunity for Negroes in all kinds of work. Nor do the alleged cases of racial discrimination under State and municipal Fair Employment Practices laws provide a good index, because their volume depends on individual complaints and the adequacy of enforcement of the law.

However, some indication of the extent of discrimination in employment is provided by a 1952 survey, covering 1,229 firms that employed 900,000 workers and were located in 44 communities in Pennsylvania. Conducted by the Governor's Commission on Industrial Race Relations, it was based on interviews with persons in those firms who were most knowledgeable about their hiring and promotional policies, plus an examination of the files of the local public employment office. Most of the discrimination covered by the study was against Negroes, but it included also any job exclusion or limitation against qualified workers in hiring, upgrading, promotion, or use in all job classifications, for nonoccupational reasons of race, color, religion, or national origin.

The study found that 89 per cent of the 1,229 firms practiced some degree of discrimination; one or more occupations was not completely open to all qualified workers. The restrictions were progressively more prevalent and stringent the higher the level of skill, responsibility, and pay. Where a minority group was not completely barred from all employment in the firm, it was often confined to jobs in the lower skill brackets. Only 38 per cent of the companies discriminated in any way against a minority in hiring workers for unskilled work and for entry jobs requiring little or no training or experience; 48 per cent of them would not employ a member of a minority group in semiskilled occupations; and 67 per cent barred such a person from skilled jobs. For office, engineering, and sales jobs, nine-tenths of the firms would not hire minorities.[45] Interestingly, of the 1,086 firms that showed some evidence of discrimination, only four had double wage standards for male workers, with a lower pay scale for those in a minority group.[46]

Experience with State and Municipal Legislation[47]

A total of twenty-one States have enacted antidiscrimination statutes and established agencies to investigate complaints and obtain compliance. Beginning with the New York and New Jersey laws passed in 1945, these statutes make it unlawful for an employer to discriminate in employment or pay because of race, religion, or nationality. Many of them also forbid employment agencies or labor unions to discriminate in any way against racial, religious, or ethnic minorities. Beginning with Philadelphia in 1948, seven major cities have enacted similar laws.

The State or municipal agency tries to negotiate with the firm's management a settlement of any individual complaint that it considers upon investigation to be valid. From such conciliation sessions, it seeks to obtain a signed statement or agreement of compliance with the spirit of the law. If unsuccessful, the agency may hold a public hearing and after that make a finding and issue an order of compliance, which can be accepted or modified and enforced by a court. Some States and cities (especially New York, New Jersey, and Philadelphia) have also used informal investigations and studies to disclose the existence of discrimination. By that means, they can demonstrate patterns of employment discrimination in an industry and achieve more general acceptance of the public policy of nondiscrimination.

Operating on individual complaints alone has certain drawbacks.

---

[45] *Ibid.*, pp. 1–6 and Appendix Table 3.

[46] *Ibid.*, p. 30.

[47] This section and the next one on Federal executive orders draw heavily from Paul H. Norgren and Samuel E. Hill, *Toward Fair Employment* (New York: Columbia University Press, 1964).

State experience shows that refusal to hire accounts for about two-thirds of all complaints, and alleged discrimination in training, transfer, and promotion represents only around one-tenth of the cases. That seems out of proportion in view of the Pennsylvania study's figures showing increasing discrimination in jobs up the line, many of which are filled by on-the-job training and promotion from within. Negro workers employed in low-level jobs apparently hesitate to complain about discrimination in training and promotion for fear of injuring their long-run employment at that firm. Negro job applicants who are rejected and complain have little to lose, for they have as yet no stake with the company to injure. Furthermore, individual complaints can be settled without much correction of over-all practice. The best administration in the States not only obtains an agreement from the employer to comply generally with the spirit of the law, but also conducts follow-up reviews of employment practices and patterns of new hires and promotions to check on compliance.

Because of budget and staff limitations, only New York State and Philadelphia have approached adequate administration and enforcement of their laws. New York's fair employment commission has been the only one with full-time commissioners. In 1960, its annual budget was about one million dollars, and it had a professional staff of eighty persons. The next most adequately staffed States were California, Michigan, New Jersey, Ohio, and Pennsylvania with ten to fifteen professionals and budgets at that time of $150,000 to $200,000 a year. The Philadelphia staff and budget were slightly larger than those for any of those five States.

One cannot determine from statistics just how much the antidiscrimination laws and the agencies administering them are responsible for any improvements in the occupational distribution of Negro workers. Census figures, corrected for population developments, show that between 1950 and 1960 Negroes in New York State advanced much more rapidly into higher-level jobs than they did in States like Illinois which enacted its fair employment law in 1961. Also, the statistics submitted by Federal contractors in their 1962 compliance reports show that the percentage of Negro workers in those firms employed in professional and technical occupations were three times as high for New York City, and twice as high for Philadelphia, as they were for Chicago and for three other major cities in States without antidiscrimination laws in 1962.

The State laws have not been too successful in preventing the placement and execution of discriminatory job orders by public and private employment offices. The State and local employment services conceive of their function largely as supplying requested services, and in referrals they try to meet the employer's desires so as to maintain his "business."[48]

Experience under Federal Executive Orders

In the absence of a Federal fair employment practices law, action by the Federal Government has taken the form of executive orders that have applied to Federal employment and to private employment on Federal contracts, both military and civilian items.

The first such executive order against discrimination was issued by President Roosevelt in 1941. It required Federal contractors to obligate themselves under the contract not to discriminate against any job applicant or employee because of race, color, creed, or national origin. For its administration, a Committee on Fair Employment Practices was established, composed of prominent persons who came occasionally to Washington for its meetings. Although a series of executive orders against discrimination in employment have been issued since 1941, that pattern still prevails under Executive Order 10925 issued by President Kennedy in March 1961, and administered by the President's Committee on Equal Employment Opportunity, of which Vice-President Johnson was chairman.

The agencies to administer these executive orders have been hampered by quite restricted budgets and funds. Since the early fifties, the Federal agency has not had half the budget and staff of the New York State agency. Each President's committee has been forced to rely heavily on the staffs of the contracting agencies themselves, because Congress has not made a direct appropriation

---

[48] For a survey and analysis of this matter, see *Employment, 1961 Commission on Civil Rights Report*, Book 3 (Washington: United States Government Printing Office, 1961); and also Paul H. Norgren and Samuel E. Hill, *op. cit.*

for the committees administering the successive executive orders.

Sanctions for violation of the antidiscrimination clause in Federal contracts include the threat to cancel the contract or bar the contractor from Federal business. Also, any discrimination can be one of the factors taken into account in allocating negotiated contracts among firms.

Negroes have obtained a growing share of Federal employment, but convincing evidence is lacking that Federal contractors have made more progress in lowering barriers to Negro employment and promotion than comparable noncontractor firms, at least prior to 1961. That does not mean that the Federal programs were completely ineffective in private industry. It could mean that, through publicity and the establishment of Federal standards, their influences were fairly general, and special results are hard to discover in the 1960 Census figures. One difficulty for all antidiscrimination programs between 1957 and 1963 was the existence of widespread unemployment and the lack of employment expansion in many industries. As a result, rivalry for jobs increased and, in many instances, Negroes could only be hired by displacing employed white workers.

More progress in lowering barriers to Negro employment and promotion among Federal contractors seems to have been made from 1961 through 1963 than during any three years in the previous decade.[49] The Federal program, however, continued to suffer from lack of a comprehensive Federal antidiscrimination law and from inadequate staff and funds for the administration of the restricted program under Executive Order 10925. A Federal fair employment statute, applying to interstate commerce, would have the advantage of greater coverage, more direct and effective remedies, the promise of more adequate financing, and much greater moral influence throughout the country. In the absence of such a statute, Negroes in 1963 in many cities took direct action against employers and building unions in the form of customer boycotts, picketing, and sitdowns and lie-downs, in order to call attention to presumed discrimination and to try to hamper operations of the business until remedial action was promised.

---

[49] See *The First Nine Months*, Report of the President's Committee on Equal Employment Opportunity, January 15, 1962.

SUMMARY

This chapter has centered on governmental actions to correct inequities, discrimination, and lack of standards in wages and in employment opportunities, for women and for Negroes.

1. Minimum-wage studies indicate both a lack of standards in low-wage industries and the lack of a consistent relationship between the relative impact of an increased minimum on particular firms and their subsequent employment. A considerable variety in the channels of employer adjustment is evident from the studies.

2. Because the impact of increases in the minimum under the Fair Labor Standards Act has been different for each firm, industry, and locality, and because only a small fraction of total employment in most industries has been directly affected, such increases have served to stimulate productivity advances. The impact of increases in the national minimum has been too small to have any evident effect on the level of prices or on total consumer spending.

3. Sex discrimination in the form of dual pay scales for the same job performance is especially prevalent in office work and other employment not subject to systematic job evaluation. It is evident that competition is not a fully effective force in eliminating manifest sex discrimination in the wage structure.

4. The 1963 amendment to the Fair Labor Standards Act, forbidding wage differentials not based on job-related factors, will involve knotty problems of measuring and compensating for employment-connected sex differentials.

5. Barriers to Negro employment and occupational advancement are based on a number of economic and noneconomic factors. Generally, the barriers increase as one moves up the occupational ladder.

6. Action by the government may be necessary to break through such barriers by reducing the assumed costs of nondiscrimination for employers and by putting pressure on government contractors to follow a policy of equal employment opportunity. Fair employment practice legislation has a definite economic justification.

7. State and Federal antidiscrimination programs have generally

lacked the staff and funds (and a proper conception of their role) in order to be really effective instruments in reducing employment discrimination based on race, particularly in the midst of widespread unemployment.

DISCUSSION QUESTIONS

1. What is the economic justification for minimum-wage legislation?
2. Contrast the probable effects on wage structures, labor productivity, and the price level, of a 15 per cent rise in the national minimum under the Fair Labor Standards Act and a 15 per cent general increase in all wages throughout the country.
3. Discuss the probable effects on employment in different industries resulting from a 15 per cent increase in the minimum under the Fair Labor Standards Act, effective five years after the previous increase.
4. Discuss the implications of experience with minimum-wage legislation for the theory of the firm (theory of management).
5. What economic justification is there for equal-pay laws?
6. Discuss the problems of determining whether genuine sex discrimination in pay scales actually exists.
7. What is the economic justification for State and Federal fair employment practices legislation?
8. What kind of a governmental program do you consider desirable to meet the problem of discrimination in employment? Support your program with an economic analysis of benefits and costs.

SELECTED READINGS

Cullen, Donald E., *Minimum Wage Laws*, Bulletin 43, New York State School of Industrial and Labor Relations at Cornell University, Ithaca, N.Y., February 1961.

Economic Indicators Relating to Equal Pay, 1962, Women's Bureau, United States Department of Labor (Washington: United States Government Printing Office, 1962).

Employment, 1961 Commission on Civil Rights Report, Book 3 (Washington: United States Government Printing Office, 1961).

Employment Practices in Pennsylvania, Report of the Governor's Commission on Industrial Race Relations, Commonwealth of Pennsylvania, Harrisburg, February 1953.

Equal Pay Act, Hearings before a Special Subcommittee on Labor of the Committee on Education and Labor on H. R. 3861 and Related Bills, House of Representatives, Eighty-eighth Congress, 1st session, March 15–27, 1963, Washington, D.C.

Norgren, Paul H. and Samuel E. Hill, *Toward Fair Employment* (New York: Columbia University Press, 1964).

Studies of the Economic Effects of the $1 Minimum Wage, Effects in Selected Low Wage Industries and Localities, Wage and Hour and Public Contracts Divisions, United States Department of Labor, January 1959.

17.

Unemployment: Facts, Analysis, and Insurance

SINCE 1957, UNEMPLOYMENT has been a serious economic problem for the United States. Our rate of job growth has slowed down while industrial and occupational shifts in employment have been accelerating. The result has been a general increase in joblessness (surplus labor), with a marked expansion in the number of long-term unemployed—those out of work half a year or more.

Unemployment means wasted manpower resources. It holds production below capacity and reduces the buying power of workers. The role of different causal factors in explaining our widespread and persistent joblessness may be in dispute but, in the contest of politicoeconomic systems for men's minds and loyalties, unemployment has become an important indicator of success or weakness. In terms of political implications, the unemployment rate is probably the most important statistic released by the Federal Government.

This chapter focusses on the nation's unemployment problem. First the facts about unemployment and their implications are discussed. Then different explanations for the high level of joblessness are considered. Finally, the present and potential effectiveness of unemployment compensation in meeting the problem is discussed.

THE FACTS

Between 1957 and 1962, the annual rate of employment growth was but half the yearly rate of expansion from 1947 to 1957. That slowdown in the growth of employment opportunities was general throughout private industry. During the five years beginning with 1957, the total number of jobs declined in manufacturing, mining, contract construction, transportation, and public utilities. Even in the industries that were experiencing employment expansion (trade and finance, insurance, real estate, and service and miscellaneous), the yearly rate of increase was 2.5 per cent compared with 2.7 per cent in the 1947–57 period. Whereas during the pre-1957 decade, an average of 900,000 new jobs (including government) was being added to nonfarm employment each year, during the five subsequent years the yearly increase was about 485,000.

In addition, the composition of employment growth changed markedly after 1957. A speed-up occurred in the shift away from employment in goods-production toward service-type industries. Indeed, the only major section with a greater rate of employment expansion from 1957 to 1962 than in the 1947–57 decade was State and local government. The difference reflected mainly the relative expansion in the school systems. Thus, although 76 per cent of the job growth was in the private sector of the nonfarm economy during the 1947–57 period, that sector supplied only 36 per cent of the job expansion between 1957 and 1962.

Upward Trends

Since 1929, unemployment in this country has varied widely. As indicated in Table 25, during 1933 it averaged 24.9 per cent, or one out of every four persons in the labor force. Eleven years later in 1944, under the pressure of war production, unemployment reached the remarkably low figure of 1.2 per cent. That year, job vacancies undoubtedly far exceeded the number of jobless seeking employment.

TABLE 25

Civilian Labor Force and Unemployment, 1929–1963

Year	Civilian Labor Force (in 000's)	Unemployed (in 000's)	Unemployed as Per Cent of Labor Force
1929	49,180	1,550	3.2
1930	49,820	4,340	8.7
1931	50,420	8,020	15.9
1932	51,000	12,060	23.6
1933	51,590	12,830	24.9
1934	52,230	11,340	21.7
1935	52,870	10,610	20.1
1936	53,440	9,030	16.9
1937	54,000	7,700	14.3
1938	54,610	10,390	19.0
1939	55,230	9,480	17.2
1940	56,640	8,120	14.6
1941	55,910	5,560	9.9
1942	56,410	2,660	4.7
1943	55,540	1,070	1.9
1944	54,630	670	1.2
1945	53,860	1,040	1.9
1946	57,520	2,270	3.9
1947	60,180	2,356	3.9
1948	61,442	2,325	3.8
1949	62,105	3,682	5.9
1950	63,099	3,351	5.3
1951	62,884	2,099	3.3
1952	62,966	1,932	3.1
1953	63,815	1,870	2.9
1954	64,468	3,578	5.6
1955	65,848	2,904	4.4
1956	67,530	2,822	4.2
1957	67,946	2,936	4.3
1958	68,647	4,681	6.8
1959	69,394	3,813	5.5
1960	70,612	3,931	5.6
1961	71,603	4,806	6.7
1962	72,011	4,012	5.6
1963	72,975	4,166	5.7

Source: *Economic Report of the President,* Transmitted to the Congress, January 1963, Table C–9, p. 194; and *Monthly Report on the Labor Force* for 1963 figures. Data for 1947 forward adjusted for new definitions. Beginning 1960, Alaska and Hawaii are included. And beginning 1953, corrections were made for the 1950 Census and beginning 1962, for the 1960 Census.

During the Korean War period, especially in 1952 and 1953, unemployment returned to minimal levels of around 3 per cent of the labor force. After a recession dip in 1954, it leveled off at annual averages of 4.2 to 4.4 per cent during the next three years. A figure of around 4 per cent unemployment came to be accepted as a sort of normal amount that is necessary in order to adjust to fluctuations and shifts in production and to allow for the movement of workers between jobs and into and out of the labor force.

However, from 1957 on, the rates of unemployment in Table 25 appear to have an upward trend. After the recession of 1958, the (seasonally adjusted) monthly figures declined only to a low of 5 per cent for a few months in 1959 and 1960; and after the 1960–61 recession the rate settled down around 5.5 per cent and then began to rise to an average of about 6 per cent for the first half of 1963. These successively higher plateaus after each recession have resulted in a higher rate of unemployment during the recovery year of 1963 than during the recession year of 1954.

That the upward trend in unemployment rates was general, affecting all major occupational groups, is indicated by Table 26. That table also shows that unskilled laborers had the highest unemployment rate and that the second highest rate was among operatives (largely semiskilled production workers in manufacturing and machine operators in other industries). But even the occupational groups with the lowest jobless rates (managers and professional and technical workers) had rates in 1962 about 1.5 times as high as those in 1957.[1]

The rise of unemployment after 1957 occurred largely in the form of longer spells of unemployment. Although between 1957 and 1962 total unemployment increased about 40 per cent, unemployment lasting fifteen weeks or more rose by 100 per cent, and long-term unemployment of half a year or more rose almost 150 per cent. Although the average duration of unemployment increased from 10.4 to 14.7 weeks between 1957 and 1962, a

---

[1] Even for shortage occupations like high-school and grade-school teachers and stenographers, typists, and secretaries, the jobless rates were about 1.5 times as large in 1962 as in 1957. That unemployment data for the years in the postwar era were comparable was verified by the President's Committee to Appraise Employment and Unemployment Statistics. See the Committee's report, *Measuring Employment and Unemployment* (Washington: United States Government Printing Office, 1962).

TABLE 26

Unemployment Rates by Major Occupation Groups, 1947–62

Major Occupation Group	1962	1957	1947
White-collar workers			
Professional and technical	1.7	1.2	1.9
Managers, officials, and proprietors	1.5	1.0	1.2
Clerical workers	3.9	2.8	2.9
Sales workers	4.1	2.6	2.6
Blue-collar workers			
Craftsmen and foremen	5.1	3.8	3.8
Operatives	7.5	6.3	5.1
Nonfarm laborers	12.4	9.4	7.5
Service workers			
Private household	4.9	3.7	3.4
All other	6.4	5.1	4.7
Farm workers	4.3	3.7	2.7
Total	5.6	4.3	3.6

Source: *Manpower Report of the President,* Transmitted to the Congress March 1963, Table A–9, p. 145.

considerable amount of turnover continued to occur among the un-employed. Partly that is because, in an average month, some three to four million persons enter the labor force and only a slightly smaller number leave it.[2] Studies show that in the course of a year about 15 per cent of the nation's families are affected to some extent by unemployment.

During the 1957–62 period, the severity and the trends in unemployment in European countries were in sharp contrast to experience in the United States. Table 27 contains comparative unemployment rates for this country and seven others for the year 1960. The rates have been made comparable to the figures for this country by adjustment of each country's data to conform to our definitions of unemployment and our survey methods.[3]

Not only is the United States' rate higher than that for any other country except Canada, but also none of the other countries (except Canada) shows an upward trend in unemployment rates

---

[2] See *Mobility and Worker Adaptation to Economic Change in the United States,* Office of Manpower, Automation and Training, United States Department of Labor, January 1963, p. 6.

[3] See Robert J. Myers, article cited in Table 27, p. 140.

TABLE 27

Rates of Unemployment in 1960 and Average Yearly Increase
*in Industrial Production (1951–60), Eight Industrial Countries**

	Unemployment Rate (per cent)	Annual Increase in Industrial Production (per cent)
United States	5.6	3.2
Canada	7.0	4.3
France	1.9	6.6
West Germany	1.0	8.8
Great Britain	2.4	3.2
Italy	4.3	8.5
Japan	1.1	14.5
Sweden	1.5	3.7

* All data adjusted to conform to United States definitions for purposes of comparability. The figure for Sweden is for 1961.

Source: Robert J. Myers, "What Can We Learn from European Experience," in *Unemployment and the American Economy*, Proceedings of a Conference Held in Connection with the Research and Evaluation Project on Unemployment and the American Economy, April 18–20, 1963, Institute of Industrial Relations, University of California, Tables 1 and 2, pp. 142 and 148 (mimeo).

between 1957 and 1962.[4] Perhaps one factor in the higher United States figure is the large-scale movement into and out of the labor force in this country to a degree unparalleled in European nations. More rapid increase in the labor supply does not seem to be part of the explanation for our high unemployment rate, for Germany, Japan, and Canada experienced appreciably higher increases in their labor forces than did this country. The rate of productivity increase and of increase in technological change seem to have been as rapid in the other countries as here. Only the marked decline in our agricultural employment and the acute minorities problem would seem to be significant structural factors that aggravate our unemployment problem compared with European countries.

The main explanation for our high unemployment rate and the upward trend in it appears to be the slow rate of economic growth in the United States. As indicated in Table 27, from 1951 to 1960 industrial production was expanding more rapidly in all other countries except Great Britain. Basically, differences in the rate of expansion in the demand for labor seem to have been largely

---

[4] *Ibid.*, p. 141.

responsible for the significant variation in unemployment rates and trends.

Some evidence indicates that, in recent upswings of the business cycle, increases in real GNP have been associated with smaller expansions in employment than was the case during the earlier post-war period.[5] If that is true, it would require a greater increase in output to provide a given expansion in employment.

Severely-Affected Groups

Normally, in periods of high unemployment the incidence is especially heavy in certain groups (youth and nonwhite, unskilled, and older workers) and in certain industries and areas. During the period 1957–63 there seems to be little evidence of abnormal concentration of unemployment in particular sections of the labor force. Nor does the distressed-area component of unemployment appear to have increased as a proportion of total joblessness during that period.

Unemployment is always higher among young persons than among adults, but the disparity was pronounced in the early sixties. In 1962, persons under twenty-five represented only one-fifth of the labor force, but they constituted over one-third of the unemployed and over one-fourth of those who had been unemployed fifteen weeks or longer.

Some of the reasons for the relatively high incidence of unemployment among youth are obvious. A high proportion of them are new entrants into the labor force. They are largely unskilled, inexperienced, and vulnerable to lay-off because of lack of much seniority. In addition, young people normally have a high turn-over as they "shop around" for the "right" job, but that process is much more risky in periods of high unemployment.

The relative reduction in unskilled jobs and the accelerated increase in the population seventeen to twenty-four years of age suggests that employment opportunities may be particularly poor in the next few years for young persons who do not acquire special

---

[5] See Richard C. Wilcock and Walter H. Franke, *Unwanted Workers: Permanent Layoffs and Long-Term Unemployment* (New York: The Free Press of Glencoe, 1963), pp. 280–83.

skills and training or a good educational foundation. The total number of young people who will enter the labor force between 1960 and 1970 has been estimated at 26 million, a far greater number than the country has had to absorb into the labor force in any previous decade.[6]

The incidence of unemployment is much heavier among non-whites (mainly Negroes) than among white workers, and the gap increased from 1957 to 1962. In the latter year, nonwhite workers, who represented 11 per cent of the labor force, constituted 22 per cent of the unemployed and 28 per cent of the long-term jobless (out of work 27 weeks or more). For nonwhite boys and girls fourteen to nineteen years of age, the unemployment rates in 1962 were double those for whites in the same age class.

As was observed in the preceding chapter, nonwhite workers are largely employed in unskilled and semiskilled occupations, where unemployment rates generally are highest (see Table 26). For the same occupations, the nonwhite rate of unemployment averages about 50 per cent higher; it is especially high for clerical and sales workers and skilled craftsmen.[7] Also it appears that once nonwhite workers lose a job, they are less likely soon to become reemployed.

The older worker generally is protected against early lay-off by high seniority. However, once he loses a job, he has extra difficulties in finding another. Often his skill has been made obsolete by a rapidly changing economy and, for the most part, he is less mobile, less well educated, and less adaptable than a younger man. Although men forty-five to sixty-four years of age constituted only 17 per cent of the unemployed men in 1962, they were 27 per cent of those jobless 27 weeks or longer. Long duration explains why unemployment among male workers fifty-five to sixty-four years old was 4.6 per cent, compared with a rate of 3.8 per cent for men thirty to fifty-four years of age.

---

[6] *Manpower Report of the President and A Report on Manpower Requirements, Resources, Utilization, and Training by the United States Department of Labor,* Transmitted to the Congress March 1963 (Washington: United States Government Printing Office, 1963), p. 90, hereafter referred to as *Manpower Report of the President,* 1963.

[7] See Matthew A. Kessler, "Economic Status of Non-White Workers, 1955–62," *Monthly Labor Review,* LXXXVI (July 1963), Table 5, p. 783.

Certain industries are subject to a high risk of unemployment. Among them are building construction, which has marked seasonal fluctuations, and mining, in which long-term unemployment has been high because mining communities are generally rather isolated and offer few alternative employment opportunities. In 1962, the unemployment rate for construction was 12 per cent and for mining 8.6 per cent, compared with an average of 5.6 per cent for all workers with previous work experience.

The impact of unemployment has been particularly heavy in certain widely distributed communities. For the most part, they are "distress areas," which suffer from chronic unemployment because of the shutdown of industrial plants and the migration of industry away from the area with changes in technology, consumer tastes, population distribution, or transportation, or the depletion of natural resources locally. The consequent sharp decline in much of the area's manufacturing industry has resulted in a high level of unemployment, which may tend to be cumulative.

In 1961, Congress passed the Area Redevelopment Act to help areas of substantial and persistent unemployment take effective steps in planning and financing their economic redevelopment so as to increase employment opportunities in the area. In addition to financial assistance, the law provides for the training and retraining of unemployed and underemployed workers in the area and the payment of subsistence allowances to persons participating in such training.

ANALYSIS OF TWO THESES

The specific causes of unemployment are many and varied. Often they occur in combination. A jobless worker may not know the extent to which his unemployment was caused by the business cycle, seasonal variation in business, technological change, product or international competition, or a hundred other conceivable factors. And what caused his disemployment may be less significant than what is preventing his reemployment.

Various explanations have been offered for the high rates of unemployment from 1957 to 1963. Most of them can be grouped under two general headings: (1) a deficiency in aggregate demand and (2) enhanced difficulties of adjustment to change. The difficulties of adjustment may have increased because changing technology is accelerating job shifts or because the impediments to adjustment have become more serious.

Implications

The relative stress that one places on those two explanations has important implications for public policy. A strong supporter of the thesis of inadequate demand would emphasize measures to raise consumption, business, and government spending by such means as a low interest-rate policy, monetary expansion, tax reduction, increases in government spending. Those who place considerable weight on the thesis of greater adjustment difficulties would press for such measures as early warning and preparation for major technological changes, increased training and vocational guidance, programs to facilitate geographic and industrial mobility by relaxing worker ties, reduction in race discrimination and barriers to the employment of older workers.

If structural changes in the economy and employment practices have created greater difficulties of adjustment, there would be a poorer matching of unemployed workers and job vacancies. More labor bottlenecks would exist at a given level of unemployment so that unfilled vacancies would increase, and the duration of unemployment would also increase. In other words, the level of frictional unemployment would be higher as a consequence of increased adjustment problems.

The Evidence

The weight of evidence seems to support the thesis that deficiency of aggregate demand explains most of the unemployment in excess of 4 per cent of the labor force from 1957 through 1963. That view finds substantiation in the figures for industrial production in Table 27, and in the data for growth in real GNP for a variety of countries. The United States has been lagging behind most industrial countries in the rate of economic growth. In this country, a noticeable retardation in the rate of increase in aggregate demand (in real terms) has been associated with a substantially lower rate of private domestic investment than occurred prior to 1957.

The thesis of deficiency in aggregate demand also finds support in the unemployment statistics. They show that the rise in joblessness has been general, affecting all industries and occupations in roughly the same proportions. The widespread nature of the unemployment increase has resembled the spread during a recession.

Some evidence is consistent with either thesis. The high rate of unemployment (and especially long-term unemployment) among youth and unskilled workers is characteristic of recession periods. It could also be strong evidence in support of the claim that labor supply was failing to adjust to the shift in manpower requirements away from unskilled work in factories and elsewhere. The higher rate of lay-offs in manufacturing from 1958 to 1963 than in the preceding five years, is also characteristic of recession periods. Certainly, the high level for all five years would seem to support the thesis that structural changes in manufacturing were either more rapid or more radical than formerly, thus causing a high rate of lay-off.

If increased impact of structural changes and stronger mobility-reducing practices were largely responsible for the abnormally high unemployment, one would expect a given high level of joblessness among the unskilled and semiskilled to be accompanied by a relative increase of vacancies unable to be filled in expanding occupations. That, however, appears not to have been the case. Although labor shortages did exist in some job categories, help-wanted advertisements in the newspapers and records of unfilled job vacancies in interstate clearance under the Federal-State employment service do not reveal any evidence of an unusual piling up of unfilled jobs compared with earlier experience.[8]

---

[8] See *Employment and Unemployment*, Report of the Subcommittee on Economic Statistics of the Joint Economic Committee, February 2, 1962, Eighty-seventh Congress, 2nd session (Washington: United States Government Printing Office, 1962), pp. 7–8. The Council of Economic Advisers states in its January 1963 report that "the index of help-wanted advertisements compiled by the National Industrial Conference Board . . . indicates a substantially smaller volume of such advertisements in 1962 than in 1957 after adjustment is made for growth of the labor force." See *Economic Report of the President, Together with the Annual Report of the Council of Economic Advisers* (Washington: United States Government Printing Office, January 1963), p. 25.

Productivity statistics for manufacturing lend some support to the thesis of increasing difficulties of adjustment growing out of structural changes. If technological change was more rapid or radical, it should increase the output per man-hour of labor. For manufacturing that figure did increase 18 per cent during the five-year period 1957 to 1962 compared with 12.5 per cent from 1952 to 1957.

It is hard to think of statistics that would be appropriate for testing the other part of the thesis of increasing difficulties of adjustment, namely, that the adaptability of the total labor force to current industrial changes has decreased. In support of such a thesis, Sar Levitan, who was Research Director to the Special Committee on Unemployment Problems of the United States Senate, states: "There is ample evidence that large sections of the labor force are not adjusting to our changing economic structure."[9] The data he gives indicate the seriousness of the problem, but they do not constitute proof that the difficulties actually increased after 1957. Severe shortages of certain types of skill may exist in areas with considerable chronic unemployment, but the question is whether that condition is more prevalent than in comparable earlier periods.

On the basis of statistical data and the analysis obtained from experts, the Subcommittee on Economic Statistics to the Joint Economic Committee of the Congress concluded: "Thus the symptoms of growing unemployment resulting from unusual structural change in recent years have not been found. A small part of the rise in unemployment—perhaps two- or three-tenths of 1 per cent of the labor force—may have been due to structural changes, but the bulk of the increase over 4 per cent in recent years reflects a failure of demand forces to keep pace with the rise in the Nation's potential output at full employment. . . ."[10]

The Subcommittee did not try to test whether the adaptability of the labor force to current economic changes had been reduced because of shifts in the type of change or stronger ties to a firm and locality because of such factors as seniority, benefits, and home

---

[9] "Structural Unemployment and Public Policy," *Labor Law Journal*, XII (July 1961), p. 578.

[10] *Employment and Unemployment, op. cit.*, p. 8. For a seemingly different opinion see the minority views of Congressman Thomas B. Curtis, *idem.*, pp. 19–21.

ownership. Generally it seemed to share the view that hard core unemployment tends to melt away with sufficient expansion in total demand. That happened in World War II, aided by Federal manpower programs and cost-plus contracts. It is true that relatively full employment leads to lower hiring standards and incentives for employers to provide training, whereas in periods of high unemployment management can be more selective, raising hiring standards and insisting on more preemployment training.

How much current unemployment is solely due to adjustment difficulties arising from structural changes in the economy probably will not be known until this country again approaches full employment, defined (say) as 96 per cent of the work force gainfully occupied and an average of 4 per cent temporarily unemployed. Then if adjustment difficulties have increased, job vacancies and other labor bottlenecks will expand significantly as the economy crowds the 4 per cent unemployment rate.

UNEMPLOYMENT COMPENSATION

Recent increases in long-term unemployment and expansion in the proportion of the workforce likely to have only intermittent or casual attachment (i.e., students, housewives, and pensioners) have raised questions concerning the aims of unemployment insurance and its relationship to retraining and other programs.

Unemployment compensation, as the program is commonly called in this country, has been subject to sharp differences of opinion. Payment of benefits to jobless workers may affect work incentives and the operation of market forces in the labor area. Establishment of a social program, financed by taxes in order to provide a minimum level of income security, may also seem to reduce individual responsibility and has been questioned as part of an expanding welfare state or "creeping socialism."

In order to evaluate criticisms of the program and proposals for revision, it is necessary to understand the basic characteristics of our present system. Therefore, consideration will be given to the aims and structure of unemployment compensation and experience with its financing and benefits, before analyzing the economic effects and considering proposals for reform.

Objectives and Framework

Unemployment compensation was initially visualized as a short-term program under which workers, who have a record of employment and are regularly attached to the labor force, would receive, when involuntarily unemployed, benefits as a matter of right. Eligibility and benefit amounts are specified in the law in terms of objective criteria, without regard to personal circumstances or needs. Primarily, the benefits are intended as partial compensation for the wage loss of jobless persons willing and able to work, with the worker's weekly benefit geared to his normal weekly wage.

Other objectives secondary to the main aim of partial wage-loss compensation are: (1) to contribute to general economic stability by underpinning workers' purchasing power; (2) to stimulate regularity of employment on the part of individual firms through incentive tax provisions; (3) to provide some general sharing of the burdens of involuntary unemployment; (4) to preserve work skills during brief periods of joblessness; and (5) to maintain normal economic incentives. It is evident that, in practice, aims (1) and (5), or (2) and (3), or (4) and (5), might conflict. Therefore, in drafting laws it was necessary to draw a balance between different objectives and to work out practical compromises.

The program has been a limited one, particularly designed for short-term unemployment, mostly frictional and cyclical in character. Primarily for financial reasons, but also because of possible effects on workers' incentives, absolute limits were put on the size and duration of weekly benefits, with wage-loss compensation, geared to normal pay, operating only within those limits.

The Social Security Act of 1935 did not create a system of unemployment compensation. Largely because of doubts about the constitutionality of such action, a Federal payroll tax of 3 per cent was levied on covered employers, with the proviso that States could save 90 per cent of the Federal tax for jobless benefits in the State or (through tax-reduction credits) for industry within the State, if the State enacted an approved unemployment compensation law. The tax-offset arrangement was sufficient to encourage all States to pass laws. Thus, each State has its own provisions with regard to employer tax rates and tax credits and benefit amounts and duration, and each State has its own reserve fund specifically for benefit payments. We have, therefore, a so-called Federal-State system, with the Federal Government paying the full cost of administration in each State.

No Federal standards exist with respect to the benefit levels or duration in a State program. Consequently, wide variation exists among States with respect to benefit eligibility, benefit schedules, and the maximum number of benefit payments a jobless worker can draw in any one year. Such variation is encouraged by the provision in the Federal Act that permits individual employers partial or even complete exemption from 90 per cent of the Federal payroll tax through a State program of experience rating. Experience rating is usually based on the amount of benefits drawn by a company's employees. Thus, management is encouraged to keep benefits charged to the company's account low by such means as avoiding lay-offs, contesting claims, and resisting improvements in benefit levels. The Federal tax was intended to eliminate unemployment benefits as an element in competition between States for industry, but experience rating has provided encouragement of interstate competition in low benefit levels and high disqualification ratios.

Financing

Benefit costs are financed by State payroll taxes. The fraction of the Federal payroll tax not offset by the State taxes or exemptions under experience rating is used for administrative costs.

When the Social Security Act was passed, it was expected that 2.7 per cent of total payrolls would be needed by the States to finance unemployment benefits. However, as indicated by the last column of Table 28, State taxes on employers averaged only half that rate in 1962, and were less than a third of it during much of the fifties. Although the United States average in 1962 was 1.38 per cent, six States has an average unemployment tax of 2.0 to 2.3 per cent, and five States had average employer tax rates of only 0.5 or 0.6 per cent of total payrolls. Experience rating and differences between States in benefit standards help to explain how a firm, with a certain number of benefit checks charged to its ac-

TABLE 28

Unemployment Compensation Benefits and Financial Ratios, 1940–62

Year	Average Weekly Benefits	Average Actual Duration of Benefits in Weeks	Average Weekly Benefit as Per Cent of Average Weekly Wages in Covered Employment	Total Benefits as Per Cent of Total Wage and Salary Income	Employer State Taxes as Per Cent of Total Wages in Covered Employment
1940	$10.56	9.8	39.1	.68	2.63
1945	18.77	8.5	41.6	.34	1.74
1950	20.76	13.0	34.4	.64	1.16
1955	25.04	12.4	32.1	.52	.81
1958	30.58	14.8	35.3	1.17	.86
1960	32.87	12.7	35.2	.75	1.17
1962	34.56	13.1	34.9	.72	1.38

Sources: Calculated from data in *Handbook of Unemployment Insurance Financial Data, 1938–1958,* plus supplementary tables for 1959–61, Bureau of Employment Security, United States Department of Labor, April 1960; "Financial Developments under State Unemployment Insurance Programs in Calendar Year 1962," *Labor Market and Employment Security,* July 1963, pp. 15–23; and *Economic Report of the President,* January 1963, p. 200.

count, could have three or four times as high an unemployment tax in one State as in another.

Within some States the range of variation in company tax rates under experience rating is more pronounced. In most of the State laws, the highest tax rate is at least nine times the lowest rate (in 29 States 0.0 or 0.1 per cent of the first $3,000). For competing firms, the difference between a tax of 0.1 and 2.7 per cent can make a real difference. With firms in an industry at both extremes of the tax-rate schedule, it is not likely that much of the State taxes under experience rating can be shifted forward to customers in prices. Most of such a highly differentiated tax undoubtedly is absorbed by the companies.[11]

As it has operated in practice, experience rating gives the highest tax rewards for employment stability during a period when the accent should be on employment expansion. With the present volume of unemployment and the unprecedented number

---

[11] For a further discussion of the incidence of State payroll taxes under experience rating see Richard A. Lester, *The Economics of Unemployment Compensation,* Industrial Relations Section, Princeton University, Princeton, N.J., 1962, pp. 60–68.

of youths who each year in the sixties will begin looking for jobs, it is passé to have an incentive-type unemployment tax that contains no incentive for employment expansion, but, on the contrary, tends to penalize it.

Since 1939, the Federal Unemployment Tax has been applied to only the first $3,000 earned by a person in any one year in covered employment. Most of the States also limit their tax base to $3,000, although nine States have bases of $3,600 to $7,200. The result is that, in a year like 1962, taxable wages were only 60 per cent of total wages; 40 per cent of total payrolls was exempt from any tax for financing unemployment benefits.

The tax base in the States should be adjusted for changes in the wage level. Average weekly wages are four times the 1939 figure. In many States, the wage base for benefits far exceeds $3,000 a year. Benefits should be at least half normal earnings, but $3,000 a year is only $58 a week, compared with an average weekly benefit of $34.56 for 1962 as indicated in Table 28.

Generally speaking, high-wage firms with fairly steady employment have opposed raising the tax base for unemployment compensation. Basically, the reason is that their managements desire to use the low tax base as a means of keeping their tax burden down and to increase the relative burden on low-wage, less stable firms through raising the top tax rates for companies with a poor experience rating. In view of the fact that, in most States, the top tax rate is at least nine times the bottom rate, representaives of the large, stable corporations would seem to be pushing an incentive tax theory to almost ridiculous extremes to the detriment of an adequate benefit program.

Benefits

Two important questions with respect to unemployment benefits are eligibility and adequacy. The eligibility question centers around whether people are drawing benefits who should not in view of the objectives of the program. If it aims to provide benefits only to persons who are regularly attached to the labor force and are seeking year-around employment, then the requirements for benefits should be drawn so as to eliminate persons who wish, and customarily engage in, part-year work. In most States, the eligibility requirements (drawn in dollars of wages or weeks of work) are too low for that purpose. In many States, a high-wage worker can gain eligibility with seven or eight weeks of work. The twenty weeks a number of States require, and that constitute the criterion for employer liability for the Federal Unemployment Tax, would seem necessary for screening out students working during vacations and housewives wishing only intermittent or seasonal work. Of course, the requirement that beneficiaries regularly report to the public employment offices for work and, in many States, actively seek employment by inquiring at firms in the community, also helps prevent malingering.

There should be some relationship between eligibility requirements and benefit duration. The longer the period a jobless worker can draw benefits, the higher the total earnings and weeks of work for eligibility should be. Otherwise, many workers may, year after year, draw more in benefits than in wages. Also some seasonal industries, in recruiting workers, offer them a certain wage plus so many weeks of unemployment benefits. That is a perversion of the system.

Difficulties of Defining Benefit Adequacy

Since the States began to pay benefits in the late thirties, benefit levels have not kept pace with wage levels. That is evident from the third column in Table 28. In the late thirties and early forties, average weekly benefits were around 40 per cent of the average wage in covered employment. In recent years, the ratio has fluctuated around 35 per cent.

One of the greatest shortcomings of the benefit schedules in the State laws has been the low benefit ceilings. In 1963, eighteen States (including five in the North) had weekly benefit ceilings of $35 or less. Assuming a 50 per cent compensation for wage loss, a $35 ceiling prevents any earnings above $70 a week from counting in the calculation of benefits. A low ceiling means the same flat benefit for a large proportion of all beneficiaries in that State. In 1962, for the country as a whole, 44 per cent of all beneficiaries were eligible for the State's maximum benefit. In fourteen States three-fifths or more of all beneficiaries were eligible for the maximum, and in Iowa, four-fifths. If the bulk of the beneficiaries in a State are to receive weekly compensation equal to half their gross weekly loss from unemployment, no more than one-third of all beneficiaries should be bumping the benefit ceiling. In order to keep their maximums in line with wage-level changes, nine States provide for automatic yearly adjustment of the benefit ceiling to 50, 52.5, or 55 per cent of average weekly wages in covered employment in the State.

Some writers have argued that, with the high taxes on personal income, unemployment benefits can be at a reduced percentage of normal wages because they are tax-free. By and large, however, the disemployed workers' losses of fringe benefits (including paid vacations, holidays, and sick leave) offset the savings that beneficiaries have on personal income taxes.[12]

The benefit ceilings and formulas in the States had such an adverse effect on wage-loss compensation for workers in certain high-wage industries that, in 1955 and 1956, the Automobile Workers, the Steelworkers, and the Rubber Workers negotiated programs of supplemental unemployment benefits paid for by the companies. Under such private s.u.b. programs, the weekly State benefit is supplemented by a company benefit equal to, say, 60 or 65 per cent of the worker's normal weekly wage, limited by a maximum of, say, $40 of s.u.b. a week.[13] The programs cover as much as 52 weeks of benefits, with the company fund paying the full amount after the laid-off employee exhausts his rights to State benefits.

As spells of unemployment have lengthened, particularly in recessions, pressures have mounted to extend benefit duration. The increase in average actual duration is indicated in Table 28. The maximum potential duration for beneficiaries rose from an average of twenty weeks in 1946 to twenty-four weeks in 1961, indicating the extent to which State laws had improved with respect to benefit duration during those fifteen years. In 1962, two-thirds of the insured claimants were eligible for 26 weeks or more of benefits. Most State laws vary duration with the amount of the worker's earnings or weeks of employment during the twelve months on which his

---

[12] For an elaboration of that point see Richard A. Lester, "The Economic Significance of Unemployment Compensation, 1948–1959," *Review of Economics and Statistics*, XLII (November 1960), pp. 350–51.

[13] For a summary of plans, see *Digest of Nine Supplemental Unemployment Benefit Plans, Early 1963*, Bulletin No. 1365, Bureau of Labor Statistics, United States Department of Labor, 1963.

benefits are based. States with short duration of benefits in their laws generally have high percentages of beneficiaries who exhaust their benefit rights before obtaining reemployment. For the country as a whole in 1962, over one-quarter of the beneficiaries became "exhaustees."

Because of the severity of long-term unemployment in the 1958 and 1961 recessions, benefit duration was extended 50 per cent (i.e., from 26 to 39 weeks) for a period of over a year under emergency programs. In each period some two million jobless received such "extended benefits." In 1958–59, the financing was by Federal loan to be repaid by the States entering the program. In 1961–62, the extended benefits were paid completely from Federal funds. Because the "extended benefits" were not provided as part of a regular program but were suddenly-adopted "emergency measures," they represented a departure from the insurance principle of benefits as a matter of right, based on previous contributions.

Economic Effects

Because many benefits are inadequate and the coverage of unemployment compensation is rather restricted, the program has not been as effective as an "automatic stabilizer" as it should. It has the distinct advantage that benefits expand and contract automatically in a countercyclical fashion. However, because of experience rating and the narrow tax base, the burden of unemployment taxes tends to have a cyclically-accentuating effect.[14]

It is estimated that over forty million workers are in employment covered by the State laws, with some fourteen million exempt from coverage by various exclusions (small firms, agriculture, State and local government, nonprofit institutions, etc.). However, eligibility requirements, disqualifications (e.g., for quitting a job or refusing suitable work), and exhaustions have meant that only about half the unemployed were drawing benefits at any one time in most postwar years. Since the benefits drawn have averaged less than 50 per cent of the wage loss that beneficiaries were experiencing as a result of unemployment, it is understandable that

---

[14] For further discussion of this point see Lester, *The Economics of Unemployment Compensation, op. cit.*, pp. 69–73.

no more than around 20 per cent of the total wage loss in the country from unemployment has, in the past, been compensated by the various public insurance programs.[15]

The year of the largest total of benefit payments was 1958, when $4.2 billion was paid out under all public programs including extended benefits. To put total benefits in perspective, they have been expressed in Table 28 in percentage of total wage and salary income. Even in 1958, total benefits amounted to only a little over 1 per cent as much as total employment income. Consequently, unemployment compensation has been a very minor factor in sustaining consumption. Exactly how the guarantee of benefits affects different items of consumption is unkown.

Experience rating undoubtedly has encouraged employer efforts to stabilize employment, although other factors (such as savings on labor turnover and transfer costs) generally provide a greater incentive for a management to make steady use of its workforce. From a public-policy viewpoint, however, the problem has been one of insufficient expansion, and experience rating tends to discourage that. To that extent, the program has its tax priorities out of step with the economy's needs. Experience rating has the further disadvantage of accentuating cyclical savings and encouraging interstate competition in saving on unemployment taxes by unduly restricting benefits. Encouragement of employer-policing of the program through experience rating does help to avoid some abuse, but it also stimulates employer opposition to adequate benefits.

Proposals for Reform

Various weaknesses in our Federal-State system of unemployment compensation have been mentioned. Some students of the subject believe that structural reform of the whole program is necessary because the tax-offset method is too awkward and too ill-suited for the achievement of certain objectives. It is claimed, for example, that national objectives (i.e., improvement in unemployment compensation as an automatic stabilizer for the economy) are bound

---

[15] For detailed monthly estimates of compensation ratios for the period 1948 through 1959, see Lester, "The Economic Significance of Unemployment Compensation, 1948–1959," *op. cit.*, pp. 349–72.

to be neglected under a framework that encourages States to concentrate on their own self-interest. Separate State systems, with the full tax load on employer payrolls, are not well designed for meeting the problem of long-term unemployment. Experience-rating provisions embodied in the tax-offset method, by emphasizing employer blame for unemployment, are based on unsound employment theory and misdirect the program. The tax-offset method is not well adapted to broadening the sources of funds for the program, nor for achieving some measure of national sharing of the uneven incidence of unemployment among States. Separate State systems mean independent State reserves, some of which are in danger of depletion while others are excessive.

Most of those who stress the shortcomings of the present system would, as a general proposition, favor a straight national program of unemployment insurance. That is the arrangement in most industrial countries. However, any such change is unlikely, unless and until the present scheme either breaks down in some States or becomes obviously unsatisfactory. Too many vested interests have been built into the present arrangements to permit any basic structural change just on the basis of economic analysis.

A set of proposals to improve the unemployment compensation program within the present Federal-State framework was offered by the Kennedy Administration in 1963. Introduced in Congress as the McCarthy-King bill, it would provide: (1) Federal adjustment benefits from the twenty-seventh up to the fifty-second week for all those who exhaust their State benefit rights and have had a substantial labor-force attachment during the preceding three years; (2) Federal equalization grants to the States with heavy unemployment in any year, the grants to amount to two-thirds of the State's benefit costs in excess of 2.7 per cent of taxable wages; (3) an increase of 0.3 per cent in the Federal Unemployment Tax rate to finance the adjustment benefits and equalization grants, which would make the total Federal tax not subject to offset 0.7 per cent; (4) a Federal requirement that State weekly benefit amounts be at least 50 per cent of the individual's average weekly wage up to a ceiling that must rise by steps to two-thirds of the State's average weekly wage in covered employment (if a State failed to meet that standard, the Federal tax could be offset only by the percentage that the State's total benefit costs were of taxable wages, measured over a four-year period); (5) an increase in the taxable wage base to $5,200 of annual earnings per employee; (6) extension of coverage to three million more workers; and (7) establishment of a Special Advisory Commission to review the Federal-State program of unemployment compensation and make recommendations for improvement.

Under the first proposal, responsibility for the first 26 weeks of a worker's joblessness would be left to the States. Unemployment of longer duration is made a Federal responsibility on the grounds (a) that long-term unemployment is a national problem resulting from economic factors (e.g., technological change, shifts in industry) that transcend State lines, and (b) that such unemployment is more effectively treated under programs that include a national approach. In this connection, the McCarthy-King bill proposes to deny tax credits to employers in States which do not amend their laws to permit workers to continue eligibility for benefits while taking training with the approval of the State agency, even though that may mean a beneficiary's refusal to accept suitable work. Such a mixing of unemployment compensation and training, although provided in twenty-two State laws, violates the basic concept in social insurance of benefits as a matter of right. Training programs should be separately operated and financed, with separate allowances for necessary living expenses during the training period.

SUMMARY

This chapter has analyzed our increasing unemployment problem and the role of unemployment compensation in meeting it. The conclusions can be condensed as follows:

1. Job expansion has been slowing down and the rate of unemployment has risen generally throughout the country. Since 1957, the spells of unemployment have lengthened.

2. The incidence of unemployment is heaviest among young persons, nonwhites, and the unskilled and semiskilled factory workers; it is high in certain industries like construction and mining.

3. Deficiency in aggregate demand appears to be largely responsible for the increased rates of unemployment; some scraps of evidence support the thesis that structural changes in the economy and added impediments to adjustment are responsible for a small fraction of the increase in unemployment.

4. Our Federal-State system of unemployment compensation was designed for short-term unemployment. Largely because of restricted coverage, inadequate benefit levels, and limited duration of benefits, the program compensates for only about one-fifth of the wage loss caused by total unemployment.

5. Many of the shortcomings of the present system stem from separate State programs under the tax-offset device with provision for experience rating.

6. Improvements can be made within the present framework to guide the whole program more in the direction of national interest. However, such steps involve an increase in Federal requirements and more Federal tax income, which are resisted by the States and the employers.

DISCUSSION QUESTIONS

1. What are the various factors that explain the high rate of unemployment among persons seventeen to twenty-four years of age?
2. Explain how you assess the responsibility for the increased rate of unemployment after 1957.
3. Explain what you think the objectives of unemployment compensation should be and in what order of priority.
4. Discuss the arguments that can be made for and against expanding the tax base from $3,000 to $7,200 of earnings in a year.
5. Discuss the question of the adequacy of state unemployment benefits from the point of view of (a) an employer, (b) a labor union official, and (c) the President of the United States.
6. What do you consider to be the most serious shortcomings of the present Federal-State program of unemployment compensation? Explain the basis for your conclusions.
7. Which of the reforms in the McCarthy-King bill do you think

should be adopted or adopted as you would propose to modify them? Explain the case that can and would be made against the reforms you favor.

SELECTED REFERENCES

Burns, Eveline M., "New Guidelines for Unemployment Insurance," *Employment Security Review*, XXIX (August 1962), pp. 5–9.

Knowles, James W., *Higher Unemployment Rates, 1957–60: Structural Transformation or Inadequate Demand*, Report of Subcommittee on Economic Statistics of the Joint Economic Committee, February 2, 1962, Eighty-seventh Congress, 2nd session (Washington: United States Government Printing Office, 1962).

Lester, Richard A., *The Economics of Unemployment Compensation*, Industrial Relations Section, Princeton University, Princeton, N.J., 1962.

Manpower Report of the President and *A Report on Manpower Requirements, Resources, Utilization, and Training by the United States Department of Labor* (Washington: United States Government Printing Office, 1963).

Measuring Employment and Unemployment, President's Committee to Appraise Employment and Unemployment Statistics (Washington: United States Government Printing Office, 1962).

Report of the Special Committee on Unemployment Problems, Senate Report No. 1206, Eighty-sixth Congress, 2nd session (Washington: United States Government Printing Office, March 30, 1960).

Somers, Herman M., "Some Issues in the Improvement of the Federal-State Unemployment Insurance Program" and "Discussion," in *Proceedings of the Twelfth Annual Meeting of the Industrial Relations Research Association*, David B. Johnson (ed.), Madison, Wisconsin, 1960, pp. 92–114.

Wilcock, Richard C., and Walter H. Franke, *Unwanted Workers: Permanent Layoffs and Long-Term Unemployment* (New York: The Free Press of Glencoe, 1963).

18.

Manpower Planning and the Training Act

WITH THE ENACTMENT of the Manpower Development and Training Act of 1962, this country took a significant step toward comprehensive manpower planning. Such planning had occurred in World War II under the War Manpower Commission. In a sense, it was implied in the Employment Act of 1946, which stipulates a goal of "maximum employment, production, and purchasing power."

The Manpower Development and Training Act, however, specifically sets forth the over-all planning function to be performed and makes the national manpower program a specific instrument of national policy. After mentioning "improved planning" the act's "Statement of Findings and Purpose" ends with the sentence: "It is therefore the purpose of this Act to require the Federal Government to appraise the manpower requirements and resources of the Nation, and to develop and apply the information and methods needed to deal with the problems of unemployment resulting from automation and technological change and other types of persistent unemployment." The act requires the President to transmit to

Congress each March "a report pertaining to manpower requirements, resources, utilization, and training."

In this country during World War II and in a number of European countries during the postwar era, manpower planning developed principally in order to anticipate and overcome labor shortages
in certain occupations and areas. Planning under the Manpower
Act, on the other hand, grew mainly out of the need to adapt
unemployed workers with obsolete or few skills to the changing
job requirements caused by technological advance and economic
shifts.

This chapter first analyzes the economics of national manpower
programming. It then discusses the instruments for manpower planning and the problems of attaining a coordinated program in a free
economy with national, State, and local levels of government.
Finally, the experience with retraining the unemployed under
Title II of the Manpower Act is examined.

ECONOMICS OF MANPOWER POLICY

Traditionally, people have been largely left on their own in
selecting careers, taking training, and locating jobs. It may be difficult, therefore, to understand why the Federal Government should:
(1) engage in planning so as to help adapt labor supply to meet
shifts in demand; (2) provide special facilities for counseling and
testing workers and referring them to jobs; and (3) pay for preemployment training in occupations where individuals have customarily financed their own preparation.

What economic justification is there for such government intervention and expenditures in the "labor market?" Why not leave
the adaptation of supply and the matching of demand and supply
to individual action, unaided except by the guidance of market
forces?

Improvement in Allocation and Adjustment

The chief basis for government services for workers and employers
in the employment area is to improve the functioning of "the
market." This the Federal, State, and local governments can do in
a variety of ways. The first is by supplying information and advice.

The public employment service can gather, analyze, and forecast demand and supply in terms of particular kinds of jobs and their preemployment requirements, not only locally but on a national basis. Serving as a job clearinghouse helps the employment service gather and analyze job information and sharpens the staff's awareness of job developments. On the basis of such information and of aptitude and other tests, students and adults can be counseled so that their career and job choices are more intelligent and can be made early enough, before age has foreclosed occupational areas for which they may have real aptitude.

A second way in which the government can improve the functioning of "the market" is by helping to adapt supply to demand through vocational training and education. Vocational education for high-school youth has been a traditional public service. For unskilled or semiskilled older workers out of work and handicapped by a low level of education, some capital investment in training may be necessary as "handicap removal" in order to open up employment opportunities for them. The alternative may be long-term joblessness and dependency, with the consequent economic waste and social costs. The chief barriers to retraining are the cost to the trainee, the lack of appropriate training facilities, and the lack of any kind of assurance of prospective employment if the individual undertakes training on his own. A government program can help in reducing each of those three barriers.

The third way that government can aid "market" adjustments is by developing a staff of experts in job placement, who can facilitate needed mobility and proper matching of workers with job openings. By screening workers for referral and by arranging for interstate transfer of workers to fill vacancies elsewhere, much wasteful and disorderly search for jobs can be avoided. Also, referral on a merit basis can reduce the wastes of discrimination. This clearinghouse function should help in the optimum allocation of the nation's labor resources among jobs and ought to aid in reducing the average loss of time between jobs.

Possible Gains and Costs

By performing satisfactorily those three functions—supplying information, training, and matching—the government can contribute to increasing productivity and economic growth. In general, people would be aided in moving to more productive jobs (measured by compensation). An adequate, free retraining program with living allowances (as under the Manpower Act) might help to lower worker resistance to technological change and reduce the propensity to develop restrictive, job-protection practices (popularly known as "featherbedding"). If government facilitates the adjustment of supply to areas of expanding demand, bottlenecks from labor shortage should be reduced, thus decreasing bottleneck pressures upward on wage scales. To the extent that a retraining program reduces the dependency costs of long-term, dispirit-producing unemployment, savings in relief and other social costs could be made.

A government manpower program also has a number of less direct benefits. It can, for example, provide companies with labor-supply information as a factor in deciding on plant location and expansion. It tends to stimulate thinking and research on manpower problems and, as explained below, helps to coordinate different activities.

Thus, the benefits or gains may accrue to individual workers, to individual managements, to taxpayers in the form of reduced unemployment compensation and relief costs (not to mention other costs of long-term unemployment), and to the economy as a whole. Against such gains must be weighed the costs or resources used to provide these government employment services.

How can one measure such uncertain and disparate gains and balance them against the cost of providing the services? In our present state of knowledge, this does not seem possible for the program as a whole, although some attempts are being made with respect to particular elements such as training.

The test of what individuals and companies are willing to pay for the service is not a satisfactory one in most cases. That may be an appropriate yardstick for private, fee-charging employment agencies, but they do not and cannot supply the kind of services mentioned above. Charging on the basis of ability to pay or cost of service would restrict the services by eliminating the elements of individual need and community or public service. As a result, some of the economies of scale would be lost. It is evident that the government must provide part of the organization for performing the informational function. Also, some machinery in the employment area is necessary for other governmental programs. For example, a public employment service is needed for the unemployment compensation program in order to help test availability for work and willingness to accept suitable employment; it is needed also for the Area Redevelopment program, both in the determination of distress areas and in the selection of training projects and workers for training.

Economists have come to recognize and give proper weight to the importance of investment in people as a means of promoting productivity and economic growth.[1] They are also beginning to stress the contribution to the production process made by the gathering, use, and dissemination of information.[2] In both areas—training and information—a government manpower program can make significant contributions. In addition, it can facilitate production by centralizing and systematizing the job-matching function so as to reduce the costs of search and recruiting and loss of time and proper utilization of labor from lack of matching or misplacement. Furthermore, economic waste can be reduced by proper planning and coordination of the different manpower-affecting activities of government at various levels—national, State, and local.

Manpower planning and coordination need to be directed from the national level. Many occupations have a national labor-market area in the sense that employers recruit for them on a nation-wide basis. Also, for reasons of national safety and well-being, it is important that we have an adequate national supply of people trained in certain occupational areas such as science, mathematics, engineering, social science, medicine, military operations, and public administration. In other occupations, Federal aid may be necessary because private employers, for reasons of anticipated turnover, may not provide sufficient on-the-job training for certain groups, especially youth and women. And States and localities may hesitate to provide sufficient preemployment training in certain occupations because of anticipated loss from migration of the trained personnel

---

[1] See Theodore W. Schultz, "Reflections on Investment in Man," *Journal of Political Economy*, LXX (October 1962), *Supplement on Investment in Human Beings*, and other papers in that Supplement.

[2] See George J. Stigler, "Information in the Labor Market," *ibid.*, pp. 94–105; and Fritz Machlup, *The Production and Distribution of Knowledge in the United States* (Princeton: Princeton University Press, 1962).

to other States and localities. In addition, a national program can achieve economies of scale in such matters as interstate job clearance, statistics, and research.

THE REPORT AND OVER-ALL PROGRAM

The Manpower Development and Training Act commits the Federal Government to a comprehensive and integrated approach to the nation's manpower problems. Through research and advance planning, changes in job requirements are to be anticipated, and preparations are to be made for the most effective use of the nation's manpower resources in the light of anticipated changes.

In the Manpower Act, a sharp distinction is drawn between the planning, information, and research activities under Title I and the training program and operations under Title II, which are discussed in the next section. The annual manpower reports of the President and the Secretary of Labor, provided for in Title I, are part of the planning and programming activities. They supply the ideas, guidelines, and the direction; execution is to be accomplished through operating branches of different government agencies.

A significant aspect of manpower planning is coordination of programs and some determination of relative priorities. Without coordination, separate programs may not mesh but instead may work at cross-purposes. Without some scale of relative importance, a particular employer may be pressed by government agencies, at the same time and with equal vigor, to fill particular jobs by hiring youth, older workers, Negroes, women, handicapped, and long-term unemployed who have been retrained.

The President's annual report sets forth general policy directions and guidelines. The Office of Manpower, Automation, and Training in the Department of Labor prepares materials for the reports of the President and the Secretary of Labor. OMAT has the responsibility for developing a comprehensive manpower program, including the analysis of manpower resources and requirements, the coordination and appraisal of policies, and the evaluation of results in terms of present and foreseeable needs.

The President's Manpower Report

The annual Manpower Report of the President provides a vehicle for analyzing the present manpower situation and the various programs of the Federal Government in this field. It also provides the occasion for offering new proposals or expansions of existing programs as part of a comprehensive, integrated plan.

President Kennedy devoted his first Manpower Report in 1963 largely to manpower trends, manpower philosophy, a catalogue of needs (with particular attention called to certain disadvantaged groups), and a glance into the future. He pointed to the shift away from employment in goods production (explained in Chapter 1), with production workers in manufacturing down 7 per cent and mining employment down over 20 per cent between 1957 and 1962, and agricultural employment disappearing at a rate of about 200,000 a year. At the same time the labor force is expected to grow in the sixties at a rate over 50 per cent greater than in the fifties. In 1965, some 3,800,000 persons will turn eighteen years of age—46 per cent above the corresponding 1960 figure. With the flood of new entrants, one-third of the labor force in 1970 will consist of persons who started work in the sixties.

The President pointed to the long-range aspects and consequences of much manpower planning. Indeed, one reason that a comprehensive plan is needed is because manpower policy has to look to the future in terms of a generation or more. For example, the lead time for the production of physicians and advanced scientists is at least a decade.

In the Report, the President stated that he looked to manpower research, provided for under the act, to develop new tools and approaches as part of our "social inventiveness" to help solve problems and realize our full manpower potential. As one example, he cited the need to explore the degree of occupational, industrial, and geographic mobility desirable under modern conditions of rapid technological and other change.

The 1963 Report contained no new proposals or programs, nor did it suggest ways to coordinate and integrate present Federal programs more effectively. Presumably, future reports will deal with such matters as the development of a set of policy criteria for coordinating different Federal programs and operations at all three levels of government, some standards for determining the success of and economic limits for each program, the efficacy of different types of attack on critical labor shortages, improvements in the techniques of forecasting occupational requirements, an "early warning" system for anticipating and preparing for major job displacements arising from technological change, the concept of an optimum amount of mobility and its implications for employment service operations and company benefit programs, an analysis of the economic and social implications of work hours, an evaluation of experience under the manpower program and the results of manpower research under the act, and the need to train more experts in the manpower field itself.

Central Role of the Employment Service[3]

The main operating agency of a manpower program is the nationwide network of over 1,900 employment offices, which are financed by the Federal Government from the Federal Unemployment Tax and administered by the States. The local offices should serve as community manpower centers, and the State agencies should be coordinated as part of a national manpower program.

Under a proper concept of its role the joint Federal-State Employment Service has a number of important manpower functions to perform. They include: (1) reporting, analyzing, and forecasting labor supply and demand on a local and national basis in order to aid in worker, company, and government planning and programs; (2) serving as an employment exchange by registering, screening, and referring workers and accepting and servicing the job orders of employers; (3) testing and counseling workers and selecting them for government training programs; and (4) assisting in the preparation and placement in jobs of handicapped groups so that their abilities are utilized. These four general areas of operation will be discussed in order to indicate what each involves. From a mere listing, however, it is evident that the staff of the

---

[3] For factual information, this subsection draws heavily from *Public Employment Service in the Nation's Job Market, 1933–1963, Employment Security Review,* XXX (June 1963), entire issue of 116 pages.

Employment Service must be experts in job analysis, job trends, workers' capabilities, and employer manpower needs.

1. INFORMATION AND ANALYSIS. For the organization and dissemination of labor demand and supply information it is necessary first to have a standard occupational classification so that requirements and available manpower can be measured, occupation by occupation. That has been accomplished by the preparation of a Dictionary of Occupational Titles (3rd ed., 1964), defining the content, tools, physical demands and training, aptitudes, and criteria for successful performance of some eight thousand separate occupational units. By grouping occupations according to skill relationships, programs of upgrading workers into higher-skill positions are facilitated. Indeed, many local employment office functions, such as selection and referral, testing and counseling, and reporting of information, depend on accurate delineation of occupations. So do the area skill surveys made every two or three years in major communities, analyzing by occupation the current and future requirements reported by employers and the local labor resources available and in prospect, in order to see how well resources will meet the requirements. Such surveys serve as a major device for community manpower planning.

The manpower information gathered and analyzed by the Employment Service provides a basis for anticipating requirements and for planning, both locally and nationally, with respect to training, counseling, interarea transfer, and other means for overcoming present and prospective occupational shortages. In addition, a system of classification of 150 major labor market areas into six labor-supply categories on the basis of percentage of unemployment and the manpower outlook permits interarea comparisons, which can be used for Federal programs to alleviate localized unemployment.

2. JOB EXCHANGE. The Employment Service provides a clearinghouse for registering and matching demand and supply. This is performed for each labor market and for the country as a whole through interarea recruitment and clearance.

To carry out this function satisfactorily, employers must use the Employment Service in recruiting workers and workers must do so in seeking jobs. Studies show that, for the nation as a whole, the job placements made through the Employment Service constitute about 15 per cent of all new hires. The percentage of all new hires supplied by the Employment Service—its "penetration rate"—varies by industry and occupation. For industries except agriculture, the rate varies from 21 per cent for manufacturing to 6 per cent for mining; by major occupational groups, the range is from 30 per cent for unskilled workers to 8 per cent for skilled workers and 10 per cent for professional workers.[4] For major metropolitan areas, the penetration rate ranges from 43 to 50 per cent for Minneapolis, Phoenix, and Memphis (and 37 per cent for New York City) to 15 to 17 per cent for upstate New York cities (Buffalo, Rochester, and Syracuse).

The percentages are not higher for a number of reasons. Most job seekers prefer informal channels for locating employment. Studies show that some three-fifths of all jobs are obtained through direct application at the company or through recruitment by relatives, friends, or others employed with the company. Advertisements amount for perhaps 10 per cent, and private fee-charging employment agencies about 4 per cent of the new hires.

Employers may be reluctant to use the public Employment Service for a variety of reasons. Informal methods of recruitment mean that the workers have expressed preference for the company, such methods permit management more easily to discriminate among applicants by selecting "our type of worker" (public agencies must implement nondiscriminatory policies), and the management can thereby obtain a better "feel" of "the market" from the company's viewpoint. Small and medium-sized firms tend to use the Employment Service more than do large firms, which have their own employment offices. Also, at times employers have complained about the quality of referrals from the Employment Service, which has been tied up with unemployment compensation; all beneficiaries have to be registered with the Service, which has helped to overrepresent unskilled workers on its rolls. To reduce that handicap and provide a more specialized service, employment

---

[4] The data in this and the next three paragraphs have been taken mostly from *Employment Service Participation in the Labor Market,* United States Employment Service, Department of Labor, Washington, D.C., February 1963, 14 pp. (mimeo.).

offices separate from unemployment compensation have been established on an industrial-occupational basis in almost all of the 55 major metropolitan areas, and 122 professional employment offices have been set up, linked by direct communication to speed up interarea placement.

The penetration rate of our Employment Service appears to be not too different from that of the public employment services in the United Kingdom and Western Germany. However, it is well below that for Sweden, which has more coordinated manpower planning and a more extensive program of training and transfer for unemployed workers than we have in this country. There 20 to 29 per cent of all hires are made through the public employment service, and private employment agencies are prohibited.

Agricultural workers constitute the largest element in the placement program of the Employment Service. In 1962, farm placements represented eight and a half million out of fifteen million job placements made by the Service that year. Exclusive of agriculture, the penetration rate is around 11 per cent.

One reason for the high number of farm placements is that agricultural workers are typically employed seasonally, mostly on large farms. A new labor force is assembled annually by each farmer for the short, critical cultivation and harvest seasons. The bulk of farm labor is recruited locally under day-haul programs. For migrant farm workers, the Employment Service has developed "The Annual Worker Plan," scheduling workers where and when they are needed so as to avoid the wastes of unsystematic individual search for work. As labor-saving machinery is increasingly applied in agriculture, the hired farm worker must possess the skills needed to operate and maintain farm equipment.

The Employment Service fulfills its job-exchange function not only by matching unemployed workers and jobs but also by placing employed workers in higher level positions so that their skills and talents are more fully utilized. Effective development and utilization of workers' capabilities is as much a part of efficient allocation of labor resources as is finding full-time work for jobless and underemployed workers. That explains why occupational testing and vocational counseling and guidance are a vital part of the Employment Service operations.

3. TESTING AND COUNSELING. The Employment Service has developed a variety of tests as a means of determining a worker's job potential and of supplying employers with test-selected workers for specific jobs. A General Aptitude Test Battery consisting of twelve tests is designed to measure intelligence, verbal aptitude, numerical aptitude, spatial aptitude, form perception, clerical perception, motor coordination, finger dexterity, and manual dexterity. An individual's test results can be compared with aptitude norms for different groups of occupations. A series of proficiency tests, such as typing and stenography, is designed to measure skills already acquired as an aid in selection and referral of experienced workers.

The Employment Service each year gives the Aptitude Battery to 150,000 applicants and tests some 60,000 individuals for proficiency. The results are used not only for placement but also for vocational counseling. Furthermore, the tests of the Service are used by a large number of schools, colleges, and other counseling organizations. Increasingly, there has been recognition of the need for early identification of talent and for educational-vocational counseling in the lower high-school grades.

In the 1963 Manpower Report, President Kennedy said: "Worker selection of occupations is now often haphazard or influenced by incentives unrelated to the best interests of the individuals or of the Nation."[5] The primary aim of counseling is to help the individual make intelligent vocational decisions by a broad assessment of his potential abilities, personal traits, and interests, plus a knowledge of occupational trends and future needs. The counselor should be particularly aware of shifting occupational requirements and the possibilities for transfer of skills, because it is estimated that, with rapid technological change, each worker can expect to make at least three career choices during his working life. Also counseling is important for mature women who are entering or reentering the labor force after years spent as housewives.

Each year over a million persons receive counseling service in local offices of the Employment Service. More than one-half of them are youths under twenty-two years of age, two-fifths are women, and one-seventh are handicapped workers. In order to

---

[5] *Manpower Report of the President*, March 1963, p. XX.

improve the quality of its counseling, the Employment Service has established educational and experience standards and arranged professional training courses.

4. ASSISTANCE TO DISADVANTAGED GROUPS. As a tax-supported agency, the Employment Service has some responsibility for helping in the economic rehabilitation of handicapped workers so that they do not lapse into permanent dependency. The physically handicapped (e.g., blind, deaf, or partially disabled veterans) and older workers who are handicapped by a lack of education or training constitute disadvantaged groups who need special attention and assistance. New job applications from physically handicapped persons at the Employment Service offices total about half a million a year. Training may be of particular importance to them, along with educational efforts to eliminate prejudices and other nonmerit factors in hiring and promotion. In the case of disemployed workers over forty-five years of age, special testing, counseling, and training may be required, together with demonstration by experience to dispel misconceptions and unfounded fears.

5. SHORTCOMINGS OF THE SERVICE. Our Federal-State Employment Service itself suffers from certain handicaps. With the organization and administration divided into fifty State units, national viewpoints and interests often fail to receive proper attention and emphasis. Also State boundaries are not well designed for employment service operations, which should be oriented in terms of labor market areas. For example, northern New Jersey should be part of a New York Metropolitan unit and southern New Jersey part of a Philadelphia area unit. Most industrial countries have a national employment service.

The Employment Service at the State and local levels has been handicapped by the quality of the staff. State salaries have been too low to recruit and hold promising employees. A high turnover has meant a continuous training problem and difficulties in maintaining staff relations with employers.

In most States, the staff of the Employment Service needs to have a more professional concept of its work, if it is to become a community and national manpower agency and not just a placement or an unemployment office. In order to serve as a manpower agency for technical and professional occupations, the Service needs to develop more knowledge of hiring and job requirements in those fields.

Strong opposition to expansion of the Employment Service beyond a placement agency for unemployed workers has been expressed by the fee-charging private agencies, which have been expanding in numbers recently. They see the Service as competition subsidized by an employer payroll tax. The United States Chamber of Commerce also has favored restriction of the Employment Service, not only to keep the Federal Unemployment Tax low but also to maintain the organization and operation of the employment process largely in private hands. Basically, such groups are opposed to central planning for the more effective use of manpower under arrangements that involve no encroachment on freedom of choice for the individual.

Vocational Education

An important factor in our total national output is the formal instruction that both youth and adults receive in the form of vocational education, including technical training. Two out of three youths enter the labor force without any college education or any vocational training in school.[6] Although a general high-school diploma is sufficient preemployment training for some occupations, lack of adequate preparation in school for subsequent employment handicaps some youngsters in locating and holding a job and in occupational advancement. Absence of adequate facilities in the high schools for vocational education with which to gain marketable skills is a major reason that more than a third of our youth drop out before completing a high-school education.

In the sixties, it is estimated that 26 million youths and three million wives or widows will enter the labor force. In addition, many millions of adults will need retraining in new occupations because automation and other changes have eliminated their cus-

---

[6] This section draws heavily from *Education for a Changing World of Work, Report of the Panel of Consultants on Vocational Education*, Office of Education, United States Department of Health, Education, and Welfare (Washington: United States Government Printing Office, 1963). Helpful also has been a pamphlet by Sar A. Levitan, *Vocational Education and Federal Policy*, W. E. Upjohn Institute for Employment Research, Kalamazoo, Michigan, May 1963.

tomary occupation or altered it so that some updating or refresher training is needed.

Present vocational training programs and facilities are inadequate for the task and, to a considerable extent, are misdirected. Each year, about six million persons, one-third of them adults, receive some vocational training in schools at a cost of about half a billion dollars. Some four million of them are in programs aided by Federal funds, which are used almost entirely for teachers' salaries. The cost is distributed roughly as follows: Federal, 20 per cent; State, 35 per cent; local, 45 per cent. The trainees are almost equally divided between youth in day-school programs and adults and out-of-school youths in extension programs. Of the four million, some 1.6 million are in homemaking courses as preparation for family and household responsibilities and not in courses aimed at participation in the labor force. Of the remaining 2.4 million, some 800,000, or one-third, are being prepared for agricultural work, which, as already noted, is an industry where jobs are disappearing at the rate of 200,000 a year. It is estimated that only about a third of the high school graduates in vocational agriculture enter farming.

The areas of expanding employment are largely in office work, retail distribution, finance, and service lines. Under the Federally aided programs, only 300,000 a year are trained in distributive occupations (retail and wholesale trade, finance, insurance, and real estate), partly because legislation restricts vocational education to persons already employed in those lines. Office work is excluded from Federal aid, but it is estimated that half of all high-school students in vocational courses are training in clerical occupations under programs that rely on State and local financing. Under the Federally supported programs, only a little over 100,000 students get technical training. In only nine States can one learn to be an office-machine repairman, and in only eleven States to be an electric-appliance repairman.

Clearly, vocational education in our schools badly needs reorientation. It should be much more closely geared to supplying the needs of expanding industries and occupations and the retraining needs of adults who, because of an inadequate educational background, are handicapped for work in nonfactory employment or for jobs in highly mechanized plants. President Kennedy pointed out in his 1963 Manpower Report that "We must modernize and enlarge our vocational and technical education programs for all age groups—and focus them on occupations with future opportunities."[7]

The Problem of Coordination

In the same Report, the President expressed the need for national manpower planning and for coordination in its application and execution, as follows: "Public and private welfare, education, health, research, cultural, defense, and other major policies have significant and perhaps conflicting implications for our Nation's manpower future. They should be appraised in an overall framework from the standpoint of their long-range manpower effects to point directions for more rational coordination and meshing."[8]

Vocational education well illustrates the need for cooperation and coordination between Federal agencies and Federally supported activities at the national, State, and local levels. The data presented above clearly show that much vocational training is not well designed for future manpower requirements as projected by the Department of Labor. The curriculum and course content of vocational education should be reshaped to take account of information supplied by the Employment Service with respect to the directions of occupational development. And the counseling that is part of the training process should be coordinated with the counseling that the worker receives from the Employment Service before and after his training.

The need for coordination can also be illustrated by unemployment compensation. The duration of benefits should be related to the extent to which disemployed workers should be encouraged to remain in their present occupations without any additional training. Eligibility provisions should take account of the need to attract workers into the labor force for seasonal work. With a training program for unemployed workers, should there be any direct relationship between unemployment compensation benefits and the size of weekly allowances to support a trainee and his family during the training period? Also the question arises whether the receipt of unemployment compensation should be conditioned upon the

---

[7] *Manpower Report of the President*, March 1963, p. XVIII.

[8] *Ibid.*, p. XX.

beneficiary's willingness to engage in a retraining program. Tying strings to the receipt of unemployment benefits tends to transform such compensation from an insurance to a labor-control program.

A country with a well-coordinated, national manpower program is Sweden. Practically all matters dealing with manpower planning, unemployment, and labor-mobility aids are concentrated in the hands of a national Labor Market Board and its twenty-five County Labor Boards. The national Board of ten members has both employer and union representation. It has central authority and control over the public employment service (with two hundred and fifty local offices), vocational guidance, vocational rehabilitation, long-term and short-term forecasting of labor requirements, and an early warning system of impending lay-offs, which, under agreements with employers' organizations, provides for two months' advance notice of reductions in a firm's work force. The national Board estimates the need for vocational training and, in consultation with the National Board of Vocational Training, works out the training courses.

In addition, the national Labor Market Board has a variety of funds at its disposal that can be used to aid in stimulating geographic mobility of labor and to provide employment for unemployed workers in their locality. To encourage unemployed workers to accept a job in another locality, the employment service at its discretion can offer one or more of the following: a travel allowance to go and consider the opening, a family allowance if the worker accepts a job but cannot for a time relocate his family and therefore has two dwellings to maintain, a starting allowance to cover the period from the time he commences employment until he receives his first pay check, and a grant to help meet the costs of moving his household. Also, the Board has funds with which it can build temporary housing in case shortage of housing is a hindrance to geographic mobility to meet labor shortages. The Swedish authorities consider all of these measures economical in terms of the gain in Gross National Product.

The national Board also has reserves of public works and work relief that can be expanded to provide temporary employment in particular localities. In addition, the Board supervises the reserve of private investment funds set aside by companies under a tax abatement scheme that permits the government to determine the timing of the construction of plant and the purchase of equipment with those funds. In other words, these are private investment funds whose actual use is governed by employment needs from a public viewpoint.

The influence and authority of the national Board reach also into other areas. The unemployment insurance system is a government-subsidized union program, yet it is well coordinated with the Labor Market Board's over-all program. The Board also has a say in deferment of workers from military service because of the need for their skills in industry or government.

Not only is the Swedish manpower program well centralized and coordinated, but it also has been given a high status to match its powers, and considerable effort has been expended to have a high quality staff in the employment service. In the twenty-five Counties (somewhat analogous to our States), the Governor of the County is usually chairman of the County Board, and the County Board is in charge of the public employment service in its County.

Although Sweden has had a few years of increasing unemployment, throughout the postwar era that country has enjoyed remarkably full employment. Manpower planning and programs are viewed as a means of achieving effective utilization of the nation's manpower resources and of considerably increasing its Gross National Product.

TRAINING THE UNEMPLOYED

In Title II of the Manpower Development and Training Act, a three-year program of training for jobless and underemployed workers is established. The act envisions that training as part of an over-all manpower planning operation. Coordinated planning between the Employment Service and the vocational education authorities is necessary at each level of government.

The Program

The act provides for both institutional (or in-school) training and on-the-job training. In the selection of trainees, priority is given to unemployed and underemployed persons (including those in farm families with less than $1,200 annual net family income). Priority is also extended to persons to be trained for skills needed within the labor market area in which they reside and, after that, within the State.

While in training, weekly allowances are paid equal to at least the average unemployment insurance benefit in the State for a period not to exceed fifty-two weeks.[9] However, eligibility for such training allowances is limited to unemployed heads of households with at least three years of employment. Young people nineteen to twenty-one years of age may also receive training allowances up to fifty-two weeks but at a rate not exceeding $20 a week, and no more than one-twentieth of the total of training allowances may be spent for such youth training allowances. A special program of counseling and training is provided, without any training allowance, for youths sixteen through twenty-one years of age. Where trainees are required to travel beyond commuting distance to get the training, a transportation expenditure is provided as well as subsistence payments up to $35 a week for living away from home.

During the first two years the Federal Government paid the full cost of the training (teachers, facilities, and administration). Thereafter, the States were to match the Federal training contribution. However, amendments to the law in 1963 extended the 100 per cent Federal support for the third fiscal year until more State legislatures have an opportunity to meet and act on the training program, especially those with regular sessions early in 1965. In extending the act for two additional years, the requirement was included that participating States shall match one-third and one-half of the costs, respectively, in fiscal years 1966 and 1967.

As a Federal-State program, the Secretary of Labor enters into an agreement with each State for the effective administration of

---

[9] Workers eligible for unemployment compensation receive as training allowance the amount of benefit for which they are eligible under unemployment compensation, with the State being reimbursed for any unemployment benefits paid during the training period.

Any earnings from gainful employment outside the training program are deducted from the trainee's weekly allowance. That destroys the incentive to take part-time work while in training, and makes the training program with its relatively low allowances rather unattractive to a man with a large family whose training would require a considerable period of time.

the Employment Service aspects of the program, and the Secretary of Health, Education, and Welfare makes an agreement with the appropriate State vocational education agencies to provide the training. All States except Louisiana entered into the program.

An important aspect of the program is determination of the occupations in which the unemployed are trained. Before selecting a person for training, the act requires that the Secretary of Labor (through the Employment Service) "shall determine that there is a reasonable expectation of employment in the occupation for which the person is to be trained." Indeed, the act makes the training program part of a broad effort to achieve more effective utilization of the nation's manpower resources. It states: "In carrying out the purposes of this act, the Secretary of Labor shall determine the skill requirements of the economy, develop policies for the adequate occupational development and maximum utilization of the skills of the Nation's workers, promote and encourage the development of broad and diversified training programs, including on-the-job training, designed to qualify for employment the many persons who cannot reasonably be expected to secure full-time employment without such training, and to equip the Nation's workers with new and improved skills that are or will be required."

During the three-year period, a total of 400,000 persons are to be trained under the program at an estimated cost of $435 million. The program was somewhat delayed in starting in 1962.

Experience

In fiscal year of 1962–63, over 1,500 training projects were approved to train 60,000 persons. For 30,000 of them, training had commenced by June 30, 1963. There were only 117 on-the-job training projects averaging fourteen workers per project. Allowance and training costs for the 1,500 institutional projects amounted to about $71 million. The average cost per trainee (covering allowance and instruction costs but excluding administrative expenses) was $1,230, divided between $664 for allowances and $566 for instruction. The average duration of training on approved institutional projects was twenty-two weeks.

The Employment Service has the responsibility for selection and referral of trainees and their placement when the training is completed. As soon as the act was passed, the State employment services embarked on an extensive program of screening, counseling, and testing of potential trainees, referring suitable candidates to specific training projects. By June 1963, a total of 305,000 screening interviews and 89,000 counseling interviews had been held under the act. The testing had included 52,000 of the General Aptitude Test Battery and 48,000 specific aptitude tests. On the basis of such interviews and tests, 32,000 persons were referred for training during the first year.

The persons selected for training were not a representative sample of the unemployed. The poorly educated, long-term unemployed were underrepresented. However, close to half of the trainees had been unemployed for fifteen weeks prior to training, and nearly one-fifth had been jobless for fifty-two weeks or more. About two-fifths of the trainees have not completed high school. One out of every ten had only a grade-school education or less. Over three-fifths of the trainees were heads of families or households.

Some 245 occupations were included in the 1,500 training projects. The principal occupations were: general machine operator, automobile mechanic, auto body repairman, electronics mechanic, welder, solderer, sewing-machine operator, stenographer, typist, clerk-typist, licensed practical nurse, nurse aides, and hospital orderlies. Especially in the repair occupations an attempt is being made to build on skills already acquired in previous training and work experience.

Seventy per cent of the trainees completing training courses under the act had obtained employment by July 1, 1963, almost wholly in training-related occupations. State employment service agencies accounted for eight out of every ten job placements among these trainees.

Problems

The first year's experience revealed certain shortcomings and problems. They fell largely into three categories: (1) hampering restrictions written into the law, (2) difficulties of selecting appropriate training projects, and (3) lack of research findings to answer a number of fundamental questions.

Economics of Labor

Three limits in the act need relaxing. Restricting allowances for youths nineteen to twenty-one years of age to $20 a week and, especially, to 5 per cent of the estimated total training allowances has proved to be too confining. Some liberalization is needed to meet more adequately the training needs of school drop-outs in that age group. The training allowances for adults who have large families have in many cases been so small as to discourage family heads from entering or continuing training over a long period such as forty to fifty-two weeks. There is no reason why training allowances should be tied to unemployment compensation and previous earnings. They serve a different purpose and should be influenced by such factors as family size, value of the training, and the prospective savings to the community and government from training the person. The fifty-two weeks' limit on training for any person may be too short, where the individual has serious deficiencies in educational background and perhaps in personality and attitudes, generated by persistent unemployment.[10]

The training projects have been too focussed on short-run needs, on the immediate local requirements, and on projects for which vocational training facilities were already available locally. The act itself gives low priority to training in which the needs are nation-wide rather than tied to specific localities. Too little of the training has been of a basic character, producing skills, abilities, and understandings that would support further personal growth and development. Too much has been specialized training with low skill requirements that is likely to become obsolete in the near future as

---

[10] The Manpower Development and Training Act was amended late in 1963 to meet these three criticisms. The youth training program was expanded by lowering the age limit for youth training allowances from 19 to 17 years (subject to a restriction of a one-year waiting period for school dropouts) and by increasing to 25 per cent the proportion of total training allowances that may be received by youth. Provision is made for the training allowance to be increased by as much as ten dollars a week above the current average level of unemployment compensation in the State, and trainees are permitted to engage in part-time work up to 20 hours a week without a reduction in the training allowance. For those who cannot enter occupational training because of inadequate education, provision is made for extending the period during which training allowances can be paid for another 20 weeks so that basic education skills can, when necessary, be acquired first in order that the person can qualify for occupational training. Also, the amended law provides for a pilot program of limited experimentation with relocation allowances for unemployed workers who have job prospects in another area.

a result of technological change. Partly, the difficulty has been a lack of imagination and leadership at the local level, plus pressures to get large numbers trained in a short time. However, the program has suffered from the basic handicap that forecasts of manpower requirements have not been made in detail by occupation either nationally or by labor market areas. Long-range projections need to be translated into specific occupational-outlook data in a form usable by local training directors, local employment service counselors, and local labor-management public advisory committees.

A series of research projects is underway to help answer basic questions and to evaluate the operations of the program itself. The act correctly places considerable emphasis on factual studies and research that gives promise of furthering its objectives. One study is attempting to measure in quantitative terms, (1) the private benefits and the various costs to individuals who participate in training programs, (2) the social benefits and costs to the national economy as a result of the program, and (3) the impact of the program on government budgets at all levels, including effects on government tax receipts from the subsequent earnings of the trainees and on public expenditures, particularly for the training.

Such a study should provide criteria for judging the proper limits to a government training program. In considering such limits, there is the question of the most advantageous division of labor in training between private industry and public-supplied training. That question is a fundamental one for government. The answer to it depends to a considerable extent on the objectives of the government program and the character of the preemployment training it provides.

SUMMARY

This chapter has dealt with manpower policy—the instruments for planning and operating a program and the need for creative thinking and coordination. It explained why we cannot rely completely on wage differentials and unguided individual choice for the proper amount of training, or for the best allocation and utilization of the nation's manpower resources.

1. Manpower planning is designed to make adjustments of supply to demand more rapid, certain, and successful than would occur through reliance on market forces alone.

2. In weighing potential gains against the costs of government manpower activities, one must include long-term gains to the community and the nation as well as individual and company benefits. The collection, organization, and distribution of manpower information by itself contributes to increased productivity and economic growth, and proper investment in training can be highly productive.

3. Under the Manpower Act, the Federal Government is committed to a comprehensive, analytical approach to the nation's manpower problems. The President's 1963 Manpower Report dealt mainly with trends and needs, leaving to future reports the tough problems of analysis, planning, and coordination.

4. The Employment Service performs important informational, clearinghouse, testing, and guidance functions, with special service for handicapped groups. Its operations are restricted by worker and management preferences for informal, private means of job seeking and employee recruitment.

5. The Employment Service has been handicapped by division into fifty State units, low State salaries, and too narrow a conception of its role in various quarters.

6. Programs of vocational education for high-school students and adults need to be restructured to meet developing occupational and industrial requirements.

7. The training program for unemployed workers under the Manpower Act is designed as part of a broad effort to adjust labor supply to changing occupational requirements. The program should place more stress on national interests, developing occupational requirements, and long-term objectives.

DISCUSSION QUESTIONS

1. Why is any sort of government manpower program necessary? Why shouldn't we rely completely on private enterprise to supply any needed organization of "the labor market" and any vocational training?

2. What should be the objectives and scope of the President's Manpower Report? Support your views with reasons.
3. What is the proper role of a public employment service? What economic limits should guide its expansion? Should employers be required to register vacancies with the public employment service, and should any restrictions be placed on private fee-charging employment agencies? Explain.
4. Would you favor or oppose a national employment service such as most countries have? Explain with reasons.
5. Explain the possible advantages and disadvantages of national manpower planning and a national manpower program such as Sweden has.
6. How would you answer the charge that a government training program for unemployed workers does not increase employment but only helps unemployed trainees get jobs that other unemployed would otherwise have obtained and been trained for by the employers?

SELECTED REFERENCES

Bakke, E. Wight, *A Positive Labor Market Policy: Policy Premises for the Development, Operation, and Integration of the Employment and Manpower Services* (Columbus, Ohio: Charles E. Merrill, 1963).

Education for a Changing World of Work, Report of the Panel of Consultants on Vocational Education, United States Department of Health, Education and Welfare (Washington: United States Government Printing Office, 1963).

Investment in Human Beings, Papers presented at a conference called by the Universities—National Bureau of Economic Research Committee for Economic Research, *Journal of Political Economy*, LXX (Supplement: October 1962).

Manpower Report of the President and A Report on Manpower Requirements, Resources, Utilization, and Training by the U. S. Department of Labor (Washington: United States Government Printing Office, March 1963).

Nation's Manpower Revolution, Hearings before the Subcommittee on Employment and Manpower of the Committee on Labor and Public Welfare, Relating to the Training and Utilization of the Manpower Resources of the Nation, United States Senate,

Eighty-eighth Congress, 1st session, Parts 1, 2, 3, 4, 5, 6, and 7, May–November, 1963.

Public Employment Service in the Nation's Job Market, 1933–1963, Employment Security Review, XXX (June 1963).

Report of the Secretary of Labor to the Congress on Research and Training Activities in Accordance with Section 309 of the Manpower Development and Training Act (Washington: United States Government Printing Office, 1963).

Reynolds, Lloyd G., *The Structure of Labor Markets* (New York: Harper, 1951), Chapter 10, "The Objectives of Labor Market Policy."

Training Activities Under the Manpower Development and Training Act, Report of the Secretary of Health, Education, and Welfare (Washington: United States Government Printing Office, March 1963).

Unemployment and the American Economy, Proceedings of a conference held in connection with the Research and Evaluation Project on Unemployment and the American Economy, Institute of Industrial Relations, University of California at Berkeley, April 1963.

Part FOUR

CONCLUSION

19.
Problems and Policies in Perspective

THIS BOOK HAS attempted to develop an economic analysis based on modern concepts of employment and collective action. It has sought to bring economic thinking in the labor area into line with developments in employment, management, and unions, and to demonstrate the interaction between institutional change and policy. A realistic analysis of management, unions, and wage and benefit determination, including interfirm differentials and latitudes for adjustment, provides the economic basis for government programs for minimum wages, nondiscrimination in employment, and more effective use of the nation's manpower resources.

Three Bases of Judgment

New modes of economic analysis, however, clash with entrenched theory and policy norms. Ours is a mixed economy, and we are prone to mix our ways of thinking about it. In the labor area, all three elements—workers, management, and government—have moved away from competitive practices and norms, away from commodity patterns of thought. Nevertheless, most of us still, to some extent, inhabit two intellectual worlds—the competitive theory with its policy prescriptions and the collective analysis with its policy implications. Recognizing the advantages of each for particular sets of circumstances, we hesitate to make a sharp choice between them.

Chapter 13 discussed three philosophies of public policy in the labor field. The values that the competitive ideology stresses are basically freedom for the individual and limited government. The market decentralizes decisions; competitive forces are impersonal. Objective wage determination and labor distribution by market indicators permit individuals and firms to make optimum adjustments; central direction according to a national program is unnecessary. Politics is subordinated to economics.

The ideology of collective bargaining emphasizes a different set of values. Starting with the shortcomings of the market mechanism for many labor problems, it points to the virtues of industrial democracy and settlement of differences by negotiation. Work rules and employee security are part of a total package under a welfare concept of employment. With large economic units, collective bargaining permits representation and participation, yet individual protection under the grievance procedure. Self-settlement by labor and management, with mutual acceptability, still means private rather than governmental decisions.

The third ideology believes that the other two leave out an element of increasing importance in our economy, namely, national and community interests for which some planning and programming are necessary. Collective bargaining is limited in its coverage and is not well suited to solving certain labor problems, such as unemployment or the preparation of labor supply for developing demands. Its results in terms of wages, hours, and benefits may not be in the national interest. Competition as a method of solving labor problems has similar handicaps. In addition, it would require reversal of the evolutionary trends since World War I and especially since 1932.

Recognition of these three ideological positions raises questions concerning the terms or standards by which unions, managements, and government policy should be judged. Should they be assessed according to competitive norms, which are directed mainly to consumer interests? Or should the test be how well they meet collective bargaining norms, which stress workers' on-the-job needs and the virtues of negotiated settlements as well as contribution to total output? And how much weight should be given to considerations of national interest, such as full and effective use of the nation's labor resources, elimination of discrimination in employment, price-level stability, and the country's position in international trade, including our balance of payments?

From the analysis of various subject areas, it is evident that no one of these three sets of norms can be the sole basis for evaluating our institutional arrangements and public policy in the labor field. Naturally, business leaders, union leaders, and leaders in the Federal Government tend to stress the norms and values that are in accord with their interests and seem to suit the problems they face. Of course, changes in the economy and in international affairs affect the emphasis that the public and opinion leaders place on different sets of norms, both in the short run and in the long run. A recession or a war brings national interests to the fore; the change to a welfare concept of employment in large sections of the economy reduces the appeal of the competitive ideology. As the economy and industrial relations practices change, new balances (or compromises) are drawn among the three sets of values. Such balancing is a vital part of the art of government.

Unions

In attempting to arrive at a set of conclusions concerning the economic consequences of union policies, one has to bear in mind the wide differences among unions. The craft organizations in the building trades in a city like New York may create unemployment by pushing wage scales up so high as to cause building space to be comparatively high-priced. Since building is a local market industry and the building unions tend to control commercial construction in large cities, they can pursue such policies without the competitive and other pressures that force moderation in cost increases in most manufacturing lines. The craft unions in railroading, airlines, and ocean shipping have their interunion rivalries and special circumstances, and, of course, the Teamsters union is extraordinary in a number of respects. Thus, it is necessary to make one's analysis in terms of the bulk of the labor movement and to recognize that there will be many exceptions to almost any generalization. In fact, after three years of field work the late Sumner H. Slichter and his two Harvard colleagues concluded that generalizations about the economic effects of unions are "highly hazardous" and that, for many purposes, understanding the differences between unions is more important than questionable generalizations about unions.[1]

How have unions in this country affected production and employment? Have they served to increase or decrease the Gross National Product?

It has been charged on the one hand that American unions tend to reduce the nation's total output by restricting the use of labor-saving devices, by requiring excessively large work crews, by enforcing other make-work (featherbedding) practices, and by distorting the wage structure so that labor resources are misallocated. The building trades and the railroad unions have been frequently cited as "horrible" examples.

On the other hand, it is claimed that unions have enhanced total output by increasing the efficiency of management, by improving employees' work attitudes, by causing business to be allocated to the more efficient firms, and by helping to increase consumption and, thus, markets. Unions like the Automobile Workers, the Amalgamated Clothing Workers, and the Communications Workers are cited in support of this view.

In manufacturing, collective bargaining and union pressures have probably forced improvements in management that have, on balance, contributed to increased efficiency and output. With the stimulus of union demands and employee grievances under the contract, managements have developed systematic procedures, written manuals of industrial relations policies for uniform application, maintained good employee records, and improved methods of communication with employees. As a result of the elimination of inequities and foreman favoritism, employee attitudes and morale generally have improved. Broadly speaking, unions in manufacturing lines have not increased employee resistance to technological

---

[1] S. H. Slichter, James J. Healy, and E. Robert Livernash, *The Impact of Collective Bargaining on Management* (Washington: Brookings Institution, 1960), pp. 954–55.

change. In industries like automobile and aircraft assembly, changes in equipment and jobs are an accepted part of industrial life. In steel, the question of work rules and crew sizes was injected into the 116-day strike in 1959–60, well after it began; but some managements explained that the issue was of no concern in their companies or plants. It is true that collective agreements in this country are detailed and lengthy (often running fifty to one hundred pages), and that arbitrations and grievance settlements under them help to strengthen resistance to any change in content or wording.

Whether unions, on balance, facilitate or impede technological change is a bit difficult to determine. To the extent that unions independently raise wages, they increase the cost of using labor and, thus, stimulate the use of labor-saving machinery. Also, the grievance procedure and various benefits aid in gaining employee acceptance of technological change and in achieving a cooperative effort during the trial period of new equipment.[2] On the other hand, should higher wages squeeze profits, managements may have less money to invest in new capital equipment. As representation agencies, unions can strengthen employee resistance to the introduction of new equipment and, under certain provisions of an agreement (requiring widespread bumping with lay-offs, supplemental unemployment benefit costs, etc.), unions may be considered responsible for making it more difficult or costly to introduce rapidly, new labor-saving equipment. It is evident that answers concerning union effects on capital investment are not easy. By citing specific cases, one can support either side of the issue.

The charge that unions distort the wage structure and, thus, cause misallocation of labor resources is based largely on competitive theory. However, as indicated in Chapter 10, within a range of 10 to 15 per cent, the differential-range approach seems more appropriate under both union and nonunion conditions. Of course, local building unions may raise their wage scales beyond the applicability of that approach, so that competitive theory would be more appropriate to apply in their case.

From an extensive study of changes in wage structures from 1907 to 1954, Lloyd G. Reynolds and Cynthia H. Taft concluded

---

[2] See, for example, Richard A. Lester and Robert L. Aronson, *Job Modifications under Collective Bargaining*, Industrial Relations Section, Princeton University, Princeton, N.J., 1950.

that the "net effect" of collective bargaining on wage differentials "has been beneficial," and that "countries with the strongest union movements appear to have a wage structure which is more orderly and defensible than the wage structure of countries where unionism has been weak."[3] Those conclusions appear to be based, in considerable measure, upon a labor-supply test, namely, that differentials have been "narrowed without disrupting the supply of labor to particular occupations and industries."[4] That, however, is not a good test where the differential-range approach applies, as job evaluation has revealed. On the basis of job evaluation, the wage structure in this country is more orderly and defensible than in countries with more tradition-influenced wage structures like England.

Unions have served to increase the extent of uniformity of wages within firms, industries, and local labor-market areas. Such uniformity has tended to raise the efficiency of laggard managements or, where that has not happened, to shift resources toward the more efficiently-operated firms. That is a net gain for the economy as a whole.

Unions are charged with responsibility for the work time and production lost as a result of work stoppages. Often, however, there are two sides to a labor dispute, so that management may share the blame. Also, as the discussion in Chapter 15 indicated, some strikes serve a constructive purpose and are not, therefore, pure waste. Table 21 indicated that the time lost directly as a result of work stoppages in recent years has been less than two days a year per union member. That is not a net loss, however, because the strike may have resulted mainly in reducing inventories. To the extent that strikes create shortages and lost time that are not really made up by additional employment and output after the strike, they may have an impact on employment and the Gross National Product beyond that implied by the figures in Table 21.

The claim that unions have increased or improved consumer markets through collective bargaining is open to some question. They could have some beneficial effects within the 10- to 15-percent range, but, of course, that is on an individual firm basis and does not apply to general movements in the whole wage level. The

---

[3] Lloyd G. Reynolds and Cynthia H. Taft, *The Evolution of the Wage Structure* (New Haven: Yale University Press, 1956), pp. 194 and 195.

[4] *Ibid.*, p. 370.

effects of unions on consumer markets partly depends on whether the employment-curtailing effects of any extra, union-caused increase in labor cost are more than offset by the employment-increasing effects of added wage income for the workers who continue to be employed full time. So much depends on the particular circumstances that any broad, general conclusion is unwarranted.

Trade unionism may have some more general economic importance. Collective bargaining, by providing worker participation and protections, by reducing class distinctions between wage-earners and salary-receivers, and by resulting in apparent economic gains, may strengthen the commitment of workers to the economic system. Also, collective bargaining may provide employees with added security (through seniority, benefit programs, etc.), which is a net gain if not accompanied by significant adverse effects on incentive or discipline. In addition, unions can serve as training grounds in democratic practice and in the development of self-respecting citizens, both of which have economic as well as political implications.

In recent years there has, however, been a feeling among union leaders[5] and students of the labor movement, that our unions are achieving less in terms of values and benefits than was true in the earlier stages of their development. Questions have been raised about the return that workers are getting for the costs of operating unions. The view that members now receive less for their dues' dollar seems to be based largely on the following assumptions: (1) that, by past successes in reforming management and in eliminating distinctions between wage-earners and salaried employees, unions have reduced their opportunities for making new gains for the membership; (2) that, as unions have grown in size, their functions have become more centralized and their operations more routinized and the possibilities of achieving certain values for individual members have been reduced; and (3) that many of the important

---

[5] See, for example, Solomon Barkin, *The Decline of the Labor Movement and What Can Be Done about It,* Center for the Study of Democratic Institutions, Santa Barbara, California, 1961; and *Labor Looks at Labor, Some Members of the United Auto Workers Undertake a Self-Examination,* Center for the Study of Democratic Institutions, Fund for the Republic, Santa Barbara, California, September 1963.

problems of labor today and in the future either exceed the reach of collective bargaining or are so broad that collective bargaining, operating chiefly on a company-by-company basis with cost limitations, is not too useful in solving them. To a considerable extent they are matters of national economic policy, such as the level of unemployment, planning for the consequences of automation, training the labor supply to meet shortages, and labor adjustments to shifts in international trade and to changes in tariffs.

With respect to national economic problems, the union movement finds itself in an ambivalent position. It favors economic planning for full employment under monetary-fiscal policies and manpower programming, yet labor leaders oppose government planning with respect to wages and others terms and conditions of employment.[6] Those, the labor movement insists, should be left entirely to free collective bargaining.

How does this all balance out? Are unions as a whole a net advantage to the economy? Is their net advantage diminishing or growing? And how about particular individual unions?

The only frank answer is that there are too many imponderables and variations among unions for a single, all-embracing conclusion. Even with much more factual information and analysis, one's answer would, in the end, depend to a considerable extent on his own scale of values. For what it is worth, the author's opinion is that most unions do make a contribution to the economy and to our society that justifies the economic resources devoted to the business of the union.

Management

The economic questions that can be raised about management's labor policies center around the issues of (1) restrictions on labor mobility, (2) discrimination in employment and pay, and (3) disregard of or injury to over-all, national economic interests. The first concerns the consequences of management efforts to tie workers to the firm by means of company benefit programs, promotion from within, antipirating arrangements, and other anticompetitive practices in the labor area. The second involves the inequities that can develop with management's latitude of discretion, such as

---

[6] The British labor movement has been suffering from the same sort of schizophrenia. See *The New York Times*, September 5, 1963, p. 18.

racial, sex, and pro-white-collar discriminations in employment, pay, benefits, and other privileges. The third is partly implied in the other two; the company focus has meant that inadequate attention has been given to the general problem of unemployment, and that opposition, for example, has been developed to improvements in unemployment compensation, to legislation for the elimination of discrimination in employment, and to revision of the emergency disputes sections of the Taft-Hartley Act.

Management policies under each of the three headings can result in a reduction in the Gross National Product. Company restrictions on labor mobility, for instance, can prevent the most efficient distribution of the work force among firms from a national viewpoint. Whether it does, and to what extent, cannot be determined until there is a thorough analysis of labor mobility and a careful definition of desirable and undesirable mobility in operational and measurable terms. Much labor turnover is costly to the individual firm, although some is desirable as a weeding-out process in the early days of employment with a particular company. The most costly part of labor turnover from a social viewpoint is the loss of the investment in training and other knowledge gained at one firm that is not transferrable to and useful in other firms.

Clearly, therefore, it may be an advantage to the nation (in terms of Gross National Product) to have most of the labor mobility concentrated among the relatively inexperienced workers and among skilled workers whose training has been largely of a craft-type, so that it is generally useful among different employers. That, for example, would be the case for skilled trades like electrician, machinist, and printer, or for white-collar occupations like secretary, nurse, and aeronautical engineer. For the latter group, the training is largely in school, prior to employment in the occupation.

As explained in Chapter 11, company benefit programs and other mobility-restricting practices do serve to tie employees to a particular company. How much they do so, however, has not been determined and is in dispute.[7] Until the company-attachment

---

[7] With respect to the company holding-power of private pensions, see, for example, Herbert S. Parnes, "Workers' Attitudes to Job Changing: The Effect of Private Pension Plans," in Gladys L. Palmer, *et al., The Reluctant Job Changer, Studies in Work Attachments and Aspirations* (Philadelphia: University of Pennsylvania Press, 1962), pp. 45–80; and Hugh Folk, "Effects of Private Pension Plans on Labor Mobility," *Monthly Labor Review*, LXXXVI (March 1963), pp. 285–88.

effect of various employer practices has been established and until there is more analysis and concensus on the amount and kinds of mobility that are desirable from a national viewpoint under various conditions (e.g., different rates of unemployment, rates of job displacement, amounts of training for new jobs), it is not possible to determine how detrimental to Gross National Product company restrictions on labor mobility are. Under the Manpower Development and Training Act the Secretary of Labor is to "establish a program of factual studies of practices of employers and unions which tend to impede the mobility of workers or which facilitate mobility."

Discrimination in employment and pay was discussed in Chapter 16. There reference was made to the estimate of the President's Council of Economic Advisers that the elimination of racial discrimination in employment (assuming no change in workers' education levels) would add about thirteen billion dollars a year to the nation's Gross National Product.[8] That, of course, is based on an over-all, national viewpoint. As the discussion in that chapter indicated, management is not solely responsible for racial, sex, or other discriminations in employment and pay. On the other hand, the managements of American business firms must assume a share of the responsibility where genuine discrimination does exist.

The consequences to Gross National Product as a result of management's concentration on individual-firm interests to the detriment of national interests is difficult to determine. As an example, we lack sufficient studies from which to make some assessment of the effects of business opposition to more adequate unemployment compensation upon the total Gross National Product over (say) a ten-year period. Is the nation's total output for a decade lower because unemployment benefits compensate for only about one-fifth of the wage loss from unemployment rather than one-third of that loss? Would changes in unemployment compensation opposed by management reduce the depth of recessions without curtailing prosperity? Do experience rating and the narrow tax base, both strongly supported by dominant business elements, serve to curtail the Gross National Product by tending to accentuate slightly the cyclical swings in business?

Valid answers to such questions would require much more

---

[8] See footnote 1, p. 505. One may, of course, question the assumptions on which such an estimate rests.

study and analysis than have yet been made. However, the discussion in Chapter 17 would seem to indicate the likelihood of some loss to Gross National Product from management-supported restrictions and tax arrangements in unemployment compensation.

A similar set of questions could be raised with respect to the emergency disputes sections of the Taft-Hartley Act. As explained in Chapter 15, ill-conceived provisions in those sections have undoubtedly hampered and delayed the settlement of some big disputes. Spokesmen for American management have played a significant role in the opposition to revision of those sections of the Act.

Since the twenties American management has made great progress in the industrial relations area. Business leaders have been quick to apply the results of social science research to employee problems. Undoubtedly the improvements in the industrial relations policies and practices of American industry have added significantly to the Gross National Product, but just how much would be impossible to determine. Nevertheless, because of differences in viewpoint between managers and managed, there may continue to be a real need for the checks and balances provided by a union and the grievance procedure.

Government

Even more difficult are the questions in Chapter 1 with respect to the consequences of government policies. The short-run and long-range effects of different types of government intervention upon both the Gross National Product and the international economic position of the country are a part of the great issues of our times.

Government policy needs to adapt to significant developments in the economy and in international affairs. As we have observed, recent decades have witnessed great changes in the character of employment, in organized labor, and in union-management relations. Furthermore, the heavy obligations that have been placed on this nation by world developments have brought new emphasis on the international aspects of labor problems. The relationship between national policies and collective bargaining is, therefore, under reassessment, and the same is true of national manpower programs.

Unemployment beyond the amount necessary for adjustment

to change in a dynamic economy has constituted the largest loss to Gross National Product. How much responsibility demand deficiency and structural impediments have for the volume of unnecessary joblessness was discussed in Chapter 17. Whatever the relative responsibility of those two factors, the Federal Government has some of the chief instruments for an attack on the problem of excessive unemployment, namely, monetary, tax, and budgetary policy and vocational training, vocational guidance, and job placement programs.

The need for a more coordinated and rational program of manpower planning, partly as a measure to reduce unemployment but also as a means of improving labor productivity, was explained in Chapter 18. Such planning involves skilled forecasting of occupational requirements, the distribution and use of such information in vocational guidance, government aid for vocational education to meet present and prospective manpower shortages, and an employment service that serves as the central arm of the whole program for skillful matching of supply to developing demand on a nationwide basis.

Such manpower planning (government-sponsored training, guidance, and placement facilities) is fully compatible with free choice of occupation and job and with uncontrolled operation of collective bargaining in industry. National needs and programs do involve limits on the use of economic power by unions and management, but that is not something new. Past experience has demonstrated that collective bargaining and the labor movement can adapt to a legal framework and to national economic circumstances. As we have observed, collective bargaining has been shifting from short-term crisis negotiations to rather continuous study and discussion. The bargaining process has adjusted to legal limits in ways that have not involved any significant loss of the self-governing and mutual-acceptance values of collective bargaining. Indeed, organized labor, with some notable exceptions, has strongly favored a greater measure of the type of economic planning under discussion.

The labor parts of any program of economic planning do need to be coordinated so that separate Federal agencies and Federal and State agencies are not working at cross purposes. Also, each element in the program should meet the economic test of the added gain or contribution weighed against the added cost. The gain may be difficult to measure, partly because of uncertainties, incommensurables, and the length of time required for full returns on investments in manpower. Under specific programs, such as training or retraining of the unemployed and the public employment service, the gains may be in terms of Gross National Product, tax revenues, savings to unemployment compensation and relief funds, and individual and family morale and development. In other words, the over-all gains may extend far beyond reckoning in terms of employment and pay.

With respect to government regulation of labor organizations and union-management relations, continuous or repeated examination is desirable to determine whether a particular program is currently worth the cost of its administration. Its worth presumably would be measured in terms of gains to the economy and society after allowing for any adverse effects. Such a test should be applied, for example, to parts of the Tart-Hartley Act and the Landrum-Griffin Act.

The same sort of test should, of course, be applied to proposals for additional regulation. As explained in Chapter 15, the suggestion for government-administered strike votes seems definitely unsupportable in terms of the costs compared with any possible gains. Proposals for the application of the Federal antitrust laws to labor unions must be rejected on the broader basis set forth in Chapter 14. Such a program would mean national labor policy made by decisions in individual court cases under a vague attempt to turn the clock back to the days when a commodity concept of employment prevailed throughout the economy.

Such proposals for radical change in government policy in the labor area do raise the question of the objectives and over-all impact of the nation's labor legislation and government intervention as a whole. The answer to that question, in turn, hinges on the kind of economic system the American people desire.

Clearly there is need for more analysis and discussion of the respective roles of national labor policies and private decision-making in our economy. More understanding and more bridges need to be developed between private programs including collective bargaining and national economic programs including manpower. But how far and how fast the country should move in the direction of the sort of economic and manpower planning discussed in this book is a basic issue of economic philosophy.

Involved are profound questions concerning the very nature of our society. Such questions each person must answer for himself. Hopefully, this volume has supplied the factual background and the analytical basis for that kind of personal decision.

INDEX